THE BARBOUR COLLECTION
OF CONNECTICUT TOWN
VITAL RECORDS

THE BARBOUR COLLECTION
OF CONNECTICUT TOWN
VITAL RECORDS

FAIRFIELD 1639–1850

FARMINGTON 1645–1850

Compiled by

Nancy E. Schott

General Editor

Lorraine Cook White

GENEALOGICAL PUBLISHING Co., Inc.

INTRODUCTION

As early as 1640 the Connecticut Court of Election ordered all magistrates to keep a record of the marriages they performed. In 1644 the registration of births and marriages became the official responsibility of town clerks and registrars, with deaths added to their duties in 1650. From 1660 until the close of the Revolutionary War these vital records of birth, marriage, and death were generally well kept, but then for a period of about two generations until the mid-nineteenth century, the faithful recording of vital records declined in some towns.

General Lucius Barnes Barbour was the Connecticut Examiner of Public Records from 1911 to 1934 and in that capacity directed a project in which the vital records kept by the towns up to about 1850 were copied and abstracted. Barbour previously had directed the publication of the Bolton and Vernon vital records for the Connecticut Historical Society. For this new project he hired several individuals who were experienced in copying old records and familiar with the old script.

Barbour presented the completed transcriptions of town vital records to the Connecticut State Library where the information was typed onto printed forms. The form sheets were then cut, producing twelve small slips from each sheet. The slips for most towns were then alphabetized and the information was then typed a second time on large sheets of rag paper, which were subsequently bound into separate volumes for each town. The slips for all towns were then interfiled, forming a statewide alphabetized slip index for most surviving town vital records.

The dates of coverage vary from town to town, and of course the records of some towns are more complete than others. There are many cases in which an entry may appear two or three times, apparently because that entry was entered by one or more persons. Altogether the entire Barbour Collection--one of the great genealogical manuscript collections and one of the last to be published--covers 137 towns and comprises 14,333 typed pages.

TABLE OF CONTENTS

ABBREVIATIONS

ae. -------------- age
b. ----------------born, both
bd.---------------buried
B.G.-------------Burying Ground
d.----------------died, day, or daughter
decd.------------deceased
f.---------------- father
h.----------------hour
J.P.--------------Justice of Peace
m.---------------married or month
res.-------------resident
s. ----------------son
st. ---------------stillborn
w. ---------------wife
wid. ------------widow
wk. -------------week
y. ---------------year

THE BARBOUR
COLLECTION
OF CONNECTICUT TOWN
VITAL RECORDS

FAIRFIELD VITAL RECORDS
1639-1850

	Vol.	Page
ABEL, Elijah, s. Samuel, of Norwich, m. Grissell **BURR**, d.		
Capt. Nath[anie]ll, Dec. 31, 1761	1	269
Elijah, Col. had negroes Amos, s. Robin & Dorcas, b.		
Feb. 11, 1780 & Phillip, s. Robin & Dorcas, b. May		
8, 1782	1	464
ADAIR, [see under **ADIAR**]		
ADAMS, Abigail, d. Samuel, b. Mar. 25, 1682	LR-A2	681
Abigail, d. Nath[anie]ll & Ann, b. Nov. 2, 1748	1	76
Abigail, m. John **HIDE**, Mar. 22, 1837* *(Intended for		
1737)	1	50
Abraham, s. Sam[ue]ll, b. Feb. 1, 1685	LR-A2	676
Ann, d. Nath[anie]ll, & Ann, b. Feb. 19, 1740	1	76
Ann, d. Stephen & Sarah, b. Aug. 10, 1742	1	59
Ann, w. Nath[anie]ll, d. Nov. 14, 1748	1	76
Avis, m. Daniel **CROFOOT**, of Reading, [ ]	1	62
Benjamin, s. Sam[ue]ll, b. Dec. 28, 1690	LR-A2	676
Daniell, s. Samuell, b. May 17, 1679	LR-A2	663
David, s. Samuell, b. June 24, 1689	LR-A2	676
Ebenezer B., m. Mary S. **DAVIS**, Sept. 24, 1839, by Rev.		
Thomas F. Davis	1-M	68
Elizabeth, d. Sam[ue]ll, b. Feb. 3, 1684	LR-A2	676
Elizabeth, m. John **MALLERY**, Apr. 15, 1735	1	89
Elizabeth, d. Stephen & Sarah, b. Oct. 9, 1744	1	59
Harriet, m. John S. **HYDE**, Feb. 21, 1837, by Rev.		
Tho[ma]s F. Davis	1-M	62
John, s. Sam[ue]ll, b. Sept. 6, 1692	LR-A2	676
John, s. Stephen & Sarah, b. Apr. 9, 1732; d. Mar. 11,		
1733	1	59
John, of Norfield, m. Eunice **RAYMOND** of Greenfield,		
Nov. 16, [1823], by Hez[ekia]h Ripley, V.D.M.	1-M	13
Jonathan, s. Samuell, b. Oct. the last, 1686	LR-A2	676
Mary, d. Stephen & Sarah, b. Oct. 18, 1728	1	59
Mary, d. Nath[anie]ll & Ann, b. Feb. 1, 1744	1	76
Nathan, s. Stephen & Sarah, b. Oct. 26, 1736	1	59
Nath[anie]ll, m. Ann **SILLIMAN**, Oct. 3, 1739	1	76
Nath[anie]ll, s. Nath[anie]ll & Ann, b. Feb. 19, 1746	1	76
Nath[anie]ll, his servant Dorcas, b. Dec. 27, 1792	1	60
Rebecca, d. Nath[anie]ll & Ann, b. June 3, 1742	1	76
Samuell, s. Samuell, b. Jan. 1, 1677	LR-A2	663
Samuell, m. Mary **McKENZIE**, d. of Dr. [ ],		
July 15, 1677	LR-A2	664
Sarah, d. Sam[ue]ll, b. Oct. 3, 1680	LR-A2	681
Sarah, m. Benjamin **STURGIS**, Feb. 9, 1715	1	120
Sarah, d. Stephen & Sarah, b. Sept. 15, 1733	1	59
Stephen, m. Sarah **FINCH**, Oct. 17, 1727	1	59
ADDIS, Orrin H. m. Mrs. Harriet **FERRIS**, b. of New Milford,		
Dec. 31, 1848, by Rev. N. E. Cornwall	1-M	94
ADIAR, Andrew, s. James & Ann, b. Apr. 23, 1745	1	244
Ann. d. James & Ann, b. Feb. 2, 1752	1	244

1

	Vol.	Page
ADIAR (cont.)		
Esther, d. James & Ann, b. July 2, 1749	1	244
James, m. Ann **CARTER***, June 3, 1744		
*(**McCARTY?**)	1	244
James, s. James & Ann, b. Aug. 26, 1757	1	244
Mary, d. James & Ann, b. Jan. 3, 1747	1	244
Sarah, d. James & Ann, b. Mar. 1, 1755	1	244
ALDEN, Solomon E. of Rochester, N. Y., m. Ann E.		
CORNWALL, of Westport, Aug. 10, [1846], by		
Rev. N. E. Cornwall	1-M	85
ALLEN, Abigaile, [d. Gideon], b. June [ ], 1705	LR-2	458
Abigail, d. Gideon, m. Joseph **WAKEMAN**, s. Joseph,		
Oct. 31, 1727	1	148
Abigail, d. John & Abigail, b. Mar. 13, 1753	1	28
Alanson, m. Nancy **OLMSTEAD**, b. of Fairfield, Nov.		
27, 1823, by Nath[anie]ll Hewit	1-M	13
Ann, d. John & Sarah, b. Dec. 20, 1739	1	157
Ann, d. David & Sarah, b. Sept. 28, 1741	1	50
Ann, d. John & Abigail, b. Jan. 19, 1757	1	28
Ann, d. Dr. John, m. William **SILLIMAN**, s. Gold		
Selleck, Sept. 22, 1774, by Rev. Andrew Eliot	1	280
Ann Tweed of Fairfield, m. James A. **THORNE**, of		
Kentucky, Sept. 25, 1838, by Rev. Edward Allen	1-M	67
Annah, [d. Gideon], b. June 6, 1700	LR-2	458
Benjamin, s. Joseph & Rachel, b. Oct. 4, 1743	1	155
Caroline, m. Gould **GREGORY**, b. of Westport, Sept.		
27, 1841, by Rev. Lyman H. Atwater	1-M	72
Cynthia, of Fairfield, m. Frederick **DONEWELL**, of		
Norwalk, Mar. 23, 1834, by Rev. C. A. Boardman,		
of Saugatuck	1-M	52
David, s. Lieut. Gideon, m. Sarah **GOLD**, d. John, Oct.		
11, 1739	1	50
David, s. David & Sarah, b. Nov. 13, 1743	1	50
David, Jr., s. David, m. Sarah **HULL**, d. Cornelius, Nov.		
10, 1768	1	270
David, s. David & Sarah, b. Sept. 22, 1773	1	270
Deborah, d. Ebenezer & Deborah, b. Oct. 8, 1744	1	160
Ebenezer, s. Gideon, m. Deborah **BENNET**, d. John,		
Nov. 12, 1731	1	160
Ebenezer, s. Ebenezer & Deborah, b. July 21, 1739	1	160
Edward, s. David & Sarah, b. Feb. 7, 1757	1	50
Edward, s. David & Sarah, b. June 22, 1778	1	270
Elizabeth, d. David & Sarah, b. Apr. 13, 1749	1	50
Elizabeth, of Black Rock, m. David **SMITH**, of		
Greenfield, Nov. 30, 1846, by Rev. Lyman H.		
Atwater	1-M	86
Ellen, d. David & Sarah, b. Nov. 19, 1754	1	50
Ellen, d. David & Sarah, b. July 27, 1775	1	270
Elnathan, s. Joseph & Rachel, b. June 23, 1729	1	155
Elnathan, m. Sallome **KNOT**, Dec. 28, 1751	1	224
Eunice, d. John & Sarah, b. May 4, 1748	1	157
Gabriel, s. Elnathan & Sallome, b. Jan. 23, 1755	1	224

	Vol.	Page
ALLEN (cont.)		
George, s. David & Sarah, b. July 26, 1760	1	50
Gershom, H. of Fairfield, m. Ann Burr **NASH**, of		
Westport, Feb. 28, 1841, by Rev. Dan[ie]l C. Curtiss	1-M	71
Gideon, m. Annah **BURR**, d. Nathaniel, Jan. 20, 1696	LR-2	458
Gideon, s. Gideon, b. Jan. 17, 1702	LR-2	458
Gideon, Jr., d. May 28, 1748	1	32
Gideon, Sr., d. Jan. 25, 1750/1	1	32
Gideon, s. John & Abigail, b. Oct. 19, 1751	1	28
Gideon, s. David & Sarah, b. Mar. 1, 1772	1	270
Hannah, d. Joseph & Rachel, b. Sept. 20, 1727	1	155
Hannah, d. David & Sarah, b. May 29, 1747	1	50
Henrietta, m. Benjamin **PENFIELD**, Oct. 8, 1832, by T.		
F. Davis	1-M	48-9
Henry, m. Mary B. **NASH**, b. of Fairfield, Sept. 9, 1827,		
by Rev. E. W. Hooker	1-M	29
James, s. John & Abigail, b. July 14, 1762	1	28
John, s. Gideon, b. Dec. 1, 1710	LR-2	458
John, s. Joseph & Rachel, b. June 16, 1736	1	155
John, m. Sarah **BENNET**, d. Deliverance, Mar. 23, 1739	1	157
John, s. Gideon, m. Abigail **JESSUP**, d. Edw[ar]d, Jan.		
17, 1750/1	1	28
John, s. John & Abigail, b. Aug. 14, 1759	1	28
John Gold, s. David & Sarah, b. Jan. 22, 1771	1	270
Joseph, s. Gideon, b. June 25, 1702; m. Rachel **BENNIT**,		
d. John, Mar. 26, 1724	1	155
Joseph, s. Joseph & Rachel, b. Feb. 6, 1725	1	155
Joseph, s. David & Sarah, b. Dec. 25, 1784	1	270
Joseph J., m. Lydia A. **STURGIS**, b. of Fairfield, Jan. 20,		
1851, by Rev. W. W. Brewer	1-M	91
Mahala, of Greens Farms, m. Aaron A. **HUTCHINSON**,		
of Trenton, N.J., Oct. 27, 1834, by T. F. Davis	1-M	55
Martha, d. Ebenezer & Deborah, b. Aug. 19, 1737	1	160
Martha, d. John & Sarah, b. July 4, 1746	1	157
Martha, d. John & Abigail, b. Apr. 1, 1755	1	28
Martha, d. Dr. John, m. John **FAIRCHILD**, s. John, of		
Durham, Feb. 17, 1773	1	277
Mary, d. Gideon, b. Aug. 6, 1708	LR-2	458
Mary, m. Peter **PENFIELD**, May 28, 1730	1	6
Mary, d. Joseph & Rachel, b. Aug. 24, 1732	1	155
Mary, [twin with Thomas], d. Joseph & Rachel, b. July 2,		
1733	1	155
Mary, m. Abraham **HIGGINS**, s. Abraham, May [ ],		
1739	1	193
Mary, d. David & Sarah, b. May 6, 1752	1	50
Mary, m. Daniel **NICHOLS**, Oct. 18, 1756	1	161
Mercy, d. Elnathan & Sallome, b. Dec. 12, 1757	1	224
Molly, d. John & Sarah, b. Sept. 1, 1742	1	157
Moses, s. Ebenezer & Deborah, b. Sept. 27, 1742	1	160
Nancy, of Greens Farms, m. Bradford **PATRICK**, of		
Redding, Aug. 26, 1823, by Hez[ekia]h Ripley,		
V.D.M.	1-M	12

	Vol.	Page
ALVORD (cont.)		
Sarah, m. John H. **GORHAM**, b. of Fairfield, Mar. 7,		
1842, by Rev. Daniel C. Curtiss	1-M	73
Urania, m. Edward Merton **BULKLEY**, b. of Southport,		
Nov. 4, 1850, by Rev. Sam[ue]l J. M. Merwin	1-M	90
ANDERSON, James, of Trenton, N.J., m. Thirza **ALLEN**, of		
Fairfield, Sept. 24, 1823, by Hezekiah Ripley,		
V.D.M.	1-M	12
ANDREWS, ANDRUS, ANDRUSS, Abigail, [d. Ens. John],		
b. June 17, 1709	LR-2	455
Abigail, d. John & Sarah, b. Dec. 13, 1736	1	34
Abigail, d. John, m. Daniel **SHERWOOD**, Jan. 28, 1760	1	305
Abraham, [s. Ens. John], b. July 21, 1717	LR-2	455
Abraham, s. John & Sarah, b. Aug. 23, 1735	1	34
Alithea, of Fairfield, m. William **HOBBY**, of New York,		
Sept. 11, 1832, by Tho[ma]s F. Davis	1-M	45-6
Ann, d. Dan[ie]ll & Sarah, b. June 15, 1743	1	104
Catharine M., m. Ezra C. **PORTER**, of Bridgeport, Jan.		
3, 1829, by John Hunter	1-M	32
Daniell, [s. Ens. John], b. Feb. 20, 1714	LR-2	455
Daniel, m. Sarah **SILLIMAN**, Feb. 8, 1741	1	104
Daniel, s. Dan[ie]ll & Sarah, b. Apr. 27, 1754	1	104
Daniel, m. Kezia **RANALL**, b. of Green's Farms, July		
16, 1820, by Hez[ekiah] Ripley, V.D.M.	1-M	1
Eben[eze]r, [s. Ens. John], b. May 12, 1720	LR-2	455
Ebenezer, m. Sarah **STURGIS**, d. Peter, Jan. [ ], 1746	1	172
Ebenezer, s. Eben[eze]r & Sarah, b. Dec. 9, 1752	1	172
Ebenezer, m. Rachel **HYDE**, b. of Greens Farms, Aug.		
15, [1825], by Rev. E. W. Hooker	1-M	19
Ellinor, d. John & Sarah, b. Aug. 4, 1738	1	34
Eunice, d. Eben[eze]r & Sarah, b. Aug. 31, 1750	1	172
Francis, s. Eben[eze]r & Sarah, b. July 8, 1754	1	172
Hellynah, [d. Ens. John], b. Oct. 9, 1711	LR-2	455
Isabell, d. John & Sarah, b. Sept. 20, 1742	1	34
John, s. John, b. Oct. 24, 1679	LR-A	682
John, [s. Ens. John], b. Aug. 6, 1707	LR-2	455
John, s. John, m. Sarah **COUCH**, d. Simon, Oct. 28, 1730	1	34
John, s. John & Sarah, b. Mar. 17, 1734	1	34
John Silliman, s. Dan[ie]ll & Sarah, b. Apr. 16, 1741	1	104
John Silliman, s. Dan[ie]ll, m. Eunice **LYON**, d.		
Ephraim, Feb. 4, 1764	1	266
Mabel, d. Dan[ie]ll & Sarah, b. Apr. 2, 1756	1	104
Molly, d. Eben[eze]r & Sarah, b. June 15, 1746	1	172
Peter, s. Eben[eze]r & Sarah, b. Aug. 12, 1757	1	172
Rachel, d. Dan[ie]ll & Sarah, b. Mar. 28, 1748	1	104
Samuel, s. John & Sarah, b. Feb. 23, 1740	1	34
Sarah, d. John, b. Jan. 12, 1680	LR-A	682
Sarah, d. John & Sarah, b. Aug. 6, 1731	1	34
Simon, s. John & Sarah, b. Oct. 28, 1744	1	34
Stephen, s. Eben[eze]r & Sarah, b. Dec. 21, 1747	1	172
ANDRUS, ANDRUSS, [see under **ANDREWS**]		

	Vol.	Page
[ANNABLE], ANNABIL, ANNIBIL, Ann, d. Anthony &		
Sarah, b. Oct. 3, 1761	1	143
Anthony, m. Sarah MIDLEBROOK, d. Jonathan, Jan.		
16, 1748	1	143
David, s. Anthony & Sarah, b. Jan. 19, 1753 N. S.	1	143
Ebenezer, s. Anthony & Sarah, b. July 16, 1756	1	143
Mary, d. Anthony & Sarah, b. June 3, 1759	1	143
Samuel, s. Anthony & Sarah, b. June 29, 1751, O.S.	1	143
Sarah, d. Anthony & Sarah, b. Dec. 25, 1754	1	143
Sarah, d. Anthony, m. Levi MALLERY, s. Eben[eze]r,		
Aug. 3, 1772	1	48
ARNOLD, Isaac, of Wilton, m. Eliza LOCKWOOD, of		
Weston, Aug. 19, 1832, by William Bonney	1-M	44
ASH, John B., m. Mary E. STURGIS, b. of Fairfield, Apr. 13,		
1851, by Rev. W. W. Brewer	1-M	91
ATKINS, Emeline E., m. Peter B. STURGIS, b. of Fairfield,		
Mar. 24, 1844, by Rev. Anson F. Beach	1-M	76
ATWATER, Benjamin, of Ithaca, N.Y., m. Sally Ann		
PHELPS, of Fairfield, [Oct,] 15, [1840], by N. E.		
Cornwall	1-M	70
AVERY, Edward, of Weston, O., m. Jennett M. BUSH, of		
Fairfield, Feb. 3, 1834, by Rev. C. A. Boardman, of		
Saugatuck	1-M	52
Mary, m. Benjamin BAKER, Aug. 14, 1718	1	160
BABBETT, Francis L., m. Bradley ZIMMERMAN, b. of		
Fairfield, Oct. 10, 1836, by Rev. T. F. Davis	1-M	60
BAKER, Abigail H., m. W[illia]m BATTERSON, June 11,		
1821, by Hezekiah Ripley, V.D.M.	1-M	4
Avery, s. Benjamin & Mary, b. Oct. 22, 1734	1	160
Benjamin, m. Mary AVERY, Aug. 14, 1718	1	160
Benjamin, s. Benjamin & Mary, b. May 10, 1728	1	160
Benjamin, s. James & Thankfull, b. Jan. 9, 1756	1	230
Caroline, m. Joseph WANZER, [June] 19, [1831], by		
Rev. Ch[arles] Smith	1-M	41
David, s. Sam[ue]ll & Sarah, b. Oct. 16, 1757	1	136
Ebenezer, s. Benjamin & Mary, b. Dec. 9, 1736	1	160
James, s. Benj[ami]n & Mary, b. June 30, 1722	1	160
James, m. Thankfull COLEY, Mar. 13, 1755	1	230
Joshua, s. Benjamin & Mary, b. Apr. 22, 1740	1	160
Lewis, m. Rachel MILLS, b. of Fairfield, Sept. 21, 1828,		
by Rev. E. W. Hooker, of Greens Farms	1-M	31
Lockwood, m. Jane CHAPMAN, b. of Greens Farms,		
Apr. 10, 1825, by Hez[ekia]h Ripley, V.D.M.	1-M	22
Mary, d. Benjamin & Mary, b. July 24, 1732	1	160
Mary, d. Benj[ami]n, m. Sam[ue]ll TURNEY, s. Thomas,		
Nov. 5, 1750	1	256
Mary, d. Sam[ue]ll & Sarah, b. Nov. 2, 1755	1	136
Matilda, m. Henry WILLIAMS, May 26, 1833, by T. F.		
Davis	1-M	50
Nancy, of Fairfield, m. Allen PRINDLE, of Norwalk,		
Apr. 1, 1825, by Rev. E. W. Hooker	1-M	17
Samuel, s. Benj[ami]n & Mary, b. Mar. 28, 1724	1	160

	Vol.	Page
BAKER (cont.)		
Samuel, m. Sarah **BARLOW**, Feb. 28, 1754	1	136
William, m. Polly **JEWET**, Apr. 25, 1824, by Rev. E. W.		
Hooker	1-M	14
BALDWIN, Alonzo, s. Gabriel & Sarah, b. Jan. 5, 1801	1	280
Anna, d. Gabriel & Sarah, b. July 28, 1790	1	280
Burr, s. Gabriel & Sarah, b. Jan. 19, 1789	1	280
Charles, s. Gabriel & Sarah, b. July 4, 1797	1	280
David, s. Gabriel & Sarah, b. Mar. 10, 1792	1	280
Eliza, d. Gabriel & Sarah, b. Dec. 7, 1804	1	280
Gabriel, s. Jared & Damaris (**BOOTH**), m. Sarah		
SUMMERS, d. Zachariah & Martha (**BURR**), May		
2, 1788, by Rev. James Johnson	1	280
Henry, of Greenfield, m. Martha **ALVORD**, of Southport,		
Oct. 7, 1841, by Rev. Lyman H. Atwater	1-M	72
Ira, s. Gabriel & Sarah, b. Apr. 8, 1799	1	280
James, s. Gabriel & Sarah, b. Aug. 27, 1802	1	280
Josiah, m. Sarah D. **BEERS**, May 11, 1831, by Rev. John		
H. Hunter	1-M	41
Morris Warren, s. Gabriel & Sarah, b. Sept. 16, 1806	1	280
Sarah Maria, d. Gabriel & Sarah, b. Jan. 4, 1811	1	280
Stephen, s. Gabriel & Sarah, b. Sept. 18, 1795	1	280
Summers, s. Gabriel & Sarah, b. Jan. 24, 1794	1	280
Venus, s. Jack & Judah, b. Oct. 28, 1793	1	290
BANKS, Aaron, [twin with Moses], s. John & Elizabeth, b.		
Sept. 25, 1747	1	219
Abigail, m. Dan[ie]l **KNAP**, Mar. 5, 1710	1	46
Alanson, of Fairfield, m. Lorinda **HALL**, of Weston,		
Mar. 7, 1838, by Hull Bradley, J.P.	1-M	67
Alson, m. Lucy **CHAPMAN**, b. of Fairfield, Oct. 19,		
1823, by Hezekiah Ripley, V.D.M.	1-M	12
Amelia, m. Anson **WHEELER**, Feb. 4, 1821, by Rev.		
William Belden, of Greenfield	1-M	2
Ann, d. Eben[eze]r & Sarah, b. Aug. 5, 1749	1	217
Beniimin, 1st s. John, m. Hannah **LYON**, 2nd d. Richard,		
decd., Jan. 29, 1679	LR-A2	663
Beniamin, s. Beniamin, b. Oct. 30, 1682	LR-A2	680
Benjamin, Jr., s. Benj[ami]n & Ruth (**HIAT**), b. Aug. 8,		
1705	1	241
Benjamin, Jr., m. Mary **TREADWELL**, Nov. [ ], 1729	1	236
Benjamin, m. Ellen **BRADLEY**, June 20, 1744	1	236
Benjamin, s. Benj[ami]n & Ellen, b. Dec. 21, 1746	1	236
Betsey, Mrs. m. Thomas **MERWIN**, b. of Greenfield,		
Jan. 31, 1841, by Rev. Matthew Batcheldor	1-M	71
Daniel, s. Gershom & Mary, b. Dec. 5, 1739	1	127
Daniel, s. Gershom, m. Hannah **THORP**, d. Nathan, Dec.		
10, 1761	1	271
Dan[ie]ll, s. Dan[ie]ll & Hannah, b. July 18, 1764	1	271
David, m. Emeline **OSBORN**, b. of Fairfield, [Jan.] 20,		
[1833], by Rev. Charles Smith	1-M	48-9

	Vol.	Page
BANKS (cont.)		
John, Sergt., d. Jan. 22, 1684	LR-A2	680
John, s. Benj[ami]n, & Ruth, b. Dec,. 13, 1717	1	241
John, m. Elizabeth **BRADLEY**, May 14, 1740	1	219
John, s. John & Elizabeth, b. Aug. 23, 1745	1	219
Joseph, Jr., s. Joseph, m. Joanna **BANKS**, d. Benj[ami]n, Mar. 29, 1737	1	91
Joseph, s. Gershom & Mary, b. Nov. 2, 1754	1	127
Joseph, s. Eben[eze]r & Sarah, b. Nov. 7, 1756	1	217
Justice, s. Dan[ie]ll & Hannah, b. Oct. 14, 1770; d. Nov. 21, 1770	1	271
Lyman, s. Dan[ie]ll & Hannah, b. May 17, 1768	1	271
Lyman, Capt., m. Mrs. Esther **MOREHOUSE**, Feb. 14, 1830, by Tho[ma]s F. Davis in Greens Farms	1-M	38
Mabel, d. Benj[ami]n & Ellen, b. Oct. 31, 1751	1	236
Mariana, d. Gershom & Hannah, b. Dec. 22, 1745	1	127
Marilla, of Fairfield, m. Charles **WAKEMAN**, of Weston, Oct. 24, 1821, by Nath[anie]l Hewit, V.D.M.	1-M	5
Mary, w. Gershom, d. May [ ], 1741	1	127
Mary, d. Benjamin, Jr., m. Samuel **OGDEN**, s. John, June 19, 1753	1	216
Mary, d. Dan[ie]ll & Hannah, b. Nov. 16, 1762	1	271
Mary T., m. Dennis **GALLAGHER**, b. of Fairfield, Feb. 18, 1844, by Rev. N. E. Cornwall	1-M	76
Mercy, d. Benj[ami]n & Mary, b. Sept. [ ], 1730	1	236
Molly, d. Benj[amin] & Ellen, b. Apr. 7, 1745	1	236
Moses, [twin with Aaron], s. John & Elizabeth, b. Sept. 25, 1747	1	219
Noah, s. Gershom & Mary, b. June 1, 1760	1	127
Peter, s. John & Elizabeth, b. Nov. 9, 1749	1	219
Polly Wakeman, m. Samuel B. **GOODSELL**, b. of Fairfield, Jan. 17, 1834, by Rev. Geo[rge] H. Hulin	1-M	58
Rhode, d. Benj[ami]n & Mary, b. Oct. 11, 1741	1	236
Ruth, d. Benj[ami]n & Ellen, b. Apr. [ ], 1755	1	236
Sallema, of Greens Farms, m. Philo **WAKELEE**, of Huntington, Aug. 2, [1820], by Hezekiah Ripley, V.D.M.	1-M	1
Sam[ue]ll, s. Dan[ie]ll & Hannah, b. July 2, 1766	1	271
Sarah, d. Jos[eph], m. Gershom **BULKLEY**, s. Gershom, May 17, 1736	1	233
Sarah, d. Joseph & Joanna, b. Dec. 26, 1743	1	91
Sarah, of Greenfield, m. Reuben E. **THOMAS**, of Litchfield, Oct. 17, 1836, by Lyman H. Atwater	1-M	60
Sarah, m. Seymour **BANKS**, b. of Greenfield, June 20, 1848, by Rev. Lyman H. Atwater	1-M	90
Sarah E., m. Napoleon **CLARK**, b. of Saugatuck, Apr. 24, 1833, by T. F. Davis	1-M	56
Seymour, m. Sarah **BANKS**, b. of Greenfield, June 20, 1848, by Rev. Lyman H. Atwater	1-M	90

	Vol.	Page
BANKS (cont.)		
Talcott, Dr. m. Polly **BURR**, b. of Greens Farms, Sept. 20, 1821, by Hezekiah Ripley, V.D.M.	1-M	5
Thomas, s. Gershom & Hannah, b. Oct. 14, 1747	1	127
BARLOW, Aaron, s. Sam[ue]ll & Esther, b. Feb. 11, 1750	1	105
Ann, d. [John], b. Oct. 6, 1699	LR-2	461
Ann, m. Jeremiah **STURGIS**, Sept. 1, 1720	1	206
Benjamin, s. David & Esther, b. Oct. 23, 1755	1	242
Daniel, s. Sam[ue]ll & Eunice, b. Nov. 24, 1734	1	105
David, s. Samuel, m. Susannah **HUBBART**, d. Zach[ariah], Dec. 27, 1743	1	242
David, s. David & Susannah, b. Jan. 10, 1745	1	242
David, m. Esther **STURGIS**, d. Jeremiah, Nov. 29, 1750	1	242
Deborah, d. [John], b. Jan. 10, 1705/6	LR-2	461
Deborah, m. Joseph **GORHAM**, Jan. 13, 1725/6	1	187
Edmund, s. Jabez & Elizabeth, b. May 4, 1749	1	64
Elizabeth, d. John, b. May 11, 1677	LR-A2	664
Elizabeth, d. [John], b. June 3, 1697	LR-2	461
Elizabeth, d. David & Esther, b. Jan. 14, 1758	1	242
Francis, s. [John], b. July 11, 1702	LR-2	461
George, m. Mehetable **STAPLES**, Apr. 1, 1722	1	175
Hezekiah, s. George & Mehetable, b. Dec. 19, 1725; d. 1 3/4 y. after	1	175
Jabez, s. Sam[ue]ll & Eunice, b. Mar. 21, 1742	1	105
Jabez, m. Elizabeth **HUNT**, Mar. 1, 1744	1	64
Jabez, s. Jabez & Elizabeth, b. Feb. 21, 1746/7	1	64
Jabez, d. Nov. 23, 1750	1	64
James, s. Sam[ue]ll & Eunice, b. Jan. 29, 1739	1	105
Jemima, d. Nehemiah & Jemima, b. Sept. 25, 1752	1	176
Joel, s. Sam[ue]ll & Esther, b. Mar. 24, 1754	1	105
John, s. John, b. Sept. 6, 1693	LR-2	461
John, s. Jabez & Elizabeth, b. Oct. 22, 1744	1	64
Joseph, s. John, b. Sept. 1, 1677	LR-A2	664
Joseph, s. [John], b. Apr. 14, 1701	LR-2	461
Joseph, s. David & Esther, b. Aug. 24, 1751	1	242
Mabel, d. Nehemiah & Jemima, b. Feb. 16, 1757	1	176
Mary, d. George & Mehetable, b. Mar. [ ], 1730; d. 8 mos., after	1	175
Mary, m. James **BURR**, Jan. [ ], 1746	1	201
Nathaniel, s. Sam[ue]ll & Esther, b. May 13, 1745	1	105
Nehemiah, s. George & Mehetable, b. May 11, 1723	1	175
Nehemiah, s. George, m. Jemima **TURNEY**, d. Tho[ma]s, Jan. 25, 1751	1	176
Ruhamah, d. Sam[ue]ll & Eunice, b. Jan. 22, 1737	1	105
Ruhamah, d. Sam[ue]ll, m. John **GRAY**, s. John, Aug. 7, 1759	1	263
Samuell, s. [John], b. Nov. 14, 1695	LR-2	461
Samuel, s. Sam[ue]ll, m. Eunice **BRADLEY**, d. Dan[ie]ll, Aug. 2, 1731	1	105
Samuel, m. 2nd w. Esther **HULL**, d. Nath[anie]ll, Aug. 7,		

	Vol.	Page
BARLOW (cont.)		
1744	1	105
Samuel, s. Sam[ue]ll & Esther, b. Apr. 3, 1752	1	105
Samuel, m. Lucy **MILLS**, b. of Greens Farms, July 23,		
1820, by Rev. William Belden of Greenfield	1-M	2
Sarah, d. John, b. July [ ], 1675	LR-A2	664
Sarah, d. [John], b. Feb. 27, 1703	LR-2	461
Sarah, d. George & Mehetable, b. Mar. 28, 1732	1	175
Sarah, m. Samuel **BAKER**, Feb. 28, 1754	1	136
Susannah, w. David, d. Oct. 15, 1745	1	242
Susannah, d. David & Esther, b. Feb. 2, 1754	1	242
Suse, d. David & Esther, b. Dec. 10, 1752; d. Feb. 17,		
1753	1	242
BARNES, BARNS, Charles, m. Betsey **FOLLIETT**, b. of		
Norwalk, Aug. 23, [1821], by Rev. E. W. Hooker	1-M	5
Mary, m. Samuel **COMSTOCK**, Apr. 27, 1834, by James		
C. Loomis, J.P.	1-M	53
BARNUM, Ann Jennett, of Bridgeport, m. Albert Sherwood		
WILSON, of Fairfield, Oct. 11, 1846, by Rev.		
James Scott, of Stratfield	1-M	85
BARTLETT, BARTLET, Angeline, m. Ebenezer S.		
DISBROW, b. of Greens Farms, Oct. 15, 1820, by		
Hezekiah Ripley, V.D.M.	1-M	2
Daniel Collins, s. Nath[anie]ll & Eunice, b. Jan. 12, 1757	1	159
Nathaniel, m. Mrs. Eunice **RUSSELL**, June 13, 1753	1	159
Russell, s. Nath[anie]ll & Eunice, b. June 3, 1754	1	159
BARTRAM, Abigail, w. Job, d. Jan. 14, 1776, aged 27 yrs., 4		
mos.	1	25
Barnabus, s. Eben[eze]r & Elizabeth, b. Sept. 20, 1739	1	223
Daniel, s. David & Mabel, b. Oct. 23, 1745	1	240
Daniel Starr, s. Job & Abigail, b. Jan. 2, 1776	1	25
David, m. Mabel **JOHNSON**, Dec. 14, 1730	1	240
David, s. David & Mabel, b. May 18, 1735	1	240
Ebenezer, s. John, b. Apr. 29, 1699	LR-A2	674
Ebenezer, m. Elizabeth **WILLIAMS**, May 15, 1728	1	223
Ebenezer, s. Eben[eze]r & Elizabeth, b. June 13, 1732	1	223
Ebenezer, Jr., s. Ebenezer, m. Mary **BURR**, d. Capt. John,		
Nov. 1, 1759	1	248
Elizabeth, [twin with Sarah], d. David & Mabel, b. Sept.		
6, 1743	1	240
Elizabeth, d. Jos[eph] & Rebecca, b. Oct. 6, 1755	1	234
Elizabeth, d. Joseph, of Fairfield, m. John **WATSON**, s.		
Robert, of Norwalk, Apr. 18, 1779	1	289
Eulilia, d. Eben[eze]r & Elizabeth, b. June 24, 1737	1	223
Eulilia, d. Jos[eph] & Rebecca, b. Dec. 1, 1757	1	234
Hannah, d. David & Mabel, b. Nov. 18, 1733	1	240
Isaac, s. David & Mabel, b. Jan. 7, 1740/1; d. June [ ],		
1747	1	240
Isaac, s. David & Abigail, b. July 24, 1748; d. [ ]	1	240
James, s. David & Mabel, b. Apr. 18, 1738	1	240
Jerusha, w. Job, d. Nov. 24, 1773	1	25

	Vol.	Page
BARTRAM (cont.)		
Job, s. Eben[eze]r & Elizabeth, b. Mar. 20, 1735	1	223
Job, s. Eben[eze]r, m. Jerusha **THOMPSON**, d. David, Nov. 18, 1762	1	25
Job, Jr., s. Eben[eze]r, Jr. & Mary, b. May 10, 1767	1	25
Job, m. 2nd w. Abigail **STARR**, wid. of Daniell, Jr. & d. Wakefield **DIBBLE**, of Danbury, Nov. 7, 1774	1	25
Job, s. Eben[eze]r, m. Elizabeth **SCUDDER**, d. Isaac, of Norwalk, Aug. 27, 1776	1	281
John, s. [John], b. Feb. 23, 1690/1	LR-A2	676
John, his d. [ ], b. May 10, 1692	LR-A2	676
John, s. John, b. Jan. 9, 1693/4	LR-A2	676
John, s. David & Mabel, b. Oct. 17, 1731	1	240
John, s. David, m. Charity **BULKLEY**, d. Dan[ie]ll, Mar. 9, 1757	1	246
John, s. John, b. [ ]	LR-A2	676
Joseph, s. John, b. Aug. 8, 1696	LR-A2	674
Joseph, s. Eben[eze]r & Elizabeth, b. Feb. 21, 1728/9	1	223
Joseph, s. Ebenezer, m. Rebecca **SQUIER**, d. Sam[ue]ll, Nov. 7, 1754	1	234
Mabel, d. John & Charity, b. Oct. 15, 1757	1	246
Mary B., m. William H. **NICHOLS**, July 16, 1822, by Rev. Nathan[ie]ll Hewit	1-M	8
Paul, s. David & Mabel, b. Oct. 12, 1736	1	240
Sarah, d. John, m. Joseph **RUMSEY**, s. Robert, Aug. 16, 1738	1	178
Sarah, [twin with Elizabeth], d. David & Mabel, b. Sept. 6, 1743	1	240
BATES, Elias, m. Sarah **PLATT**, Jan. 17, 1734	1	148
Ezra, s. John & Esther, b. July 20, 1753; d. Mar. 15, 1754	1	211
John, s. Nicholas, m. Esther **BANKS**, d. Tho[ma]s, June 11, 1752	1	211
Justus, s. Elias & Sarah, b. Feb. 5, 1736; d. Feb. 8, [1736]	1	148
Justus, s. Elias & Sarah, b. July 20, 1737	1	148
Martha, d. Elias & Sarah, b. July 20, 1739	1	148
Mary, d. John & Esther, b. Mar. 14, 1755	1	211
Ruth, d. John & Esther, b. Nov. 1, 1757	1	211
Sarah, d. Elias & Sarah, b. Nov. 7, 1741	1	148
BATTERSON, Anna, m. Boaz **TILTON**, May 27, 1832, by T. F. Davis	1-M	44
George, m. Elizabeth **OYSTERBANKS**, Dec. 1, 1752	1	215
Naomi, d. George & Elizabeth, b. Mar. 19, 1753	1	215
W[illia]m, m. Abigail H. **BAKER**, June 11, 1821, by Hezekiah Ripley, V.D.M.	1-M	4
BEACH, BEECH, Charity, m. Jabez **WHEELER**, Dec. 9, 1742	1	117
David, of Trumbull, m. Ruth **BULKLEY**, of Fairfield, [Mar.] 18, [1832], by Rev. Charles Smith	1-M	44
Lazarus, s. John, m. Lydea **SANFORD**, June 20, 1756	1	63
Lucy, d. John & Sarah, b. Oct. 8, 1746	1	63
Phebe, d. John, m. Daniel **HILL**, s. W[illia]m, Oct. 31, 1748	1	93

	Vol.	Page
BEACH, BEECH (cont.)		
Sheldon, of Bridgeport, m. Miranda **SUMMERS**, of		
Fairfield, Apr. 26, 1837, by Lyman H. Atwater	1-M	62
BEADLE, Ansell Lathrop, s. W[illia]m & Lydia, b. Feb. 2,		
1771	1	273
William, s. Samuel, of the Points of Great Bursted,		
County of Essex, England, m. Lydia **LATHROP**, d.		
Ansell, of Plimouth, Apr. 15, 1770	1	273
BEARDSLEY, BEARDSLEE, Dan[ie]ll, s. Jesse & Ruth, b.		
Oct. 16, 1761	1	268
Jesse, s. W[illia]m, m. Ruth **LYON**, d. Daniel, Jr., Nov.		
26, 1760	1	268
Obadiah, m. Esther J. **BENSON**, b. of Fairfield, July 24,		
1831, by Rev. John Blatchford	1-M	42-3
BEBBENS, [see under **BIBBINS**]		
BEDIENT, Adoniram, twin with Azariah, s. John & Mary, b.		
Apr. 9, 1734	1	220
Azariah, twin with Adoniram, s. John & Mary, b. Apr. 9,		
1734	1	220
Azariah, s. John, m. Phebe **HOLLEBERT**, Mar. 28, 1756	1	200
Elizabeth, d. John & Mary, b. Oct. 30, 1731	1	220
Elizabeth, d. John, m. Luke **GUYSE**, s. Luke, Apr. 14,		
1757	1	110
Eunice, d. John & Mary, b. Mar. 9, 1740	1	220
Gilead, s. John & Mary, b. Jan [ ], 1743	1	220
Jesse, s. John & Mary, b. Jan. 13, 1745	1	220
John, m. Mary **MOR[E]HOUSE**, May 28, 1723	1	220
John, s. John & Mary, b. June 4, 1730	1	220
Mardica, s. John & Mary, b. Oct. 7, 1737	1	220
Mary, d. John & Mary, b. Feb. 23, 1727	1	220
Thomas, s. John & Mary, b. Nov. 11, 1724	1	220
BEEBEE, James, s. James, b. Dec. 29, 1677	LR-A2	683
Joseph, s. James, b. July 11, 1679	LR-A2	683
Rebecca, d. Ralph, m. Beniamin **TURNEY**, Nov. 16,		
1671	LR-A2	683
[BEECHER], BEACHER, Elizabeth, m. John **CLINTON**,		
Nov. [ ], 1746	1	201
BEERS, Aaron, s. David & Mary, b. Aug. 14, 1750	1	94
Abell, s. David & Mary, b. May 18, 1748	1	94
Abigail, d. Joseph, b. Apr. 24, 1662	LR-A2	674
Abigail, d. Joseph & Hannah, b. Oct. 11, 1721	1	93
Abigail, d. James & Olive, b. Apr. 2 1731	1	95
Abigail, m. Abram **PULLING,** Nov. 10, 1743	1	101
Abigail, m. Peter **BLACKMAN**, Oct. 18, 1746	1	225
Abigail, d. Joseph & Elizabeth, b. Apr. 24, 1747	1	94
Abigail, d. Nathan & Ann, b. Dec. 20, 1754	1	173
Abigail, m. James **HALL**, Apr. 3, 1755	1	54
Ann, d. Nathan & Ann, b. Nov. 17, 1756	1	173
Augustine P., m. Catharine **MILLS,*** b. of Fairfield,		
Dec. 30, 1828, by John Hunter *(MILK?)	1-M	32
Daniel, s. Sam[ue]ll & Thankfull, b. July 22, 1753	1	95
Dan[ie]ll, s. Ephraim, m. Abigail **DICKMAN**, d.		
Cor[neliu]s (?), Sept. 3, 1760	1	260

	Vol.	Page
BEERS (cont.)		
David, s. Joseph & Hannah, b. Apr. 27, 1717	1	93
David, s. Joseph, m. Mary **LIVESAY**, Nov. 10, 1743	1	94
David, s. David & Mary, b. Mar. 17, 1746	1	94
David, s. Eph[rai]m & Mary, b. Apr. 27, 1756	1	164
David, m. Mabel **PERRY**, b. of Fairfield, Sept. 21, 1834, by Nath[anie]l E. Cornwell	1-M	54
Elizabeth, d. Joseph & Elizabeth, b. Apr. 28, 1752	1	94
Elizabeth, of Fairfield, m. John M. **PHILLIPS**, of Newark, N.J., July 3, 1848, by Rev. J. H. Perry	1-M	90
Ellen, d. Eph[rai]m & Mary, b. Feb. 11, 1764	1	164
Ephraim, s. Ephraim, m. Mary **FANTON**, d. Jonathan, Dec. 24, 1745	1	164
Ephraim, s. Ephraim & Mary, b. Dec. 23, 1748	1	164
Esther, d. Nathan & Ann, b. Apr. 24, 1753	1	173
Eunice, d. David & Mary, b. Aug. 14, 1744	1	94
Eunice, d. Nehemiah & Eunice, b. Apr. 15, 1760; d. June 22, 1781	1	228
Ezra, s. Eph[rai]m & Mary, b. Aug. 15, 1761	1	164
Fanton, s. Nehemiah & Eunice, b. Jan. 11, 1756	1	228
Hannah, d. James & Olive, b. June 8, 1726	1	95
Hannah, d. Lieut. James, m. Nath[anie]ll **PIERSON**, Oct. 14, 1746	1	58
Hannah, d. Nehemiah & Eunice, b. Feb. 24, 1769	1	228
Hannah, w. James, d. Mar. 17, [ ]	1	95
Hezekiah, s. Ephraim & Mary, b. Apr. 16, 1754	1	164
Huldah, d. Dan[ie]ll & Abigail, b. Sept. 12, 1761	1	260
Isaac, s. Nehemiah & Eunice, b. Feb. 20, 1758	1	228
Isabel, d. Joseph & Elizabeth, b. July 14, 1745	1	94
Isabel, d. Joseph, Jr., m. Ansel **TRUBEE**, s. Andrew, Nov. [ ], 1769	1	138
James, m. Hannah **RAMSEY**, Jan. 20, 1716	1	95
James, m. 2nd, w. Olive **BULKLEY**, Aug. 5, 1725	1	95
James, s. James & Olive, b. July 4, 1728	1	95
James, d. Apr. 29, 1772	1	95
James, m. Eliza **SHERWOOD**, b. of Fairfield, July 11, 1842, by N. E. Cornwall	1-M	74
James, s. Joseph, b. [ ]	LR-A2	674
Jonathan, s. Ephraim & Mary, b. Dec. 22, 1746	1	164
Jonathan, of Bridgeport, m. Mary F. **NICHOLS**, of Fairfield, Sept. 13, 1847 by Rev. Lyman H. Atwater	1-M	87
Joseph, s. Joseph, b. Mar. 18, 1688/9	LR-A2	674
Joseph, m. Hannah **WHITLOCK**, Mar. 1, 1711	1	93
Joseph, s. Joseph & Hannah, b. Dec. 19, 1711	1	93
Joseph, Jr., s. Joseph, m. Elizabeth **LIVESAY**, Sept. 21, 1738	1	94
Joseph, s. Joseph & Elizabeth, b. May 28, 1754	1	94
Julia Maria, d. Thomas P., m. Ebenezer **BURR**, Jr., b. of Fairfield, Nov. 22, 1846, by Rev. N. E. Cornwall	1-M	86
Louis, d. Eph[rai]m & Mary, b. Jan. 12, 1759	1	164
Mary, d. James & Hannah, b. Nov. 29, 1722	1	95
Mary, d. James, m. Daniel **STURGIS**, s. Peter, Nov. 5, 1741	1	145

	Vol.	Page
BEERS (cont.)		
Mary, d. Sam[ue]ll & Thankfull, b. July 15, 1748	1	95
Mary, d. Ephraim & Mary, b. Aug. 16, 1751	1	164
Mary, d. David & Mary, b. July 9, 1754	1	94
Mehetabel P., m. George **OGDEN**, b. of Fairfield, [Oct.] 16, [1832], by Rev. Charles Smith	1-M	47
Munson H., m. Sarah A. **MEEKER**, b. of Fairfield, Apr. 23, 1826, by Nath[anie]ll Hewit	1-M	23
Nathan, s. James & Olive, b. Oct. 6, 1734	1	95
Nathan, s. Eph[rai]m, m. Ann **BURR**, d. Peter, Jan. 16, 1750	1	173
Nathan, s. James, m. Abigail **SQUIER**, wid. July 22, 1756	1	127
Nathan, s. Nathan & Abigail, b. June 3, 1757	1	127
Nehemiah, m. Eunice **FANTON**, June 27, 1753	1	228
Nehemiah, s. Nehemiah & Eunice, b. Dec. 23, 1771;d. Mar. 13, 1775	1	228
Nehemiah, s. Nehemiah & Eunice, b. July 11, 1781	1	228
Olive, wid. James, d. Oct. 5, 1774	1	95
Pinkney, s. Nathan & Ann, b. Nov. 8, 1751	1	173
Rachel, d. Nehemiah & Eunice, b. Aug. 12, 1778	1	228
Rebecca of Bridgeport, m. Bronson **HAWLEY**, May 7, 1826, by Rev. H. R. Judah, of Bridgeport	1-M	28
Reuben, s. Joseph & Elizabeth, b. Nov. 21, 1739	1	94
Rhoda, d. Nehemiah & Eunice, b. Apr. 27, 1762	1	228
Sally, of Fairfield, m. John **PLUMB**, of Bridgeport, Dec. 25, 1826, by William Shelton	1-M	26-7
Samuel, s. James & Hannah, b. June 2, 1708	1	95
Samuel, s. James, m. Thankfull **OSBORN**, d. John, Nov. 10, 1743	1	95
Samuel, s. Sam[ue]ll & Thankfull, b. Sept. 4, 1744	1	95
Sarah, d. Joseph & Hannah, b. Nov. 12, 1714	1	93
Sarah, d. Eph[rai]m, m. Ebenezer **GUYSE**, s. Luke, Apr. 20, 1742	1	209
Sarah, d. Joseph & Elizabeth, b. Sept. 19, 1743	1	94
Sarah, d. Nehemiah & Eunice, b. Feb. 3, 1754	1	228
Sarah D., m. Josiah **BALDWIN**, May 11, 1831, by Rev. John H. Hunter	1-M	41
Uriah, s. Nehemiah & Eunice, b. July 20, 1764	1	228
William, m. Jane Eliza **BOOTH**, b. of Fairfield, Nov. 21, 1847, by Rev. N. E. Cornwall	1-M	88
Zillah, d. Nehemiah & Eunice, b. Oct. 23, 1766	1	228
BELL, John, m. Elizabeth **HIDE**, d. Dr. [ ], June 10, 1736	1	57
BENEDICT, Cornelius, of Bridgeport, m. Harriet E. **WELLS**, of Black Rock, [Dec.] 14, [1845], by Rev. Cha[rle]s R. Adams	1-M	83
George, W., Prof. of Burlington, Vt. , m. Mrs. Ebeline **KELLOGG**, of West Stockbridge, Mass., Aug. 8, 1842, by Rev. Lyman H. Atwater	1-M	74
Henderson, of Huntington, m. Eliza **ROBINSON**, of Fairfield, June 4, 1851, by Rev. Lyman H. Atwater	1-M	93

	Vol.	Page

BENEDICT (cont.)

Joseph S., of Ridgefield, m. Deborah **DISBROW**, of
Greens Farms, June 30, 1824, by Hez[ekiah] Ripley,
V.D.M.   1-M   15

BENHAM, Elias P., m. Rachel M. **DIMON**, b. of Fairfield,
Sept. 16, 1835, by Lyman H. Atwater   1-M   57

BENNET, BENNIT, BENNITT, BENNET, Abigail, d.
W[illia]m & Abigail, b. Dec. 30, 1749   1   139

Adaline, of Fairfield, m. William H. **CHAPMAN**, of
New York, Sept. 15, 1834, by Rev. C. A. Boardman,
of Saugatuck   1-M   54

Alethea, of Greens Farms, m. Edwin **HURLBAULT**, of
Norwalk, Apr. 15, 1827, by Rev. E. W. Hooker   1-M   26-7

Alman, [twin with Amos] negro, b. July 20, 1797   1   298

Amos, [twin with Alman] negro, b. July 20, 1797   1   298

Andrew, s. Nathan & Hannah, b. Mar. 11, 1750   1   161

Ann, d. W[illia]m & Hannah, b. Nov. [ ], 1738   1   117

Ann, [d. Joseph], b. Apr. 17, 1791   1   297

Anna D., of Fairfield, m. W[illia]m F. **CROFUT**, of
Norwalk, Nov. 11, 1840, by Rev. Cyrus Silliman   1-M   70

Beel, of Weston, m. Anna **DAVIS**, of Green Farms, Sept.
17, 1820, by Hezekiah Ripley, V.D.M.   1-M   2

Benjamin, s. Deliverance & Mary, b. July 2, 1721   1   141

Damaries, d. W[illia]m & Hannah, b. Dec. 15, 1741   1   117

Damaris, d. Dea. William, m. Francis **JACKSON**, s.
Gabriel, Aug. 24, 1758   1   258

Daniel, s. Deliverance & Mary, b. Nov. 11, 1711   1   141

Daniel, s. W[illia]m & Hannah, b. Apr. 26, 1732   1   117

Daniel, s. Nathan & Hannah, b. Apr. 1, 1754   1   161

Deborah, d. John, m. Ebenezer **ALLEN**, s. Gideon, Nov.
12, 1731   1   160

Deliverance, m. Mary **BIGGS**, Mar. 15, 1708   1   141

Deliverance, d. W[illia]m & Abigail, b. Feb. 27, 1738   1   139

Edward, m. Mary Burr **STURGIS**, b. of Fairfield, Oct.
18, 1820, by Nath[anie]l Hewit, V.D.M.   1-M   3

Elias, s. Nathan & Hannah, b. May 10, 1752   1   161

Eunice, d. Deliverance & Mary, b. Oct. 24, 1718   1   141

Eunice, d. W[illia]m & Hannah, b. Dec. 17, 1734   1   117

Eunice, d. Moses & Eunice, b. Jan. 21, 1751   1   142

Hannah, d. Thomas, b. Aug. 20, 1680   LR-A2   683

Hannah, d. Tho[ma]s & Mary, b. Oct. [ ], 1721   1   123

Hannah, d. Tho[ma]s, m. Humphrey **OGDEN**, Nov. 22,
1743   1   164

Hannah, w. William, d. Nov. 27, 1743   1   117

Hannah, d. W[illia]m & Katherine, b. Dec. 11, 1745   1   117

Hannah, d. Moses & Eunice, b. Aug. 11, 1756   1   142

Henry, m. Susan **MOREHOUSE**, b. of Fairfield, June 10,
1844; by Rev. Lyman H. Atwater   1-M   77

Hezekiah, s. Nathan & Hannah, b. Apr. 7, 1756   1   161

Ire, negro b. May 26, 1795   1   298

James, s. Thomas, b. Aug. 6, 1675   LR-A2   663

James, s. Tho[ma]s & Mercy, b. July 15, 1743   1   123

	Vol.	Page
BENNET, BENNIT, BENNITT, BENNET (cont.)		
James, s. Thomas, m. Sarah **READ**, d. Tho[ma]s, of		
Norwalk, Apr. 7, 1762	1	254
Joseph, of Stratfield, m. Elizabeth **WHEDDON**, d.		
Richard & Sarah, late of Fairfield, Jan. 22, 1705/6,		
by Rev. Joseph Webb	LR-2	460
Joseph, of Stratfield, m. Elizabeth **WHEDDON**, of		
Fairfield, Jan. 22, 1705/6, by Rev. Joseph Webb	LR-2	460
Joseph, m. Elizabeth **WIDOW**,* b. of Fairfield, Jan. 22,		
1708 *(Probably "**WHEDDON**")	LR-2	459
Joseph, s. W[illia]m & Abigail, b. Sept. 17, 1745	1	139
Joseph S., [s. Joseph], b. Apr. 26, 1787	1	297
Katharine, d. W[illia]m & Katharine, b. Apr. 7, 1751	1	117
Lucretia S. of Fairfield, m. Andrew W. **DeFORREST**, of		
Humphreyville, Oct. 30, 1844, by Rev. Lyman H.		
Atwater	1-M	78-80
Lydea, d. Moses & Eunice, b. Feb. 10, 1749	1	142
Martha, d. Will[ia]m & Katharine, b. Nov. 5, 1747	1	117
Mary, d. Thomas, b. Jonathan **CABLE**, s. John, Sept. 3,		
1728	1	213
Mary, w. Thomas, d. Apr. 17, 1733	1	123
Mary, d. Will[ia]m & Katharine, b. Aug. 6, 1749	1	117
Mary, d. W[illia]m & Abigail, b. Aug. 25, 1743; d. Oct. 4,		
1754	1	139
Mary, m. Abraham**SHERWOOD**, [1], 1829, by Rev.		
Thomas F. Davis	1-M	37
Mary S., m. Robert **PERRY**, b. of Fairfield, Nov. 10,		
1841, by Rev. Lyman H. Atwater	1-M	72
Mercy, d. W[illia]m & Katharine, b. Jan. 1, 1753	1	117
Molley, d. Moses & Eunice, b. June 5, 1747	1	142
Moses, s. Deliverance & Mary, b. Apr. 8, 1727	1	141
Moses, s. Deliverance, m. Eunice **HOLLIBERT**, d.		
Gideon, June 17, 1746	1	142
Moses, s. Moses & Eunice, b. Apr. 12, 1754	1	142
Nabby, [d. Joseph], b. Dec. 23, 1793	1	297
Nathan, d. Tho[ma]s & Mary, b. Mar. 4, 1725	1	123
Nathan, m. Hannah **STURGIS**, d. John, June 17, 1746	1	161
Nathan, s. Nathan & Hannah, b. Mar. 30, 1747	1	161
Phillis, m. David **SMITH**, b. of Fairfield (colored), June		
29, [1823], by Rev. E. W. Hooker	1-M	11
Rachel, d. John, b. Mar. [ ], 1702; m. Joseph **ALLEN**, s.		
Gideon, Mar. 26, 1724	1	155
Rachel, d. Deliverance & Mary, b. Oct. 11, 1729	1	141
Rebecca, d. Will[ia]m & Hannah, b. Jan. 14, 1736/7	1	117
Sally Read, m. Alpha **TAYLOR**, b. of Greens Farms, Jan.		
28, 1823, by Rev. E. W. Hooker	1-M	10
Samuel, s. Deliverance & Mary, b. Aug. 24, 1723	1	141
Sarah, d. Deliverance & Mary, b. Apr. 8, 1716	1	141
Sarah, d. W[illia]m & Abigail, b. Mar. 17, 1734	1	139
Sarah, d. Deliverance, m. John **ALLEN**, Mar. 23, 1739	1	157
Sarah, d. W[illia]m, m. Jabez **LOCKWOOD**, s. John,		
Oct. 17, 1754	1	235

	Vol.	Page
BENNET, BENNIT, BENNITT, BENNET (cont.)		
Sarah, m. Selleck **BURR**, b. of Greens Farms, May 29,		
1825, by Hez[ekia]h Ripley, V.D.M.	1-M	22
Stephen, s. W[illia]m & Abigail, b. Dec. 18, 1747	1	139
Stephen, [s. Joseph], b. Nov. 11, 1799	1	297
Tabitha, d. Tho[ma]s & Mary, b. Apr. [ ], 1718	1	123
Thaddeus, d. [sic] W[illia]m & Abigail, b. June 22, 1736	1	139
Thomas, m. Mary **ROWLAND**, Mar. 17, 1717	1	123
Thomas, s. Tho[ma]s & Mary, b. Mar. 8, 1727	1	123
Thomas, m. 2nd w. Mercy **SCOFIELD**, Oct. 14, 1741	1	123
Thomas, Jr., s. Thomas, m. Mary **COUCH**, d. Sam[ue]ll,		
Apr. 1, 1754	1	122
Thomas B., [s. Joseph], b. July 24, 1789	1	297
William, s. Deliverance & Mary, b. Jan. 8, 1708 [sic]	1	141
William, s. Isaac, m. Hannah **SEELEY**, d. James, July		
26, 1731	1	117
William, m. Abigail **HIECOCK**, d. Benj[amin], Aug. [ ],		
1733	1	139
William, s. W[illia]m & Abigail, b. July 5, 1741	1	139
William, s. W[illia]m & Hannah, b. Nov. 11, 1743; d.		
May 12, 1744	1	117
William, m. 2nd w. Katharine **HAWLEY**, d. Thomas,		
Dec. 3, 1744	1	117
William, s. W[illia]m & Katharine, b. Aug. 29, 1756; d.		
Sept. 15, 1757	1	117
William Ward, negro b. June 26, 1793	1	298
BENSON, Esther, J., m. Obadiah **BEARDSLEY**, b. of		
Fairfield, July 24, 1831, by Rev. John Blatchford	1-M	42-3
BERLIN, Melinda, of Patterson, N.Y., m. Boston **SMEDLEY**,		
of Fairfield, (colored), Dec. 5, 1824, by Nath[anie]l		
Hewit	1-M	16
BETTS, Hannah, m. Peter **FAIRCHILD**, Nov. 7, 1751	1	99
Mary, d. Stephen, m. Daniel **HULL**, s. Ebenezer, Nov. 2,		
1748	1	125
Mary H.F., of Fairfield, m. John H. **LEWIS**, of		
Huntsville, Ala., Nov. 21, 1824, by Rev. Nath[anie]l		
Hewit	1-M	16
BIBBINS, BEBBENS, Billy, m. Sarah **MOREHOUSE**, b. of		
Fairfield, Dec. 11, 1825, by Nath[anie]l Hewit	1-M	21
Elijah, s. Israel & Hannah, b. Aug. 25, 1770	1	34
Elijah, m. Eunice Burr **ELLIOT**, b. of Fairfield, Feb. 26,		
1821, by Nath[anie]l Hewit, V.D.M.	1-M	3
Israel, s. Arter, of Windham, m. Hannah **SILLEMAN**, d.		
Capt. Nath[anie]l, Nov. 9, 1769	1	34
Mary, of Fairfield, m. Charles **FRENCH**, of Trumbull,		
May 13, 1850, by Rev. Lyman H. Atwater	1-M	92
Seeley, of Fairfield, m. Ann Eliza **HILL**, of Greenfield,		
Dec. 29, 1841, by Rev. Lyman H. Atwater	1-M	73
BIGGS, Mary, m. Deliverance **BENNIT**, Mar. 15, 1708	1	141
BINGHAM, Abel, m. Elizabeth **ODELL**, May 10, 1694	LR-A2	674
Abigaile, d. Abel, b. June 7, 1695	LR-A2	674
BIXBY, [see also **HAXBEY**], Daniel, [twin with John], s.		
Jon[a]th[an] & Martha, b. May 15, 1757	1	212

	Vol.	Page
BIXBY (cont.)		
John, [twin with Daniel], s. Jon[a]th[an] & Martha, b. May 15, 1757	1	212
Jonathan, s. Elias, m. Martha **HULL**, d. George, July 4, 1752	1	212
Lydea, d. Jon[a]th[an] & Martha, b. Feb. 19, 1753	1	212
Sarah, d. Jon[a]th[an] & Martha, b. Feb. 9, 1755	1	212
BLACKLEACH, Sarah, m. Edward **JESSUP**, Dec. 7, 1724	1	194
BLACKMAN, [see also **BLAKEMAN**], Eunice, d. Peter & Abigail, b. June 10, 1747	1	225
George, m. Eliza **RICHMOND**, b. of Fairfield, Mar. 24, 1834, by Rev. C. A. Boardman, of Saugatuck	1-M	52
John, s. Peter & Abigail, b. July 15, 1749	1	225
Julia, m. Airldon **GOULD**, b. of Fairfield, Apr. 6, 1847, by Rev. James Scott, of Stratfield	1-M	86
Martha, b. Oct. [ ], 1708; m. Ephraim **JACKSON**, June [ ], 1730	1	73
Nabbe, d. Peter & Abigail, b. Feb. 16, 1755	1	225
Peter, m. Abigail **BEERS**, Oct. 18, 1746	1	225
Rebecca, m. William **JACOBS**, Jan. 25, 1735	1	173
BLAKEMAN, [see also **BLACKMAN**], Charles C., s. Eli, b. Mar. 31, 1822	1	273
Edwards, of Fairfield, m. Mrs. Rebecca **GILBERT**, of Sherman, Nov. 10, 1844, by Rev. James Scott, of Stratfield	1-M	78-9-80
Mary, of Fairfield, m. Levi B. **STILLSON**, of Weston, Dec. 25, 1835, by Rev. William Denison	1-M	58
Susan, of Fairfield, m. Benjamin W. **WARD**, of Weston, Jan. [ ], 1837, by Rev. Enoch E. Chase, of Stratfield	1-M	61
BOOTH, Abner, s. Nath[anie]ll & Mary, b. Feb. 25, 1745/6	1	90
David H., of Bridgeport, m. Anna Eliza **GOULD**, d. Abram, decd., of Fairfield, Oct. 24, 1849, by Rev. N. E. Cornwall	1-M	94
Eunice, d. Joseph, m. John **BURR**, s. Capt. John, Apr. 1, 1750	1	126
Eunice, d. Nath[anie]ll & Mary, b. Jan. 27, 1751	1	90
Hannah, m. Nath[anie]l **SILLEMAN**, May 2, 1723	1	15
Jane Eliza, m. William **BEERS**, b. of Fairfield, Nov. 21, 1847, by Rev. N. E. Cornwall	1-M	88
Mary, d. Nath[anie]ll & Mary, b. Sept. 23, 1742	1	90
Nathaniel, m. Mary **FOOT**, Oct. 4, 1739	1	90
Nath[anie]ll, s. Nath[anie]ll & Mary, b. May 22, 1755	1	90
Sarah, d. Nath[anie]ll & Mary, b. Feb. 24, 1748/9	1	90
Solomon, s. Nath[anie]ll & Mary, b. Oct. 13, 1740	1	90
BOSTWICK, Abigail, d. Sam[ue]ll & Sarah, b. Sept. 25, 1761	1	246
Abigail, d. Sam[ue]ll & Sarah, b. Sept. 25, 1761	1	276
David, s. Sam[ue]ll & Sarah, b. Sept. 27, 1763	1	246
David, s. Sam[ue]ll & Sarah, b. Sept. 27, 1763	1	276
Elizabeth, d. Sam[ue]ll & Sarah, b. Jan. 8, 1758	1	246
Elizabeth, d. Sam[ue]ll & Sarah, b. Jan. 8, 1758	1	276
Esther, d. Sam[ue]ll & Sarah, b. Aug. 20, 1756	1	246
Esther, d. Sam[ue]ll & Sarah, b. Aug. 20, 1756	1	276

	Vol.	Page
BOSTWICK (cont.)		
Henry, s. Sam[ue]ll & Sarah, b. Nov. 28, 1767	1	246
Henry, s. Sam[ue]ll & Sarah, b. Nov. 28, 1767	1	276
Sam[ue]ll, s. David, m. Sarah **JENNINGS**, d. Isaac, Mar.		
[ ], 1756	1	246
Samuel, s. David, m. Sarah **JENNINGS**, d. Isaac, Mar.		
[ ], 1756	1	276
Sarah, d. Sam[ue]ll & Sarah, b. Aug. 14, 1759	1	246
Sarah, d. Sam[ue]ll & Sarah, b. Aug. 14, 1759	1	276
William, s. Sam[ue]ll & Sarah, b. Feb. 27, 1771	1	246
William, s. Sam[ue]ll & Sarah, b. Feb. 27, 1771	1	276
BRADLEY, Abigail, m. Solomon **STURGES**, Mar. 3, 1725	1	102
Abigail, d. Dan[ie]ll & Esther, b. Apr. 25, 1725	1	81
Abigail, d. Francis & Mary, b. May 20, 1737	1	82
Abigail, d. Francis & Ruth, b. Mar. 24, 1757	1	158
Ann, d. Joseph & Mary, b. Jan. 11, 1747/8	1	57
Asa, s. Onessimus & Emitt, b. June 26, 1756	1	144
Benjamin, s. Joseph & Olive, b. Apr. 1, 1749	1	144
Bette, d. David & Damaries, b. July 9, 1753	1	77
Charry A., m. Rufus **NICHOLS**, b. of Fairfield, July 2,		
1839, by N. E. Cornwall	1-M	67
Damaries, d. David & Damaries, b. Dec. 2, 1742	1	77
Daniel, m. Esther **BURR**, June [ ], 1724	1	81
Dan[ie]ll, s. Dan[ie]ll & Esther, b. May 20, 1729	1	81
Daniel, m. 2nd, w. Mary **FITCH**, Mar. [ ] 1743	1	81
Dan[ie]ll, m. 3rd, w. Sarah **BRADLEY**, Mar. [ ], 1749	1	81
David, m. Damaris **DAVIS**, Apr. 25, 1731	1	77
David, s. David & Damaries, b. Sept. 12, 1740	1	77
Ebenezer, s. Francis & Mary, b. Oct. 5, 1723	1	82
Ellenor, m. Benjamin **SHERWOOD**, Feb. 9, 1723	1	192
Eleanor, d. Francis & Mary, b. Oct. 7, 1725	1	82
Eleanor, of Fairfield, m. Isaac **COLEY**, of Redding, Nov.		
21, [1821], by Rev. E. W. Hooker	1-M	6
Elisha, s. Joseph & Jerusha, b. May 20, 1745	1	57
Elizabeth, d. Francis & Mary, b. Aug. 30, 1721	1	82
Elizabeth, m. John **BANKS**, May 14, 1740	1	219
Elizabeth, d. Dan[ie]ll & Esther, b. Dec. 22, 1741	1	81
Ellen, d. David & Damaries, b. June 16, 1736	1	77
Ellen, m. Benjamin **BANKS**, June 20, 1744	1	236
Elnathan, s. Francis & Mary, b. Jan. 21, 1729/30	1	82
Esther, m. Sam[ue]l **GOLD**, Dec. 7, 1716	1	13
Esther, d. Dan[ie]ll & Esther, b. Mar. 30, 1733	1	81
Esther, w. Dan[ie]ll, d. Dec. [ ], 1741	1	81
Esther, d. Francis, m. John **WAKEMAN**, Jr., s. John,		
Oct. 3, 1754	1	120
Esther, m. Ezekiel O. **BANKS**, Oct. 1, 1826, by William		
Shelton	1-M	24
Eunice, d. Dan[ie]ll, m. Samuel **BARLOW**, s. Sam[ue]ll,		
Aug. 2, 1731	1	105
Eunice, d. Joseph & Olive, b. Jan. 2, 1732	1	144
Eunice, d. David & Damaries, b. Mar. 15, 1732	1	77
Eunice, d. Dan[ie]ll & Sarah, b. July 22, 1752	1	81

	Vol.	Page
BRADLEY (cont.)		
Eunice, d. David, m. John **HENDRICK**, Jr., s. John, Nov. 13, 1753	1	159
Francis, b. May 29, 1699; m. Mary **STURGIS**, d. John, Apr. 29, 1719	1	82
Francis, s. Francis & Mary, b. Jan. 11, 1727/8	1	82
Francis, s. Francis, m. Ruth **HULL**, d. Eliphalet, Feb. 20, 1750	1	158
Francis, s. Francis & Ruth, b. Oct. 25, 1753	1	158
George, m. Eliza **OSBORN**, b. of Fairfield, Apr. 16, 1828, by William Shelton	1-M	31
Gershom, m. Jane **DIMON**, d. Moses, Dec. [ ]	1	116
Hannah, d. John, m. Gershom **BANKS**, Oct. 14, 1743; d. Oct. 14, 1749	1	127
Hester, d. Francis & Mary, b. Sept. 2, 1735	1	82
Hezekiah, s. Sam[ue]ll & Sarah, b. July 28, 1735	1	·70
Hezekiah, s. Samuel, m. Abigail **SHERWOOD**, d. Samuel, Jan. 1, 1756	1	111
Hezekiah, s. Hezekiah & Abigail, b. June 23, 1757	1	111
Hezekiah, had negroes Diana, b. Mar. 13, 1790 & Ire, b. Dec. 14, 1792	1	464
Huldah, d. Sam[ue]ll & Sarah, b. Jan. 22, 1741	1	70
Increase, s. Joseph & Jerusha, b. May 29, 1736	1	57
Isaac, s. Joseph & Olive, b. Jan. 15, 1738	1	144
Jabez, s. Dan[ie]ll & Esther, b. Feb. 20, 1726/7	1	81
Jane, d. Francis & Mary, b. [ ] 21, 1733	1	82
Jane, d. Francis, m. Increase **BURR**, s. Joseph, Jan. 3, 1753	1	82
Jerusha, d. Joseph & Jerusha, b. Apr. 19, 1739	1	57
Jerusha, w. Joseph, d. Jan. 16, 1746/7	1	57
Joseph, m. Olive **HUBBEL**, June 20, 1724	1	144
Joseph, Jr., m. Jerusha **TURNEY**, d. Robert, Nov. 9, 1732	1	57
Joseph, s. Joseph & Olive, b. Oct. 22, 1736	1	144
Joseph, Jr., m. Mary **SQUIRE**, d. Dr. Sam[ue]ll, Apr. 11, 1747	1	57
Justus, d. David & Damaries, b. Mar. 7, 1734; d. Feb. 1, 1745/6	1	77
Justus, s. David & Damaries, b. Oct. 22, 1745	1	77
Legrand, m. Mary **MOREHOUSE**, b. of Fairfield, July 10, 1823, by Hez[ekia]h Ripley, V.D.M.	1-M	11
Lois, m. Joseph **GILBERT**, s. John, Oct. 3, 1744	1	107
Mabel, d. Sam[ue]ll & Sarah, b. May 5, 1729	1	70
Mable, d. Joseph & Mary, b. Mar. 30, 1753	1	57
Martha, d. Joseph & Olive, b. Sept. 2, 1737	1	144
Mary, d. Ffrancis, b. Dec. 5, 1677	LR-A2	664
Mary, d. Francis & Mary, b. Sept. 13, 1719; d. Apr. 24, 1741	1	82
Mary, d. Joseph & Jerusha, b. June 21, 1733	1	57
Mary, d. Francis, m. Gershom **BANKS**, s. Benjamin, May [ ], 1739; d. May [ ], 1741	1	127
Mary, w. Dan[ie]ll, d. Dec. [ ],1747	1	81
Mary, d. David & Damaries, b. [ ] 28, 1750	1	77
Mary, d. Francis & Ruth, b. May 11, 1751	1	158

	Vol.	Page
BRADLEY (cont.)		
Mary, m. Gershom **HUBBEL**, May 2, 1754; d. Feb. 23,		
1756	1	38
Mary, d. Joseph & Mary, b. Feb. 6, 1757	1	57
Naomi, d. Joseph & Mary, b. Nov. 22, 1749	1	57
Nathan, s. Joseph & Olive, b. July 20, 1740	1	144
Nathan, s. David & Damaries, b. Feb. 5, 1747/8	1	77
Nehemiah, s. Francis & Mary, b. May 20, 1737; d. May		
22, 1737	1	82
Olive, d. David & Damaries, b. Sept. 21, 1738	1	77
Onessimus, s. Joseph & Olive, b. July 17, 1730	1	144
Onessmus, s. Joseph, m. Emitt **CABLE**, Aug. 1, 1754	1	144
Peter, s. David & Damaries, b. Apr. 1, 1756	1	77
Philip, s. Dan[ie]ll & Esther, b. Mar. 26, 1738	1	81
Rocky, Mrs., m. Ephraim **MIDDLEBROOKS**, Aug. 7,		
1831, by Rev. E. Loomis	1-M	42-3
Ruhanah, d. Dan[ie]ll & Mary, b. July 31, 1745	1	81
Ruth, d. Joseph & Olive, b. Feb. 24, 1734	1	144
Ruth, d. Joseph & Mary, b. July 18, 1751	1	57
Samuel, b. Sept. 29, 1702; m. Sarah **WHELPLEY**, Nov.		
[ ], 1724	1	70
Samuel, s. Samuel & Sarah, b. Jan. 4, 1734	1	70
Samuel, Jr., m. Sarah **WAKEMAN**, Sept. 10, 1751	1	110
Samuel, s. Sam[ue]ll & Sarah, b. Sept. 9, 1757	1	110
Sarah, d. Sam[ue]ll & Sarah, b. Nov. 27, 1726	1	70
Sarah, m. Dan[ie]ll **BRADLEY**, Mar. [ ], 1749	1	81
Sarah, d. Samuel, m. John **READ**, Dec. 19, 1750	1	2
Sarah, d. Joseph & Mary, b. Dec. 17, 1754	1	57
Sarah Ann, m. Edward **PACOCK**, May 4, 1834, by Rev.		
David L. Ogden	1-M	52
Seth M., m. Mary **OGDEN**, July 16, 1835, by Rev. T. F.		
Davis	1-M	56
Stephen, s. Dan[ie]ll & Esther, b. Dec. 14, 1734	1	81
Stephen, m. Lucy **ODELL**, of Greenfield, July 10, 1822,		
by Hezekiah Ripley, V.D.M.	1-M	8
Thaddeus, s. Joseph & Olive, b. May 25, 1727	1	144
Thaddeus, s. Francis & Ruth, b. May 14, 1755	1	158
Walter, of Newtown, m. Julia A. **TURNEY**, of Fairfield,		
Sept. 25, 1836, by Lyman H. Atwater	1-M	59
William, Jr., m. Eleanor Maria **NICHOLS**, b. of		
Fairfield, Dec. 25, 1844, by Rev. N. E. Cornwall	1-M	81
Zalmon, s. Sam[ue]ll & Sarah, b. Dec. 31, 1754	1	110
BREWSTER, Ann, [d. Caleb & Anna], b. July 22, 1790	1	292
Benjamin, [s. Caleb & Anna], b. Aug. 17, 1796	1	292
Caleb, m. Anna [ ], Apr. 18, 1784	1	292
Caleb, had negroes Dinah, b. Dec. 12, 1791, York, b. July		
31, 1793 & Charles, b. Dec. 27, 1794	1	463
Jonathan Lewis, [s. Caleb & Anna], b. Nov. 5, 1786	1	292
Lucy A., of Greenfield, m. Geo[rge] B. **KISSAM**, of New		
York, Aug. 8, 1843, by Rev. N. E. Cornwall	1-M	75
Racilia, [child Caleb & Anna], b. Apr. 17, 1794	1	292
Sarah, [d. Caleb & Anna], b. Mar. 5, 1785	1	292
Sturgis, [s. Caleb & Anna], b. Jan. 20, 1789	1	292

	Vol.	Page
BRINMAID, Sarah, m. John **GUYRE**, Nov. 22, 1750	1	68
BROTHERTON, BROTHERTOWN, Abigail, of Greens Farms, m. William **ELWOOD**, of Norwalk, Apr. 11, 1827, by Rev. E. W. Hooker	1-M	26-7
Anson, m. Sarah A. **NICHOLS**, b. of Fairfield, Dec. 31, 1844, by Rev. Lyman H. Atwater	1-M	78-9-80
Betsey, m. Benjamin **GODFREY**, Dec. 28, 1834, by T. F. Davis	1-M	55
David, of Westport, m. Luritta **LYON**, of Fairfield, Mar. 30, 1845, by Rev. Moses Hill	1-M	81
Elizabeth, m. Lewis **SMITH**, b. of Fairfield, July 27, 1842, by Rev. Anson T. Beach	1-M	74
Jerusha, of Fairfield, m. Henry **PARTRICH**, of Norwald (?), [Nov.] 27, [1822], by Rev. E. W. Hooker	1-M	9
Walter, m. Emily **GREGORY**, b. of Fairfield, Mar. 26, 1848, by Rev. Lyman H. Atwater	1-M	89
BROUGHTON, Burr, of Ridgefield, m. Flora **TREADWELL**, of Weston, Apr. 25, 1832, by Tho[ma]s F. Davis	1-M	44
BROWN, Admon, m. Temma **ALLEN**, b. of Greens Farms, Mar. 24, 1826, by Rev. E. W. Hooker	1-M	22
Harry, m. Lorinda **WOOD**, b. of Norfield, Nov. 25, 1821, by Hezekiah Ripley, V.D.M.	1-M	6
Sarah, of Greenfield, m. Isaac Chauncey **GODFREY**, of Fairfield, Nov. 10, 1822, by Nathaniel Hewit	1-M	9
Thomas N., of North Kingston, R. I., m. Amanda **BULKLEY**, of Fairfield, Mar. 1, 1840, by N. E. Cornwall	1-M	69
BRUSH, Charlotte F., of Greens Farms, m. Burr **NOYES**, M.D., of Weston, Oct. 5, 1828, by Rev. E. W. Hooker	1-M	32
BRYAN, Titus, of Washington, m. Harriet **SEELEY**, of Fairfield, Feb. 10, 1836, by W[illia]m Denison, (Rev.)	1-M	58
BULKLEY, BULKELEY, Aaron, s. Peter & Elizabeth, b. Feb. 22, 1748	1	170
Abigail, d. Tho[ma]s, m. John **OSBORN**, s. John, Apr. 15, 1741	1	171
Abigail, d. Peter & Ann, b. Apr. 12, 1743	1	170
Abigail, d. Jonathan & Hannah, b. Aug. 30, 1769	1	262
Abigail, d. Eben[eze]r & Hannah, b. Mar. 16, 1781; d. Apr. 7, 1788	1	278
Abigail, m. Timothy **BULKLEY**, Jan. 23, 1831, by Thomas F. Davis	1-M	39-40
Abraham, s. Peter & Ann, b. June 15, 1755	1	170
Amanda, of Fairfield, m. Thomas N. **BROWN**, of North Kingston, R. I., Mar. 1, 1840, by N. E. Cornwall	1-M	69
Amelia, d. Gershom & Sarah, b. Oct. 19, 1738; d. May 29, 1754	1	233
Andrew, s. Peter & Elizabeth, b. Aug. 27, 1743	1	170
Andrew, 2nd, m. Maria L. **HUBBELL**, b. of Fairfield, Feb. 22, 1844, by Rev. N. E. Cornwall	1-M	76
Ann, d. Hez[ekiah] & Catherine, b. Sept. 15, 1739	1	206

	Vol.	Page
BULKLEY, BULKELEY (cont.)		
Anna, m. Primus **SANFORD**, b. of Fairfield (colored),		
Feb. 10, 1822, by Nath[anie]l Hewit	1-M	7
Catharine, m. Moses **BULKLEY**, b. of Fairfield, Dec. 14,		
1825, by Rev. Nath[anie]l Hewit	1-M	21
Charity, d. Dan[ie]ll, m. John **BARTRAM**, s. David,		
Mar. 9, 1757	1	246
Charles, m. Elizabeth **BURR**, b. of Fairfield, Jan. 4, 1831,		
by Rev. Charles Smith	1-M	39-40
Cloe,* of Southport, m. W[illia]m **KENNEDY**, of		
Southport, Jan. 17, 1836, by Nath[anie]l E.		
Cornwall *(Chloe)	1-M	58
Clarina, m. Joseph B. **OSBORN**, b. of Fairfield, Nov. 22,		
1829, by John Hunter	1-M	37
Deborah, d. Sam[ue]ll & Bulah, b. Jan. 26, 1761	1	119
Deborah, d. Isaac, m. Abel **TURNEY**, s. Stephen, Dec.		
26, 1784	1	287
Ebenezer, s. Joseph, m. Hannah **MALTBIE**, d. Jonathan,		
of Stamford, Dec. 11, 1765	1	278
Eben[eze]r, s. Eben[eze]r & Hannah, b. Nov. 19, 1766	1	278
Eben[eze]r, d. Sept. 22, 1786 ae 54 y. 9 m. 8 d.	1	278
Edward, m. Mary **WILLIAMS** (colored), Mar. 23, 1828,		
by Cha[rle]s G. Lee	1-M	31
Edward Merton, m. Urania **ALVORD**, b. of Southport,		
Nov. 4, 1850, by Rev. Sam[ue]l J. M. Merwin	1-M	90
Edwin, s. [Edwin & Mary], b. Dec. 4, 1737* *(Arnold		
copy has "1837")	1	232
Edwin, of New York, m. Helen **PERRY**, of Southport,		
July 7, 1846, by Samuel J. M. Merwin	1-M	84
Ellenor, d. Peter & Ann, b. July 24, 1759	1	170
Eliza Ann, m. Francis **PERRY**, b. of Fairfield, June 20,		
1831, by Rev. John H. Hunter	1-M	41
Elizabeth, d. Peter & Elizabeth, b. Aug. 27, 1741	1	170
Elizabeth, d. Peter & Ann, b. Dec. 13, 1746	1	170
Elizabeth, w. Peter, d. [ ]	1	170
Emily, of Fairfield, m. Isaac **CHIDSEY**, of Boston, Jan.		
1, 1845, by Rev. N. E. Cornwall	1-M	81
Esther, m. John **HILL**, Jan. 27, 1729	1	61
Esther, d. Capt. Dan[ie]ll, m. Talcott **BULKLEY**, s. Capt.		
Gershom, June 19, 1753	1	54
Esther, d. Talcott & Esther, b. Feb. 6, 1754	1	54
Esther, d. Sam[ue]ll & Bulah, b. Dec. 7, 1755	1	119
Esther, d. Nathan & Sarah, b. Aug. 1, 1763	1	232
Esther, d. Abner & Sarah, b. Aug. 1, 1763	1	283
Esther, d. Nathan, m. David **JUDSON**, s. Abner, of		
Stratford, Nov. 13, 1783, by Rev. Andrew Eliot	1	283
Eunice, d. Peter & Ann, b. Apr. 11, 1753	1	170
Francis, m. Hester **BULKLEY**, b. of Fairfield, Mar. 31,		
1839, by N. E. Cornwall	1-M	67
Frances, m. Mary **NICHOLS**, b. of Southport, June 26,		
1842, by Rev. N. E. Cornwall	1-M	74
George, s. Eben[eze]r & Hannah, b. Aug. 3, 1784	1	278

	Vol.	Page
BULKLEY, BULKELEY (cont.)		
Gershom, s. Gershom, m. Sarah **BANKS**, d. Jos[eph],		
May 17, 1736	1	233
Gershom, s. Peter & Ann, b. May 9, 1748	1	170
Gershom, s. Gershom & Sarah, b. Sept. 19, 1751	1	233
Gershom, s. Peter & Elizabeth, b. Feb. 6, 1753	1	170
Gershom, Capt., d. Apr. 9, 1753	1	36
Gershom B., of Southport, m. Mary Elizabeth		
GRIFFETH, of Danbury, Nov. 9, 1851, by Rev.		
Samuel J. M. Merwin	1-M	93
Grace, d. Gershom, m. John **BURR**, Nov. 9, 1741	1	169
Grace, d. Peter & Ann, b. Apr. 7, 1745	1	170
Hannah, d. Peter, m. Eleazer **OSBORN**, June 29, 1738	1	174
Hannah, d. Dan[ie]ll, m. Benjamin **HAMBLETON**, Apr.		
6, 1754	1	145
Hannah, d. Peter & Hannah, b. Jan. 12, 1761	1	170
Hannah, d. Sam[ue]ll & Bulah, b. Apr. 4, 1763	1	119
Hannah, d. Eben[eze]r & Hannah, b. Oct. 14, 1768	1	278
Hannah, d. Jonathan & Hannah, b. Sept. 1, 1773	1	262
Henretta, m. Samuel **PERRY**, b. of Fairfield, Dec. 4,		
1825, by Nath[anie]l Hewit	1-M	20
Henry Stanley, s. Jonathan & Hannah, b. Mar. 18, 1776	1	262
Hester, m. Francis **BULKLEY**, b. of Fairfield, Mar. 31,		
1839, by N. E. Cornwall	1-M	67
Hezekiah, m. Catharine **HILL**, Jan. 4, 1739	1	206
Hezekiah, s. Hez[ekiah] & Catharine, b. Oct. 17, 1749	1	206
James, s. Peter, m. Elizabeth **WHITHEAD**, Apr. 8,		
1756	1	205
James, m. Eleanor **SHERWOOD**, Nov. 6, 1825, by Rev.		
H. R. Judah, of Bridgeport	1-M	28
James Chester, s. Jonathan & Hannah, b. May 24, 1779	1	262
Jerusha, d. Peter & Ann, b. June 26, 1757	1	170
Joel Burr, m. Priscilla **STURGIS**, b. of Fairfield, Dec. 13,		
1824, by Nath[anie]l Hewit	1-M	16
John, s. Joseph & Esther, b. Sept. 14, 1711 O.S.; d. July		
25, 1784 N.S., aged 72 yrs. 10 m.	1	36
John, s. Eben[eze]r & Hannah, b. Oct. 28, 1778	1	278
John, m. Catharine **MOREHOUSE**, Jan. 17, 1836, by		
James H. Linsley	1-M	58
Jonathan, s. Peter & Ann, b. Nov. 15, 1751	1	170
Jonathan, s. Peter, m. Hannah **HOYT**, d. James, of		
Norwalk, Jan. 21, 1762	1	262
Jonathan, s. Jonathan & Hannah, b. Mar. 9, 1767	1	262
Jonathan, of Huntington, m. Anna **OSBORNE**, of		
Fairfield, Dec. 25, 1844, by N. E. Cornwall	1-M	81
Joseph, s. Joseph, b. May 9, 1682	LR-A2	678
Joseph, s. Gershom & Sarah, b. Nov. 2, 1741; d. Apr. 22,		
1742	1	233
Joseph, 2nd, m. Charlotte **MASON**, b. of Fairfield, June		
7, 1829, by John H. Hunter	1-M	34
Julia Ann, m. Philo **SMITH**, Aug. 7, 1825, by Rev. H. R.		
Judah, of Bridgeport	1-M	28

26 BARBOUR COLLECTION

	Vol.	Page
BULKLEY, BULKELEY (cont.)		
Peter, s. Jonathan & Hannah, b. Apr. 3, 1765	1	262
Priscilla, m. William **GRIFFIN**, b. of Fairfield, Oct. 21,		
1841, by Rev. Lyman H. Atwater	1-M	72
Rachel, d. Peter & Ann, b. Mar. 30, 1750	1	170
Ruth, m. Samuel **BURR**, Mar. 14, 1754	1	89
Ruth, of Fairfield, m. David **BEACH**, of Trumbull,		
[Mar.] 18, [1832], by Rev. Charles Smith	1-M	44
Samuel, s. Joseph, m. Beulah **HENRY**, d. Sam[ue]ll,		
Sept. 2, 1754	1	119
Sam[ue]ll, s. Sam[ue]ll & Bulah, b. Dec. 19, 1757	1	119
Samuel, b. Mar. 1, 1725/6 O.S.; d. Aug. 17, 1772, N.S.	1	119
Sarah, d. Peter, m. Joseph **PERRY**, s. Joseph, Nov. 11,		
1736	1	142
Sarah, d. Peter & Elizabeth, b. Dec. 29, 1750	1	170
Sarah, d. Nathan & Sarah, b. Jan. 26, 1768	1	232
Sarah, d. Eben[eze]r & Hannah, b. May 2, 1773	1	278
Sarah Banks, of Greens Farms, m. Daniel **CROSSMAN**,		
of Weston, Feb. 22, 1835, by T. F. Davis	1-M	55
Stiles, m. Catharine Ann **JUDSON**, b. of Fairfield, Jan.		
15, 1826, by Nath[anie]l Hewit	1-M	21
Susan, d. [Edwin & Mary], b. Sept. 4, 1735* *(Arnold		
copy has "1835")	1	232
Talcott, s. Capt. Gershom, b. Aug. 21, 1724	1	36
Talcott, s. Capt. Gershom, m. Esther **BULKLEY**, d. Capt.		
Dan[ie]ll, June 19, 1753	1	54
Tho[ma]s, s. Jonathan & Hannah, b. Nov. 23, 1771	1	262
Timothy, of Greenfield, m. Susannah **OSBORN**, of		
Greens Farms, Oct. 19, 1823, by Nath[anie]l Hewit	1-M	12
Timothy, m. Abigail **BULKLEY**, Jan. 23, 1831, by		
Thomas F. Davis	1-M	39-40
Turney, s. Peter & Elizabeth, b. June 9, 1755	1	170
Walter, s. Edwin & Mary, b. Nov. 12, 1728	1	232
William, s. Peter & Ann, b. Sept. 17, 1741	1	170
BUNNELL, Giles, of Weston, m. Abigail **OGDEN**, of Greens		
Farms, Oct. 10, 1825, by Rev. E. W. Hooker	1-M	20
BURGIS, Jane Hall, m. Isaac **HALL**, Jan. 24, 1689	LR-2	458
BURLING, Laura Louisa, of Norwalk, m. William **COUCH**,		
of Readding, Mar. 26, 1846, by Rev. N. E. Cornwall	1-M	83
BURR, Aaron, s. David & Abigail, b. Oct. 6, 1749	1	168
Abel, s. Joseph & Hannah, b. Sept. 8, 1728	1	84
Abell, s. Joseph, m. Sarah **CADWELL**, d. Jacob, Jan. 16,		
1751	1	84
Abell, s. Abell & Sarah, b. Dec. 19, 1751	1	84
Abigaill, d. Daniell, b. May 14, 1671	LR-A2	682
Abigail, m. John **WHEELER**, Mar. 22, 1692	1	8
Abigail, d. Major Peter, m. Ephraim **BURR**, Jan. 7,		
1724/5	1	12
Abigail, d. Major Peter, m. Ephraim **BURR**, Jan.		
[ ],1724/5	LR-2	456
Abigail, d. Thaddeus & Abigail, b. Mar. 24, 1729	1	30
Abigail, d. John [& Katherine], b. July 27, 1736	1	3
Abigail, d. Eph[rai]m & Abigail, b. Feb. 14, 1740/1	1	12

	Vol.	Page
BURR (cont.)		
Abigail, d. David & Abigail, b. Apr. 8, 1747	1	168
Abigail, d. Thaddeus, m. Lyman **HALL**, May 20, 1752	1	36
Abigail, w. Thaddeus, d. June 26, 1753	1	30
Abigail, d. James & Mary, b. Aug. 18, 1755	1	201
Abigail, d. Increase & Jane, b. Dec. 10, 1756	1	82
Abigail, d. Dan[ie]ll & Ann, b. Oct. 6, 1758	1	133
Abigail, d. Capt. John, m. Moses **JENNINGS**, s. Isaac, Oct. 11, 1759	1	251
Abigail, d. David & Eunice, b. Sept. 29, 1763	1	31
Amos, s. John & Katharine, b. Sept. 8, 1741; d. Sept. 27, 1743	1	3
Andrew, s. Jno, b. Sept. 27, 1696	LR-B	C
Andrew, s. John, b. Sept. 27, 1696	1	11
Andrew, m. Sarah **STURGIS**, Apr. 30, 1719	LR-B	C
Andrew, s. John, m. Sarah **STURGIS**, d. Jonathan, Apr. 30, 1719	1	11
Andrew, s. And[re]w, b. July 24, 1724	LR-B	C
And[re]w, s. And[re]w & Sarah, b. July 24, 1724	1	11
Andrew, m. 2nd w. Sarah **STANLEY**, of Hartford, Aug. 6, 1747	1	11
Andrew, d. Nov. 9, 1763, "being 67 yrs. old the 8th of Oct. before, New Style"	1	11
Andrew, s. David & Eunice, b. Apr. 7, 1768	1	31
Andrew Eliot, s. Gershom & Elizabeth, b. Aug. 9, 1802	1	294
Ann, d. And[re]w, b. Feb. 6, 1719/20	LR-B	C
Ann, d. And[re]w & Sarah, b. Feb. 6, 1719/20	1	11
Ann, d. John & Katharine, b. Sept. 7, 1726	1	3
Ann, d. Ephraim & Abigail, b. Jan. 16, 1731/2	1	12
Ann, d. And[re]w, m. Sam[ue]l **STURGIS**, Jan. 17, 1739/40	1	7
Ann, d. David & Abigail, b. Feb. 24, 1742	1	168
Ann, w. Gershom, d. Sept. 29, 1747	1	32
Ann, d. Peter, m. Nathan **BEERS**, s. Eph[rai]m, Jan. 16, 1750	1	173
Ann, d. Dan[ie]ll & Ann, b. Dec. 9, 1756	1	133
Ann, d. George & Mabel, b. Apr. 3, 1766	1	266
Ann, of Easton, m. George **WAKEMAN**, of Fairfield, June 28, 1846, by Rev. E. C. Bull, at Southport	1-M	84
Annah, d. Nathaniel, m. Gideon **ALLEN**, Jan. 20, 1696	LR-2	458
Catharine, d. Capt. John, m. Robert **WILLSON**, s. Nath[anie]ll, Sept. 7, 1741	1	29
Catharine, m. Benjamin **MEAKER**, Aug. 20, 1745	1	242
Catharine, d. John & Eunice, b. Nov. 5, 1753	1	126
Charity, d. W[illia]m & Charity, b. Mar. 4, 1744/5	1	44
Charles, s. Sam[ue]ll & Elizabeth, b. Aug. [ ], 1741	1	89
Daniell, s. Daniell, b. July 30, 1670	LR-A2	682
Dan[ie]ll, s. Sam[ue]ll & Elizabeth, b. July 2, 1730	1	89
Daniel, s. John & Elizabeth, b. Mar. 5, 1737	1	169
Daniel, s. James & Mary, b. Dec. 25, 1748	1	201
Daniel, s. Sam[ue]ll, m. Ann **SILLIMAN**, d. Nath[anie]ll, Jan. 22, 1756	1	133
David, s. And[re]w, b. July 5, 1722	LR-B	C

	Vol.	Page
BURR (cont.)		
David. s. Andrew & Sarah, b. July 5, 1722	1	11
David, s. Dan[ie]ll, m. Abigail **SILLIMAN**, d. John, Apr. 8, 1741	1	168
David, s. David & Abigail, b. Sept. 29, 1751	1	168
David, s. Col. Andrew, m. Eunice **OSBORN**, d. Samuel, Dec. 11, 1751	1	31
David, s. David & Eunice, b. Aug. 8, 1757	1	31
David, Col., d. Dec. 3, 1773	1	31
Deborah, d. John & Katharine, b. May 14, 1730	1	3
Deborah, d. Capt. John, m. Ichabod **WHEELER**, s. John, Jan. 1, 1757	1	118
Desire, b. Feb. 19, 1782; m. Justin **HOBART**, July 1, 1804	1	302
Eben, m. Hannah A. **OSBORN**, b. of Fairfield, Apr. 23, 1825, by Nath[anie]l Hewit	1-M	17
Ebenezer, s. John, b. Feb. 7, 1681	LR-A2	681
Ebenezer, s. John, d. Jan. [ ], 1684	LR-A2	680
Ebenezer, s. Sam[ue]ll & Elizabeth, b Oct. [ ], 1732	1	89
Eben[eze]r, s. Ephraim & Abigail, b. May 23, 1738	1	12
Ebenezer, s. Timothy, m. Sarah **SHERWOOD**, d. Benjamin, Jan. 17, 1754	1	45
Ebenezer, s. Capt. John, m. Amelia **SILLIMAN**, d. Ebenezer, Feb. 26, 1759	1	248
Ebenezer, s. Ebenezer & Sarah, b. Dec. 14, 1760	1	45
Ebenezer, s. Nehe[mia]h & Sarah, b. Dec. 31, 1766	1	274
Ebenezer, 2nd, had negroes Dinah, b. Apr. 18, 1784 & Primus, b. Jan. 16, 1787	1	292
Ebenezer, m. Abby Jane **MILLS**, Apr. 28, 1833, by Tho[ma]s F. Davis	1-M	50
Ebenezer, Jr., m. Julia Maria **BEERS**, d. Thomas P., b. of Fairfield, Nov. 22, 1846, by Rev. N. E. Cornwall	1-M	86
Eleazer, s. Nehe[mia]h & Sarah, b. Jan. 8, 1773	1	274
Eliphalet, s. Joseph & Hannah, b. Jan. 11, 1739	1	84
Elizabeth, d. And[re]w, b. June 22, 1726	LR-B	C
Elizabeth, d. Andrew & Sarah, b. June 22, 1726	1	11
Elizabeth, d. Stephen & Elizabeth, b. Jan. 17, 1728	1	178
Elizabeth, [twin with Mary], d. John & Katharine, b. Apr. 7, 1732	1	3
Elizabeth, d. Sam[ue]ll & Elizabeth, b. Sept. [ ], 1738	1	89
Elizabeth, w. John, d. Mar. 29, 1740	1	169
Elizabeth, d. John & Grace, b. Sept. 16, 1743	1	169
Elizabeth, w. Samuel, d. June 16, 1753	1	89
Elizabeth, d. Capt. John, m. Abram **GOLD**, s. Sam[ue]l, Jan. 1, 1754	1	49
Elizabeth, d. Sam[ue]ll & Eunice, b. July 1, 1754	1	21
Elizabeth, d. Sam[ue]ll, m. Samuel **SILLIMAN**, s. Nath[anie]ll, Jan.21, 1756	1	181
Elizabeth, d. Andrew, m. Daniel **OSBORN**, s. Sam[ue]ll, Jan. 19, 1758	1	247
Elizabeth, m. Charles **BULKLEY**, b. of Fairfield, Jan. 4, 1831, by Rev. Charles Smith	1-M	39-40
Ellin, d. Daniell, b. Oct. 26, 1680	LR-A2	682

	Vol.	Page

BURR (cont.)

Elin, d. Ephraim & Abigail, b. Feb. 23, 1733/4	1	12
Elen, d. Sam[ue]ll & Elizabeth, b. Nov. [ ], 1736	1	89
Ellen, d. Capt. Samuell, m. Abell **GOLD**, s. Sam[ue]ll, Dec. 19, 1754	1	25
Ellen, d. Ebenezer & Sarah, b. Mar. 18, 1758	1	45
Ellen, d. Ephraim, m. James **PENFIELD**, s. Peter, Apr. 23, 1758	1	259
Ellen, d. David & Eunice, b. Aug. 12, 1761	1	31
Ephraim, m. Abigail **BURR**, d. Major Peter, Jan. 7, 1724/5	1	12
Ephraim, m. Abigail **BURR**, d. Major Peter, Jan. [ ],1724/5	LR-2	456
Ephraim, s. Ephraim & Abigail, b. Mar. 5, 1735/6	1	12
Ephraim H., of Fairfield, m. Eunice **SHERWOOD**, of Greens Farms, May 18, 1823, by Rev. Nath[anie]ll Hewit	1-M	11
Esther, m. Daniel **BRADLEY**, June [ ],1724	1	81
Esther, d. Peter, m. Joshua **JENNINGS**, s. Joshua, Dec. 24, 1754	1	166
Esther, d. Ebenezer & Sarah, b. May 29, 1755	1	45
Eunice, d. Ephraim & Abigail, b. Feb. 8, 1729/30	1	12
Eunice, d. Major Peter, of Fairfield, m. Benjamin **WYNKOOP**, s. Benjamin, of New York, Nov. 22, 1730	1	85
Eunice, d. John & Eunice, b. Oct. 5, 1750	1	126
Eunice, d. Eph[rai]m, m. Daniel **JENNINGS**, Jr., s. Dan[ie]ll, Dec. 10, 1752	1	251
Eunice, d. John & Grace, b. Sept. 24, 1755	1	169
Eunice, d. David & Eunice, b. Dec. 29, 1755	1	31
Eunice, wid. Col. David, d. Dec. 1, 1789	1	31
Evelina, of Greens Farms, m. Henry J. **LAMBERTON**, of Windsor, Dec. 14, 1828, by Rev. E. W. Hooker	1-M	33
George, s. Andrew & Sarah, b. May 26, 1736	1	11
George, s. Col. Andrew, m. Mabel **WAKEMAN**, d. Jabez, Dec. 30, 1762	1	266
Gershom, s. Thaddeus & Abigail, b. June 10, 1744	1	30
Gershom, s. Gershom & Priscilla, of Fairfield, m. Susannah **YOUNG**, d. Daniel & Margaret, of Stratford, Sept. 10, 1789, by Rev. Andrew Eliot	1	294
Gershom, had negroes Dorcas, d. Dinah, b. June 13, 1792 & Ned, s. Dinah, b. July 19, 1794	1	294
Gershom, m. 2nd w. Elizabeth **ELIOT**, d. Rev. Andrew & Mary, Oct. 13, 1801	1	294
Grace, d. Stephen & Elizabeth, b. Dec. 12, 1724	1	178
Grace, d. John & Grace, b. Feb. 2, 1753	1	169
Grissell, d. Nath[anie]ll & Mary, b. Nov. 15, 1741	1	68
Grissell, d. Capt. Nath[anie]ll, m. Elijah **ABEL**, s. Samuel, of Norwich, Dec. 31, 1761	1	269
Grissell, m. Joseph **MOTT**, of Fairfield, Mar. 9, 1823, by Rev. Philo Shelton	1-M	10
Hannah, d. Dan[ie]ll, b. Jan. 16, 1681	LR-A2	681
Hannah, w. James, d. Aug. 11, 1743	1	201

	Vol.	Page
BURR (cont.)		
Hannah, d. Increase & Jane, b. Dec. 25, 1754	1	82
Hester, d. Stephen & Elizabeth, b. Feb. 5, 1743	1	178
Hezekiah, s. Stephen & Elizabeth, b. Sept. 1, 1730	1	178
Hezekiah, s. Nath[anie]ll & Mary, b. Feb. 28, 1737/8; d, Jan. 7, 1787	1	68
Ichabod, s. Joseph & Hannah, b. May 1, 1736	1	84
Increase, s. Joseph & Hannah, b. May 1, 1736	1	84
Increase, s. Joseph, m. Jane **BRADLEY**, d. Francis, Jan. 3, 1753	1	82
Isaac, s. Nath[anie]ll & Mary, b. Dec. 13, 1733	1	68
Isaac, s. Nath[anie]ll & Mary, d. Mar. 28, 1738	1	68
Isaac, s. James & Hannah, b. May 18, 1738	1	201
Isaac, s. Nath[anie]ll & Mary, b. Apr. 11, 1744	1	68
Isaac Lathrop, s. Gershom & Susanna, b. July 12, 1794	1	294
Isabel, d. James & Hannah, b. Jan. 8, 1733	1	201
James, m. Hannah **OSBORN**, wid., Dec. 12, 1731	1	201
James, m. Mary **BARLOW**, Jan. [ ],1746	1	201
James, s. James & Mary, b. May 25, 1751	1	201
Jane, m. Samuel **SHERWOOD**, Mar. 8, 1722	1	75
Jerusha, d. Andrew & Sarah, b. Dec. 3, 1749	1	11
Jerusha, d. Col. Andrew, m. Hezekiah **FITCH**, s. Hon. Tho[ma]s, of Norwalk, Sept. 21, 1767	1	270
Jesse, s. John & Eunice, b. Dec. 30, 1755	1	126
John, s. John, b. May 2, 1673	LR-A2	681
John, Jr., m. Katharine **WAKEMAN**, Oct. 18, 1722	1	3
John, s. John & Katharine, b. June 13, 1728	1	3
John, s. Andrew & Sarah, b. Mar. 11, 1731/2	1	11
John, s. Dan[ie]ll, m. Elizabeth **NASH**, d. Tho[ma]s, Oct. 14, 1735	1	169
John, s. John & Elizabeth, b. Oct. 9, 1739; d. Oct. 9, 1749	1	169
John, m. 2nd w. Grace **BULKLEY**, d. Gershom, Nov. 9, 1741	1	169
John, s. Capt. John, m. Eunice **BOOTH**, d. Joseph, Apr. 1, 1750	1	126
John, s. John & Grace, b. Feb. 9, 1751	1	169
Jonathan, s. Abell & Sarah, b. Dec. 25, 1753	1	84
Jonathan Strugis, [s. Gershom & Elizabeth], b. Mar. 6, 1804	1	294
Joseph, m. Hannah **HIDE**, Mar. 3, 1725	1	84
Joseph, s .Joseph & Hannah, b. Oct. 22, 1733	1	84
Josiah, s. Andrew & Sarah, b. July 15, 1738	1	11
Julia, m. Henry C. **SMITH**, b. of Fairfield, Jan. 16, 1842, by Rev. Lyman H. Atwater	1-M	75
Justus, s. John & Katharine, b. Sept. 2, 1734	1	3
Katharine, d. John & Katharine, b. Oct. 26, 1723	1	3
Lewis, m. Eliza **OLMSTEAD**, b. of Fairfield, Oct. 25, 1829, by John H. Hunter	1-M	35-6
Lucreacy, d. And[re]w & Sarah, b. May 23, 1728	1	11
Lucretia, d. David & Eunice, b. Mar. 10, 1754	1	31

	Vol.	Page
BURR (cont.)		
Mance* Titus, freeman, negro, of Fairfield, m. Castile or		
Lusteel **NICHOLS**, Freeman, of Weston, [ ],		
1822, by David Hill, J.P. *(Or Nancy)	1-M	6
Marretta, m. George **HAWLEY**, Nov. 30, 1820, by Rev.		
Elijah Waterman	1-M	3
Martha, d. Stephen & Elizabeth, b. Mar. 24, 1735	1	178
Martha, [twin with Mary], d. Nath[anie]ll & Martha, b.		
June 13, 1740	1	69
Martha, w. Nathaniel, d. Mar. 18, 1753	1	69
Mary, d. John, b. Aug. 19, 1683	LR-A2	680
Mary, m. Tho[ma]s **HILL**, Dec. 9, 1715	1	10
Mary, d. Andrew & Sarah, b. May 22, 1730	1	11
Mary, [twin with Elizabeth], d. John & Katharine, b. Apr.		
7, 1732	1	3
Mary, [twin with Martha], d. Nath[anie]ll & Martha, b.		
June 13, 1740	1	69
Mary, w. W[illia]m, d. Mar. 19, 1743	1	44
Mary, d. James & Mary, b. June[ ], 1746	1	201
Mary, d. W[illia]m & Charity, b. Mar. 23, 1749	1	44
Mary, d. David & Abigail, b. Apr. 2, 1755	1	168
Mary, d. Capt. John, m. Ebenezer **BARTRAM**, Jr., s.		
Ebenezer, Nov. 1, 1759	1	248
Mary, d. Peter, m. Seth **STURGIS**, s. Benj[ami]n, Jr.,		
Feb. 5, 1761	1	256
Mary, d. Nath[anie]ll, m. Aaron **HUBBELL**, s. David,		
Nov. 29, 1761	1	39
Mary A., m. George **MOREHOUSE**, b. of Fairfield,		
Sept. 23, 1832, by John H. Hunter	1-M	45-6
Mehetabel, s. Sam[ue]ll & Elizabeth, b. May 28, 1723	1	89
Moses, s. Joseph & Hannah, b. Aug. 22, 1742	1	84
Moses, s. David & Abigail, b. Apr. 5, 1744	1	168
Nathan, s. Nath[anie]ll & Martha, b. Sept. 19, 1733	1	69
Nathaniell, d. Feb. 26, 1712	LR-2	456
Nath[anie]ll, m. Martha **SILLIMAN**, Nov. 10, 1726	1	69
Nathaniel, Jr., m. Mary **TURNEY**, Nov. 23, 1732	1	68
Nathaniel, Capt., d. Nov. 8, 1784	1	68
Nehemiah, s. Sam[ue]ll & Elizabeth, b. Apr. 18, 1734	1	89
Nehemiah, s. Capt. Sam[ue]ll, m. Sarah **OSBORN**, d.		
Eleazer, Apr. 21, 1763	1	274
Nehe[mia]h, s. Nehe[mia]h & Sarah, b. Aug. 2, 1765; d.		
June 5, 1766	1	274
Nehem[ia]h, s. Nehe[mia]h & Sarah, b. Feb. 16, 1769	1	274
Oliver, s. Andrew & Sarah, b. Nov. 10, 1745	1	11
Ozias, s. John & Katharine, b. May 1, 1739	1	3
Patience, d. Jehu, m. Elnathan **GRIFFEN**, Nov. 26, 1750	1	134
Peter, s. Thaddeus & Abigail, b. Apr. 27, 1731	1	30
Peter, s. Eph[rai]m & Abigail, b. Nov. 2, 1745	1	12
Polly, m. Dr. Talcott **BANKS**, b. of Greens Farms, Sept.		
20, 1821, by Hezekiah Ripley, V.D.M.	1-M	5
Priscella, d. George & Mabel, b. Sept. 26, 1763	1	266
Prisc[i]lla Lathrop, [d. Gershom & Elizabeth], b .July 6,		
1806	1	294

	Vol.	Page
BURR (cont.)		
Prudence, m. Ebenezer **GILBERT**, May 12, 1756	1	107
Rachel, d. Joseph & Hannah, b. Sept. 3, 1730	1	84
Rebecca, d. Nath[anie]ll & Martha, b. Apr. 13, 1736	1	69
Rebecca, d. Stephen & Elizabeth, b. Nov. 2, 1739	1	178
Rebeckah, d. Stephen, m. Seth **SANFORD**, s. Sam[ue]ll, Apr. 18, 1759	1	261
Ruth, d. Nath[anie]ll & Martha, b. Sept. 20, 1727	1	69
Sally G., m. David **LOCKWOOD**, b. of Fairfield, Feb. 18, 1833, by Rev. Stephen Martindale	1-M	48-9
Samuell, s. John, b. Apr. 2, 1679	LR-A2	681
Sam[ue]ll, s. Dan[ie]ll, b. June 20, 1694	LR-B	C
Sam[ue]ll, m. Elizabeth **WAKEMAN**, June [ ], 1722	1	89
Sam[ue]ll, s. Sam[ue]ll & Elizabeth, b. Nov [ ], 1728	1	89
Samuel, s. Joseph & Hannah, b. Mar. 9, 1746	1	84
Sam[ue]ll, Jr., s. Sam[ue]ll, m. Eunice **STURGIS**, d. Solomon, May 31, 1753	1	21
Samuel, m. 2nd w. Ruth **BULKLEY**, Mar. 14, 1754	1	89
Samuel, d. Mar. 20, 1791	1	21
Sarah, m. Rev. Charles **CHAUNCEY**, June 29, 1692	LR-2	460
Sarah, d. John & Katharine, b. Feb. 7, 1724/5	1	3
Sarah, d. Thaddeus & Abigail, b. Sept. 5, 1726	1	30
Sarah, d. Nath[anie]ll & Martha, b. Apr. 19, 1729	1	69
Sarah, d. Stephen & Elizabeth, b. Nov. 9, 1732	1	178
Sarah, d. Andrew & Sarah, b. Sept. 23, 1742	1	11
Sarah, d. Eph[rai]m & Abigail, b. July 5, 1743	1	12
Sarah, d. John, m. Daniel **SILLIMAN**, s. Robert, Mar. 13, 1746	1	167
Sarah, d. James & Mary, b. Dec. 17, 1753	1	201
Sarah, d. Ephraim, m. Eleazer **OSBORN**, Jr. s. Eleazer, June 3, 1764	1	105
Sarah, d. David & Eunice, b. Apr. 21, 1766; d. June 2, 1787	1	31
Sarah, d. George & Mabel, b. May 15, 1770	1	266
Sarah, d. Nehem[ia]h & Sarah, b .Mar. 29, 1771	1	274
Sarah, m. Edward **HYDE**, b. of Greens Farms, Sept. 11, 1826, by Rev. E. W. Hooker	1-M	23
Sarah Ann, m. W[illia]m **SMITH**, Dec. 10, 1826, by Nath[anie]l Hewit	1-M	25
Selleck, m. Sarah **BENNIT**, May 29, 1825, b. of Greens Farms, by Hez[ekia]h Ripley, V.D.M.	1-M	22
Seth, s. Sam[ue]l & Elizabeth, b. Jan. [ ],1726/7	1	89
Seth, s. Dan[ie]ll & Ann, b. Mar. 2, 1761	1	133
Silliman, s. David & Abigail, b. Aug. 12, 1753; d. Jan. 29, 1754	1	168
Stephen, m. Elizabeth **HALL**, d. Cornelius, June 8, 1721	1	178
Susan, m. Daniel **SHERWOOD**, Jr. b. of Fairfield, Apr. 24, 1825, by Rev. E. W. Hooker	1-M	18
Susaniah, d. Andrew & Sarah, b. Apr. 29, 1734	1	11
Susanna, d. Gershom & Susannah, b. Jan. 7, 1793; d. Feb. 4, 1797	1	294
Susanna, w. Gershom, d. Feb. 12, 1797	1	294

	Vol.	Page
BURR (cont.)		
Susanna Young, [d. Gershom & Elizabeth], b. Feb. 6, 1808	1	294
Talcott, s. John & Grace, b. Oct. 20, 1746	1	169
Thad, s. Gershom & Susannah, b. Nov. 13, 1790	1	294
Thaddeus, s. Peter, m. Abigail **STURGIS**, d. Jonathan, Nov. 26, 1725	1	30
Thaddeus, s. Thaddeus & Abigail, b. Aug. 22, 1735	1	30
Thaddeus, d. Mar. 28, 1755	1	30
Thaddeus, s. Thad[deus], m. Eunice **DENNIE**, d. James, Mar. 22, 1759	1	249
Thaddeus, had negroes Tom **CUFFE**, s. Luce, b. Sept. 9, 1785; & Mercy, d. Luce, b. Mar. 5, 1790	1	462
Tho[ma]s, s. Nehemiah & Sarah, b. Feb. 2, 1764	1	274
Wakeman, s. John & Katharine, b. Oct. 3, 1743	1	3
Walter, s. Andrew & Sarah, b. Sept. 9, 1740	1	11
Walter, s. David & Eunice, b. Dec. 25, 1752	1	31
Will[ia]m, s. Col. John, m. Mary **WAKEMAN**, d. Capt. Joseph, Aug. 4, 1736	1	44
Will[ia]m, s. W[illia]m & Mary, b. July 23, 1740	1	44
William, m. 2nd w. Charity **STRONG**, wid. Joseph & d. John **WELLS** of Stratford, May 16, 1744	1	44
William, s. David & Eunice, b. July 27, 1759	1	31
William, of Hudson, N.Y., m. Mary **WAKEMAN**, of Greens Farms, Jan. 8, 1826, by Rev. E. W. Hooker	1-M	22
William H., of Westport, m. Mary A. **JENNINGS**, of Fairfield, Nov. 27, 1845, by Rev. L. B. Burr, of Ridgebury	1-M	83
BURRIT, Abigail, m. Timothy **WHEELER**, s. Timothy, Aug. 9, 1744	1	51
BURTON, Ruth, d. Solomon, m. Hezekiah **OSBORN**, s. W[illia]m, Oct. 18, 1764	1	269
BURWELL, Robera, d. Stephen & Ann, b. May 24, 1741	1	16
Will[ia]m, s. Stephen & Ann, b. May 6, 1740	1	16
BUSH, Jennett M., of Fairfield, m. Edward **AVERY**, of Weston, O., Feb. 3, 1834, by Rev. C. A. Boardman, of Saugatuck	1-M	52
BUSKIRK, George, of New York City, m. Elizabeth **TURNEY**, of Fairfield, Oct. 27, 1847, by Rev. Lyman H. Atwater	1-M	87
BUTLER, Francis M., of Southport, m. John **HULL**, of New York, Aug. 5, 1840, by N. E. Cornwall	1-M	70
[CABELL], **CABLE**, Abigail, d. Jon[a]th[an] & Mary, b. Apr. 6, 1729	1	213
Abigail, d. George & Sarah, b. May 19, 1737	1	129
Abigail, d. Dan[ie]ll & Sarah, b. Nov. 22, 1751	1	222
Abijah, s. Dan[ie]ll & Sarah, b. June 24, 1742	1	222
Ann, d. George & Sarah, b. May 19, 1730	1	129
Ann, d. John & Ann, b. Nov. 4, 1750	1	44
Bettey, d. Jon[atha]n & Mary, b. Nov. 12, 1737	1	213
Damaries, d. Jon[atha]n & Mary, b. Apr. 29, 1745	1	213
Daniel, s. John, m. Sarah **CRANE**, June 7, 1739	1	222
Daniel, s. Dan[ie]ll & Sarah, b. Mar. 7, 1746	1	222

	Vol.	Page
[CABELL], CABLE (cont.)		
Elijah, s. Dan[ie]ll & Sarah, b. Sept. 18, 1755	1	222
Elizabeth, d. John & Ann, b. Sept. 12, 1746	1	44
Emet, d. John & Ann, b. June 28, 1734	1	44
Emitt, m. Onessmus **BRADLEY**, s. Joseph, Aug. 1, 1754	1	144
Eunice, d. Jon[a]th[an] & Mary, b. Nov. 4, 1731	1	213
Eunice, m. David **SHERWOOD**, Jr., Jan. 16, 1749/50	1	231
George, m. Sarah **SHAW**, Feb. 17, 1729	1	129
George, s. George & Sarah, b. Aug. 14, 1742	1	129
George, of Norwalk, m. Esther P. **MEEKER**, of Fairfield,		
June 12, 1825, by Rev. E. W. Hooker	1-M	18
Isaac, s. John & Ann, b. Sept. 7, 1744	1	44
Jabez, s. George & Sarah, b. Apr. 14, 1733	1	129
James, s. John & Ann, b. July 1, 1761	1	184
Jane, d. John & Ann, b. Apr. 19, 1759	1	184
Jerusha, d. Dan[ie]ll & Sarah, b. May 18, 1753	1	222
John, s. George & Sarah, b. Aug. 15, 1731	1	129
John, m. Ann **DAVIS**, Sept. 26, 1733	1	44
John, s. John & Ann, b. Apr. 29, 1753	1	44
John, s. George, m. Ann **LABARIE**, May 1st Monday,		
1756	1	184
John, s. John & Ann, b. Feb. 27, 1757	1	184
John, d. Mar. 24, 1760	1	44
Jonathan, s. John, m. Mary **BENNET**, d. Thomas, Sept. 3,		
1728	1	213
Jonathan, s. George & Sarah, b. Aug. [ ], 1751	1	129
Josiah, s. Dan[ie]ll & Sarah, b. Apr. 15, 1744	1	222
Margary, d. Jon[atha]n & Mary, b. Oct. 1, 1741; d. July		
10, following	1	213
Margary, d. George & Sarah, b. Jan. 1, 1744	1	129
Nathaniel, s. George & Sarah, b. Nov. 14, 1740	1	129
Nehemiah, s. John & Ann, b. July 19, 1736	1	44
Sarah, d. Jon[a]th[an] & Mary, b. Aug. 19, 1734	1	213
Sarah, d. George & Sarah, b. July [ ],1746	1	129
Sarah, d. Dan[ie]ll & Sarah, b. Jan. 10, 1749	1	222
Temperance, d. George & Sarah, b. Jan. 16, 1739	1	129
Thaddeus, s. John & Ann, b. Mar. 21, 1742	1	44
Thaddeus, d. Mar. 13, 1760	1	44
Thomas, s. George & Sarah, b. Aug. 16, 1735	1	129
William, s. John & Ann, b. Sept. 19, 1739	1	44
CADWELL, Sarah, d. Jacob, m. Abell **BURR**, s. Joseph, Jan.		
16, 1751	1	84
CALLON, Caroline, of Fairfield, m. Rufus **FANSHER**, of		
New Canaan, Dec. 11, 1836, by Lyman H. Atwater	1-M	60
Jane, M., m. Archibald **COGSWELL**, b. of Fairfield, Jan.		
20, 1822, by Nath[anie]l Hewit, V.D.M.	1-M	6
CAMPBELL, Robert, m. Mary Jane **HAYS**, b. of Fairfield,		
May 8, 1842, by Rev. Lyman H. Atwater	1-M	74
CAPEN, Charles W[illia]m, s. W[illia]m, of St. Helena S.C. &		
Abigail (**BURR**), d. Gershom & Priscilla, of		
Fairfield, b. Nov. 25, 1794	1	297

	Vol.	Page
CAPEN (cont.)		
Nath[anie]ll Lothrop, [s. W[illia]m, of St. Helena, S.C. & Abigail (**BURR**, d. Gershom & Priscilla, of Fairfield), b. Dec. 5, 1798	1	297
CAREW, Edward, m. Rebecca **OSBORN**, b. of Fairfield, June 29, 1823, by Rev. Philo Shelton	1-M	11
CARR, Mary Ann, m. Thomas **SMITH**, b. of Fairfield, Oct. 10, 1847, by Rev. N. E. Cornwall	1-M	87
CARTER,* Ann, m. James **ADIAR**, June 3, 1744 *(McCarty?)	1	244
Samuel, of Brooklyn, N. Y., m. Harriet H. **DAVIS**, of Southport, this day [ ], by Rev. G. S. Gilbert: Recorded Mar. 3, 1853	1-M	96
CARTLEDGE, Eliza, of Fairfield, m. Herbert Q. Ferguson, of New York, Oct. 21, 1846, by Rev. N. E. Cornwall	1-M	85
Maria, d. Charles, m. Jonathan **GODFREY**, Jr., b. of Fairfield, Oct. 21, 1849, by Rev. N. E. Cornwall	1-M	94
CASE, Frances, m. Thaddeus **WILLIAMS**, s. David, Nov. 28, 1747	1	134
CASTLE, Mabel, of Fairfield, m. Isaac **THOMPSON**, of Bridgeport, Nov. 1, 1843, by Rev. A. F. Beach	1-M	75
CHAPMAN, Abigail, d. Dennie, m. Simon **COUCH**, s. Simon, Nov. 25, 1779	1	112
Abigail, [d. James & Abigail], b. Apr. 25, 1782	1	291
Albert, s. Phinheas & Sarah, b. Dec. 13, 1748	1	196
Anna, m. Benjamin W. **ROGERS**, Sept. 8, 1830, by T. F. Davis	1-M	39-40
Betsey, of Fairfield, m. Hansom **NICHOLS**, of Weston, Jan. 15, 1828, by Rev. E. W. Hooker	1-M	30
Daniel, s. Phineheas & Sarah, b. Aug. 19, 1743	1	196
Dennil, s. Dan[ie]ll, m. Desire **LOVEL**, Oct. 4, 1750	1	183
Dennil, s. Dennil & Desire, b. Aug. 28, 1757	1	183
Elizabeth, d. Dennil & Desire, b. Aug. 12, 1751	1	183
Ellen, wid., m. Aaron **TURNEY**, b. of Fairfield, Nov. 9, 1829, by C. G. Lee	1-M	35-6
Grissel, d. Phineheas & Sarah, b. Apr. 16, 1755	1	196
Grizzell, [d. James & Abigail], b. May 20, 1788	1	291
James, s. Phinehas & Sarah, b. Apr. 8, 1750	1	196
James, m. Abigail **SHERWOOD**, Mar. 4, 1779	1	291
James, [s. James & Abigail], b. Mar. 28, 1784	1	291
James, had negroes Alson, b. Feb. 10, 1795 & Eli, b. Dec. 4, 1797	1	291
Jane, m. Lockwood **BAKER**, b. of Greens Farms, Apr. 10, 1825, by Hez[ekia]h Ripley, V.D.M.	1-M	22
Jeremiah Sherwood, [s. James & Abigail], b. Oct. 8, 1780	1	291
John, s. Phineheas & Sarah, b. Sept. 14, 1757	1	196
Joseph, s. Phinehas & Sarah, b. Aug. 29, 1745	1	196
Lovel, s. Dennil & Desire, b. Jan. 14, 1755	1	183
Lucy, [d. James & Abigail], b. Apr. 1, 1795	1	291
Lucy, m. Alson **BANKS**, b. of Fairfield, Oct. 19, 1823, by Hezekiah Ripley, V.D.M.	1-M	12
Mary, d. Dennil & Desire, b. May 2, 1753	1	183
May [d. James & Abigail], b. June 25, 1786	1	291

	Vol.	Page
CHAPMAN (cont.)		
Molly, d. Phineheas & Sarah, b. June 10, 1752	1	196
Moses, [s. James & Abigail], b. Nov. 30, 1790	1	291
Phineheas, s. Dan[ie]ll, m. Sarah **KETCHUM**, d. Nathaniel, Sept. 22, 1742	1	196
Samuel S., of Greens Farms, m. Eunice **BANKS**, of Greenfield, [Mar.] 14, [1822], by Rev. E. W. Hooker	1-M	7
Samuel Sherwood, [s. James & Abigail], b. Oct. 15, 1797	1	291
Sarah, d. Robert, of East Haddam, m. Ebenezer **SANFORD**, s. Tho[ma]s, of Fairfield, Feb. 14, 1739/40	1	252
Sarah, [d. James & Abigail], b. Nov. 12, 1792	1	291
Susan, m. David B. **STURGIS**, b. of Fairfield, Jan. 20, 1830, by John H. Hunter	1-M	38
William H., of New York, m. Adaline **BENNETT**, of Fairfield, Sept. 15, 1834, by Rev. C. A. Boardman, of Saugatuck	1-M	54
-----, of Greens Farms, m. Paul L. **TAYLOR**, of Norwalk, Apr. 3, 1827, by Rev. E. W. Hooker	1-M	26-7
CHAUNCEY, CHANEY, CHAUNEY, [CHANCY], Abiah, d. Rev. Charles, b. Jan. 22, 1699/1700	LR-2	460
Charles, Rev., m. Sarah **BURR**, June 29, 1692	LR-2	460
Charles, Rev. of Stratfield, m. Mrs. Sarah **WOOLCOTT**, d. Henry, of Windsor, Mar. 16, 1698	LR-2	460
Eleanor, m. Gurdon **MERCHANT**, Dec. 9, 1747	1	203
Ichabod Woolcott, s. Rev. Charles, of Stratfield, b. Jan. 5, 1703/4	LR-2	461
Israel, s. Charles, b. June 29, 1693	LR-2	460
John, s. [Rev. Charles], b. Nov. 7, 1695	LR-2	460
Robert, s. Rev. Charles, b. Oct. 30, 1701	LR-2	460
Sarah, [w. Rev. Charles, d. [ ] 15, 1697/8	LR-2	460
Sarah, formerly a **WOOLCOTT**, now w. Rev. Charles, of Stratfield, d. Jan. 5, 1703/4	LR-2	461
-----, Rev., m. 2nd w. Mrs. Sarah **WOOLCOT**, Mar. 16, 1698	LR-2	460
CHIDSEY, Isaac of Boston, m. Emily **BULKLEY**, of Fairfield, Jan. 1, 1845, by Rev. N. E. Cornwall	1-M	81
CHRISTMAS, Charles Henry, of New York, m. Emily Davis, d. Jos. **WAKEMAN**, of Fairfield, June 5, 1848, by Rev. N. E. Cornwall	1-M	89
CHUB, Harriet, m. Burr S. **NASH**, May 8, 1834, by T. F. Davis	1-M	53
CLAGSTONE, [see also **CLUQSTON**], Elizabeth, 1st. w. of John, d. Sept. 1, 1745	1	211
John, m. Elizabeth **ROWLINSON**, Mar. 23, 1749	1	211
CLAPHAM, Abigail, m. [ ], Mar. [ ],1675	LR-A2	663
CLARKE, CLARK, Amelia Ann, of Bridgeport, m. Francis Malbone **JENKINS**, of Rochester, Dec. 2, 1828, by William Shelton	1-M	32
Napoleon, m. Sarah E. **BANKS**, b. of Saugatuck, Apr. 24, 1833, by T. F. Davis	1-M	56
CLAYTON, David, s. Sam[ue]ll & Deborah, b. Nov. 21, 1759	1	249

	Vol.	Page

CLAYTON (cont.)

Sam[ue]ll, s. John, m. Deborah **MALLORY**, d.
Jonathan, Feb. 11, 1758 — 1 — 249

CLINTON, David, s. John & Elizabeth, b. Oct. 9, 1747 — 1 — 201

Elizabeth, d. John & Elizabeth, b. May 10, 1754 — 1 — 201

John, m. Elizabeth **BEACHER**, Nov. [ ], 1746 — 1 — 201

John, s. John & Elizabeth, b. May 4, 1752 — 1 — 201

CLUQSTON, [see also **CLAGSTONE**], Mary, see Mary
EDWARDS — 1 — 10

COE, Charles, of Monroe, m. Pamelia **WAKEMAN**, of
Fairfield, (colored), Nov. 27, 1828, by Chauncey G.
Lee — 1-M — 32

Phebe, m. John **HENDRICK**, [ ], 1728 — 1 — 163

COGSHALL, [see also **COGSWELL**], Mary, m. David
TREADWELL, Nov. 4, 1756 — 1 — 115

COGSWELL, [see also **COGSHALL**], Archibald, m. Jane M.
CALLON, b. of Fairfield, Jan. 20, 1822, by
Nath[anie]l Hewit, V.D.M. — 1-M — 6

John S., m. Julia Ann **PHIPPENNY**, d. Hannah, [ ] — 1 — 35

Osmond, of Cincinnati, O., m. Eliza F. **ROWLAND**, of
Fairfield, Apr. 24, 1825, by Nath[anie]l Hewit — 1-M — 17

COLEMAN, William, of New York, m. Eleanor **BANKS**, of
Fairfield, Mar. 7, 1837, by Nath[anie]l E. Cornwall — 1-M — 61

COLEY, **COOLEE**, Abigail, m. William **GRAY**, Dec. 23,
1714 — 1 — 185

Abigail, d. David & Mary, b. Apr. 29, 1758 — 1 — 64

Abigail H., m. Talcott B. **WAKEMAN**, Dec. 17, 1838,
by Rev. Tho[ma]s F. Davis — 1-M — 67

Ann, d. Peter, b. Jan. 13, 1673 — LR-A2 — 682

Ann, d. Jon[a]th[an] & Lucey, b. Nov. 17, 1745 — 1 — 207

Daniel, m. Sarah **SANFORD**, Apr. 16, 1754 — 1 — 119

Dan[ie]ll, s. Jon[a]th[an] & Lucy, b. May 24, 1759 — 1 — 207

David, b. Jan. 29, 1715; m. Mary **HIDE**, Dec. 16, 1740 — 1 — 64

David, m. Mary **HIDE**, Dec. 16, 1740 — 1 — 64

David, s. David & Mary, b. July 29, 1743 — 1 — 64

David, m. Sally **NASH**, Apr. 30, 1826, b. of Greens
Farms, by Hez[ekia]h Ripley, V.D.M. — 1-M — 22

Ebenezer, s. David & Mary, b. Oct. 19, 1741 — 1 — 64

Ebenezer, s. Gershom & Abigail, b. Feb. 24, 1751 — 1 — 125

Eliphalet, s. John & Mercy, b. Aug. 3, 1746 — 1 — 208

Elizabeth, d. Peter, b. Dec. 1, 1680 — LR-A2 — 682

Elizabeth, m. Jeremiah **JENNINGS**, Dec. 15, 1726 — 1 — 167

Ellen, d. Jon[a]tha]n & Lucey, b. July 17, 1748 — 1 — 207

Eunice, d. Gershom & Abigail, b. Feb. 26, 1754 — 1 — 125

Gershom, s. Sam[ue]ll, m. Abigail **HULL**, d. Ebenezer,
Nov. 15, 1748 — 1 — 125

Hannah, d. Jon[a]th[an] & Lucy, b. May 5, 1741 — 1 — 207

Hezekiah, s. John & Mercy, b. Apr. 23, 1742 — 1 — 208

Isaac, of Redding, m. Eleanor **BRADLEY**, of Fairfield,
Nov. 21, [1821], by Rev. E. W. Hooker — 1-M — 6

John, s. Samuel, m. Mercy **GREGORY**, d. Benj[ami]n,
July 22, 1728 — 1 — 208

John, s. John & Mercy, b. Dec. 31, 1738 — 1 — 208

	Vol.	Page
COLEY, COOLEE (cont.)		
Jonathan, s. Peter, m. Lucy **STURGIS**, d. John, Dec. 6, 1739	1	207
Jonathan, s. Jon[a]tha]n & Lucy, b. Sept. 21, 1754	1	207
Lois, d. John & Mercy, b. Jan. 7, 1736	1	208
Lucey, d. Jon[atha]n & Lucey, b. Jan. 26, 1751	1	207
Mary,* d. Peter, b. Apr. 23, 1677 *{Mercy?)	LR-A2	682
Mary, d. John & Mercy, b. Aug. 13, 1732	1	208
Mary, d. David & Mary, b. Mar. 2, 1756	1	64
Peter, s. Peter, b. June 12, 1671	LR-A2	682
Rachel, d. David & Mary, b. Mar. 18, 1746	1	64
Sarah, d. Jon[a]th[an] & Lucey, b. June 8, 1743	1	207
Stephen, s. Dan[ie]ll & Sarah, b. Oct. 21, 1754	1	119
Thankfull, m. James **BAKER**, Mar. 13, 1755	1	230
COLWELL, Daniel S., of New York, m. Julia **ROGERS**, of Fairfield, Sept. 22, 1840, by Rev. Lyman H. Atwater	1-M	69
COMSTOCK, Eloesa, of Fairfield, m. Edwin **RIPLEY**, of Lebanan, May 6, 1824, by Hez[ekia]h Ripley, V.D.M.	1-M	14
Samuel, m. Mary **BARNES**, Apr. 27, 1834, by James C. Loomis, J.P.	1-M	53
COOLEE, [see under **COLEY**]		
CORNWALL, Ann E., of Westport, m. Solomon E. **ALDEN**, of Rochester, N.Y., Aug. 10, [1846], by Rev. N. E. Cornwall	1-M	85
COUCH, Abigail, m. Nathaniel **HEBBARD**, Apr. 24, 1740	1	175
Abigail, d. Sam[ue]ll & Elizabeth, b. June 10, 1741	1	156
Abigail, d. Simon & Abigail, b. Aug. 14, 1782	1	112
Abigail, d. Simon, m. William **SHERWOOD**, s. Daniel, Jan. 5, 1800	·1	305
Abraham, of Redding, m. Mary **PATTERSON**, of Greens Farms, Mar. 27, 1831, by Oliver Sykes	1-M	41
Adria, d. Sam[ue]ll, m. Joseph **FROST**, Aug. 27, 1724	1	208
Adria, d. Eben[eze]r & Ann, b. Sept. 12, 1742	1	215
Benjamin, s. Joseph & Hannah, b. Mar. 26, 1748	1	72
Benjamin, [twin (?) with Solomon], s. Sam[ue]ll & Elizabeth, b. Mar. 26, 1749	1	156
Betsey, m. Stephen B. **WAKEMAN**, Mar. 8, 1835, by T. F. Davis	1-M	56
Clary, of Greens Farms, m. Horace **STAPLES**, of Westport, Oct. 23, 1837, by Rev. Tho[ma]s F. Davis	1-M	63-4
Daniel, s. Eben[eze]r & Ann, b. July 20, 1739	1	215
David, s. Sam[ue]ll & Elizabeth, b. June 25, 1733	1	156
Ebenezer, s. Sam[ue]ll, m. Ann **CRANE**, d. Jonathan, May 18, 1731	1	215
Ebenezer, s. Eben[eze]r & Ann, b. Jan. 20, 1733	1	215
Eli, m. Matilda **JENNINGS**, Jan. 7, 1827, by E. W. Hooker	1-M	25
Elijah, s. Eben[eze]r & Ann, b. July 29, 1747	1	215
Elizabeth, d. Sam[ue]ll & Elizabeth, b. June 13, 1735	1	156
Elizabeth, d. Tho[ma]s & Elizabeth, b. Jan. 23 1756	1	149
Elizabeth, d. Sam[ue]ll, m. Timothy **PIERSON**, s. Thomas, Mar. 9, 1756	1	185

	Vol.	Page
COUCH (cont.)		
Elizabeth, d. Sam[ue]ll & Rachel, b. Aug. 20, 1756	1	186
Elizabeth, d. Stephen & Ann, b. Apr. 20, 1785	1	284
Gideon, s. Tho[ma]s & Elizabeth, b. Sept. 14, 1757	1	149
Hannah, m. Sam[ue]ll **OSBORN**, Nov. 4, 1724	LR-2	457
Hannah, m. Sam[ue]ll **OSBORN**, Nov. 4, 1724	1	24
Hannah, d. Joseph & Hannah, b. June 8, 1756	1	72
Isabel, d. Simon, m. Benjamin **RUMSEY**, [ ], 1729; d. Nov. 7, 1754	1	193
Jonathan, s. Eben[eze]r & Ann, b. July 16, 1736	1	215
Joseph, m. Hannah **SHERWOOD**, May 7, 1747	1	72
Joseph, s. Joseph & Hannah, b. Feb. 5, 1751	1	72
Josiah, s. Sam[ue]ll & Elizabeth, b. Apr. [ ], 1743	1	156
Martha, m. Ephraim **JACKSON**, Nov. [ ], 1727	1	73
Martha, d. Eben[eze]r & Ann, b. Dec. 25, 1744	1	215
Martha, m. Nathan **GODFREY**, June 11, 1747	1	156
Mary, d. Sam[ue]ll & Elizabeth, b. Mar. 28, 1728	1	156
Mary, d. Benj[ami]n, b. Nov. 15, 1732	1	171
Mary, d. Benj[ami]n, m. Jabez **GORHAM**, s. Joseph, Nov. 27, 1752	1	171
Mary, d. Sam[ue]lll, m. Thomas **BENNIT**, Jr., s. Thomas, Apr. 1, 1754	1	122
Mary, bp. May 15, 1760	1	149
Miriam, d. Sam[ue]ll & Elizabeth, b. Apr. 11, 1727; d. Nov. 13, 1728	1	156
Meriam, d. Sam[ue]ll & Elizabeth, b. Apr. 14, 1737	1	156
Naomi, d. Sam[ue]ll & Elizabeth, b. Dec. 13, 1751	1	156
Nehemiah, s. Sam[ue]ll & Elizabeth, b. May 25, 1739	1	156
Samuel, s. Sam[ue]ll & Elizabeth, b. May 5, 1731	1	156
Samuel, s. Sam[ue]lll, m. Elizabeth **STURGIS**, d. John, Sept. 13, 1726	1	156
Samuel, s. Samuel, m. Rachel **ALLEN**, d. Joseph, Feb. 22, 1756	1	186
Sarah, d. Tho[ma]s, b. Dec. 1, 1723	LR-B	C
Sarah, d. Simon, m. John **ANDREWS**, s. John, Oct. 28, 1730	1	34
Sarah, d. Tho[ma]s & Elizabeth, b. Mar. 30, 1754	1	149
Sarah, d. Joseph & Hannah, b. Sept. 13, 1758	1	72
Simon, Capt., s. Simon, m. Abigail **JENNINGS**, d. Joshua, May 18, 1721	1	71
Simon, s. Tho[ma]s & Elizabeth, b. Nov. 6, 1752	1	149
Simon, s. Thomas, m. Rebecca **NASH**, d. Tho[ma]s, Jan. 27, 1753	1	239
Simon, s. Simon & Rebecca, b. May 18, 1756	1	239
Simon, s. Simon, m. Abigail **CHAPMAN**, d. Dennie, Nov. 25, 1779	1	112
Simon, s. Simon & Abigail, b. Oct. 16, 1783	1	112
Simon, decd., had negro Tobias, s. Gin, b. May 23, 1801	1	78
Solomon, [twin (?), with Benjamin], s. Sam[ue]ll & Elizabeth, b. Mar. 26, 1749	1	156
Stephen, s. Tho[ma]s m. Ann **EDMOND**, d. Robert, Jan. 29, 1784	1	284
Theody, d. Eben[eze]r & Ann, b. Jan. 24, 1755	1	215

	Vol.	Page
COUCH (cont.)		
Tho[ma]s, m. Sarah **ALLEN**, Dec. 7, 1721	LR-B	C
Tho[ma]s, s. Tho[ma]s, b. Nov. 28, 1725	LR-B	C
Thomas, s. Tho[ma]s, m. Elizabeth **JESSUP**, d. Edward, Feb. 22, 1749/50	1	149
Thomas, s. Tho[ma]s & Elizabeth, b. Feb. 1, 1751	1	149
William, s. Simon & Abigail, b. May 8, 1786	1	112
William, of Reading, m. Laura Louisa **BURLING**, of Norwalk, Mar. 26, 1846, by Rev. N.E. Cornwall	1-M	83
Zebulon, s. Sam[ue]ll & Elizabeth, b. Aug. 28, 1745	1	156
CRAFT, Julia B. of Fairfield, m. Edmund B. **SMITH**, of Norwalk, this day, [Nov. 13, 1839], by Rev. Cyrus Silliman	1-M	69
Mary, m. Joshua J. **THORP**, Aug. 21, 1826, by Marvin Richardson	1-M	23
CRANE, Abigail, m. Andris **TRUBE**, Sept. 14, 1744	1	28
Ann, d. Jonathan, m. Ebenezer **COUCH**, s. Sam[ue]ll, May 18, 1731	1	215
Sarah, m. Daniel **CABLE**, s. John, June 7, 1739	1	222
CRAPO, Samuel A., of New York, m. Cornelia **WAKEMAN**, of Southport, Oct. [ ], 1837, by Lyman H. Atwater	1-M	65
CROFOOT, CROWFOOT, Daniel, of Reading, m. Avis **ADAMS**, [ ]	1	62
David, s. James & Catharine, b. Oct. 21, 1753	1	249
Jemima, d. James & Catharine, b. Feb. 22, 1755	1	249
John, s. Dan[ie]l & Avis, b. May 6, 1735	1	62
John, s. Dan[ie]ll, m. Esther **SANFORD**, d. Eben[eze]r, June 16, 1756	1	141
Nathan, s. David & Mary, b. July 20, 1738	1	81
Stephen, s. Dan[ie]ll & Avis, b. Apr. 28, 1740	1	62
Stephen, s. John & Esther, b. Mar. 27, 1757	1	141
Thankfull, d. James & Catharine, b. July 12, 1759	1	249
W[illia]m F., of Norwalk, m. Anna D. **BENNET**, of Fairfield, Nov. 11, 1840, by Rev. Cyrus Silliman	1-M	70
CROSSMAN, Daniel, of Weston, m. Sarah Banks **BULKLEY**, of Greens Farms, Feb. 22, 1835, by T. F. Davis	1-M	55
David, m. Betsey **THORP**, Oct. 3, 1822, by Rev. Aaron Hunt	1-M	8
Inbridge, of Weston, m. Phebe **ALLEN**, of Fairfield, Dec. 31, 1820, by Rev. Phineas Cook	1-M	3
CURRANT, Emenuel, of Boston, Mass., m. Mary Ann **BULKELEY**, d. W[illia]m, of Fairfield, Sept. 10, 1848, by Rev. N. E. Cornwall	1-M	90
CURRIER, John, m. Nancy **PIERCE**, b. of New York, Jan. 23, 1828, by Rev. E. W. Hooker	1-M	30
CURTIS, CURTISS, Caroline, of Fairfield, m. Charles G. **KELLOGG**, of New York, June 15, 1839, by Rev. Lyman H. Atwater	1-M	68
Phebe, m. Daniel **MORHOUSE**, s. Stephen, Dec. 25, 1751	1	49
Prudence, wid., m. Dan[ie]l **MORRISS**, Dec. 29, 1761	1	33
DARLING, Benjamin, m. Mary **HIDE**, Jan. 6, 1725/6	1	162

	Vol.	Page
DARLING (cont.)		
David, s. John, m. Sarah**MOR[E]HOUSE**, d. Jehu, Dec.		
14, 1756	1	234
Elizabeth, m. Nathan **GUYRE**, s. Luke, Mar. [ ], 1749	1	92
Isaac, s. Joseph & Aurelia, b. May 21, 1786	1	267
Jessup, s. David & Sarah, b. June 20, 1758	1	234
Joseph, Dr. of Fairfield, m. Mrs.* Aurelia **MILLS**, of		
Ripton, Mar. 24 last, [1784], by David Ely		
*(Note says "Miss")	1	267
Rachel, m. Benjamin **STURGIS**, s. Benjamin, Dec. 10,		
1746	1	123
Sarah, d. David & Sarah, b. Feb. 9, 1760	1	234
DARROW, Minerva, of Fairfield, m. Samuel **WILMOT**, of		
Georgetown, S.C. Oct. 12, 1841, by Rev. N. E.		
Cornwall	1-M	72
DAVENPORT, Martha, m. Gold Selleck **SILLIMAN**, s.		
Eben[eze]r, Jan.21, 1754	1	61
DAVIS, Ann, m. John **CABLE**, Sept. 26, 1733	1	44
Anne, of Green Farms, m. Beel **BENNIT**, of Weston,		
Sept. 17, 1820, by Hezekiah Ripley, V.D.M.	1-M	2
Aquila, d. Jabez & Rebecca, b. May 28, 1737	1	174
Betty, d. Jabez & Rebecca, b. May 29, 1741	1	174
Cornelia, of Fairfield, m. W[illia]m **PARKS**, of New		
York, Oct. 16, 1843, by Rev. N. E. Cornwall	1-M	75
Damaris, m. David **BRADLEY**, Apr. 25, 1731	1	77
Ebenezer, s. James & Hannah, b. June 9, 1736	1	152
Elinor, d. Jos[eph] & Elizabeth, b. Aug. 11, 1733	1	214
Emily, d. Jos. Wakeman, of Fairfield, m. Charles Henry		
CHRISTMAS, of New York, June 5, 1848, by Rev.		
N. E. Cornwall	1-M	89
Eunice, d. Jabez & Rebecca, b. Nov. 15, 1730	1	174
Experience, d. Jabez & Rebecca, b. Aug. 29, 1733	1	174
Grace, d. Jabez & Rebecca, b. June 25, 1739	1	174
Hannah, d. Jabez & Rebecca, b. May 26, 1728	1	174
Hannah, w. James, d. Apr. 15, 1755	1	152
Hannah, d. John & Elizabeth, b. Nov. 17, 1756; d. Feb. 2		
following	1	195
Hannah, d. John & Elizabeth, b. Dec. 3, 1757	1	195
Harriet H., of Southport, m. Samuel **CARTER**, of		
Brooklyn, N.Y., this day [ ], by Rev.		
G.S. Gilbert. Recorded Mar. 3, 1853	1-M	96
Hezekiah, m. Harriet **HUBBELL**, b. of Mill River, May		
10, 1829, by William Shelton	1-M	34
Jabez, m. Rebecca **ROWLAND**, Aug. 3, 1726	1	174
James, m. Hannah **THORP**, July 16, 1729	1	152
James, s. John & Elizabeth, b. July 27, 1755	1	195
James, m. 2nd w. Sarah **MORHOUSE**, Oct. 3, 1755	1	152
Jehiel, s. Jos[eph] & Elizabeth, b. Mar. 31, 1742	1	214
John, s. James & Hannah, b. July 2, 1730	1	152
John, m. Elizabeth **MEAKER**, Jan. 3, 1752	1	195
Joseph, m. Elizabeth **SMITH**, Jan. 11, 1733	1	214
Joseph, s. Jos[eph] & Elizabeth, b. Feb. 16, 1738	1	214

	Vol.	Page
DAVIS (cont.)		
Lydea, d. Jabez & Rebecca, b. June 19, 1735	1	174
Lydia, d. John & Elizabeth, b. June 17, 1754; d. Sept. 15, following	1	195
Lidea, d. Jabez, m. Nehemiah **PHIPENNY**, s. James, of Stratford, Feb. 14, 1771	1	35
Mary, d. John, m. Samuel **LYON**, s. Sam[ue]ll, May 8, 1718	1	189
Mary, d. James & Hannah, b. Nov. 2, 1732	1	152
Mary, m. Peter **LYON**, s. Sam[ue]ll, Dec. 13, 1749	1	189
Mary S., m. Ebenezer B. **ADAMS**, Sept. 24, 1839, by Rev. Thomas F. Davis	1-M	68
Nathan, s. Jos[eph] & Elizabeth, b. Mar. 25, 1754	1	214
Phebe, d. Jos[eph] & Elizabeth, b. Nov. 26, 1747	1	214
Rachel, m. Richard **ELWOOD**, Feb. 20, 1742	1	227
Sarah, d. Sam[ue]ll, m. Caleb **DISBROW**, s. Thomas, Nov. 19, 1740	1	132
DEAN, Benjamin, m. Mary **SQUIER**, Dec. 6, 1753	1	243
Esther, d. Benj[ami]n & Mary, b. Nov. 8, 1755	1	243
Margaret, m. William **MURRAY**, b. of Black Rock, Mar. 16, 1851, at Black Rock, by Rev. W[illia]m Jesup Jennings	1-M	91
Sarah, d. Benj[ami]n & Mary, b. Jan. 31, 1754	1	243
DeFOREST, DeFORREST, Andrew W., of Humphreyville, m. Lucretia S. **BENNETT**, of Fairfield, Oct. 30, 1844, by Rev. Lyman H. Atwater	1-M	78-80
Rufus, of New Canaan, m. Eunice **TURNEY**, of Fairfield, Aug. 7, 1823, by Rev. Philo Shelton	1-M	12
DENISON, Jeremiah T., Dr., m. Esther Judson **GOODSELL**, Mar. 15, 1842, by Rev. Lyman H. Atwater	1-M	74
Marinda, of Fairfield, m. Russell **GREEN**, of Huntington, L.I., Apr. 11, 1823, by Rev. Philo Shelton	1-M	10
DENNIE, Eunice, w. James, d. Oct. 16, 1740	1	16
Eunice, d. James, m. Thaddeus **BURR**, s. Thad[deus], Mar. 22, 1759	1	249
James, m. Eunice **STURGIS**, Apr. 13, 1731, by Rev. Henry Caner	1	16
DIBBLE, Abigail, see Abigail Starr	1	25
DICKERSON, Elizabeth, d. Thomas, b. Jan. 12, 1681	LR-A2	681
Mary, d. Thomas, b. May 26, 1679	LR-A2	683
DICKMAN, Abigail, d. Cor[neliu]s (?), m. Dan[ie]ll **BEERS**, s. Ephraim, Sept. 3, 1760	1	260
DIMON, DIMOND, Abigail, d. Moses, b. Aug. 20, 1676	LR-A2	664
Abigail, d. Moses & Hannah, b. June 4, 1729; d. soon after	1	79
Àbigail, d. Moses, m. Joseph **HILL**, s. William, Mar. 30, 1731	1	152
Abigail, d. John & Elizabeth, b. Mar. 1, 1740/1	1	80
Abigail, d. Ebenezer, m. Hezekiah **STURGES**, s. Solomon, Nov. 21, 1751	1	103
Abigail, d. W[illia]m & Esther, b. Mar. 10, 1775	1	282
Ann, d. John & Elizabeth, b. Apr. 12, 1734	1	80
Damaries, d. Moses & Hannah, b. Mar. 23, 1744/5	1	79

	Vol.	Page
DIMON, DIMOND (cont.)		
Daniel, s. John & Elizabeth, b. Mar. 20, 1747	1	80
David, s. Moses & Hannah, b. July 5, 1726; d. Apr. 3, 1727	1	79
David, s. W[illia]m & Esther, b. July 28, 1779	1	282
Eben, s. W[illia]m & Esther, b. Feb. 29, 1784	1	282
Ebenezer, Jr., b. Feb. 29, 1784; m. Catharine **SHERWOOD**, Aug. 19, 1810	1	301
Eliza, [d. Ebenezer, Jr. & Catharine], b. Mar. 15, 1812	1	301
Eliza P., m. Thomas **ROBINSON**, July 8, 1834, by T. F. Davis	1-M	53
Eliza Perry, [d. Ebenezer, Jr. & Catharine], b. July 8, 1813	1	301
Elizabeth, d. John & Elizabeth, b. Oct. 11, 1738	1	80
Elizabeth, d. W[illia]m & Esther, b. Jan. 28, 1768	1	282
Elizabeth H., m. Tho[ma]s B. **OSBORN**, Sept. 6, 1826, by Rev. H. R. Judah, of Bridgeport	1-M	28
Esther, d. John & Elizabeth, b. May 11, 1728	1	80
Esther, d. John, m. Joseph **FROST**, s. Jos[eph], Oct. 19, 1747	1	219
Esther, d. W[illia]m & Esther, b. Jan. 10, 1770	1	282
Esther, b. Jan. 28, 1770; m. Joseph **WAKEMAN**, May 29, 1796, by Rev. A. Eliot	1	303
Grace, d. John & Elizabeth, b. Mar. 1, 1735/6	1	80
Hannah, d. Moses & Hannah, b. Apr. 20, 1730; d. 12 hrs. after	1	79
Hannah, d. Moses & Hannah, b. Sept. 15, 1731; d. 1 mo. after	1	79
Hannah, d. Moses & Hannah, b. May 24, 1733; d. 6 wks. after	1	79
Jane, d. Moses & Hannah, b. Aug. 1, 1722; d. Feb. 3, 1754	1	79
Jane, d. Moses, m. Gershom **BRADLEY**, Dec. [ ]	1	116
John, m. Elizabeth **WHEELER**, May 10, 1727	1	80
John, s. John & Elizabeth, b. July 5, 1720	1	80
Jonathan, s. Moses & Hannah, b. Apr. 21, 1738	1	79
Jonathan, s. Moses, m. Hannah **ROWLAND**, d. Joseph, Feb. 14, 1760	1	265
Jon[a]th[an], s. Jon[a]th[an] & Hannah, b. Mar. 14, 1761	1	265
Martha W., d. Bradley, m. Nathaniel S. **BULKELEY**, b. of Fairfield, May 25, 1851, by Rev. N. E. Cornwall	1-M	95
Mary, wid., m. James **SMEDLEY**, Jan. 4, 1747/8	1	197
Mary, d. Ebenezer, m. Benjamin **OSBORN**, s. Sam[ue]ll, Oct. 6, 1753	1	96
Mary, of Fairfield, m. Otis **KELLOGG**, of Troy, N.Y., [Nov.] 24, [1831], by Rev. Charles Smith	1-M	44
Moses, s. Moses, b. Oct. 7, 1672	LR-A2	664
Moses, s. Moses, b. Apr. 4, 1698; m. Hannah **GILBERT**, Apr. 27, 1721	1	79
Moses, s. Moses & Hannah, b. Mar. 2, 1734/5	1	79
Pinkney, s. John & Elizabeth, b. Sept. 12, 1743	1	80
Priscilla, d. W[illia]m & Esther, b. Apr. 2, 1777	1	282

	Vol.	Page
DIMON, DIMOND (cont.)		
Rachel M., m. Elias P. **BENHAM**, b. of Fairfield, Sept.		
16, 1835, by Lyman H. Atwater	1-M	57
Sarah, d. Moses & Hannah, b. July 16, 1724; d. Apr. 15,		
1727	1	79
Sarah, d. Moses & Hannah, b. May 6, 1728	1	79
Sarah, d. W[illia]m & Esther, b. July 29, 1766; d. Sept.		
21, 1778	1	282
Sarah, d. W[illia]m & Esther, b. Nov. 10, 1781	1	282
Thomas, s. Moses, b. Sept. 15, 1678	LR-A2	663
Thomas, s. John & Elizabeth, b. Apr. 1, 1732	1	80
William, s. Eben[eze]r, m. Esther **STURGIS**, d. Solomon,		
Jan. 3, 1765	1	282
William Burr, s. W[illia]m & Esther, b. Feb. 10, 1773	1	282
DISBROW, Abigail, w. of Asahel, b. Nov. 23, 1743 O.S.; m.		
Nov. 20, 1775	1	286
Abigail, d. Nathan & Weight, b. Nov. 25, 1743	1	172
Abigail, w. Thomas, d. Apr. 17, 1756	1	146
Abig[ai]l, d. Asael & Abig[ai]l, b. Nov. 28, 1780	1	286
Andrew, s. Nathan & Weight, b. Oct. 8, 1751	1	172
Ann, d. Tho[ma]s & Jane, b. Aug. 24, 1742	1	146
Anna, [twin with Deborah], d. Asael & Abig[ai]l b. Nov.		
4, 1787	1	286
Asa, s. Caleb & Sarah, b. June 13, 1753	1	132
Asahel, b. Mar. 28, 1746 O.S.; m. Abigail [ ], Nov. 20,		
1775	1	286
Asael, s. Joseph & Abigail, b. Mar. 28, 1747	1	131
Asael, s. Asael & Abigail, b. June 17, 1782	1	286
Asael, had negro Nancy, d. Lilly, b. Dec. 10, 1791	1	463
Betsey, m. George N. **HURLBUTT**, b. of Fairfield,		
[Oct.] 12, [1823], by Rev. E. W. Hooker	1-M	12
Betty, d. Joseph & Abigail, b. Nov. 18, 1738; d. Sept. 13,		
1748	1	131
Betty, d. Joshua & Mary, b. Apr. 21, 1754	1	150
Betty, d. Jabez & Mabel, b. Nov. 10, 1756	1	131
Caleb, s. Tho[ma]s & Abigail, b. Aug. 1, 1719	1	146
Caleb, s. Thomas, m. Sarah **DAVIS**, d. Sam[ue]ll, Nov.		
19, 1740	1	132
Caleb, s. Caleb & Sarah, b. Dec. 10, 1749	1	132
Damaries, d. Caleb & Sarah, b. June 24, 1747	1	132
Deborah, [twin with Anna], d. Asael & Abigail, b. Nov. 4,		
1787	1	286
Deborah, of Greens Farms, m. Joseph S. **BENEDICT**, of		
Ridgefield, June 30, 1824, by Hez[ekiah] Ripley,		
V.D.M.	1-M	15
Ebenezer, s. Joshua & Mary, b. Aug. 20, 1748; d. Sept.		
16, 1757	1	150
Ebenezer S., m. Angeline **BARTLETT**, b. of Greens		
Farms, Oct. 15, 1820, by Hezekiah Ripley, V.D.M.	1-M	2
Elias, s. Joseph & Abigail, b. Nov. 26, 1750	1	131
Ezra, s. Asael & Abig[ai]l, b. Nov. 4, 1785	1	286
George, s. Asael & Abig[ai]l, b. May 5, 1784	1	286
Henry, s. Caleb & Sarah, b. Apr. 19, 1756	1	132

	Vol.	Page

DISBROW (cont.)

	Vol.	Page
Isaac, s. Joshua & Mary, b. Aug. 2, 1757	1	150
Jabez, s. Joseph & Abigail, b. June 23, 1734	1	131
Jabez, s. Joseph, m. Mabel **JEACOCKS**, d. Joshua, Nov. 3, 1754	1	131
Jacob, s. Nathan & Weight, b. Jan. 28, 1753/4	1	172
James, s. Caleb & Sarah, b. Mar. 24, 1743	1	132
Jason, s. Joseph & Abigail, b. Apr. 30, 1736	1	131
Jesse, s. Caleb & Sarah, b. May 24, 1745	1	132
Johanna, d. Nathan & Weight, b. Jan. 6, 1739/40	1	172
John, s. Joseph & Abigail, b. Jan. 15, 1732/3; d. May 11, following	1	131
John, s. Tho[ma]s & Jane, b. Oct. 22, 1749	1	146
Joseph, s. Tho[ma]s & Abigail, b. Dec. 15, 1712	1	146
Joseph, s. Thomas, m. Abigail **MEAKER**, d. John, Oct. 27, 1731	1	131
Joseph, s. Joseph & Abigail, b. Feb. 28, 1744/5	1	131
Joseph, of Westport, m. Mary Ann **GRAY**, of Weston, [ ], by Cyrus Silliman. Recorded Feb. 22, 1838	1-M	66
Joshua, s. Tho[ma]s & Abigail, b. [}, 1723	1	146
Joshua, s. Tho[ma]s, m. Mary **GRAY**, d. Isaac, June 7, 1743	1	150
Joshua, s. Joshua & Mary, b. Jan. 27, 1745	1	150
Joshua, s. Joshua & Mary, d. May 13, 1747	1	150
Joshua, s. Joshua & Mary, b. Sept. 29, 1750	1	150
Justus, s. Caleb & Sarah, b. June 24, 1751	1	132
Lois, d. Joseph & Abigail, b. Jan. 29, 1742/3	1	131
Lydea, d. Nathan & Weight, b. Apr. 1, 1756	1	172
Mary, d. Joshua & Mary, b. Nov. 26, 1746	1	150
Meaker, s. Asael & Abig[ai]l, b. Apr. 18, 1777	1	286
Nathan, s. Tho[ma]s & Abigail, b. June 10, 1715	1	146
Nathan, s. Tho[ma]s, m. Weight **SCRIBNER**, d. Tho[ma]s, Nov. 21, 1738	1	172
Nathan, s. Nathan & Weight, b. Apr. 6, 1741	1	172
Noah, s. Joseph & Abigail, b. Feb. 8, 1740/1	1	131
Patte, d. Nathan & Weight, b. Aug. 31, 1742	1	172
Peter, s .Nathan & Weight, b. Feb. 23, 1746/7	1	172
Polly, d. Asael & Abig[ai]l, b. Sept. 27, 1789	1	286
Rhoda, of Fairfield, m. Epenetus J. **WEBB**, of Norwalk, Nov. 30, 1823, by Hezekiah Ripley, V.D.M.	1-M	13
Russel, s. Jabez & Mabel, b. June 20, 1755	1	131
Ruth, d. Nathan & Weight, b. Jan. 10, 1744/5	1	172
Sam[ue]ll, s. Caleb & Sarah, b. Sept. 30, 1741	1	132
Sarah, d. Tho[ma]s & Abigail, b. Apr. [ ], 1726	1	146
Sarah, m. William **GRAY**, s. William, Jan. 25, 1742	1	209
Sarah, d. Nathan & Weight, b. Feb. 19, 1745/6; d. Mar. 23, 1746	1	172
Sarah, d. Tho[ma]s & Jane, b. June 10, 1747	1	146
Solomon, s. Nathan & Weight, b. July 8, 1757	1	172
Susannah, d. Tho[ma]s & Abigail, b. May [ ], 1717	1	146
Susannah, d. Tho[ma]s, m. Josiah **WEBB**, Nov. [ ], 1729	1	232
Susannah, d. Nathan & Weight, b. July 4, 1750	1	172

	Vol.	Page
DISBROW (cont.)		
Thaddeus, s. Joseph & Abigail, b. May 3, 1749	1	131
Thomas, m. Abigail **GODING**, Oct. [ ], 1708	1	146
Thomas, s. Thomas & Abigail, b. Dec. 6, 1710	1	146
Thomas, s. Thomas, m. Jane **SHERWOOD**, d. Isaac, Aug. 4, 1741	1	146
Thomas, s. Tho[ma]s & Jane, b. May 24, 1744	1	146
Thomas, [ ] 1757	1	83
Thomas, d. Sept. 30, 1757	1	146
Thomasa S., s. Asael & Abig[ai]l, b. June 26, 1778	1	286
Weight, d. Nathan & Weight, b. Oct. 10, 1748	1	172
Wate, d. Asael & Abig[ai]l, b. Aug. 5, 1779	1	286
DONEWELL, Frederick, of Norwalk, m. Cynthia **ALLEN**, of Fairfield, Mar. 23, 1834, by Rev. C. A. Boardman, of Saugatuck	1-M	52
DOWNS, DOWN, Abigail, d. Edward & Mary, b. Jan. 24, 1743/4	1	19
David, m. Elizabeth **ROWLAND**, Jan. 3, 1733/4	1	136
David, s. David & Elizabeth, b. Aug. 20, 1750	1	136
David, m. Mary **WILLIAMS**, b. of Fairfield, Dec. 31, 1837, by N.E. Cornwall	1-M	65
Elizabeth, d. David & Elizabeth, b. Aug. 5, 1737	1	136
Elizabeth, d. David, m. Gershom **WAKEMAN**, s. John, Apr. 17, 1757	1	257
Elizabeth, m. David **STURGIS**, July 9, 1826, by William Shelton	1-M	24
Hannah, d. Edw[ar]d & Marcy, b. Jan. 5, 1741/2	1	19
Mary, d. David & Elizabeth, b. July 10, 1746	1	136
Mary E., of Weston, m. Stephen P. **SAUNDERSON**, of Norwalk, Dec. 22, 1832, by T. F. Davis	1-M	48-9
Seth, s. David & Elizabeth, b. Dec. 10, 1734	1	136
Thiah, m. Jabel **STURGIS**, [ ], 1752	1	239
DUNCOMBE, Charles, s. William, of Barleyend, near Joinghoe, in the County of Bucks, m. Elizabeth **HULBART**, d. Zachariah, Mar. 10, 1744/5 by Rev. Henry Caner, of Fairfield	1	186
Charles, s. Charles & Elizabeth, b. Apr. 24, 1747	1	186
Elizabeth, d. Charles & Elizabeth, b. July 23, 1753	1	186
John, s. Charles & Elizabeth, b. Apr. 18, 1751	1	186
Thomas, s. Charles & Elizabeth, b. Sept. [ ], 1756	1	186
William, s. Charles & Elizabeth, b. Apr. 5, 1749	1	186
DUNKINS, Mary, m. Ebenezer **MUNROE**, Jan. 1, 1751/2	1	187
DUTTON, Henry, of Newtown, m. Elizabeth Elliott **JOY**, of Fairfield, Sept. 8, 1823, by Nath[anie]l Hewit	1-M	12
DWIGHT, Timothy, Rev. had negro Maria, b. Oct. 14, 1789; York, b. May 31, 1794; next youngest b. June 1, 1797	1	293
EDMOND, Ann, d. Robert, m. Stephen **COUCH**, s. Tho[ma]s, Jan. 29, 1784	1	284
EDWARDS, Elizabeth, d. Feb. 22, 1709/10	LR-2	456
Mary, w. Capt. Tho[ma]s of Stratford, formerly w. of Joseph **PERRY**, of Fairfield, d. of Michael **CLUQSTON**, of Fairfield, d. Nov. 8, 1773	1	10

	Vol.	Page
EGAN, William, m. Mary **MILLER**, b. of Southport, May 25, 1851, by Rev. Sam[ue]l J. M. Merwin	1-M	91
ELDREDGE, Joseph, s. Abell & Abigail, b. July 2, 1753	1	29
ELLIOT, ELIOT, Andrew, Rev. of Fairfield, s. Rev. Andrew, D.D., of Boston, m. Mary **PYNCHON** (Mrs.?) of Cambridge, d. Hon. Joseph Pynchon, of Boston, July 19, 1774, at Cambridge, by Rev. Dr. Appleton	1	279
Andrew, s. And[re]w & Mary, b. Aug. 15, 1780	1	279
Andrew, Rev. of New Milford, m. Sophia **WASSON**, of Fairfield, Sept. 17, 1820, by Nath[anie]l Hewit, V.D.M.	1-M	2
Elizabeth, d. Andrew & Mary, b. Oct. 29, 1776	1	279
Elizabeth, d. Rev. Andrew & Mary, m. Gershom **BURR**, Oct. 13, 1801	1	294
Eunice Burr, d. And[re]w & Mary, b. Aug. 16, 1778	1	279
Eunice Burr, m. Elijah **BIBBINS**, b. of Fairfield, Feb. 26, 1821, by Nath[anie]l Hewit, V.D.M.	1-M	3
Mary, d. Rev. And[re]w & Mary, b. July 4, 1775	1	279
Rutha Martha, d. And[re]w & Mary, b. July 25, 1785	1	279
Sarah, d. Rev. Andrew, D.D., of Boston, m. Joseph **SQUIER**, s. Capt. Joseph, of Fairfield, Oct. 5, 1778, by Rev. John Lathrop, of Boston	1	282
Sarah, d. And[re]w & Mary, b. Nov. 2 1782	1	279
Susanna, of Boston, m. Dr. David **HALL**, of Fairfield, Nov. 10, 1789, by Rev. John Eliot, of Boston	1	288
Susanna, d. And[re]w & Mary, b. Dec. 1, 1790	1	279
ELLS, James of New Canaan, m. Louisa Ann **TREDWELL**, of Fairfield, Nov. 29, 1832, by Rev. Stephen Martindale	1-M	47
ELWELL, Esther, m. John **FINCH**, s. Samuel, Dec. 11, 1745	1	198
ELWOOD, Abraham, s. Rich[ar]d & Rachel, b. Dec. 19, 1756	1	227
Arin, m. Hannah **GREGORY**, b. of Saugatuck, Mar. 21, 1827, by Rev. E. W. Hooker	1-M	26-7
Eliakim, s. Rich[ar]d & Rachel, b. Feb. 6, 1750	1	227
Hannah, m. John **ROBERD**, Mar. [ ], 1757 [sic]	1	48
Happy Frances, m. James **LEFFERTY**, May 8, 1836, by Rev. T. F. Davis	1-M	59
John, s. Richard & Rachel, b. May 15, 1745	1	227
Joseph, s. Rich[ar]d & Rachel, b. Apr. 15, 1742	1	227
Munson, m. Emily **GODFREY**, Sept. 29, 1833, by T. F. Davis	1-M	51
Richard, m. Rachel **DAVIS**, Feb. 20, 1742	1	227
Samuel, s. Rich[ar]d & Rachel, b. Sept. 14, 1747	1	227
Shelton, m. Maria **NASH**, Jan. 29, 1837, by Rev. Tho[ma]s F. Davis	1-M	62
Thomas, s. Rich[ar]d & Rachel, b. July 13, 1754	1	227
William, of Norwalk, m. Abigail **BROTHERTOWN**, of Greens Farms, Apr. 11, 1827, by Rev. E. W. Hooker	1-M	26-7
ELY, W., M.D., m. Sarah Anne **ALLEN**, Oct. 13, 1834, by Amos Savage	1-M	54
EVITTS, William M., of Bridgeport, m. Eliza J. **JENNINGS**, of Southport, July 11, 1852, by Rev. Sam[ue]l J. M. Merwin	1-M	95

	Vol.	Page
FAIRCHILD, Abraham, m. Rachel **SCRIBNER**, Nov. 7, 1742	1	179
Abraham, s. Abraham & Rachel, b. Jan. 1, 1745	1	179
Alexander, s. Tho[ma]s & Rachel, b. Dec. 5, 1753	1	238
Andrew m. Abigail **HILL**, Apr. 26, 1752	1	153
Billee [twin with Timothy], s. Thomas & Mary, b. Oct. 22, 1738 (Timothy being the eldest)	1	17
Catharine, m. Joseph **SANFORD**, Feb. 11, 1724/5	1	222
Charles, m. Polly **NASH**, b. of Fairfield, May 8, 1825, by Rev. E. W. Hooker	1-M	18
Daniel, s. Abraham & Rachel, b. Dec. 26, 1748	1	179
David, s. Abraham & Rachel, b. June 19, 1753	1	179
Ezekiel, s. Abraham & Rachel, b. Oct. 26, 1746	1	179
George, of Westport, m. Polly Ann **NASH**, of Fairfield, Feb. 14, 1841, by Rev. Dan C. Curtiss	1-M	71
Gershom, s. Alexander, m. Mary **KNAP**, d. Moses, Nov. 19, 1754	1	124
Huldah, d. Tho[ma]s & Rachel, b. Apr. 20, 1757	1	238
Isaac, s. Abraham & Rachel, b. Mar. 6, 1751	1	179
Joanna, d. Joseph, m. Samuel **HULL**, s. Samuel, Feb. 3, 1727	1	57
John, s. Tho[ma]s & Rachel, b. Jan. 26, 1755	1	238
John, s. John, of Durham, m. Martha **ALLEN**, d. Dr. John, Feb. 17, 1773	1	277
John, d. Sept. 10, 1777	1	277
Mary, d. Andrew & Abigail, b. Mar. 7, 1754	1	153
Mary, w. Gershom, d. Dec. 9, 1756	1	124
Peter, m. Hannah **BETTS**, Nov. 7, 1751	1	99
Phebe, d. Andrew & Abigail, b. Nov. 12, 1756	1	153
Robert, s. John & Martha, b. Jan. 19, 1775	1	277
Samuel, s. Abraham & Rachel, b .July 9, 1755	1	179
Tho[ma]s, m. Mary **HALL**, Sept. 22, 1737	1	17
Thomas, s. Alexander, m,. Rachel **SHERWOOD**, d. John, June 17, 1753	1	238
Timothy, [twin with Billee], s. Thomas & Mary, b. Oct. 22, 1738 (Timothy being the eldest)	1	17
FANNING, Bridget, of Stamford, m. Patrick **FARRELL**, of Norwalk, Dec. 22, 1847, by S. M. TenBrouch, J.P.	1-M	88
FANSHER, Rufus, of New Canaan, m. Caroline **CALLON**, of Fairfield, Dec. 11, 1836, by Lyman H. Atwater	1-M	60
FANTON, Abigail, d. John & Mary, b. Feb. 10, 1736	1	190
Ann, d. John & Mary, b. Sept. 10, 1740	1	190
Ellen, m. Ebenezer **LYON**, Jan. 9, 1717	1	99
Esther, d. John & Mary, b. Oct. 10, 1753	1	190
Eunice, m. Nehemiah **BEERS**, June 27, 1753	1	228
Hannah, d. John & Mary, b. July 15, 1734	1	190
Hezekiah, s. John & Mary, b. Nov. 14, 1743	1	190
John, s. Jonathan, m. Mary **ROWLAND**, Nov. [ ], 1731	1	190
John, s. John & Mary, b. Mar. 15, 1745	1	190
John, m. Eunice **LYON**, wid., Feb. 12, 1755	1	190
Jonathan, s. John & Mary, b. Nov. 2, 1738	1	190
Mary, d. Jonathan, m. Ephraim **BEERS**, s. Ephraim, Dec. 24, 1745	1	164
Mary, d. John & Mary, b. Oct. 10, 1751	1	190

	Vol.	Page
FANTON (cont.)		
Nehemiah, s. John & Mary, b. Jan. 10, 1748	1	190
FARRELL, Patrick, of Norwalk, m. Bridget **FANNING**, of		
Stamford, Dec. 22, 1847, by S. M. Ten Brouch, J.P.	1-M	88
FAYERFIELD, William, m. Abigail **OSBORN**, d. David, of		
East Chester, decd., Oct. 7, 1691, by Mr. John Bare	LR-A2	676
FAYERWEATHER, Hannah, d. Joseph & Abigail, b .Nov.		
30, 1731	1	20
Penelope, m. Rich[ar]d **HUBBLE**, Jr., Dec. 9, 1735	1	9
FERGUSON, Herbert Q., of New York, m. Eliza		
CARTLEDGE, of Fairfield, Oct. 21, 1846, by Rev.		
N. E. Cornwall	1-M	85
FERRIS Charles R., of Stamford, m. Sarah B. **PERRY**, of		
Fairfield, Mar. 18, 1850, by Rev. Lyman H. Atwater	1-M	92
Harriet, Mrs. m. Orrin H. **ADDIS**, b. of New Milford,		
Dec. 31, 1848, by Rev. N. E. Cornwall	1-M	94
FERRY, Sarah, d. Ebenezer, m. Stephen **GREY**, s. John, Sept.		
3, 1758	1	263
FILLIO, Elizabeth, m. Jabez **SHERWOOD**, Oct. [ ], 1742	1	229
FINCH, Abigail, d. John [Sam[ue]ll in copy], & Esther, b. June		
30, 1746	1	198
Alva, of Norwalk, m. Anna **SHERWOOD**, of Greens		
Farms, Feb. 25, 1829, by John Hunter	1-M	33
Esther, d. John & Esther, b. Oct. 28, 1750	1	198
Harriet, m. William D. **GILBERT**, b. of Norwalk, Oct.		
29, 1826, by Rev. E. W. Hooker	1-M	24
John, s. Samuel, m. Esther **ELWELL**, Dec. 11, 1745	1	198
John, s. John & Esther, b. Mar. 15, 1748	1	198
Phebe, d. John & Esther, b. Nov. 25, 1754	1	198
Sarah, m. Stephen **ADAMS**, Oct. 17, 1727	1	59
Sarah, m. Richard **KING**, Oct. 28, 1742	1	243
FISHER, Edward, of Bridgeport, m. Julia Ann **REED**, of		
Fairfield, Mar. 9, 1845, by Rev. Lyman H. Atwater	1-M	81
William, of Nottingham, Eng., m. Sarah **SMITH**, of		
Fairfield, [Dec.] 8, [1844], by Rev. Cha[rle]s R.		
Adams	1-M	78-80
FITCH, Hezekiah, s. Hon. Tho[ma]s, of Norwalk, m. Jerusha		
BURR, d. Col. Andrew, Sept. 21, 1767	1	270
James D., of New York, m. Martha Ann **GLOVER**, d.		
John, of Fairfield, Apr. 19, 1849, by Rev. N. E.		
Cornwall	1-M	94
Mary, m. Daniel **BRADLEY**, Mar. [ ], 1743	1	81
FOLLIETT, Betsey, m. Charles **BARNS**, b. of Norwalk, Aug.		
23, [1821], by Rev. E. W. Hooker	1-M	5
FOOT, Abiah, d. Nathan & Abiah, b. Jan. 15, 1751	1	108
Dorotha, m. Reuben **SALMON**, Nov. 16, 1752	1	245
Hannah, d. Nathan & Abiah, b. May 12, 1754	1	108
Mary, m. Nathaniel **BOOTH**, Oct. 4, 1739	1	90
Nathan, m. Abiah **GILBERT**, July 3, 1750	1	108
Phebe, d. John, m. Timothy **TREADWELL**, s. Benjamin,		
Dec. 4, 1751	1	122

	Vol.	Page
FOOT (cont.)		
Phebe, of Norwalk, m. William P. **SNAGG**, of Philadelphia, Pa., June 11, 1826, by Rev. E. W. Hooker	1-M	23
FORESTER, John R., of Danbury, m. M. Angeline **PERRY**, of Westport, Jan. 16, 1848, by Rev. Lyman H. Atwater	1-M	88
FOUNTAIN, Sarah, d. Aaron, m. David **RAYMAN**, s. W[illia]m, Nov. 24, 1760	1	27
FOWLER, Sarah A., m. Zalmon B. **WAKEMAN**, b. of Fairfield, Mar. 3, 1829, by John Hunter	1-M	33
FREEMAN, Edmond, s. Isaac & Bethiah, b. Jan. 4, 1725/6	LR-A2	457
Phebe, d. Eace & Nancy (negro), b. Sept. [ ], 1814	1	302
FRENCH, Abigail, m. Hezekiah **WHEELER**, Dec. 19, 1754	1	51
Charles of Trumbull, m. Mary **BIBBINS**, of Fairfield, May 13, 1850, by Rev. Lyman H. Atwater	1-M	92
FROST, Abigail, d. Isaac, m. Samuel **MORHOUSE**, s. Gideon, Aug. 20, 1743	1	154
Adria, w. Joseph, d. July 23, 1753	1	208
Dimon, s. Jos[eph] & Esther, b. Apr. 17, 1757	1	219
Eunice, d. Jos[eph] & Adria, b. Sept. 16, 1742	1	208
Grissel, d. Jos[eph] & Adria, b. Oct. 24, 1732	1	208
Grissel, d. Joseph, m. Benjamin **WYNKOOPE**, Jr., s. Benjamin, Mar. 6, 1754	1	58
Jabez, s. Jos[eph] & Adria, b. Aug. 4, 1725	1	208
Joseph, m. Adria **COUCH**, d. Sam[ue]ll, Aug. 27, 1724	1	208
Joseph, s. Jos[eph] & Adria, b. Nov. 8, 1726	1	208
Joseph, s. Jos[eph], m. Esther **DIMON**, d. John, Oct. 19, 1747	1	219
Joseph, s. Jos[eph] & Esther, b. May 22, 1755	1	219
Mary, m. Ebenezer **MEAD**, Aug. 1, 1744	1	199
Sarah, d. Jos[eph] & Esther, b. Dec. 15, 1747	1	219
GALLAGHER, Dennis, m. Mary T. **BANKS**, b. of Fairfield, Feb. 18, 1844, by Rev. N. E. Cornwall	1-M	76
GIBBS, George, of Turks Island, m. Ann Mills **JUDSON**, of Fairfield, Oct. 7, 1832, by Rev. John H. Hunter	1-M	47
GILBERT, Abiah, d. John & Jemima, b. Dec. 6, 1731	1	106
Abiah, m. Nathan **FOOT**, July 3, 1750	1	108
Abigail, d. Joseph & Lois, b. Dec. 19, 1746	1	107
Andrew, s. Thaddeus & Deborah, b. Oct. 10, 1743	1	106
Burr, s. Ebenezer & Prudence, b. Oct. 17, 1757	1	107
Caleb, s. Josiah & Sarah, b. Mar. 12, 1789	1	53
Catharine, m. John **WAKEMAN**, Apr. 8, 1730	1	147
David, s. Eben[eze]r & Joanna, b. Nov. 13, 1746	1	107
Ebenezer, s. John & Jemima, b. Mar. 31, 1724	1	106
Ebenezer, s. John, m. Joanna **NORTHROP**, Apr. 18, 1744	1	107
Ebenezer, s. Eben[eze]r & Joanna, b. June 9, 1754	1	107
Ebenezer, m. Prudence **BURR**, May 12, 1756	1	107
Elizabeth, b. Sept. 11, 1731	1	88
Elizabeth, m. Ebenezer **GREEN**, Mar. 24, 1748	1	88
Elmor, s. Thaddeus & Deborah, b. May 6, 1757	1	106
Eunice, d. John & Lydea, b. Apr. 16, 1757	1	108

	Vol.	Page
GILBERT (cont.)		
Hannah, b. Dec. 29, 1700; m. Moses **DIMON**, Apr. 27, 1721	1	79
Hannah, d. Josiah & Sarah, b. Apr. 16, 1737; d. Jan. 30, 1740	1	53
Hannah, d. Joseph & Lois, b. Apr. 13, 1756	1	107
Hezekiah, s. Eben[eze]r & Joanna, b. Dec. 9, 1744	1	107
Ichabod, s. Josiah & Sarah, b. June 3, 1741	1	53
Joanna, d. Eben[eze]r & Joanna, b. May 9, 1748	1	107
Joanna, w. Eben[eze]r, d. Feb. 27, 1756	1	107
John, m. Jemima **WILLIAMS**, June 29, 1721	1	106
John, s. John & Jemima, b. Aug. 11, 1735	1	106
John, Jr., s. John, m. Lidea **MERWIN**, June 17, 1756	1	108
John B., of Bridgeport, m. Louisa **WHEELER**, of Fairfield, May 7, 1848, by Rev. J. H. Perry, Southport	1-M	89
Joseph, s. John & Jemima, b. June 14, 1726	1	106
Joseph, s. John, m. Lois **BRADLEY**, Oct. 3, 1744	1	107
Josiah, m. Sarah **LORD**, June 14, 1722	1	53
Josiah, s. Josiah & Sarah, b. July 3, 1731	1	53
Josiah, d. Dec. 4, 1760	1	53
Martha, d. John & Jemima, b. June 25, 1728	1	106
Mary, d. Josiah & Sarah, b. Nov. 11, 1726	1	53
Moses, s. Josiah & Sarah, b. Mar. 7, 1723	1	53
Phinehas, s. Josiah & Sarah, b. Aug. 6, 1734	1	53
Rebecca, Mrs. of Sherman, m. Edwards **BLAKEMAN**, of Fairfield, Nov. 10, 1844, by Rev. James Scott, of Stratfield	1-M	78-80
Reuben, s. Joseph & Lois, b. Oct. 17, 1752	1	107
Richard, s. Josiah & Sarah, b. Oct. 14, 1725; d. 1748	1	53
Ruth, d. Thaddeus & Deborah, b. Sept. 15, 1748	1	106
Sarah, d. Joseph & Lois, b. Mar. 29, 1745	1	107
Seth, s. Thaddeus & Deborah, b. May 31, 1742	1	106
Stephen, s. Joseph & Lois, b. Nov. 11, 1749	1	107
Thaddeus, s. John & Jemima, b. Aug. 5, 1722	1	106
Thaddeus, s. John, m. Deborah **WINTON**, d. John, July 7, 1741	1	106
Thaddeus, s. Thaddeus & Deborah, b. Mar. 28, 1753	1	106
William D., m. Harriet **FINCH**, b. of Norwalk, Oct. 29, 1826, by Rev. E. W. Hooker	1-M	24
GLOVER, Martha Ann, d. John, of Fairfield, m. James D. **FITCH**, of New York, Apr. 19, 1849, by Rev. N. E. Cornwall	1-M	94
GODFREY, GODFREE, Abraham, s. Nathan & Martha, b. May 13, 1748	1	156
Andrew B., of Weston, m. Arete **MEEKER**, of Fairfield, Dec. 3, 1826, by Rev. E. W. Hooker	1-M	25
Ann, d. David & Mary, b. May 16, 1740	1	137
Benjamin, m. Betsey **BROTHERTON**, Dec. 28, 1834, by T. F. Davis	1-M	55
Bette, d. Stephen & Elizabeth, b. Feb. 16, 1747	1	188
Bette, d. Stephen, m. Eben[eze]r **LEWIS**, s. Charles, Feb. [ ], 1763	1	268

	Vol.	Page
GODFREY, GODFREE (cont.)		
Christopher, m. Margary **STURGIS**, Feb. 11, 1711	1	188
Daniel, s. David & Mary, b. Mar. 30, 1739	1	137
David, s. Christopher & Margary, b. Feb. 20, 1713	1	188
David, s. Christopher, m. Mary **SILLIMAN**, d. Dan[ie]ll, June 24, 1738	1	137
David, s. David & Mary, b. Sept. 1, 1743	1	137
Ebenezer, s. Christopher & Margary, b. June 27, 1727	1	188
Edward B., of Weston, m. Eunice **JENNINGS**, of Greens Farms, Apr. 8, 1835, by T. F. Davis	1-M	56
Eleazer, s. Christopher & Margary, b. Mar. 15, 1721	1	188
Eliza, of Greens Farms, m. Samuel A. **WOOD**, of Weston, Sept. 30, 1821, by Hezekiah Ripley, V.D.M.	1-M	5
Eliza, of Fairfield, m. Luther **SALE**, of Fairfield, Oct. 24, 1836, by Nath[anie]l E. Cornwall	1-M	60
Emily, m. Munson **ELWOOD**, Sept. 29, 1833, by T. F. Davis	1-M	51
Eunice, d. Stephen & Elizabeth, b. Nov. 5, 1749	1	188
Francis, m. Sarah **NASH**, June 21, 1836, by Rev. T. F. Davis	1-M	59
Isaac, s. Christopher & Margary, b. Dec. 25, 1724	1	188
Isaac Chauncey, of Fairfield, m. Sarah **BROWN**, of Greenfield, Nov. 10, 1822, by Nathaniel Hewit	1-M	9
John, m. Polly **GODFREY**, Aug. 7, 1827, South Salem, by Jesse Keeler, J.P.	1-M	29
Jonathan, s. David & Mary, b. Dec. 23, 1754	1	137
Jona[th]an, m. Elizabeth **HUBBELL**, b. of Fairfield, Jan. 19, 1823, by Rev. Philo Shelton	1-M	10
Jonathan, Jr., m. Maria **CARTLEDGE**, d. Charles, b. of Fairfield, Oct. 21, 1849, by Rev. N. E. Cornwall	1-M	94
Laura, of Fairfield, m. S. **WILSON**, of Boston, Nov. 1, 1829, by John H. Hunter	1-M	35-6
Martha, d. Nathan & Martha, b. May 24, 1752	1	156
Mary, d. Stephen & Elizabeth, b. Nov. 12, 1751	1	188
Mary, d. David & Mary, b. Feb. 24, 1752	1	137
Nathan, s. Christopher & Margary, b. Sept. 25, 1719	1	188
Nathan, s. Stephen & Elizabeth, b. Apr. 30, 1743	1	188
Nathan, m. Martha **COUCH**, June 11, 1747	1	156
Nathan, s. Nathan & Martha, b. Aug. 19, 1754	1	156
Polly, m. John **GODFREY**, Aug. 7, 1827, South Salem, by Jesse Keeler, J.P.	1-M	29
Priscilla, of Weston, m. Horace **PORTER**, of Ridgefield, Sept. 7, 1824, by Rev. E. W. Hooker	1-M	15
Samuel, m. Betsey Ann **TREDWELL**, b. of Fairfield, July 5, 1822, by Rev. Asa Bronson, of Stratfield	1-M	7
Sarah, d. Stephen & Elizabeth, b. May 17, 1741	1	188
Sarah, d. Christopher, m. Gideon **MOR[E]HOUSE**, s. Gideon, Feb. 3, 1742	1	182
Sarah, d. David & Mary, b. Feb. 12, 1757	1	137
Silliman, s. David & Mary, b. May 1, 1750	1	137
Stephen, s. Christopher & Margary, b. Sept. 8, 1715	1	188

	Vol.	Page
GODFREY, GODFREE (cont.)		
Stephen, s. Christopher, m. Elizabeth **LEWIS**, June 11, 1739	1	188
Stephen, s. Stephen & Elizabeth, b. Oct. 4, 1745	1	188
Zalmon, m. Sally **HUBBELL**, Dec. 19, 1830, by Elisha Cushman	1-M	39-40
GODING, Abigail, m. Thomas **DISBROW**, Oct. [ ], 1708	1	146
GOLD, [see also **GOULD**], Aaron, S. Oneprimus* & Eunice, b. Jan. 18, 1740/1 *(Onessimus)	1	23
Aaron, s. Onessimus, m. Rebeckah **SCUDDER**, d. Peter, of Huntington, L.I., Jan. 27, 1761	1	102
Abell, s. Sam[ue]l & Esther, b. Sept. 14, 1727	1	13
Abell, s. Sam[ue]ll, m. Ellen **BURR**, d. Capt. Samuell, Dec. 19, 1754	1	25
Abel, s. Abel & Ellen, b. Oct. 18, 1756	1	25
Abel, d. Nov. 11, 1789	1	25
Abigail, d. Nathan, b. Feb. 14, 1687	LR-B	C
Abigail, d. Sam[ue]l & Esther, b. Apr. 27, 1721	1	13
Abigail, d. Abraham & Elizabeth, b. Nov. 15, 1754	1	49
Abraham, s. Sam[ue]l & Esther, b. Oct. 12, 1730; d. 6wks. 3 das. after	1	13
Abraham, 2nd, s. Sam[ue]l & Esther, b. May 10, 1732	1	13
Abram, s. Sam[ue]ll, m. Elizabeth **BURR**, d. Capt. John, Jan. 1, 1754	1	49
David, s. Sam[ue]l & Esther, b. July 11, 1717	1	13
Esther, d. Sam[ue]l & Esther, b. Oct. 13, 1719	1	13
Esther, d. Sam[ue]ll, m. John **TURNEY**, s. Robert, Dec. 28, 1742	1	65
Hezekiah, s. Abra[ha]m & Elizabeth, b. Dec. 9, 1756	1	49
John, s. [Nathan], b. Apr. 25, 1688/9	LR-B	C
John, s. Abel & Ellen, b. Oct. 2, 1755; d. Dec. 15, 1755	1	25
Nathan, s. [Nathan], b. Apr. 6, 1690	LR-B	C
Nathan, Major d. Mar. 4, 1693/4	LR-A2	676
Rebecca, d. Onesimus, m. Ephraim **NICHOLS**, s. Ignacius, July 5, 1741	1	87
Samuell, s. [Nathan], b. Dec. 27, 1692	LR-B	C
Sam[ue]l, m. Esther **BRADLEY**, Dec. 7, 1716	1	13
Sarah, Mrs. d. Oct. 17, 1711	LR-2	456
Sarah, d. John, m. David **ALLEN**, s. Lieut. Gideon, Oct. 11, 1739	1	50
Sarah, d. Daniel, m. David **TURNEY**, s. Stephen, Oct. 4, 1766	1	130
Scudder, s. Aaron & Rebeckah, b. Mar. 27, 1762	1	102
Tho[ma]s, s. Hez[ekiah], m. Anna **SMITH**, d. Sam[ue]ll, Feb. 13, 1755	1	198
GOLDEN, [see also **GOULDEN**], Charlotte, m. George **PENFIELD**, b. of Fairfield, May 2, 1839, by Lyman H. Atwater	1-M	67
Margaret A., of Fairfield, m. James H. **TAYLOR**, of Trumbull, Sept. 17, 1845, by Rev. Lyman H. Atwater	1-M	82
GOODSELL, Bradley, m. Sarah Anna **SILLIMAN**, b. of Fairfield, Dec. 30, 1841, by Rev. Cyrus Silliman	1-M	73

	Vol.	Page
GOODSELL (cont.)		
Esther Judson, m. Dr. Jeremiah T. **DENISON**, Mar. 15, 1842, by Rev. Lyman H. Atwater	1-M	74
Hannah, d. John, m. Elisha **ALVORD**, May 9, 1745	1	139
Molly, d. John, m. Moses **WAKEMAN**, s. Sam[ue]ll, Aug. 22, 1745	1	153
Samuel B., m. Polly Wakeman **BANKS**, b. of Fairfield, Jan. 17, 1834, by Rev. Geo[rge] H. Hulin	1-M	58
GOOKIN, Warren D., of New York, m. Hetty D. **WAKEMAN**, of Southport, Jan. 11, 1847, by Rev. Samuel J. M. Merwin	1-M	86
GORDON, George, of New Haven, m. Caroline **STEENBOUGH**, d. J. B., of Fairfield, June 5, 1850, by Rev. Samuel Cooke	1-M	95
GORHAM, Abigail, d. Jos[eph] & Deborah, b. Apr. 7, 1728	1	187
Abigail, 2nd, d. Jos[eph] & Deborah, b. Apr. 7, 1744	1	187
Abigail, d. Lockwood, m. Ralph **SHERWOOD**, Aug. 21, 1788, by Rev. Hez[ekiah] Ripley, of Greens Farms	1	299
Ann, d. Isaac & Ann, b. Sept. 29, 1754	1	180
Daniel, s. Joe[eph] & Abigail, b. Nov. 10, 1717	1	187
Dan[ie]l, s. Lockwood & Abigail, b. Oct. 9, 1752	1	83
David, s. Lockwood & Abigail, b. Jan. 1, 1743/4	1	83
Deborah, d. John & Abigail, b. Mar. 10, 1755	1	227
Ebenezer, s. Shubal & Rebecca, b. Sept. 1, 1749	1	145
Elizabeth, d. Lockwood & Abigail, b. Jan. 4, 1749/50	1	83
Hannah, d. Jos[eph] & Deborah, b. May 4, 1737	1	187
Hannah, d. Lockwood & Abigail, b. Sept. 27, 1745	1	83
Hannah, d. Isaac & Ann, b. Nov. 15, 1752	1	180
Ichabod, s. Jos[eph] & Abigail, b. Jan. 31, 1724/5	1	187
Isaac, s. Jos[eph] & Deborah, b. Nov. 14, 1730	1	187
Isaac, s. Joseph, m. Ann **WAKEMAN**, d. Joseph, July 25, 1752	1	180
Jabez, s. Jos[eph] & Abigail, b. Mar. 22, 1718/19	1	187
Jabez, s. Joseph, m. Mary **COUCH**, d. Benj[ami]n, Nov. 27, 1752	1	171
John, s. Jos[eph] & Deborah, b. July 4, 1732	1	187
John, s. Joseph, m. Abigail **WAKEMAN**, d. Joseph, Oct. 5, 1754	1	227
John, s. John & Abigail, b. May 22, 1756	1	227
John H., m. Sarah **ALVORD**, b. of Fairfield, Mar. 7, 1842, by Rev. Daniel C. Curtiss	1-M	73
Joseph, m. Abigail **LOCKWOOD**, May 11, 1715	1	187
Joseph, m. Deborah **BARLOW**, Jan. 13, 1725/6	1	187
Joseph, s. Jos[eph] & Deborah, b. Nov. 20, 1741	1	187
Joseph, s. Lockwood & Abigail, b. June 18, 1755	1	83
Lockwood, s. Jos[eph] & Abigail, b. Jan. 1, 1720/1	1	187
Lockwood, s. Joseph, m. Abigail **MEAKER**, d. David, Sept. 20, 1742	1	83
Lockwood, s. Lockwood & Abigail, b. Nov. 9, 1747	1	83
Lydea, d. Jabez & Mary, b. May 29, 1756	1	171
Martha, d. Jabez & Mary, b. Aug. 13, 1753	1	171
Mary, d. Jos[eph] & Deborah, b. Dec. 25, 1739	1	187
Mary, d. Jabez & Mary, b. Nov. 29, 1754	1	171

	Vol.	Page
GORHAM (cont.)		
Rebeckah, d. Shubal & Rebeckah, b. [ ]	1	145
Shubal, s. Jos[eph] & Deborah, b. Oct. 28, 1726	1	187
Shubal, s. Joseph, m. Rebecca **HOLLEBERT**, d. Gideon, Jan. 22, 1746/7	1	145
Shubal, s. Shubal & Rebecca, b. July 4, 1752	1	145
Shubal, at his house, a child named Lydia was b. Dec. 14, 1763, and left there to be brought up	1	145
Stephen, s. Shubal & Rebecca, b. Dec. 19, 1747	1	145
GOULD, [see also **GOLD**], Airldon, m. Julia **BLACKMAN**, b. of Fairfield, Apr. 6, 1847, by Rev. James Scott, of Stratfield	1-M	86
Alden, m. Sarah H. **WAKEMAN**, b. of Fairfield, Mar. 27, 1831, by Hull Bradley, J.P.	1-M	41
Anna Eliza, d. Abram, decd., of Fairfield, m. David H. **BOOTH**, of Bridgeport, Oct. 24, 1849, by Rev. N. E. Cornwall	1-M	94
Caroline W., m. Edward B. **STURGES**, b. of Fairfield, June 26, 1850, by Rev. Lyman H. Atwater	1-M	92
Harriet, of Fairfield, m. Walter **WILSON**, of Weston, Oct. 7, 1827, by Nath[anie]l Hewit	1-M	29
Henry, m. Esther **JENNINGS**, b. of Fairfield, Dec. 9, 1841, by Rev. Geo[rge] Waterbury	1-M	73
John, m. Mary **THORP**, b. of Fairfield, Nov. 3, 1822, by Rev. Nath[anie]l Hewit	1-M	9
Luther, m. Mary A. **HALL**, b. of Fairfield, Jan. 11, 1843 [sic], by Rev. A. S. Beach [1844?]	1-M	76
GOULDEN, GOULDON, [see also **GOLDEN & GOULEN**], John W. of Bridgeport, m. Emily Francis **PENNOGER**, of New Canaan, [Oct.] 6, [1844], by Rev. Charles B. Adams	1-M	77
W[illia]m, of Bridgeport, m. Harriet L. **STURGIS**, of Fairfield, [Mar. 26, 1846], by Rev. Cha[rle]s R. Adams	1-M	83
GOULEN, [see also **GOULDEN & GOLDEN**], Elizabeth B., of Fairfield, m. Alphonzo D. **PECK**, of New York City, Nov. 10, 1847, by Rev. Lyman H. Atwater	1-M	88
GRANT, Samuel, m. Sally Ann **JENNINGS**, Oct. 7, 1832, by T. F. Davis	1-M	48-9
GRAY, Abigail, d. W[illia]m & Elizabeth, b. May 7, 1719	1	185
Abigail, d. John & Hannah, b. Dec. 28, 1745	1	151
Abigail, d. Hez[ekia]h & Abigail, b. May 22, 1761	1	257
Abijah, s. Nathan & Mary, b. Nov. 16, 1747	1	138
Abraham, s. John & Hannah, b. June 22, 1737	1	151
Amos, s. W[illia]m & Sarah, b. Mar. 17, 1753	1	209
An[n], d. John & Hannah, b. Aug. 2, 1732	1	151
Ann, d. John, m. Timothy **HALL**, s. John, Dec. 14, 1749	1	179
Daniel, s. Nathan & Mary, b. Oct. 29, 1744	1	138
Ebenezer, s. W[illia]m & Elizabeth, b. Mar. 29, 1723	1	185
Elias, s. W[illia]m & Sarah, b. Apr. 4, 1746	1	209
Eliphalet, s. Nathan & Mary, b. May 4, 1753	1	138
Elisha, s. W[illia]m & Elizabeth, b. June 1, 1735	1	185
Elizabeth, d. W[illia]m & Elizabeth, b. Apr. 12, 1721	1	185

	Vol.	Page
GRAY (cont.)		
Elizabeth, d. W[illia]m & Sarah, b. Jan. 8, 1755	1	209
Esther, m. Abraham **MOREHOUSE**, b. of Fairfield, Apr. 6, 1828, by Rev. E. W. Hooker	1-M	31
Eunice, d. John & Hannah, b. Dec. 21, 1754; d. Sept. 2, 1755	1	151
Eunice, d. Nathan & Mary, b. Jan. 19, 1756	1	138
Eunice, d. John & Ruhamah, b. Mar. 15, 1760	1	263
Gideon, s. Nathan & Mary, b. Mar. 7, 1751	1	138
Hannah, d. Sam[ue]ll & Ellenor, b. Nov. 12, 1736	1	147
Hannah, d. John & Hannah, b. June 25, 1744	1	151
Hezekiah, s. John & Hannah, b. Oct. 1, 1738	1	151
Hezekiah, s. Sam[ue]ll & Ellenor, b. Nov. 14, 1738	1	147
Hezekiah, s. Sam[ue]ll, m. Abigail **WATERBURY**, d. Capt. David, of Stanford, Apr. 24, 1760	1	257
Huldah, d. Stephen & Sarah, b. Nov. 9, 1760	1	263
Isaac, s. Nathan & Mary, b. May 7, 1739	1	138
Jabez, s. W[illia]m & Elizabeth, b. Oct. 11, 1728	1	185
Jacob, s. Jacob, b. Dec. 10, 1677	LR-A2	680
Jacob, Sr., d. Mar. 6, 1712	LR-2	456
Joel, s. John & Ruhamah, b. July 27, 1763	1	263
John, m. Hannah **SCRIBNER**, Sept. 19, 1730	1	151
John, s. John & Hannah, b. Feb. 17, 1734	1	151
John, s. Nathan & Mary, b. Sept. 3, 1749	1	138
John, d. May 10, 1755	1	151
John, s. John, m. Ruhamah **BARLOW**, d. Sam[ue]ll, Aug. 7, 1759	1	263
Joseph, s. Joseph, b. Nov. 15, 1706	LR-2	459
Joseph, s. W[illia]m & Elizabeth, b. Oct. 11, 1732	1	185
Joseph, s. John & Hannah, b. July 7, 1753	1	151
Joseph, s. Nathan & Mary, b. Nov. 9, 1754	1	138
Joshua, s. W[illia]m & Elizabeth, b. Sept. 22, 1738	1	185
Lydea, d. W[illia]m & Sarah, b. Jan. 18, 1757	1	209
Martha, of Fairfield, m. John **KNOT**, of Weathersfield, [ ], 1731	1	245
Mary, d. Jacob, b. July 7, 1679	LR-A2	680
Mary, d. Isaac, m. Joshua **DISBROW**, s. Tho[ma]s, June 7, 1743	1	150
Mary, d. Nathan & Mary, b. Mar. 11, 1745 [sic]	1	138
Mary, d. Sam[ue]ll & Ellenor, b. Mar. 8, 1746	1	147
Mary Ann of Weston, m. Joseph **DISBROW**, of Westport, [ ], by Cyrus Silliman. Recorded Feb. 22, 1838	1-M	66
Moses, s. W[illia]m & Sarah, b. Aug. 1, 1743	1	209
Nathan, s. Isaac, m. Mary **HOLLEBERT**, d. Gideon, June 24, 1735	1	138
Nathan, s. Nathan & Mary, b. Sept. 29, 1737	1	138
Nathaniel, s. John & Hannah, b. July 20, 1741	1	151
Ollive, d. W[illia]m & Sarah, b. Dec. 3, 1748	1	209
Rebekca, d. Jacob (?), b. June 1, 1670	LR-A2	664
Samuel, s. Henry, m. Elliner **STURGIS**, d. Christopher, Oct. 24, 1734	1	147
Samuel, s. Sam[ue]ll & Ellenor, b. July 10, 1742	1	147

	Vol.	Page
GRAY (cont.)		
Sanford, s. Sam[ue]ll & Ellenor, b. Sept. 23, 1735; d.		
Nov. 23, following	1	147
Sarah, d. Jacob, b. Oct. 9, 1675	LR-A2	664
Sarah, d. Joseph, b. Sept. 10, 1708	LR-2	459
Sarah, m. Benjamin **SMITH**, Jan. 1, 1730	1	221
Sarah, d. Sam[ue]ll & Ellenor, b. Feb. 11, 1743/4	1	147
Sarah, d. W[illia]m & Sarah, b. Apr. 3, 1751	1	209
Solomon, s. Nathan & Mary, b. Apr. 21, 1740	1	138
Solomon, m. Abigail H. **THORP**, July 3, 1820, by		
Hez[ekiah] Ripley, V.D.M.	1-M	1
Stephen, s. W[illia]m & Abigail, b. Nov. 7, 1715	1	185
Stephen, s .John & Hannah, b. Dec. 7, 1735	1	151
Stephen, s. John, m. Sarah **FERRY**, d. Ebenezer, Sept. 3,		
1758	1	263
Thaddeus, s. W[illia]m & Elizabeth, b. Oct. 27, 1730	1	185
Thomas, s. Nathan & Mary, b. Dec. 7, 1742	1	138
William, m. Abigail **COLEY**, Dec. 23, 1714	1	185
William, m. Elizabeth **MEAKER**, Oct. 31, 1716	1	185
William, m. W[illia]m & Elizabeth, b. Aug. 17, 1717	1	185
William, s. William, m. Sarah **DISBROW**, Jan. 25, 1742	1	209
GREEN, Ebenezer, b. Oct. 25, 1723	1	88
Ebenezer, m. Elizabeth **GILBERT**, Mar. 24, 1748	1	88
Ebenezer, s. Eben[eze]r & Elizabeth, b. Apr. 16, 1757	1	88
Hannah, d. Ebenezer & Elizabeth, b. Sept. 14, 1749	1	88
Mary, d. Ebenezer & Elizabeth, b. Aug. 8, 1751	1	88
Russell, of Huntington, L.I., m. Marinda **DENISON**, of		
Fairfield, Apr. 11, 1823, by Rev. Philo Shelton	1-M	10
Tho[ma]s, m. Ann **HULL**, Apr. 7, 1720	LR-B	146
Thomas, s. Ebenezer & Elizabeth, b. May 11, 1753	1	88
William, s Eben[eze]r & Elizabeth, b. Apr. 12, 1755	1	88
GREGORY, Abigail, m. Edward **LACY**, July 23, 1702	LR-2	462
Abigail, m. Samuel **MEAKER**, Aug. 1, 1722	1	228
Emily, m. Walter **BROTHERTON**, b. of Fairfield, Mar.		
26, 1848, by Rev. Lyman H. Atwater	1-M	89
Gould, m. Caroline **ALLEN**, b. of Westport, Sept. 27,		
1841, by Rev. Lyman H Atwater	1-M	72
Hannah, m. Arin **ELWOOD**, b. of Saugatuck, Mar. 21,		
1827, by Rev. E. W. Hooker	1-M	26-7
John, m. Mary E. **OSBORNE**, b. of Fairfield, Feb. 6,		
1848, by Rev. N. E. Cornwall	1-M	88
Mercy, d. Benj[ami], m. John **COLEY**, s. Samuel, July		
22, 1728	1	208
Plumb B., m. Mary Ann **SEELEY**, Nov. 23, 1820, by		
Rev. Elijah Waterman	1-M	3
Samuell, of Fairfield, m. Mary **SILLAMAN**, Dec. 28,		
1699, by Rev. Charles Chaney	LR-2	461
GRIFFIN, GRIFFEN, Elnathan, m. Patience **BURR**, d. Jehu,		
Nov. 26, 1750	1	134
Hezekiah, s. Elnathan & Patience, b. Aug. 30, 1753	1	134
Huldah, d. Elnathan & Patience, b. Dec. 26, 1755	1	134
Sarah, d. Elnathan & Patience, b. Sept. 8, 1751	1	134

	Vol.	Page
GRIFFIN, GRIFFEN (cont.)		
William, m. Priscilla **BULKLEY**, b. of Fairfield, Oct. 21, 1841, by Rev. Lyman H. Atwater	1-M	72
GRIFFETH, Mary Elizabeth, of Danbury, m. Gershom B. **BULKELEY**, of Southport, Nov. 9, 1851, by Rev. Samuel J. M. Merwin	1-M	93
GRUMMAN, GUMMAN, Abigaill, d. John, b. Aug. 1, 1685	LR-A2	680
Abigail, m. Joseph **JENNINGS**, Jan. 20, 1709	1	69
Eben[eze]r, [s. John], b. July 7, 1720	LR-2	458
Elizabeth, [d. John], b. July 3, 1717	LR-2	458
Esther, [d. John], b. Jan. 10, 1704	LR-2	458
John, [s. John], b. July 3, 1710	LR-2	458
Samuell, d. Mar. 12, 1690/1	LR-2	463
Sarah, d. Thomas, b. Mar. 6, 1690/1	LR-2	463
Sarah, d. Thomas, d. Mar. 30, 1690/1	LR-2	463
Silence, [d. John], b. Apr. 15, 1708	LR-2	458
Thankfull, [d. John], b. Jan. 5, 1712/13	LR-2	458
Thomas, d. Mar. 10, 1690/1	LR-2	463
GUION, William H., of New York City, m. Elizabeth P. **PERRY**, of Southport, Sept. 20, 1841, by Rev. Lyman H. Atwater	1-M	72
[GUIRE], [see under **GUYER**]		
GUMMAN, [see under **GRUMMAN**]		
GUTHRIE, Austin A., of Putnam, O., m. Amelia **STURGIS**, of Fairfield, Sept. 26, 1825, by Nathan[ie]l Hewit	1-M	19
GUYER, GUYRE, Abigail, d. Luke, m. Nehemiah **SEELEY**, Jr., s. Nehemiah, Apr. 12, 1755	1	91
Ann, d. Eben[eze]r & Sarah, b. May 17, 1746	1	209
Bette, d Eben[eze]r & Sarah, b. Feb. 15, 1748	1	209
Daniel, s. Eben[eze]r & Sarah, b. Aug. 27, 1755	1	209
Eben, s. Eben[eze]r & Sarah, b. Jan. 16, 1750	1	209
Ebenezer, s. Luke, m. Sarah **BEERS**, d. Eph[rai]m, Apr. 20, 1742	1	209
Jesse, s. Eben[eze]r & Sarah, b. Feb. 3, 1743	1	209
Joanna, d. Luke, m. Enos **LEE**, s. William, Oct. 1, 1740	1	118
John, m. Sarah **BRINMAID**, Nov. 22, 1750	1	68
John Darling, s. Nathan & Elizabeth, b. Mar. 16, 1750	1	92
Joseph, s. John & Sarah, b. Nov. 11, 1755	1	68
Lazarus, s. Nathan & Elizabeth, b. Apr. 12, 1757	1	92
Luke, s. John & Sarah, b. Oct. 27, 1751	1	68
Luke, s. Luke, m. Elizabeth **BEDIENT**, d. John, Apr. 14, 1757	1	110
Mary, d. Nathan & Elizabeth, b. Aug. 4, 1754	1	92
Nathan, s. Luke, m. Elizabeth **DARLING**, Mar. [ ], 1749	1	92
Nathaniel, s. Nathan & Elizabeth, b. Nov. 19, 1751	1	92
Peter, s. Eben[eze]r & Sarah, b. Apr. 6, 1744	1	209
Rebecca B., m. Giles **SEYMOUR**, b. of Norwalk, Nov. 29, 1829, by Rev. Tho[ma]s F. Davis	1-M	37
Ruth, d. Luke, m. Daniel **STURGIS**, Jr., s. John, Dec. 11, 1752; d. Sept. 29, 1755	1	168
Sarah, d. Eben[eze]r & Sarah, b. Aug. 1, 1759	1	209
Susanna, d. Eben[eze]r & Sarah, b. Jan. 31, 1752	1	209
Thad, s. John & Sarah, b. Oct. 22, 1753	1	68

	Vol.	Page
H-----, Samuell, b. Jan. 19, [ ]	LR-A2	664
HADDON, Benjamin, of New York, m. Mary Ann **STREET**, of Fairfield, residing in Southport, Nov. 16, 1836, by Nath[anie]l E. Cornwall	1-M	61
HADLEY, Esther, of Fairfield, m. Ephraim **RHICALS**, of Stratford, Oct. 17, 1682	LR-A2	674
HALL, [see also **HULL**], Abigaill, d. Josiah, b. Apr. 1, 1683	LR-A2	682
Abigail, d. Apr. 27, 1712	LR-2	456
Abigail, w. Lyman, d. July 8, 1753	1	36
Ann, [d. Isaac], b. Dec. 26, 1710	LR-2	458
Ann, m. Zachariah **SANFORD**, Oct. 7, 1736	1	60
Asa, [s. Isaac], b. Feb. 9, 1706	LR-2	458
David, [s. Isaac], b. Jan. 2, 1689/90	LR-2	458
David, Dr., of Fairfield, m. Susanna **ELIOT**, of Boston, Nov. 10, 1789, by Rev. John Eliot, of Boston	1	288
Edward, s. Sam[ue]ll, b. Jan. 8, 1685	LR-A2	677
Edward, s. Sam[ue]ll, d. Mar. 12, 1686	LR-A2	677
Eleazer, s. Francis, b. Mar. 19, 1732	1	5
Elizabeth, w. Francis, "had a piece of land in England, to which she fell heir, Mar. 9, 1664"	LR-A2	678
Elizabeth, w. Frances, d. July 6, 1665	LR-A2	677
Elizabeth, d. Isaac, b. Nov. 11, 1672	LR-A2	682
Elizabeth, d. Cornelius, m. Stephen **BURR**, June 8, 1721	1	178
Eunice, d. Timo[thy] & Ann, b. Aug. 20, 1757	1	179
Ezra, s. Timo[thy] & Ann, b. Feb. 14, 1756	1	179
Ffrancis, s. Isaac, b. Apr. 26, 1676	LR-A2	682
Francis, s. Sam[ue]ll, b. Feb. 27, 1683	LR-A2	677
Francis, d. Mar. 5, 1689/90	LR-A2	677
Francis, s. Samue]ll, d. Dec. 17, 1690	LR-A2	677
Francis, [Twin with James], s. Francis, b. Mar. 7, 1730	1	5
George, [s. Isaac], b. Nov. 3, 1701	LR-2	458
Hannah, m. Sam[ue]ll **HALL**, Mar. 16, 1686/7	LR-A2	677
Hannah, w. Sam[ue]ll, d. Nov. 17, 1687	LR-A2	677
Hannah, d. Timo[thy] & Ann, b. July 27, 1751	1	179
Henry, m. Catharine **LACEY**, b. of Bridgeport, July 2, 1843, by Rev. N. E. Cornwall	1-M	75
Isaac, s. Ffrancis, m. Lydea **KNAP**, d. Nicolas, Jan. 16, 1666	LR-A2	682
Isaac, s. Isaac, b. Nov. 8, 1667	LR-A2	682
Isaac, m. Jane Hall **BURGIS**, Jan. 24, 1689	LR-2	458
Isaac, [s. Isaac], b. Oct. 14, 1692	LR-2	458
James, [twin with Francis], s. Francis, b. Mar. 7, 1730	1	5
James, m. Abigail **BEERS**, Apr. 3, 1755	1	54
Jane, d. Isaac, Jr., b. Nov. 15, 1712; d. July 24, 1714	LR-2	458
Jane, d. Isaac, b. Oct. 9, 1714	LR-2	458
Jena, [child of Isaac], b. Dec. 19, 1703	LR-2	458
John, s. Isaac, b. Feb. 8, 1677; lived a few hours	LR-A2	682
John, s. Isaac, b. Jan. 3, 1679	LR-A2	682
Jonathan, s. Josiah, b. Dec. 2, 1684	LR-A2	682
Joshua, [s. Isaac], b. Nov. 4, 1708	LR-2	458
Lorinda, of Weston, m. Alanson **BANKS**, of Fairfield, Mar. 7, 1838, by Hull Bradley, J.P.	1-M	67
Lidea, d. Isaac, b. Sept. 21, 1670	LR-A2	682

	Vol.	Page
HALL (cont.)		
Lydia, [d. Isaac], b. Sept. 25, 1698	LR-2	458
Lyman, m. Abigail **BURR**, d. Thaddeus, May 20, 1752	1	36
Lyman, had negroes Amos, b. June 7, 1755; d. Dec. 8,		
1756 & Primus, b. June 7, 1757	1	36
Margaret, d. Francis, m. Gabriel **JACKSON**, s.		
Sam[ue]ll, May 24, 1727	1	258
Mary, d. Isaac, b. Aug. 7, 1681	LR-A2	682
Mary, w. Sam[ue]ll, d. Feb. 1, 1685	LR-A2	677
Mary, m. Tho[ma]s **FAIRCHILD**, Sept. 22, 1737	1	17
Mary, d. Sam[ue]ll, m. Silvanus **MORHOUSE**, s.		
Abraham, Nov. 3, 1747	1	149
Mary A., m. Luther **GOULD**, b. of Fairfield, Jan. 11,		
1843 [sic], by Rev. A. S. Beach [1844?]	1-M	76
Meriam, m. Timothy **LYON**, s. Dan[ie]ll, July 1, 1752	1	114
Rebeckah, d. Francis, d. Mar. 28, 1690	LR-A2	677
Rebeckah, [d. Isaac], b. Jan. 13, 1691; d. Feb. 3, 1691	LR-2	458
Rebeckah, of Fairfield, m. John M. **MIDDLEBROOKS**,		
of Bridgeport, Nov. 23, 1825, by Rev. Marvin		
Richardson	1-M	20
Samuell, s. Isaac, b. Sept. 14, 1674	LR-A2	682
Sam[ue]ll, s. Frances, m. Mary [ ], Mar. 20, 1682/3	LR-A2	677
Sam[ue]ll, m. Hannah **HALL**, Mar. 16, 1686/7	LR-A2	677
Sam[ue]ll, s. Frances & Elizabeth, filed claim Sept. 7,		
1687 to a piece of land in England, to which his		
mother fell heir Mar. 9, 1664	LR-A2	678
Sam[ue]ll, [s. Isaac], b. Oct. 21, 1695	LR-2	458
Sarah, d. Isaac, b. May 3, 1668	LR-A2	682
Sarah, d. Frances, b. July 10, 1734	1	5
Sarah, d. Timo[thy] & Ann, b. Apr. 5, 1753	1	179
Sarah, d. James & Abigail, b. Feb. 8, 1756	1	54
Susan E., of Fairfield, m. John **SANFORD**, of		
Greenwich, June 5, 1826, by Nath[aniel]l Hewit	1-M	24
Timothy, s. John, m. Ann **GRAY**, d. John, Dec. 14, 1749	1	179
HALSTEAD, Thomas, m. Milla **WOCKEY**, b. of Fairfield		
(colored), Apr. 21, 1822, by Nath[anie]l Hewit	1-M	7
HAMBLETON, Benjamin, m. Hannah **BULKLEY**, d.		
Dan[ie]ll, Apr. 6, 1754	1	145
Hannah, d. Benj[amin] & Hannah, b. Nov. 28, 1756	1	145
Isaac, s. Benj[amin] & Hannah, b. Sept. 22, 1754	1	145
HAMMOND, Aaron, of New York City, m. Julia B.		
NICHOLS, of Fairfield, Oct. 27, 1851, by Rev.		
Lyman H. Atwater	1-M	92
Catharine, of New York, m. Timothy **WILLIAMS**, of		
Fairfield, Sept. 16, 1849, by Rev. Jacob L. Clark	1-M	94
HANFORD, Albert, m. Delia Ann **NASH**, June 6, 1830, by T.		
F. Davis	1-M	39-40
Charles, of Norwalk, m. Elizabeth A. **HOLMES**, of		
Wilton, Sept. 4, 1836, by Rev. Tho[ma]s F. Davis	1-M	59
Elnathan, m. wid. Abigail **LOCKWOOD**, June 26, 1700,		
by Nathan Gold	LR-2	459
Sarah, m. Eben[eze]r **WAKEMAN**, May 10, 1752	1	19
HANLY, Elizabeth, d. Ebenezer, b. May 6, 1679	LR-A2	663

	Vol.	Page
HARDING, Maria Ann, m. George Rowland **HITCHINS**, b.		
of Fairfield, Aug. 26, 1838, by N. E. Cornwall	1-M	66
HARPER, Mary, d. John, of Martha's Vineyard, m. John		
SQUIER, Aug. 22, 1754	1	272
HATHOUSE, George C., of Williamsburgh, L. I., m. Elizabeth		
TAYLOR, of Fairfield, Jan. 4, 1835, by Rev. C. A.		
Boardman, of Saugatuck	1-M	55
HAWKINS, David M., m. Sarah Ann **OSBORN**, b. of		
Southport, Oct. 18, 1837, by N. E. Cornwall, in		
Southport	1-M	63-4
HAWLEY, HALLEY, Bronson, m. Rebecca **BEERS**, of		
Bridgeport, May 7, 1826, by Rev. H. R. Judah, of		
Bridgeport	1-M	28
Eunice, d. Joseph & Hannah, b. Sept. 6, 1750	1	90
George, m. Marretta **BURR**, Nov. 30, 1820, by Rev.		
Elijah Waterman	1-M	3
Joseph, s. W[illia]m & Lydia, b. June 3, 1762	1	114
Katharine, d. Thomas, m. William **BENNIT**, Dec. 3,		
1744	1	117
Mary, d. John, of Stratford, m. John **READ**, of Reading,		
Sept. 26, 1723	1	2
Mary, d. Joseph & Hannah, b. Feb. 2, 1741/2	1	90
Ruth, d. Joseph & Hannah, b. Oct. 26, 1745	1	90
Samuel, s. Joseph & Hannah, b. Aug. 2, 1744	1	90
William, s. Joseph, m. Lydea **NASH**, d. Tho[ma]s, July		
12, 1758	1	114
HAXBEY, [see also **BIXBY**], Abigail, [d. Josiah], b. Jan. 8,		
1671	LR-A2	677
Hannah, [d. Josiah], b. June 7, 1675	LR-A2	677
Martha, [d. Josiah], b. Oct. 12, 1677	LR-A2	677
Mary, [d. Josiah], b. May 25, 1669	LR-A2	677
Thomas, [s. Josiah], b. Jan. 23, 1680	LR-A2	677
HAYES, HAYS, Irena, d. Abraham, m. George **SQUIER**, s.		
Sam[ue]ll, Nov. 7, 1781	1	281
Jane, m. Albert **LEWIS**, Apr. 29, 1823, by Rivers		
Morrell, J. P.	1-M	11
Johnson, m. Ellen **TURNEY**, b. of Fairfield, Oct. 4, 1835,		
by Nath[anie]l E. Cornwall	1-M	58
Mary Jane, m. Robert **CAMPBELL**, b. of Fairfield, May		
8, 1842, by Rev. Lyman H. Atwater	1-M	74
HAZARD, John, m. Mary **WAKEMAN**, d. Joseph, Apr. 9,		
1752	1	140
Joseph, s. John & Mary, b. Mar. 13, 1753	1	140
Mary, d. John & Mary, b. Nov. 21, 1754	1	140
Samuel, s. John & Mary, b. Nov. 3, 1756	1	140
HEDENBERG, Francis L., of Newark, N. J., m. Mary B.		
THORP, of Fairfield, Mar. 26, 1826, by Rev. E. W.		
Hooker	1-M	22
HENDRICK, Andrew, s. John & Phebe, b. [ ], 1732	1	163
Andrew, s. Sam[ue]ll & Mary, b. Oct. 15, 1771	1	252
Benj[ami]n, s. Sam[ue]ll & Mary, b. May 24, 1763	1	252
Deborah Phileas, d. John & Phebe, b. [ ], 1746	1	163
Elizabeth, d. John & Phebe, b. [ ], 1744	1	163

	Vol.	Page
HENDRICK (cont.)		
James, s. John & Phebe, b. [ ], 1742	1	163
James, s. Sam[ue]ll & Mary, b. Mar. 27, 1767	1	252
John, m. Phebe **COE**, [ ], 1728	1	163
John, s. John & Phebe, b. [ ], 1730	1	163
John, Jr., s. John, m. Eunice **BRADLEY**, d. David, Nov. 13, 1753	1	159
Joseph, s. Sam[ue]ll & Mary, b. Sept. 14, 1769	1	252
Justus, s. John & Eunice, b. Jan. 20, 1757	1	159
Nancy, d. Sam[ue]ll & Mary, b. Apr. 14, 1765	1	252
Peter, s. John & Phebe, b. [ ], 1738	1	163
Phebe, d. John & Phebe, b. [ ], 1740	1	163
Phebe, d. John & Eunice, b. Nov. 5, 1754	1	159
Samuel, s. John & Phebe, b. [ ], 1734	1	163
Samuel, s. John, m. Mary **RUMSEY**, d. Benj[ami]n, Aug. 30, 1759	1	252
Sam[ue]ll, s. Sam[ue]ll & Mary, b. May 22, 1761	1	252
Sarah, d. John & Phebe, b. [ ], 1736	1	163
Sarah, m. Rowland **HUGH**, Mar. 17, 1757	1	163
HENDRICKSON, Abraham, of Bridgeport, m. Junia M. **TREADWELL**, of Weston, this day [July 4, 1847], by Rev. James H. Perry, Southport	1-M	87
HENRIETTA, Charlotte Ruth, m. Curtis **RAYMOND**, b. of Fairfield, Jan. 1, 1849, by Rev. N. E. Cornwall	1-M	94
HENRY, Beulah, d. Sam[ue]l, m. Samuel **BULKLEY**, s. Joseph, Sept. 2, 1754	1	119
HERING, James D., of New York City, m. Caroline E. **PHELPS**, of Fairfield, Sept. 1, 1846, by Rev. Lyman H. Atwater	1-M	85
[HIBBARD], **HEBBARD**, Abigail, d. Nath[anie]ll & Abigail, b. Feb. 22, 1741	1	175
Deborah, d. Nath[anie]ll & Abigail, b. Sept. 7, 1748	1	175
Elisha, s. Nath[anie]ll & Abigail, b. May 20, 1746	1	175
Grissel, d. Nath[anie]ll & Abigail, b. Feb. 20, 1752	1	175
Nathaniel, m. Abigial **COUCH**, Apr. 24, 1740	1	175
Sarah, d. Nath[anie]ll & Abigail, b. Feb. 24, 1756	1	175
HICOCK, Benjamin E., of Danbury, m. Almyra **TAYLOR**, of Fairfield, May 11, 1825, by Rev. E. W. Hooker	1-M	18
HIDE, Damaries, m. Thomas **WHITLOCK**, Jan. 24, 1716	1	207
Elizabeth, d. Dr. [ ], m. John **BELL**, June 10, 1736	1	57
Elizabeth, d. Joseph & Betty, b. Dec. 5, 1753	1	39
Eunice, d. John & Rachel, b. Feb. 10, 1719	1	50
Eunice, m. John **WILLSON**, Feb. 27, 1740	1	25
Hannah, m. Joseph **BURR**, Mar. 3, 1725	1	84
John, m. Rachel **HOMES**, Apr. 22, 1718	1	50
John, s. John & Rachel, b. Nov. 25, 1724	1	50
John, Jr., s. John, m. Abigail **OGDEN**, d. David, Jan. 21, 1748	1	216
John, s. Joseph & Betty, b. Aug. 17, 1755	1	39
John, had negroes Jimmy, b. Oct. 17, 1788; Jesse, b. Nov. 19, 1789 & Ned, b. Aug. [ ], 1791	1	60
John, m. Abigail **ADAMS**, Mar. 22, 1837* *(Intended for "1737")	1	50

	Vol.	Page
HIDE (cont.)		
Joseph, s. John & Rachel, b. Dec. 5, 1729	1	50
Joseph, s. John, m. Betty **SHERWOOD**, d. Sam[ue]ll,		
Aug. 1, 1753	1	39
Joseph, s. Joseph & Betty, b. Jan. 3, 1761	1	39
Joseph, his negro Michael, b. Sept. 14, 1790	1	60
Mabel, d. John, b. Aug. 23, 1668	LR-A2	664
Mary, d. John, b. July 26, 1672	LR-A2	664
Mary, d. John & Rachel, b. Sept. 30, 1720	1	50
Mary, m. Benjamin **DARLING**, Jan. 6, 1725/6	1	162
Mary, m. David **COLEY**, Dec. 16, 1740	1	64
Rachel, d. John & Rachel, b. Feb. 29, 1736	1	50
Rachel, d. John, m. Sam[ue]ll **SHERWOOD**, s.		
Sam[ue]ll, June 6, 1754	1	40
Rachel, d. Joseph & Betty, b. Oct. 30, 1762	1	39
Salome, d. Joseph & Betty, b. Aug. 30, 1757	1	39
Sarah, d. John, b. Sept. 25, 1670	LR-A2	664
Sarai, d. John & Rachel, b. Nov. 27, 1727	1	50
Sarah, m. Ebenezer **BANKS**, s. Jos[eph], June 17, 1746	1	217
HIECOCK, Abigail, d. Benj[amin], m. William **BENNETT**,		
Aug. [ ], 1733	1	139
HIGGINS, Abraham, s. Abraham, m. Mary **ALLEN**, May [ ],		
1739	1	193
Ebenezer, s. Abraham & Mary, b. Dec. 12, 1745	1	193
Gabriel, s. Abraham & Mary, b. Mar. 16, 1741	1	193
John, s. Abraham & Mary, b. Mar. 5, 1740	1	193
Joseph, s. Abraham & Mary, b. Apr. 4, 1751	1	193
Moses, s. Abraham & Mary, b. Mar. 1, 1747	1	193
Phebe, d. Abraham & Mary, b. Sept. 23, 1743	1	193
Sarah, m. Nathaniel **SQUIER**, Jan. 20, 1723	1	226
HILL, Aaron, s. Nathan & Eunice, b. Dec. 12, 1755	1	52
Abel, s. Dan[ie]ll & Phebe, b. Jan. 10, 1750	1	93
Abegaile, d. William, b. Feb. 8, 1694	LR-A2	674
Abigail, d. Tho[ma]s & Mary, b. May 9, 1718	1	10
Abigail, d. Jos[eph] & Abigail, b. Mar. 21, 1732/3	1	152
Abigail, d. W[illia]m & Mary, b. May 6, 1734	1	199
Abigail, m. Andrew **FAIRCHILD**, Apr. 26, 1752	1	153
Abigail, wid. m. Sam[ue]ll **STURGIS**, s. Capt. Sam[ue]ll,		
Jan. 9, 1771	1	262
Andrew, s. Tho[ma]s & Mary, b. Oct. 22, 1739	1	10
Andrew, s. Capt. Tho[ma]s, m. Abigail **LEWIS**, d.		
Nath[anie]ll, of Barnstable, Dec. 1, 1763	1	262
Andrew, d. Oct. 25, 1769	1	262
Andrew Lane, s. Dan[ie]ll & Elizabeth, b. Dec. 14, 1755	1	93
Ann, d. Tho[ma]s & Mary, b. May 6, 1729	1	10
Ann, d. Will[ia]m, m. Peter **BULKLEY**, s. Gershom,		
Apr. 9, 1740	1	170
Ann, m. Ebenezer **WAKEMAN**, Sept. 4, 1768, by Rev.		
Noah Hobart	1	19
Ann, d. Ezekiel & Elizabeth, b. Jan. 19, 1754	1	101
Ann Eliza, of Greenfield, m. Seeley **BIBBINS**, of		
Fairfield, Dec. 29, 1841, by Rev. Lyman H. Atwater	1-M	73
Catharine, m. Hezekiah **BULKLEY**, Jan. 4, 1739	1	206

	Vol.	Page
HILL (cont.)		
Catharine, m. Peter Burr **JENNINGS**, b. of Greens Farms, Sept. 24, 1821, by Hezekiah Ripley, V.D.M.	1-M	5
Daniel, s. W[illia]m & Hannah, b. Jan. 26, 1726	1	199
Daniel, s. W[illia]m, m. Phebe **BEACH**, d. John, Oct. 31, 1748	1	93
Dan[ie]l, m. 2nd, w. Elizabeth **LANE**, Apr. [ ], 1752	1	93
David, s. William, b. Apr. 3, 1719	LR-2	459
David, s. Joseph & Abigail, b. Apr. 22, 1737	1	152
David, s. Ezekiel & Elizabeth, b. Mar. 11, 1757	1	101
Ebenezer, s. Joseph & Abigail, b. Feb. 26, 1741/2	1	152
Eliphalet, m. Esther **NICHOLLS**, d. Will[ia]m Ward, Nov. [ ], 1691	LR-A2	676
Eliphalet, s. Eliphalet, b. Jan. 11, 1694/5	LR-A2	674
Elizabeth, d. Tho[ma]s & Mary, b. Dec. 27, 1726	1	10
Elizabeth, d. Capt. Thomas, m. David **ROWLAND**, Feb. 14, 1749/50	1	26
Esther, d. John & Esther, b. Apr. 21, 1738	1	61
Esther, m. William **SHERWOOD**, Jr., b. of Fairfield, [Sept.] ll, [1832], by Rev. Charles Smith	1-M	45-6
Esther, d. Jabez & Sarah, m. William **SHERWOOD**, s. W[illia]m & Abigail, Sept. 11, 1832	1	306
Esther, d. Jabez & Sarah, m. William **SHERWOOD**, s. William & Abigail, Sept. 11, 1832	1-M	85
Eunice, d. Nathan & Eunice, b. June 5, 1754, d. [ ]	1	52
Eunice, w. Nathan, d. Jan. 29, 1765	1	52
Ezekiel, s. W[illia]m & Mary, b. Feb. 16, 1732	1	199
Ezekiel, m. Elizabeth **MORHOUSE**, June 3, 1750	1	101
Hannah, d. W[illia]m & Hannah, b. June 8, 1728	1	199
Hannah, [w, William, of Reading], d. Aug. 10, 1729	1	199
Hannah, d. W[illia]m, m. David **MEAKER**, Jr., s. David, Oct. 31, 1744	1	83
Horace, m. Eleanor **LYON**, Jan. 7, 1830, by Rev. Nehemiah Ruggles	1-M	37
Ira, of Reading, m. Eliza **MONROE**, Nov. 9, 1834, by T. F. Davis	1-M	55
Isaac, s. John & Esther, b. Sept. 25, 1745	1	61
Jabez, s. Joseph & Abigail, b. June 17, 1744	1	152
John, m. Esther **BULKLEY**, Jan. 27, 1729	1	61
John, d. Dec. 17, 1759	1	61
John, s. Nathan & Elizabeth, b. June 5, 1767	1	52
Joseph, s. William, b. Apr. 1, 1699	LR-A2	674
Joseph, s. William, m. Abigail **DIMON**, d. Moses, Mar. 30, 1731	1	152
Joseph, s. John & Esther, b. May 2, 1752	1	61
Martha, w. Nathan, d. Mar. 9, 1766	1	52
Mary, d. Tho[ma]s & Mary, b. Aug. 5, 1724	1	10
Mary, d. W[illia]m & Mary, b. Feb. 13, 1739	1	199
Mary, d. W[illia]m, m. Elnathan **PARRUCH**, s. John, Nov. 22, 1750	1	116
Mary, w. Capt. Thomas, d. Dec. 19, 1763	1	10
Moses, s. Joseph & Abigail, b. Jan. 11, 1748/9	1	152
Nathan, s. John & Esther, b. Oct. 9, 1731	1	61

	Vol.	Page

HILL (cont.)

	Vol.	Page
Nathan, s. John, m. Eunice **WAKEMAN**, d. Stephen, July 3, 1753	1	52
Nathan, m. 2nd w. Martha **WAKEMAN**, Aug. 26, 1765	1	52
Nathan, m. 3rd w. Elizabeth **WHITEHEAD**, d. Gershom, Dec. [ ], 1766	1	52
Rebecca, d. W[illia]m & Rebecca, b. Nov. 9, [1730]; d. Mar. 22, 1749	1	199
Rebecca, d. Ezekiel & Elizabeth, b. Mar. 13, 1751	1	101
Sarah, m. Richard **WHEDDON**, Apr. 15, 1686	LR-A2	677
Sarah, w. William, d. Mar. 28, 1715	LR-2	456
Sarah, d. John, m. Gershom **MOR[E]HOUSE**, s. John, Apr. 22, 1725	1	235
Sarah, d. Joseph & Abigail, b. Aug. 21, 1733	1	152
Sarah, d. Tho[ma]s & Mary, b. July 2, 1734	1	10
Sarah, d. John & Esther, b. Apr. 28, 1742	1	61
Sarah, d. Joseph, m. William **WAKEMAN**, s. Jabez, June 21, 1753	1	73
Sarah, d. Nathan & Eunice, b. Nov. 17, 1760	1	52
Stephen, s. Nathan & Eunice, b. Nov. 16, 1762	1	52
Thaddeus, s. Tho[ma]s & Mary, b. June 19, 1720	1	10 ·
Tho[ma]s, m. Mary **BURR**, Dec. 9, 1715	1	10
Tho[ma]s, s. Tho[ma]s & Mary, b. Nov. 30, 1732	1	10
Thomas, s. Capt. Thomas, m. Ellen **STURGIS**, d. Peter, Jan. 20, 1757	1	48
Thomas, s. And[re]w & Abigail, b. Jan. 13, 1766	1	262
William, d. Dec. 19, 1684	LR-A2	680
William, s. Eliphalet, b. Nov. 17, 1692	LR-A2	676
William, of Reading, m. Hannah **MOR[E]HOUSE**, Apr. 28, 1725	1	199
William, m. Rebecca **SANFORD**, Feb. 28, [1730]* *(Date crossed out)	1	199
William, m. Mary **OGDEN**, May 6, 1731	1	199
Will[ia]m, s. Will[ia]m, b. May 16, 17[ ]	LR-B	C
HINE, Henry M. of Bridgeport, m. Martha **ALVORD**, of Southport, May 22, 1848, by Rev. Sam[ue]l J. M. Merwin	1-M	90
HITCHENS, George Rowland, m. Maria Ann **HARDING**, b. of Fairfield, Aug. 26, 1838, by N. E. Cornwall	1-M	66
HOBART, Edmund [s. Justin & Desire], b. July 29, 1814	1	302
Ellen, d. Noah & Ellen, b. Oct. 15, 1741	1	24
Ellen, w. Rev. Noah, d. Aug. 19, 1753	1	24
Ellen, d. Justin & Hannah, b. Jan. 18, 1764	1	23
Hannah, d. Justin & Hannah, b. Nov. 7, 1777	1	23
Hannah, w. Justin, d. Jan. 7, 1809	1	23
Hannah, [d. Justin & Desire], b. Dec. 18, 1817	1	302
Jane Ann, [d. Justin & Desire], b. Feb. 2, 1809	1	302
Jerome, s. Justin & Hannah, b. Feb. 26, 1768; d. Mar. 9, 1768	1	23
John Sloss, s. Noah & Ellen, b. May 6, 1738	1	24
John Sloss, s. Justin & Hannah, b. Feb. 12, 1781; d. Aug. 10, 1803, in New York	1	23

	Vol.	Page
HOBART (cont.)		
Justin, s. Nehemiah, of Hingham, m. Hannah		
PENFIELD, d. Peter, Mar. 18, 1762	1	23
Justin, s. Justin & Hannah, b. Mar. 26, 1772	1	23
Justin, b. Mar. 26, 1772; m. Desire **BURR**, July 1, 1804	1	302
Justin, d. Apr. 7, 1809	1	23
Lydia, d. Justin & Hannah, b. Mar. 12, 1774	1	23
Mary, d. Justin & Hannah, b. Dec. 21, 1765	1	23
Noah, Rev., m. Ellen **SLOP**,* Sept. 22, 1735 *SLOSS	1	24
Noah, s. Noah & Ellen, b. June 18, 1743	1	24
Noah, s. Justin & Hannah, b. Mar. 23, 1769	1	23
Noah, Rev., d. Dec. 6, 1773	1	24
Peter, s. [Justin & Desire], b. Oct. 8, 1811	1	302
Rebecca, d. [Justin & Desire], b. Oct. 22, 1806	1	302
HOBBY, William of New York, m. Alithea **ANDRUS**, of		
Fairfield, Sept. 11, 1832, by Tho[ma]s F. Davis	1-M	45-6
HODGDEN, Benj[ami]n, s. David & Sarah, b. Dec. 24, 1750	1	163
David, s. Will[ia]m, m. Sarah **LACEY**, d. John, June [ ],		
1750	1	163
HOLBERTON, John, s. Thomas & Ruth, b. Oct. 13, 1770	1	41
Thomas, s. John, m. Ruth **WILLSON**, d. Robert, May 31,		
1770	1	41
HOLLIBERT, [see under HURLBURT]		
HOLLINGSWORTH, HOLLINGWORTH, Abigail, d.		
Joseph & Ann, b. Jan. 16, 1743	1	96
Ann, d. Joseph & Ann, b. Dec. 9, 1744	1	96
Elizabeth, d. Joseph & Ann, b. Jan. 18, 1748	1	96
Joseph, m. Ann **JENNINGS**, Nov. 4, 1734	1	96
Mary, d. Joseph & Ann, b. June 26, 1737	1	96
Ruth, d. Joseph & Ann, b. June 6, 1741	1	96
Sarah, d. Joseph & Ann, b. Mar. 31, 1736	1	96
Sarah, m. Abel **JENNINGS**, s. John, [ ], 1756	1	304
HOLMES, HOMES, Elizabeth A. of Wilton, m. Charles		
HANFORD, of Norwalk, Sept. 4, 1836, by Rev.		
Tho[ma]s F. Davis	1-M	59
Rachel, m. John **HIDE**, Apr. 22, 1718	1	50
HOPKINS, Charles, of Long Island, m. Elizabeth S.		
JENNINGS, of Greenfield, Oct. 17, 1841, in		
Greenfield, by Rev. John Noyes	1-M	72
Eli, Jr., of New York, m. Martha Ann **OSBORN**, of		
Southport, Aug. 12, 1852, by Rev. Sam[ue]l J. M.		
Merwin	1-M	95
James, m. Mary **SHERWOOD**, b. of Fairfield, Nov.		
[1837], by [Enoch E. Chase]	1-M	65
HOUGH, Elizabeth H., of Fairfield, m. John L.		
VANDERWOORT, of New York City, Oct. 1,		
1839, by Rev. Lyman H. Atwater	1-M	68
HOWELL, George, of Brooklyn, N.Y., m. Elizabeth		
TRUBEE, Apr. 10, 1837, by Lyman H. Atwater	1-M	62
HOYT, Hannah, d. James, of Norwalk, m. Jonathan		
BULKLEY, s. Peter, Jan. 21, 1762	1	262
W[illia]m, of New Canaan, m. Angeline **OGDEN**, of		
Fairfield, Apr. 26, 1829, by John H. Hunter	1-M	34

	Vol.	Page
HUBBART, Susannah, d. Zach[ariah], m. David **BARLOW**, s.		
Samuel, Dec. 27, 1743	1	242
Zachariah, had negro James, m. Sarah **CEASER**, d.		
Joseph, Nov. 1752. Children: Sarah, b. Apr. 27,		
1753; Phebe, b. Mar. 24, 1755; d. Jan. 24, 1756	1	9
HUBBELL, HUBBLE, HUBBEL, Aaron, s. David, m. Mary		
BURR, d. Nath[anie]ll, Nov. 29, 1761	1	39
Abigaile, [d. Richard], b. Sept. 19, 1709	LR-2	459
Anne, d. Hezekiah & Annah, b. Mar. 6, 1753	1	43
Asa, s. Hezekiah & Annah, b. Jan. 9, 1757	1	43
Benjamin, s. Rich[ar]d & Penelopy, b. May 11, 1726	1	9
Christian, m. Joseph **SILLIMAN**, s. Capt. Nath[anie]ll,		
Oct. 14, 1762	1	253
Christopher, s. Rich[ar]d & Penelopy, b. July 6, 1729	1	9
David, s. Aaron & Mary, b. Aug. 1, 1768	1	39
Deborah, m. Moses **JACKSON**, Oct. 24, 1672	LR-A2	663
Ebenezer, s. Richard, Jr., b. Sept. 20, 1687	LR-A2	678
Ebenezer, [s. Richard, Jr.,], b. Sept. 19, 1687	LR-2	459
Eleazer, [s. Richard], b. Aug. 15, 1700	LR-2	459
Elizabeth, [d. Richard, Jr.], b. Oct. 23, 1689	LR-2	459
Elizabeth, m. Jona[tha]n **GODFREY**, b. of Fairfield, Jan.		
19, 1823, by Rev. Philo Shelton	1-M	10
Gershom, m. Mary **BRADLEY**, May 2, 1754	1	38
Gershom, m. Sarah **WAKEMAN**, Nov. 3, 1756	1	38
Grezel, d. Rich[ar]d & Penelopy, b. Aug. 12, 1733	1	9
Hannah, [d. Richard], b. July 7, 1698	LR-2	459
Harriet, m. Hezekiah **DAVIS**, b. of Mill River, May 10,		
1829, by William Shelton	1-M	34
Hez[ekiah], s. Rich[ar]d & Penelopy, b. Feb. 24, 1728	1	9
Hezekiah, s. Richard, m. Annah **PATTERSON**, d.		
William, May 14, 1752	1	43
Jonathan, [s. Richard, Jr.,], b. Mar. 25, 1692	LR-2	459
Margary, [d. Richard], b. Jan. 17, 1705	LR-2	459
Maria, m. James **LEWIS**, Apr. 13, 1846, by David C.		
Comstock	1-M	83
Maria, L., m. Andrew **BULKLEY**, 2nd, b. of Fairfield,		
Feb. 22, 1844, by Rev. N. E. Cornwall	1-M	76
Martha, d. Aaron & Mary, b. May 2, 1762	1	39
Mary, d. Gershom & Mary, b. July 10, 1755; d. Dec.		
following	1	38
Mary, w. Gershom, d. Feb. 23, 1756	1	38
Mary, d. Gershom & Sarah, b. Aug. 15, 1757	1	38
Mary, d. Richard, m. Isaac **YONGS**, Sept. 1, 1757	1	267
Mary, d. Aaron & Mary, b. July 2, 1767; d. Oct. 26, 1768	1	39
Mary, d. Aaron & Mary, b. Jan. 29, 1769	1	39
Mary, m. Eli B. **NICHOLS**, June 12, 1836, by Rev.		
Nath[anie]l E. Cornwall	1-M	59
Nathaniell, [s. Richard], b. Aug. 11, 1702	LR-2	459
Olive, m. Joseph **BRADLEY**, June 20, 1724	1	144
Penelopy, d. Rich[ar]d & Penelopy, b. July 22, 1732	1	9
Peter, s. Richard, Jr. & Rebecca (**MOREHOUSE**), b.		
Aug. 10, 1686, Stratfield Parish (3rd generation)	1	308
Peter, s. Richard, Jr., b. Aug. 10, 1686	LR-2	459

	Vol.	Page
HUBBELL, HUBBLE, HUBBEL (cont.)		
Peter, s. Richard, Jr., b. Aug. 10, 1686	LR-A2	678
Polly, m. Roswell **SEELEY**, Sept. 12, 1821, by Rev.		
Daniel Wildman	1-M	6
Rebeckah, w. Richard, d. Apr. 2, 1692	LR-2	459
Richard, Sr., b. [ ], 1628, in Great Britain or		
Plymouth Wales (1st generation)	1	308
Richard, Jr., s. Richard, Sr. & Elizabeth (**MEIGS**), b.		
[ ], 1654, in Guilford, Conn. (2nd		
generation)	1	308
Richard, Jr., m. Rebeckah **MOREHOUSE**, Nov. 4, 1685	LR-A2	678
Richard, of Fairfield, m. Hannah **SILAWAY**, of		
Mauldon, Mass., Oct. 12, 1692, by Major Nathan		
Gold	LR-2	459
Richard, [s. Richard], b. Oct. 20, 1696	LR-2	459
Rich[ar]d, Jr., m. Penelopy **FAYERWEATHER**, Dec. 9,		
1735	1	9
Sally, m. Zalmon **GODFREY**, Dec. 18, 1830, b Elisha		
Cushman	1-M	39-40
Sarah, m. John **PARRETT**, Jan. 7, 1752	1	167
Sarah, m. John **PARRETT**, Jan. 17, 1752	1	241
Silas, s. Peter & Katharine (**WHEELER**), b. Feb. 24,		
1738, in Newtown, Conn. (4th generation)	1	308
Truman Mallory, s. Silas & Hannah Wheeler (nee		
FRENCH), b. Sept. 18, 1788, in Montgomery		
Hampshire Co., Mass., (5th generation)	1	308
Uriah, m. Mabel **HULL**, b. of Greenfield, Feb. 19,		
[1822], by Rev. E. W. Hooker	1-M	7
Uriah, m. Sally **STERLING**, Nov. 24, 1829, by G.		
Pierce, Elder	1-M	38
Walter, s. William & Elizabeth Catharine (**PAMILLEE**),		
b. Apr. 25, 1851, in Philadelphia, Pa. (7th		
generation)	1	308
Will[ia]m, s. Hezekiah & Annah, b. July 24, 1755	1	43
William, m. Sarah **SHUTE**, b. of Bridgeport, [July] 13,		
[1845], by Rev. Cha[rle]s R. Adams	1-M	82
William Wheeler, s. Truman Mallory & Mary Ann		
(**FLOWER**), b. Mar. 4, 1821, [in], Philadelphia, Pa.		
(6th generation)	1	308
Zachariah, [s. Richard], b. Aug. 25, 1694	LR-2	459
HUESTER, Esther, m. Kenneth **SAGE**, of Norwalk, Mar. 10,		
1833, by Tho[ma]s F. Davis	1-M	50
HUGH, Rowland, m. Sarah **HENDRICK**, Mar. 17, 1757	1	163
HULL, [see also **HALL**], Abigail, d. Cornelius & Abigail, b.		
Apr. 26, 1742	1	220
Abigail, d. Ebenezer, m. Gershom **COLEY**, s. Sam[ue]ll,		
Nov. 15, 1748	1	125
Ann, m. Tho[ma]s **GREEN**, Apr. 7, 1720	LR-B	146
Anna, d. Peter & Jerusha, b. Aug. 17, 1760	1	247
Charles W[illia]m, m. Sally Wakeman **MEEKER**, Apr. 5,		
1821, by Hezekiah Ripley, V.D.M.	1-M	4
Cornelius, m. Abigail **RUMSEY**, d. Rob[er]t, Aug. 24,		
1731	1	220

	Vol.	Page
HULL (cont.)		
Daniel, s. Ebenezer, m. Mary **BETTS**, d. Stephen, Nov. 2, 1748	1	125
David, s. Seth & Hannah, b. Dec. 5, 1760	1	140
Eliphalet, s. Cornelius & Abigail, b. Apr. 16, 1737	1	220
Eliphalet, s. Seth & Hannah, b. Dec. 4, 1749	1	140
Elip[hale]t, Dr. had negro Annis, d. Ceazer & Hagar, b. June 14, 1789, Phillip, s. [Ceazer] & Hagar, b. Feb. 7, 1791	1	290
Esther, d. Nath[anie]ll, m. Samuel **BARLOW**, Aug. 7, 1744	1	105
Esther, d. John, m. Dan[ie]ll **SANFORD**, s. Sam[ue]ll, Apr. 18, 1758	1	261
Eunice, d. Cornelius & Abigail, b. Mar. 6, 1733	1	220
Grace, d. Cornelius & Abigail, b. July 16, 1736	1	220
Hezekiah, s. Dan[ie]ll & Mary, b. May 29, 1753	1	125
Jedediah, s. Cornelius & Abigail, b. July 24, 1732	1	220
John, of New York, m. Francis M. **BUTLER**, of Southport, Aug. 5, 1840, by N. E. Cornwall	1-M	70
Julia, of Greenfield, m. Joel **BANKS** of Easton, Sept. 29, 1852, by Rev. Martin Dudley, of Easton	1-M	93
Justus, s. Dan[ie]ll & Mary, b. July 5, 1755	1	125
Lide, d. Theophilus & Sarah, b. Dec. 31, 1720	1	6
Mabel, m. Uriah **HUBBELL**, b. of Greenfield, Feb. 19, [1822], by Rev. E. W. Hooker	1-M	7
Martha, d. Dan[ie]ll & Mary, b. Feb. 2, 1751	1	125
Martha, d. George, m. Jonathan **BIXBY**, s. Elias, July 4, 1752	1	212
Mary, d. Theophilus & Sarah, b. Sept. 12, 1723	1	6
Mary, d. Eliphalet, m. Seth **JENNINGS**, s. Isaac, Mar. 13, 1754	1	233
Peter, s. Nath[anie]ll, m. Jerusha **STURGIS**, d. Solomon, [ ]	1	247
Rebecca, m. Thomas **NASH**, s. Tho[ma]s, Sept. 28, 1731	1	104
Ruey, d. Cornelius & Abigail, b. Dec. 16, 1751	1	220
Ruth, d. Eliphalet, m. Francis **BRADLEY**, s. Francis, Feb. 20, 1750	1	158
Sally, m. Cyrus **SHERWOOD**, Mar. 6, 1831, by Tho[ma]s F. Davis	1-M	42-3
Samuel, s. Samuel, m. Joanna **FAIRCHILD**, d. Joseph, Feb. 3, 1727	1	57
Sarah, m. John **LANE**, Nov. 5, 1735	1	92
Sarah, d. Cornelius & Abigail, b. Apr. 15, 1745	1	220
Sarah, d .Cornelius, m. David **ALLEN**, Jr., s. David, Nov. 10, 1768	1	270
Seth, s. Eliphalet, m. Hannah **RUMSEY**, d. Robert, Dec. 24, 1747	1	140
Seth, s. Seth & Hannah, b. Feb. 12, 1755	1	140
Theophilus, Capt., d. June 5, 1710	LR-2	456
Theophilus, s. Theophilus & Sarah, b. Feb. 21, 1735/6	1	6
Thomas, had negroes Amos, b. Nov. 15, 1795 & Nancy, b. Sept. 25, 1797	1	462

	Vol.	Page

HUNT, Edmund, s. Thomas, m. Abigail **SMEDLEY**, d. James,
    Aug. 12, 1756 — 1 — 229
  Elizabeth, m. Jabez **BARLOW**, Mar. 1, 1744 — 1 — 64
  Jane, d. Edmund & Abigail, b. Mar. 21, 1757 — 1 — 229
  Jesse, m. Sarah **STAPLES**, Mar. 22, 1753 — 1 — 60
  Mary, d. Jesse & Sarah, b. Dec. 6, 1756 — 1 — 60
  Sarah, d. Jesse & Sarah, b. May 10, 1755 — 1 — 60
  Thomas, s. Jesse & Sarah, b. Mar. 8, 1754 — 1 — 60
HUNTER, George, of Fairfield, m. Catharine **NASH**, of
    Saugatuc, (colored), Feb. 28, 1827, by Nath[anie]l
    Hewit — 1-M — 25
HURD, Jane, of Black Rock, m. Wakeman **WILSON**, of
    Greenfield, Jan. 3, 1841, by Rev. Lyman H. Atwater — 1-M — 71
HURLBURT, HURLBERT, HURLBUTT, HURLBAULT,
HULBART, HOLLIBERT, HOLLEBERT, Charles, m.
    Eunice **PERRY**, Dec. 29, 1833, by Tho[ma]s F.
    Davis — 1-M — 51
  Edwin, of Norwalk, m. Alethea **BENNITT**, of Greens
    Farms, Apr. 15, 1827, by Rev. E. W. Hooker — 1-M — 26-7
  Elizabeth, d. Zachariah, m. Charles **DUNCOMBE**, s.
    William, of Barleyend, near Joinghoe, in the County
    of Bucks, Mar. 10, 1744/5, by Rev. Henry Caner, of
    Fairfield — 1 — 186
  Eunice, d. Gideon, m. Moses **BENNIT**, s. Deliverance,
    June 17, 1746 — 1 — 142
  George N., m. Betsey **DISBROW**, b. of Fairfield, [Oct.]
    12, [1823], by Rev. E. W. Hooker — 1-M — 12
  Gideon, s. Gideon, m. Hannah **TAYLOR**, d. John, of
    Norwalk, Nov. 14, 1751 — 1 — 203
  Gideon, s. Gideon & Hannah, b. Nov. 3, 1752 — 1 — 203
  Hannah, d. Gideon & Hannah, b. Oct. 22, 1754 — 1 — 203
  James, s. Gideon & Hannah, b. Nov. 3, 1756 — 1 — 203
  Martha, m. David **LYON**, June 12, 1745 — 1 — 157
  Mary, d. Gideon, m. Nathan **GRAY**, s. Isaac, June 24,
    1735 — 1 — 138
  Phebe, m. Azariah **BEDIENT**, s. John, Mar. 28, 1756 — 1 — 200
  Rebecca, d. Gideon, m. Shubal **GORHAM**, s. Joseph,
    Jan. 22, 1746/7 — 1 — 145
HUTCHINSON, Aaron A., of Trenton, N.J., m. Mahala
    ALLEN, of Greens Farms, Oct. 27, 1834, by T. F.
    Davis — 1-M — 55
HYATT, Lewis, of Wilton, m. Amanda L. **MILLS**, of
    Fairfield, Mar. 4, 1824, by Rev. Samuel Codner — 1-M — 14
HYDE, Edward, m. Sarah **BURR**, b. of Greens Farms, Sept.
    11, 1826, by Rev. E. W. Hooker — 1-M — 23
  John S., m. Harriet **ADAMS**, Feb. 21, 1837, by Rev.
    Tho[ma]s F. Davis — 1-M — 62
  Mary Augusta, m. Edwin **SHERWOOD**, Dec. 12, 1837,
    by Rev. Tho[ma]s F. Davis — 1-M — 65
  Rachel, m. Ebenezer **ANDREWS**, b. of Greens Farms,
    Aug. 15, [1825], by Rev. E. W. Hooker — 1-M — 19

	Vol.	Page
IVES, George W., of Bridgeport, m. Sarah L. JONES, of Black Rock, Feb. 20, 1848, by Rev. Lyman H. Atwater	1-M	88
JACKSON, Benj[ami]n, s. Gabriel & Margaret, b. July 30, 1743; d. Nov. 20, 1744	1	258
Bille, s. Francis & Damaris, b. Aug. 21, 1759	1	258
Daniel, s. Ephraim & Martha, b. May 16, 1733	1	73
David, s. Ephraim & Martha, b. Oct. 28, 1736	1	73
Deborah, m. Samuel SMITH, Oct. 27, 1699	LR-2	460
Deborah, d. Moses, b. Feb. 8, 1778	LR-A2	663
Ephraim, b. Oct. [ ], 1704; m. Martha COUCH, Nov. [ ], 1727	1	73
Ephraim, m. 2nd w. Martha BLACKMAN, June [ ], 1730	1	73
Ephraim, s. Ephraim & Martha, b. Sept. 10, 1741	1	73
Francis, s. Gabriel & Margaret, b. Mar. 11, 1736	1	258
Francis, s. Gabriel & Margaret, b. Mar. 11, 1736; d. Jan. [ ], 1738	1	258
Francis, s. Gabriel & Margaret, b. June 3, 1740	1	258
Francis, s. Gabriel, m. Damaris BENNETT, d. Dea. Will[ia]m, Aug. 24, 1758	1	258
Gabriel, s. Sam[ue]ll, m. Margaret HALL, d. Francis, May 24, 1727	1	258
Gershom, s. Moses, Jr., b. Nov. 23, 1689	LR-A2	678
Hannah, d. Samuell, b. Nov. 17, 167[ ]	LR-A2	664
Joseph, s. Ephraim & Martha, b. Nov. [ ], 1728	1	73
Martha, d. Ephraim & Martha, b. Sept. 8, 1731	1	73
Mahetable, d. Gabriel & Margaret, b. Mar. 27, 1730; d. Jan. [ ], 1738	1	258
Mehitable, d. Gabriel & Margaret, b. Sept. 30, 1745	1	258
Moses, m. Deborah HUBBEL, Oct. 24, 1672	LR-A2	663
Patience, d. Gabriel & Margaret, b. Sept. 25, 1733	1	258
Patience, d. Gabriel, m. Nehemiah JENNINGS, s. John, Sept. 11, 1752	1	56
Rebecka, d. Moses, b. May 10, 1674	LR-A2	663
Sam[ue]ll, s. Gabriel & Margaret, b. Mar. 19, 1728	1	258
Thankfull, d. Samuell, b. May 6, 167[ ]	LR-A2	664
JACOBS, [see also JEACOCKS], Abigail, d. W[illia]m & Rebecca, b. Aug. 19, 1739	1	173
Ann, d. W[illia]m & Rebecca, b. Feb. 3, 1750/1	1	173
Bowers, s. W[illia]m & Rebecca, b. July 13, 1745	1	173
Gershom, s. W[illia]m & Rebecca, b. Mar. 12, 1757	1	173
Grissel, d. W[illia]m & Rebecca, b. Apr. 5, 1743	1	173
Jemima, d. W[illia]m & Rebecca, b. Sept. 5, 1741	1	173
Joshua, s. W[illia]m & Rebecca, b. July 4, 1755	1	173
Mary, d. W[illia]m & Rebecca, b. Aug. 20, 1737	1	173
Olive, d. W[illia]m & Rebecca, b. Oct. 17, 1735	1	173
Rebecca, d. W[illia]m & Rebecca, b. Jan. 25, 1747	1	173
Samuel, s. W[illia]m & Rebecca, b. Jan. 24, 1753	1	173
William, m. Rebecca BLACKMAN, Jan. 25, 1735	1	173
JARVIS, Isaac, s. Isaac & Lydia, of Norwalk, b. Jan. 20, 1756	1	42
Lydea, wid. Isaac, of Norwalk, m. John SQUIER, June 10, 1762	1	272

	Vol.	Page
JARVIS (cont.)		
Nelson, m. Mary **RAYMOND**, Nov. 24, 1825, by Rev. H. R. Judah, of Bridgeport	1-M	28
Noah, s. Isaac & Lydea, b. Nov. 18, 1757; d. May 19, 1766	1	42
JEACOCKS, [see also **JACOBS**], Mabel, d. Joshua, m. Jabez **DISBROW**, s. Joseph, Nov. 3, 1754	1	131
JELLEPP, [see also **JELLIFF**], Mary, m. Selleck **SHERMAN**, b. of Southport, Nov. 26, 1837, by N. E. Cornwall, in Southport	1-M	63-4
JELLIFF [see also **JELLEPP**], Francis, of Southport, m. Juliet **WOOD**, of New London, Apr. 10, 1842, by Rev. N. E. Cornwall	1-M	74
JENKINS, Francis Malbone, of Rochester, m. Amelia Ann **CLARKE**, of Bridgeport, Dec. 2, 1828, by William Shelton	1-M	32
JENNINGS, Aaron, s. John & Sarah, b. Sept. 8, 1734	1	128
Abel, s. John, s. Sarah **HOLLINGWORTH**, [ ], 1756	1	304
Abel, [s. Abel & Sarah], b. July 26, 1772	1	304
Abel, s. John, grandson of Joseph, who was the s. of Joshua	1	304
Abigail, d. Joshua, m. Capt. Simon **COUCH**, s. Simon, May 18, 1721	1	71
Abigail, d. Joseph & Abigail, b. Jan. 18, 1712; d. Aug. 7, 1721	1	69
Abigail, d. Joseph & Abigail, b. Sept. 22, 1721	1	69
Abigail, d. Joshua & Esther, b. Jan. 1, 1757	1	166
Abigail, d. Joseph & Elizabeth, b. Jan. 19, 1757	1	80
Abigail, d. Dan[ie]ll & Eunice, b. Aug. 8, 1757	1	251
Abigail H., of Fairfield, m. Lewis B. **SHEPHARD**, of Danbury, Sept. 7, 1845, by Rev. James Scott, of Stratfield	1-M	82
Abijah, [s. Abel & Sarah], b. Oct. 7, 1762	1	304
Abraham, s. Zach[ariah] & Sarah, b. [ ], 1750	1	221
Alathea, m. Walter **SHERWOOD**, Sept. 19, 1824, by Hezekiah Ripley, V.D.M.	1-M	15
Andrew, s. Joseph & Abigail, b. Mar. 17, 1729	1	69
Andrew W., of Greens Farms, m. Ellen O. **MOREHOUSE**, of Fairfield, Feb. 23, 1848, by Rev. Lyman H. Atwater	1-M	89
Ann, m. Joseph **HOLLINGSWORTH**, Nov. 4, 1734	1	96
Ann, [d. Abel & Sarah], b. Apr. 11, 1768	1	304
Augustus, [s. Isaac & Phebe], b. July 4, 1745; d. next day	1	14
Augustus, s. Isaac & Phebe, b. Feb. 26, 1747/8	1	14
Augustus, m. Sophronia **ROBINSON**, b. of Southport, Nov. 21, 1837, by Lyman H. Atwater	1-M	65
Benjamin, s. Joseph & Abigail, b. July 20, 1713; d. Aug. 6, 1720	1	69
Benjamin, s. Joseph & Abigail, b. Nov. 7, 1723	1	69
Betsey, m. Hezekiah C. **TAYLOR**, b. of Greens Farms, Aug. 29, 1824, by Rev. E. W. Hooker	1-M	15
Catharine, d. Zach[ariah] & Sarah, b. [ ], 1747	1	221

	Vol.	Page
JENNINGS (cont.)		
Charles, s. Joseph & Elizabeth, b. Jan. 23, 1749/50	1	80
Daniel, s. Nathan, b. [ ], 1700	LR-2	459
Daniel, Jr., s. Dan[ie]ll, m. Eunice **BURR**, d. Eph[rai]m,		
Dec. 10, 1752	1	251
David, [s. Isaac], b. Sept. 6, 1714	LR-2	459
David, s. Joseph & Hannah, b. June 7, 1742	1	18
David, s. John & Sarah, b. June 27, 1746	1	128
David, s. Joshua & Esther, b. Oct. 9, 1755	1	166
Dorothy, d. Sam[ue]ll, b. Nov. 11, 1709	LR-2	459
Edmond, s. Zach[ariah] & Sarah, b. [ ], 1754	1	221
Edward, m. Abba Jane **WHITEHEAD**, b. of Fairfield,		
Sept. 16, 1832, by Gershom Pierce	1-M	47
Eliza J., of Southport, m. William M. **EVITTS**, of		
Bridgeport, July 11, 1852, by Rev. Sam[ue]l J. M.		
Merwin	1-M	95
Elizabeth, d. Nathan, b. [ ], 1697	LR-2	459
Elizabeth, d. Jeremiah & Elizabeth, b. Oct. 15, 1727	1	167
Elizabeth S., of Greenfield, m. Charles **HOPKINS**, of		
Long Island, Oct. 17, 1841, in Greenfield, by Rev.		
John Noyes	1-M	72
Ellen, d. Joseph & Elizabeth, b. Aug. 29, 1753	1	80
Emeline, m. Lot **BULKLEY**, b. of Fairfield, Mar. 8,		
1830, by John H. Hunter	1-M	38
Emma, m. Joseph H. **WAKEMAN**, b. of Fairfield, Mar.		
6, 1815, by Rev. E. W. Hooker	1-M	16
Esther, d. Seth & Mary, b. Mar. 2, 1755	1	233
Esther, m. Henry **GOULD**, b. of Fairfield, Dec. 9, 1841,		
by Rev. Geo[rge] Waterbury	1-M	73
[E]unis, d. [Samuell], b. Dec. 13, 1704	LR-2	462
Eunice, d. Joseph & Elizabeth, b. Oct. 9, 1751	1	80
Eunice, d. Nehemiah & Patience, b. Apr. 20, 1753	1	56
Eunice, [d. Abel & Sarah], b. Nov. 24, 1763	1	304
Eunice, of Greens Farms, m. Edward B. **GODFREY**, of		
Weston, Apr. 8, 1835, by T. F. Davis	1-M	56
Gershom, s. Joseph & Abigail, b. Jan. 16, 1710	1	69
Gershom, s. Dan[ie]ll, m. Rhoda **SANFORD**, d.		
Zachariah, Nov. 18, 1762	1	265
Gideon M., m. Betsey **SHERWOOD**, b. of Fairfield,		
[Nov.] 9, [1823] by Rev. E. W. Hooker	1-M	13
Grissell, [d. Abel & Sarah], b. July 7, 1766	1	304
Hannah, d. Micall, b. Dec. 13, 1717	LR-2	456
Hannah, d. Mathew, m. John **KNAP**, s. Dan[ie]ll, June		
29, 1738	1	52
Hannah, d. Jeremiah & Elizabeth, b. May 20, 1745	1	167
Henry, m. Marinda **WHEELER**, Jan. 16, 1822, by		
Nath[anie]l Hewit, V.D.M.	1-M	6
Hezekiah, s. Jeremiah & Elizabeth, b. Oct. 1, 1733; d.		
May 20, 1789	1	167
Isaac, s. Isaac, b. July 11, 1692	LR-2	459
Isaac, Jr., m. Phebe **STAPLES**, June 1, 1731	1	14
Isaac, s. Isaac & Phebe, b. May 7, 1743	1	14
Isaac, d. Mar. 16, 1760	1	14

	Vol.	Page
JENNINGS (cont.)		
Jabez, s. Joseph & Elizabeth, b. July 19, 1748	1	80
Jacob, s. Isaac & Phebe, b. Dec. 5, 1739	1	14
Jeremiah, s. Nathan, b. [ ], 1703	LR-2	459
Jeremiah, m. Elizabeth **COLEY**, Dec. 15, 1726	1	167
Jeremiah, s. Jeremiah & Elizabeth, b. Sept. 14, 1740	1	167
Jeremiah, Jr., s. Jeremiah, m. Elizabeth **SMITH**, d. John, Dec. 8, 1762	1	129
Joel, s. John & Sarah, b. July 13, 1753	1	128
John, s. Isaac, b. Mar. 24, 1706	LR-2	459
John, s. John, b. Jan. 17, 1710/11	LR-2	459
John, s. Isaac, m. Sarah **WINTON**, d. John, Jan. 20, 1731	1	128
John, s. Nehemiah & Patience, b. Jan. 12, 1757	1	56
John, s. Joseph, grandson of Joshua	1	304
John M., m. Mary **OSBORN**, b. of Fairfield, Jan. 25, 1829, by Leonard Bacon	1-M	33
Joseph, m. Abigail **GRUMMAN**, Jan. 20, 1709	1	69
Joseph, s. Joseph & Abigail, b. July 11, 1716	1	69
Joseph, Jr., m. Elizabeth **BOSTWICK**, Aug. 30, 1744	1	80
Joseph, [s. Abel & Sarah], b. Aug. 27, 1770	1	304
Joseph, see Abel **JENNINGS**	1	304
Joshua, s. Joshua, m. Esther **BURR**, d. Peter, Dec. 24, 1754	1	166
Joshua, see Abel **JENNINGS**	1	304
Josiah, [s. Isaac], b. Apr. 1, 1711	LR-2	459
Josiah, s. John & Sarah, b. Sept. 15, 1748	1	128
Julia M., m. Isaac S. **BANKS**, b. of Westport, Sept. 22, 1850, by Rev. Lyman H. Atwater	1-M	92
Justin, s. Joseph & Elizabeth, b. June 11, 1745	1	80
Levi, s. Isaac & Phebe, b. Oct. 27, 1735	1	14
Lucinda S., of Fairfield, m. Truman **SLUBUCK**, of Princeton, N. J., Mar. 6, 1837, by Lyman H. Atwater	1-M	62
Lucrece, d. Isaac & Phebe, b. Oct. 8, 1737	1	14
Lyman, s. Dan[ie]ll & Eunice, b. Nov. 16, 1753	1	251
Marcham, m. Sally Ann **WHITEHOUSE**, Sept. 18, 1825, by Rev. H. Humphreys	1-M	19
Mary, m. George **STANTON**, Dec. 16, 1680	LR-A2	683
Mary, d. Isaac, b. July 4, 1695	LR-2	459
Mary, d. Nathan, b. [ ], 1705	LR-2	458
Mary, m. John **OGDEN**, Jan. 1, 1730	1	214
Mary, d. Jeremiah & Elizabeth, b. Aug. 21, 1730	1	167
Mary, d. John & Sarah, b. Dec. 11, 1743	1	128
Mary, d. Nehemiah & Patience, b. Nov. 25, 1754	1	56
Mary A., of Fairfield, m. William H. **BURR**, of Westport, Nov. 27, 1845, by Rev. L. B. Burr, of Ridgebury	1-M	83
Matilda, m. Eli **COUCH**, Jan. 7, 1827, by E. W. Hooker	1-M	25
Michael, s. Samuell, b. Dec. 3, 1693	LR-2	462
Micall, m. [ ], Mar. 6, 1716/17	LR-2	456
Moses, s. Isaac & Phebe, b. Aug. 19, 1733	1	14
Moses, s. Isaac, m. Abigail **BURR**, d. Capt. John, Oct. 11, 1759	1	251
Nathan, s. Nathan, b. [ ], 1695	LR-2	459
Nathan, s. Sam[ue]ll, b. Mar. 13, 1710/11	LR-2	459

	Vol.	Page
JENNINGS (cont.)		
Nehemiah, s. John, b. [ ], 1718	LR-2	459
Nehemiah, s. John, m. Patience **JACKSON**, d. Gabriel, Sept. 11, 1752	1	56
Noah, [s. Abel & Sarah], b. Mar. 30, 1760	1	304
Peter, s. Jeremiah & Elizabeth, b. June 12, 1743	1	167
Peter Burr, m. Catharine **HILL**, b. of Greens Farms, Sept. 24, 1821, by Hezekiah Ripley, V.D.M.	1-M	5
Rebecca, m. Jonathan **MIDLEBROOK**, s. Jonathan, June 2, 1734	1	133
Ruebin, s. Joseph & Elizabeth, b. Aug. 20, 1746	1	80
Robert, [s. Abel & Sarah], b. Apr. 5, 1759	1	304
Robert, m. Mary **PERRY**, b. of Fairfield, Apr. 29, 1838, by Lyman H. Atwater	1-M	66
Ruth, d. Jeremiah & Elizabeth, b. Nov. 13, 1735	1	167
Ruth, [d. Abel & Sarah], b. July 3, 1761	1	304
Sally Ann, m. Samuel **GRANT**, Oct. 7, 1832, by T. F. Davis	1-M	48-9
Samuell, [s. Samuell], b. Mar. 16, 1702/3	LR-2	462
Sarah, [d. Samuell], b. Feb. 9, 1699	LR-2	462
Sarah, m. Daniel **LYON**, Aug. 7, 1718	1	118
Sarah, d. John, b. [ ], 1723	LR-2	458
Sarah, d. Jeremiah & Elizabeth, b. July 26, 1738	1	167
Sarah, d. John & Sarah, b. Apr. 14, 1751	1	128
Sarah, d. Isaac, m. Sam[ue]ll **BOSTWICK**, s. David, Mar. [ ], 1756	1	246
Sarah, d. Isaac, m. Samuel **BOSTWICK**, s. David, Mar. [ ], 1756	1	276
Seth, s. Isaac & Phebe, b. Dec. 20, 1731	1	14
Seth, s. Isaac, m. Mary **HULL**, d. Eliphalet, Mar. 13, 1754	1	233
Seth, s. Isaac & Phebe, d. May 5, 1757	1	14
Stephen, s. Joseph & Abigail, b. Feb. 11, 1714	1	69
Stephen, s. Joseph, m. Hannah **STURGIS**, d. Peter, Aug. 20, 1741	1	18
Stephen, s. Joseph & Hannah, b. Sept. 21, 1750; d. July 20, 1753	1	18
Stephen, s. Joseph & Hannah, b. Jan. 27, 1755	1	18
Susan, d. John & Sarah, b. Mar. 28, 1741	1	128
Susannah, d. Joseph & Hannah, b. Sept. 30, 1746	1	18
Thaddeus, s. John & Sarah, b. Aug. 31, 1732	1	128
William, s. Joseph & Hannah, b. Oct. 4, 1744	1	18
William, s. Zach[ariah] & Sarah], b. [ ], 1752	1	221
William, s. Jeremiah & Elizabeth, b. July 8, 1766	1	129
Zachariah, s. John, b. Jan. [ ], 1720	LR-2	458
Zachariah, s. Zachariah, m. Sarah **MOR[E]HOUSE**, June [ ], 1743	1	221
Zachariah, s. Zach[ariah] & Sarah, b. Mar. 25, 1745	1	221
JESSUP, JESUP, Abigail, d. Edw[ar]d & Sarah, b. May 9, 1731	1	194
Abigail, d. Edw[ar]d, m. John **ALLEN**, s. Gideon, Jan. 17, 1750/1	1	28

	Vol.	Page

JESSUP, JESUP (cont.)

Angeline, of Greens Farms, m. Edward M. **MORGAN**, of Westfield, Mass., June 19, 1827, by Rev. E. W. Hooker — 1-M — 26-7

Blackleach, s. Edw[ar]d & Sarah, b. Dec. 14, 1735 — 1 — 194

Blackleach, s. Edward, m. Sarah **STEBBENS**, Feb. 23, 1757 — 1 — 194

Charles, m. Abigail **SHERWOOD**, b. of Greens Farms, [Sept.] 9, [1821], by Rev. E. W. Hooker — 1-M — 5

Ebenezer, s. Edw[ar]d & Sarah, b. Mar. 14, 1739 — 1 — 194

Edward, m. Sarah **BLACKLEACH**, Dec. 7, 1724 — 1 — 194

Edward, d. Sept. last day, 1750 — 1 — 194

Elizabeth, d. Edw[ar]d & Sarah, b. Feb. 13, 1727/8 — 1 — 194

Elizabeth, d. Edward, m. Thomas **COUCH**, s. Tho[ma]s, Feb. 22, 1749/50 — 1 — 149

Martha, of Greens Farms, m. John **WOOFINDELE**, of New York, [Nov.] 6, [1822], by Rev. E. W. Hooker — 1-M — 9

Mary, d. Edw[ar]d & Sarah, b. Sept. 28, 1729 — 1 — 194

Mary, d. Edward, m. John **MOR[E]HOUSE**, s. Gideon, May 16, 1745 — 1 — 180

Sarah, d. Edw[ar]d & Sarah, b. July 14, 1726 — 1 — 194

JEWET, Polly, m. William **BAKER**, Apr. 25, 1824, by Rev. E. W. Hooker — 1-M — 14

JOHNSON, Amanda, of Fairfield, m. Michael **NICHOLS**, of Easton, (colored), Nov. 17, 1851, by Rev. N. D. Benedict — 1-M — 93

Fanny B., m. Anthony **SMITH**, b. of Fairfield (colored), Nov. 24, 1846, by Rev. Samuel J. M. Merwin — 1-M — 86

Jeremiah, s. Nath[anie]ll & Sarah, b. May 6, 1756 — 1 — 176

Joseph, s. Nath[anie]ll & Sarah, b. Nov. 8, 1750 — 1 — 176

Lyman, of Derby, m. Catharine **SHERWOOD**, of Fairfield, Aug. 6, 1821, by William Belden — 1-M — 4

Mabel, m. David **BARTRAM**, Dec. 14, 1730 — 1 — 240

Nathaniel, m. Sarah **NICHOLS**, Jan. 11, 1749/50 — 1 — 176

Sarah, d. Moses, m. Daniel **MEAKER**, s. Joseph, July 19, 1744 — 1 — 240

Solomon, s. Nath[anie]ll & Sarah, b. June 7, 1753 — 1 — 176

JONES, JOANS, Esther, m. John **RUMSEY**, s. Robert, Mar. 19, 1752 — 1 — 158

Hewlet, m. Eliza **MILLS**, Oct. 6, 1833, by T. F. Davis — 1-M — 51

Martha, d. Thomas, b. Oct. 25, 1683 — LR-A2 — 680

Mary, m. Ebenezer **THORP**, s. John, June 24, 1746 — 1 — 124

Obadian William, of New York, m. Elizabeth Mallbie **ROWLAND**, of Fairfield, Nov. 10, 1820, by Nath[anie]l Hewit, V.D.M. — 1-M — 2

Sarah L., of Black Rock, m. George W. **IVES**, of Bridgeport, Feb. 20, 1848, by Rev. Lyman H. Atwater — 1-M — 88

Thomas, m. Abigaill **ROLAND**, d. Henry, Mar. 5, 1670/1 — LR-A2 — 680

JOY, Elizabeth Elliott, of Fairfield, m. Henry **DUTTON**, of Newtown, Sept. 8, 1823, by Nath[anie]ll Hewit — 1-M — 12

Nancy, of Fairfield, m. Henry **TUTHILL**, of Norwalk, Oct. 11, 1829, by John H. Hunter — 1-M — 35-6

	Vol.	Page
JUDD, Ard B., of Ridgebury, m. Fanny **SHERWOOD**, of		
Greenfield, Dec. 25, 1832, by T. F. Davis	1-M	50
Ebenezer, of Danbury, m. Abby Jane **STURGIS**, of		
Fairfield, Apr. 23, 1846, by Rev. Lyman H. Atwater	1-M	84
Hiram, of Danbury, m. Mana **THORP**, of Fairfield, Dec.		
8, 1841, by Rev. N. E. Cornwall	1-M	73
Nelson, H., of Fairfield, m. Jane **SOULES**, of Bridgeport,		
Aug. 10, [1846] by Rev. N. E. Cornwall	1-M	85
JUDSON, Ann Mills, of Fairfield, m. George **GIBBS**, of Turks		
Island, Oct. 7, 1832, by Rev. John H. Hunter	1-M	47
Catharine Ann, m. Stiles **BULKLEY**, b. of Fairfield, Jan.		
15, 1826, by Nath[anie]l Hewit	1-M	21
David, s. Abner & Hannah, b. Aug. 11, 1757	1	283
David, s. Abner, of Stratford, m. Esther **BULKLEY**, d.		
Nathan, Nov. 13, 1783, by Rev. Andrew Eliot	1	283
KAM,* Emily, of Huntington, m. Frederic **WAKEMAN**, of		
Fairfield, Nov. 30, 1841, by Rev. Lyman H. Atwater		
*[Perhaps "**KAIN**"?]	1-M	73
KEELER, Rufus, of New York, m. Jane L. **STURGIS**, of		
Fairfield, Oct. 10, 1826, by Nath[anie]l Hewit	1-M	23
KELLOGG, Charles G., of New York, m. Caroline **CURTIS**,		
of Fairfield, June 15, 1839, by Rev. Lyman H.		
Atwater	1-M	68
Ebeline, Mrs. of West Stockbridge, Mass., m. Prof.		
George W. **BENEDICT**, of Burlington, Vt., Aug. 8,		
1842, by Rev. Lyman H. Atwater	1-M	74
Margaret, of Fairfield, m. Charles E. **OSBORN**, of		
Corning, N.Y., Sept. 24, 1839, by Rev. Lyman H.		
Atwater	1-M	68
Otis, of Troy, N.Y., m. Mary **DIMON**, of Fairfield,		
[Nov.] 24, [1831],by Rev. Charles Smith	1-M	44
KENNEDY, W[illia]m, of Southport, m. Cloe **BULKLEY**, of		
Southport, Jan. 17, 1836, by Nath[anie]l E.		
Cornwall	1-M	58
KETCHUM, Sarah, d. Nathaniel, m. Phineheas **CHAPMAN**,		
s. Dan[ie]ll, Sept. 22, 1742	1	196
KING, Daniel, s. Richard & Sarah, b. Nov. 8, 1751	1	243
David, s. Richard & Sarah, b. Dec. 17, 1746	1	243
Jemima, d. Rich[ar]d & Sarah, b. June 29, 1757	1	243
Richard, m. Sarah **FINCH**, Oct. 28, 1742	1	243
Samuel, s. Rich[ar]d & Sarah, b. Sept. 22, 1754	1	243
Sarah, d. Richard & Sarah, b. Jan. 24, 1748	1	243
KIPPEN, George, of Bridgeport, m. Jane **NICHOLS**, of		
Fairfield, Sept. 9, 1845, by Rev. Lyman H. Atwater	1-M	82
KISSAM, Geo[rge] B., of New York, m. Lucy A.		
BREWSTER, of Greenfield, Aug. 8, 1843, by Rev.		
N. E. Cornwall	1-M	75
KNAPP, KNAP, Abel, s. Dan[ie]l & Elinor, b. May 21, 1742	1	59
Abigail, d. Dan[ie]ll & Abigail, b. Dec. 20, 1719	1	46
Abigail, d. John & Hannah, b. Mar. 3, 1754	1	52
Ann, d. Dan[ie]ll & Abigail, b. July 11, 1721	1	46
Ann, [twin with Hannah], d. John & Hannah, b. June 2,		
1744	1	52

	Vol.	Page
KNAPP, KNAP (cont.)		
Anna, d. David & Anna, b. July 29, 1737	1	100
Aquila, s. David & Anna, b. Dec. 20, 1738	1	100
Catharine, m. Alden WILSON, Jr., b. of Fairfield, Nov. 3, 1840, by Rev. Matthew Batchelder	1-M	70
Christopher, d. Jan. 17, 1709/10	LR-2	456
Clara, Mrs. m. Alden WILSON, Sr., b. of Fairfield, Nov. 22, 1840, by Rev. Matthew Batcheldor	1-M	70
Dan[ie]l, m. Abigail BANKS, Mar. 5, 1710	1	46
Daniel, s. Dan[ie]ll & Abigail, b. Aug. 4, 1717	1	46
Dan[ie]l, Jr., s. Dan[ie]ll, m. Elenor LYON, d. Ebenezer, Jan. 9, 1740	1	59
Dan[ie]l, s. Dan[ie]l & Elinor, b. May 21, 1744; d. May 26, 1754	1	59
David, m. Anna MEAKER, Oct. 24, 1736	1	100
David, s. David & Anna, b. May 18, 1745	1	100
Eben, s. Eben & Elizabeth, b. June 29, 1755	1	38
Eben[eze]r, s. Dan[ie]ll & Abigail, b. May 24, 1724	1	46
Ebenezer, s. Dan[ie]l, m. Elizabeth MCRAA, d. Hugh, Dec. 31, 1750	1	38
Elinor, d. Dan[ie]l & Elinor, b. Nov. 3, 1740; d. Nov. 3, 1740	1	59
Eliza, of Fairfield, m. Elnathan J. WEBB, of Stratford, Dec. 5, 1825, by Rev. Nath[anie]l Hewit	1-M	20
Elizabeth, d. Dan[ie]ll & Abigail, b. Sept. 27, 1736; d. Sept. 27, 1755	1	46
Elizabeth, d. Eben[eze]r & Elizabeth, b. Sept. 10, 1753	1	38
Eunice, b. [ ], 1728	1	100
Eunice, m. Jabez WILLIAMS, [ ], 1753	1	100
Grace, d. Dan[ie]l & Elinor, b. Apr. 6, 1749; d. June 26, 1749	1	59
Hannah, [twin with Ann], d. John & Hannah, b. June 2, 1744	1	52
Henry, m. Caroline SHERWOOD, b. of Fairfield, Apr. 23, 1846, by Rev. N. E. Cornwall	1-M	84
James, s. John & Hannah, b. July 7, 1739	1	52
John, s. Dan[ie]ll & Abigail, b. May 25, 1713	1	46
John, s. Dan[ie]ll, m. Hannah JENNINGS, d. Mathew, June 29, 1738	1	52
John, s. John & Hannah, b. Mar. 24, 1753 (?)* *(Probably 1743)	1	52
John, m. Mary KNAPP, b. of Fairfield, [ ], in Stratfield, by E. E. Chase. Recorded Apr. 2, 1838	1-M	66
Jonathan, s. Jona[tha]n, b. Apr. 21, 1690	LR-A2	682
Jonathan, s. David & Anna, b. Mar. 6, 1750	1	100
Joseph, s. Dan[ie]ll & Abigail, b. July 20, 1731	1	46
Lois, d. David & Anna, b. Jan. 1, 1743/4	1	100
Lydea, d. Nicholas, m. Isaac HALL, s. Ffrancis, Jan. 16, 1666	LR-A2	682
Mary, d. Josiah, b. Nov. 7, 167[ ]	LR-A2	683
Mary, d. Dan[ie]ll & Abigail, b. Mar. 7, 1711	1	46
Mary, m. John KNAPP, b. of Fairfield, [ ], in Stratfield, by E. E. Chase. Recorded Apr. 2, 1838	1-M	66

	Vol.	Page
KNAPP, KNAP (cont.)		
Mary, d. Moses, m. Gershom **FAIRCHILD**, s.		
Alexander, Nov. 19, 1754	1	124
Nehemiah, s. John & Hannah, b. Nov. 9, 1740	1	52
Primus, m. Elizabeth Ann **OWEN**, b. of Fairfield, July		
29, 1851, by Rev. W. W. Brewer	1-M	92
Priscilla, d. David & Anna, b. Mar. 8, 1741	1	100
Rachel, b. June 7, 1726; m. Josiah **WHITLOCK**, s. John,		
[ ]	1	99
Rufus, m. Caroline **TRUBER**, b. of Fairfield, Oct. 28,		
1840, by Rev. Lyman H. Atwater	1-M	70
Ruth, d. Dan[ie]l & Elinor, b. July 5, 1747; d. Sept. 1,		
1747	1	59
Ruth, d. Dan[ie]l & Elinor, b. Jan. 5, 1754	1	59
Sarah, d. Dan[ie]ll & Abigail, b. May 26, 1726	1	46
Sarah, d. Eben[eze]r & Elizabeth, b. Oct. 20, 1751	1	38
Stephen, s. Dan[ie]l & Elinor, b. July 7, 1751; d.		
[ ]	1	59
William, m. Harriet **TRUBEE**, b. of Fairfield, July 11,		
1849, by Rev. Lyman H. Atwater	1-M	92
KNOT, Gershom, s. John & Martha, b. Mar. 7, 1737	1	245
John, s. John & Martha, b. Sept. 24, 1731	1	245
John, of Weathersfield, m. Martha **GRAY**, of Fairfield,		
[ ], 1731	1	245
Nath[anie]ll, s. John & Martha, b. Jan. 26, 1747	1	245
Ollive, d. John & Martha, b. Feb. 13, 1744	1	245
Salome, s. [sic] John & Martha, b. July 10, 1735		
(Probably a dau.)	1	245
Sallome, m. Elnathan **ALLEN**, Dec. 28, 1751	1	224
Thomas, s. John & Martha, b. June 23, 1741	1	245
William, s. John & Martha, b. Sept. 24, 1739	1	245
KNOWLES, Joshua, d. Jan. 26, 1711	LR-2	456
Rebecka, m. Jonathan **MOREHOUSE**, Apr. 16, 1690	LR-A2	677
KUNDSON, Gilbert A., of New York City, m. Elizabeth B.		
ALVORD, of Southport, Mar. 20, 1844, by Rev.		
Lyman H. Atwater	1-M	77
LABARIE, Ann, m. John **CABLE**, s. George, May 1st		
Monday, 1756	1	184
LACEY, LACY, Catharine, m. Henry **HALL**, b. of		
Bridgeport, July 2, 1843, by Rev. N. E. Cornwall	1-M	75
Ebenezer, s. Edward, Jr., b. Mar. 12, 1703/4	LR-2	462
Edward, m. Abigail **GREGORY**, July 23, 1702	LR-2	462
Sarah, d. John, m. David **HODGDEN**, s. Will[ia]m, June		
[ ], 1750	1	163
Urban, m. Mary Ann **SHERWOOD**, Feb. 15, 1835, by		
James H. Linsley	1-M	56
LAFORGE, Geo[rge] H., of Trumbull, m. Eliza B. **LINES**, of		
New Haven, [May] 7, [1845], by Rev. Charles R.		
Adams	1-M	81
LAMBERTON, Henry J., of Windsor, m. Evelina **BURR**, of		
Greens Farms, Dec. 14, 1828, by Rev. E. W. Hooker	1-M	33
LAMSON, Alithea, d. Joseph & Alithea, b. Oct. 27, 1749	1	85

	Vol.	Page
LAMSON (cont.)		
Anna, d. Joseph & Alethea, b. May 18, 1748; d. July 10, 1753	1	85
Anna, d. Joseph & Alithea, b. Jan. 28, 1754	1	85
Elizabeth, d. Joseph & Alithea, b. May 5, 1756	1	85
Esther, d. Joseph & Alithea, b. Feb. 25, 1751	1	85
Joseph, m. Mrs. Alethea **WETMORE**, July 26, 1747	1	85
William, s. Joseph & Alithea, b. Oct. [ ], 1752	1	85
LANE, Elizabeth, m. Dan[ie]l **HILL**, Apr. [ ], 1752	1	93
James, s. John & Sarah, b. Oct. 15, 1738	1	92
Jeane, d. John & Sarah, b. May 15, 1747	1	92
Jerusha, d. John & Sarah, b. Feb. 18, 1755	1	92
John, m. Sarah **HULL**, Nov. 5, 1735	1	92
Martha, d. John & Sarah, b. Oct. 15, 1736	1	92
Mary, d. John & Sarah, b. June 10, 1743	1	92
Sarah, d. John & Sarah, b. July 15, 1751	1	92
LANGTREE, Samuel Daly, m. Mary Juana **O'SULLIVAN**, July 30, 1834, by Rev. George Carrington	1-M	53
LATHROP, Lydia, d. Ansell, of Plimouth, m. William **BEADLE**, s. Samuel, of the Points of Great Bursted, County of Essex, England, Apr. 15, 1770	1	273
LEE, Ann, d. Enos & Joanna, b. Feb. 9, 1743	1	118
Enos, s. William, m. Joanna **GUYRE**, d. Luke, Oct. 1, 1740	1	118
Enos, s. Enos & Joanna, b. Nov. 25, 1757	1	118
John, s. Enos & Joanna, b. Dec. 20, 1748	1	118
Mary, d. Enos & Joanna, b. Dec. 4, 1746	1	118
Nathan, s. Enos & Joanna, b. Mar. 21, 1751	1	118
Rebecca, d. Enos & Joanna, b. Apr. 2, 1754	1	118
Sarah, d. William, m. Daniel **MALLORY**, Nov. 30, 1748	1	177
Silas, s. Enos & Joanna, b. Apr. 30, 1745	1	118
William, s. Enos & Joanna, b. July 25, 1741	1	118
LEFFERTY, James, m. Happy Frances **ELWOOD**, May 8, 1836, by Rev. T. F. Davis	1-M	59
LEONARD, W[illia]m B., of New York, m. Louisa D. **BULKELEY**, d. Andrew, of Southport, July 6, 1847, by Rev. N. E. Cornwall	1-M	87
LEWIS, LEWISS, Abigail, d. Nath[anie]ll, of Barnstable, m. Andrew **HILL**, s. Capt. Tho[ma]s, Dec. 1, 1763	1	262
Albert, m. Jane **HAYES**, Apr. 29, 1823, by Rivers Morrell, J. P.	1-M	11
Deborah, d. Lathrop & Sarah, b. Nov. 21, 1742	1	22
Deborah, d. Lothrop, m. Jonathan **STURGIS**, s. Capt. Sam[ue]ll, Oct. 26, 1760	1	253
Eben[eze]r, s. Charles, m. Betty **GODFREE**, d. Stephen, Feb. [ ], 1763	1	268
Elizabeth, m. Stephen **GODFREY**, s. Christopher, June 11, 1739	1	188
Elizabeth, m. Samuel **PENFIELD**, s. Peter, Sept. 2, 1757	1	184
Hiram, of Bridgeport, m. Elizabeth M. **MILLER**, of Fairfield, Mar. 1, 1830, by John Hunter	1-M	38
James, m. Maria **HUBBELL**, Apr. 13, 1846, by David C. Comstock	1-M	83

	Vol.	Page

LEWIS, LEWISS (cont.)

John H., of Huntsville, Ala., m. Mary H. F. **BETTS**, of
    Fairfield, Nov. 21, 1824, by Rev. Nath[anie]l Hewit — 1-M — 16

Jonathan, s. Lathrop & Sarah, b. Sept. 1, 1728 — 1 — 22

Jonathan, s. Lathrop Lewis, m. Sarah **OSBORN**, d. Capt.
    John, Jan. 10, 1754 — 1 — 42

Lathrop, m. Mrs. Sarah **WAKEMAN**, July 26, 1727 — LR-B — C

Lathrop, m. Mrs. Sarah **WAKEMAN**, July 26, 1727 — 1 — 22

Sarah, d. Lathrop & Sarah, b. June 28, 1735 — 1 — 22

Sarah, d. Lathrop, m. Seth **OSBORN**, s. Samuel, July 12,
    1752 — 1 — 113

Sarah, d. Jonathan & Sarah, b. Nov. 17, 1754 — 1 — 42

Sarah, w. Lathrop, d. May 15, 1756 — 1 — 22

Sturgis, s. Lathrop & Sarah, b. Aug. 28, 1731 — 1 — 22

Sturgis, s. Lathrop & Sarah, d. Aug. 19, 1753 — 1 — 22

Sturgis, s. Jonathan & Sarah, b. Mar. 13, 1756 — 1 — 42

LINES, Eliza B., of New Haven, m. Geo[rge] H. **LaFORGE**,
    of Trumbull, [May] 7, [1845], by Rev. Charles R.
    Adams — 1-M — 81

Ruhamah, d. Benj[ami]n, m. John **ROBERSON**, May 3,
    1762 — 1 — 236

LIVESAY, Elizabeth, m. Joseph **BEERS**, Jr., s. Joseph, Sept.
    21, 1738 — 1 — 94

Mary, m. David **BEERS**, s. Joseph, Nov. 10, 1743 — 1 — 94

LIVINGSTONE, Robert Cambridge, of New York, m. Maria
    Bronson **MURRAY**, of Fairfield, July 29, [1846],
    by Rev. N. E. Cornwall — 1-M — 85

LOCKWOOD, Abigaile, d. Daniel, m. Samuel **ROBINSON**,
    Aug. 20, 1691 — LR-A2 — 676

Abigaill, d. Daniell, b. May 28, 1694 — LR-A2 — 674

Abigail, wid. m. Elnathan **HANFORD**, June 26, 1700, by
    Nathan **GOLD** — LR-2 — 459

Abigail, m. Joseph **GORHAM**, May 11, 1715 — 1 — 187

Abigail, d. John & Abigail, b. Nov. 7, 1738 — 1 — 162

Albert, s. John & Abigail, b. July 10, 1757 — 1 — 162

Anna, d. John & Abigail, b. Apr. 18, 1734 — 1 — 162

Benjamin, m. Mary **WHEELER**, b. of Fairfield, July 5,
    1837, by Enoch E. Chase — 1-M — 63-4

David, m. Sally G. **BURR**, b. of Fairfield, Feb. 18, 1833,
    by Rev. Stephen Martindale — 1-M — 48-9

Eleazer, s. John & Abigail, b. Aug. 27, 1755 — 1 — 162

Eliza, of Weston, m. Isaac **ARNOLD**, of Wilton, Aug.
    19, 1832, by William Bonney — 1-M — 44

Elizabeth, d. Joseph & Agnes, b. Aug. 29, 1743 — 1 — 21

Elizabeth, d. John & Abigail, b. Mar. 13, 1748 — 1 — 162

Ephraim, s. John & Abigail, b. Jan. 4, 1741 — 1 — 162

Esther, d. John & Abigail, b. Feb. 9, 1749 — 1 — 162

Gideon, s. John & Abigail, b. Oct. 23, 1753 — 1 — 162

Jabez, s. John & Abigail, b. Feb. 6, 1732 — 1 — 162

Jabez, s. John, m. Sarah **BENNET**, d. W[illia]m, Oct. 17,
    1754 — 1 — 235

	Vol.	Page
LOCKWOOD (cont.)		
John, s. John, m. Abigail **MOR[E]HOUSE**, d. Gideon, Feb. 8, 1731	1	162
John, s. John & Abigail, b. Oct. 12, 1736	1	162
Joseph, Sergt., d. Apr. 14, 1717	LR-2	456
Joseph, of Fairfield, m. Agnes **MONEY**, of Ireland, Nov. 1, 1737	1	21
Joseph, s. Jos. & Agnes, b. June 25, 1738	1	21
Lucinda, of Westport, m. Edward **WHEELER**, of New York City, Sept. 28, 1840, by Rev. Lyman H. Atwater	1-M	70
Mary, d. Daniell, b. Jan. 15, 1698	LR-A2	674
Mary, d. John & Abigail, b. Jan. 20, 1743	1	162
Michel, s. John & Abigail, b. Oct. 2, 1744	1	162
Sarah, d. Joseph & Agnes, b. Jan. 24, 1739/40	1	21
Susannah, d. John & Abigail, b. Jan. 2, 1752	1	162
Walter, s. Joseph & Agnes, b. Sept. 1, 1741	1	21
William F., of Weston, m. Mary H. **WAKEMAN**, of Fairfield, Mar. 18, 1844, by Rev. E. O. Beers	1-M	76
LORD, Sarah, m. Josiah **GILBERT**, June 14, 1722	1	53
LOVELL, LOVEL, Anna, d. James, of Barnstable, m. David **RUMSEY**, s. Benj[ami]n, Dec. 26, 1764	1	275
Desire, m. Dennil **CHAPMAN**, s. Dan[ie]ll, Oct. 4, 1750	1	183
LYON, Abel, s. Timothy & Meriam, b. Dec. 12, 1747 [sic]	1	114
Abell, m. Sarah **OLMSTEAD**, May 11, 1757	1	115
Abigail, m. Samuel **SMITH**, Jan. 9, 1696	LR-2	460
Abigail, m. Daniel **MOR[E]HOUSE**, Jan. 2, 1724	1	202
Abigail, d. James & Abigail, b. Aug. 24, 1743	1	165
Abigail, w. James, d. Mar. 26, 1752	1	165
Abigail, d. Joseph & Lois, b. Aug. 4, 1760	1	166
Ann, d. Peter & Abigail, b. Apr. 1, 1757	1	151
Asa, s. Timothy & Meriam, b. Dec. 12, 1754	1	114
Asahel, s. Peter & Abigail, b. Aug. 31, 1755	1	151
Caleb, s. Sam[ue]ll, m. Abiah **PARRUCK**, d. John, Aug. 24, 1738	1	135
Daniell, [s. Richard], b. Oct. 3, 1697	LR-2	462
Daniel, m. Sarah **JENNINGS**, Aug. 7, 1718	1	113
Daniel, s. Dan[ie]ll & Sarah, b. Aug. 1, 1719	1	113
David, m. Martha **HURLBERT**, June 12, 1746	1	157
David, s. David & Martha, b. Feb. 23, 1754	1	157
David, s. Nathan, m. Hannah **SANFORD**, d. Eph[rai]m, Sept. 19, 1756	1	210
Ebenezer, [s. Richard], b. Aug. 15, 1694	LR-2	462
Ebenezer, m. Ellen **FANTON**, Jan. 9, 1717	1	99
Ebenezer, s. Eben[eze]r & Ellen, b. June 10, 1722	1	99
Elenor, d. Ebenezer, m. Dan[ie]ll **KNAP**, Jr., s. Dan[ie]ll, Jan. 9, 1740	1	59
Eleanor, m. Horace **HILL**, Jan. 7, 1830, by Rev. Nehemiah Ruggles	1-M	37
Eliphalet, s. James & Abigail, b. May 4, 1738	1	165
Eliphalet, s. Caleb & Abiah, b. Sept. 13, 1754; d. Nov. 10, 1756	1	135
Elizabeth, d. John & Elizabeth, b. July 7, 1754	1	204

	Vol.	Page
LYON (cont.)		
Ellen, d. Eben[eze]r & Ellen, b. Nov. 27, 1718	1	99
Eunice, d. Dan[ie]ll & Sarah, b. Apr. 8, 1721	1	113
Eunice, wid. m. John **FANTON**, Feb. 12, 1755	1	190
Eunice, d. Ephraim, m. John Silliman **ANDREWS**, s. Dan[ie]ll, Feb. 4, 1764	1	266
Gershom, s. Dan[ie]ll & Sarah, b. July 10, 1725	1	113
Gideon, s. Caleb & Abiah, b. Feb. 2, 1750; d. Sept. 28, 1751	1	135
Gideon, s. Caleb & Abiah, b. Jan. 16, 1752	1	135
Hannah, 2nd d. Richard, decd., m. Beniimin **BANKS**, 1st s. John, Jan. 29, 1679	LR-A2	663
Hannah, [d. Richard], b. May 14, 1701	LR-2	462
Harriet, of Fairfield, m. Daniel **MOREHOUSE**, of Dutchess County, N.Y., Nov. 20, 1843, by Rev. James Scott	1-M	75
Hester, d. David & Hannah, b. Apr. 2, 1757; d. 6th day of same month	1	210
Hezekiah, s. James & Abigail, b. Feb. 6, 1735/6	1	165
Hezekiah, s. Caleb & Abiah, b. Oct. 21, 1739	1	135
Hezekiah, s. Joseph & Lois, b. Aug. 3, 1757	1	166
Huldah, d. Caleb & Abiah, b. Dec. 12, 1741	1	135
Jabez, s. John & Elizabeth, b. Mar. 18, 1747	1	204
James, b. Mar. 21, 1704; m. Abigail **ROWLAND**, Dec. 14, 1732	1	165
John, m. Elizabeth **WAKEMAN**, d. Sam[ue]ll, Jan. 23, 1745/6	1	204
John, s. Caleb & Abiah, b. Jan. 21, 1748	1	135
John, s. John & Elizabeth, b. Aug. 30, 1752; d. 9th day following	1	204
John, s. John & Elizabeth, b. Apr. 19, 1756	1	204
Jonathan, s. Dan[ie]ll & Sarah, b. May 6, 1741	1	113
Joseph, s. James & Abigail, b. Oct. 1, 1733	1	165
Joseph, m. Lois **THORP**, Dec. 22, 1756	1	166
Joseph, s. Nathan, m. Lois **SANFORD**, d. Ephraim, May 21, 1761	1	255
Luritta, of Fairfield, m. David **BROTHERTON**, of Westport, Mar. 30, 1845, by Rev. Moses Hill	1-M	81
Lydia, d. David & Martha, b. June 12, 1749	1	157
Margary, m. John **MEAKER**, Aug. 9, 1727	1	196
Martha, d. Sam[ue]ll, m. Thomas **TURNEY**, Jr., s. Tho[ma]s, Dec. 28, 1746	1	135
Martha, d. David & Martha, b. Aug. 3, 1751	1	157
Mary, [d. Wyllys], b. Oct. 1, 1822	1-M	96
Michel, s. Dan[ie]ll & Sarah, b. Feb. 28, 1728	1	113
Nathan, [s. Richard], b. Nov. 23, 1703	LR-2	462
Nathan, s. David & Hannah, b. Dec. 23, 1759	1	210
Peter, s. Sam[ue]ll & Mary, b. Nov. 27, 1727	1	189
Peter, s. Sam[ue]ll, m. Mary **DAVIS**, Dec. 13, 1749	1	189
Peter, s. Nathan, m. Abigail **SHERWOOD**, May 10, 1753	1	151
Rebecca, d. Sam[ue]ll & Mary, b. July 23, 1722	1	189
Rebecca, d. Peter & Mary, b. Feb. 13, 1755	1	189

	Vol.	Page
LYON (cont.)		
Rebecca, d. David & Martha, b. Sept. 9, 1756	1	157
Rhoda, d. Caleb & Abiah, b. Mar. 12, 1743	1	135
Ruth, d. Caleb & Abiah, b. Apr. 12, 1745	1	135
Ruth, d. Daniel, Jr., m. Jesse **BEARDSLEE**, s.		
W[illia]m, Nov. 26, 1760	1	268
Samuell, s. Richard, b. Dec. 27, 1688	LR-2	462
Samuel, s. San[ue]ll, m. Mary **DAVIS**, d. John, May 8,		
1718	1	189
Samuel, s. Peter & Mary, b. Apr. 17, 1751	1	189
Samuel, m. Elizabeth **McLANE**, May 12, 1757	1	114
Sarah, d. Richard, b. Feb. 14, 1691	LR-2	462
Sarah, d. Sam[ue]ll & Mary, b. Oct. 8, 1719	1	189
Sarah, d. Dan[ie]ll & Sarah, b. Nov. 18, 1720	1	113
Sarah, d. Samuel, m. John **ROWLAND**, Dec. 13, 1738	1	204
Sarah, d. James & Abigail, b. Jan. 1, 1745/6; d. Apr. 4,		
1757 [sic]	1	165
Sarah, d. David & Martha, b. July 4, 1747	1	157
Sarah, d. James & Abigail, b. June 30, 1748 [sic]	1	165
Sarah, d. Timothy & Meriam, b. June 7, 1753	1	114
Seth, s. James & Abigail, b. Dec. 22, 1740	1	165
Thomas, s. John & Elizabeth, b. Oct. 9, 1749	1	204
Timothy, s. Dan[ie]ll & Sarah, b. Nov. 5, 1734	1	113
Timothy, s. Dan[ie]ll, m. Meriam **HALL**, July 1, 1752	1	114
Walker, s. Peter & Abigail, b. May 13, 1754	1	151
William B., m. Amelia S. **WILSON**, b. of Fairfield, Oct.		
14, 1835, by W[illia]m Denison	1-M	57
Wyllis, m. Pamela **WILLSON**, Dec. 30, 1821, by Rev.		
Daniel Wildman	1-M	7
McBERNEY, Thomas, of Pointed Post, N.Y., m. Jane A.		
MILLS, of Fairfield, June 4, 1840, by Rev. Lyman		
H. Atwater	1-M	69
McCOY, Letitia, m. John **ROACH**, Oct. 8, 1848, by Rev. N.		
E. Cornwall	1-M	90
McCUE, MACHUGH, John, see John **MAHUE**	LR-A2	680
John, see John **MAHUE**	LR-A2	680
McKAN, Paul, of Ireland, m. Sarah **STAPLES**, of Fairfield,		
Nov. 13, 1824, by Nathaniel Hewit	1-M	15
MACKENZIE, McKENZIE, Abigail, d. Dugald, b. Aug. 4,		
1700	LR-2	459
Ann, [d. Dugald], b. Feb. 17, 1704/5	LR-2	459
Danniel, [s. Dugald], b. Apr. 30, 1703	LR-2	459
Dugald, m. Sarah **WAKEMAN**, wid. of Samuell, Nov.		
18, 1696	LR-2	459
John, s. [Dugald], b. Oct. 18, 1701	LR-2	459
Mary, d. of Dr. [ ], m. Samuell **ADAMS**, July 15,		
1677	LR-A2	664
MACKHARD, Sarah, d. Benjamin Fairweather, of Fairfield,		
m. Dan[ie]ll **MORRIS**, of Fairfield, July 9, 1741	1	33
McLANE, Elizabeth, m. Samuel **LYON**, May 12, 1757	1	114
McRAA, Archibald, s. Hugh & Ann, b. Aug. 5, 1745	1	43
Elizabeth, d. Hugh & Ann, b. July 21, 1730	1	43

	Vol.	Page
McRAA (cont.)		
Elizabeth, d. Hugh, m. Ebenezer **KNAP**, s. Dan[ie]l, Dec. 31, 1750	1	38
Hugh, m. Ann **SPEERS**, Feb. [ ], 1727	1	43
Hugh, s. Hugh & Ann, b. Aug. 21, 1742	1	43
Isabella, d. Hugh & Ann, b. Aug. 5, 1728	1	43
James, s. Hugh & Ann, b. Aug. 15, 1739	1	43
Margaret, d .Hugh & Ann, b. Aug. 15, 1737	1	43
MAHUE, * John, alias **CAHUE**, d. Jan. 19, 1685 *(**McCUE?** or **MacHUGH?**)	LR-A2	680
MALLET, David, s. John, b. Jan. 10, 1704	LR-2	457
Joannah, d. John, b. Mar. 10, 1710	LR-2	457
John, s. John, b. Oct. 16, 1712	LR-2	457
Lewiss, d. John, b. Aug. 14, 1708	LR-2	457
Peter, s. John, b. Mar. 31, 1711	LR-2	457
MALLORY, MALLERY, Abigail, d. Dan[ie]ll & Sarah, b. Mar. 12, 1757	1	177
Daniel, m. Sarah **LEE**, d. William, Nov. 30, 1748	1	177
Daniel, s. Dan[ie]ll & Sarah, b. Oct. 13, 1750	1	177
Deborah, d. Jonathan, m. Sam[ue]ll **CLAYTON**, s. John, Feb. 11, 1758	1	249
Eben[eze]r, s. Levi & Sarah, b. Feb. 11, 1773	1	48
Elizabeth, d. John & Elizabeth, b. Dec. 11, 1738	1	89
John, m. Elizabeth **ADAMS**, Apr. 15, 1735	1	89
John, s. John & Elizabeth, b. Jan. 7, 1736	1	89
Jonathan, s. John & Elizabeth, b. Oct. 12, 1744	1	89
Levi, s. Eben[eze]r, m. Sarah **ANNIBIL**, d. Anthony, Aug. 3, 1772	1	48
Nathan, s. Dan[ie]ll & Sarah, b. Aug. 16, 1754	1	177
Priscilla, d. Levi & Sarah, b. Sept. 6, 1774	1	48
Samuel, s. Dan[ie]ll & Sarah, b. June 21, 1752	1	177
MALTBIE, Abigail, d. Jonathan, m. Samuel **SQUIRE**, Jr., s. Lieut., Feb. 27, 1743	1	63
Hannah, d. Jonathan, of Stamford, m. Ebenezer **BULKLEY**, s. Joseph, Dec. 11, 1765	1	278
Sally, d. Jonathan & Elizabeth, m. Samuel **ROWLAND**, s. Andrew & Elizabeth, Oct. 30, 1794, by Rev. Andrew Eliot	1	296
MANSFIELD, William N., of Lyme,* Mass., m. Emeline C. **THORP**, of Greenfield, Nov. 7, 1839, by Rev. Lyman H. Atwater *(Arnold copy says, "Lynn")	1-M	58
MARSH, Samuel D., of Ware, Mass., m. Mary S. **SKINNER**, of Fairfield, Aug. 31, 1847, by Rev. Lyman H. Atwater	1-M	87
MARWIN, [see under **MERWIN**]		
MARYUAND, Frederick, m. Mehetable alias "Hetty" **PERRY**, Sept. 3, 1822, by Rev. Nathaniel Hewit	1-M	8
MASON, Charlotte, m. Joseph **BULKLEY**, 2nd, b. of Fairfield, June 7, 1829, by John H. Hunter	1-M	34
MEAD, Daniel, s. Even[eze]r & Mary, b. June 20, 1747	1	199
Ebenezer, m. Mary **FROST**, Aug. 1, 1744	1	199
Ebenezer, s. Eben[eze]r & Mary, b. Nov. 29, 1748	1	199

	Vol.	Page
MEAD (cont.)		
Ezra, s. Stephen & Rachel, b. Dec. 31, 1754	1	86
Hannah, d. Stephen & Rachel, b. May 2, 1756	1	86
Jeremiah, s. Stephen & Rachel, b. Apr. 2, 1752	1	86
Mary, d. Eben[eze]r & Mary, b. Sept. 2, 1755	1	199
Seeley, s. Eben[eze]r & Mary, b. Dec. 17, 1752	1	199
Stephen, m. Rachel **SANFORD**, Oct. 31, 1751	1	86
MEEKER, MEAKER, Abigail, d. Sam[ue]ll & Abigail, b.		
Jan. 15, 1725	1	228
Abigail, d. David, b. June 10, 1725; m. Lockwood		
GORHAM, s. Joseph, Sept. 20, 1742	1	83
Abigail, d. John, m. Joseph **DISBROW**, s. Thomas, Oct.		
27, 1731	1	131
Anna, d. John & Margary, b. Nov. 14, 1725	1	196
Anna, m. David **KNAP**, Oct. 24, 1736	1	100
Anna, d. Peter & Anna, b. Sept. 20, 1796	1	284
Arete, of Fairfield, m. Andrew B. **GODFREY**, of		
Weston, Dec. 3, 1826, by Rev. E. W. Hooker	1-M	25
Benjamin, s. Sam[ue]ll & Abigail, b. Nov. [ ], 1741	1	228
Benjamin, m. Catharine **BURR**, Aug. 20, 1745	1	242
Betsey, d. Peter & Anna, b. June 9, 1792	1	284
Daniel, s. Sam[ue]ll & Abigail, b. Aug. 10, 1739	1	228
Dan[ie]ll, s. Jonathan & Abigail, b. Dec. 26, 1739	1	88
Daniel, s. Joseph, m. Sarah **JOHNSON**, d. Moses, July		
19, 1744	1	240
Dan[ie]ll, s. David & Hannah, b. June 13, 1747	1	83
David, Jr., s. David, m. Hannah **HILL**, d. W[illia]m, Oct.		
31, 1744; d. July 30, 1755	1	83
David, s. David & Hannah, b. Apr. 22, 1755	1	83
Edward, m. Lucinda **NASH**, May 21, 1837, by Rev.		
Tho[ma]s F. Davis	1-M	63-4
Elizabeth, m. William **GRAY**, Oct. 31, 1716	1	185
Elizabeth, d. John & Margary, b. Aug. 5, 1732	1	196
Elizabeth, m. John **DAVIS**, Jan. 3, 1752	1	195
Elnathan, s. Dan[ie]ll & Sarah, b. Aug. 19, 1747; d. Jan.		
10, following	1	240
Esther, [twin with Eunice], d. Benjamin & Catharine, b.		
Aug. 7, 1755	1	242
Esther P., of Fairfield, m. George **CABLE**, of Norwalk,		
June 12, 1825, by Rev. E. W. Hooker	1-M	18
Eunice, [twin with Esther], d. Benjamin & Catharine, b.		
Aug. 7, 1755	1	242
Hannah, d. David & Hannah, b. Nov. 1, 1745	1	83
Harriet, m. John **THORP**, b. of Fairfield, Oct. 29, 1826		
by Rev. E. W. Hooker	1-M	24
Jared, s. Dan[ie]ll & Sarah, b. Jan. 25, 1749	1	240
John, m. Margary **LYON**, Aug. 9, 1727	1	196
John, s. Jonathan & Abigail, b. Aug. 30, 1744	1	88
Jonathan, b. May 25, 1707; m. Abigail **PARRIE**, Jan. 18,		
1731	1	88
Jonathan, s. Jonathan & Abigail, b. Jan. 25, 1733	1	88
Joseph, s. Dan[ie]ll & Sarah, b. July 11, 1745	1	240
Josiah, s. Dan[ie]ll & Sarah, b. July 15, 1757	1	240

	Vol.	Page
MEEKER, MEAKER (cont.)		
Julia Frances, of Southport, m. William R. **TAYLOR**, of		
Bridgeport, Nov. 7, 1837, by Rev. Thomas F. Davis	1-M	65
Lois, d. Benj[ami]n & Catharine, b. Mar. 27, 1754	1	242
Mabel, d. John & Margary, b. June 29, 1730	1	196
Mary, m. Dan[ie]l **MURWIN**, Feb. 15, 1740	1	33
Mary, d. David & Hannah, b. Dec. 11, 1750	1	83
Mary, d. Peter & Anna, b. Sept. 14, 1787	1	284
Mary, of Fairfield, m. George **MIDDLEBROOKS**, of		
Bridgeport, [Feb. 16, 1838, in Stratfield], by Rev.		
Enoch E. Chase	1-M	65
Matilda Jennings, of Southport, m. John **SIMPSON**, of		
York, May 25, 1845, by Rev. Samuel J. M. Merwin	1-M	82
Molly, d. Sam[ue]ll & Abigail, b. Sept. 28, 1743	1	228
Peter, s. Ebenezer, m. Anne **WHEELER**, Nov. 1, 1785	1	284
Polly, of Norfield, m. Alva **RAYMOND**, of Greenfield,		
Nov. 19, 1826, by Hezekiah Ripley, V.D.M.	1-M	24
Rebecca, d. Joseph, m. Nehemiah **SMITH**, s. Eleazer,		
Oct. 8, 1747	1	177
Rebecca, d. Dan[ie]ll & Sarah, b. Dec. 6, 1750	1	240
Sally Wakeman, m. Charles W[illia]m **HULL**, Apr. 5,		
1821, by Hezekiah Ripley, V.D.M.	1-M	4
Samuel, m. Abigail **GREGORY**, Aug. 1, 1722	1	228
Sarah, d. John, m. David **SHERWOOD**, Mar. 16, 1709	1	224
Sarah, d. John & Margary, b. May 27, 1726	1	196
Sarah, m. Samuel **SANFORD**, Jan. 11, 1732/3	1	111
Sarah, d. Jonathan & Abigail, b. Mar. 25, 1736	1	88
Sarah, m. David **MUNROW**, Nov. 11, 1742	1	195
Sarah, d. David & Hannah, b. Feb. 27, 1753	1	83
Sarah A., m. Munson H. **BEERS**, b. of Fairfield, Apr. 23,		
1826, by Nath[anie]l Hewit	1-M	23
Seth, s. Sam[ue]ll & Abigail, b. Sept. 12, 1731	1	228
Seth, s. Benj[ami]n & Catharine, b. Nov. 18, 1749	1	242
Solomon, s. Peter & Anne, b. Aug. 13, 1794	1	284
Stephen, s. John & Margary, b. Apr. 23, 1736	1	196
Stephen, s. Sam[ue]ll & Abigail, b. Oct. 3, 1745	1	228
Susan, d. Peter & Anna, b. Dec. 27, 1798	1	284
Witley, d. Benj[ami]n & Catharine, b. May 8, 1747	1	242
MERCHANT, Ann, d. Gurdon & Eleanor, b. Jan. 31, 1749	1	203
Chauncey, s. Gurdon & Eleanor, b. Feb. 13, 1753	1	203
Eleanor, d. Gurdon & Eleanor, b. Nov. 27, 1757	1	203
Gurdon, m. Eleanor **CHAUNCEY**, Dec. 9, 1747	1	203
Gurdon, b. Feb. 9, 1760	1	10
Gurdon, s. Gurdon & Eleanor, b. Feb. 9, 1760	1	203
Joel, s. Gurdon & Eleanor, b. May 1, 1762	1	203
John, s. Gurdon & Eleanor, b. Aug. 2, 1755	1	203
Phebe, d. Gurdon & Eleanor, b. Apr. 19, 1764	1	203
Sarah, d. Gurdon & Eleanor, b. Jan. 19, 1751	1	203
MERWIN, MARWIN, MURWIN, Abigail, [twin with		
Lydea], d. Sam[ue]ll, & Abigail, b. Dec, [ ], 1730	1	191
Abijah, s. Dan[ie]l & Mary, b. Apr. 7, 1747	1	33
Daniel, s. Thomas, b. May 21, 1719	1	33
Dan[ie]l, m. Mary **MEAKER**, Feb. 15, 1740	1	33

	Vol.	Page
MERWIN, MARWIN, MURWIN (cont.)		
David, s. Sam[ue]ll & Abigail, b. Dec. [ ], 1728	1	191
Eunice, m. Walter **PERRY**, b. of Greenfield Parish, July		
12, 1821, by Rev. Nath[anie]l Hewit	1-M	14
J.S.M., Rev. m. Mary Francis **BULKELEY**, b. of		
Southport, Jan. 20, 1846, in Southport, by Samuel		
Merwin	1-M	84
John, s. Tho[ma]s & Ruth, b. [ ]	1	217
Lydea, [twin with Abigail], d. Sam[ue]ll & Abigail, b.		
Dec. [ ], 1730	1	191
Lidea, m. John **GILBERT**, Jr., s. John, June 17, 1756	1	108
Mary, d. Sam[ue]ll & Abigail, b. [ ], 1739; d. July		
[ ], 1742	1	191
Mary, d. Tho[ma]s & Mary, b. July 5, 1744	1	217
Nathan T., of Weston, m. Eunice **NICHOLS**, of Fairfield,		
Aug. 5, 1838, by N. E. Cornwall, in Southport	1-M	66
Peter, s. Dan[ie]l & Mary, b. Oct. 9, 1744	1	33
Ruth, d. Dan[ie]l & Mary, b. July 17, 1741	1	33
Samuel, s. Thomas, m. Abigail **WHEELER**, July 5, 1722	1	191
Samuel, s. Sam[ue]ll & Abigail, b. Jan. [ ], 1735	1	191
Seth, s. Sam[ue]ll & Abigail, b. Nov. 5, 1726	1	191
Seth, s. Sam[ue]ll, m. Ann **SHERWOOD**, d. Dan[ie]ll,		
Feb. 13, 1755	1	191
Thomas, m. Ruth **MOR[E]HOUSE**, Aug. [ ], 1717	1	217
Thomas, m. Mary **SMITH**, wid., July [ ], 1742	1	217
Thomas, m. Mrs. Betsey **BANKS**, b. of Greenfield, Jan.		
31, 1841, by Rev. Matthew Batcheldor	1-M	71
Thomas, s. Sam[ue]ll & Abigail, b. [ ]	1	191
MIDDLEBROOK, MIDLEBROOK, MIDDLEBROOKS,		
Daniell, s. Joseph, b. Aug. 22, 1704	LR-2	462
Elizabeth, d. Jonathan & Rebecca, b. Jan. 18, 1735	1	133
Elizabeth, d. Jonathan, m. Jacob **WHITE**, May 5, 1754	1	231
Ellen, d. Jonathan & Rebecca, b. Mar. 1, 1738	1	133
Ellen, d. Mar. 27, 1813	1	23
Ephraim, m. Mrs. Rocky **BRADLEY**, Aug. 7, 1831, by		
Rev. E. Loomis	1-M	42-3
George, of Bridgeport, m. Mary **MEEKER**, of Fairfield,		
[Feb. 16, 1838, in Stratfield], by Rev. Enoch E.		
Chase	1-M	65
Hannah, d. Joseph, b. June 25, 1677	LR-A2	683
Hester, m. Stephen **TURNEY**, Nov. 5, 1744	1	67
John, s. [sic] Joseph, b. Oct. 25, 1678	LR-A2	683
John M., of Bridgeport, m. Rebeckah **HALL**, of Fairfield,		
Nov. 23, 1825, by Rev. Marvin Richardson	1-M	20
Jonathan, m. Martha **SQUIER**, d. Sergt. Thomas, of		
Woodbury, Jan. 31, 1712	LR-2	457
Jonathan, s. Jonathan, m,. Rebecca **JENNINGS**, June 2,		
1734	1	133
Joseph, s. Joseph, Jr., b. Apr. 15, 1680	LR-A2	682
Joseph, d. [sic] Joseph, b. Apr. 15, 1680	LR-A2	683
Mary, d. John, m. Benjamin **WHEELER**, s. Timothy,		
Apr. 20, 1749, by Rev. James Beebee, of North		
Stratford	1	276

	Vol.	Page

MIDDLEBROOK, MIDLEBROOK, MIDDLEBROOKS
(cont.)

	Vol.	Page
Mary, m. Hiram **THORP**, May 4, 1834, by Rev. David L. Ogden	1-M	53
Oliver, s. Jonathan & Rebecca, b. Oct. 19, 1746	1	133
Rebecca, d. Jonathan & Rebecca, b. Oct. 22, 1740	1	133
Sallome, d. Jonathan & Rebecca, b. Sept. 27, 1752	1	133
Sarah, d. Joseph, b. Nov. 12, 1675	LR-A2	683
Sarah, d. Jonathan, m. Anthony **ANNABIL**, Jan. 16, 1748	1	143
Sarah, d. Eben[eze]r, m. Paul **NICHOLS**, s. Ephraim, Aug. 14, 1766	1	40
Silvanus, s. Jonathan & Rebecca, b. Sept. 13, 1743	1	133

MILK, Catharine, see Catharine **MILLS**

MILLER, Elizabeth, M., of Fairfield, m. Hiram **LEWIS**, of

	Vol.	Page
Bridgeport, Mar. 1, 1830, by John Hunter	1-M	38
Mary, m. William **EGAN**, b. of Southport, May 25, 1851, by Rev. Sam[ue]l J. M. Merwin	1-M	91
Zephaniah M., of Bedford, N.Y., m. Jane A. **TRUBEE**, of Fairfield, Dec. 3, 1835, by Lyman H. Atwater	1-M	57

MILLS, Abby Jane, m. Ebenezer **BURR**, Apr. 28, 1833, by

	Vol.	Page
Tho[ma]s F. Davis	1-M	50
Amanda L., of Fairfield, m. Lewis **HYATT**, of Wilton, Mar. 4, 1824, by Rev. Samuel Codner	1-M	14
Aurelia, Mrs.,* of Ripton, m. Dr. Joseph **DARLING**, of Fairfield, Mar. 24, last [1784], by David Ely *(Note says "Miss")	1	267
Catharine,* m. Augustine P. **BEERS**, b. of Fairfield, Dec. 30, 1828, by John Hunter *(Perhaps "Catharine **MILK**"?)	1-M	32
Eliza, m. Hewlet **JONES**, Oct. 6, 1833, by T. F. Davis	1-M	51
Jane A., of Fairfield, m. Thomas **McBERNEY**, of Pointed Post, N.Y., June 4, 1840, by Rev. Lyman H. Atwater	1-M	69
Lucy, m. Samuel **BARLOW**, b. of Greens Farms, July 23, 1820, by Rev. William Belden, of Greenfield	1-M	2
Rachel,* m. Lewis **BAKER**, b. of Fairfield, Sept. 21, 1828, by Rev. E. W. Hooker *("Rachel **MILK**"?)	1-M	31
Rebecca, m. Levi **SNOW**, b. of Fairfield, Nov. 27, 1836, by Nath[anie]l E. Cornwall	1-M	61
Samuel, m. Mary **SNIFFING**, Oct. 13, 1833, by T. F. Davis	1-M	51
Sarah Ann, of Westport, m. Bradley **NICHOLS**, of Fairfield, July 25, 1847, by Rev. Lyman H. Atwater	1-M	87

MITCHELL, Abiah, wid., d. Josiah Tredwell, m. Stephen

	Vol.	Page
TURNEY, Feb. 9, 1773	1	67
Samuel, s. John & Esther, b. May 24, 1782	1	295

MIX, Elizabeth, m. Ephraim **SANFORD**, Oct. 7, 1730 — 1 — 71

MONEY, Agnes, of Ireland, m. Joseph **LOCKWOOD**, of

	Vol.	Page
Fairfield, Nov. 1, 1737	1	21

	Vol.	Page
MONROE, MUNROW, MUNRO, Benaiah, s. David & Sarah,		
b. Aug. 15, 1743	1	195
David, m. Sarah **MEAKER**, Nov. 11, 1742	1	195
David, s. David & Sarah, b. May 15, 1747	1	195
Ebenezer, m. Mary **DUNKINS**, Jan. 1, 1751/2	1	187
Eliza, m. Ira **HILL**, of Reading, Nov. 9, 1834, by T. F.		
Davis	1-M	55
Elizabeth, d. Eben[eze]r & Mary, b. Feb. 14, 1754	1	187
Ellen, d. David & Sarah, b. Mar. 31, 1757	1	195
Harvey, J., of Norwalk, m. Laura **WILSON**, of Fairfield,		
June 23, 1844, by Rev. James Scott	1-M	77
John, s. David & Sarah, b. Jan. 2, 1755	1	195
Joseph, s. David & Sarah, b. Mar. 31, 1759	1	195
Lydia, d. David & Sarah, b. Feb. 11, 1745	1	195
Mary, d. David & Sarah, b. Apr. 1, 1749	1	195
Mary, d. Eben[eze]r & Mary, b. May 22, 1757	1	187
Sarah, d. David & Sarah, b. Jan. 4, 1751; d. Mar. 20,		
following	1	195
Sarah, d. David & Sarah, b. Dec. 5, 1752	1	195
MOODEY, Elizabeth, of Fairfield, m. James **POTTER**, of		
Gap Grove, Lee Co., Ill., Sept. 24, 1849, by Rev.		
William Read	1-M	91
MOREHOUSE, MORHOUSE, A. W., says in note following		
the record of the family of Zechariah Jennings &		
Sarah Morehouse, "The Jennings record is partly if		
not entirely wrong"	1	221
Aaron, s. Gershom & Anna, b. June 2, 1758	1	86
Aaron, [s. Abijah & Mary], b. Sept. 10, 1773	1	295
Abel, s. Stephen & Abigail, b. July 15, 1741	1	97
Abel S., m. Eliza C. **SHERWOOD**, of Fairfield, Nov. 2,		
1843, by Rev. James Scott	1-M	76
Abigail, d. Gideon, m. John **LOCKWOOD**, s. John, Feb.		
8, 1731	1	162
Abigail, d. Stephen & Abigail, b. May 8, 1731	1	97
Abigail, d. Sam[ue]ll & Abigail, b. Mar. 22, 1744	1	154
Abigail, d. Zacheas & Abigail, b. Aug. 1, 1757	1	75
Abigail, w. Daniel, d. Sept. [ ], 1757	1	202
Abijah, s. Gideon & Sarah, b. Oct. 27, 1747; d. Oct. 14,		
1751	1	182
Abijah, s. Gideon & Sarah, b. Apr. last day, 1751	1	182
Abijah, [s. Abijah & Mary], b. May 8, 1778	1	295
Abraham, m. Elizabeth **PATTERSON**, Apr. 12, 1722	1	47
Abraham, s. Daniel & Sarah, b. Nov. [ ], 1755; d. [ ]	1	65
Abraham, s. Sam[ue]l & Ruth, b. Mar. 26, 1758	1	41
Abraham, m. Esther **GRAY**, b. of Fairfield, Apr. 6, 1828,		
by Rev. E. W. Hooker	1-M	31
Alice, d. Thaddeus & Martha, b. June 14, 1756	1	169
Andrew, s. Abraham & Elizabeth, b. July 21, 1740	1	47
Andrew, s. Silvanus & Mary, b. May 5, 1766	1	149
Ann, b. Sept. 14, 1718; m. James **MORGAN**, Apr. 7,		
1736	1	130
Ann, d. Stephen & Abigail, b. Dec. 15, 1737	1	97
Ann, d. Nathan & Elizabeth, b. Sept. 25, 1741	1	137

	Vol.	Page
MOREHOUSE, MORHOUSE (cont.)		
Benjamin, [s. Abijah & Mary], b. May. 9, 1785	1	295
Betty, d. Zacheas & Abigail, b. Nov. 8, 1745	1	75
Bille, s. Gershom & Anna, b. June 12, 1756	1	86
Catharine, d. Thomas, decd. was 13 years old Jan. 22, 1704	1	462
Catharine, m. John **BULKLEY**, Jan. 17, 1836, by James H. Linsley	1-M	58
Charles, m. Lydia E. **PORTER**, b. of Fairfield, July 16, 1843, by Rev. James Scott, Stratfield	1-M	75
Cretia, [d. Abijah & Mary], b. Aug. 5, 1788	1	295
Daniel, m. Abigail **LYON**, Jan. 2, 1724	1	202
Daniel, s. Dan[ie]ll & Abigail, b. Mar. 19, 1726* *(Probably 1736)	1	202
Dan[ie]ll, s. Stephen & Abigail, b. July 21, 1726	1	97
Dan[ie]ll, s. Abraham & Elizabeth, b. Apr. 27, 1732	1	47
Daniel, s. Jehu & Lavinah, b. July 5, 1746	1	200
Daniel, s. David, m. Mary **STURGIS**, d. John, Oct. 17, 1751	1	197
Daniel, s. Stephen, m. Phebe **CURTISS**, Dec. 25, 1751	1	49
Daniel, s. Abraham, m. Sarah **STURGIS**, d. Solomon, Apr. 15, 1755	1	65
Daniel, of Dutchess County, N.Y., m. Harriet **LYON**, of Fairfield, Nov. 20, 1843, by Rev. James Scott	1-M	75
David, s. Jehu & Lavinah, b. Aug. 8, 1735	1	200
David, s. Jabez & Sarah, b. Aug. 14, 1740	1	210
David, s. Dan[ie]ll & Abigail, b. Mar. 31, 1744	1	202
David, s. Joseph & Elizabeth, b. Oct. 25, 1759	1	97
Eben[eze]r, s. Gideon & Sarah, b. Jan. 1, 1743	1	182
Edward, s. John & Mary, b. Apr. 13, 1748	1	180
Edward Allen, [s. Abijah & Mary], b. Oct. 5, 1775	1	295
Elias, s. Thaddeus & Martha, b. Mar. 6, 1747	1	169
Eliphalet, s. Jabez & Sarah, b. Dec. 22, 1742; d. May [ ], 1756	1	210
Elizabeth, d. John, b. Mar. 24, 1705	LR-2	460
Elizabeth, d. John, d. Mar. 24, 1706	LR-2	460
Elizabeth, d. Stephen & Abigail, b. Nov. 1, 1728	1	97
Elizabeth, d. Gershom & Sarah, b. Jan. 3, 1730	1	235
Elizabeth, d. Dan[ie]ll & Abigail, b. Dec. 19, 1740	1	202
Elizabeth, m. Nehemiah **SANFORD**, Mar. 5, 1747	1	223
Elizabeth, m. Ezekiel **HILL**, June 3, 1750	1	101
Elizabeth, d. Sam[ue]l & Ruth, b. Aug. 15, 1753; d. Aug. 12, 1756	1	41
Elizabeth, d. Joseph & Elizabeth, b. July 8, 1757	1	97
Ellen, [d. Abijah & Mary], b. Feb. 16, 1794	1	295
Ellen O., of Fairfield, m. Andrew W. **JENNINGS**, of Greens Farms, Feb. 23, 1848, by Rev. Lyman H. Atwater	1-M	89
Enos, s. Thaddeus & Martha, b. Feb. 2, 1751	1	169
Ephenetus, s. Dan[ie]ll & Abigail, b. Mar. 20, 1734; d. Apr. [ ], following	1	202
Esther, d. Daniel & Sarah, b. Feb. 15, 1757	1	65

	Vol.	Page
MOREHOUSE, MORHOUSE (cont.)		
Esther, Mrs., m. Capt. Lyman **BANKS**, Feb. 14, 1830, by		
Tho[ma]s F. Davis, in Greens Farms	1-M	38
Eunice, d. Jabez & Sarah, b. Aug. 26, 1753	1	210
Eunice, d. Sam[ue]l & Ruth, b. Aug. 6, 1756	1	41
Eunice, d. Gideon & Eunice, b. Jan. 8, 1761	1	182
Ezra, s. Gershom & Anna, b. Apr. 15, 1754	1	86
George, [s. Abijah & Mary], b. Mar. 21, 1796	1	295
George, m. Mary A. **BURR**, b. of Fairfield, Sept. 23,		
1832, by John H. Hunter	1-M	45-6
Gershom, s. John, b. Nov. 18, 1703	LR-2	460
Gershom, s. John, m. Sarah **HILL**, d. John, Apr. 22, 1725	1	235
Gershom, s. Gershom & Sarah, b. Nov. 5, 1727	1	235
Gershom, Jr., m. Anna **SANFORD**, Jan. 18, 1749/50	1	86
Gideon, s. Gideon, m. Sarah **GODFREY**, d. Christopher,		
Feb. 3, 1742	1	182
Gideon, s. Gideon & Sarah, b. Aug. 5, 1746	1	182
Gideon, s. John & Mary, b. Dec. 7, 1746	1	180
Gideon, d. May 12, 1753	1	154
Gideon, m. Eunice **STURGIS**, d. Eleazer, Sept. 13, 1756	1	182
Gideon, m. Eunice **ROBINSON**, Dec. 28, 1828, by		
William Shelton	1-M	32
Gould, [s. Abijah & Mary], b. Feb. 23, 1781	1	295
Gramman, s. Gideon & Sarah, b. Sept. 19, 1744	1	182
Hannah, m. William **HILL**, of Reading, Apr. 28, 1725; d.		
Aug. 10, 1729	1	199
Hannah, d. Abraham & Elizabeth, b. Nov. 18, 1729	1	47
Hannah, d. Jabez & Sarah, b. May 2, 1750	1	210
Hannah, d. Gideon & Sarah, b. Oct. 12, 1753	1	182
Henry, [s. Abijah & Mary], b. May. 26, 1783	1	295
Isaac, s. Sam[ue]l & Ruth, b. Aug. 31, 1749	1	41
Jabez, s. Nathan, m. Sarah **OGDEN**, d. Joseph, Sept. 18,		
1738	1	210
James, s. John, b. Mar. 21, 1710	LR-2	461
Jane, d. Gershom & Anna, b. Nov. 7, 1760	1	86
Jehu, m. Lavinah **ROW**, Mar. 10, 1727	1	200
Jehu, s. Jehu & Lavinah, b. Apr. 1, 1730	1	200
Jeremiah, [s. Abijah & Mary], b. Nov. 27, 1791	1	295
Jerusha, d. Dan[ie]ll & Abigail, b. Nov. 1, 1730	1	202
Jesse, s. Jehu & Lavinah, b. June 6, 1742	1	200
Jesse, s. Dan[ie]ll & Abigail, b. Sept. 9, 1742	1	202
Jesse, s. Gideon & Sarah, b. Sept. 7, 1750	1	182
Jethro, s. Jeheu & Lavinah, b. Dec. 10, 1727; d. Sept. 20,		
1756	1	200
John, s. Thomas, b. Sept. 20, 1698	LR-2	462
John, s. Stephen & Abigail, b. Dec. 1, 1739	1	97
John, s. Jehu & Lavinah, b. Dec. 20, 1744	1	200
John, s. Gideon, m. Mary **JESSUP**, d. Edward, May 16,		
1745; d. June 13, 1753	1	180
John, s. John & Mary, b. Aug. 25, 1751	1	180
John, s. Zacheas & Abigail, b. May 26, 1763	1	75
John, m. Clary **OGDEN**, b. of Fairfield, May 27, 1821,		
by Nath[anie]l Hewit, V.D.M.	1-M	4

	Vol.	Page
MOREHOUSE, MORHOUSE (cont.)		
Jonathan, s. Jonathan, b. Jan. 1, 1677	LR-A2	682
Jonathan, m. Rebecka **KNOWLES**, Apr. 16, 1690	LR-A2	677
Joseph, s. Stephen & Abigail, b. Feb. 17, 1723/4	1	97
Joseph, s. Stephen & Abigail, m. Elizabeth **SILLIMAN**, d. Nath[anie]ll, Mar. 26, 1747	1	97
Joseph, s. Jehu & Lavinah, b. Sept. 20, 1750	1	200
Joseph, s. John & Mary, b. June 11, 1753	1	180
Joseph, s. Joseph & Elizabeth, b. June 13, 1754	1	97
Joseph, m. Mary **WILLSON**, b. of Fairfield, Jan. 1, 1834, by Chester Tilden	1-M	52
Joseph M., m. Mary A. **MOREHOUSE**, [Sept.] 8, [1833], by J. M. Rowland	1-M	50
Lavinah, d. Jehu & Lavinah, b. Apr. 19, 1737	1	200
Lockwood, s. Jabez & Sarah, b. Oct. 29, 1745; d. Sept. [ ], 1752	1	210
Lockwood, s. Jabez & Sarah, b. Aug. 4, 1755	1	210
Lois, d. Abraham & Elizabeth, b. Mar. 27, 1739; d. June 24, 1739	1	47
Lois, d. Sam[ue]l & Ruth, b. Feb. 24, 1746	1	41
Lois, m. Peter **PERSONS**, Mar. 25, 1756	1	165
Mabel, d. Nathan & Elizabeth, b. Apr. 29, 1750	1	137
Marcy, d. Dan[ie]ll & Abigail, b. Oct. 15, 1738	1	202
Martha, d. Jonathan, b. Nov. 2, 1679	LR-A2	682
Martha, d. Thaddeus & Martha, b. Apr. 5, 1754	1	169
Mary, d. Thomas, b. June last day,1696	LR-2	462
Mary, m. John **BEDIENT**, May 28, 1723	1	220
Mary, d. Dan[ie]ll & Abigail, b. Dec. 25, 1724	1	202
Mary, d. Nathan & Elizabeth, b. Nov. 14, 1741 [sic]	1	137
Mary, m .Daniel **WHITLOCK**, May 4, 1746	1	205
Mary, d. Dan[ie]ll, m. John **STALKER**, July 10, 1746	1	27
Mary, d. John & Mary, b .Nov. 23, 1749	1	180
Mary, wid., m. Gershom **STURGIS**, s. Jer[emiah], July 30, 1754	1	181
Mary, m. Robert **SILLIMAN**, Dec. 14, 1756	1	72
Mary, d. Gideon & Eunice, b. Aug. 26, 1757	1	182
Mary, eldest child [Abijah & Mary], b. Nov. 16, 1771	1	295
Mary, m. Legrand **BRADLEY**, b. of Fairfield, July 10, 1823, b Hez[ekia]h Ripley, V.D.M.	1-M	11
Mary A., m. Joseph M. **MOREHOUSE**, [Sept.] 8, [1833], by J. M. Rowland	1-M	50
Molly, d. Zacheas & Abigail, b. Apr. 30, 1759	1	75
Nathan, s. Nathan, m. Elizabeth **OGDEN**, d. Joseph, Mar. 4, 1740	1	137
Nathan, s. Nathan & Elizabeth, b. Feb. 28, 1755	1	137
Olive, d. Thaddeus & Martha, b. Sept. 28, 1748	1	169
Othniel, s. Dan[ie]ll & Abigail, b. Oct. 9, 1726	1	202
Peter, s. Gershom & Anna, b. Feb. 27, 1750	1	86
Phebe, d. Joseph & Elizabeth, b. May 3, 1763	1	97
Rebeckah, m. Richard **HUBELL**, Jr., Nov. 5, 1685	LR-A2	678
Rebeckah, d. Thomas, decd., b. Apr. 26, 1693	LR-2	462
Rebecca, m. Stephen **WAKEMAN**, Apr. 28, 1727	1	70
Rebecca, d. Abraham & Elizabeth, b. Feb. 20, 1736/7	1	47

	Vol.	Page
MOREHOUSE, MORHOUSE (cont.)		
Rhoda, d. Gideon & Sarah, b. May 16, 1755	1	182
Ruth, d. John, b. Apr. 21, 1699	LR-2	460
Ruth, m. Thomas **MARWIN**, Aug. [ ], 1717	1	217
Ruth, d. Gershom & Sarah, b. Dec. 23, 1733	1	235
Ruth, d. Sam[ue]l & Ruth, b. Aug. 15, 1753	1	41
Samuel, s. Gideon & Marry, b. Oct. 10, 1710	1	154
Sam[ue]ll, s. Abraham & Elizabeth, b. Apr. 8, 1724	1	47
Samuel, s. Dan[ie]ll & Abigail, b. Oct. 27, 1732; d. Dec. [ ], 1753	1	202
Samuel, s. Abraham, m. Ruth **WILLSON**, d. Nath[anie]ll, July 8, 1741	1	41
Samuel, s. Gideon, m. Abigail **FROST**, d. Isaac, Aug. 20, 1743	1	154
Sam[ue]ll, s. Gideon & Eunice, b. Feb. 11, 1759	1	182
Samuel, Jr., m. Elizabeth **OGDEN**, b. of Fairfield, Nov. 29, 1829, by John H. Hunter	1-M	37
Sarah, d. Abraham & Elizabeth, b. Nov. 28, 1727	1	47
Sarah, d. Jehu & Lavinah, b. Oct. 24, 1733	1	200
Sarah, m. Zachariah **JENNINGS**, s. Zachariah, June [ ], 1743	1	221
Sarah, d. Jabez & Sarah, b. Nov. 19, 1746	1	210
Sarah, d. Gideon & Sarah, b. Apr. 14, 1749	1	182
Sarah, m. James **DAVIS**, Oct. 3, 1755	1	152
Sarah, w. Gideon, d. June 12, 1756	1	182
Sarah, d .Jehu, m. David **DARLING**, s. John, Dec. 14, 1756	1	234
Sarah, d. Zacheas & Abigail, b. Nov. 14, 1760	1	75
Sarah, m. Billy **BIBBINS**, b. of Fairfield, Dec. 11, 1825, by Nath[anie]l Hewit	1-M	21
Sarah Ann, of Fairfield, m. Silvester **RANDAL**, of Port Jefferson, L .I., Apr. 19, 1841, by Rev. Lyman H. Atwater	1-M	71
Sarah W., m. George **OSBORN**, b. of Fairfield, Dec. 11, 1820, by Nath[anie]l Hewit, V.D.M.	1-M	3
Seth, s. Abraham & Elizabeth, b. July 8, 1734	1	47
Silas, s. Silvanus & Mary, b. July 20, 1763	1	149
Silvanus, s. Abraham & Elizabeth, b. Dec. 14, 1725	1	47
Silvanus, s. Abraham, m. Mary **HALL**, d. Sam[ue]ll, Nov. 3, 1747	1	149
Solomon, s. Jehu & Lavinah, b. Nov. 28, 1731	1	200
Stephen, [s. John], b. July 12, 1701	LR-2	460
Stephen, m. Abigail **TREADWELL**, Mar. 1, 1722	1	97
Stephen, s. Stephen & Abigail, b. Sept. 25, 1733	1	97
Sturgis, s. Zacheas & Abigail, b. Nov. 11, 1754	1	75
Susan, m. John H. **NICHOLS**, b. of Fairfield, Jan. 31, 1828, by Rev. Asa Bronson	1-M	29
Susan, m. Henry **BENNETT**, b. of Fairfield, June 10, 1844, by Rev. Lyman H. Atwater	1-M	77
Tabbe, d. Gershom & Anna, b. July 4, 1752	1	86
Thaddeus, s. Dan[ie]ll & Abigail, b. Oct. 14, 1728; d. Apr. [ ], 1747	1	202

	Vol.	Page

MOREHOUSE, MORHOUSE (cont.)

	Vol.	Page
Thaddeus, s. Nathan, m. Martha **WILLIAMS**, Apr. 2, 1746	1	169
Thaddeus, s. Dan[ie]ll & Abigail, b. Oct. 11, 1746	1	202
Thomas, s. Thomas, b. Nov. 18, 1695	LR-2	462
Thomas, s. Jehu & Lavinah, b. Feb. 24, 1739	1	200
Walter, m. Ruth **SCOTT**, Sept. 13, 1829, by Rev. Elisha Cushman	1-M	35-6
Zacheas, s. Gideon, m. Abigail **STURGIS**, d. John, Dec. 24, 1744	1	75
Zacheas, s. Zacheas & Abigail, b. June 4, 1753	1	75
MORGAN, Abbey, d. James & Ann, b. Mar. 2, 1738/9	1	130
Abijah, s. James & Ann, b. Apr. 11, 1744	1	130
Ann, d. James & Ann, b. Jan. 25, 1741/2	1	130
Ann, w. James, d. Nov. 5, 1755	1	130
Edward M., of Westfield, Mass., m. Angeline **JESUP**, of Greens Farms, June 19, 1827, by Rev. E. W. Hooker	1-M	26-7
James, b. Apr. 2, 1716; m. Ann **MORHOUSE**, Apr. 7, 1736	1	130
James, s. James & Ann, b. Mar. 16, 1747/8	1	130
John, s. James & Ann, b. Dec. 27, 1736	1	130
Joseph, s. James & Ann, b. Aug. 20, 1743	1	130
Stephen, s. James & Ann, b. June 19, 1741	1	130
MORRIS, MORRISS, Amos. s. Dan[ie]l & Prudence, b. Sept. 28, 1762	1	33
Dan, s. Dan[ie]l & Sarah, b. Dec. 13, 1750	1	33
Dan[ie]ll, of Fairfield, m. Sarah **MACKHARD**, d. Benjamin Fairweather, of Fairfield, July 9, 1741	1	33
Dan[ie]ll, m. 2nd, w. wid. Prudence **CURTISS**, Dec. 29, 1761	1	33
James, s. Dan[ie]l & Sarah, b. June 14, 1753	1	33
Mary, d. Dan[ie]l & Sarah, b. Dec. 1, 1742	1	33
Matthew M. Hurd, s. Dan[ie]l & Sarah, b. July 25, 1757	1	33
Sarah, d. Dan[ie]l & Sarah, b. Sept. 1, 1745	1	33
Sarah, w. Dan[ie]ll, d. Apr. 16, 1761	1	33
MORISON, William, of Florida, m. Catharine A. **WILSON**, of Fairfield, June 24, 1846, by Rev. Lyman H. Atwater	1-M	84
MOTT, Joseph, m. Grissell **BURR**, b. of Fairfield, Mar. 9, 1823, by Rev. Philo Shelton	1-M	10
MOULTON, Elizabeth J., of Fairfield, m. James **PINE**, of Rye, N.Y., Sept. 9, 1833, by Rev. C. A. Boardman, of Saugatuck	1-M	50
MUNGER, Benj[ami]n, s. Jonath[a]n, of Woodberry, m. Mercy **NORTHRUP**, d. Dec. Benj[ami]n, of Newton, Dec. 11, 1759	1	10
Benjamin, s. Jonathan, of Woodbury, m. Mercy **NORTHROP**, d. Dea. Benjamin, of Newtown, Dec. 11, 1759	1	250
MURRAY, Maria Bronson, of Fairfield, m. Robert Cambridge **LIVINGSTONE**, of New York, July 29, [1846], by Rev. N. E. Cornwall	1-M	85

	Vol.	Page
MURRAY (cont.)		
William, m. Margaret **DEAN**, b. of Black Rock, Mar. 16, 1851, at Black Rock, by Rev. W[illia]m Jesup Jennings	1-M	91
MURWIN, [see under **MERWIN**]		
NASH, Ann Burr, of Westport, m. Gershom H. **ALLEN**, of Fairfield, Feb. 28, 1841, by Rev. Dan[ie]l C. Curtiss	1-M	71
Burr S., m. Harriet **CHUB**, May 8, 1834, by T. F. Davis	1-M	53
Catherine, of Saugatuc, m. George **HUNTER**, of Fairfield, (colored), Feb. 28, 1827, by Nath[anie]ll Hewit	1-M	25
Delia Ann, m. Albert **HANFORD**, June 6, 1830, by T. F. Davis	1-M	39-40
Elizabeth, d. Tho[ma]s & Rebecca, b. Aug. 23, 1734	1	104
Elizabeth, d. Tho[ma]s, m. John **BURR**, s. Dan[ie]ll, Oct. 14, 1735	1	169
Elizabeth, of Fairfield, m. Levi **STILSON**, of Norwalk, [Mar.] 7, [1824], by Rev. E. W. Hooker	1-M	14
Eunice, d. Tho[ma]s & Rebecca, b. Mar. 27, 1737	1	104
Harriet, m. William **SMITH**, b. of Fairfield, Feb. 12, 1826, by Rev. E. W. Hooker	1-M	21
Lucinda, m. Edward **MEEKER**, May 21, 1837, by Rev. Tho[ma]s F. Davis	1-M	63-4
Lydia, d. Tho[ma]s & Rebecca, b. Mar. 26, 1740	1	104
Lydea, d. Tho[ma]s, m. William **HAWLEY**, s. Joseph, July 12, 1758	1	114
Maria, m. Shelton **ELWOOD**, Jan. 29, 1837, by Rev. Thomas F. Davis	1-M	62
Mary, d. Tho[ma]s & Rebecca, b. Dec. 11, 1747; d. Dec. 25, 1747	1	104
Mary B., m. Henry **ALLEN**, of Fairfield, Sept. 9, 1827, by Rev. E. W. Hooker	1-M	29
Polly, m. Charles **FAIRCHILD**, b. of Fairfield, May 8, 1825, by Rev. E. W. Hooker	1-M	18
Polly Ann, of Fairfield, m. George **FAIRCHILD**, of Westport, Feb. 14, 1841, by Rev. Dan C. Curtiss	1-M	71
Rebecca, d. Tho[ma]s & Rebecca, b. Nov. 18, 1732	1	104
Rebecca, d. Tho[ma]s, m. Simon **COUCH**, s. Thomas, Jan. 27, 1753	1	239
Sally, m. David **COOLEY**, b. of Greens Farms, Apr. 30, 1826, by Hez[ekia]h Ripley, V.D.M.	1-M	22
Sarah, m. Francis **GODFREY**, June 21, 1836, by Rev. T. F. Davis	1-M	59
Thomas, s. Tho[ma]s, m. Rebecca **HULL**, Sept. 28, 1731	1	104
Thomas, s. Tho[ma]s & Rebecca, b. May 21, 1743	1	104
NEWTON, Dorothy, d. James, b. Mar. 22, 1681	LR-A2	681
NICHOLS, NICOLLS, NUKOLS, Abel, s. Benj[ami]n & Elizabeth, b. May 24, 1732	1	145
Benjamin, s. John, m. Elizabeth **TROWBRIDGE**, Oct. 13, 1730	1	145
Bradley, of Fairfield, m. Sarah Ann **MILLS**, of Westport, July 25, 1847, by Rev. Lyman H. Atwater	1-M	87

	Vol.	Page

NICHOLS, NICOLLS, NUKOLS (cont.)

	Vol.	Page
Castile,* freeman, negro, of Weston, m. Mance, or Nancy, Titus **BURR**, freeman, of Fairfield, [ ], 1822, by David Hill, J.P. *("Lusteel"?)	1-M	6
Dan[ie]ll, s. Benj[ami]n & Elizabeth, b. Apr. 15, 1735	1	145
Daniel, m. Mary **ALLEN**, Oct. 18, 1756	1	161
Dan[ie]ll, s. Ignatius & Deborah, b. June 13, 1759	1	87
David, s. Ephraim & Rebecca, b. Mar. 29, 1746	1	87
Debora, d. Eph[rai]m, b. Jan. 1, 1685	LR-A2	674
Deborah, m. Joseph **WHEELER**, Dec. 7, 1705	1	4
Ebenezer, s. Ephraim & Rebecca, b. Nov. 4, 1741	1	87
Ebenezer, s. Paul & Sarah, b. Oct. 21, 1769	1	40
Eleanor Maria, m. William **BRADLEY**, Jr., b. of Fairfield, Dec. 25, 1844, by Rev. N. E. Cornwall	1-M	81
Eli B., m. Mary **HUBBELL**, June 12, 1836, by Rev. Nath[anie]l E. Cornwall	1-M	59
Eliza S., d. Sturgis, m. Samuel **PIKE**, b. of Fairfield, Oct. [ ], 1850, by Rev. N.E. Cornwall	1-M	95
Ephraim, s. Ignacius, m. Rebecca **GOLD**, d. Onesimus, July 5, 1741	1	87
Esther, d. Eph[rai]m, b. Dec. 18, 1689	LR-A2	674
Esther, d. Will[ia]m Ward, m. Eliphalet **HILL**, Nov. [ ], 1691	LR-A2	676
Esther, m. David **WHEELER**, Mar. 20, 1716/17	1	4
Esther, d. Ignatius & Deborah, b. June 5, 1756	1	87
Eunice, d. Benj[ami]n & Elizabeth, b. Dec. 16, 1738	1	145
Eunice, d. Ephraim & Rebecca, b. Apr. 4, 1748	1	87
Eunice, d. Benjamin, m. Samuel **ALLEN**, s. Ebenezer, Jan. 17, 1757	1	155
Eunice, of Fairfield, m. Nathan T. **MERWIN**, of Weston, Aug. 5, 1838, by N. E. Cornwall, in Southport	1-M	66
Gershom, s. Benj[ami]n & Elizabeth, b. Mar. 23, 1753	1	145
Grace, d. Ignatius & Deborah, b. Mar. 26, 1761	1	87
Hansom, of Weston, m. Betsey **CHAPMAN**, of Fairfield, Jan. 15, 1828, by Rev. E. W. Hooker	1-M	30
Hezekiah, s. Ephraim & Rebecca, b. Jan. 25, 1744	1	87
Huldah, d. John & Rebecca, b. May 7, 1741; d. Aug. 12, 1752	1	76
Huldah, of Stratford, m. John **NICHOLS**, Dec. 25, 1751	1	76
Ignatius, s. Eph[rai]m, b. Dec. 17, 1683	LR-A2	674
Ignatius, m. Deborah **WHEELER**, Mar. 27, 1755	1	87
Ignatius, d. May 23, 1764	1	87
James, s. Paul & Sarah, b. May 31, 1772	1	40
Jane, of Fairfield, m. George **KIPPEN**, of Bridgeport, Sept. 9, 1845, by Rev. Lyman H. Atwater	1-M	82
Jesse, s. Benj[ami]n & Elizabeth, b. Jan. 27, 1748	1	145
Jesse, s. Ephraim & Rebecca, b. Apr. 26, 1757	1	87
John, m. Rebecca **SHERWOOD**, Dec. 1, 1737	1	76
John, s. John & Rebecca, b. Feb. 27, 1745	1	76
John, m. 2nd. w. Huldah **NICHOLS**, of Stratford, Dec. 25, 1751	1	76
John, s. Ephraim & Rebecca, b. Aug. 2, 1754	1	87

	Vol.	Page
NICHOLS, NICOLLS, NUKOLS (cont.)		
John C., m. Catharine **OSBORN**, b. of Fairfield, May 13, 1841, by Rev. Lyman H. Atwater	1-M	71
John H., m. Susan **MOREHOUSE**, b. of Fairfield, Jan. 31, 1828, by Rev. Asa Bronson	1-M	29
Josiah, s. Benj[ami]n & Elizabeth, b. Sept. 29, 1746	1	145
Julia B., of Fairfield, m. Aaron **HAMMOND**, of New York City, Oct. 27, 1851, by Rev. Lyman H. Atwater	1-M	92
Lydia, d. Dan[ie]ll & Mary, b. July 10, 1756 (sic)* *(1757?)	1	161
Mary, m. Frances **BULKLEY**, b. of Southport, June 26, 1842, by Rev. N. E. Cornwall	1-M	74
Mary Ann, m. George **ROBINSON**, b. of Southport, Nov. 29, 1837, by N. E. Cornwall in Southport	1-M	63-4
Mary F., of Fairfield, m. Jonathan **BEERS**, of Bridgeport, Sept. 13, 1847, by Rev. Lyman H. Atwater	1-M	87
Michael, of Easton, m. Amanda **JOHNSON**, of Fairfield (colored), Nov. 17, 1851, by Rev. N. D. Benedict	1-M	93
Paul, s. Ephraim, m. Sarah **MIDDLEBROOK**, d. Eben[eze]r, Aug. 14, 1766	1	40
Peter, s. Ephraim & Rebecca, b. Sept. 29, 1750	1	87
Rebecca, d. John & Rebecca, b. May 7, 1743	1	76
Rufus, m. Charry A. **BRADLEY**, b. of Fairfield, July 2, 1839, by N. E. Cornwall	1-M	67
Sarah, d. John & Rebecca, b. May 3, 1739	1	76
Sarah, d. Benj[amin] & Elizabeth, b. May 3, 1743	1	145
Sarah, m. Nathaniel **JOHNSON**, Jan. 11, 1749/50	1	176
Sarah, d. Ephraim & Rebecca, b. July 28, 1752	1	87
Sarah, d. Ignatius & Deborah, b. Mar, 13, 1763	1	87
Sarah A., m. Anson **BROTHERTON**, b. of Fairfield, Dec. 31, 1844, by Rev. Lyman H. Atwater	1-M	78-80
Selleck, of Fairfield, m. Angeline **RUGGLES**, of Weston, Dec. [ ], 1834, by Rev. C. A. Boardman of Saugatuck	1-M	55
Squier, s. Paul & Sarah, b. Feb. 20, 1767	1	40
Susan, m. Zalmon **WAKEMAN**, b. of Fairfield, May 1, 1839, by N. E. Cornwall	1-M	67
William H., m. Mary B. **BARTRAM**, July 16,* 1822, by Rev. Nathan[ie]l Hewit *(Perhaps "Apr. 16")	1-M	8
NOGNIER*, Anthony, d. Oct. 23, 1740 *("Nougeire")	1	17
NORRIS, Cible, see under Sybil		
David A., m. Sarah A. **SEELEY**, b. of Fairfield, Dec. 12, 1847, by Rev. William Read	1-M	91
Hannah, d. John & Experience, b. June 4, 1733	1	18
Sarah, d. John & Experience, b. June 24, 1736	1	18
Stephen, s. John & Experience, b. Mar. 10, 1738	1	18
Cible,* d. John & Experience, b. Mar. 10, 1740/1 *(Sybil)	1	18
NORTHROP, NORTHRUP, Ann, m. Samuel **WHITNEY**, May 14, 1740	1	74
Joanna, m. Ebenezer **GILBERT**, s. John, Apr. 18, 1744	1	107
Mercy, d. Dea. Benj[amin], of Newtown, m. Benj[amin] **MUNGER**, s. Jonath[a]n, of Woodberry, Dec. 11, 1759	1	10

	Vol.	Page
NORTHROP, NORTHRUP (cont.)		
Mercy, d. Dea. Benjamin, of Newtown, m. Benjamin		
MUNGER, s. Jonathan, of Woodbury, Dec. 11, 1759	1	250
NORTON, Lucy A., of Southbury, m. Samuel S. **TWEEDY**, of		
Bridgeport, May 27, 1838, by Enoch E. Chase	1-M	66
NOUGEIRE*, Anthony, d. Oct. 23, 1740 *(Arnold copy has		
"Nognier")	1	17
NOYES, Burr, M.D., of Weston, m. Charlotte F. **BRUSH**, of		
Greens Farms, Oct. 5, 1828, by Rev. E. W. Hooker	1-M	32
Mary, Mrs. of New Haven, m. Col. Gold Selleck		
SILLIMAN, of Fairfield, May 24, 1775, at		
Stonington, by Rev. Joseph Fish, of Stonington	1	61
OAKLEY, Abigail, d. Jeremiah, m. Nathan **WHEELER**, Jr., s.		
Capt. Jabez, Oct. 19, 1775	1	285
ODELL, [see also **ODLE**], Ann, d. Capt. Sam[ue]ll, m. William		
WORDAIN, s. Tho[ma]s, Feb. 13, 1755	1	103
Bethyah, d. John, Jr., b. Feb. 27, 1692	LR-A2	674
Deborah, d. John, b. Aug. 28, 1682	LR-A2	681
Elizabeth, m. Abel **BINGHAM**, May 10, 1694	LR-A2	674
Hannah, d. John, b. Oct. 20, 1679	LR-A2	682
Lucy, m. Stephen **BRADLEY**, b. of Greenfield, July 10,		
1822, by Hezekiah Ripley, V.D.M.	1-M	8
Samuell, s. John, b. Mar. 10, 1677	LR-A2	682
Sarah, d. John, Jr., b. Aug. 10, 1694	LR-A2	674
ODLE, [see also **ODELL**], James, m. Lucy **TREDWELL**, b. of		
Fairfield, Apr. 13, 1828, by Rev. Asa Bronson, at his		
house	1-M	10
OGDEN, Abby Jane, m. Judson **STURGIS**, b. of Fairfield, Feb.		
3, 1828, by Rev. William Shelton	1-M	30
Abigail, d. David & Abigail, b. Oct. 14, 1725; d. Mar. 15,		
1726/7	1	98
Abigail, d. David & Abigail, b. Feb. 9, 1729/30	1	98
Abigail, d. David, m. John **HIDE**, Jr., s. John, Jan. 21, 1748	1	216
Abigail, d. David & Jane, b. Feb. 2, 1750/1	1	98
Abigail, of Greens Farms, m. Giles **BUNNELL**, of Weston,		
Oct. 10, 1825, by Rev. E. W. Hooker	1-M	20
Abigail H., of Fairfield, m. Stephen **WATERMAN**, of		
Hillsdale, N. Y., Jan. 29, [1823], by Hez[ekia]h		
Ripley, V.D.M.	1-M	9
Angeline, of Fairfield, m. W[illia]m **HOYT**, of New		
Canaan, Apr. 26, 1829, by John H. Hunter	1-M	34
Ann, d. Humphrey & Hannah, b. Nov. 2, 1744	1	164
Clary, m. John **MOREHOUSE**, b. of Fairfield, May 27,		
1821, by Nath[anie]l Hewit, V.D.M.	1-M	4
David, m. Abigail **OSBORN**, Dec. 14, 1724	1	98
David, s. David & Abigail, b. June 16, 1727	1	98
David, Jr., s. David, m. Jane **STURGIS**, d. Solomon, Apr.		
5, 1750	1	98
Ebenezer, s. John & Mary, b. Apr. 24, 1738	1	214
Edmund, s. Humphrey & Hannah, b. Feb. 12, 1755	1	164
Elizabeth, d. Joseph, m. Nathan **MORHOUSE**, s. Nathan,		
Mar. 4, 1740	1	137

	Vol.	Page
OGDEN (cont.)		
Elizabeth, m. Samuel **MOREHOUSE**, Jr., b. of Fairfield,		
Nov. 29, 1829, by John H. Hunter	1-M	37
Eunice, d. David & Jane, b. Jan. 5, 1753	1	98
Eunice, d. Humphrey & Hannah, b. Dec. 28, 1756	1	164
Eunice, d. David, m. John **PENFIELD**, s. Peter, Nov. 1,		
1770	1	17
George, m. Mehetabel P. **BEERS**, b. of Fairfield, [Oct.]		
16, [1832], by Rev. Charles Smith	1-M	47
Hezekiah, s. John & Mary, b. June 9, 1745	1	214
Humphrey, m. Hannah **BENNIT**, d. Tho[ma]s, Nov. 22,		
1743	1	164
Humphrey, s. Humphrey & Hannah, b. Feb. 21, 1751	1	164
John, m. Mary **JENNINGS**, Jan. 1, 1730	1	214
John, s. John & Mary, b. Apr. 24, 1736	1	214
John H., m. Abby G. **SHERWOOD**, b. of Fairfield, Dec.		
31, 1826, by Rev. E. W. Hooker	1-M	25
Jonathan, s. David & Abigail, b. Aug. 7, 1735	1	98
Joseph, s. Humphrey & Hannah, b. Mar. 1, 1749	1	164
Joseph, m. Sarah **THORP**, [Jan.] 12, [1823], by		
Hez[ekia]h Ripley, V.D.M.	1-M	9
Mabel, d. Sam[ue]ll & Mary, b. Nov. 29, 1765	1	216
Mary, m. William **HILL**, May 6, 1731	1	199
Mary, d. Sam[ue]ll & Mary, b. June 26, 1761	1	216
Mary, m. Seth M. **BRADLEY**, July 16, 1835, by Rev. T.		
F. Davis	1-M	56
Mercy, d. Humphrey & Hannah, b. Apr. 3, 1747	1	164
Moses, m. Sarah **WHITNEY**, b. of Greenfield, June 27,		
1820, by Rev. William Belden, of Greenfield	1-M	1
Nathaniel, m. Rachel **OGDEN**, Sept. 16, 1832, by		
Tho[ma]s F. Davis	1-M	45-6
Rachel, m. Nathaniel **OGDEN**, Sept. 16, 1832, by		
Tho[ma]s F. Davis	1-M	45-6
Rhoda, d. Sam[ue]ll & Mary, b. Apr. 9, 1769	1	216
Salome, m. Darius **WILLIAMS**, b. of Fairfield, Dec. 14,		
1823, by Hez[ekia]h Ripley, V.D.M.	1-M	13
Samuel, s. John & Mary, b. Oct. 24, 1732	1	214
Samuel, s. John, m. Mary **BANKS**, d. Benjamin, Jr., June		
19, 1753	1	216
Samuel, s. Sam[ue]ll & Mary, b. Apr. 25, 1758	1	216
Sarah, d. Joseph, m. Jabez **MOR[E]HOUSE**, s. Nathan,		
Sept. 18, 1738	1	210
Sarah, d. John & Mary, b. May 24, 1740	1	214
Sarah, d. Humphrey & Hannah, b .Jan. 24, 1753	1	164
Sarah, d. Sam[ue]ll & Mary, b. Mar. 1, 1757	1	216
Sturgis, s. David & Jane, b. Apr. 9, 1757; d. Apr. 10, 1757	1	98
OLDS, David, s. David & Hannah, b. Sept. 20, 1747	1	25
Sarah, d. David & Hannah, b. Aug. 8, 1745	1	25
OLMSTEAD, OLMSTED, Eliza, m. Lewis **BURR**, b. of		
Fairfield, Oct. 25, 1829, by John H. Hunter	1-M	35-6
Nancy, m. Alanson **ALLEN**, b. of Fairfield, Nov. 27,		
1823, by Nath[anie]l Hewit	1-M	13
Sarah, m. Abell **LYON**, May 11, 1757	1	115

	Vol.	Page
OSBORN, OSBORNE, OSBURN, Aaron, s. Jonathan &		
Catharine, b. May 17, 1740	1	46
Abigail, d. David, of East Chester, decd., m. William		
FAYERFIELD, Oct. 7, 1691, by Mr. John Bare	LR-A2	676
Abigail, m. Eleazer STURGIS, Apr. 23, 1724	1	238
Abigail, m. David OGDEN, Dec. 14, 1724	1	98
Abigail, d. Sam[ue]ll & Hannah, b. Sept. 1, 1729	1	24
Abigail, of Fairfield, m. Cornelius WYNKOOP, Jr., of		
New York, Mar. 12, 1758, by Rev. Noah Hobart	1	237
Albert, m. Maria STAPLES, b. of Fairfield, Dec. 24,		
1835, by Lyman H. Atwater	1-M	57
Anna, d. Eleazer & Sarah, b. Oct. 22, 1764	1	105
Anna, of Fairfield, m. Jonathan BULKLEY, of		
Huntington, Dec. 25, 1844, by N. E. Cornwall	1-M	81
Benjamin, s. Sam[ue]ll & Abigail, b. Feb. 24, 1723/4	1	62
Benjamin, s. Sam[ue]ll, m. Mary DIMON, d. Ebenezer,		
Oct. 6, 1753	1	96
Catharine, m. John C. NICHOLS, b. of Fairfield, May		
13, 1841, by Rev. Lyman H. Atwater	1-M	71
Charles E., of Corning, N.Y., m. Margaret KELLOGG,		
of Fairfield, Sept. 24, 1839, by Rev. Lyman H.		
Atwater	1-M	68
Dan[ie]l, s. Sam[ue]l & Hannah, b. Oct. 10, 1725	1	24
Daniel, s. Sam[ue]ll & Hannah, b. Oct. 10, 1725	LR-2	457
Daniel, s. Sam[ue]ll, m. Elizabeth BURR, d. Andrew,		
Jan. 19, 1758	1	247
Dan[ie]ll, s. Dan[ie]ll & Eliza[be]th, b. June 25, 1760	1	247
David, s. Eleazer & Hannah, b. Sept. 3, 1743	1	174
Dorothy, d. David, m. Nathan THROP, s. John, May 3,		
1738	1	212
Ebenezer, s. John & Abigail, b. Jan. 19, 1747	1	171
Eben[eze]r, s. Eleazer & Hannah, b. [ ]	1	174
Eleazer, m .Hannah BULKLEY, d. Peter, June 29, 1738	1	174
Eleazer, s. Eleazer & Hannah, b. Apr. 11, 1739	1	174
Eleazer, Jr., s. Eleazer, m. Sarah BURR, d. Ephraim, June		
3, 1764	1	105
Eleazer, s. Eleazer & Sarah, b. Jan. 21, 1770	1	105
Eleazer, d. May 20, 1788	1	174
Eliza, m. George BRADLEY, b. of Fairfield, Apr. 16,		
1828, by William Shelton	1-M	31
Ellen, d. Sam[ue]ll & Hannah, b. Feb. 8, 1738	1	24
Ellen, d. Eleazer & Hannah, b. Dec. 18, 1754	1	174
Emeline, m. David BANKS, b. of Fairfield, [Jan.] 20,		
[1833], by Rev. Charles Smith	1-M	48-9
Esther, d. Jonathan & Catharine, b. Apr. 11, 1753	1	46
Eunice, d. Sam[ue]ll & Hannah, b. Feb. 16, 1728	1	24
Eunice, d. Samuel, m. David BURR, s. Col. Andrew,		
Dec. 11, 1751	1	31
Eunice, d. Eleazer & Sarah, b. June 24, 1766	1	105
George, m. Sarah W. MOREHOUSE, b. of Fairfield,		
Dec. 11, 1820, by Nath[anie]l Hewit, V.D.M.	1-M	3
Gershom, s. Eleazer & Hannah, b. Apr. 23, 1746	1	174
Grissel, d. Eleazer & Hannah, b. Mar. 14, 1751	1	174

	Vol.	Page
OSBORN, OSBORNE, OSBURN (cont.)		
Hanna, d. John, b. July 26, 1677	LR-A2	663
Hannah, wid., m. James **BURR**, Dec. 12, 1731	1	201
Hannah, d. Eleazer & Hannah, b. Nov. 21, 1748	1	174
Hannah A., m. Eben **BURR**, b. of Fairfield, Apr. 23, 1825, by Nath[anie]l Hewit	1-M	17
Hawes, s. John, m. Mary **BULKLEY**, d. Peter, Feb. 6, 1755	1	192
Hezekiah, s. W[illia]m, m. Ruth **BURTON**, d. Solomon, Oct. 18, 1764	1	269
Isabel, d. Samuell & Hannah, b. Feb. 1, 1731	1	24
Jane, m. Henry A. **STURGIS**, b. of Fairfield, Oct. 28, 1834, by Rev. Amos Savage	1-M	54
Jeremiah, s. Sam[ue]ll & Hannah, b. Sept. 30, 1734	1	24
Jeremiah, s. Samuell & Hannah, d. Oct. 8, 1757	1	24
Jeremiah, s. Dan[ie]ll & Eliza[be]th, b. Dec. 10, 1763	1	247
John, Capt. d. July 15, 1709	LR-2	456
John, s. John, m. Abigail **BULKLEY**, d. Tho[ma]s, Apr. 15, 1741	1	171
John, s. Hawes & Mary, b. June 24, 1756	1	192
Jonathan, s. Capt. John, m. Catharine **WHEELER**, d. Joseph, Sept. [ ], 1733	1	46
Jonathan, s. Jonathan & Catharine, b. May 26, 1738	1	46
Joseph, s. Sam[ue]ll & Hannah, b. Feb. 22, 1733	1	24
Joseph B., m. Clarina **BULKLEY**, b. of Fairfield, Nov. 22, 1829, by John H. Hunter	1-M	37
Martha, d. Sam[ue]ll & Hannah, b. May 17, 1739; d. Mar. 7, 1788	1	24
Martha Ann, of Southport, m. Eli **HOPKINS**, Jr., of New York, Aug. 12, 1852, by Rev. Sam[ue]l J. M. Merwin	1-M	95
Mary, d. Sam[ue]ll & Hannah, b. Aug. 8, 1736	1	24
Mary, d. Capt. John, m. Nath[anie]ll **PERRY**, s. Joseph, Nov. 5, 1740	1	45
Mary, d. John & Abigail, b. Apr. 23, 1742	1	171
Mary, m. John M. **JENNINGS**, b. of Fairfield, Jan. 25, 1829, by Leonard Bacon	1-M	33
Mary E., m. John **GREGORY**, b. of Fairfield, Feb. 6, 1848, by Rev. N. E. Cornwall	1-M	88
Rebecca, m. Edward **CAREW**, b. of Fairfield, June 29, 1823, by Rev. Philo Shelton	1-M	11
Reuben, s. Jonathan & Catharine, b. Mar. 4, 1735/6	1	46
Sam[ue]ll, m. Hannah **COUCH**, Nov. 4, 1724	LR-2	457
Sam[ue]ll, m. Hannah **COUCH**, Nov. 4, 1724	1	24
Sam[ue]ll, s. Sam[ue]ll & Abigail, b. Mar. 1, 1740; d. Nov. 19, 1752	1	62
Samuell, d. Apr. 2, 1752	1	24
Sam[ue]ll, d. June 7, 1754	1	62
Sarah, m. Joseph **SHERWOOD**, Feb. 17, 1731	1	213
Sarah, d. Eleazer & Hannah, b. May 27, 1741	1	174
Sarah, d. Capt. John, m. Jonathan **LEWIS**, s. Lathrop, Jan. 10, 1754	1	42

	Vol.	Page
OSBORN, OSBORNE, OSBURN (cont.)		
Sarah, d. Eleazer, m. Nehemiah **BURR**, s. Capt.		
Sam[ue]ll, Apr. 21, 1763	1	274
Sarah, d. Eleazer & Sarah, b. Mar. 6, 1768	1	105
Sarah Ann, m. David M. **HAWKINS**, b. of Southport,		
Oct. 18, 1837, by N. E. Cornwall, in Southport	1-M	63-4
Seth, s. Sam[ue]ll & Abigail, b. Dec. 31, 1727	1	62
Seth, s. Samuel, m. Sarah **LEWIS**, d. Lathrop, July 12,		
1752	1	113
Stratton, s. Seth & Sarah, b. Oct. 17, 1752	1	113
Susannah, d. Dan[ie]ll & Eliza[be]th, b. Nov. 17, 1758	1	247
Susannah, of Greens Farms, m. Timothy **BULKLEY**, of		
Greenfield, Oct. 19, 1823, by Nath[anie]l Hewit	1-M	12
Thaddeus, s. Samuell & Hannah, b. Dec. 1, 1726	1	24
Thankfull, d. John, m. Samuel **BEERS**, s. James, Nov.		
10, 1743	1	95
Tho[ma]s B., m. Elizabeth H. **DIMON**, Sept. 6, 1826, by		
Rev. H. R. Judah, of Bridgeport	1-M	28
O'SULLIVAN, Mary Juana, m. Samuel Daly **LANGTREE**,		
July 30, 1834, by Rev. George Carrington	1-M	53
OWEN, Elizabeth Ann, m. Primus **KNAP[P]**, b. of Fairfield,		
July 29, 1851, by Rev. W. W. Brewer	1-M	92
OYSTERBANKS, Elizabeth, m. George **BATTERSON**, Dec.		
1, 1752	1	215
PACOCK, Edward, m. Sarah Ann **BRADLEY**, May 4, 1834,		
by Rev. David L. Ogden	1-M	52
PARKS, W[illia]m, of New York, m. Cornelia **DAVIS**, of		
Fairfield, Oct. 16, 1843, by Rev. N. E. Cornwall	1-M	75
PARRET, Abraham, s. [John & Sarah], b. May 15, 1752	1	167
Abraham, s. John & Sarah, b. May 15, 1752	1	241
David, s. John & Sarah, b. Aug. 30, 1758	1	241
Ebenezer, s. John & Sarah, b. July 29, 1765	1	241
Eunice, d. John & Sarah, b. Feb. 6, 1768	1	241
Hannah, d. John & Sarah, b. Feb. 2, 1778	1	241
James, s. John & Sarah, b .July 17, 1774	1	241
John, m. Sarah **HUBBELL**, Jan. 7, 1752	1	167
John, m. Sarah **HUBBELL**, Jan. 17, 1752	1	241
John, [s. John & Sarah], b. May 30, 1756	1	167
John, s. John & Sarah, b. May 30, 1756	1	241
Mary, d. John & Sarah, b. Nov. 20, 1767	1	241
Sarah, [d. John & Sarah], b. May 1, 1754	1	167
Sarah, d. John & Sarah, b. May 1, 1754	1	241
William, s. John & Sarah, b. Jan. 26, 1770	1	241
PARRIE, Abigail, b. Sept. 18, 1712; m. Jonathan **MEAKER**,		
Jan. 18, 1731	1	88
PARRUCH, PARRUCK, Abiah, d. John, m. Caleb **LYON**, s.		
Sam[ue]ll, Aug. 24, 1738	1	135
Abigail, d. Elnthan & Mary, b. Dec. 27, 1755	1	116
Elnathan, s. John, b. Feb. 18, 1724; m. Mary **HILL**, d.		
W[illia]m, Nov. 22, 1750	1	116
Ruhamah, d. Elnathan & Mary, b. Oct. 24, 1752	1	116
Sarah, d. Elnathan & Mary, b. July 18, 1751	1	116

	Vol.	Page
PARSONS, PERSONS, David, s. Peter & Lois, b. Oct. 31, 1756	1	165
Peter, m. Lois **MOR[E]HOUSE**, Mar. 25, 1756	1	165
PARTON, Amanda, m. David **PLATT**, b. of Bridgeport, Aug. 21, 1832, by Tho[ma]s F. Davis	1-M	45-6
PARTRICH, [see also **PATRICK**], Henry, of Norwald, m. Jerusha **BROTHERTON**, of Fairfield, [Nov.] 27, [1822], by Rev. E. W. Hooker	1-M	9
[PARTRIDGE], [see under **PARTRICH**]		
PATCHEN, PATCHIN, Abigail, m. William **STERLING** [ ], 1714	1	183
Charity, of Fairfield, m. John **ROBINSON**, of Long Island, May 19, [1822], by Rev. Asa Bronson, of Stratfield	1-M	7
PATRICK, [see also **PARTRICH**], Bradford, of Redding, m. Nancy **ALLEN**, of Greens Farms, Aug. 26, 1823, by Hez[ekia]h Ripley, V.D.M.	1-M	12
PATTERSON, Annah, d. William, m. Hezekiah **HUBBELL**, s. Richard, May 14, 1752	1	43
Elizabeth, m. Abraham **MORHOUSE**, Apr. 12, 1722	1	47
Mary, of Greens Farms, m. Abraham **COUCH**, of Redding, Mar. 27, 1831, by Oliver Sykes	1-M	41
[PEACOCK], [see under **PACOCK**]		
PECK, Alphonzo D., of New York City, m. Elizabeth B. **GOULEN**, of Fairfield, Nov. 10, 1847, by Rev. Lyman H. Atwater	1-M	88
PEET, W[illia]m L., m. Hannah **PENFIELD**, May 20, 1827, by Rev. H. R. Judah, of Bridgeport	1-M	28
PENFIELD, Ann, d. Peter & Mary, b. July 12, 1745	1	6
Ann, d. James & Ellen, b. June 28, 1775	1	259
Benjamin, m. Henrietta **ALLEN**, Oct. 8, 1832, by T. F. Davis	1-M	48-9
David, s. James & Ellen, b. Sept. 10, 1769	1	259
Elizabeth, d. Sam[ue]ll & Elizabeth, b. Jan. 6, 1760	1	184
Ellen, d. James & Ellen, b. June 10, 1767	1	259
Ephraim, s. James & Ellen, b. Feb. 18, 1763	1	259
Eunice, d. James & Ellen, b. Feb. 28, 1773	1	259
George, m. Charlotte **GOLDEN**, b. of Fairfield, May 2, 1839, by Lyman H. Atwater	1-M	67
Hannath, d. Peter & Mary, b. Nov. 10, 1737	1	6
Hannah, d. Sam[ue]ll & Elizabeth, b. Dec. 28, 1761	1	184
Hannah, d. Peter, m. Justin **HOBART**, s. Nehemiah, Mar. 18, 1762	1	23
Hannah, m. W[illia]m L. **PEET**, May 20, 1827, by Rev. H. R. Judah, of Bridgeport	1-M	28
James, s. Peter & Mary, b. Apr. 28, 1732	1	6
James, s. Peter, m. Ellen **BURR**, d. Ephraim, Apr. 23, 1758	1	259
James, s. James & Ellen, b. Feb. 24, 1761	1	259
John, s. Peter & Mary, b. Nov. 25, 1747	1	6
John, s. Peter, m. Eunice **OGDEN**, d. David, Nov. 1, 1770	1	17
Lydia, d. Peter & Mary, b. Feb. 14, 1741 [sic]	1	6

	Vol.	Page
PENFIELD (cont.)		
Mary, d. Peter & Mary, b. Apr. 18, 1731; d. July 16, 1753	1	6
Mary, d. James & Ellen, b. Mar. 10, 1759	1	259
Nathaniel, s. Sam[ue]ll & Elizabeth, b. Mar. 19, 1758	1	184
Peter, m. Mary **ALLEN**, May 28, 1730	1	6
Peter, s. Peter & Mary, b. Sept. 13, 1743	1	6
Sam[ue]l, s. Peter & Mary, b. Nov. 5, 1734	1	6
Samuel, s. Peter, m. Elizabeth **LEWIS**, Sept. 2, 1757	1	184
Sarah, d. Peter & Mary, b. May 23, 1740	1	6
Sarah, d. John & Eunice, b. Feb. 10, 1771	1	17
Thaddeus, s. James & Ellen, b. May 7, 1765	1	259
PENNOGER*, Emily Francis, of New Canaan, m. John W.		
GOULDON, of Bridgeport, [Oct.] 6, [1844], by		
Rev. Charles R. Adams ***(PENNOYER?)**	1-M	77
PERRY, Abigail, m. Joseph **WHEELER**, Sept. 10, 1729	1	20
Abigail, d. Nathaniel & Mary, b. Nov. 20, 1743; d. Aug.		
4, 1753	1	45
Catharine T., of Fairfield, m. John **SKINNER**, of		
Brooklyn, N.Y., Dec. 16, 1844, by Rev. Lyman H.		
Atwater	1-M	78-80
Daniel, s. Joseph, m. Mary **STURGIS**, d. Peter, Oct. 8,		
1740	1	53
Dan[ie]ll, m. Sarah **WILLSON**, Jan. 1, 1744/5	1	53
Dan[ie]ll, s. Dan[ie]ll & Sarah, b. Apr. 15, 1747	1	53
Deborah, d. Dan[ie]ll & Sarah, b. Oct. 15, 1750	1	53
Drusilla, m. Zenus **WHETNEY**, b. of Fairfield, [probably		
1837], by [Enoch E. Chase]	1-M	65
Eben[eze]r, s. Joseph, m. Martha **SHERWOOD**, d.		
Daniel, Dec. 24, 1760	1	254
Elizabeth P., of Southport, m. William H. **GUION**, of		
New York City, Sept. 20, 1841, by Rev. Lyman H.		
Atwater	1-M	72
Emily, of Southport, m. Chandler **SMITH**, of Danbury,		
Nov. 21, 1831, by Rev. John H. Hunter	1-M	42-3
Emily, of Fairfield, m. George **RIDER**, of Danbury, Nov.		
13, 1850, by Rev. Lyman H. Atwater	1-M	93
Eunice, d. Sam[ue]ll, m. Eliphalet **THORP**, s. David,		
May 8, 1760	1	260
Eunice, m. Charles **HURLBURT**, Dec. 29, 1833, by		
Tho[ma]s F. Davis	1-M	51
Francis, m. Eliza Ann **BULKLEY**, b. of Fairfield, June		
20, 1831, by Rev. John H. Hunter	1-M	41
George, s. Dan[ie]ll & Sarah, b. Nov. 26, 1752	1	53
Grissel, d. Dan[ie]ll & Sarah, b. Feb. 20, 1745/6	1	53
Helen, of Southport, m. Edwin **BULKLEY**, of New		
York, July 7, 1846, by Samuel J. M. Merwin	1-M	84
Henry, m. Henrietta **STURGIS**, b. of Mill River, [Apr.]		
20, [1831], by Rev. Charles Smith	1-M	39-40
Isaac, s. Dan[ie]ll & Sarah, b .Nov. 3, 1754	1	53
John, s. Dan[ie]ll & Sarah, b. Dec. 30, 1748	1	53
John, s. Nathaniel & Mary, b. Mar. 4, 1760	1	45
Joseph, s. Joseph, m. Sarah **BULKLEY**, d. Peter, Nov.		
11, 1736	1	142

PERRY (cont.)

Joseph, s. Joseph & Sarah, b. Apr. 11, 1741; d. May 9,
    1743   1   142

	Vol.	Page
Joseph, s. Joseph & Sarah, b. Apr. 11, 1741; d. May 9, 1743	1	142
Joseph, s. Joseph & Sarah, b. Aug. 4, 1748	1	142
Joseph, d. Aug. 20, 1753	1	142
M. Angeline, of Westport, m. John R. **FORESTER**, of Danbury, Jan. 16, 1848, by Rev. Lyman H. Atwater	1-M	88
Mabel, m. David **BEERS**, b. of Fairfield, Sept. 21, 1834, by Nath[anie]l E. Cornwell	1-M	54
Mary, see Mary **EDWARDS**	1	10
Mary, w. Daniel, d. Oct. 31, 1742	1	53
Mary, d. Nathaniel & Mary, b. Nov. 16, 1747	1	45
Mary, d. Joseph, m. Gershom **BANKS**, Jan. [ ], 1751	1	127
Mary, w. Nathaniel, d. Dec. 29, 1787	1	45
Mary, m. Robert **JENNINGS**, b. of Fairfield, Apr. 29, 1838, by Lyman H. Atwater	1-M	66
Mehetable, d. Nathaniel & Mary, b. Mar. 26, 1753	1	45
Mehetable, alias "Hetty", m. Frederick **MARYUAND**, Sept. 3, 1822, by Rev. Nathaniel Hewit	1-M	8
Narcissa, of Fairfield, m. Joseph **WHETTEMORE**, of Boston, Nov. 21, 1821, by Nath[anie]l Hewit	1-M	6
Nath[anie]ll, s. Joseph, m. Mary **OSBORN**, d. Capt. John, Nov. 5, 1740	1	45
Nath[anie]ll, Jr., s. Nathaniel & Mary, b. Jan. 19, 1746; d. July 23, 1753	1	45
Nath[anie]l, Jr., s. Nathaniel & Mary, b. Mar. 15, 1756	1	45
Peter, s. Joseph & Sarah, b. Feb. 24, 1738/9	1	142
Robert, m. Mary S. **BENNETT**, b. of Fairfield, Nov. 10, 1841, by Rev. Lyman H. Atwater	1-M	72
Samuel, m. Henretta **BULKLEY**, b. of Fairfield, Dec. 4, 1825, by Nath[anie]l Hewit	1-M	20
Sarah, d. Joseph & Mary, b. Jan. 30, 1727/8	1	232
Sarah, d Joseph & Sarah, b. July 25, 1744	1	142
Sarah, d. Joseph, m. Nathan **BULKLEY**, s. Joseph, Apr. 15, 1756	1	232
Sarah B., of Fairfield, m. Charles R. **FERRIS**, of Stamford, Mar. 18, 1850, by Rev. Lyman H. Atwater	1-M	92
Thaddeus, s. Nathaniel & Mary, b. Mar. 23, 1750	1	45
Thankfull, d. Nathaniel & Mary, b. Oct. 26, 1741	1	45
Thankfull, d. Nath[anie]ll, m. Ebenezer **STURGIS**, s. Elnathan, Dec. 17, 1761	1	264
Thomas, s. Dan[ie]ll & Sarah, b. Feb. 21, 1757	1	53
Walter, m. Eunice **MERWIN**, b. of Greenfield Parish, July 12, 1821, by Rev. Nath[anie]l Hewit	1-M	4
PHELPS, Caroline E., of Fairfield, m. James D. **HERING**, of New York City, Sept. 1, 1846, by Rev. Lyman H. Atwater	1-M	85
Sally Ann, of Fairfield, m. Benjamin **ATWATER**, of Ithaca, N.Y. [Oct.] 15, [1840], by N. E. Cornwall	1-M	70
PHILLIPS, John, m. Caroline **RAY**, b. of Fairfield, Apr. 3, 1844, by Rev. Anson F. Beach	1-M	76

	Vol.	Page

PHILLIPS (cont.)

	Vol.	Page
John M., of Newark, N.J., m. Elizabeth **BEERS**, of Fairfield, July 3, 1848, by Rev. J. H. Perry	1-M	90
PHIPPENNY, PHIPENNY, Hannah, d. Nehemiah & Lidea, b. Oct. 13, 1771	1	35
Hannah, had d. Julia Ann, b. July 29, 1807	1	35
Julia Ann, d. Hannah, b. July 29, 1807; m. John S. COGSWELL, [ ]	1	35
Nehemiah, s. James, of Stratford, m. Lidea **DAVIS**, d. Jabez, Feb. 14, 1771	1	35
PICKENS, James, m. Susan **TYLER**, b. of Fairfield, May 2, 1848, by Rev. Lyman H. Atwater	1-M	89
PICKERING, Joseph, m. Laura **WILLSON**, b. of Southport, July 25, 1836, by Nath[anie]l E. Cornwall	1-M	60
PIERCE, Nancy, m. John **CURRIER**, b. of New York, Jan. 23, 1828, by Rev. E. W. Hooker	1-M	30
PIERSON, Eunice, d. Nath[anie]ll & Hannah, b. Feb. 27, 1747	1	58
John, s. Nath[anie]ll & Hannah, b. Sept. 7, 1748	1	58
Nath[anie]ll, m. Hannah **BEERS**, d. Lieut. James, Oct. 14, 1746	1	58
Olive, d. Nath[anie]ll & Hannah, b. Oct. 4, 1756	1	58
Timothy, s. Thomas, m. Elizabeth **COUCH**, d. Sam[ue]ll, Mar. 9, 1756	1	185
PIKE, Samuel, m. Eliza S. **NICHOLS**, d. Sturgis, b. of Fairfield, Oct. [ ], 1850, by Rev. N. E. Cornwall	1-M	95
PINE, James, of Rye, N.Y., m. Elizabeth J. **MOULTON**, of Fairfield, Sept. 9, 1833, by Rev. C. A. Boardman, of Saugatuck	1-M	50
PLATT, Abel, s. Obediah & Mary, b. Aug. 2, 1723	1	109
Abigail, d. Timothy & Margary, b. Apr. 14, 1736	1	143
Ame, d. Timothy & Margary, b. Aug. 25, 1739	1	143
Ann, d. Obediah & Mary, b. Nov. 5, 1731	1	109
David, s. Obediah & Mary, b. Sept. 15, 1734	1	109
David, of Weston, m. Mary **SANFORD**, of Fairfield, [Oct.] 7, [1822], by Rev. E. W. Hooker	1-M	8
David, m. Amanda **PARTON**,* b. of Bridgeport, Aug. 21, 1832, by Tho[ma]s F. Davis *(**PARTOW**?)	1-M	45-6
Elizabeth, d. Obediah & Mary, b. May 10, 1739	1	109
Hezekiah, s. Timothy & Margary, b. Apr. 22, 1732	1	143
Jesse, s. Timothy & Margary, b. July 4, 1741	1	143
Jonas, s. Obediah & Mary, b. Oct. 9, 1727	1	109
Mary, d. Obediah & Mary, b. Jan. 7, 1736	1	109
Obediah, m. Mary **SMITH**, Aug. 10, 1722	1	109
Obediah, s. Obediah & Mary, b. Aug. 8, 1729	1	109
Sarah, d. Obediah & Mary, b. June 25, 1725	1	109
Sarah, m. Elias **BATES**, Jan. 17, 1734	1	148
Timothy, s. Jonas, m. Margary **SMITH**, d. John, Aug. 22, 1728	1	143
Timothy, s. Timothy & Margary, b. June 26, 1729	1	143
Zebulon, s. Timothy & Margary, b. Feb. 28, 1743	1	143
PLUMB, John, of Bridgeport, m. Sally **BEERS**, of Fairfield, Dec. 25, 1826, by William Shelton	1-M	26-7

	Vol.	Page
POMEROY, Benjamin, Jr., of New York, m. Mary Josephine BULKLEY, d. Andrew, of Fairfield, June 7, 1848, by Rev. N. E. Cornwall	1-M	89
PORTER, Ezra C., of Bridgeport, m. Catharine M. ANDREWS, Jan. 3, 1829, by John Hunter	1-M	32
Horace, of Ridgefield, m. Priscilla GODFREY, of Weston, Sept. 7, 1824, by Rev. E. W. Hooker	1-M	15
Lide, of Winsor, m. John WHEELER, Oct. 17, 1712	1	8
Lydia E., m. Charles MOREHOUSE, b. of Fairfield, July 16, 1843, by Rev. James Scott, Stratfield	1-M	75
POTTER, James, of Gap Grove, Lee Co., Ill., m. Elizabeth MOODEY of Fairfield, Sept. 24, 1849, by Rev. William Read	1-M	91
PRINDLE, Allen, of Norwalk, m. Nancy BAKER, of Fairfield, Apr. 1, 1825, by Rev. E. W. Hooker	1-M	17
PULLING, Abell, s. Abram & Abigail, b. Oct. 8, 1752; d. [ ], aged 10 m. 7 das.	1	101
Abel, s. Abraham & Abigail, b. May 23, 1760	1	101
Abigail, d. Abram & Abigail, b. Nov. 12, 1756	1	101
Abraham, s. Abram & Abigail, b. Aug. 14, 1758	1	101
Abram, m. Abigail BEERS, Nov. 10, 1743	1	101
Augustus, s. Abram & Abigail, b. Aug. 21, 1747	1	101
Mary, d. Abram & Abigail, b. Sept. 5, 1744	1	101
William, s. Abram & Abigail, b. Aug. 21, 1750	1	101
PYNCHON, Mary, Mrs.? of Cambridge, d. Hon. Joseph Pynchon, of Boston, m. Rev. Andrew ELIOT, of Fairfield, s. Rev. Andrew, D.D., of Boston, July 19, 1774, at Cambridge, by Rev. Dr. Appleton	1	279
RAMSEY,* Hannah, m. James BEERS, Jan. 20, 1716 *("RUMSEY"?)	1	95
RANALL, [see also RANDAL], Kezia, m. Daniel ANDREWS, b. of Greens Farms, July 16, 1820, by Hez[ekiah] Ripley, V.D.M	1-M	1
Sam[ue]ll, had negroes Lucy, b. Jan. 8, 1787 & Rose, b. Feb. 8, 1789	1	275
RAND, Richard, of Middletown, m. Sarah WETMORE, of Bridgeport, Oct. 17, 1824, by Rev. Nath[anie]l Hewit	1-M	15
RANDAL, [see also RANALL], Silvester, of Port Jefferson, L.I., m. Sarah Ann MOREHOUSE, of Fairfield, Apr. 19, 1841, by Rev. Lyman H. Atwater	1-M	71
RAY, Caroline, m. John PHILLIPS, b. of Fairfield, Apr. 3, 1844, by Rev. Anson F. Beach	1-M	76
RAYMOND, RAYMAN, Alva, of Greenfield, m. Polly MEEKER, of Norfield, Nov. 19, 1826, by Hezekiah Ripley, V.D.M.	1-M	24
Curtis, m. Charlotte Ruth HENRIETTA, b. of Fairfield, Jan. 1, 1849, by Rev. N. E. Cornwall	1-M	94
David, s. W[illia]m, m. Sarah FOUNTAIN, d. Aaron, Nov. 24, 1760	1	27
Elizabeth, d. David & Sarah, b. Nov. 22, 1761	1	27

	Vol.	Page
RAYMOND, RAYMAN (cont.)		
Elizabeth, of Greenfield, m. Benjamin J. **WHITEHEAD**, of Weston, July 9, 1826, by Hezekiah Ripley, V.D.M.	1-M	24
Eunice, of Greenfield, m. John **ADAMS**, of Norfield, Nov. 16, [1823], by Hez[ekia]h Ripley, V.D.M.	1-M	13
Mary, m. Nelson **JARVIS**, Nov. 24, 1825, by Rev. H. R. Judah, of Bridgeport	1-M	28
Sturgis, m. Jenetta **BANKS**, b. of Greenfield, Apr. 18, 1821, by Hezekiah Ripley, V.D.M.	1-M	4
READ, REED, Abigail, d. William, b. Feb. 1, 1677/8	LR-A2	664
Deborah, d. John & Sarah, b. Apr. 5, 1756	1	2
Hez[ekiah], s. John & Mary, b. Feb. 23, 1734/5	1	2
Hezekiah, s. John & Sarah, b. Feb. 23, 1753	1	2
John, s. Will[ia]m, b. Jan. 29, 1679	LR-A2	682
John, of Reading, m. Mary **HALLEY**, d. John, of Stratford, Sept. 26, 1723	1	2
John, s. John & Mary, b. Jan. 16, 1725/6	1	2
John, m. 2nd w. Sarah **BRADLEY**, d. Samuel, Dec. 19, 1750	1	2
Julia Ann, of Fairfield, m. Edward **FISHER**, of Bridgeport, Mar. 9, 1845, by Rev. Lyman H. Atwater	1-M	81
Mary, d. John & Mary, b. Sept. 2, 1724	1	2
Mary, w. John, d. Feb. 14, 1748	1	2
Ruth, d. John & Sarah, b. Sept. 25, 1754	1	2
Sarah, d. John & Sarah, b. Nov. 27, 1751	1	2
Sarah, d. Tho[ma]s, of Norwalk, m. James **BENNIT**, s. Thomas, Apr. 7, 1762	1	254
Thurza Maria, m. W[illia]m S. **TURNEY**, b. of Fairfield, Jan. 31, 1841, by Rev. Lyman H. Atwater	1-M	71
William, s. John & Mary, b. Jan. 31, 1730/1	1	2
REDFIELD, David, s. John & Sarah, b. May 8, 1760	1	255
Grace, m. John **SEEGAR**, Apr. 15, 1713	LR-B	146
John, s. James, m. Sarah **SMITH**, d. Benj[ami]n, Oct. 20, 1757	1	255
John, s. John & Sarah, b. Feb. 26, 1763	1	255
Mary, d. John & Sarah, b. July 17, 1758	1	255
RHICALS(?), Ephraim, of Stratford, m. Esther **HADLEY**, of Fairfield, Oct. 17, 1682	LR-A2	674
RICE, Francis, m. [ ] **SINGLETON**, Apr. 6, 1850, by Rev. Lyman H. Atwater	1-M	92
RICHMOND, Eliza, m. George **BLACKMAN**, b. of Fairfield, Mar. 24, 1834, by Rev. C. A. Boardman, of Saugatuck	1-M	52
RIDER, George, of Danbury, m. Emily **PERRY**, of Fairfield, Nov. 13, 1850, by Rev. Lyman H. Atwater	1-M	93
RIPLEY, Edwin, of Lebanon, m. Eloesa **COMSTOCK**, of Fairfield, May 6, 1824, by Hez[ekia]h Ripley, V.D.M.	1-M	14
RISLEY, Cornelia A., of Fairfield, m. Charles A. **WHITTINGHAM**, of New York, Oct. 2, 1825, by Rev. Edward Rutledge, of Stratford	1-M	19

	Vol.	Page
ROACH, John, m. Letitia Mc**COY**, Oct. 8, 1848, by Rev. N. E.		
Cornwall	1-M	90
Peter R., of New York, m. Jane **THROCKMORTON**, of		
Fairfield, Jan. 2, 1828, by Rev. William Shelton	1-M	29
[**ROBERTS**], **ROBERDS, ROBERD**, Abigail, d. John &		
Hannah, b. Sept. 27, 1751	1	48
Grace, d. John & Hannah, b. Feb. 17, 1748	1	48
John, m. Hannah **ELWOOD**, Mar. [ ], 1757 [sic]	1	48
Mary, d. John & Hannah, b. May 22, 1754	1	48
ROBERTSON, ROBERSON, Damaris, d. Samuell, b. Apr. 13,		
1696	LR-A2	674
Daniel, s. Jon[atha]n & Lucretia, b. June 8, 1756	1	230
John, m. Ruhamah **LINES**, d. Benj[amin], May 3, 1762	1	236
John, s. John & Ruhamah, b. Mar. 27, 1763	1	236
Jonathan, m. Lucretia **THORP**, Apr. 12, 1752	1	230
Sam[ue]ll, s. Jonathan & Lucretia, b. May 31, 1753	1	230
Seth, s. Jonathan & Lucretia, b. Aug. 11, 1754	1	230
William, of Fairfield, m. Mrs. Anna **RUGGLES**, of		
Brookfield, Nov. 27, 1828, by William Shelton	1-M	32
ROBINSON, Eliza, of Fairfield, m. Henderson **BENEDICT**, of		
Huntington, June 4, 1851, by Rev. Lyman H. Atwater	1-M	93
Eunice, m. Gideon **MOREHOUSE**, Dec. 28, 1828, by		
William Shelton	1-M	32
George, m. Mary Ann **NICHOLS**, b. of Southport, Nov.		
29, 1837, by N. E. Cornwall, in Southport	1-M	63-4
Jerusha P., d. William, decd., of Fairfield, m. Charles		
ROCKWELL, of New York, Oct. 16, 1848, by Rev.		
N. E. Cornwall	1-M	94
Jerusha T., d. W[illia]m, decd., of Fairfield, m. Charles		
ROCKWELL, of New York City, Oct. 16, 1848, by		
Rev. N. E. Cornwall	1-M	93
John, of Long Island, m. Charity **PATCHIN**, of Fairfield,		
May 19, [1822], by Rev. Asa Bronson, of Stratfield	1-M	7
Samuel, m. Abigaile **LOCKWOOD**, d. Daniel, Aug. 20,		
1691	LR-A2	676
Sophronia, m. Augustus **JENNINGS**, b. of Southport, Nov.		
21, 1837, by Lyman H. Atwater	1-M	65
Thomas, m. Eliza P. **DIMON**, July 8, 1834, by T. F. Davis	1-	53
ROCKWELL, Charles, of New York City, m. Jerusha T.		
ROBINSON, d. W[illia]m, decd., of Fairfield, Oct.		
16, 1848, by Rev. N. E. Cornwall	1-M	93
Charles, of New York, m. Jerusha P. **ROBINSON**, d.		
William, decd., of Fairfield, Oct. 16, 1848, by Rev. N.		
E. Cornwall	1-M	94
ROGERS, Benjamin W., m. Anna **CHAPMAN**, Sept. 8, 1830,		
by T. F. Davis	1-M	39-40
Julia, of Fairfield, m. Daniel S. **COLWELL**, of New York		
City, Sept. 22, 1840, by Rev. Lyman H. Atwater	1-M	69
ROOT, Mary, d. John, b. Jan. 19, 1679	LR-A2	683
Susannah, d. John, b. May 13, 1678	LR-A2	683
ROW, Lavinah, m. Jehu MOR[E]**HOUSE**, Mar. 10, 1727	1	200
ROWLAND, ROLAND, Abigaill, d. Henry, m. Thomas		
JOANS, Mar. 5, 1670/1	LR-A2	680

	Vol.	Page
ROWLAND, ROLAND (cont.)		
Abigail, m. James **LYON**, Dec. 14, 1732	1	165
Abigail, d. Samuel & Abigail, b. Feb. 23, 1742/3	1	66
Andrew, s. Sam[ue]ll & Abigail, b. Jan. 17, 1736/7	1	66
Andrew, [s. Samuel & Sally], b. May 6, 1810	1	296
Charles, [s. Samuel & Sally], b. May 6, 1800	1	296
Dan[ie]ll, s. Jos[eph] & Sarah, b. Apr. 21, 1750	1	225
David, m. Mrs. Deborah **SLOP**,* Dec. 1, 1745		
*(SLOSS?)	1	26
David, m. 2nd w. Elizabeth **HILL**, d. Capt. Thomas, Feb. 14, 1749/50	1	26
David, d. Aug. 27, 1768	1	26
Deborah, m. Thomas **STAPLES**, Sr., May 24, 1723	1	55
Deborah, w. David, d. Sept. 29, 1748	1	26
Edward S., [s. Samuel & Sally], b. Sept. 26, 1812	1	296
Eliza F., of Fairfield, m. Osmond **COGSWELL**, of Cincinnati, O., Apr. 24, 1825, by Nath[anie]l Hewit	1-M	17
Elizabeth, m. David **DOWNS**, Jan. 3, 1733/4	1	136
Elizabeth, w. David, d. July 18, 1753	1	26
Elizabeth, [d. Samuel & Sally], b. Apr. 1, 1802	1	296
Elizabeth Mallbie, of Fairfield, m. Obadian William **JONES**, of New York, Nov. 10, 1820, by Nath[anie]l Hewit, V.D.M.	1-M	2
Esther, d. David & Deborah, b. Sept. 17, 1746; d. Sept. 25, 1748	1	26
Esther, d. David & Elizabeth, b. Oct. 29, 1751	1	26
Esther, d. David, m. Sam[ue]ll **SMEDLEY**, s. Col. James, Apr. 9, 1771	1	277
George, [s. Samuel & Sally], b. Dec. 3, 1796	1	296
Grace, d. Samuel & Abigail, b. Sept. 30, 1738	1	66
Grace, Mrs., d. Sam[ue]ll Rowland, of Fairfield, m. Asa **SPALDING**, of Fairfield, s. Benj[amin] & Deborah of Plainfield, Sept. 4, 1755	1	32
Hannah, d. Jos[eph] & Sarah, b. Aug. 7, 1742	1	225
Hannah, d. Joseph, m. Jonathan **DIMON**, s. Moses, Feb. 14, 1760	1	265
Henry, [s. Samuel & Sally], b. Mar. 25, 1806	1	296
Isaac, s. John & Sarah, b. Nov. 20, 1755	1	204
James, [s. Samuel & Sally], b. May 6, 1808	1	296
James, of New York City, m. Mary Eliza **SMITH**, of Fairfield, Sept. 15, 1844, by Rev. Lyman H. Atwater	1-M	77
Jane, [twin with Samuel], d. Jos[eph] & Sarah, b. Sept. 19, 1755	1	225
John, m. Sarah **LYON**, d. Samuel, Dec. 13, 1738	1	204
John, s. John & Sarah, b. Mar. 20, 1747	1	204
Jonathan, [s. Samuel & Sally], b. Jan. 6, 1804	1	296
Joseph, m. Sarah **SHERWOOD**, Nov. 3, 1741	1	225
Joseph, s. Jos[eph] & Sarah, b. Aug. 5, 1745	1	225
Julia Ann B., [d. Samuel & Sally], b. Nov. [ ], 1819	1	296
Mary, m. Thomas **BENNIT**, Mar. 17, 1717	1	123
Mary, m. John **FANTON**, s. Jonathan, Nov. [ ], 1731	1	190
Mary, d. John & Sarah, b. June 7, 1750	1	204
Noah, s. Jos[eph] & Sarah, b. Apr. 15, 1757	1	225

	Vol.	Page
ROWLAND, ROLAND (cont.)		
Rebecca, m. Jabez **DAVIS**, Aug. 3, 1726	1	174
Samuel, m. Abigail **SQUIRE**, Aug. 13, 1736	1	66
Samuel [twin with Jane], s. Jos[eph] & Sarah, b. Sept. 19, 1755	1	225
Samuel, s. Andrew & Elizabeth, b. Mar. 15, 1769; m. Sally **MALTBIE**, d. Jonathan & Elizabeth, Oct. 30, 1794, by Rev. Andrew Eliot	1	296
Samuel, [s. Samuel & Sally], b. Sept. 24, 1798	1	296
Samuel T., of Weston, m. Emily C. **THORP**, of Fairfield, Nov. 17, 1852, by Z. B. Burr	1-M	95
Sarah, d. John & Sarah, b. Dec. 25, 1744	1	204
Seth, s. John & Sarah, b. June 7, 1742	1	204
William, [s, Samuel & Sally], b. June 25, 1795	1	296
ROWLINSON, Elizabeth, m. John **CLAGSTONE**, Mar. 23, 1749	1	211
RUGGLES, Angeline, of Weston, m. Selleck **NICHOLS**, of Fairfield, Dec. [ ], 1834, by Rev. C. A. Boardman, of Saugatuck	1-M	55
Anna, Mrs. of Brookfield, m. William **ROBERSON**, of Fairfield, Nov. 27, 1828, by William Shelton	1-M	32
RUMSEY, Abigail, d. Rob[er]t, m. Cornelius **HULL**, Aug. 24, 1731	1	220
Abigail, d. Benj[ami]n & Isabel, b. Sept. 15, 1747	1	193
Abigail, d. John & Esther, b. Jan. 12, 1752/3	1	158
Ann, d. Benj[ami]n & Isabel, b. Dec. 10, 1744	1	193
Benjamin, m. Isabel **COUCH**, d. Simon, [ ], 1729	1	193
Benjamin, s. Benj[ami]n & Isabel, b. July 28, 1732	1	193
Daniel, s. Benj[ami]n & Isabel, b. Feb. 22, 1736	1	193
Daniel, s. Jos[eph] & Sarah, b. Oct. 6, 1747	1	178
Daniel, s. David & Anna, b. July 11, 1768	1	275
David, s. Benj[ami]n & Isabel, b. Oct. 22, 1738	1	193
David, s. Benj[ami]n, m. Anna **LOVELL**, d. James, of Barnstable, Dec. 26, 1764	1	275
David, s. David & Anna, b. May 20, 1770	1	275
Ephraim, s. Jos[eph] & Sarah, b. Feb. 1, 1753	1	178
Hannah,* m. James **BEERS**, Jan. 20, 1716 *(Arnold copy has "Hannnah **RAMSEY**")	1	95
Hannah, d. Robert, m. Seth **HULL**, s. Eliphalet, Dec. 24, 1747	1	140
Hezekiah, s. Jos[eph] & Sarah, b. Apr. 9, 1756	1	178
Isaac, s. Joseph & Sarah, b. May 24, 1739	1	178
Isabel, [w. Benjamin], d. Nov. 7, 1754	1	193
John, s. Robert, m. Esther **JONES**, Mar. 19, 1752	1	158
Joseph, s. Benj[ami]n & Isabel, b. Jan. 15, 1730; d. Jan. 20, 1750	1	193
Joseph, s. Robert, m. Sarah **BARTRAM**, d. John, Aug. 16, 1738	1	178
Joseph, s. Jos[eph] & Sarah, b. Oct. 29, 1743	1	178
Lewis, s. Benj[ami]n & Isabel, b. Aug. 21, 1741	1	193
Mary, d. Benj[ami]n & Isabel, b. July 28, 1734	1	193
Mary, d. Benj[ami]n, m. Samuel **HENDRICK**, s. John, Aug. 30, 1759	1	252

	Vol.	Page
RUMSEY (cont.)		
Nathan, s. John & Esther, b .June 15, 1756	1	158
Puella, d. David & Anna, b. Aug. 1, 1766	1	275
Rachel, d. John & Esther, b. Jan. 22, 1754	1	158
Sarah, d. Jos[eph] & Sarah, b. Nov. 24, 1740	1	178
William, s. Jos[eph] & Sarah, b. June 22, 1750	1	178
RUSSELL, Elizabeth, Mrs., m. Rev. Joseph **WEBB**, Jan. 8,		
1691, at Stratford, by Rev. William Corliss	LR-2	462
Eunice, Mrs., m. Nathaniel **BARTLET**, June 13, 1753	1	159
RUST, James Morgan, of Poughkeepsie, N.Y., m. Ruilla		
STURGIS, of Fairfield, [Mar.] 9, [1823], by William		
Belden	1-M	10
SAGE, Kenneth, of Norwalk, m. Esther **HUESTER**, Mar. 10,		
1833, by Tho[ma]s F. Davis	1-M	50
SALE, Luther, m. Eliza **GODFREY**, b. of Fairfield, Oct. 24,		
1836, by Nath[anie]l E. Cornwall	1-M	60
SALMON, Gershom, s. Reuben & Dorotha, b. Sept. 26, 1753	1	245
Reuben, m. Dorotha **FOOT**, Nov. 16, 1752	1	245
Reuben, s. Reuben & Dorotha, b. Aug. 17, 1756	1	245
SANFORD, SANDFORD, Abigail, d. Ephraim, b. May 10, 1735	1	71
Abigail, d. Sam[ue]ll & Sarah, b. Jan. 16, 1742/3	1	111
Abigail, d. Zachariah & Ann, b. Aug. 27, 1747; d. Dec. 1,		
1747	1	60
Ann, d. Jos[eph] & Catharine, b. Feb. 15, 1731/2	1	222
Ann, d. Zachariah & Ann, b. Feb. 6, 1739/40	1	60
Ann, d. Nehemiah & Elizabeth, b. Oct. 2, 1755	1	223
Anna, d. Lemuel & Rebecca, b. Oct. 19, 1736; d. Dec. 4,		
1743	1	112
Anna, d. Lemuel & Rebecca, b. Oct. 7, 1744	1	112
Anna, m. Gershom **MORHOUSE**, Jr., Jan. 18, 1749/50	1	86
Augustus, s. Eph[rai]m, b. July 12, 1753	1	71
Catharine, d. Nehemiah & Elizabeth, b. Oct. 31, 1759	1	223
Daniel, s. Sam[ue]ll & Sarah, b. Feb. 25, 1733/4	1	111
Dan[ie]ll, s. Sam[ue]ll, m. Esther **HULL**, d. John, Apr. 18,		
1758	1	261
David, s. Sam[ue]ll & Sarah, b. Nov. 16, 1739	1	111
Deborah, d. Eben[eze]r & Sarah, b. Aug. 25, 1754	1	252
Ebenezer, s. Tho[ma]s, of Fairfield, m. Sarah **CHAPMAN**,		
d. Robert, of East Haddam, Feb. 14, 1739/40	1	252
Eben[eze]r, s. Eben[eze]r & Sarah, b. Apr. 25, 1748	1	252
Eli, s. Dan[ie]ll & Esther, b. July 23, 1761	1	261
Elias, s. Seth & Rebeckah, b. Sept. 18, 1760	1	261
Elihu, Jr., of New Haven, m. Cornelia **TURNEY**, of		
Fairfield, Mar. 26, 1838, by Lyman H. Atwater	1-M	66
Elizabeth, d. Ezekiell, b. Sept. 6, 1679	LR-A2	681
Elizabeth, d. Ephraim, b. July 3, 1731	1	71
Elnathan, s. Jos[eph] & Catharine, b. Oct. 11, 1727	1	222
Ephraim, s. [Ezekiell], b. Feb. 12, 1708/9	LR-2	462
Ephraim, m. Elizabeth **MIX**, Oct. 7, 1730	1	71
Ephraim, s. Ephraim, b. May 25, 1750	1	71
Esther, d. Sam[ue]ll & Sarah, b. Apr. 9, 1749	1	111
Esther, d. Eben[eze]r, m. John **CROFOOT**, s. Dan[ie]ll,		
June 16, 1756	1	141

	Vol.	Page
SANFORD, SANDFORD (cont.)		
Eunice, d. Zachariah & Ann, b. Oct. 23, 1741	1	60
Eunice, d. Lemuel & Rebecca, b. Sept. 12, 1746	1	112
Ezekiell, m. Rebecca WICKLEE, Apr. 25, 1665	LR-A2	681
Ezekiell, s. Ezekiell, b. Mar. 6, 1668	LR-A2	681
Ezekiell, s. [Ezekiell], b July 27, 1704	LR-2	462
Ezekiel, s. Lemuel & Rebecca, b. June 30, 1742	1	112
Ezra, s. Sam[ue]ll & Sarah, b. Feb. 26, 1750/1	1	111
Gershom, s. Nehemiah & Elizabeth, b. Aug. 26, 1748	1	223
Hannah, d. Eph[raim], b. Mar. 3, 1737	1	71
Hannah, d. Eben[eze]r & Sarah, b. Feb. 25, 1744	1	252
Hannah, d. Eph[rai]m, m. David LYON, s. Nathan, Sept. 19, 1756	1	210
Hezekiah, s. Lemuel & Rebecca, b. Mar. 1, 1731	1	112
Huldah, d. Zachariah & Ann, b. Apr. 15, 1744	1	60
Huldah, d. Eph[rai]m, b. Apr. 25, 1748	1	71
James, s. Jos[eph] & Catharine, b. Dec. 14, 174[1]	1	222
Jared W., of Wellsborough, m. Henrietta STURGIS, of Fairfield, Sept. 6, 1829, by John H .Hunter	1-M	34
Jeremiah, s. Dan[ie]ll & Esther, b. Mar. 10, 1759	1	261
John, s. Ephraim, b. Apr. 26, 1739	1	71
John, of Greenwich, m. Susan E. HALL, of Fairfield, June 5, 1826, by Nath[anie]l Hewit	1-M	24
Joseph, m. Catharine FAIRCHILD, Feb. 11, 1724/5	1	222
Joseph, s. Jos[eph] & Catharine, b. June 20, 1736	1	222
Josiah, s. Eben[eze]r & Sarah, b. June 29, 1746	1	252
Lemuel, s. Ezekiell, b. Dec. 16, 1699	LR-2	462
Lemuel, m. Rebecca SQUIER, May 12, 1730	1	112
Lemuel, s. Lemuel & Rebecca, b. Apr. 18, 1740	1	112
Lipka, d. Nehemiah & Elizabeth, b. Aug. 30, 1750	1	223
Lois, d. Ephraim, b. Sept. 14, 1743	1	71
Lois, d. Ephraim, m. Joseph LYON, s. Nathan, May 21, 1761	1	255
Lydea, d. Lemuel & Rebecca, b. May 19, 1738	1	112
Lydea, m. Lazarus BEACH, s. John, June 20, 1756	1	63
Marthah, d. Ezekiell, b. June 29, 1677	LR-A2	681
Mary, d. Ezekiell, b. Apr. 3, 1670	LR-A2	681
Mary, d. Sam[ue]ll & Sarah, b. Feb. 16, 1737/8	1	111
Mary, d. Eben[eze]r & Sarah, b .July 25, 1750; d. same day	1	252
Mary, d. Eben[eze]r & Sarah, b. June 15, 1752	1	252
Mary, of Fairfield, m. David PLATT, of Weston, [Oct.] 7, [1822], by Rev. E. W. Hooker	1-M	8
Nathan, s. Jos[eph] & Catharine, b. Aug. 15, 1738	1	222
Nehemiah, s. Jos[eph] & Catharine, b. Jan. 10, 1725/6	1	222
Nehemiah, m. Elizabeth MOR[E]HOUSE, Mar. 5, 1747	1	223
Oliver, s. Ephraim, b. Sept. 17, 1741	1	71
Peter, s. Sam[ue]ll & Sarah, b. May 18, 1756	1	111
Phebe, d. Jos[eph] & Catharine, b. Nov. 11, 1729	1	222
Phebe, d .Nehemiah & Elizabeth, b. Aug. 20, 1752	1	223
Primus, m. Anna BULKLEY, b. of Fairfield (colored), Feb. 10, 1822, by Nath[anie]l Hewit	1-M	7
Rachel, d. Ephraim, b. July 23, 1733	1	71
Rachel, m. Stephen MEAD, Oct. 31, 1751	1	86

	Vol.	Page
SANFORD, SANDFORD (cont.)		
Rachel, d. Sam[ue]ll & Sarah, b. Feb. 2, 1753	1	111
Rebecca, d. Ezekiell, b. Dec. 13, 1672	LR-A2	681
Rebeckah, [d. Ezekiell], b. Nov. 21, 1710	LR-2	462
Rebecca, m. William **HILL**, Feb. 28, [1730]* *(Date crossed out)	1	199
Rebecca, d. Lemuel & Rebecca, b. Oct. 29, 1732	1	112
Rhoda, d. Zachariah & Ann, b. Feb. 28, 1742/3	1	60
Rhodoah, d. Lemuel & Rebecca, b. Feb. 20, 1749	1	112
Rhoda, d. Zachariah, m. Gershom **JENNINGS**, s. Dan[ie]ll, Nov. 18, 1762	1	265
Ruth, d. Zachariah & Ann, b. June 19, 1737	1	60
Samuell, [s. Ezekiell], b. Feb. 20, 1706/7	LR-2	462
Samuel, m. Sarah **MEAKER**, Jan. 11, 1732/3	1	111
Samuel, s. Sam[ue]ll & Sarah, b. Apr. 24, 1745	1	111
Sarah, d. Ezekiell, b. Mar. 25, 1666	LR-A2	681
Sarah, d. Lemuel & Rebecca, b. Sept. 11, 1734	1	112
Sarah, d. Eben[eze]r & Sarah, b. Mar. 1, 1741; d. May 18, 1741	1	252
Sarah, d. Eben[eze]r & Sarah, b. June 13, 1742	1	252
Sarah, d. Sam[ue]ll & Sarah, b. May 6, 1747	1	111
Sarah, m. Daniel **COLEY**, Apr. 16, 1754	1	119
Seth, s. Sam[ue]ll & Sarah, b. Aug. 18, 1735	1	111
Seth, s. Sam[ue]ll, m. Rebeckah **BURR**, d. Stephen, Apr. 18, 1759	1	261
Stephen, s. Jos[eph] & Catharine, b. July 16, 1743	1	222
Tabitha, d. Ephraim, b. Feb. 28, 1745/6	1	71
Thomas, s. Ezekiell, b. May 2, 1675	LR-A2	681
Timothy, s. Jos[eph] & Catharine, b. Feb. 8, 1733/4	1	222
Tom, s. Ezekiel, b. Mar. 27, 16[ ]	LR-B	C
Zachariah, s. [Ezekiell], b. Nov. 24, 1701	LR-2	462
Zachariah, m. Ann **HALL**, Oct. 7, 1736	1	60
Zachariah, s. Zachariah & Ann, b. Mar. 19, 1739; d. [Mar.] 20, [1739]	1	60
SAUNDERSON, Stephen P., of Norwalk, m. Mary E. **DOWN**, of Weston, Dec. 22, 1832, by T. F. Davis	1-M	48-9
SCOFIELD, Mercy, m. Thomas **BENNIT**, Oct. 14, 1741	1	123
SCOTT, Jesup W., of Chester, Ga., m. Susan **WAKEMAN**, of Fairfield, May 3, 1824, by Nath[anie]l Hewit	1-M	14
Ruth, m. Walter **MOREHOUSE**, Sept. 13, 1829, by Rev. Elisha Cushman	1-M	35-6
SCRIBNER, Hannah, m. John **GRAY**, Sept. 19, 1730	1	151
Rachel, m. Abraham **FAIRCHILD**, Nov. 7, 1742	1	179
Weight, d. Tho[ma]s, m. Nathan **DISBROW**, s. Tho[ma]s, Nov. 21, 1738	1	172
SCUDDER, Elizabeth, d. Isaac, of Norwalk, m. Job **BARTRAM**, s. Eben[eze]r,. Aug. 27, 1776	1	281
Rebeckah, d. Peter, of Huntington, L.I., m. Aaron **GOLD**, s. Onessimus, Jan. 27, 1761	1	102
SEEGAR, John, m. Grace **REDFIELD**, Apr. 15, 1713	LR-B	146
SEELEY, Abell, s. Nehemiah & Abigail, b. Oct. 16, 1755	1	91
Ephraim, s. Joseph, b. Sept. 9, 1684	LR-A2	680
Hannah, d. Nath[anie]ll, b. July 10, 1663	LR-A2	680

	Vol.	Page
SEELEY (cont.)		
Hannah, d. James, m. William **BENNIT**, s. Isaac, July 26, 1731	1	117
Harriet, of Fairfield, m. Titus **BRYAN**, of Washington, Feb. 10, 1836, by Rev. W[illia]m Denison	1-M	58
James, s. Nathaniell, b. Apr. 19, 1681	LR-A2	681
Mary Ann, m. Plumb B. **GREGORY**, Nov. 23, 1820, by Rev. Elijah Waterman	1-M	3
Nathaniell, s. Nathaniell, b. May 24, 1678	LR-A2	681
Nehemiah, Jr., s. Nehemiah, m. Abigail **GUYRE**, d. Luke, Apr. 12, 1755	1	91
Roswell, m. Polly **HUBBELL**, Sept. 12, 1821, by Rev. Daniel Wildman	1-M	6
Samuell, s. Joseph, b. Apr. 12, 1686	LR-A2	680
Sarah A., m. David A. **NORRIS**, b. of Fairfield, Dec. 12, 1847, by Rev. William Read	1-M	91
Seth, m. Charity **WILSON**, b. of Fairfield, Dec. [ ], 1836, [by Rev. Enoch E. Chase, of Stratfield]	1-M	61
SELLECK, Abigail, m. Ebenezer **SILLIMAN**, Oct. 8, 1728	1	66
SELLEMAN, [see under **SILLIMAN**]		
SEYMOUR, Giles, m. Rebecca B. **GUYER**, b. of Norwalk, Nov. 29, 1829, by Rev. Tho[ma]s F. Davis	1-M	37
SHARP, Eleanor, m. Almond **ALVORD**, b. of Greens Farms, Aug. 22, [1820], by Hezekiah Ripley, V.D.M.	1-M	1
SHAW, Sarah, m. George **CABLE**, Feb. 17, 1729	1	129
Sarah, m. Joseph Wakeman **SHERWOOD**, Nov. 18, 1838, by Lyman H. Atwater	1-M	67
SHELTON, Maria, d. Rev. Philo & Lucy, b. Jan. 4, 1787; m. Jeremiah **STURGIS**, s. Seth & Mary, Nov. 18, 1807, by Rev. Philo Shelton	1	300
SHEPHARD, Lewis B., of Danbury, m. Abigail H. **JENNINGS**, of Fairfield, Sept. 7, 1845, by Rev. James Scott, of Stratfield	1-M	82
SHERMAN, Charles Coley, of Eaton, m. Amelia **WAKEMAN**, of Greenfield, Dec. 31, 1851, by Rev. Martin Dudley, of Easton	1-M	93
Selleck, m. Mary **JELLEP**, of Southport, Nov. 26, 1837, by N. E. Cornwall, in Southport	1-M	63-4
SHERWOOD, Aaron, s. [Daniel & Abigail], b. Nov. 28, 1766	1	305
Aaron, Jr., m. Mary B. **ALVORD**, Nov. 28, 1833, by Thomas F. Davis	1-M	51
Aaron Moses, s. W[illia]m & Abigail, b. Aug. 25, 1812	1	305
Abby G., m. John H. **OGDEN**, b. of Fairfield, Dec. 31, 1826, by Rev. E. W. Hooker	1-M	25
Abel, s. David & Sarah, b. Dec. 20, 1720	1	224
Abel, s. Jos[eph] & Sarah, b. Dec. 14, 1750	1	213
Abigail, d. Sam[ue]ll & Jane, b. May 10, 1736	1	75
Abigail, w. Daniel, b. Dec. 13, 1736; d. Dec. 27, 1793	1	305
Abigail, m. Peter **LYON**, s. Nathan, May 10, 1753	1	151
Abigail, d. Jeremiah & Abigail, b. June 6, 1753	1	190
Abigail, d. David & Eunice, b. Apr. 19, 1754	1	231
Abigail, d. Samuel, m. Hezekiah **BRADLEY**, s. Samuel, Jan. 1, 1756	1	111

	Vol.	Page
SHERWOOD (cont.)		
Abigail, d. Daniel & Abigail, b. Apr. 21, 1760	1	305
Abigail, m. James **CHAPMAN**, Mar. 4, 1779	1	291
Abigail, [d. Ralph & Abigail], b. Mar. 16, 1806	1	299
Abigail, d. W[illia]m & Abigail, b. July 4, 1809	1	305
Abigail, m. Charles **JESUP**, b. of Greens Farms, [Sept.] 9, [1821], by Rev. E. W. Hooker	1-M	5
Abraham, s. [Daniel & Abigail], b. May 15, 1763	1	305
Abraham, s. [Daniel & Abigail], d. Oct. 18, 1799	1	305
Abraham, m. Mary **BENNETT**, [ ] 1, 1829, by Rev. Thomas F. Davis	1-M	37
Albert, s. William & Abigail, b. May 12, 1818	1	305
Andrew, s. David & Sarah, b. Oct. 10, 1716	1	224
Ann, d. Dan[ie]ll, m. Seth **MARWIN**, s. Sam[ue]ll, Feb. 13, 1755	1	191
Anna, of Greens Farms, m. Alva **FINCH**, of Norwalk, Feb. 25, 1829, by John Hunter	1-M	33
Benjamin, m. Ellenor **BRADLEY**, Feb. 9, 1723	1	192
Benjamin, s. Benj[amin] & Ellenor, b. Dec. 22, 1732	1	192
Benjamin, s. Benjamin, "will be six years old Mar. 1, next" *(Written between the dates 1696 and 1702)	LR-2	461
Betsey, [d. Ralph & Abigail], b. Nov. 18, 1790	1	299
Betsey, m. Gideon M. **JENNINGS**, b. of Fairfield, [Nov.] 9, [1823], by Rev. E. W. Hooker	1-M	13
Betty, d. Sam[ue]l, m. Joseph **HIDE**, s. John, Aug. 1, 1753	1	39
Caroline, m. Henry **KNAPP**, b. of Fairfield, Apr. 23, 1846, by Rev. N. E. Cornwall	1-M	84
Catharine, b. Aug. 11, 1790; m. Ebenezer **DIMON**, Jr., Aug. 19, 1810	1	301
Catharine, of Fairfield, m. Lyman **JOHNSON**, of Derby, Aug. 6, 1821, by William Belden	1-M	4
Charles, [s. Ralph & Abigail], b. June 18, 1796	1	299
Clarrissa, [d. Ralph & Abigail], b. Feb. 11, 1789	1	299
Cyrus, s. William & Abigail, b. Aug. 24, 1807	1	305
Cyrus, m. Sally **HULL**, Mar. 6, 1831, by Tho[ma]s F. Davis	1-M	42-3
Daniel, [Sr.], b. Nov. 20, 1735; d. [ ]	1	305
Daniel, s. Daniel, m. Abigail **ANDREWS**, d. John, Jan. 28, 1760	1	305
Daniel, s. Daniel & Abigail, b. June 8, 1761	1	305
Daniel, Jr., m. Susan **BURR**, b. of Fairfield, Apr. 24, 1825, by Rev. E. W. Hooker	1-M	18
David, m. Sarah **MEAKER**, d. John, Mar. 16, 1709	1	224
David, s. David & Sarah, b. Mar. 15, 1718; d. Mar. 16, 1722	1	224
David, s. David & Sarah, b. Oct. 1, 1723	1	224
David, s. Jos[eph] & Sarah, b. May 21, 1745	1	213
David, Jr., m. Eunice **CABLE**, Jan. 16, 1749/50	1	231
Edwin, s. William & Abigail, b. Feb. 24, 1805	1	305
Edwin, m. Mary August **HYDE**, Dec. 12, 1837, by Rev. Tho[ma]s F. Davis	1-M	65
Ellenor, d. Benj[ami]n & Ellenor, b. Aug. 16, 1740	1	192

	Vol.	Page
SHERWOOD (cont.)		
Eleanor, s.* [Daniel & Abigail], b. Apr. 16, 1775		
*(Probably a dau.)	1	305
Ellenor, [d. Ralph & Abigail], b. Nov. 24, 1808	1	299
Eleanor, m. James **BULKELEY**, Nov. 6, 1825, by Rev. H.		
R. Judah, of Bridgeport	1-M	28
Eleazer, s. Jos[eph] & Sarah, b. Oct. 18, 1733	1	213
Eliza, m. James **BEERS**, b. of Fairfield, July 11, 1842, by		
N. E. Cornwall	1-M	74
Eliza C., m. Abel S. **MOREHOUSE**, b. of Fairfield, Nov.		
2, 1843, by Rev. James Scott	1-M	76
Elizabeth, d. Sam[ue]ll & Jane, b. Feb. 14, 1732	1	75
Elizabeth, d. Jabez & Elizabeth, b. Feb. 10, 1750	1	229
Elizabeth, d. [Daniel & Abigail], b. July 24, 1770	1	305
Elizabeth, d. W[illia]m & Abigail, b. Mar. 15, 1821	1	305
Elizabeth, d. [Daniel & Abigail], d. Sept. 11, 1826	1	305
Emeline, Mrs. of Fairfield, m. Philo **WELLS**, of		
Vermillion, O., Oct. 1, 1851, by Rev. N. E. Cornwall	1-M	95
Eunice, of Greens Farms, m. Ephraim H. **BURR**, of		
Fairfield, May 18, 1823, by Rev. Nath[anie]l Hewit	1-M	11
Fanny, of Greenfield, m. Ard B. **JUDD**, of Ridgebury, Dec.		
25, 1832, by T. F. Davis	1-M	50
Frederick, m. Emily **BANKS**, b. of Greens Farms, Oct. 30,		
1839, by Rev. Lyman H. Atwater	1-M	69
Grace, s. Jos[eph] & Sarah, b. Oct. 20, 1731	1	213
Grissel, s. Jos[eph] & Sarah, b. Dec. 7, 1743	1	213
Hannah, d. David & Sarah, b. Mar. 4, 1728	1	224
Hannah, m. Joseph **COUCH**, May 7, 1747	1	72
Hannah, m. Josiah **WEBB**, Oct. [ ], 1750	1	232
Hannah, d. John, of Newtown, m. Peter **BULKLEY**, Feb.		
14, 1760	1	170
Henry, m. Hester **WAKEMAN**, b. of Fairfield, Feb. 17,		
1828, by Rev. E. W. Hooker	1-M	30
Huldah, d. Sam[ue]ll & Rachel, b. May 4, 1755	1	40
Jabez, s. David & Sarah, b. Apr. 8, 1714	1	224
Jabez, m. Elizabeth **FILLIO**, Oct. [ ], 1742	1	229
Jabez, s. Jabez & Elizabeth, b. July 4, 1744	1	229
James, s. David & Eunice, b. Mar. 16, 1756	1	231
Jane, d. Isaac, m. Thomas **DISBROW**, s. Thomas, Aug. 4,		
1741	1	146
Jehiel, s. Jos[eph] & Sarah, b. Mar. 1, 1739	1	213
Jeremiah, s. Sam[ue]ll & Jane, b. Feb. 23, 1726	1	75
Jeremiah, s. Sam[ue]ll, m. Abigail **STURGIS**, d. Peter, Feb.		
3, 1747	1	190
John, s. Benj[amin] & Ellenor, b. Sept. 27, 1730	1	192
John, s. Jabez & Elizabeth, b. Dec. 2, 1746	1	229
Joseph, [s. Benjamin], b. Nov. 21, 1702	LR-2	461
Joseph, s. David & Sarah, b. May 16, 1712	1	224
Joseph, m. Sarah **OSBORN**, Feb. 17, 1731	1	213
Joseph, s. Jos[eph] & Sarah, b. Dec. 31, 1735	1	213
Joseph Wakeman, m. Sarah **SHAW**, Nov. 18, 1838, by		
Lyman H. Atwater	1-M	67
Justus, s. [Daniel & Abigail], b. Aug. 13, 1768	1	305

	Vol.	Page
SHERWOOD (cont.)		
Mabel, d. Benj[ami]n & Ellinor, b. Jan. 6, 1745/6	1	192
Marietta, m. William **SHERWOOD**, 3rd, b. of Fairfield,		
Apr. 17, 1825, by Nath[anie]l Hewit	1-M	17
Marietta, d. Abel & Mary, m. William **SHERWOOD**, s.		
William & Abigail, Apr. 17, 1825	1-M	85
Marietta, d. Abel & Mary, m. William **SHERWOOD**, s.		
W[illia]m & Abigail, Apr. 17, 1825	1	306
Marietta, d. William & Marietta, b. Dec. 5, 1827	1-M	85
Marietta, d. W[illia]m & Marietta, b. Dec. 5, 1827	1	306
Marietta, w. William, d. Dec. 25, 1827	1-M	85
Marietta, w. W[illia]m, d. Dec. 25, 1827	1	306
Martha, d. Daniel, m. Eben[eze]r **PERRY**, s. Joseph, Dec.		
24, 1760	1	254
Mary, d. Benjamin, b. Jan. 8, 1692	LR-2	461
Mary, d. David & Sarah, b. Aug. 10, 1725	1	224
Mary, m. James **HOPKINS**, b. of Fairfield, Nov. [1837], by		
[Enoch E. Chase]	1-M	65
Mary Ann, m. Urban **LACY**, Feb. 15, 1835, by James H.		
Linsley	1-M	56
Mary Couch, d. William & Abigail, b. June 19, 1815	1	305
Matthew, s. Jabez & Elizabeth, b. Jan. 27, 1748	1	229
Mercy, m. Jeffrey **WAKEMAN**, b. of Fairfield, [June 28,		
1845], by Rev. Cha[rle]s R. Adams	1-M	82
Micajah, s. David & Eunice, b. May 3, 1758	1	231
Mindwell, [d. Benjamin], b. Sept. 8, 1696	LR-2	461
Moses, s. Jeremiah & Abigail, b. May 28, 1749	1	190
Moses, had negroes Ned, b. Aug. 13, 1784; Ezekiel, b. July		
15, 1786 & Massey, b. May 11, 1790	1	464
Nehemiah, s. Benj[amin] & Ellenor, b. Apr. 7, 1728; d. in		
his 9th year	1	192
Nehemiah, s. Benj[amin] & Ellenor, b. July 27, 1738; d. in		
his 5th year	1	192
Nehemiah, s. Benj[amin] & Ellenor, b. Oct. 5, 1747; d. in		
his 7th year	1	192
Noah, s. Benjamin, b. May 8, 1707	LR-2	461
Paulina, m. Burr **WHITEHOUSE**, b. of Greens Farms,		
Dec. 9, 1832, by Rev. H. A. Boardman	1-M	47
Phineas, s. Jabez & Elizabeth, b. Feb. 27, 1752	1	229
Rachel, d. John, m. Thomas **FAIRCHILD**, s. Alexander,		
June 17, 1753	1	238
Ralph, s. [Daniel & Abigail], b. Nov. 19, 1764	1	305
Ralph, m. Abigail **GORHAM**, d. Lockwood, Aug. 21,		
1788, by Rev. Hez[ekia]h Ripley, of Greens Farms	1	299
Ralph, [s. Ralph & Abigail], b. June 13, 1793	1	299
Rebecca, m. John **NICHOLS**, Dec. 1, 1737	1	76
Reuben, s. Jos[eph] & Sarah, b. May 29, 1753	1	213
Sally, d. Albert, decd., m. Robert **WILLSON**, May 29,		
1807	1	301
Samuel, m. Jane **BURR**, Mar. 8, 1722	1	75
Sam[ue]ll, s. Sam[ue]ll & Jane, b. Feb. 10, 1730	1	75
Sam[ue]ll, s. Sam[ue]ll, m. Rachel **HIDE**, d. John, June 6,		
1754	1	40

	Vol.	Page
SHERWOOD, (cont.)		
Sarah, d. David & Sarah, b. Jan. 8, 1710	1	224
Sarah, d. Sam[ue]ll & Jane, b. Dec. 30, 1722	1	75
Sarah, d. Benj[amin] & Ellenor, b. Feb. 16, 1725/6	1	192
Sarah, d. Benj[amin] & Ellenor, b. May 13, 1736	1	192
Sarah, m. Joseph **ROWLAND**, Nov. 3, 1741	1	225
Sarah, d. David & Eunice, b. Oct. 21, 1750	1	231
Sarah, d. Capt. John, m. Thaddeus **STAPLES**, s. Thomas, Apr. 24, 1753	1	55
Sarah, d. Benjamin, m. Ebenezer **BURR**, s. Timothy, Jan. 17, 1754	1	45
Sarah Esther, d. William & Esther, b. Dec. 14, 1833	1-M	85
Sarah Esther, d. W[illia]m & Esther, b. Dec. 14, 1833	1	306
Seth, s. Benj[ami]n & Ellenor, b. Dec. 6, 1742	1	192
Silas B., m. Ann C. **TAYLOR**, b. of Greens Farms, May 31, 1829, by John H. Hunter	1-M	34
Simon, s. William & Abigail, b. Mar. 7, 1801	1	305
Stephen, s. [Daniel & Abigail], b. Mar. 2, 1779	1	305
Walker, of Weston, m. Caroline **WILLSON**, of Fairfield, Dec. 21, 1820, by Nath[anie]l Hewit, V.D.M.	1-M	3
Walter, s. [Daniel & Abigail], b. Sept. 12, 1773	1	305
Walter, [s. Ralph & Abigail], b. Sept. 12, 1799	1	299
Walter, s. [Daniel & Abigail]. d. Oct. 20, 1799	1	305
Walter, m. Alathea **JENNINGS**, Sept. 19, 1824, by Hezekiah Ripley, V.D.M.	1-M	15
William, s. [Daniel & Abigail], b. Mar. 23, 1777	1	305
William, s. Daniel, m. Abigail **COUCH**, d. Simon, Jan. 5, 1800	1	305
William, s. William & Abigail, b. Mar. 5, 1803	1	305
William, 3rd, m. Marietta **SHERWOOD**, b. of Fairfield, Apr. 17, 1825, by Nath[anie]l Hewit	1-M	17
William, s. William & Abigail, m. Marietta **SHERWOOD**, d. Abel & Mary, Apr. 17, 1825	1-M	85
William, s. W[illia]m & Abigail, m. Marietta **SHERWOOD**, d. Abel & Mary, Apr. 17, 1825	1	306
William, s. William & Abigail, m. Esther **HILL**, d. Jabez & Sarah, Sept. 11, 1832	1-M	85
William, Jr., m. Esther **HILL**, b. of Fairfield, [Sept.] 11, [1832], by Rev. Charles Smith	1-M	45-6
William, s. W[illia]m & Abigail, m. Esther **HILL**, d. Jabez & Sarah, Sept. 11, 1832	1	306
William, Sr., d. Mar. 30, 1844	1	305
William Couch, s. William & Esther, b. Nov. 14, 1835	1-M	85
W[illia]m Couch, s. W[illia]m & Esther, b. Nov. 14, 1835	1	306
SHUTE, Sarah, m. William **HUBBELL**, b. of Bridgeport, [July] 13, [1845], by Rev. Cha[rle]s R. Adams	1-M	82
SILAWAY, Hannah, of Mauldon, Mass., m. Richard **HUBBELL**, of Fairfield, Oct. 12, 1692, by Major Nathan Gold	LR-2	459
SILLIMAN, SELLEMAN, SILLEMAN, SILLAMAN,		
Abigail, d. John, m. David **BURR**, s. Dan[ie]ll, Apr. 8, 1741	1	168
Abigail, d. Eben[eze]r & Abigail, b. Oct. 28, 1745	1	66

	Vol.	Page
SILLIMAN, SELLEMAN, SILLEMAN, SILLAMAN		
(cont.)		
Amelia, d. Eben[eze]r & Abigail, b. Oct. 30, 1736	1	66
Amelia, d. Ebenezer, m. Ebenezer **BURR**, s. Capt. John,		
Feb. 26, 1759	1	248
Ann, d. Nathaniel & Hannah, b. Aug. 29, 1730	1	15
Ann, m. Nath[anie]ll **ADAMS**, Oct. 3, 1739	1	76
Ann, d. Nath[anie]ll, m. Daniel **BURR**, s. Sam[ue]ll, Jan.		
22, 1756	1	133
Ann, w. William, d. Jan. 14, 1776	1	280
Benjamin, s. Gold Selleck & Mary, b. Aug. 8, 1779	1	61
Catharine, d. Dan[ie]ll & Sarah, b. July 15, 1754	1	167
Dan[ie]l, s. Robert & Ruth, b. Dec. 31, 1722	1	72
Daniel, s. Robert, m. Sarah **BURR**, d. John, Mar. 13,		
1746	1	167
Daniel, s. Dan[ie]ll & Sarah, b. June 14, 1752	1	167
David, s. Nathaniel & Hannah, b. Oct. 2, 1737	1	15
Deodate, s. Eben[eze]r & Abigail, b. Dec. 13, 1749	1	66
Ebenezer, m. Abigail **SELLECK**, Oct. 8, 1728	1	66
Ebenezer, s. Eben[eze]r & Abigail, b. June 21, 1734	1	66
Elizabeth, d. Nathaniel & Hannah, b. Feb. 1, 1725/6	1	15
Elizabeth, d. Nath[anie]ll, m. Joseph **MORHOUSE**, s.		
Stephen & Abigail, Mar. 26, 1747	1	97
Gold Selleck, s. Eben[eze]r & Abigail, b. May 7, 1732	1	66
Gold Selleck, s. Eben[eze]r, m. Martha **DAVENPORT**,		
Jan. 21, 1754	1	61
Gold Selleck, Col. of Fairfield, m. Mrs. Mary **NOYES**, of		
New Haven, May 24, 1775, at Stonington, by Rev.		
Joseph Fish, of Stonington	1	61
Gold Selleck, s. Gold Selleck & Mary, b. Oct. 26, 1777	1	61
Gold Selleck, d. July 21, 1790	1	61
Hannah, d. Nath[anie]l & Hannah, b. Apr. 18, 1724	1	15
Hannah, d. Nath[anie]l & Hannah, d. Feb. 18, 1726/7	1	15
Hannah, d. Nathaniel & Hannah, b. Jan. 23, 1744/5	1	15
Hannah, d. Capt. Nath[anie]l, m. Israel **BEBBENS**, s.		
Arter, of Windham, Nov. 9, 1769	1	34
Hezekiah, s. Eben[eze]r & Abigail, b. Mar. 11, 1738/9	1	66
Isaac, s. Dan[ie]ll & Sarah, b. Aug. 6, 1756	1	167
John, s. Robert & Ruth, b. Apr. 9, 1731	1	72
Jonathan, s. Ebenezer & Abigail, b. Aug. 31, 1742	1	66
Joseph, s. Nathaniel & Hannah, b. Dec. 19, 1732	1	15
Joseph, s. Capt. Nath[anie]ll, m. Christian **HUBBELL**,		
Oct. 14, 1762	1	253
Justus, Dea. of Weston, m. Mrs. Sally **WHITNEY**, of		
Fairfield, [Feb. 16, 1838], by Rev. Enoch E. Chase,		
in Stratfield	1-M	65
Marinda, m. Raymond **WHITNEY**, Jan. 4, 1835, by		
James H. Linsley	1-M	56
Martha, m. Nath[anie]ll **BURR**, Nov. 10, 1726	1	69
Martha, w. G. Selleck, d. Aug. 1, 1774	1	61
Mary, m. Samuell **GREGORY**, Dec. 28, 1699, by Rev.		
Charles Chaney	LR-2	461

	Vol.	Page
SILLIMAN, SELLEMAN, SILLEMAN, SILLAMAN		
(cont.)		
Mary, d. Dan[ie]ll, m. David **GODFREY**, s. Christopher,		
June 24, 1738	1	137
Mary, d. Capt. John, m. Nath[anie]ll **WILLSON**, Jr., s.		
Nath[anie]ll, Sept. 16, 1746	1	37
Mary, d. Dan[ie]ll & Sarah, b. Dec. 10, 1746	1	167
Mary, d. Jos[eph] & Christian, b. Oct. 31, 1768	1	253
Mary, had negro, Lewis, b. Sept. 10, 1781; Amos, b. June		
8, 1784; Cloe, b. Dec. 10, 1785; Job, b. Nov. 4,		
1787; Clary, b. July 11, 1789; Eli, b. Feb. 15, 1783;		
Annes, b. May 4, 1786; Rhoda, b. June 1, 1792;		
Levi, b. Jan. 28, 1794	1	462
Nath[anie]l, b. Aug. 10, 1696; m. Hannah **BOOTH**, May		
2, 1723	1	15
Nath[anie]ll, s. Jos[eph] & Christian, b. Aug. 11, 1763	1	253
Nathaniel, m. Deborah **STAPLES**, Jan. 3, 1822, by Rev.		
Daniel Wildman	1-M	6
Priscilla, d. G. Selleck & Martha, b. June 22, 1772; d.		
Nov. 23, 1773	1	61
Rhoda, d. Nathaniel & Hannah, b. Jan. 7, 1739/40	1	15
Rhoda, d. Jos[eph] & Christian, b. Oct. 10, 1770	1	253
Robert, m. Ruth **TREADWELL**, Oct. 20, 1715	1	72
Robert, s. Robert & Ruth, b. Sept. 26, 1716	1	72
Robert, m. 2nd w. Mary **MORHOUSE**, Dec. 14, 1756	1	72
Ruth, d. Nathaniel & Hannah, b. Aug. 1, 1735	1	15
Ruth, d. Dan[ie]ll & Sarah, b. Mar. 1, 1750	1	167
Ruth, w. Robert, d. Mar. 15, 1756	1	72
Ruth, d. Robert & Mary, b. Aug. 19, 1760	1	72
Sam[ue]l, s. Nath[anie]l & Hannah, b. June 1, 1728	1	15
Samuel, s. Nath[anie]ll, m. Elizabeth **BURR**, d.		
Sam[ue]ll, Jan. 21, 1756	1	181
Sam[ue]ll, s. Sam[ue]ll & Elizabeth, b. Aug. 4, 1757	1	181
Sarah, d. Robert & Ruth, b. Feb. 17, 1728/9	1	72
Sarah, m. Daniel **ANDREWS**, Feb. 8, 1741	1	104
Sarah, d. Dan[ie]ll & Sarah, b. Mar. 25, 1748	1	167
Sarah, m. Nath[anie]ll **WILLSON**, Feb. 15, 1750	1	37
Sarah, d. Jos[eph] & Christian, b. Dec. 22, 1766	1	253
Sarah Anna, m. Bradley **GOODSELL**, b. of Fairfield,		
Dec. 30, 1841, by Rev. Cyrus Silliman	1-M	73
Seth, s. Nathaniel & Hannah, b. Oct. 28, 1742	1	15
William, s. G. Selleck & Martha, b .July 22, 1756	1	61
William, s. Gold Selleck, m. Ann **ALLEN**, d. Dr. John,		
Sept. 22, 1774, by Rev. Andrew Eliot	1	280
SIMPSON, John, of New York, m. Matilda Jennings		
MEEKER, of Southport, May 25, 1845, by Rev.		
Samuel J. M. Merwin	1-M	82
SINGLETON, -----, m. Francis **RICE**, Apr. 6, 1850, by Rev.		
Lyman H. Atwater	1-M	92
SKINNER, John, of Brooklyn, N.Y., m. Catharine T. **PERRY**,		
of Fairfield, Dec. 16, 1844, by Rev. Lyman H.		
Atwater	1-M	78-80

	Vol.	Page

SILLIMAN, SELLEMAN, SILLEMAN, SILLAMAN
(cont.)

Mary S., of Fairfield, m. Samuel D. **MARSH**, of Ware,
Mass., Aug. 31, 1847, by Rev. Lyman H. Atwater — 1-M — 87

SLOP,* Deborah, Mrs. m. David **ROWLAND**, Dec. 1, 1745
*(**SLOSS**"?) — 1 — 26

Ellen,* m. Rev. Noah **HOBART**, Sept. 2, 1735
*("Ellen **SLOSS**"?) — 1 — 24

SLOSS,* Deborah, Mrs., m. David **ROWLAND**, Dec. 1, 1745
*(Arnold copy has "**SLOP**") — 1 — 26

Ellen,* m. Rev. Noah **HOBART**, Sept. 22, 1735
*(Arnold copy has "Ellen **SLOP**") — 1 — 24

SLUBUCK, Truman, of Princeton, N.J., m. Lucinda S.
JENNINGS, of Fairfield, Mar. 6, 1837, by Lyman
H. Atwater — 1-M — 62

SMEDLEY, Abigail, d. James & Jane, b. May 28, 1737 — 1 — 197

Abigail, d. James, m. Edmund **HUNT**, s. Thomas, Aug.
12, 1756 — 1 — 229

Boston, of Fairfield, m. Melinda **BERLIN**, of Patterson,
N.Y., (colored), Dec. 5, 1824, by Nath[anie]l Hewit — 1-M — 16

James, m. Jane **STURGIS**, Oct. 20. 1731 — 1 — 197

James, s. James & Jane, b. June 25, 1732; d. July 6, 1736 — 1 — 197

James, s. James & Jane, b. July 4, 1739; d. July 25, 1755 — 1 — 197

James, m. wid. Mary **DIMON**, Jan. 4, 1747/8 — 1 — 197

Jane, w. [James], d. Sept. 22, 1747 — 1 — 197

John, s. James & Jane, b. Nov. 11, 1734; d. June 10, 1786 — 1 — 197

Nathan, had negro Boston, s. York & Catharine, b. Apr.
18, 1790; Edward, s. York & Catharine, b. Aug. 9,
1794 — 1 — 290

Samuel, s. James & Mary, b. Mar. 5, 1753 — 1 — 197

Sam[ue]ll, s. Col. James, m. Esther **ROWLAND**, d.
David, Apr. 9, 1771 — 1 — 277

SMITH, Abigaill, d. Joseph, b. Sept. 18, 1679 — LR-A2 — 683

Abigaile, d. Samuel, b. Sept. 23, 1696 — LR-2 — 460

Abigaile, w. Sam[ue]ll, d. Mar. 6, 1698 — LR-2 — 460

Anna, d. Sam[ue]ll, m. Tho[ma]s **GOLD**, s. Hez[ekiah],
Feb. 13, 1755 — 1 — 198

Anthony, m. Fanny B. **JOHNSON**, b. of Fairfield
(colored), Nov. 24, 1846, by Rev. Samuel J. M.
Merwin — 1-M — 86

Benjamin, m. Sarah **GRAY**, Jan. 1, 1730 — 1 — 221

Benjamin, s. Benj[ami]n & Sarah, b. Apr. 20, 1747 — 1 — 221

Bette, d. Benj[ami]n & Sarah, b. Mar. 3, 1742 — 1 — 221

Chandler, of Danbury, m. Emily **PERRY**, of Southport,
Nov. 21, 1831, by Rev. John H. Hunter — 1-M — 42-3

David, s. Jos[eph] & Eunice, b. June 16, 1757 — 1 — 221

David, m. Phillis **BENNETT**, b. of Fairfield (colored),
June 29, [1823], by Rev. E. W. Hooker — 1-M — 11

David, of Greenfield, m. Elizabeth **ALLEN**, of Black
Rock, Nov. 30, 1846, by Rev. Lyman H. Atwater — 1-M — 86

Deborah, [d. Samuel]. b. Nov. 15, 1699 — LR-2 — 460

Deborah, [d. Samuel], d. June [ ], 1700 — LR-2 — 460

Deborah, [d. Samuel], b. Mar. 28, 1702 — LR-2 — 460

	Vol.	Page
SMITH (cont.)		
Deborah, m. John **SQUIER**, s. Samuel, Feb. 24, 1747; d.		
Aug. 9, 1748	1	272
Edmund B., of Norwalk, m. Julia B. **CRAFT**, of		
Fairfield, this day [Nov. 13, 1839], by Rev. Cyrus		
Silliman	1-M	69
Eleanor, d. Sam[ue]ll & Mary, b. May 17, 1745	1	237
Eleazer, s. John, b. Feb. 15, 1701	LR-2	462
Eleazer, s. Eleazer, m. Lucy **STURGIS**, d. Eleazer, Nov.		
14, 1752	1	218
Elizabeth, m. Joseph **DAVIS**, Jan. 11, 1733	1	214
Elizabeth, d. John, m. Jeremiah **JENNINGS**, Jr., s.		
Jeremiah, Dec. 8, 1762	1	129
Ephraim, s. Sam[ue]ll & Mary, b. Dec. 18, 1739	1	237
Esther P., of Greens Farms, m. Cornelius **SPINANET**, of		
New York State, [July] 21, [1822], by Rev. E. W.		
Hooker	1-M	8
Hanford, s. Nehemiah & Rebecca, b. Apr. 25, 1754	1	177
Hannah, d. Benj[ami]n & Sarah, b. Apr. 1, 1731	1	221
Henry, of Norwalk, m. Rhoda **ALLEN**, of Westport,		
Sept. 4, 1836, by Rev. Tho[ma]s F. Davis	1-M	59
Henry C., m. Julia **BURR**, b. of Fairfield, Jan. 16, 1842,		
by Rev. Lyman H. Atwater	1-M	75
Henry M., of Bridgeport, m. Mary H. **TURNEY**, of		
Fairfield, Jan. 1, 1845, by Rev. Lyman H. Atwater	1-M	78-80
Henry M., of Bridgeport, m. Emeline **TURNEY**, of		
Fairfield, Dec. 16, 1850, by Rev. Lyman H. Atwater	1-M	93
Joel, s. Nehemiah & Rebecca, b. Nov. 10, 1761	1	177
John, s. John, b. May 17, 1692	LR-A2	674
Joseph, s. Benj[ami]n & Sarah, b. Jan. 19, 1735	1	221
Joseph, s. Benj[ami]n, m. Eunice **WILLIAMS**, Oct. 19,		
1756	1	221
Lewis, m. Elizabeth **BROTHERTON**, b. of Fairfield,		
July 27, 1842, by Rev. Anson T. Beach	1-M	74
Margary, d. John, m. Timothy **PLATT**, s. Jonas, Aug.		
22, 1728	1	143
Martha, d. John, b. Mar. 16, 1694	LR-A2	674
Mary, m. Obediah **PLATT**, Aug. 10, 1722	1	109
Mary, wid., m. Thomas **MARWIN**, July [ ], 1742	1	217
Mary Eliza, of Fairfield, m. James **ROWLAND**, of New		
York City, Sept. 15, 1844, by Rev. Lyman H.		
Atwater	1-M	77
Merrett, d. June 13, 1762	1	29
Nehemiah, s. Eleazer, m. Rebecca **MEAKER**, d. Joseph,		
Oct. 8, 1747	1	177
Peter, s. Sam[ue]ll & Mary, b. Apr. 30, 1747	1	237
Philo, m. Julia Ann **BULKLEY**, Aug. 7, 1825, by Rev.		
H. R. Judah, of Bridgeport	1-M	28
Rachel, d. Benj[ami]n & Sarah, b. Mar. 23, 1738	1	221
Rebeckah, [d. Samuel], b. Mar. 2, 1704	LR-2	460
Reuben, s. Sam[ue]ll & Mary, b. July 24, 1750	1	237
Samuel, m. Abigail **LYON**, Jan. 9, 1696	LR-2	460
Samuel, m. Deborah **JACKSON**, Oct. 27, 1699	LR-2	460

	Vol.	Page
SMITH (cont.)		
Samuell, d. Dec. 19, 1711	LR-2	456
Samuel, s. John, m. Mary **WINTON**, d. John, Nov. 10, 1737	1	237
Samuel, s. Eleazer & Lucy, b. Apr. 14, 1756	1	218
Samuel, s. Sam[ue]ll & Mary, b. July 29, 1756	1	237
Sarah, [d. Samuel], b. Dec. 23, 1697	LR-2	460
Sarah, d. Sam[ue]ll, d. Mar. [ ], 1700	LR-2	460
Sarah, [d. Samuel], b. Jan. 2, 1706/7	LR-2	460
Sarah, d. Benj[ami]n & Sarah, b. Dec. 18, 1732	1	221
Sarah, d. Benj[ami]n, m. John **REDFIELD**, s. James, Oct. 20, 1757	1	255
Sarah, of Fairfield, m. William **FISHER**, of Nottingham, Eng., [Dec.] 8, [1844], by Rev. Cha[rle]s R. Adams	1-M	78-80
Thomas, m. Mary Ann **CARR**, b. of Fairfield, Oct. 10, 1847, by Rev. N. E. Cornwall	1-M	87
William, m. Harriet **NASH**, b. of Fairfield, Feb. 12, 1826, by Rev. E. W. Hooker	1-M	21
W[illia]m, m. Sarah Ann **BURR**, Dec. 10, 1826, by Nath[anie]l Hewit	1-M	25
SNAGG, William P., of Philadelphia, Pa., m. Phebe **FOOT**, of Norwalk, June 11, 1826, by Rev. E. W. Hooker	1-M	23
SNIFFING, Mary, m. Samuel **MILLS**, Oct. 13, 1833, by T. F. Davis	1-M	51
SNOW, Levi, m. Rebecca **MILLS**, b. of Fairfield, Nov. 27, 1836, by Nath[anie]l E. Cornwall	1-M	61
Rebecca, m. Henry **WILSON**, b. of Fairfield, Mar. 14, 1842, by Rev. Daniel C. Curtiss	1-M	73
SOULES, Jane, of Bridgeport, m. Nelson H. **JUDD**, of Fairfield, Aug. 10, [1846], by Rev. N. E. Cornwall	1-M	85
SPALDING, Abigail, d. Asa & Grace, b. May 9, 1772; d. Oct. 10, 1790	1	32
Alpheas, s. Asa & Grace, b. Aug. 31, 1756; d. same day	1	32
Asa, of Fairfield, s. Benj[ami]n & Deborah, of Plainfield, m. Mrs. Grace **ROWLAND**, d. Sam[ue]ll, of Fairfield, Sept. 4, 1755	1	32
David, s. Asa & Grace, b. July 24, 1768	1	32
Esther, d. Asa & Grace, b. Jan. 31, 1766	1	32
Grace, d. Asa & Grace, b. July 30, 1770	1	32
Pollythea, d. Asa & Grace, b. Jan. 30, 1764, at Greenwich; d. Feb. 18, 1774	1	32
Rowland, s. Asa & Grace, b. Nov. 19, 1762	1	32
Samuel, s. Asa & Grace, b. May 7, 1759; d. Nov. 29, 1778	1	32
SPEERS, Ann, m. Hugh **McRAA**, Feb. [ ], 1727	1	43
SPINANET, Cornelius, of New York, m. Esther P. **SMITH**, of Greens Farms, [July] 21, [1822], by Rev. E. W. Hooker	1-M	8
SPRAGE, Ann, d. Will[ia]m, b. Mar. 12, 1683	LR-A2	680
Humphrey, s. Will[ia]m, b. June 8, 1680	LR-A2	683
Humphrey, s. Will[ia]m, b. June 8, 1680	LR-A2	683
SQUIRE, SQUIER, Abigail, m. Samuel **ROWLAND**, Aug. 13, 1736	1	66

	Vol.	Page
SQUIRE, SQUIER (cont.)		
Abigail, d. Nath[anie]ll & Sarah, b. Oct. 5, 1741; d. Mar.		
5, following	1	226
Abigail, d. Nath[anie]ll & Sarah, b. May 14, 1743	1	226
Abigail, d. Dan[ie]ll & Abigail, b. Feb. 22, 1753	1	126
Abigail, d. Sam[ue]ll & Abigail, b. Feb. 26, 1755	1	63
Abigail, wid., m. Nathan **BEERS**, s. James, July 22, 1756	1	127
Andrew Eliot, s. Jos[eph] & Sarah, b. Aug. 13, 1779	1	282
Benjamin, s. John, m. Elizabeth **WHITHEAD**, d		
.Nath[anie]ll, Feb. 1, 1749	1	218
Benjamin, s. Benj[ami]n & Elizabeth, b. Sept. 21, 1757	1	218
Charity, of Greens Farms, m. Aaron **STURGIS**, of		
Greenfield, Apr. 3, 1826, by Nath[anie]ll Hewit	1-M	22
Charles, [s. Joseph & Sarah], b. Apr. 5, 1790	1	282
Daniel, s. Dan[ie]ll & Abigail, b. May 12, 1751	1	126
David, s. Sam[ue]ll & Abigail, b. Nov. 16, 1751	1	63
Deborah, w. John, d. Aug. 9, 1748	1	272
Deborah, d. John & Mary, b. Oct. 12, 1755	1	272
Ebenezer, s. Nath[anie]ll & Sarah, b. Dec. 6, 1726	1	226
Elizabeth, d. John, m. David **WINTON**, s. John, Nov. 16,		
1748	1	128
Elizabeth, [d. Joseph & Sarah], b. Feb. 15, 1786	1	282
Esther, d. Benj[ami]n & Elizabeth, b. Apr. 13, 1753	1	218
Eunice, d. George & Irena, b. Apr. 9, 1782	1	281
Francis, [child of Joseph & Sarah], b. Oct. 1, 1795	1	282
George, s. Sam[ue]ll & Abigail, b. Nov. 18, 1758	1	63
George, s. Sam[ue]ll, m. Irena **HAYES**, d. Abraham,		
Nov. 7, 1781	1	281
Grace, d. Benj[ami]n & Elizabeth, b. May 24, 1755	1	218
Hannah, d. Benj[ami]n & Elizabeth, b. Dec. 13, 1750	1	218
James, s. John & Lydea, b. Feb. 18, 1772	1	272
John, s. Samuel, m. Deborah **SMITH**, Feb. 24, 1747	1	272
John, s. Sam[ue]ll & Abigail, b. Apr. 12, 1750	1	63
John, m. Mary **HARPER**, d. John, of Marthas Vineyard,		
Aug. 22, 1754	1	272
John, s. John & Mary, b. Aug. 19, 1759	1	272
John, m. Lydea **JARVIS**, wid. of Isaac, of Norwalk, June		
10, 1762	1	272
Jonathan, s. Nath[anie]ll & Sarah, b. Oct. 6, 1739	1	226
Joseph, s. Capt. Joseph, of Fairfield, m. Sarah **ELIOT**, d.		
Rev. Andrew, D.D., of Boston, Oct. 5, 1778, by		
Rev. John Lathrop, of Boston	1	282
Joseph, [s. Joseph & Sarah], b. June 10, 1781	1	282
Lydeea, d. John & Lydia, b. Nov. 22, 1763; d. next day	1	272
Lydea, d. John & Lydia, b. June 30, 1769	1	272
Martha, d. Sergt. Thomas, of Woodbury, m. Jonathan		
MIDDLEBROOK, Jan. 31, 1712	LR-2	457
Mary, d. Nath[anie]ll & Sarah, b. Oct. 12, 1735	1	226
Mary, d. Dr. Sam[ue]ll, m. Joseph **BRADLEY**, Jr., Apr.		
11, 1747	1	57
Mary, d. Dan[ie]ll & Abigail, b. Sept. 22, 1748	1	126
Mary, m. Benjamin **DEAN**, Dec. 6, 1753	1	243
Mary, d. John & Mary, b. July 3, 1757	1	272

	Vol.	Page
SQUIRE, SQUIER (cont.)		
Mary, w. John, d. Feb. 7, 1761	1	272
Mary Ann, [d. Joseph & Sarah], b. Dec. 21, 1793	1	282
Mehetable, [d. Joseph & Sarah], b. Dec. 4, 1791	1	282
Nathan, s. Benj[ami]n & Elizabeth, b. Apr. 15, 1760	1	218
Nathaniel, m. Sarah **HIGGINS**, Jan. 20, 1723	1	226
Nathaniel, s. Nath[anie]ll & Sarah, b. July 16, 1724	1	226
Peter, s. John & Lydea, b. Aug. 19, 1765	1	272
Phineheas, s. Nath[anie]ll & Sarah, b. Aug. 12, 1737; d.		
Aug. 17, 1756	1	226
Rebecca, m. Lemuel **SANFORD**, May 12, 1730	1	112
Rebecca, d. Sam[ue]ll, m. Joseph **BARTRAM**, s.		
Ebenezer, Nov. 7, 1754	1	234
Sam[ue]ll, Capt., d. Nov. 6, 1711	LR-2	456
Samuel, Jr., s. Lieut. Sam[ue]ll, m. Abigail **MALTBIE**,		
d. Jonathan, Feb. 27, 1743	1	63
Sam[ue]ll, s. Sam[ue]ll & Abigail, b. Jan. 15, 1745/6	1	63
Samuel, [s. Joseph & Sarah], b. May 21, 1784	1	282
Sarah, d. Nath[anie]ll & Sarah, b. June 6, 1730; d. July		
31, 1730	1	226
Sarah, d. Nath[anie]ll & Sarah, b. Nov. 9, 1731	1	226
Sarah, d. Dan[ie]ll & Abigail, b. Jan. 23, 1747	1	126
Sarah, d. Sam[ue]ll & Abigail, b. Oct. 26, 1747	1	63
Sarah, m. Stephen **TURNEY**, Dec. 17, 1747	1	67
Sarah, [d. Joseph & Sarah], b. Oct. 11, 1782	1	282
Seley, s. Nath[anie]ll & Sarah, b. Oct. 6, 1728	1	226
Thaddeus, s. Nath[anie]ll & Sarah, b. Sept. 12, 1733	1	226
Thomas, s. Nath[anie]ll & Abigail, b. June 2, 1725	1	226
William, s. Sam[ue]ll & Abigail, b. Sept. 12, 1762	1	63
STALKER, John, m. Mary **MOREHOUSE**, d. Dan[ie]ll, July		
10, 1746	1	27
John, s. John & Mary, b. July 19, 1749	1	27
Peter, s. John & Mary, b. May 31, 1754	1	27
Seth, s. John & Mary, b. June 23, 1751	1	27
Thaddeus, s. John & Mary, b. May 15, 1747	1	27
STANLEY, Sarah, of Hartford, m. Andrew **BURR**, Aug. 6,		
1747	1	11
STANTON, George, m. Mary **JENNINGS**, Dec. 16, 1680	LR-A2	683
STAPLES, Abigail, d. Tho[ma]s & Deborah, b. Apr. 24, 1724	1	55
Deborah, m. Nathaniel **SILLIMAN**, Jan. 3, 1822,		
by Rev. Daniel Wildman	1-M	6
Horace, of Westport, m. Clary **COUCH**, of Greens		
Farms, Oct. 23, 1837, by Rev. Tho[ma]s F. Davis	1-M	63-4
John, s. Tho[ma]s & Deborah, b. Oct. 4, 1737	1	55
Maria, m. Albert **OSBORN**, b. of Fairfield, Dec. 24,		
1835, by Lyman H. Atwater	1-M	57
Mary, d. Tho[ma]s & Deborah, b. Oct. 7, 1742	1	55
Mehetable, m. George **BARLOW**, Apr. 1, 1722	1	175
Phebe, m. Isaac **JENNINGS**, Jr., June 1, 1731	1	14
Sam[ue]ll, s. Thaddeus & Sarah, b. Dec. 9, 1753	1	55
Sarah, m. Jesse **HUNT**, Mar. 22, 1753	1	60
Sarah, of Fairfield, m. Paul **McKAN**, of Ireland, Nov. 13,		
1824, by Nathaniel Hewit	1-M	15

	Vol.	Page
STAPLES (cont.)		
Thaddeus, s. Tho[ma]s & Deborah, b. Apr. 15, 1726	1	55
Thaddeus, s. Thomas, m. Sarah **SHERWOOD**, d. Capt. John, Apr. 24, 1753	1	55
Thomas, Sr., m. Deborah **ROWLAND**, May 24, 1723	1	55
STARR, Abigail, wid. Daniel, Jr. & Wakefield **DIBBLE**, of Danbury, m. Job **BARTRAM**, Nov. 7, 1774	1	25
STEBBINS, Sarah, m. Blackleach **JESSUP**, s. Edward, Feb. 23, 1757	1	194
STEENBOUGH, Caroline, d. J. B., of Fairfield, m. George **GORDON**, of New Haven, June 5, 1850, by Rev. Samuel Cooke	1-M	95
STERLING, Abigail, d. W[illia]m & Abigail, b. Mar. 20, 1718	1	183
Daniel, s. W[illia]m & Abigail, b. Aug. 20, 1732	1	183
Grace, d. W[illia]m & Abigail, b. July 20, 1736	1	183
Isaac, s. W[illia]m & Abigail, b. Feb. 1, 1734/5	1	183
Nath[anie]ll, s. W[illia]m & Abigail, b. Sept. 20, 1725; d. in the 21st y. of his age	1	183
Sally, m. Uriah **HUBBELL**, Nov. 24, 1829, by G. Pierce, Elder	1-M	38
Samuel, s. W[illia]m & Abigail, b. Apr. 20, 1721	1	183
William, m. Abigail **PATCHEN**, [ ], 1714	1	183
William, s. W[illia]m & Abigail, b. Oct. 10, 1716	1	183
STILSON, STILLSON, Levi, of Norwalk, m. Elizabeth **NASH**, of Fairfield, [Mar.] 7, [1824], by Rev. E. W. Hooker	1-M	14
Levi B., of Weston, m. Mary **BLAKEMAN**, of Fairfield, Dec. 25, 1835, by Rev. William Denison	1-M	58
STREET, Mary Ann, of Fairfield, residing in Southport, m. Benjamin **HADDON**, of New York, Nov. 16, 1836, by Nath[anie]ll E. Cornwall	1-M	61
STRONG, Charity, wid. Joseph & d. John **WELLS**, of Stratford, m. William **BURR**, May 16, 1744	1	44
STURGIS, Aaron, of Greenfield, m. Charity **SQUIER**, of Greens Farms, Apr. 3, 1826, by Nath[anie]l Hewit	1-M	22
Abby Jane, of Fairfield, m. Ebenezer **JUDD**, of Danbury, Apr. 23, 1846, by Rev. Lyman H. Atwater	1-M	84
Abigail, d. Jonathan, b. Sept. 9, 1702	LR-B	C
Abigail, [d. Christopher], b. July 10, 1708	LR-2	458
Abigail, d. Jonathan, m. Thaddeus **BURR**, s. Peter, Nov. 26, 1725	1	30
Abigail, d. Elnathan & Rebecca, b. Mar. 7, 1737	1	121
Abigail, d. Jer[emiah] & Ann, b. Nov. 29, 1743	1	206
Abigail, d. John, m. Zacheas **MORHOUSE**, s Gideon Dec. 24, 1744	1	75
Abigail, d. Peter, m. Jeremiah **SHERWOOD**, s. Sam[ue]ll, Feb. 3, 1747	1	190
Abigail, d. Benjamin & Rachel, b. Nov. 6, 1753	1	123
Abigail, d. Jabel & Thiah, b. Oct. [ ], 1757	1	239
Abigail D., m. Judson **STURGIS**, b. of Fairfield, Oct. 9, 1837, by Lyman H. Atwater	1-M	63-4
Amelia, of Fairfield, m. Austin A. **GUTHRIE**, of Putnam, O., Sept. 26, 1825, by Nathan[ie]l Hewit	1-M	19

	Vol.	Page
STURGIS (cont.)		
Andrew, s. Sam[ue]l & Ann, b. Nov. 12, 1741	1	7
Ann, d. Jer[emiah] & Ann, b. Feb. 3, 1737	1	206
Ann, d. Peter, m. Jabez **THORP**, s. Peter, Mar. 7, 1754	1	244
Ann, d. Gershom & Mary, b. Mar. 18, 1755	1	181
Benjamin, m. Sarah **ADAMS**, Feb. 9, 1715	1	120
Benjamin, s. Benjamin & Sarah, b. Dec. 17, 1726	1	120
Benjamin, s. Benjamin, m. Rachel **DARLING**, Dec. 10, 1746	1	123
Daniel, s. Peter, m. Mary **BEERS**, d. James, Nov. 5, 1741	1	145
Dan[ie]ll, s. Dan[ie]ll & Mary, b. Oct. 15, 1745	1	145
Daniel, Jr., s. John, m. Ruth **GUYRE**, d. Luke, Dec. 11, 1752	1	168
David, s. Jonathan, b. Jan. 7, 1695	LR-B	C
David, s. Eleazer & Abigail, b. Feb. 2, 1727	1	238
David, s. Sam[ue]l & Ann, b. Nov. 19, 1747	1	7
David, m. Elizabeth **DOWNS**, July 9, 1826, by William Shelton	1-M	24
David B., m. Susan **CHAPMAN**, b. of Fairfield, Jan. 20, 1830, by John H. Hunter	1-M	38
Dimon, s. Hezekiah & Abigail, b. Oct. 29, 1754	1	103
Ebenezer, s. Elnathan & Rebecca, b. May 14, 1739	1	121
Ebenezer, s. Hezekiah & Abigail, b. Aug. 8, 1752	1	103
Ebenezer, s. Elnathan, m. Thankfull **PERRY**, d. Nath[anie]ll, Dec. 17, 1761	1	264
Edward B., m. Caroline W. **GOULD**, b. of Fairfield, June 26, 1850, by Rev. Lyman H. Atwater	1-M	92
Helenor,* [d. Christopher], b. Oct. 19, 1704 *(Eleanor)	LR-2	458
Elliner, d. Christopher, m. Samuel **GRAY**, s. Henry, Oct. 24, 1734	1	147
Eleazer, m. Abigail **OSBORN**, Apr. 23, 1724	1	238
Eliphalet, s. Jer[emiah] & Ann, b. June 22, 1726	1	206
Elizabeth, d. John, m. Samuel **COUCH**, s. Sam[ue]ll, Sept. 13, 1726	1	156
Elizabeth, d. Solomon & Abigail, b. Nov. 10, 1735; d. [ ], in the 6th y. of her age	1	102
Elizabeth, d. David, decd., m. Samuel **STURGIS**, s. Peter, Nov. 1, 1737, by Rev. Daniel Chapman [b. of Fairfield]. Witnesses Simon Couch, Abigail Couch	1	7
Elizabeth, w. Samuel, d. Feb. 9, 1738/9	1	7
Elizabeth, d. Elnathan & Rebecca, b. Nov. 15, 1741; d. Feb. 3, 1748	1	121
Elizabeth, d. Elnathan & Rebecca, b. June 10, 1752; d. June 20, 1752	1	121
Elizabeth, d. Elnathan & Rebecca, b. Jan. 27, 1756; d. Mar. 13, following	1	121
Ellen, d. Peter, m. Thomas **HILL**, s. Capt. Thomas, Jan. 20, 1757	1	48
Elnathan, s. John, b. Jan. 20, 1710/11, m. Rebecca **TURNEY**, Mar. 14, 1733	1	121
Elnathan, s. Elanthan & Rebecca, b. Aug. 16, 1743	1	121
Esther, d. Jer[emiah] & Ann, b. May 29, 1722	1	206
Esther, d. Solomon & Abigail, b. Aug. 16, 1744	1	102

	Vol.	Page
STURGIS (cont.)		
Esther, d. Jeremiah, m. David **BARLOW**, Nov. 29, 1750	1	242
Esther, d. Solomon, m. William **DIMON**, s Eben[eze]r,		
Jan. 3, 1765	1	282
Eunice, d. Jonathan, b. Jan. 3, 1709	LR-B	C
Eunice, d. Solomon & Abigail, b. Feb. 18, 1731	1	102
Eunice, m. James **DENNIE**, Apr. 13, 1731, by Rev.		
Henry Caner	1	16
Eunice, d. Solomon, m. Sam[ue]ll **BURR**, Jr., s.		
Sam[ue]ll, May 31, 1753	1	21
Eunice, d. Eleazer, m. Gideon **MOR[E]HOUSE**, Sept.		
13, 1756	1	182
Eunice, d. Eleazer & Abigail, b. Aug. 16, [ ]	1	238
Gershom, s. Jer[emiah] & Ann, b. Sept. 8, 1730	1	206
Gershom, s. Jer[emiah], m. wid. Mary **MOR[E]HOUSE**,		
July 30, 1754	1	181
Gershom, d. Mar. 15, 1762	1	181
Hannah, d. Peter, m. Stephen **JENNINGS**, s. Joseph,		
Aug. 20, 1741	1	18
Hannah, d. John, m. Nathan **BENNET**, June 17, 1746	1	161
Hannah, d .Dan[ie]ll & Mary, b. Dec. 5, 1755	1	145
Harriet L., of Fairfield, m. W[illia]m **GOULDEN**, of		
Bridgeport, [Mar.] 26, [1846], by Rev. Cha[rle]s R.		
Adams	1-M	83
Henrietta, [d. Jeremiah & Maria], b. July 9, 1815	1	300
Henrietta, of Fairfield, m. Jared W. **SANFORD**, of		
Wellsborough, Sept. 6, 1829, by John H. Hunter	1-M	34
Henrietta, m. Henry **PERRY**, b. of Mill River, [Apr.] 20,		
[1831], by Rev. Charles Smith	1-M	39-40
Henry, s. [Jeremiah & Maria], b. Oct. 4, 1810	1	300
Henry A., m. Jane **OSBORN**, b. of Fairfield, Oct. 28,		
1834, by Rev. Amos Savage	1-M	54
Hezekiah, s. Solomon & Abigail, b. Nov. 23, 1725	1	102
Hezekiah, s. Solomon, m. Abigail **DIMON**, d. Ebenezer,		
Nov. 21, 1751	1	103
Hezekiah, s. Hezekiah & Abigail, b. Nov. 24, 1756	1	103
Isaac, s. Dan[ie]ll & Mary, b. Aug. 22, 1742	1	145
Isaac, s. Jabel & Thiah, b. Feb. 25, 1754	1	239
Jabel, s. Eleazer & Abigail, b. Feb. 26, 1729	1	238
Jabel, m. Thiah **DOWNS**, [ ], 1752	1	239
James, s. Dan[ie]ll & Mary, b. May 11, 1747	1	145
Jane, d. Solomon & Abigail, b. Apr. 26, 1729	1	102
Jane, m. James **SMEDLEY**, Oct. 20, 1731	1	197
Jane, d. Solomon, m. David **OGDEN**, Jr., s. David, Apr.		
5, 1750	1	98
Jane L., of Fairfield, m. Rufus **KEELER**, of New York,		
Oct. 10, 1826, by Nath[anie]l Hewit	1-M	23
Jeremiah, m. Ann **BARLOW**, Sept. 1, 1720	1	206
Jeremiah, s. Jer[emiah] & Ann, b. Mar. 14, 1721	1	206
Jeremiah, s. Seth & Mary, b. Apr. 30, 1779; m. Maria		
SHELTON, d. Rev. Philo & Lucy, Nov. 18, 1807,		
by Rev. Philo Shelton	1	300
Jerusha, d. Solomon & Abigail, b .Nov. 28, 1727	1	102

	Vol.	Page
STURGIS (cont.)		
Jerusha, d. Solomon, m. Peter HULL, s. Nath[anie]ll,		
[ ]	1	247
John, s. Sam[ue]l & Ann, b. Sept. 22, 1750; d. Sept. 26,		
1750	1	7
Jonathan, d. Nov. 29, 1711	LR-2	456
Jonathan, s. Sam[ue]l & Ann, b. Aug. 23, 1740	1	7
Jonathan, s. Capt. Sam[ue]ll, m. Deborah LEWIS, d.		
Lothrop, Oct. 26, 1760	1	253
Jonathan, made affidavit Nov. 15, 1790 before Sam[ue]ll		
Squier, J.P., Tom negro of Sam[ue]ll Sherwood, was		
s. of his negro Phyllys, b. about Feb. 1785, Lucy		
now with Capt. Hezekiah Wheeler's family and		
whom he had given Polly Sturgis, was d. Phyllys, b.		
about Apr. 1788; Jenne or Gin, d. Phillis, b. about		
Feb. 1, 1790	1	285
Jonathan, m. Laura WILSON, b. of Fairfield, Jan. 25,		
1847, by Rev. James Scott, of Stratfield	1-M	86
Joseph, s. Jer[emiah] & Ann, b. July 28, 1728	1	206
Joseph, s. Solomon & Abigail, b. June 25, 1739	1	102
Judson, s. Solomon & Abigail, b. Feb. 21, 1748	1	102
Judson, m. Abby Jane OGDEN, b. of Fairfield, Feb. 3,		
1828, by Rev. William Shelton	1-M	30
Judson, m. Abigail D. STURGIS, b. of Fairfield, Oct. 9,		
1837, by Lyman H. Atwater	1-M	63-4
Lucy, d. Eleazer & Abigail, b. Sept. [ ], 1734	1	238
Lucy, d. John, m. Jonathan COLEY, s. Peter, Dec. 6,		
1739	1	207
Lucy, d. Eleazer, m. Eleazer SMITH, s. Eleazer, Nov. 14,		
1752	1	218
Lydea, d. Jabel & Thiah, b. Nov. 24, 1756	1	239
Lydia A., m. Joseph J. ALLEN, b. of Fairfield, Jan. 20,		
1851, by Rev. W. W. Brewer	1-M	91
Marah, d. Christopher, b. Dec. 26, 1702	LR-2	458
Margary, m. Christopher GODFREY, Feb. 11, 1711	1	188
Mary, d. John, b. Aug. 8, 1699; m. Francis BRADLEY,		
Apr. 29, 1719	1	82
Mary, d. Sam[ue]l & Elizabeth, b. Jan. 19, 1738/9; d. Jan.		
24, 1738/9	1	7
Mary, d. Jer[emiah] & Ann, b. Feb. 12, 1739	1	206
Mary, d. Peter, m. Daniel PERRY, s. Joseph, Oct. 8,		
1740; d. Oct. 31, 1742	1	53
Mary, d. Sam[ue]l & Ann, b. Aug. [ ], 1743; d. Nov. [ ],		
1743	1	7
Mary, d. Dan[ie]ll & Mary, b. Sept. 13, 1751	1	145
Mary, d. John, m. Daniel MOR[E]HOUSE, s. David,		
Oct. 17, 1751	1	197
Mary Burr, m. Edward BENNETT, b. of Fairfield, Oct.		
18, 1820, by Nath[anie]ll Hewit, V.D.M.	1-M	3
Mary E., m. John B. ASH, b. of Fairfield, Apr. 13, 1851,		
by Rev. W. W. Brewer	1-M	91
Mercy, d. Eben[eze]r & Thankfull, b. Sept. 15, 1762	1	264
Moses, s. Dan[ie]ll & Mary, b. July 25, 1752	1	145

	Vol.	Page
STURGIS (cont.)		
Nathan, [s. Christopher], b. Aug. 29, 1710	LR-2	458
Nathan, s. Eleazer & Abigail, b .Jan. 2, 1744	1	238
Nathaniel, s. Elnathan & Rebecca, b. July 12, 1745; d. July 23, 1745	1	121
Nath[anie]ll, s. Elnathan & Rebecca, b. July 18, 1746; d. July 24, 1746	1	121
Nathaniel, s. Elnathan & Rebecca, b. Mar. 2, 1750	1	121
Nathaniel, s. Sam[ue]ll & Abigail, b. [ ]	1	262
Nehemiah, s. Elnathan & Rebecca, b. Aug. 23, 1753	1	121
Peter, s. Dan[ie]ll & Mary, b. Jan. 15, 1743	1	145
Peter B., m. Emeline E. **ATKINS**, b. of Fairfield, Mar. 24, 1844, by Rev. Anson F. Beach	1-M	76
Priscilla, m. Joel Burr **BULKLEY**, b. of Fairfield, Dec. 13, 1824, by Nath[anie]l Hewit	1-M	16
Rebecca, d. Elnathan & Rebecca, b. Sept. 15, 1747	1	121
Ruilla, of Fairfield, m. James Morgan **RUST**, of Poughkeepsie, N.Y., Mar. 9 [1823], by William Belden	1-M	10
Ruth, [w. Daniel, Jr.,], d. Sept. 29, 1755	1	168
Samuel, s. Elnathan & Rebecca, b. Feb. 9, 1734/5	1	121
Samuel, s. Peter, m. Elizabeth **STURGIS**, d. David, decd., b. of Fairfield, Nov. 1, 1737, by Rev. Daniel Chapman, Witnesses Simon Couch, Abigail Couch	1	7
Sam[ue]l, m. Ann **BURR**, d. And[re]w, Jan. 17, 1739/40	1	7
Sam[ue]l, s. Sam[ue]l & Ann, b. Mar. 17, 1744/5	1	7
Sam[ue]ll, s. Capt. Sam[ue]ll, m. wid. Abigail **HILL**, Jan. 9, 1771	1	262
Samuel, d. May 18, 1784	1	262
Samuel, s. Sam[ue]ll & Abigail, b. [ ]	1	262
Sarah, d. Jonathan, b. Dec. 22, 1701	LR-B	C
Sarah, [d. Christopher], b. Sept. 4, 1706	LR-2	458
Sarah, m. Andrew **BURR**, Apr. 30, 1719	LR-B	C
Sarah, d. Jonathan, m. Andrew **BURR**, s. John, Apr. 30, 1719	1	11
Sarah, d. Jer[emiah] & Ann, b. Jan. 8, 1724	1	206
Sarah, Mrs., m. Eben[eze]r **WAKEMAN**, b. of Fairfield, June 24, 1724, by Rob[er]t Tenny	LR-B	C
Sarah, d. Solomon & Abigail, b. Mar. 20, 1733	1	102
Sarah, d. Peter, m. Ebenezer **ANDREWS**, Jan. [ ], 1746	1	172
Sarah, d. Benjamin & Rachel, b. Mar. 20, 1748	1	123
Sarah, d. Solomon, m. Daniel **MORHOUSE**, s. Abraham, Apr. 15, 1755	1	65
Sarah, d. Gershom & Mary, b. June 19, 1760	1	181
Seth, s. Benj[ami]n, Jr., m. Mary **BURR**, d. Peter, Feb. 5, 1761	1	256
Solomon, m. Abigail **BRADLEY**, Mar. 3, 1725	1	102
Stephen, s. Jer[emiah] & Ann, b. Jan. 1, 1741	1	206
Thaddeus, s. Eleazer & Abigail, b. Dec. [ ], 1746	1	238
Thomas, s. Jer[emiah] & Ann, b. Mar. 1, 1735	1	206
William, s. Jer[emiah] & Ann, b. Mar. 8, 1733	1	206
SUMMERS, Miranda, of Fairfield, m. Sheldon **BEACH**, of Bridgeport, Apr. 26, 1837, by Lyman H. Atwater	1-M	62

	Vol.	Page
SUMMERS (cont.)		
Sarah, d. Zachariah & Martha (**BURR**), m. Gabriel		
BALDWIN, s. Jared & Damaris (**BOOTH**), May 2,		
1788, by Rev. James Johnson	1	280
TANTON, Angeline, of Weston, m. Alanson **WAKEMAN**, of		
Greenfield, Aug. 23, 1841, by Rev. Rodney G.		
Dennis	1-M	71
TAYLOR, Almyra, of Fairfield, m. Benjamin E. **HICKOCK**,		
of Danbury, May 11, 1825, by Rev. E. W. Hooker	1-M	18
Alpha, m. Sally Read **BENNETT**, b. of Greens Farms,		
Jan. 28, 1823, by Rev. E. W. Hooker	1-M	10
Ann C., m. Silas B. **SHERWOOD**, b. of Greens Farms,		
May 31, 1829, by John H. Hunter	1-M	34
Elizabeth, of Fairfield, m. George C. **HATHOUSE**, of		
Williamsburgh, L.I., Jan. 4, 1835, by Rev. C. A.		
Boardman, of Saugatuck	1-M	55
Hannah, d. John, of Norwalk, m. Gideon **HURLBERT**, s.		
Gideon, Nov. 14, 1751	1	203
Hezekiah C., m. Betsey **JENNINGS**, b. of Greens Farms,		
Aug. 29, 1824, by Rev. E. W. Hooker	1-M	15
James H., of Trumbull, m. Margaret A. **GOLDEN**, of		
Fairfield, Sept. 17, 1845, by Rev. Lyman H. Atwater	1-M	82
Paul L., of Norwalk, m. [ ] **CHAPMAN**, of Greens		
Farms, Apr. 3, 1827, by Rev. E. W. Hooker	1-M	26-7
William R., of Bridgeport, m. Julia Frances **MEEKER**,		
of Southport, Nov. 7, 1837, by Rev. Thomas F.		
Davis	1-M	65
THOMAS, Flora, of Huntington, m. Charles A. **WAKEMAN**,		
of Fairfield, Nov. 19, 1840, by Rev. Lyman H.		
Atwater	1-M	70
Reuben E., of Litchfield, m. Sarah **BANKS**, of		
Greenfield, Oct. 17, 1836, by Lyman H. Atwater	1-M	60
THOMPSON, TOMSON, Isaac, of Bridgeport, m. Mabel		
CASTLE, of Fairfield, Nov. 1, 1843, by Rev. A. F.		
Beach	1-M	75
Jerusha, d. David, m. Job **BARTRAM**, s. Eben[eze]r,		
Nov. 18, 1762	1	25
John, s. John, b. Feb. 21, 1686	LR-A2	678
John, of Huntington, m. Mary Ann **ZIMMAMAN**, of		
Fairfield, [Feb.] 11, [1828], by Cha[rle]s G. Lee	1-M	30
Martha, d. John, b. May 11, 1685	LR-A2	680
Martha, d. William, b. Sept. 3, 1688	LR-A2	678
Mary, d. William, b. Nov. 20, 1685	LR-A2	678
Sarah, d. John, b. Oct. 4, 1689	LR-A2	677
THORNE, James A., of Kentucky, m. Ann Tweed **ALLEN**, of		
Fairfield, Sept. 25, 1838, by Rev. Edward Allen	1-M	67
THORP, Aaron, s. Jabez & Ann, b. July 22, 1756	1	244
Abigail H., m. Solomon **GRAY**, July 3, 1820, by		
Hez[ekiah] Ripley, V.D.M.	1-M	1
Amanda, m. Aralzamon A. **WILLIAMS**, Mar. 6, 1831,		
by T. F. Davis	1-M	42-3
Betsey, m. David **CROSSMAN**, Oct. 3, 1822, by Rev.		
Aaron Hunt	1-M	8

	Vol.	Page
THORP (cont.)		
Ebenezer, s. John, m. Mary **JONES**, June 24, 1746	1	124
Eliphalet, s. David, m. Eunice **PERRY**, d. Sam[ue]ll,		
May 8, 1760	1	260
Emeline C., of Greenfield, m. William N. **MANSFIELD**,		
of Lyme,* Mass., Nov. 7, 1839, by Rev. Lyman H.		
Atwater *(Arnold says, "Lynn")	1-M	68
Emily C., of Fairfield, m. Samuel T. **ROWLAND**, of		
Weston, Nov. 17, 1852, by Z. B. Burr	1-M	95
Eunice, d. Nathan & Dorothy, b. Dec. 3, 1738	1	212
Grizzel, m. John **WILLIAMS**, Sept. 4, 1749	1	56
Grissel, d. Nathan & Dorothy, b. Apr. 18, 1756	1	212
Hannah, m. James **DAVIS**, July 16, 1729	1	152
Hannah, d. Nathan & Dorothy, b. July 29, 1739	1	212
Hannah, d. Peter, m. Elnathan **WILLIAMS**, s. David,		
Dec. 5, 1753	1	109
Hannah, d. Nathan, m. Daniel **BANKS**, s. Gershom, Dec.		
10, 1761	1	271
Hiram, m. Mary **MIDDLEBROOKS**, May 4, 1834, by		
Rev. David L. Ogden	1-M	53
Jabez, s. Peter, m. Ann **STURGIS**, d. Peter, Mar. 7, 1754	1	244
John, s. Eben[eze]r & Mary, b. Mar. 15, 1747	1	124
John, s. John, m. Mary **WHITLOCK**, wid. Joseph, Sept.		
[ ], 1760	1	186
John, s. John & Mary, b. Sept. 2, 1761	1	186
John, m. Harriet **MEEKER**, b. of Fairfield, Oct. 29,		
1826, by Rev. E. W. Hooker	1-M	24
Joshua J., m .Mary **CRAFT**, Aug. 21, 1826, by Marvin		
Richardson	1-M	23
Lois, m. Joseph **LYON**, Dec. 22, 1756	1	166
Lucretia, m. Jonathan **ROBERSON**, Apr. 12, 1752	1	230
Mana, of Fairfield, m. Hiram **JUDD**, of Danbury, Dec. 8,		
1841, by Rev. N. E. Cornwall	1-M	73
Mary, d. Eben[eze]r & Mary, b. Sept. 28, 1752	1	124
Mary, m. John **GOULD**, b. of Fairfield, Nov. 3, 1822, by		
Rev. Nath[anie]l Hewit	1-M	9
Mary B., of Fairfield, m. Francis L. **HEDENBERG**, of		
Newark, N. J., Mar. 26, 1826, by Rev. E. W. Hooker	1-M	22
Mary C., m. Maurice **WAKEMAN**, b. of Southport,		
[Oct.] 15, [1845], in Southport, by L. B. Burr	1-M	82
Molle, d. Eliph[ale]t & Eunice, b. Aug. 16, 1761	1	260
Nathan, s. John, m. Dorothy **OSBORN**, d. David, May 3,		
1738	1	212
Peter, s. Peter, m. Abigail **WARD**, d. Moses, Apr. 18,		
1754	1	150
Peter, s. Peter & Abigail, b. May 29, 1755	1	150
Sarah, d. Nathan & Dorothy, b. June 26, 1747	1	212
Sarah, d. Jabez & Ann, b. Jan. 10, 1755	1	244
Sarah, m. Joseph **OGDEN**, [Jan.] 12, [1823], by		
Hez[ekia]h Ripley, V.D.M.	1-M	9
THRACKMORTON, Jane, of Fairfield, m. Peter R. **ROACH**,		
of New York, Jan. 2, 1828, by Rev. William Shelton	1-M	29

	Vol.	Page
TILTON, Boaz, m. Anna **BATTERSON**, May 27, 1832, by T. F. Davis	1-M	44
TOBEY, Henry, s. Eben[eze]r, b. Dec. 14, 1669, at Seabrooke	LR-A2	664
TREADWELL, TREDWELL, Abiah, see Abiah **MITCHELL**	1	67
Abigail, m. Stephen **MORHOUSE**, Mar. 1, 1722	1	97
Anna, d. Timothy & Phebe, b. Aug. 3, 1755	1	122
Betsey Ann, m. Samuel **GODFREY**, b. of Fairfield, July 5, 1822, by Rev. Asa Bronson, of Stratfield	1-M	7
David, m. Mary **COGSHALL**, Nov. 4, 1756	1	115
Ephraim, s. Samuell, b. Mar. 7, 1691[?]	LR-A2	681
Flora, of Weston, m. Burr **BROUGHTON**, of Ridgefield, Apr. 25, 1832, by Tho[ma]s F. Davis	1-M	44
John, s. Samuell, b. Feb. 11, 1674	LR-A2	681
Junia M., of Weston, m. Abraham **HENDRICKSON**, of Bridgeport, this day [July 4, 1847], by Rev. James H. Perry, Southport	1-M	87
Louisa Ann, of Fairfield, m. James **ELLS**, of New Canaan, Nov. 29, 1832, by Rev. Stephen Martindale	1-M	47
Lucy, m. James **ODLE**, b. of Fairfield, Apr. 13, 1823, by Rev. Asa Bronson, at his house	1-M	10
Mary, m. Benjamin **BANKS**, Jr., Nov. [ ], 1729	1	236
Mary, d. Timothy & Phebe, b. Apr. 28, 1753	1	122
Ruth, d. Samuell, b. Jan. 20, 1679	LR-A2	681
Ruth, m. Robert **SILLIMAN**, Oct. 20, 1715	1	72
Ruth, m. Jabez **WAKEMAN**, June 1, 1727	1	78
Timothy, s. Benjamin, m. Phebe **FOOT**, d. John, Dec. 4, 1751	1	122
TREAT, David L., of Bridgeport, m. Eliza A. **WILCH**, of Stratford, June 5, 1844, by Rev. Anson F. Beach	1-M	77
TROWBRIDGE, Elizabeth, m. Benjamin **NICHOLS**, s. John, Oct. 13, 1730	1	145
TRUBY, TRUBEE, TRUBER, TREEBEE, Abigail, d. Ansel & Isabel, b. May 24, 1770	1	138
Alexander, s. Andris & Abigail, b. Oct. 27, 1748	1	28
Andrew, m. Sarah **TURNEY**, b. of Fairfield, Jan. 12, 1823, by Rev. Philo Shelton	1-M	10
Andris, m. Abigail **CRANE**, Sept. 14, 1744	1	28
Ansel, s. Andris & Abigail, b. May 13, 1747	1	28
Ansel, s. Andrew, m. Isabel **BEERS**, d. Joseph, Jr., Nov. [ ], 1769	1	138
Caroline, m. Rufus **KNAPP**, b. of Fairfield, Oct. 28, 1840, by Rev. Lyman H. Atwater	1-M	70
Comfort, s. Andris & Abigail, b. Nov. 9, 1754	1	28
David, s. Andris & Abigail, b. Dec. 22, 1750	1	28
Elizabeth, m. George **HOWELL**, of Brooklyn, N.Y., Apr. 10, 1837, by Lyman H. Atwater	1-M	62
Esther, d. Andris & Abigail, b. Feb. 23, 1857* *(Probably 1757)	1	28
Eunice, d. Andris & Abigail, b. July 11, 1740 [sic]	1	28
Getto, d. Andris & Abigail, b. Jan. 27, 1846*; d. Oct. 18, 1748 *(Probably intended for 1746)	1	28

	Vol.	Page
TRUBY, TRUBEE, TRUBER, TREEBEE (cont.)		
Harriet, m. William **KNAPP**, b. of Fairfield, July 11,		
1849,by Rev. Lyman H. Atwater	1-M	92
Jane A., of Fairfield, m. Zephaniah M. **MILLER**, of		
Bedford, Dec. 3, 1835, by Lyman H. Atwater	1-M	57
Sam[ue]ll Cohen, s. Andris & Abigail, b. Sept. 22, 1744		
[sic]	1	28
TUCKER, Hannah, d. Isaac & Mary, b. Aug. 20, 1768	1	119
Isaac, m. Mary **WAKEMAN**, d. Sam[ue]ll, Jr., [ ]	1	119
Mary, d. Isaac & Mary, b. Sept. 19, 1766	1	119
Sam[ue]ll **WAKEMAN**, s. Isaac & Mary, b. Nov. 27,		
1764	1	119
TURNEY, TUERNEY, Aaron, s. Stephen & Sarah, b. Apr. 7,		
1752; d. Aug. 1, 1753	1	67
Aaron, s. Stephen & Sarah, b. June 28, 1754	1	67
Aaron, m. wid., Ellen **CHAPMAN**, b. of Fairfield, Nov.		
9, 1829, by C. G. Lee	1-M	35-6
Abel, s. Stephen & Sarah, b. Sept 25, 1762	1	67
Abel, s. Stephen, m. Deborah **BULKLEY**, d. Isaac, Dec.		
26, 1784	1	287
Abigaile, d. Robert, b. Feb. 21, 1661	LR-A2	663
Abigail, d. Sam[ue]ll & Mary, b. June 9, 1754	1	256
Andrew, s. Abel & Deborah, b. Feb. 6, 1786	1	287
Ann, d. John **ODELL**, b. Mar. 6, 1688/9	LR-A2	677
Asa, s. Stephen & Sarah, b. Oct. 15, 1759	1	67
Benjamin, m. Rebecca **BEEBEE**, d. Ralph, Nov. 16,		
1671	LR-A2	683
Beniamin, s. Benjamin, b. Sept. 3, 1672	LR-A2	683
Benjamin, s. Tho[ma]s & Martha, b. Mar. 25, 1750	1	135
Beniamin, s. Robert, b. [ ]	LR-a2	683
Cornelia, of Fairfield, m. Elihu **SANFORD**, Jr., of New		
Haven, Mar. 26, 1838, by Lyman H. Atwater	1-M	66
David, s. Stephen & Sarah, b. Dec. 6, 1748	1	67
David, s. Stephen, m. Sarah **GOLD**, d. Daniel, Oct. 4,		
1766	1	130
Deborah Francis, of Fairfield, m. John **VAN**		
BUSHKIRK, of Haverstraw, N. Y., Sept. 23, 1839,		
by Rev. Lyman H. Atwater	1-M	68
Elijah, s. Stephen & Abiah, b. Nov. 30, 1773	1	67
Elizabeth, d. Robert, b. July 15, 1668	LR-A2	663
Elizabeth, d. Thomas, m. Peter **BULKLEY**, s. Peter, Jan.		
1, 1741	1	170
Elizabeth, d Stephen & Hester, b. Sept. 15, 1745; d. July		
31, 1746	1	67
Elizabeth, d. Tho[ma]s & Martha, b. July 10, 1748	1	135
Elizabeth, of Fairfield, m. George **BUSKIRK**, of New		
York City, Oct. 27, 1847, by Rev. Lyman H.		
Atwater	1-M	87
Ellen, [d. Abel & Deborah], b. May 28, 1789	1	287
Ellen, m. Johnson **HAYES**, b. of Fairfield, Oct. 4, 1835,		
by Nath[anie]ll E. Cornwall	1-M	58

	Vol.	Page
TURNEY, TUERNEY (cont.)		
Emeline, of Fairfield, m. Henry M. **SMITH**, of		
Bridgeport, Dec. 16, 1850, by Rev. Lyman H.		
Atwater	1-M	93
Esther, [d. Abel & Deborah], b. June 6, 1793	1	287
Eunice, d. Tho[ma]s & Martha, b .Jan. 19, 1752	1	135
Eunice, [d. Abel & Deborah], b. Mar. 28, 1805	1	287
Eunice, of Fairfield, m. Rufus **DeFOREST**, of New		
Canaan, Aug. 7, 1823, by Rev. Philo Shelton	1-M	12
Hannah, d. Tho[ma]s & Martha, b. Mar. 27, 1756	1	135
Hannah, [d. Abel & Deborah], b. Dec. 8, 1799	1	287
Hester, w. Stephen, d. Mar. 9, 1747	1	67
Isaac, s. John & Esther, b. Jan. [ ], 1743/4	1	65
Jemima, d. Tho[ma]s, m. Nehemiah **BARLOW**, s.		
George, Jan. 26, 1751	1	176
Jerusha, d. Robert, m. Joseph **BRADLEY**, Jr., Nov. 9,		
1732	1	57
Joel, s. Stephen & Abiah, b. Apr. 11, 1777	1	67
John, s. John **ODELL**, b. Nov. 5, 1690	LR-A2	677
John, s. Robert, m. Esther **GOLD**, d. Sam[ue]ll, Dec. 28,		
1742	1	65
John, s. David & Sarah, b. Oct. 20, 1767	1	130
Julia A., of Fairfield, m. Walter **BRADLEY**, of		
Newtown, Sept. 25, 1836, by Lyman H. Atwater	1-M	59
Levi, [s. Abel & Deborah], b. May 16, 1791	1	287
Martha, d. Robert, b. June 5, 1676	LR-A2	683
Mary, d. Robert & Ruth, b. Dec. 9, 1673	LR-A2	683
Mary, m. Nathaniel **BURR**, Jr., Nov. 23, 1732	1	68
Mary, [d. Abel & Deborah], b. Sept. 8, 1797	1	287
Mary, m. David **WAKEMAN**, b. of Fairfield, Nov. 28,		
1839, by Rev. Lyman H. Atwater	1-M	69
Mary H., of Fairfield, m. Henry M. **SMITH**, of		
Bridgeport, Jan. 1, 1845, by Rev. Lyman H. Atwater	1-M	78-80
Peter, s. Stephen & Sarah, b. Dec. 18, 1755	1	67
Rebecka, d. Robert, b. July 10, 1671	LR-A2	663
Rebecca, d. Beniamin, b. Oct. 16, 1676	LR-A2	683
Rebecca, w. Elnathan, b. Aug. 4, 1717; m. Elnathan		
STURGIS, s .John, Mar. 14, 1733	1	121
Robert, s. Beniamin, b. Mar. 6, 1673	LR-A2	683
Sam, [s. Abel & Deborah], b. Oct. 4, 1795	1	287
Samuel, s. Stephen & Sarah, b. June 24, 1750; d. Apr. 9,		
1751	1	67
Sam[ue]ll, s. Thomas, m. Mary **BAKER**, d. Benj[ami]n,		
Nov. 5, 1750	1	256
Sam[ue]ll, s. Sam[ue]ll & Mary, b. Oct. 26, 1759	1	256
Sarah, d. Robert, b. Sept. 27, 1663	LR-A2	663
Sarah, d. David & Sarah, b. Oct. 20, 1769	1	130
Sarah, m. Andrew **TREEBEE**, b. of Fairfield, Jan. 12,		
1823, by Rev. Philo Shelton	1-M	10
Sarah, w. Stephen, d. [ ]	1	67
Stephen, m. Hester **MIDDLEBROOK**, Nov. 5, 1744	1	67
Stephen, m. 2nd, w. Sarah **SQUIRE**, Dec. 17, 1747	1	67

	Vol.	Page
TURNEY, TUERNEY (cont.)		
Stephen, m. wid. Abiah **MITCHELL**, d. Josiah Tredwell,		
Feb. 9, 1773	1	67
Thomas, s. Beniamin, b. Jan. 5, 1678	LR-A2	683
Thomas, Jr., s. Tho[am]s, m. Martha **LYON**, d.		
Sam[ue]ll, Dec. 28, 1746	1	135
Thomas, s. Tho[ma]s & Martha, b. Mar. 2, 1754	1	135
William, [s. Abel & Deborah], b. Oct. 6, 1802	1	287
W[illia]m S., m. Thurza Maria **REED**, b. of Fairfield, Jan.		
31, 1841, by Rev. Lyman H. Atwater	1-M	71
TUTHILL, Henry, of Norwalk, m. Nancy **JOY**, of Fairfield,		
Oct. 11, 1829, by John H. Hunter	1-M	35-6
TWEEDY, Samuel S., of Bridgeport, m. Lucy A. **NORTON**,		
of Southbury, May 27, 1838, by Enoch E. Chase	1-M	66
TYLER, Susan, m. James **PICKENS**, b. of Fairfield, May 2,		
1848, by Rev. Lyman H. Atwater	1-M	89
VAN BUSKIRK, John, of Haverstraw, N.Y., m. Deborah		
Francis **TURNEY**, of Fairfield, Sept. 23, 1839, by		
Rev. Lyman H. Atwater	1-M	68
VANDERWOORT, John L., of New York City, m. Elizabeth		
H. **HOUGH**, of Fairfield, Oct. 1, 1839, by Rev.		
Lyman H. Atwater	1-M	68
WAKE, Martha, wid., d. June 5, 1710	LR-2	456
WAKEFIELD, Ruth, d. W[illia]m & Sarah, b. June 3, 1757	1	73
WAKELEY, WAKELEE, WICKLEE, Jane, of Fairfield, m.		
John **WILSON**, of Saugatuck, Mar. 18, 1833, by		
James H. Linsley	1-M	51
Philo, of Huntington, m. Sallema **BANKS**, Aug. 2,		
[1820], by Hezekiah Ripley, V.D.M.	1-M	1
Rebecca, m. Ezekiell **SANDFORD**, Apr. 25, 1665	LR-A2	681
WAKEMAN, Aaron, s. John & Esther, b. Mar. 7, 1764	1	120
Abel, s. Gershom & Elizabeth, b. Mar. 19, 1760	1	257
Abigail, d. Joseph & Abigail, b. Dec. 19, 1735	1	148
Abigail, d. John & Catharine, b. Sept. 22, 1741	1	147
Abigail, d. Joseph, m. John **GORHAM**, s. Joseph, Oct. 5,		
1754	1	227
Abigail, d. W[illia]m & Sarah, b. Oct. 4, 1755; d. Sept. 2,		
1786	1	73
Abigail, d. Gershom & Elizabeth, b. Mar. 10, 1758	1	257
Alanson, of Greenfield, m. Angeline **TANTON**, of		
Weston, Aug. 23, 1841, by Rev. Rodney G. Dennis	1-M	71
Amelia, of Greenfield, m. Charles Coley **SHERMAN**, of		
Easton, Dec. 31, 1851, by Rev. Martin Dudley,		
of Easton	1-M	93
Ann, d. Joseph & Abigail, b. Oct. 24, 1728	1	148
Ann, w. Eben[eze]r, d. July 31, 1749	1	19
Ann, d. Joseph, m. Isaac **GORHAM**, s. Joseph, July 25,		
1752	1	180
Asahel, m. Elizabeth **WAKEMAN**, b. of Greenfield, Apr.		
26, 1821, by Hezekiah Ripley, V.D.M.	1-M	4
Catharine, d. John & Catharine, b. Jan. 29, 1750/1	1	147
Charles, of Weston, m. Marilla **BANKS**, of Fairfield, Oct.		
24, 1821, by Nath[anie]l Hewit, V.D.M.	1-M	5

	Vol.	Page

WAKEMAN (cont.)

	Vol.	Page
Charles A., of Fairfield, m. Flora Thomas, of Huntington, Nov. 19, 1840, by Rev. Lyman H. Atwater	1-M	70
Cornelia, [d. Joseph & Esther], b. Oct. 8, 1817	1	303
Cornelia, of Southport, m. Samuel A. **CRAPO**, of New York, Oct. [ ], 1837, by Lyman H. Atwater	1-M	65
Dan[ie]ll, s. Stephen & Rebecca, b. Apr. 6, 1732	1	70
David, s. Stephen & Rebecca, b. Jan. 14, 1730	1	70
David, s. W[illia]m & Sarah, b. Apr. 5, 1766	1	73
David, m. Mary **TURNEY**, b. of Fairfield, Nov. 28, 1839, by Rev. Lyman H. Atwater	1-M	69
Ebenezer, m. Sarah **STURGIS**, June 24, 1724	LR-B	C
Eben[eze]r, m. Mrs. Sarah **STURGIS**, b. of Fairfield, June 24, 1724, by Rob[er]t Tenny	LR-B	C
Eben[eze]r, s. Eben[eze]r & Sarah, b. June 26, 1725	1	22
Ebenezer, s. John & Catharine, b. Jan. 20, 1731/2; d. June 20, [ ], aged about 1 1/2 year	1	147
Ebenezer, s. John & Catharine, b. July 20, 1737	1	147
Ebenezer, m. Ann **HILL**, Sept. 4, 1748, by Rev. Noah Hobart	1	19
Eben[eze]r, s. Eben[eze]r & Ann, b. July 20, 1749	1	19
Eben[eze]r, m. Sarah **HANFORD**, May 10, 1752	1	19
Eben[eze]r, s. John, m. Elizabeth **WEBB**, d. Josiah, May 3, 1764	1	259
Elenor, d. John & Catharine, b. Apr. 9, 1739	1	147
Elihu Diman, [s. Joseph & Esther], b. Sept. 27, 1814	1	303
Eliphalet, s. Moses & Molly, b. Mar. 16, 1749	1	153
Elizabeth, m. Sam[ue]ll **BURR**, June [ ], 1722	1	89
Elizabeth, d. Jabez & Ruth, b. Mar. 30, 1728	1	78
Elizabeth, d. Joseph & Abigail, b. Sept. 4, 1745	1	148
Elizabeth, d. Sam[ue]ll, m. John **LYON**, Jan. 23, 1745/6	1	204
Elizabeth, d. Moses & Molly, b. Mar. 17, 1751	1	153
Elizabeth, m. Asahel **WAKEMAN**, b. of Greenfield, Apr. 26, 1821, by Hezekiah Ripley, V.D.M.	1-M	4
Ellin, d. Feb. 12, 1710/11, in the 21st y. of her age	LR-2	461
Ellen, d. John & Esther, b. Jan. 30, 1762	1	120
Epaphras, s. Moses & Molly, b. May 9, 1746	1	153
Esther, d. John & Esther, b. Aug. 15, 1756	1	120
Eunice, d. Stephen & Rebecca, b. Jan. 31, 1735	1	70
Eunice, d. Jabez & Ruth, b. Oct. 2, 1746	1	78
Eunice, d. Stephen, m. Nathan **HILL**, s. John, July 3, 1753	1	52
Eunice, d. W[illia]m & Sarah, b. June 22, 1774	1	73
Frederic, of Fairfield, m. Emily **KAM**,* of Huntington, Nov. 30, 1841, by Rev. Lyman H. Atwater *(Perhaps "Kain"?)	1-M	73
George, of Fairfield, m. Ann **BURR**, of Easton, June 28, 1846, by Rev. E. C. Bull, at Southport	1-M	84
Gershom, s. John & Catharine, b. Nov. 8, 1731	1	147
Gershom, s. John, m. Elizabeth **DOWN**, d. David, Apr. 17, 1757	1	257
Gideon, s. Joseph & Abigail, b. Dec. 17, 1737	1	148
Hellen, d. Joseph & Abigail, b. Apr. 4, 1742	1	148

	Vol.	Page
WAKEMAN (cont.)		
Hester, m. Henry **SHERWOOD**, b. of Fairfield, Feb. 17, 1828, by Rev. E. W. Hooker	1-M	30
Hetty D., of Southport, m. Warren D. **GOOKIN**, of New York, Jan. 11, 1847, by Rev. Samuel J. M. Merwin	1-M	86
Hezekiah, s. W[illia]m & Sarah, b. June 19, 1768	1	73
Ira, s. W[illia]m & Sarah, b. Mar. 9, 1777	1	73
Jabez, m. Ruth **TREDWELL**, June 1, 1727	1	78
Jabez, s. Jabez & Ruth, b. Dec. 2, 1734; d. July [ ], 1738	1	78
Jabez, s. Jabez & Ruth, b. May 10, 1739	1	78
Jabez, s. W[illia]m & Sarah, b. May 10, 1761	1	73
James, s. Stephen & Rebecca, b. Mar. 19, 1743	1	70
Jane, d. John & Catherine, b. Jan. [ ], 1747/8; d. in infancy	1	147
Jeffrey, m. Mercy **SHERWOOD**, b. of Fairfield, [June 28, 1845], by Rev. Cha[rle]s R. Adams	1-M	82
Joel, s. Jabez & Ruth, b. May 17, 1752	1	78
John, d. Feb. 15, 1708/9	LR-2	456
John, m. Catharine **GILBERT**, Apr. 8, 1730	1	147
John, s. John & Catharine, b. Jan. 16, 1730/1	1	147
John, Jr., s. John, m. Esther **BRADLEY**, d. Francis, Oct. 3, 1754	1	120
John, s. John & Esther, b. Mar. 10, 1760	1	120
Joseph, s. Joseph, m. Abigail **ALLEN**, d. Gideon, Oct. 31, 1727	1	148
Joseph, s. Joseph & Abigail, b. Nov. 26, 1730; d. Jan. 1, following	1	148
Joseph, s. Joseph & Abigail, b. Dec. 4, 1733; d. Dec. 22, 1735	1	148
Joseph, s. Jabez & Ruth, b. Mar. 30, 1737; d. July [ ], 1738	1	78
Joseph, s. Joseph & Abigail, b. Feb. 25, 1739/40	1	148
Joseph, b. Feb. 12, 1771; m. Esther **DIMON**, May 29, 1796, by Rev. A. Eliot	1	303
Joseph, had negro Dinah, b. Aug. 25, 1790	1	293
Joseph Banks, [s. Joseph & Esther], b. June 17, 1806	1	303
Joseph H., m. Emma **JENNINGS**, b. of Fairfield, Mar. 6, 1815, by Rev. E. W. Hooker	1-M	16
Julia Francis, [d. Joseph & Esther], b. Sept. 23, 1811	1	303
Katherine, m. John **BURR**, Jr., Oct. 18, 1722	1	3
Levi, s. W[illia]m & Sarah, b. Mar. 13, 1764	1	73
Lyman, s. John & Esther, b. Jan. 26, 1755	1	120
Mabel, d. Jabez & Ruth, b. May 24, 1742	1	78
Mabel, d. Jabez, m. George **BURR**, s. Col. Andrew, Dec. 30, 1762	1	266
Martha, m. Nathan **HILL**, Aug. 26, 1765	1	52
Mary, d. Sam[ue]ll, Jr., m. Isaac **TUCKER**, [ ]	1	119
Mary, d. Joseph & Abigail, b. Jan. 5, 1731/2	1	148
Mary, d. Capt. Joseph, m. Will[ia]m **BURR**, s. Col. John, Aug. 4, 1736	1	44
Mary, d. Joseph, m. John **HAZARD**, Apr. 9, 1752	1	140
Mary, d. John & Esther, b. July 15, 1758	1	120

	Vol.	Page
WAKEMAN (cont.)		
Mary, of Greens Farms, m. William **BURR**, of Hudson,		
N.Y., Jan. 8, 1826, by Rev. E. W. Hooker	1-M	22
Mary H., of Fairfield, m. William F. **LOCKWOOD**, of		
Weston, Mar. 18, 1844, by Rev. E. O. Beers	1-M	76
Maurice, [s. Joseph & Esther], b. Sept. 15, 1801	1	303
Maurice, m. Mary C. **THORP**, b. of Southport, [Oct.] 15,		
[1845], by L. B. Burr, in Southport	1-M	82
Molly, d. Moses & Molly, b. July 12, 1753	1	153
Molly, w. Moses, d. July 16, 1757	1	153
Moses, s. Sam[ue]ll, m. Molly **GOODWELL**, d. John,		
Aug. 22, 1745	1	153
Noah, s. Stephen & Rebecca, b. Nov. 28, 1751	1	70
Pamelia, of Fairfield, m. Charles **COE**, of Monroe		
(colored), Nov. 27, 1828, by Chauncey G. Lee	1-M	32
Peter, d. Jabez & Ruth, b. Oct. 18, 1744	1	78
Sam[ue]ll, s. Moses & Molly, b. July 8, 1757; d. same day	1	153
Sarah, wid. of Samuell, m. Dugald **MACKENZIE**, Nov.		
18, 1696	LR-2	459
Sarah, d. Samuell, decd., b. May 13, 1691; d. Dec. 28,		
1710	LR-2	461
Sarah, Mrs., m. Lathrop **LEWISS**, July 26, 1727	1	22
Sarah, d. Stephen & Rebecca, b. Mar. 15, 1728; d. June		
11, 1728	1	70
Sarah, d. Jabez & Ruth, b. Apr. 15, 1732	1	78
Sarah, d. Stephen & Rebecca, b. Jan. 26, 1748	1	70
Sarah, m. Samuel **BRADLEY**, Jr., Sept. 10, 1751	1	110
Sarah, d. W[illia]m & Sarah, b. Jan. 24, 1754; d. Apr. 26,		
1779	1	73
Sarah, d. Moses & Molly, b. Apr. 12, 1755	1	153
Sarah, m. Gershom **HUBBEL**, Nov. 3, 1756	1	38
Sarah H., m. Alden **GOULD**, b. of Fairfield, Mar. 27,		
1831, by Hull Bradley, J.P.	1-M	41
Selina, d. W[illia]m & Sarah, b. June 8, 1771	1	73
Seth, s. John & Catharine, b. Jan. 22, 1743/4	1	147
Seth, s. Joseph & Abigail, b. Mar. 3, 1744; d. Oct. 5, 1744	1	148
Stephen, m. Rebecca **MORHOUSE**, Apr. 28, 1727	1	70
Stephen, s. Stephen & Rebecca, b. Nov. 19, 1740; d. May		
7, 1744	1	70
Stephen, s. Stephen & Rebecca, b. Oct. 23, 1745	1	70
Stephen B., m. Betsey **COUCH**, Mar. 8, 1835, by T. F.		
Davis	1-M	56
Squire, s. Stephen & Rebecca, b. June 29, 1738	1	70
Susan, [d. Joseph & Esther], b. Mar. 7, 1797	1	303
Susan, of Fairfield, m. Jesup W. **SCOTT**, of Chester, Ga.,		
May 3, 1824, by Nath[anie]l Hewit	1-M	14
Talcott B., m. Abigail H. **COLEY**, Dec. 17, 1838, by		
Rev. Tho[ma]s F. Davis	1-M	67
Thaddeus, s. John & Catharine, b. Sept. 19, 1745	1	147
Thomas Hanford, s. Eben[eze]r & Sarah, b. Sept. 25,		
1755	1	19
Timothy, s. Jabez & Ruth, b. Dec. 2, 1749	1	78
William, s. Jabez & Ruth, b. Apr. 1, 1730	1	78

	Vol.	Page
WAKEMAN (cont.)		
William, s. Jabez, m. Sarah **HILL**, d. Joseph, June 21, 1753	1	73
William, s. W[illia]m & Sarah, b. Apr. 29, 1759	1	73
William Webb, [s. Joseph & Esther]b. June 19, 1799	1	303
Zalmon, m. Susan **NICHOLS**, b. of Fairfield, May 1, 1839, by N. E. Cornwall	1-M	67
Zalmon B., m. Sarah A. **FOWLER**, b. of Fairfield, Mar. 3, 1829, by John Hunter	1-M	33
Zalmon Bradley, [s. Joseph & Esther], b. Nov. 2, 1803	1	303
WANZER, Joseph, m. Caroline **BAKER**, [June] 19, [1831], by Rev. Ch[arles] Smith	1-M	41
WARD, Abigail, d. Moses, m. Peter **THORP**, s. Peter, Apr. 18, 1754	1	150
Benjamin W., of Weston, m. Susan **BLAKEMAN**, of Fairfield, Jan. [ ], 1837, by Rev. Enoch E. Chase, of Stratfield	1-M	61
Esther,* dau of William, m. Eliphalet **HILL**, Nov. [ ], 1691 *(Esther Nicholls)	LR-A2	676
WASSON, Sophia, of Fairfield, m. Rev. Andrew Elliot, of New Milford, Sept. 17, 1820, by Nath[anie]l Hewit, V.D.M.	1-M	2
WATERBURY, Abigail, d. Capt. David, of Stanford, m. Hezekiah Gray, s. Sam[ue]ll, Apr. 24, 1760	1	257
WATERMAN, Stephen, of Hillsdale, N.Y., m. Abigail H. **OGDEN**, of Fairfield, Jan. 29, [1823], by Hez[ekia]h Ripley, V.D.M.	1-M	9
WATSON, George Augustus, s. John & Elizabeth, b. May 24, 1794	1	289
James, s. John & Elizabeth, b. Apr. 1, 1784	1	289
John, s. Robert, of Norwalk, m. Elizabeth **BARTRAM**, d. Joseph, of Fairfield, Apr. 18, 1779	1	289
John, had negro Candace, b. June 8, 1791	1	289
John Jackson, s. John & Elizabeth, b. Dec. 27, 1782	1	289
Joseph Bartram, s. John & Elizabeth, b. Sept. 10, 1781	1	289
Robert, s. John & Elizabeth, b. Oct. 10, 1791	1	289
Sophia, d. John & Elizabeth, b. June 28, 1790	1	289
WEBB, Abigail, d. Rev. Joseph, b. Mar. 23, 1704/5	LR-2	462
Abigail, d. Josiah & Susannah, b. June 6, 1747	1	232
Disbrow, s. Josiah & Susannah, b. June 3, 1738	1	232
Elizabeth, d. Rev. Joseph & Elizabeth, b. Feb. 14, 1696/7	LR-2	462
Elizabeth, d. Josiah & Susannah, b. Apr. 28, 1745	1	232
Elizabeth, d. Josiah, m. Eben[eze]r **WAKEMAN**, s. John, May 3, 1764	1	259
Elnathan J., of Stratford, m. Eliza **KNAP**, of Fairfield, Dec. 5, 1825, by Rev. Nath[anie]l Hewit	1-M	20
Epenetus J., of Norwalk, m. Rhoda **DISBROW**, of Fairfield, Nov. 30, 1823, by Hezekiah Ripley, V.D.M.	1-M	13
Grace, d. Rev. Joseph, b. Dec. 3, 1700	LR-2	462
Grace, d. Josiah & Susannah, b. Mar. 7, 1733/4	1	232
Hezekiah, s. Josiah & Hannah, b. Nov. 18, 1752	1	232
Isaac, s. Josiah & Susannah, b. Aug. 23, 1750	1	232

	Vol.	Page
WEBB (cont.)		
Joseph, Rev., m. Mrs. Elizabeth **RUSSELL**, Jan. 8, 1691,		
at Stratford, by Rev. William Corliss	LR-2	462
Jos[eph], s. Rev. Jos., b. Sept. 21, 1693	LR-B	C
Joseph, s. Rev. Joseph & Elizabeth, b. Sept. 21, 1693	LR-2	462
Joseph, s. Josiah & Susannah, b. Mar. 17, 1736	1	232
Josiah, s. Joseph, b. Mar. 15, 1706/7	LR-2	462
Josiah, m. Susannah **DISBROW**, d. Tho[ma]s, Nov. [ ],		
1729	1	232
Josiah, s. Josiah & Susannah, b. Apr. 16, 1743	1	232
Josiah, m. Hannah **SHERWOOD**, Oct. [ ], 1750	1	232
Mary, d. Rev. Joseph & Elizabeth, b. Mar. 15, 1698/9	LR-2	462
Nehemiah, s. Rev. Joseph & Elizabeth, b. Feb. 26, 1694/5	LR-2	462
Nehemiah, s. Josiah & Susannah, b. Sept. 23, 1740	1	232
Sarah, d. Rev. Joseph, b. Jan. 30/ 1702/3	LR-2	462
Seth, s. Josiah & Hannah, b. [ ], 1755	1	232
Susannah, w. Josiah, d. [ ], 1748	1	83
WELLS, Charity, see Charity **STRONG**	1	44
Eunice, d. Gideon & Catharine, b. Dec. 4, 1754	1	35
Gideon, m. Catharine **WYNKOOP**, d. Benj[ami]n, May		
1, 1754	1	35
Harriet E., of Black Rock, m. Cornelius **BENEDICT**, of		
Bridgeport, [Dec.] 14, [1845], by Rev. Cha[rle]s R.		
Adams	1-M	83
Philo, of Vermillion, O., m. Mrs. Emeline **SHERWOOD**,		
of Fairfield, Oct. 1, 1851, by Rev. N. E. Cornwall	1-M	95
WETMORE, [see also **WHETTEMORE**], Alethea, Mrs., m.		
Joseph **LAMSON**, July 26, 1747	1	85
Sarah, of Bridgeport, m. Richard **RAND**, of Middletown,		
Oct. 17, 1824, by Rev. Nath[anie]l Hewit	1-M	15
WHALEY, Ruth, m. John S. **WILLIAMS**, July 17, 1842, by		
Rev. Samuel Nichols, of Greenfield Hill	1-M	83
WHEDDON, Elizabeth, d. Richard, b. Sept. 19, 1688	LR-A2	677
Elizabeth, m. Joseph **BENNIT**, b. of Fairfield, Jan. 22,		
1708	LR-2	459
Elizabeth, of Fairfield, m. Joseph **BENNIT**, of Stratfield,		
Jan. 22, 1705/6, by Rev. Joseph Webb	LR-2	460
Elizabeth, d. Richard & Sarah, late of Fairfield, m. Joseph		
BENNIT, of Stratfield, Jan. 22, 1705/6, by Rev.		
Joseph Webb	LR-2	460
Richard, m. Sarah **HILL**, Apr. 15, 1686	LR-A2	677
Richard, d. Oct. 24, 1690	LR-A2	677
Sarah, d. Richard, b. Dec. 29, 1689	LR-A2	677
Sarah, wid. Richard, d. Mar. 28, 1697	LR-2	463
WHEELER, Abel, s. Jonathan, m. Rebeckah **WHITEAR**, d.		
John, Mar. 27, 1758	1	250
Abel, d. Mar. 26, 1772	1	250
Abigail, d. John & Abigail, b. Aug. 16, 1698	1	8
Abigail, d. John & Abigail, b. Apr. 3, 1703	1	8
Abigail, d. Feb. 7, 1712	LR-2	456
Abigail, w. John, d. Feb. 7, 1711/12	1	8
Abigail, m. Samuel **MARWIN**, s. Thomas, July 5, 1722	1	191
Ann, d. John & Abigail, b. Jan. 16, 1706	1	8

	Vol.	Page
WHEELER (cont.)		
Ann, d. Timothy & Abigail, b. Jan. 30, 1749	1	51
Anne, d. Benj[ami]n & Mary, b. Feb. 1, 1767*		
*(Probably 1757)	1	276
Anne, m. Peter **MEAKER**, s. Ebenezer, Nov. 1, 1785	1	284
Anson, m. Amelia **BANKS**, Feb. 4, 1821, by Rev.		
William Belden, of Greenfield	1-M	2
Benjamin, s. Timothy, m. Mary **MIDDLEBROOK**, d.		
John, Apr. 20, 1749, by Rev. James Beebee, of		
North Stratford	1	276
Catharine, d. Joseph & Deborah, b. Nov. 7, 1712	1	4
Catharine, d. Joseph, m. Jonathan **OSBORN**, s. Capt.		
John, Sept. [ ], 1733	1	46
Dan, s. John & Lide, b. July 15, 1718	1	8
Daniel Burr, s. Nathan & Abigail, b. Sept. 16, 1778; d.		
Dec. 31, 1782	1	285
Daniel Burrit, s. Timothy & Abigail, b. Nov. 25, 1754	1	51
David, m. Esther **NICKOLS**, Mar. 20, 1716/17	1	4
David, s. David & Esther, b. Apr. 6, 1726	1	4
Deborah, d. Joseph & Abigail, b. Jan. 14, 1730	1	20
Deborah, m. Ignatius **NICHOLS**, Mar. 27, 1755	1	87
Edward, of New York City, m. Lucinda **LOCKWOOD**,		
of Westport, Sept. 28, 1840, by Rev. Lyman H.		
Atwater	1-M	70
Eliphalet, s. Jos. & Abigail, b. June 3, 1749	1	20
Elizabeth, m. John **DIMON**, May 10, 1727	1	80
Ephraim, s. Joseph & Deborah, b. Mar. 10, 1735 [sic]	1	4
Ephraim, s. Timothy & Abigail, b. Feb. 7, 1747	1	51
Esther, d. Joseph & Deborah, b. Aug. 1, 1710; d. Apr. [ ],		
1732	1	4
Eunice, d. David & Esther, b. Dec. 24, 1737 [sic]	1	4
Hannah, Mrs., m John **WHEELER**, physician, Aug. 24,		
1708, by Nathan Gold, Dept. Gov.	LR-2	460
Hezekiah, s. Jos. & Abigail, b. July 15, 1744	1	20
Hezekiah, m. Abigail **FRENCH**, Dec. 19, 1754	1	51
Huldah, d. Abel & Rebeckah, b .June 21, 1760	1	250
Ichabod, s. John & Lide, b. Jan. 11, 1725	1	8
Ichabod, s. Jos. & Abigail, b. May 11, 1746	1	20
Ichabod, s. John, m. Deborah **BURR**, d. Capt. John, Jan.		
1, 1757	1	118
Isaac, s. Jabez & Charity, b. Dec. 17, 1743	1	117
Jabez, s. John & Lide, b. Feb. 25, 1722	1	8
Jabez, m. Charity **BEECH**, Dec. 9, 1742	1	117
Jesse, s. Nathan & Abigail, b. July [ ], 1780	1	285
John, m. Abigail **BURR**, Mar. 22, 1692	1	8
John, s. John & Abigail, b. July 20, 1694; d. Feb. 19,		
1725/6	1	8
John, physician, m. Mrs. Hannah **WHEELER**, Aug. 24,		
1708, by Nathan Gold, Dept. Gov.	LR-2	460
John, s. John, b. Nov. 12, 1709	LR-2	460
John, m. Lide **PORTER**, of Winsor, Oct. 17, 1712	1	8
John, s. John & Lide, b. June 3, 1729	1	8
Joseph, m. Deborah **NUKOLS**, Dec. 7, 1705	1	4

	Vol.	Page
WHEELER (cont.)		
Joseph, s. Joseph & Deborah, b. Nov. 18, 1706	1	4
Joseph, m. Abigail **PERRY**, Sept. 10, 1729	1	20
Joseph, s. Joseph & Abigail, b. Dec. [ ], 1734; d. Mar. 1735	1	20
Joseph, Jr., s. Joseph & Abigail, b. May 27, 1738	1	20
Levi, s. Nathan & Abigail, b. Aug. 7, 1776	1	285
Lois, d. Jos. & Abigail, b. Dec. 15, 1740	1	20
Louisa, of Fairfield, m. John B. **GILBERT**, of Bridgeport, May 7, 1848, by Rev. J. H. Perry, Southport	1-M	89
Luse, d. Hezekiah & Abigail, b. Aug. 9, 1755	1	51
Mara, d. Sergt. Samuell, of Stratfield, decd., b. July 22, 1708	LR-2	460
Marinda, m. Henry **JENNINGS**, Jan. 16, 1822, by Nath[anie]l Hewit, V.D.M.	1-M	6
Mary, d. John & Abigail, b. Nov. 4, 1701; d. Dec. 11, 1713/14	1	8
Mary, d. John & Lide, b. Oct. 11, 1713; d. Feb. 28, 1720/1	1	8
Mary, d. Timothy & Abigail, b. Oct. 21, 1744	1	51
Mary, d. Ichabod & Deborah, b. May 21, 1756 [sic]	1	118
Mary, m. Benjamin **LOCKWOOD**, b. of Fairfield, July 5, 1837, by Enoch E. Chase	1-M	63-4
Naomi, d. Timothy & Abigail, b. Aug. 4, 1751	1	51
Nathan, s. Jabez & Charity, b. May 7, 1751	1	117
Nathan, Jr., s. Capt. Jabez, m. Abigail **OAKLEY**, d. Jeremiah, Oct. 19, 1775	1	285
Obediah, s. John & Lide, b. Mar. 15, 1716	1	8
Patience, d. David & Esther, b. Oct. 1, 1723	1	4
Sarah, d. John & Abigail, b Feb. 11, 1696	1	8
Sarah, d. Joseph & Abigail, b. Dec. [ ], 1735	1	20
Sarah, d. Benj[ami]n & Mary, b. Apr. 1, [or 11th], 1753	1	276
Sarah, d. Jabez & Charity, b. Feb. 19, 1754	1	117
Sarah Burr, d. Nathan & Abigail, b. Nov. 10, 1782	1	285
Seth, s. Joseph & Deborah, b. Mar. 30, 1720	1	4
Temperance, d. David & Esther, b. Nov. 6, 1721	1	4
Tho[ma]s, s. Joseph & Deborah, b. July 16, 1708	1	4
Timothy, s. Timothy, m. Abigail **BURRIT**, Aug. 9, 1744	1	51
Timothy, s. Benj[ami]n & Mary, b. Dec. 13, 1750	1	276
WHELPLEY, WHELPHLEE, WHELPLY, Joseph, s. Joseph, b. Oct. 7, 1682	LR-A2	681
Rebecka, d. Joseph, b. Apr. 2, 1679	LR-A2	663
Rebecka, d. Apr. 19, 1709	LR-2	456
Sarah, b. Jan. 17, 1707; m. Samuel **BRADLEY**, Nov. [ ], 1724	1	70
WHETTEMORE, Joseph, of Boston, m. Narcissa **PERRY**, of Fairfield, Nov. 21, 1821, by Nath[anie]l Hewit	1-M	6
WHITE, Daniel, s. Jacob & Elizabeth, b. May 22, 1761	1	231
Jacob, m. Elizabeth **MIDLEBROOK**, d. Jonathan, May 5, 1754	1	231
Jonathan, s. Jacob & Elizabeth, b. Oct. 2, 1757	1	231
Joseph, s. Jacob & Elizabeth, b. May 1, 176[ ]	1	231

	Vol.	Page
WHITE (cont.)		
Sarah, d. Jacob & Elizabeth, b. Jan. [ ], 1769	1	231
Wright, s. Jacob & Elizabeth, b. Nov. 30, 1755	1	231
WHITEAR, Rebeckah, d. John, m. Abel **WHEELER**, s.		
Jonathan, Mar. 27, 1758	1	250
WHITEHEAD, WHITHEAD, Abba Jane, m. Edward		
JENNINGS, b. of Fairfield, Sept. 16, 1832, by		
Gershom Pierce	1-M	47
Benjamin J., of Weston, m. Elizabeth **RAYMOND**, of		
Greenfield, July 9, 1826, by Hezekiah Ripley,		
V.D.M.	1-M	24
Elizabeth, d. Nath[anie]ll, m. Benjamin **SQUIER**, s. John,		
Feb. 1, 1749	1	218
Elizabeth, m. James **BULKLEY**, s. Peter, Apr. 8, 1756	1	205
Elizabeth, d. Gershom, m. Nathan **HILL**, Dec [ ], 1766	1	52
WHITEHOUSE, [see also **WHITOEUS**], Burr, m. Paulina		
SHERWOOD, b. of Greens Farms, Dec. 9, 1832,		
by Rev. H. A. Boardman	1-M	47
Sally Ann, m. Marcham **JENNINGS**, Sept. 18, 1825, by		
Rev. H. Humphreys	1-M	19
WHITLOCK, Ann, d. Dan[ie]ll & Mary, b. Dec. 2, 1748	1	205
Bette, d. Dan[ie]ll & Mary, b. Mar. 9, 1747	1	205
Daniel, m. Mary **MOR[E]HOUSE**, May 4, 1746	1	205
Daniel, s. Dan[ie]ll & Mary, b. Sept. 8, 1751	1	205
David, s. Dan[ie]ll & Mary, b. Sept. 7, 1753	1	205
Hannah, m. Joseph **BEERS**, Mar. 1, 1711	1	93
Joseph, s. Tho[ma]s & Damaries, b. Feb. 17, 1718	1	207
Josiah, s. John, b. Apr. 17, 1727; m. Rachel **KNAP**,		
[ ]	1	99
Justus, s. Josiah & Rachel, b. Apr. 2, 1755	1	99
Mary, wid. Joseph, m. John **THORP**, s. John, Sept. [ ],		
1760	1	186
Nathan, s. Josiah & Rachel, b. May 22, 1753	1	99
Nathan, s. Dan[ie]ll & Mary, b. Aug. 16, 1755	1	205
Rachel, d. Josiah & Rachel, b. Apr. 15, 1751	1	99
Sarah, d. Tho[ma]s & Damaries, b. Jan. 14, 1734	1	207
Sarah, d. Dan[ie]ll & Mary, b. Sept. 26,* 1757		
*(Perhaps Sept. 20)	1	205
Sarah, d. Tho[ma]s, m. Lemuel **WOOD**, s. Obadiah, June		
4, 1760	1	264
Thomas, m. Damaries **HIDE**, Jan. 24, 1716	1	207
[WHITMORE], [see under **WHETTEMORE**]		
WHITNEY, WHETNEY, Aaron, s. Sam[ue]ll & Ann, b. Sept.		
25, 1745	1	74
Ann, d. Sam[ue]ll & Ann, b. June 6, 1747	1	74
Levy, s. Sam[ue]ll & Ann, b. July 11, 1757	1	74
Lyman, s. Sam[ue]ll & Ann, b. Oct. 22, 1755; d. Jan. 25,		
1756	1	74
Nehemiah, s. Sam[ue]ll & Ann, b. Aug. 9, 1749	1	74
Peter, s. Sam[ue]ll & Ann, b. Jan. 6, 1743/4	1	74
Ransford, s. Sam[ue]ll & Ann, b. Mar. 10, 1753	1	74
Raymond, m. Marinda **SILLIMAN**, Jan. 4, 1835, by		
James H. Linsley	1-M	56

	Vol.	Page
WHITNEY, WHETNEY (cont.)		
Sally, Mrs. of Fairfield, m. Dea. Justus **SILLIMAN**, of Weston, [Feb. 16, 1838], by Rev. Enoch E. Chase, in Stratfield	1-M	65
Samuel, m. Ann **NORTHROP**, May 14, 1740	1	74
Sam[ue]ll, s. Sam[ue]ll & Ann, b. Feb. 17, 1740/1	1	74
Sarah, d. Sam[ue]ll & Ann, b. May 16, 1751	1	74
Sarah, m. Moses **OGDEN**, b. of Greenfield, June 27, 1820, by Rev. William Belden, of Greenfield	1-M	1
Silas, s. Sam[ue]ll & Ann, b. July 16, 1742	1	74
Zenus, m. Drusilla **PERRY**, b. of Fairfield, [probably 1837], by [Enoch E. Chase]	1-M	65
WHITOEUS (?), [see also **WHITEHOUSE**], Jonathan, s. Jonathan, b .May 28, 1698	LR-2	461
WHITTINGHAM, Charles A., of New York, m. Cornelia A. **RISLEY**, of Fairfield, Oct. 2, 1825, by Rev. Edward Rutledge, of Stratford	1-M	19
WICKLEE [see under **WAKELEY**]		
WILCH, Eliza A., of Stratford, m. David L. **TREAT**, of Bridgeport, June 5, 1844, by Rev. Anson F. Beach	1-M	77
WILLIAMS, Alice, d. Thaddeus & Frances, b. June 17, 1754	1	134
Amelia, d. Elnathan & Hannah, b. Dec. 5, 1756	1	109
Aralzamon A., m. Amanda **THORP**, Mar. 6, 1831, by T. F. Davis	1-M	42-3
Darius, m. Salome **OGDEN**, b. of Fairfield, Dec. 14, 1823, by Hez[ekia]h Ripley, V.D.M.	1-M	13
Deborah, d. Tho[ma]s, of Reading, Oct. 26, 1710	1	5
Elizabeth, d. Tho[ma]s, of Reading, b. Aug. 31, 1719	1	5
Elizabeth, m. Ebenezer **BARTRAM**, May 15, 1728	1	223
Elnathan, s. David, m. Hannah **THORP**, d. Peter, Dec. 5, 1753	1	109
Esther, d. Thomas, b. [ ], "will be four years old Apr. 27, next"	LR-2	461
Eunice, d. Tho[ma]s, of Reading, b. May 23, 1714	1	5
Eunice, m. Joseph **SMITH**, s. Benj[ami]n, Oct. 19, 1756	1	221
Frances, d. Thaddeus & Frances, b. Aug. 24, 1749	1	134
Grace, d. Tho[ma]s, of Reading, b. Aug. 1, 1722	1	5
Hannah, d. Elnathan & Hannah, b. Sept. 28, 1754	1	109
Henry, m. Matilda **BAKER**, May 26, 1833, by T. F. Davis	1-M	50
Jabez, m. Eunice **KNAP**, [ ], 1753	1	100
Jabez, s. Jabez & Eunice, b. July 3, 1756	1	100
Jemima, m. John **GILBERT**, June 29, 1721	1	106
John, m. Grizzel **THORP**, Sept. 4, 1749	1	56
John, s. John & Grizzel, b. Nov. 19, 1752	1	56
Johns S., m. Ruth **WHALEY**, July 17, 1842, by Rev. Samuel Nichols, of Greenfield Hill	1-M	83
Martha, m. Thaddeus **MOR[E]HOUSE**, s. Nathan, Apr. 2, 1746	1	169
Mary, m. Edward **BULKLEY** (colored), Mar. 23, 1828, by Cha[rle]s G. Lee	1-M	31
Mary, m. David **DOWNS**, b. of Fairfield, Dec. 31, 1827, by N. E. Cornwall	1-M	65

	Vol.	Page
WILLIAMS (cont.)		
Sarah, d. Thomas, b. Feb. 9, 1702	LR-2	461
Thaddeus, s. David, m. Frances **CASE**, Nov. 28, 1747	1	134
Thaddeus, s. Thaddeus & Frances, b. Feb. 16, 1752	1	134
Thomas, s. Thaddeus & Frances, b. Jan. 28, 1757	1	134
Timothy, of Fairfield, m. Catharine **HAMMOND**, of		
New York, Sept. 16, 1849, by Rev. Jacob L. Clark	1-M	94
WILMOT, Samuel, of Georgetown, S.C., m. Minerva		
DARROW, of Fairfield, Oct. 12, 1841, by Rev. N.		
E. Cornwall	1-M	72
WILSON, WILLSON, Albert Sherwood, s. [Robert & Sally],		
b. Sept. 19, 1818	1	301
Albert Sherwood, of Fairfield, m. Ann Jennet **BARNUM**,		
of Bridgeport, Oct. 11, 1846, by Rev. James Scott,		
of Stratfield	1-M	85
Alden, Jr., m. Catharine **KNAPP**, b. of Fairfield, Nov. 3,		
1840, by Rev. Matthew Batchelder	1-M	70
Alden, Sr., m. Mrs. Clara **KNAPP**, b. of Fairfield, Nov.		
22, 1840, by Rev. Matthew Batcheldor	1-M	70
Amelia S., m. William B. **LYON**, of Fairfield, Oct. 14,		
1835, by W[illia]m Denison	1-M	57
Ann, d. Nath[anie]ll & Mary, b. Oct. 4, 1749; d. Oct. 27,		
1749	1	37
Ann, d. Nath[anie]ll & Sarah, b. May 12, 1751	1	37
Bradford, of Southport, m. Sarah Paulina **WILSON**, of		
Fairfield, Jan. 30, 1848, by Rev. Lyman H. Atwater	1-M	88
Caroline, of Fairfield, m. Walker **SHERWOOD**, of		
Weston, Dec. 21, 1820, by Nath[anie]l Hewit,		
V.D.M.	1-M	3
Catharine, d. Rob[er]t & Catharine, b. Feb. 6, 1751	1	29
Catharine A., of Fairfield, m. William **MORRISON**, of		
Florida, June 24, 1846, by Rev. Lyman H. Atwater	1-M	84
Charity, m. Seth **SEELEY**, b. of Fairfield, Dec. [ ],		
[1836], by [Rev. Enoch E. Chase, of Stratfield]	1-M	61
Dan[ie]ll, s. Nath[anie]ll & Mary, b. July 26, 1747	1	37
Elizabeth, [twin with Mary], d. Robert & Catharine, b.		
June 23, 1753	1	29
Eunice, d. Rob[er]t & Catharine, b. June 11, 1743	1	29
Fairchild, m. Fanny **WILSON**, b. of Fairfield, Jan. 20,		
1840, by Rev. Lyman H. Atwater	1-M	69
Fanny, m. Fairchild **WILSON**, b. of Fairfield, Jan. 20,		
1840, by Rev. Lyman H. Atwater	1-M	69
Henry, m. Rebecca **SNOW**, b. of Fairfield, Mar. 14,		
1842, by Rev. Daniel C. Curtiss	1-M	73
James, s. Rob[er]t & Catharine, b. Apr. 11, 1742	1	29
Jane, eldest d. [Robert & Sally]. b. Dec. 6. 1820	1	301
John, m. Eunice **HIDE**, Feb. 27, 1740	1	25
John, of Saugatuck, m. Jane **WAKELEY**, of Fairfield,		
Mar. 18, 1833, by James H. Linsley	1-M	51
John, s. Rob[er]t & Catharine, b. June 7, 1847*		
*(Probably 1747)	1	29
Laura, m. Joseph **PICKERING**, b. of Southport, July 25,		
1836, by Nath[anie]l E. Cornwall	1-M	60

	Vol.	Page
WILSON, WILLSON (cont.)		
Laura, of Fairfield, m. Harvey J. **MUNROE**, of Norwalk,		
June 23, 1844, by Rev. James Scott	1-M	77
Laura, m. Jonathan **STURGIS**, b. of Fairfield, Jan. 25,		
1847, by Rev. James Scott, of Stratfield	1-M	86
Mary, w. Nath[anie]ll, Jr., d. Oct. 10, 1749	1	37
Mary, [twin with Elizabeth], d. Robert & Catharine, b.		
June 23, 1753	1	29
Mary, d. Nath[anie]ll & Sarah, b. Apr. 4, 1756	1	37
Mary, m. Joseph **MOREHOUSE**, b. of Fairfield, Jan. 1,		
1834, by Chester Tilden	1-M	52
Nath[anie]ll, Jr., s. Nath[anie]ll, m. Mary **SILLEMAN**, d.		
Capt. John, Sept. 16, 1746	1	37
Nath[anie]ll, m. 2nd w. Sarah **SILLEMAN**, Feb. 15,		
1750	1	37
Pamela, m. Wyllis **LYON**, Dec. 30, 1821, by Rev. Daniel		
Wildman	1-M	7
Phebe, m. William S. **WILLSON**, b. of Fairfield, [Feb.		
16, 1838], by [Rev. Enoch E. Chase, in Stratfield]	1-M	65
Robert, s. Nath[anie]ll, m. Catharine **BURR**, d. Capt.		
John, Sept. 7, 1741	1	29
Robert, s. Robert & Catharine, b. Nov. 2, 1755	1	29
Robert, m. Sally, **SHERWOOD**, d. Albert, decd., May		
29, 1807	1	301
Ruth, d. Nath[anie]ll, m. Samuel **MORHOUSE**, s.		
Abraham, July 8, 1741	1	41
Ruth, d. Rob[er]t & Catharine, b. Oct. 5, 1744	1	29
Ruth, d. Robert, m. Thomas **HOLBERTON**, s. John,		
May 31, 1770	1	41
S., of Boston, m. Laura **GODFREY**, of Fairfield, Nov. 1,		
1829, by John H. Hunter	1-M	35-6
Sarah, m. Dan[ie]ll **PERRY**, Jan. 1, 1744/5	1	53
Sarah, d. Nath[anie]ll & Sarah, b. Oct. 27, 1752	1	37
Sarah Paulina, of Fairfield, m. Bradford **WILSON**, of		
Southport, Jan. 30, 1848, by Rev. Lyman H.		
Atwater	1-M	88
Wakeman, of Greenfield, m. Jane **HURD**, of Black Rock,		
Jan. 3, 1841, by Rev. Lyman H. Atwater	1-M	71
Walter, of Weston, m. Harriet **GOULD**, of Fairfield, Oct.		
7, 1827, by Nath[anie]l Hewit	1-M	29
William S., m. Phebe **WILSON**, b. of Fairfield, [Feb. 16,		
1838], by [Rev. Enoch E. Chase], in Stratfield	1-M	65
WINTON, Abigail, d. David & Elizabeth, b. Oct. 18, 1754	1	128
Asa, s. David & Elizabeth, b. Sept. 13, 1758	1	128
David, s. John, m. Elizabeth **SQUIER**, d. John, Nov. 16,		
1748	1	128
David, s. David & Elizabeth, b. Dec. 10, 1752	1	128
Deborah, d. John, m. Thaddeus **GILBERT**, s. John, July		
7, 1741	1	106
Elizabeth, d. David & Elizabeth, b. Dec. 18, 1756	1	128
James, s. David & Elizabeth, b. Oct. 8, 1750	1	128
Mary, d. John, m. Samuel **SMITH**, s. John, Nov. 10,		
1737	1	237

	Vol.	Page
WINTON (cont.)		
Sam[ue]ll, s. David & Elizabeth, b. Mar. 27, 1749	1	128
Sarah, d. John, m. John **JENNINGS**, s. Isaac, Jan. 20,		
1731	1	128
[**WOLCOTT**], **WOOLCOTT**, Sarah, Mrs., d. of Henry		
Woolcott, of Windsor, m. Rev. Charles		
CHAUNEY, of Stratfield, Mar. 16, 1698	LR-2	460
Sarah, Mrs., m. Rev. [ ] **CHANEY**, Mar. 16, 1698	LR-2	460
Sarah, see Sarah **CHAUNEY**	LR-2	461
WOOD, Juliet, of New London, m. Francis **JELLIFF**, of		
Southport, Apr. 10, 1842, by Rev. N. E. Cornwall	1-M	74
Lemuel, s. Obadiah, m. Sarah **WHITLOCK**, d.		
Tho[ma]s, June 4, 1760	1	264
Lemuel, s. Lem[ue]ll & Sarah, b. Nov. 16, 1764	1	264
Lorinda, m. Harry **BROWN**, b. of Norfield, Nov. 25,		
1821, by Hezekiah Ripley, V.D.M.	1-M	6
Mary F., [twin with William H.], d. Thomas & Marinda,		
b. May 28, 1844	1	274
Rachel, d. Lem[ue]ll & Sarah, b. Sept. 6, 1761; d. Jan. 16,		
1765	1	264
Samuel A., of Weston, m. Eliza **GODFREY**, of Greens		
Farms, Sept. 30, 1821, by Hezekiah Ripley, V.D.M.	1-M	5
William H., [twin with Mary F.], s. Thomas & Marinda,		
b. May 28, 1844	1	274
WOOFINDELE, John, of New York, m. Martha **JESUP**, of		
Greens Farms, [Nov.] 6, [1822], by Rev. E. W.		
Hooker	1-M	9
WOOKEY, Milla, m. Thomas **HALSTEAD**, b. of Fairfield		
(colored), Apr. 21, 1822, by Nath[anie]l Hewit	1-M	7
WORDAIN, Sam[ue]ll, s. W[illia]m & Ann, b. Jan. 20, 1757	1	103
William, s. Tho[ma]s, m. Ann **ODELL**, d. Capt.		
Sam[ue]ll, Feb. 13, 1755	1	103
W[illia]m, s. W[illia]m & Ann, b. Jan. 7, 1760	1	103
WYLMAN, John, s. George, b. Apr. 15, 1740	1	74
WYNKOOP, **WYNKOOPE**, Abraham, s. Benjamin &		
Grizzell, b. May 12, 1755	1	58
Anna, d. Benjamin & Grissell, b. Dec. 15, 1756	1	58
Benjamin, s. Benjamin, of New York, m. Eunice **BURR**,		
d. Major Peter, of Fairfield, Nov. 22, 1730	1	85
Benjamin, s. Benjamin & Eunice, b. Sept. 17, 1731	1	85
Benjamin, Jr., s. Benjamin, m. Grissell **FROST**, d.		
Joseph, Mar. 6, 1754	1	58
Benj[ami]n, s. Benj[ami]n & Grizzell, b. Apr. 10, 1769	1	58
Catharine, d. Benj[amin] & Eunice, b. Sept. 17, 1735	1	85
Catharine, d. Benj[amin], m. Gideon **WELLS**, May 1,		
1754	1	35
Cornelius, Jr., of New York, m. Abigail **OSBORN**, of		
Fairfield, Mar. 12, 1758, by Rev. Noah Hobart	1	237
Elizabeth, d. Cor[neliu]s & Abigail, b. Aug. 21, 1759	1	237
Eunice, d. Benj[ami]n & Eunice, b. Apr. 7, 1739	1	85
Grissell, d .Benjamin & Grissell, b. Aug. 12, 1760	1	58

	Vol.	Page
WYNKOOP, WYNKOOPE (cont.)		
James Van der Spiegle, s. Cornelius & Abigail, b. Oct. 1, 1767	1	237
John, s. Benjamin & Grissell, b. Feb. 24, 1763	1	58
Peter, s. Benj[amin] & Eunice, b. Oct. 6, 1733	1	85
YONGS [see under **YOUNG**]		
YOUNG, YONGS, Benj[ami]n, s. Isaac & Mary, b. July 16, 1758	1	267
Isaac, m. Mary **HUBBELL**, d. Richard, Sept. 1, 1757	1	267
Isaac, s. Isaac & Mary, b. Sept. 23, 1760	1	267
Mary, d. Isaac & Mary, b. Nov. 6, 1762	1	267
Susannah, d. Daniel & Margaret, of Stratford, m. Gershom **BURR**, s. Gershom & Priscilla, of Fairfield, Sept. 10, 1789, by Rev. Andrew Eliot	1	294
ZIMMERMAN, ZIMMAMAN, Bradley, m. Francis L. **BABBETT**, b. of Fairfield, Oct. 10, 1836, by Rev. T. F. Davis	1-M	60
Mary Ann, of Fairfield, m. John **THOMPSON**, of Huntington, [Feb.] 11, [1828], by Cha[rle]s G. Lee	1-M	30
NO SURNAME		
Anna, m. Caleb **BREWSTER**, Apr. 18, 1784	1	292
Christopher & w. Dinah, negroes, had Prince, b. June 4, 1797 & Sally, b. Mar. 6, 1799	1	462
Eli, s. Quash & Rose (colored), b. July [ ], 1782	1	283
Mary, m. Sam[ue]ll **HALL**, s. Frances, Mar. 20, 1682/3	LR-A2	677
Sarah, d. [ ], b. [ ], 167[ ]	LR-A2	664
-----, m. Abigail **CLAPHAM**, Mar. [ ], 1675	LR-A2	663

FARMINGTON VITAL RECORDS
1645-1850

	Vol.	Page
ABERNATHY, ABANATHA, ABERNETHY,		
ABANERTHA, Anna, d. Caleb, b. Mar. 14, 1754	LR9	6
Anne, d. Caleb, b. Mar. 15, 1754	LR15	B
Calleb, s. Caleb, b. Apr. 7, 1748	LR8	3
Caleb, had s. [ ], d. Nov. 3, 1751	LR8	11
Caleb, d. June 29, 1759	LR11	577
Giles, s. Caleb, b. Dec. 3, 1743	LR7	J
Giles, s. Caleb, b. Dec. 7, 1744	LR8	3
Lois, d. Caleb, b. Apr. 11, 1750	LR8	3
Lois, m. Solomon **WELTON,** Nov. 28, 1771	LR17	G
Mary, m. Daniel **BACON,** Oct. 24, 1765	LR11	594
Wright, s. Caleb, b. Dec. 14, 1745	LR7	F
ADAMS, ADDAMS, Elizabeth, w. William, d. Aug. 3, 1655	LR2	320
Erastus H., m. Almira **ROWE,** Dec. 9, 1828, by Rev.		
Noah Porter	LR42	564
Huldah, of Farmington, m. Joel **PLACE,** of Burlington,		
Mar. 7, 1828, by Rev. Noah Porter	LR42	565
John H., lately of Hartford, m. Cartini **PRINCE,** lately of		
Norfolk, Dec. 24, 1849, by Rev. Noah Porter	LR47	126
Keziah, of Mass. Bay, m. Dr. Josiah **HOLT,** of		
Farmington, May 28, 1777	LR22	480
Lewis, m. Rachel **WILLIAMS,** b. of New Britain, Dec.		
18, 1843, by Rev. Noah Porter, Int. Pub.	LR47	112
Lyman, s. Samuell, Jr., b. Feb. 24, 1779	LR21	539
Martha, m. Jonathan **GRIDLEY,** Jr., Oct. 18, 1750	LR7	46
Phebee, d. Samuell, Jr., b. Jan. 29, 1770	LR21	539
William, d. July 18, 1655	LR2	320
ADKINS, Abigail, m. Hezekiah **HART,** Jan. 10, 1757	LR11	575
Aetisa, d. Thomas, b. Oct. 28, 1741	LR6	1
David, s. John, b. Mar. 3, 1752	LR8	3
Elizabeth, d. Joseph, b. Sept. 22, 1755	LR9	6
Josiah, s. Joseph, b. July 1, 1749	LR7	F
Josiah, d. Sept. 9, 1751	LR8	11
Luther, m. Eunis **ANDRUSS,** Nov. 14, 1743	LR7	46
Mary, d. Thomas, b. Nov. 26, 1739	LR6	1
Mary, m. Isaac **PARSONS,** July 17, 1766	LR15	N
Phebe, m. Asa **BARNS,** Oct. 31, 1765	LR15	A
Samuel, s. Joseph, b. Sept. 3, 1751	LR8	3
Thomas, m. Mary **ASPINWALL,** b. of Farmington, Feb.		
8, 1738/9	LR6	27
----er, had d. [ ], b. Nov. [ ]	LR7	F
AGARD, Abigaill, m. Joshua **PARSONS,** Apr. 29, 1762	LR11	592
ALCOTT, Lois, of Wolcott, m. Jesse **GAYLORD,** of Bristol,		
[Jan. 14, 1830], by Erastus Scranton, V.D.M.	LR42	561
ALDERMAN, Eli, m. Cynthia **HUMPHREY,** Sept. 3, 1823,		
by Rev. Stephen S. Nelson	LR40	572
John, Jr., m. Charlotte **TAFT,** of Burlington, July 4, 1843,		
by Rev. B. Creagh	LR47	110

	Vol.	Page
ALDERMAN, (cont.)		
Mannah, of Burlington, m. Maria **HOWE**, of Farmington, June 2, 1847, by William Wright	LR47	119
Truman, of Burlington, m. Julia **HADSELL**, of Torrington, Dec. 27, 1820, by Ludovicus Robbins, V.D.M.	LR40	571
ALFORD, Lucy, of Farmington, Northington Soc., m. Henry **HUMPHREY**, of Canton, Feb. 27, 1828, by Rev. Isaac Kimball	LR42	565
Uriah, m. Clarissa A. **ORVIS**, Oct. 20, 1839, by Egbert Cowles, J. P.	LR47	110
ALLEN, ALLIN, [see also **ALLYN**], Augustus A., of New Britain, m. Cornelia **ROBBINS**, of Farmington, Nov. 5, 1848, by William Wright	LR47	123
Daniel, m. Huldah **CLARK**, Mar. 31, 1755	LR10	6
Harriet Louisa, m. Winthrop **WARNER**, b. of Farmington, Jan. 23, 1839, by Rev. S. H. Clark	LR47	99
Mary J., [d. Samuel & Juliaanna], b. Dec. 28, 1827	LR47	W-Y
Miron D., [s. Samuel & Juliaanna], b. Feb. 15, 1825	LR47	W-Y
Polly Emeline, m. Frederick B. **SUTLIFF**, b. of Bristol, Nov. 28, 1834, by Rev. Noah Porter	LR47	88
Rufus, C., [s. Samuel & Juliaanna], b. Oct. 26, 1831	LR47	W-Y
Samuel, b. July 21, 1795; m. Juliaanna **KING**, Jan. 2, 1817	LR47	W-Y
Samuel H., [s. Samuel & Juliaanna], b. Aug. 23, 1815 [sic] ("1819"?)	LR47	W-Y
Susannah, m. Timothy **BROWNSON**, Dec. 2, 1752	LR8	10
ALLIS, [see also **ELLIS**], Anne, d. William, b. June 14, 1724	LR4	375
John, s. William, b. Sept. 11, 1726	LR4	375
ALLYN, [see also **ALLEN**], Anne, d. John, b. Dec. 23, 1766	LR15	B
Cloe, d. John, b. Aug. 15, 1769	LR15	B
Mary, m. Nathaniel **INGRAHAM**, Nov. 18, 1765	LR15	N
Ruth, d. John, b. May 1, 1764	LR14	4
ALVORD, ALVERT, ALVORT, Arclemene, d. Thomas G., b. July 13, 1765	LR15	B
Charles, s. Thomas G., b. Aug. 27, 1769	LR15	B
David S., of Winchester, m. Sarah **ANDRUS**, of Farmington, Oct. 5, 1835, by Rev. Noah Porter	LR47	90
Ebenezer, s. Thomas G., b. Aug. 27, 1767	LR15	B
Electa, m. Elias **ROOT**, May 16, 1827, by Rev. Noah Porter	LR42	565
Rachel, d. Hannah **NORTON**, b. Dec. 22, 1761	LR22	460
Thomas Goal, s. Thomas Goal, b. Mar. 23, 1763	LR15	B
ANDREWS, ANDROS, ANDRUS, ANDRUSS, ANDREWES, ANDREUSS, Abel, s. Timothy, b. Apr. 17, 1765	LR14	4
Abell, s. Timothy, d. Aug. 24, 1777	LR21	560
Abigail, d. Jonathan, b. Sept. 19, 1738	LR6	1
Abigail, w. Thomas, d. Sept. 23, 1749	LR7	36
Abigail, d. Thomas, b. Sept. 6, 1755	LR9	6
Abigail, d. Jacob, b. June 14, 1760	LR11	578
Abigail, w. Stephen, d. Feb. 3, 1763	LR11	593

	Vol.	Page
ANDREWS, ANDROS, ANDRUS, ANDRUSS,		
ANDREWES, ANDREUSS (cont.)		
Abigail, m. Ephraim **ROYCE**, Nov. 9, 1780	LR22	480
Abigail M., m. Simon **HART**, Jr., Dec. 9, 1824, by Rev.		
Noah Porter	LR42	568
Abriham, s. John, b. Oct. 31, 1648	LR2	329
Abraham, s. Abraham, b. Nov. 26, 1705	LR1	4
Amon, m. Roxy **GOODWIN**, May 2, 1827, by Rev.		
Harry Bushnell	LR42	565
Amon, of Mereden, m. Fanny **WOODRUFF**, of		
Farmington, June 24, 1846, by Rev. Noah Porter	LR47	117
Amos, s. Samuel, b. May 27, 1722	LR5	1
Anne, d. Hezekiah, b. Sept. 6, 1760	LR11	578
Asa, s. Timothy, b. Jan. 25, 1769	LR15	B
Barzilla, s. David, b. Oct. 20, 1754	LR8	3
Barzillah, s. David, b. Oct. 20, 1754	LR9	6
Benjamin, s. John, bp. June 17, 1659	LR2	327
Benjamin, m. Mary **SMITH**, May about 26, 1682	LR1	5
Benjamin, s. Benjamin, b. Aug. 20, 1683	LR1	2
Benjamin, Sr., of Ffarmington, m. Dorcas **WETTMORE**,		
wid., of Middletown, June 14, 1710	LR2	123
Benjamin, Jr., m. Elizabeth **GRIDLEY**, b. of Farmington,		
Dec. 6, 1711	LR2	125
Benjamin, Sr., d. [ ], 1727	LR4	396
Benjamin, Jr., d. Feb. 24, 1727/8	LR4	396
Benjamin, s. James, b. June 5, 1734	LR5	1
Beriah, s. Benjamin, Jr., b. Feb. 9, 1774	LR17	430
Bethiah, d .John, s. of Benjamin, b. Mar. 12, 1716/17	LR2	81
Bulah, d. Moses, Jr., b. Apr. 6, 1784	LR22	460
Bildad, s. John, s. of Benjamin, b. May 12, 1719	LR2	83
Candasa, d. Ozias, b. Sept. 17, 1774	LR21	539
Catharine, m. Henry **STEPHENS**, b. of Farmington, Nov.		
25, 1841, by Rev. Aaron S. Hill	LR47	106
Charlotte E., of Farmington, m. Justus F. **THOMSON**, of		
Avon, Feb. 4, 1846, by Rev. Noah Porter	LR47	116
Chester, s. Oziah, b. Mar. 19, 1777	LR21	539
Clement, s. Ichabod, b. Mar. 22, 1764	LR14	4
Content, d. Jacob, b. Aug. 5, 1755	LR11	578
Daniell, s. John, b. May 25, 1649	LR2	329
Daniell, had s. [ ], b. Mar. 9, 1672/3	LR1	2
Daniell, his d. [ ], d. [ ] 10, 1680	LR1	2
Daniel, s. Benjamin, b. Sept. 7, 1693	LR2	111
Daniel, s. Benjamin, m. Mary **COWLES**, b. of		
Ffarmington, Feb. 8, 1720/1	LR2	51
Daniel, m. Mary **COWLES**, b. of Ffarmington, Feb. 9,		
1720/1	LR2	100
Daniel, Sr., d. Apr. 16, 1731	LR5	50
David, s. John (s. of Beniamin), b. June 20, 1723	LR4	375
David, m. Mary **WILLCOX**, Sept. 6, 1744	LR7	35
David, m. Mary **MILES**, Dec. 27, 1749	LR7	46

	Vol.	Page
ANDREWS, ANDROS, ANDRUS, ANDRUSS,		
ANDREWES, ANDREUSS (cont.)		
David, d. Dec. 1, 1762	LR11	593
David Ira, s. Ichabod, b. Apr. 14, 1766	LR14	4
Dorcas, 2nd w. Benjamin, d. Dec. 4, 1716	LR2	62
Ebenezer, s. Daniell, b. Aug. 28, 1792	LR1	2
Ebenezer, s. Daniell, d. Oct. 26, 1692	LR1	2
Ebenezer, s. Joseph, b. Oct. 27, 1718	LR2	88
Ebenezer, m. Mary **BECKWITH**, Nov. 4, 1742	LR6	305
Ebenezer, s. Elijah, Jr., b. Dec. 24, 1778	LR22	460
Edward, of Farmington, m. Adelia **PENFIELD**, of		
Berlin, July 5, 1840, by Rev. Aaron S. Hill	LR47	102
Eli, m. Johannah **THOMSON**, Sept. 3, 1753	LR9	286
Eli, s. Obediah, b. Dec. 13, 1755	LR9	6
Elidia, w. Thomas, d. Aug. 20, 1761	LR11	574
Elijah, s. James, b. Dec. 6, 1731	LR5	1
Elijah, m. Sarah **THOMSON**, Aug. 4, 1761	LR11	592
Elijah, 2nd, m. Rebeckah **GRIDLEY**, Mar. 2, 1775	LR21	557
Eliphas, s. John (s. of Benjamin), b. May 13, 1725	LR4	375
Eliphas, m. Mary **STIMSON**, Sept. 3, 1752	LR8	10
Elisha, s. John, b. June 29, 1733	LR6	1
Elisha, s. Samuell, b. Mar. 16, 1741	LR6	1
Elisha, s. Thomas & Elida, b. Dec. 4, 1753	LR8	3
Elizabeth, d. Timothy, b. June 12, 1743	LR8	3
Elizabeth, d. [Joseph, Jr.], b. Apr. 2, 1749	LR7	F
Elizabeth, d. Eliphas, b. July 24, 1754	LR9	6
Elizabeth, w. Joseph, d. May [ ], 1755	LR9	495
Elizabeth, d. Joseph, d. Sept. 22, 1755	LR9	495
Emma, m. Gad **YEOMANS**, June 11, 1824, by Rev.		
Noah Porter	LR42	568
Esther, m. Daniel **ROOT**, Apr. 27, 1757	LR11	576
Esther, of Farmington, m. Seth R. **SMITH**, of		
Southington, Dec. 11, 1831, by Rev. Noah Porter	LR42	559
[E]vnic[e], d. Daniel (of Benjamin), b. Jan. 4, 1724/5	LR2	65
Eunis, m. Luther **ADKIN**, Nov. 14, 1743	LR7	46
Gideon, m. Abigail **POTTER**, b. of Farmington, Apr. 11,		
1743/4	LR7	46
Hanny, d. John, b. Feb. 26, 1647	LR2	329
Hannah, b. Jan. 13, 1684	LR1	2
Hannah, d. Abraham, b. Feb. 12, 1708/9	LR2	109
Hannah, d. Joseph, Jr., b. Mar. 22, 1739/40	LR6	1
Hannah, m. James **JUDD**, July 27, 1749	LR7	35
Hannah M., of Farmington, m. George W. **WATEROUS**,		
of Hartford, Dec. 25, 1850, by Rev. Charles Kelsey	LR47	128
Henry, m. Mary Ann **GILLET**, b. of Farmington, Dec. 4,		
1836, by Rev. Noah Porter	LR47	94
Hezekiah, s. Samuel, b. July 11, 1730	LR5	1
Hezekiah, m. Anne **STEDMAN**, May 20, 1757	LR11	576
Hezekiah, s. Hezekiah, b. Jan. 11, 1758	LR11	578
Hezekiah, twin with Martha, s. Thomas, b. July 20, 1761;		
d. same day	LR11	578
Huldah, d. Eli, b. Aug. 20, 1761	LR11	578

	Vol.	Page
ANDREWS, ANDROS, ANDRUS, ANDRUSS,		
ANDREWES, ANDREUSS (cont.)		
Huldah, m. Henry **WOODFORD**, b. of Farmington, Sept.		
20, 1826, by Rev. Noah Porter	LR42	567
Icabod, s. E[ ]s, b. July 15, 1745	LR7	F
Ichabod, m. Lydia **SMITH**, Nov. 17, 1763	LR11	594
James, s. Benjamin, b. Aug. 1, 1700	LR2	111
James, of Farmington, m. Elizabeth **JELETT**, of Seffield,		
Dec. 9, 173[ ]	LR5	13
James, d. July 18, 1761	LR11	593
James, s. Elijah, b. Nov. 22, 1762	LR11	578
Jerusha, d. John, b. May 20, 1729	LR6	1
Johannah, d. Benjamin, b. May 24, 1698	LR2	111
Johannah, d. Benjamin, d. Nov. [ ], 1706	LR2	141
Joanah, d. Benjamin, Jr., b. Sept. 13, 1712	LR2	98
Job, s. John, b. Mar. 8, 1720/1	LR2	102
Joel, s. Eliphas, b. Dec. 10, 1752	LR8	3
John, s. John, b. Aug. 12, 1645	LR2	329
John, b. June 10, 1680	LR1	2
John, s. Benjamin, b. May 8, 1685	LR1	2
John, s. Benjamin, m. Elizabeth **ORUIS**, Apr. 26, 1716	LR2	94
John, s. Elephas, b. Apr. 25, 1757	LR11	578
Jonathan, s. Benjamin, Jr., b. Apr. 7, 1715	LR2	95
Jonathan, m. Susanah **RICHARDS**, b. of Farmington,		
June 5, 1735	LR5	692
Joseph, s. John, b. May 26, 1651	LR2	329
Joseph, b. Aug. 10, 1676	LR1	2
Joseph, of Farmington, m. Susanah **HOUGH**, of		
Saybrook, Feb. 10, 1707/8	LR2	93
Joseph, s. Joseph, b. Apr. 18, 1709	LR2	99
Joseph, s. Joseph, of Farmington, m. Elizabeth		
BECKWITH, of Norwich, Jan. 31, 1738/9	LR6	27
Josiah, s. Jonathan, b. Nov. 3, 1740	LR6	1
Josiah, s. Thomas, of Southington, b. Oct. 24, 1752	LR8	3
Josiah, m. Rebeckah **BISHOP**, Jan. 6, 1762	LR11	575
Lemuel, s. Joseph, Jr., b. Apr. 9, 1747	LR7	F
Lenoard, s. Ozias, b. Jan. 20, 1772	LR21	539
Lewis, d. Jonathan, b. June 30, 1736	LR6	1
Lois, m. David **CLARK**, Nov. 18, 1756	LR11	576
Lois, d. Josiah, b. Oct. 6, 1766	LR15	B
Lydia, m. Asa **BRAY**, May 12, 1763	LR11	592
Lydia, m. Asa **PORTTER**, June 13, 1764	LR11	594
Ledia, d. Samuell, Jr., b. Feb. 18, 1774	LR17	430
Lydia, of Farmington, m. Daniel **PRINDLE**, of		
Simsbury, May 28, 1829, by Rev. Noah Porter	LR42	562
Marah, d. David, d. May 12, 1753	LR8	12
Martha, b. June 17, 1682	LR1	2
Martha, d. John, b. Nov. 28, 1710	LR2	92
Martha, d. Thomas & Martha, b. Apr. 27, 1752	LR8	3
Martha, w. Thomas, d. May 2, 1752	LR8	11
Martha, d. Thomas, d. May 3, 1752	LR8	11

	Vol.	Page
ANDREWS, ANDROS, ANDRUS, ANDRUSS,		
ANDREWES, ANDREUSS (cont.)		
Martha, twin with Hezekiah, d. Thomas, b. July 20, 1761;		
d. same day	LR11	578
Mary, d. John, b. Apr. 15, 1643	LR2	329
Mary, d. Benjamin, b. Aug. 24, 1688	LR2	111
Mary, m. Isaac **COWLS**, Jan. 2, 1694	LR1	4
Mary, ye aged wife, w. John, d. May [ ], 1694	LR1	7
Mary, w. Benjamin, d. Jan. [ ], 1707/8	LR2	141
Mary, m. Nathaniel **COWLES**, b. of Farmington, Feb.		
26, 1712/13	LR2	93
Mary, d. John, s. Abraham, b. Aug. 23, 1713	LR2	99
Mary, d. Stephen (s. of Daniel), b. July 13, 1724	LR2	282
Mary, d. Daniel (s. of Benjamin), b. Oct. 29, 1727	LR4	395
Mary, w. Lieut. Samuell, d. Dec. 17, 1741	LR6	305
Mary, w. David, d. July 20, 1745	LR7	36
Mary, d. Thomas, b. Oct. 6, 1746	LR7	F
Mary, d. David, b. Feb. 31 (sic), 1750	LR8	3
Mary, d. David, b. July 8, 1760	LR11	587
Mary, m. Daniel **CURTIS**, Jr., Feb. 4, 1773	LR17	442
Mary C., of Bristol, m. William **BENNET**, of		
Farmington, Oct. 27, 1845, by William Wright	LR47	116
Miriam, d. John, b. May 20, 1735	LR6	1
Moses, s. Moses, b. Dec. 16, 1750	LR8	3
Moses, s. Moses, b. Apr. 7, 1755	LR9	6
Nancy, m. Sylvester **WOODRUFF**, b. of Farmington,		
Mar. 7, 1828, by Rev. Noah Porter	LR42	564
Noah, s. Thomas, b. Jan. 29, 1746/7	LR7	F
Noah, s. Moses, Jr., b. Mar. 19, 1782	LR22	460
Noble, of Farmington, m. Lucina **STEELE**, of Berlin,		
Apr. 13, 1838, by Rev. S. H. Clark	LR47	97
Obadiah, s. Joseph, b. Aug. 2, 1714	LR2	88
Obadiah, s. Joseph, Jr., b. May 4, 1741	LR6	1
Obadiah, m. Hannah **HART**, Oct. 3, 1765	LR11	594
Ozias, m. [ ], Dec. 29, 1768	LR21	557
Paull, b. Jan. 2, 1686	LR1	2
Phebe, d. Eli, b. June 27, 1756	LR9	6
Rachall, d. John, b. Apr. 9, 1654	LR2	329
Rachel, of Waterbury, m. Samuel **ORUIC**, Jr., of		
Farmington, Sept. 5, 1707	LR2	123
Rachall, [twin with Rhadah], d. Jacob, b. Apr. 2, 1767	LR15	B
Rebeckah, d. Abraham, b. Oct. 19, 1712	LR2	98
Ruben, s. [ ]eza[ ], b. Nov. 16, 1[ ]3	LR7	F
Rhody, d. Eli, b. Dec. 23, 1758	LR11	578
Rhodah, [twin with Rachall], d. Jacob, b. Apr. 2, 1767	LR15	B
Roger, s. John, b. Apr. 22, 1731	LR6	1
Romeo, m. Serepta **GILLET**, b. of Farmington, Jan. 1,		
1824, by Bela Kellogg	LR42	568
Romulus, m. Mary E. **GRISWOLD**, b. of Farmington,		
Sept. 24, 1837, by Rev. S. H. Clark	LR47	96
Royal, m. Julia M. **FULLER**, b. of Farmington, Dec. 3,		
1840, by Rev. Aaron S. Hill	LR47	103

	Vol.	Page
ANDREWS, ANDROS, ANDRUS, ANDRUSS,		
ANDREWES, ANDREUSS (cont.)		
Ruth, m. Giles **LANKTON**, Nov. 4, 1751	LR7	46
Ruth, d. Josiah, b. Oct. 10, 1762	LR15	B
Sabara, s. Timothy, b. July 13, 1739	LR8	3
Samuel, s. Benjamin, b. Nov. 20, 1695	LR2	111
Samuel, s. Abraham, b. May 14, 1707	LR1	4
Samuel, m. Mary **SCOTT**, Nov. 8, 1721	LR2	101
Samuel, s. Samuel, b. Apr. 14, 1725	LR5	1
Samuel, had twin children, b. Apr. 1, 1727	LR5	1
Samuel, his twin children, d. Apr. 16, 1727	LR5	50
Samuel, s. Timothy, b. Apr. 27, 1741	LR8	3
Samuell, Lieut. m. wid. Sarah **HUBBARD**, Mar. 18, 1742	LR6	305
Samuel, s. Moses, b. Nov. 2, 1749	LR8	3
Samuel, s. Ely, b. Oct. 3, 1764	LR14	4
Samuel, m. Abigall **SMITH**, Dec. 17, 1769	LR17	442
Samuel, s. Samuel, b. Mar. 7, 1772	LR17	430
Sarah, of New Haven, m. Isaac **COWLES**, of		
Ffarmington, Nov. 1, 1709	LR2	145
Sarah, d. Abraham, b. Mar. 27, 1711	LR2	97
Sarah, d. Samuel, b. Sept. 4, 1728	LR5	1
Sarah, d. Samuel, d. Aug. 13, 1729	LR5	50
Sarah, d. Samuel, b. Oct. 10, 1733	LR5	1
Sarah, m. Timothy **MARSH**, Oct. 27, 1765	LR11	594
Sarah, of Farmington, m. David S. **ALVORD**, of		
Winchester, Oct. 5, 1835, by Rev. Noah Porter	LR47	90
Selah, s. Ozias, b. Nov. 14, 1769	LR21	539
Seth, s. Capt. Obadiah, b. Mar. 13, 1762	LR11	578
Seth, s. Samuel, b. May 4, 1770	LR17	430
Sidney, s. Moses, Jr., b. Mar. 8, 1780	LR22	460
Silas, s. Jacob, b. Jan. 8, 1758	LR11	578
Sophia, m. Jesse **HILLS**, b. of Farmington, Mar. 27,		
1822, by Noah Porter, V.D.M.	LR40	571
Stephen, s. Daniell, b. Aug. 2, 1689	LR1	2
Stephen, s. Benjamin, b. Sept. 20, 1690	LR2	111
Stephen, s. Daniel, m. Abigail **PORTTER**, Dec. 29, 1720	LR2	101
Susannah, d .Joseph, b. Jan. 20, 1712/13	LR2	99
Thankfull, w. Timothy, d. Apr. 19, 1749	LR8	12
Theoda, s. David, b. Sept. 18, 1751	LR8	3
Thomas, s. Stephen (s. of Daniel), b. Nov. 27, 1721	LR2	282
Thomas, m. Abigail **NORTH**, July 18, 1744	LR7	35
Thomas, m. Abigail **NORTH**, June 18, 1744	LR7	46
Thomas, had s. [ ], b. Sept. 22, 1749; d. same day	LR7	F
Thomas, m. Martha **WOODRUFF**, July 3, 1751	LR7	46
Thomas, m. Hannah **WINTTENE** (?), Nov. 7, 1751	LR7	46
Thomas, m. Elidia **WOODFORD**, Jan. 13, 1753	LR8	10
Thomas, d. Nov. 30, 1761	LR11	574
Timothy, s. Joseph, b. Feb. 28, 1716/17	LR2	88
Timothy, m. Sarah **HUBBERT**, June 16, 1749	LR8	10
Timothy, m. Thankfull **HUNN**, Sept. 9, 1756	LR8	10
Timothy, m. Abigail **ROOT**, Apr. 18, 1764	LR11	594

	Vol.	Page
ANDREWS, ANDROS, ANDRUS, ANDRUSS,		
ANDREWES, ANDREUSS (cont.)		
Titus, s. Eli, b. Oct. 5, 1772	LR17	430
Truman, s. Elijah, 2nd, b. Jan. 23, 1776	LR21	539
Truman, of Berlin, m. Sally **BARNS**, of Burlington, Feb.		
17, 1822, by John Mix, J.P.	LR40	571
William, s. John, s. Abraham, b. Aug. 21, 1715	LR2	96
Zebulon, s. Daniel, b. Oct. 3, 1722	LR2	88
Zebulon, s. Daniel, (of Benjamin), b. Oct. 4, 1722	LR2	65
Zerech, d. Josiah, b. June 18, 1764	LR15	B
Zopher, s. John, b. Mar. 2, 1726/7	LR4	395
----as, b. June 3, 1678	LR1	2
-----, b. Dec. 9, 1674	LR1	2
ARIALL, John, s. John, b. Mar. 26, 1775	LR21	539
Luck, s. John, b. June 27, 1777	LR21	539
ASHLEY, Abigail, m. Nathaniell **LEWIS**, Nov. 25, 1699	LR1	4
Sarah, of Westfield, m. David **BULL**, of Ffarmington,		
July 4, 1717	LR2	101
ASHMAN, John, m. Martha **PORTTER**, b. of Ffarmington,		
Jan. 7, 1723/4	LR2	257
Jonathan, s. John & Martha, b. [ ], 1729	LR4	396
ASPINWALL, ASPENWAL, ASPENWALL, Mary, m.		
Thomas **ADKINS**, b. of Farmington, Feb. 8, 1738/9	LR6	27
Sarah, d. Aaron, b. Dec. 8, 1739	LR6	1
-----, s. [ ], b. Oct. 6, 17[ ]	LR7	F
ATKINS, Elbridge G., of Bristol, m. Emeline **CURTISS**, of		
Farmington, Feb. 6, 1833, by Rev. Henry Stanwood,		
of Bristol	LR42	558
Eunice, m. Tho[ma]s Will[ia]m **TALMAGE**, Jan. 27,		
1774	LR21	557
Hannah, d. Samuel, b. Feb. 27, 1776	LR21	539
Harriet, of Plymouth, m. Alson T. **WOODRUFF**, of		
Avon, Mar. 19, 1849, by J. C. Searle	LR47	124
Jerusha, m. Robert **WEBSTER**, Feb. 23, 1775	LR21	557
Lloyd, of Bristol, m. Charity **CAMPTON**, of Farmington,		
Oct. 22, 1823, by Noah Porter, V.D.M.	LR40	572
Mary Hillhouse, of Farmington, m. John Treadwell		
NORTON, of Albany, Aug. 29, 1821, by N. S.		
Wheaton	LR40	571
Thomas, s. Samuel, b. Mar. 6, 1778	LR21	539
Wethene, d. Samuel, b. Mar. 13, 1774	LR21	539
ATWATER, Lois, m. John **UPSON**, Jr., Dec. 14, 1768	LR15	N
ATWOOD, Chauncey H., of Woodbury, m. Abigail		
HAMLIN, of Farmington, Dec. 24, 1845, by Rev.		
S. H. Clark	LR47	117
AUSTIN, Elizabeth, m. Benjamin **WELTON**, Feb. 12, 1776	LR17	443
BACHELDOR, Moses, m. Rosanna **YEOMANS**, b. of		
Farmington, June 15, 1834, by Rev. Noah Porter	LR42	E
BACON, Alma, d. Moses, b. Sept. 26, 1778	LR21	540
Anna, d. Joseph, Jr., b. May 12, 1766	LR17	430
Bethiah, m. Samuel **COLE**, Nov. 27, 1759	LR11	575

	Vol.	Page
BACON (cont.)		
Bethiah, w. Joseph, d. Sept. 9, 1779, in the 73rd y. of her		
age	LR21	560
Daniel, m. Mary **ABERNATHA**, Oct. 24, 1765	LR11	594
Daniel Harvey, s. Daniel, b. Oct. 30, 1766	LR15	C
Douglass, s. Joseph, Jr., b. Oct. 26, 1767	LR17	430
John Flavell, s. Daniell, b. May 26, 1770	LR17	430
Joseph, s. Joseph, Jr., b. Sept. 24, 1777	LR21	540
Moses, m. Roseannah **RUST**, Dec. 25, 1777	LR21	557
Rhoda, d. Daniell, b. Feb. 10, 1772	LR17	430
Rosanner, d. Moses, b. Oct. 14, 1780	LR21	540
Roswell, s. Joseph, Jr., b. May 12, 1764	LR17	430
Seth, s. Daniel, b. Oct. 7, 1768	LR15	C
BAILEY, Luther, m. Margaret E. **BLAKESLEE**, Dec. 12,		
1837, by Rev. David G. Parmelee	LR47	96
BAKER, Caroline, of Farmington, m. Frederick T. **FRISBIE**,		
of Watertown, Jan. 1, 1842, by Noah Porter	LR47	109
BALDWIN, BALDING, Abiah, of Durham, m. Hezekiah		
BROWNSON, of Farmington, July 26, 1727	LR4	423
Elizabeth, m. Matthew **WOODRUFF**, Sept. 15, 1694	LR1	4
Temperance, of Milford, m. Josiah **NORTH**, of		
Ffarmington, Nov. 22, 1726	LR2	104
William, of New Haven, m. Celestial M. **STEELE**, of		
Farmington, Nov. 16, 1845, by Rev. S. H. Clark	LR47	115
BALL, Dorothy, of New Haven, m. Nathaniell		
WADSWORTH, of Ffarmington, Mar. 21, 1705	LR2	123
BANCROFT, John S., of East Windsor, m. Mary		
THOMSON, of Farmington, Nov. 20, 1834, by		
Rev. Noah Porter	LR47	88
BARBER, Abial, s. Abial, b. Mar. 21, 1754	LR8	3
Augustus L., m. Ann **THOMSON**, b. of Farmington,		
Sept. 28, 1836, by Rev. Noah Porter	LR47	94
Hector, of Harwinton, m. Diana **HINMAN**, of		
Farmington, May 27, 1850, by Rev. Noah Porter	LR47	129
Mary Ann, of Farmington, m. George W. **RISTER**, of		
Flemington, N.J., July 2, 1844, by Rev. Noah Porter	LR47	112
Noadiah, of Avon, m. Annis M. **DORMAN**, of		
Farmington, May 4, 1837, by Rev. Noah Porter	LR47	95
Romanta, m. Lydia **ROOT**, b. of Farmington, May 3,		
1829, by Rev. H. Bushnell	LR42	562
Samuel, m. Phebe **BECKWITH**, b. of Farmington, May		
25, 1825, by Rev. Harvey Bushnell	LR42	569
Sarah, m. Seth **MARSHALL**, Jan. 19, 1749/50	LR7	35
BARKER, Anna, d. Joseph, of Cornwall & Mercy, b. Dec. 2,		
1773	LR17	432
Betsey, d. Joseph, b. Feb. 2, 1776	LR21	540
Isaiah Gridley, s. Joseph, b. Jan. 29, 1786	LR22	460
Joseph, m. Mercy **GRIDLEY**, Feb. 16, 1773	LR17	443
Levi, s. Joseph, b. Feb. 19, 1780	LR21	540
Orlin, s. Joseph, b. Dec. 6, 1782	LR22	460
William, s. Joseph, b. Jan. 8, 1778	LR21	540
BARNES, BARNS, Aaron, s. Gideon, b. July 22, 1747	LR8	3
Abel, s. John, b. Nov. 7, 1754	LR9	6

	Vol.	Page
BARNES, BARNS (cont.)		
Abigail, d. Joseph, b. Feb. 18, 1689/90* *(Written "1689/10")	LR2	84
Abigail, m. Thomas **WARNER**, s. Thomas, b. of Farmington, Jan. 2, 1728/9	LR5	545
Abigail, d. Ebenezer, b. Oct. 22, 1750	LR11	579
Abigail, wid., d. June 17, 1753	LR8	12
Abijah, s. Ebenezer, b. Jan. 31, 1727	LR5	1
Allyn, s. Asa, b .July 15, 1767	LR15	B
Almira, d. John, b. Sept. 1, 1778	LR21	540
Amase, s. Ebenezer, b. Nov. 8, 1730	LR5	1
Amos, s. Judah, b .Oct. 9, 1778	LR21	540
Ann, m. Joseph **HART**, Jr., June 29, 1749	LR7	46
Ann, d. Dea. Stephen, b. Oct. 11, 1755	LR9	6
Anna, d. Ebenezer, b. June 7, 1706	LR2	92
Anne, d. Thomas, b. [ ], 1727	LR4	396
Anne, d. Dea. Stephen, b. Oct. 11, 1755	LR9	6
Asa, m. Phebe **ADKINS**, Oct. 31, 1765	LR15	A
Asa, s. Asa & Phebe, b. July 22, 1777	LR22	460
Asahel, m. Mercy **GRIDLEY**, May 2, 1769	LR17	G
Azubah, d. Stephen, b. Feb. 13, 1749/50	LR8	3
Azubah, d. William, b. Feb. 7, 1759	LR11	579
Benjamin, s. Nathaniel, b. July 23, 1745	LR7	542
Benjamin, s. William, b. Oct. 6, 1761	LR11	578
Benjamin, s. William, b. Oct. 6, 1761	LR15	C
Charles, s. Jonathan, b. Nov. 17, 1748	LR7	E
Charles, s. Jonathan, b. [ ], 1750	LR8	3
Charles, s. Jonathan, d. Sept. 17, 1751	LR8	11
Charles, 1st, s. Jonathan, d. Feb. 1, 1787	LR8	11
Clarissa, of Bristol, m. William W. **CARTER**, July 21, 1841, by Rev. Noah Porter	LR47	105
Daniel, s. Ebenezer, b. Apr. 17, 1729	LR5	1
Daniel, m. Rachel **BIRD**, Nov. 9, 1744	LR7	46
Daniel, d. Oct. 4, 1763	LR11	593
Daniel, Lieut., m. Jerusha **WEBSTER**, Jan. 13, 1779	LR22	480
Deborah, d. Ebenezer, b. July 13, 1717	LR5	1
Deborah, m. Stephen **BUCK**, Jr., June 14, 1739	LR6	27
Ebenezer, m. Deborah **ORUIC**, of Ffarmington, Apr. 8, 1699	LR2	123
Ebenezer, s. Ebenezer, b. Feb. 7, 1699/1700	LR2	92
Eli, s. Asa, b. May 21, 1775	LR21	540
Eli, s. Asa & Phebe, b. May 21, 1775	LR22	460
Elidia, d. Daniel, b. Oct. 30, 1757	LR11	579
Elijah, s. William, b. July 22, 1771	LR17	432
Elinah, d. Joseph, Jr., b. Sept. 20, 1732	LR5	307
Eliphalet, s. Ebenezer, b. Feb. 17, 1756	LR11	579
Elizabeth, d. Joseph, b. Oct. 1, 1692	LR2	84
Elizabeth, d. Thomas, b. July 21, 1695	LR2	112
Elizabeth, d. Joseph, d. about Apr. middle, 1714	LR2	62
Elizabeth, d. Jacob, b. Dec. 22, 1718	LR2	83
Elizabeth, d. Joseph, Jr., b. Oct. 30, 1726	LR2	242
Elizabeth, d. Gideon, b. Mar. 10, 1743	LR8	3
Elizabeth, m. Job **ROOT**, Jan. 3, 1754	LR8	10

	Vol.	Page
BARNES, BARNS (cont.)		
Elizabeth, d. Samuel, b. Apr. 7, 1759	LR11	578
Elizabeth, d. Jonathan, b. Oct. 21, 1764	LR15	B
Elizabeth, d. Judah, b. Oct. 21, 1775	LR21	540
Erastus, s. Judah, b. Aug. 7, 1781	LR21	540
Esther, d. Joseph, b. July 31, 1697	LR2	84
Esther, m. William **BROWNSON**, Mar. 20, 1707	LR2	145
Esther, d. Ebenezer, b. July 30, 1723	LR5	1
Esther, d. Judah, b. Aug. 12, 1777	LR21	540
[E]unice, d. Jacob, b. Nov. 25, 1721	LR2	102
Experience, d. William, b. Sept. 17, 1763	LR15	C
Farington, s. Stephen, Jr., b. Dec. 2, 1760	LR11	578
Gideon, s. Ebenezer, b. Aug. 1, 1711	LR5	1
Gideon, of Farmington, m. Mehitabel **SHAW**, of		
Windham, Nov. 2, 1732	LR6	27
Gideon, s. Gideon, b. Aug. 9, 1733	LR6	1
Hannah, d. Thomas, b. Sept. 6, 1708	LR2	112
Hannah, d. Joseph, Jr., b. Apr. 7, 1721	LR2	87
Hannah, of Brookfield, m. Isaac **PARSONS**, of		
Ffarmington, Feb. 1, 1727/8	LR4	423
Hannah, wid., m. James **BECKWITH**, 2nd, Jan. 19,		
1749	LR8	10
Hannah, d. Wise, b. June 27, 1756	LR11	579
Hanah, d. William, b. Aug. 8, 1757	LR11	579
Hannah, d. Timothy, b. June 28, 1763	LR11	578
Horrace, s. Daniel, b. Apr. 16, 1783	LR22	461
Irene, d. Thomas, [s. of Ebenezer], b. Jan. 14, 1723/4	LR5	307
Irene, d. Nov. 28, 1751	LR8	11
Israel, s. Gideon, b. Apr. 23, 1737	LR6	1
Jacob, s. Joseph, b. Sept. 18, 1687	LR1	2
Jacob, m. Grace **BROWNSON**, b. of Ffarmington, Mar.		
19, 1710/11	LR2	123
[J]ames, s. Jonathan, b. Jan. 3, 1746/7	LR7	G
Jedediah, s. Ebenezer, b. Aug. 27, 1708	LR2	92
Jedediah, m. Abigail **WARNER**, b. of Farmington, Dec.		
3, 1730	LR5	13
Jerusha, w. [Capt. Daniel?],* d. Feb. 20, 1785, in the 29th		
y. of her age *(In pencil)	LR22	482
Joana, d. Gideon, b. Nov. 2, 1741	LR8	3
Job, s. Gideon, b. Mar. 17, 1749	LR8	3
Joel, of Burlington, m. Sena **GILLET**, of Farmington,		
Jan. 10, 1822, by Noah Porter, V.D.M.	LR40	571
John, s. Jacob, b. Aug. 26, 1729	LR4	396
John, s. Ebenezer, Sr., b. Nov. 5, 1732	LR5	1
John, s. Ebenezer, Jr., b. Nov. 5, 1732	LR5	307
John, Jr., m. Rhoda [ ], Aug. 11, 1766	LR17	G
John S., of Hartford, m. Abigail R. **WOODRUFF**, of		
Avon, Jan. 6, 1850, by J. C. Searle	LR47	127
Jonathan, s. Jacob, b. May 19, 1716	LR2	96
Jonathan, s. Jacob, b. May 23, 1716	LR2	83
Jonathan, m. Deborah **ORUIS**, July 12, 1741	LR6	304
Jonathan, d. Sept. 16, 1751	LR8	11
Jonathan, m. Elizabeth [ ], Aug. 4, 1757	LR15	A

	Vol.	Page
BARNES, BARNS (cont.)		
Jonathan, s. Jonathan, b. Mar. 13, 1763	LR15	B
Joseph, s. Joseph, b. Aug. 17, 1702	LR2	84
Joseph, Jr., m. Thankfull **HOLCOM**, b. of Ffarmington,		
May 12, 1720	LR2	60
Joseph, Sr., d. Jan. 23, 1740/1	LR6	10
Joseph, d. Mar. 23, 1744	LR7	36
Josiah, m. Abigail **GIB[B]S**, July 5, 1684	LR1	5
Judah, s. Capt. Amos, b. Jan. 20, 1755	LR14	6
Judah, m. Hephsibah **WOODS**, Nov. 3, 1774	LR21	557
Juliet, of Burlington, m. Lucien **HOTCHKISS**, of		
Bristol, Aug. 21, 1836, by N. Porter	LR47	94
Lauren, s. Capt. Daniell, b. June 16, 1781	LR21	540
Lois, d. Jedadiah, b. Nov. 28, [ ]	LR5	1
Lucy, d. Ebenezer, Sr., b. Mar. 4, 1734/5	LR5	307
Lucy, m. James **LEE**, June 13, 1765	LR17	442
Lydia, d. Thomas (s. of Ebenezer), b. Jan. 13, 1734/5	LR5	307
Marble, d. Stephen, Jr., b. Jan. 29, 1768	LR17	430
Mark, s. Stephen, b .Nov. 12, 1764	LR14	5
Martha, d. Thomas, b. Mar. 8, 1702/3	LR2	112
Martha, m. Benjamin **BROWNSON**, b. of Ffarmington,		
Dec. 15, 1725	LR2	51
Martha, d. Stephen, Jr., b. Jan. [ ], 1768	LR17	430
Mary, d. Joseph, b. Feb. 6, 1694/5	LR2	84
Mary, d. Ebenezer, b. Oct. 1, 1721	LR5	1
Mary, d. Thomas, Jr., b. Apr. 12, 1737	LR6	1
Mary, d. Stephen, b. Feb. 13, 1741/2	LR6	1
Mary, m. Noah **WOODRUFF**, Dec. 5, 1752	LR11	592
Mary, d. Samuel, b. Jan. 22, 1756	LR11	579
Mary, m. John **PORTTER**, s. of Ebenezer, Feb. 9, 1758	LR11	576
Mary, d. Daniel, b. [ ], 24, 1761	LR11	578
Mary, d. Jonathan, b. Mar. 4, 1767	LR15	B
Matthew, s. Joseph, Jr., b. Oct. 29, 1729/30	LR5	1
Mehetibel, d. Gideon, b. June 5, 1735	LR6	1
Moses, s. Jacob, b. Aug., 12, 1724	LR2	46
Moses, m. Marah **WOOLCOT**, Sept. 7, 1748	LR7	35
Moses, s. Moses, b. Apr. 9, 1752	LR8	3
Naomi, d. Asa, b. Apr. 29, 1766	LR15	B
Nathan, m. Sarah **BYINGTON**, Dec. 1, 1763	LR17	G
Nathan, s. Stephen, Jr., b. Jan. 8, 1771	LR17	430
Nathaniel, s. Thomas, [b.], [ ], 1729	LR4	396
Patience, d. Thomas, b. Sept. [ ], 1705	LR2	112
Phileman, s. Stephen, Jr., b. June 26, 1757	LR11	579
Philemon, m. Anner **SCOTT**, of Waterbury, June 10,		
1779	LR22	480
Phineas, s. Thomas (s. Ebenezer), b. July 7, 1730	LR5	1
Prudence, d. Daniel, b. Apr. 8, 1764	LR11	587
Rachel, d. Joseph, b. Oct. 19, 1699	LR2	84
Rachel, d. Joseph, m. William **PARSONS**, Jr., Feb. 20,		
1715/16	LR2	94
Rachel, d. Jonathan, b. Jan. 3, 1742/3	LR6	1
Rachel, d. Daniel, b. July 31, 1752	LR8	3
Rebecca, d. Joseph, b. "June ye last", 1685	LR1	2

	Vol.	Page
BARNES, BARNS (cont.)		
Rebeckah, of Farmington, m. Thomas **SANFORD**, of		
Milford, Sept. 29, 1713	LR2	60
Rebeckah, d. Joseph, Jr., b. Jan. 8, 1723/4	LR2	87
Rebeckah, m. Thomas **PARSONS**, Aug. 17, 1743	LR6	305
Rodney, of Burlington, m. Roxanna **HORTON**, of		
Cheshire, Feb. 27, 1842, by Rev. C. D. Cowles	LR47	106
Ruth, d. Thomas, b. Oct. 23, 1692	LR2	112
Ruth, d. Asa, b. Dec. 21, 1771	LR21	540
Ruth, d. Asa & Phebe, b. Dec. 21, 1771	LR22	460
Sally, of Burlington, m. Truman **ANDROS**, of Berlin,		
Feb. 17, 1822, by John Mix, J.P.	LR40	571
Samuel, s. Thomas, b. June 4, 1700	LR2	112
Samuel, s. Jonathan, b. Nov. 14, 1744	LR7	G
Samuel, m. Temperance **BUSHNEL**, June 2, 1751	LR8	10
Samuel, s. Jonathan, d. Sept. 17, 1751	LR8	11
Sarah, m. John **SCOBELL**, Mar. 29, 1666	LR1	5
Sarah, d. Jacob, b. Sept. 29, 1712	LR4	374
Sarah, d. Daniel, b. Nov. 26, 1749	LR7	E
Sarah, m. Stephen **BARNS**, Jr., Nov. 14, 1751	LR7	35
Sarah, d. Stephen, Jr., b. Aug. 18, 1754	LR11	579
Sarah, m. John **BROWNSON**, Mar. 30, 1758	LR11	576
Sarah, m. [ ] [ ]is, Feb. 11, 1768	LR17	G
Sarah, d. Wise, Jr., b. Apr. 7, 1775	LR22	460
Seth, s. Asael, b. May 1, 1771	LR17	430
Silas, s. Timothy, b. Dec. 26, 1760	LR11	579
Stephen, s. Ebenezer, b. May [ ], 1714	LR5	1
Stephen, Jr., m. Sarah **BARNS**, Nov. 14, 1751	LR7	35
Stephen, s. Jonathan, b. Feb. 12, 1769	LR15	B
Thomas, m. Mary **JOANS**, b. of Ffarmington, June [ ],		
1690	LR2	145
Thomas, s. Ebenezer, b. June 21, 1703	LR2	92
Thomas, s. Ebenezer, of Ffarmington, m. Hannah **DAY**,		
of Hartford, May 19, 1726	LR2	100
Tho[ma]s, [s.] Stephen, b. Apr. 26, 1744	LR7	G
Thomas, s. Gideon, b. May 15, 1745	LR8	3
Thomas, s. Samuel, b. Feb. 15, 1752	LR8	3
Timothy, s. Thomas, Jr., b. Feb. 20, 1738/9	LR6	1
Timothy, m. Merriam **MILLER**, Mar. 19, 1760	LR11	575
Timothy, s. Timothy, b. Sept. 6, 1765	LR14	5
William, s. Ebenezer, b. Mar. 24, 1724/5	LR5	1
William, m. Martha **UPTON**, Jan. [ ], 1757	LR11	576
William, s. William, b. Feb. 2, 1767	LR15	C
Wise, s. Wise, b. Feb. 23, 1754	LR11	579
BARNUM, Samuel A., of Lee, Mass., m. Rhoda Ann		
INGERSOLL, of Farmington, Sept. 18, 1836, by		
Rev. Noah Porter	LR47	94
BARR, [see also BURR], Hannah, m. Elish[a] **HOSINGTON**,		
Dec. 22, 1742	LR6	305
BARRETT, BARET, BARIT, BARRIT, Esther, d. James &		
Esther, b. Oct. 28, 1753	LR8	3
James, m. Esther **BROWNSON**, Dec. 20, 1753	LR9	12
Joseph, m. Mary **COGSWELL**, Oct. 6, 1756	LR11	576

	Vol.	Page
BARRETT, BARET, BARIT, BARRIT (cont.)		
Martha, m. Charles **BROWNSON**, May 30, 1759	LR11	575
BARRINGTON, Minerva, m. Martin **DEPATUR**, of		
Northford, Oct. 5, 1851, by Rev. Nathan E. Shailer	LR47	130
BARROWS, [see also **BURROWS**], Daniel, of Mansfield, m.		
Marian **BOOTH**, of Farmington, Nov. 27, 1835, by		
Rev. Noah Porter	LR47	91
Luther, of Mansfield, m. Sally **BOOTH**, of Farmington,		
June 25, 1837, by Rev. S. H. Clark	LR47	95
BARTHOLOMEW, Ama, d. Jacob, b. Mar. 4, 1772	LR21	540
Asa, s. Jacob, b. Mar. 25, 1770(?)	LR21	540
Charles, s. Abraham, Jr., b. June [ ], 1760	LR11	578
Eli, s. Jacob, b. Jan. 7, 1774	LR21	540
Elidia, m. Joseph **HEFFORD**, Apr. 29, 1761	LR11	592
Emeline M., of Farmington, m. Charles **LEWIS**, of		
Wolcott, Oct. 30, 1827, by Rev. Noah Porter	LR42	565
Jacob, m. Sarah **GRIDLEY**, Sept. 10, 1761	LR11	575
Jacob, s. Jacob, b. Jan. 7, 1758	LR21	540
Jeremiah H., of Farmington, m. Polly **ROOT**, of Bristol,		
Sept. 15, 1834, by Rev. Noah Porter	LR42	E
Lem[ue]l, s. Jacob, b. Feb. 29, 1764	LR14	6
Lucetta, m. Stephen T. **TALMAGE**, May 8, 1842, by		
Rev. C. D. Cowles	LR47	107
Maria, of Harwinton, m. Charles F. **HAMLIN**, of		
Farmington, Oct. 26, 1835, by Rev. Noah Porter	LR47	90
Mercy, d. Jacob, b. Aug. 28, 1762	LR11	578
Rosannah, d. Jacob, b. June 2, 1770	LR21	540
Sarah, d. Jacob, b. Feb. 6, 1766	LR14	6
Sarah, of [Plainville], m. Jeremiah S. **THOMAS**, of		
Terryville, Oct. 20, 1847, by William Wright	LR47	121
BARTLETT, John N., of Avon, m. Ellen A. **STRONG**, of		
Farmington, Sept. 7, 1846, by Noah Porter	LR47	118
BASSETT, Joseph M., of Rowe, Mass., m. Nancy J. **ROOT**,		
of Farmington, Nov. 3, 1844, by Rev. S. H. Clark	LR47	113
BATES, Henry, of Southington, m. Mary Ann **HILLS**, of		
Farmington, Nov. 2, 1847, by Rev. Noah Porter	LR47	121
Mary W., of Farmington, m. Charles K. **STOW**, of		
Middletown, June 8, 1826, by Rev. Noah Porter	LR42	567
BEACH, BEECH, David, s. Aaron, b. Sept. 16, 1750	LR7	E
David, d. Sept. 18, 1752	LR8	12
Jerham,* s. A[a]ron & Esteer, b. Nov. 19, 1747 *(In		
pencil "Gershom")	LR7	G
Sarah, m. Ingham **CLARK**, Oct. 22, 1767	LR17	443
Zopher, m. Mary A. **HAZARD**, Aug. 18, 1845, by Rev.		
John R. Keep	LR47	114
BECKLEY, Abigail, m. Zachariah **HART**, Mar. [ ], 1758	LR11	576
Catharen, of Weathersfield, m. Daniel **DEWEY**, of		
Ffarmington, Sept. 27, 1706	LR2	125
Hephzibah, m. John **WOODS**, Jan. 18, 1753	LR8	10
Meriam, m. Thomas **WADSWORTH**, b. of Farmington,		
Dec. 5, 1745	LR7	35
BECKWITH, Elizabeth, of Norwich, m. Joseph **ANDRUS**, s.		
Joseph, of Farmington, Jan. 31, 1738/9	LR6	27

	Vol.	Page
BECKWITH (cont.)		
Hulda, d. James, b. Dec. 20, 1734	LR5	307
James, 2nd, m. wid. Hannah **BARNES**, Jan. 19, 1749	LR8	10
James, 3rd, m. Elida **HITCHCOCK**, May 28, 1752	LR8	10
Johannah, d. May 3, 1748	LR8	11
Mary, d. James, b. Apr. 18, 1738	LR8	3
Mary, m. Ebenezer **ANDRUSS**, Nov. 4, 1742	LR6	305
Phebe, m. Samuel **BARBER**, b. of Farmington, May 25, 1825, by Rev. Harvey Bushnell	LR42	569
Samuel, s. James, b. Sept. 10, 1732	LR5	307
Samuel, s. James, d. Nov. 11, 1732	LR5	50
Samuel, s. James, 3rd, b. May 13, 1753	LR8	3
Samuel, m. Catharine **OULDS**, b. of Farmington, Aug. 9, 1821, by Noah Porter, V.D.M.	LR40	571
Silence Lamb, d. James, b. July 23, 1743	LR8	3
BEECHER, BEACHER, BEACHOR, Delight, of Wolcott, m. Capt. Moses H. **UPSON**, of Burlington, Jan. 14, 1830, by Erastus Scranton, V.D.M.	LR42	561
Joel, of Cheshire, m. Sarah **ROOT**, of Farmington, July 21, 1833, by Rev. Noah Porter	LR42	A
John, m. Pantha **NORTH**, b. of Farmington, Sept. 27, 1823, by Amasa Woodford, J.P.	LR40	572
Leonard, m. Ruth B. **WEBSTER**, of Harwinton, June 6, 1841, by Rev. Noah Porter	LR47	105
Samuel, s. Joel, b. Oct. 31, 1808	LR32	566
BELDEN, BELDING, Ezra, m. Rebecka **DIX**, Sept. 30, 1745	LR7	35
Ezra, s. Ezra, b. Dec. 21, 1746	LR7	G
Hannah, d. Leonard, b. July 24, 1770	LR22	460
Helen E., of Farmington, m. Enos J. **HART**, of Bristol, June 7, 1849, by Rev. Noah Porter	LR47	125
Jonathan, s. Ezra, b. Jan. 11, 1750/1	LR8	3
Jonathan, of Berlin, m. Lucretia **HUNGERFORD**, of Harwinton, Nov. 23, 1825, by Rev. Noah Porter	LR42	569
Leonard, s. Leonard, b. July 13, 1778	LR22	460
Lidea, d. Leonard, b. Nov. 3, 1772	LR22	460
Olive, d. Leonard, b. Aug. 18, 1775	LR22	460
Oliver, of Vienna, O., m. Rhoda Ann **THOMSON**, of Southington, Dec. 30, 1830, by Rev. Irenus Atkins, of Southington	LR42	560
Rebecka, d. Ezra, b. Mar. 23, 1757	LR11	579
BELL, Amos, s. Solomon, b. Dec. 1, 1772	LR17	432
Elisha, s. John, b. Sept. 5, 1743	LR6	1
Harvey, s. Solomon, b. Jan. 13, 1765	LR15	C
Hellinah, d. John, b. Oct. 15, 173[ ]	LR5	1
Henry, s. Solomon, b. Jan. 13, 1765	LR14	5
Hezekiah, s. John, b .July 19, 1740	LR6	1
Hulda, d. John, b. Apr. 13, 1733	LR5	1
Jerusha, d. Solomon, b. Aug. 5, 1775	LR21	540
John, m. Rachel **WOODRUFF**, b. of Ffarmington, Dec. 7, 1727	LR4	423
John, s. John, b. Aug. 13, 1734	LR5	307
Luthene, d. Elisha, b. Feb. 11, 1775	LR21	540
Lydia, d. John, b. [ ], 1728	LR4	396

	Vol.	Page
BELL (cont.)		
Margrette, d. Elisha, b. June 2, 1772	LR21	540
Patience, d. John, Jr., b. Apr. 26, 1766	LR15	C
Phebee, d. John, Jr., b. June 28, 1765	LR15	C
Rachel, d. John, b. Mar. 2, 1735/6	LR5	692
Rachell, d. Elisha, b. June 5, 1770	LR21	540
Ruth, d. John, b. Feb. 25, 1729/30	LR5	1
Salmon, s. Salmon, b. May 3, 1765	LR15	C
Solomon, s. John, b. Sept. 25, 1738	LR6	2
BENEDICT, Amzi, Rev. of Vernon, m. Martha **COWLES**,		
Oct. 5, 1824, by Rev. Noah Porter	LR42	568
BENHAM, BENOM, BENUM, BENNUM, Amos, s. Joseph,		
b. Nov. 25, 1774	LR17	432
Joseph, s. Joseph, b .June 4, 1742	LR6	1
Lemuel, d. Nov. 12, 1753	LR8	12
Lucy, d. Lemuel & Zubah, b. Nov. 12, 1753	LR8	3
Lucy, d. Joel, b. Jan. 17, 1771	LR17	432
Mary, w. Joseph, d. Jan. 11, 1743/4	LR7	36
Merriell, d. Joel, b. Jan. 10, 1765	LR15	B
Nathan, s. Joseph & Mary, b. July 17, 1740	LR6	1
Nathan, s. Joel, b. Feb. 6, 1774	LR17	432
Samuel, m. Asubah **COOK**, Mar. 1, 1753	LR8	10
Sybel, d. Joel & Esther, b. Dec. 4, 1767	LR15	B
Thankfull, of Wallingford, m. John **LEWIS**, of		
Farmington, Nov. 1, 1739	LR6	27
BENNET, J., m. Julia A. **SMALLAGE**, Jan. 5, 1847, by Rev.		
B. Creagh	LR47	119
William, of Farmington, m. Mary C. **ANDREWS**, of		
Bristol, Oct. 27, 1845, by William Wright	LR47	116
BENTON, David, of Litchfield, m. Amy H. **ORVIS**, of		
Farmington, Apr. 25, 1831, by Rev. Noah Porter	LR42	560
Dorothy, of Hartford, m. John **GRIDLEY**, s. Samuell, of		
Farmington, May 3, 1716	LR2	94
Lidya, of Hartford, m. Stephen **COLE**, of Farmington,		
Apr. 26, 1745	LR7	35
Lidia, m. Ebenezer **HART**, Jr., Apr. 5, 1770	LR17	G
BI-----, Jonathan, [ ]	LR5	13
BIDWELL, BIDDEL, Anne, d. Isaac, b. Apr. 4, 1758	LR11	579
Cloe, d. Isaac, b. Aug. 1, 1764	LR11	587
Hannah, of Hartford, m. Joseph **JUDD**, of Ffarmington,		
Apr. 11, 1706	LR2	145
Huldah, d. Isaac, b. Aug. 20, 1755	LR9	6
Isaac, m. Anna **PORTER**, June 5, 1744	LR7	35
Isaac, twin with Oliver, s. Isaac, b. Aug. 5, 1746	LR7	G
Isaac, twin with Oliver, s. Isaac, d. Sept. 1, 1746	LR7	36
Isaac, s. Isaac, b. Dec. 6, 1749	LR7	E
Isaac, s. Isaac, d. Jan. 14, 1749/50	LR7	540
Jane E., m. Chauncey D. **COWLES**, b. of Farmington,		
Jan. 7, 1835, by Rev. Noah Porter	LR47	88
Julia Ann, of Farmington, m. Thomas R. **STOCKING**, of		
Buffalo, N.Y., May 6, 1835, by Rev. Noah Porter	LR47	89
Levina, d. Isaac, b. May 20, 1760	LR11	578
Mable, m. Uriah **JUDD**, Dec. 20, 1744	LR7	46

	Vol.	Page
BIDWELL, BIDELL (cont.)		
Oliver, twin with Isaac, s. Isaac, b. Aug. 5, 1746	LR7	G
Oliver, twin with Isaac, s. Isaac, d. Sept. 21, 1746	LR7	36
Sarah, d. Isaac, b. Nov. 9, 1747	LR7	G
Titus, s. Isaac, b. Oct. 3, 1765	LR11	587
BIRD, BURD, Abijah, s. Jonathan & Hannah, b. June 21, 1736	LR5	1
Abijah, s. Jonathan, d. Sept. 20, 1736	LR5	500
Betsey, m. Ira **HADSELL**, b. of Farmington, May 9, 1825, by Rev. Noah Porter	LR42	568
Esther, d. Samuel, b. Feb. 28, 1696/7	LR2	91
Easther, m. Samuel **WOODRUFF**, Jr., b. of Ffarmington, July 10, 1718	LR2	101
Ester, d. Samuell, b. Aug. 4, 1738	LR6	1
Esther, wid., d. Apr. 5, 1742	LR6	305
Esther, m. Eneas **COWLES**, Oct. 3, 1765	LR11	594
Esther, m. Lettes **HAMMOND**, b. of Farmington, Apr. 8, 1834, by Rev. Noah Porter	LR42	E
[E]unice, d. Samuel & [E]unice, b. Aug. 15, 1731; d. Sept. 26, 1731	LR5	645
[E]unice, 2nd, d. Samuel [& [E]unice], b. Sept. 17, 1732; d. Nov. 4, 1732	LR5	645
Eunice, m. John **GARDNER**, Jan. 3, 1776	LR21	557
George, m. Elizabeth **STANLEY**, b. of Farmington, Dec. 15, 1825, by Rev. Noah Porter	LR42	569
Herman, d. Jonathan, b. Jan. 5, 1740/1	LR6	1
James, m. Ledia **STEEL**, Mar. 31, 1657	LR2	331
John, s. Thomas, b. Apr. 15, 1695	LR2	98
Jonathan, s. Thomas, b. Dec. 28, 1699	LR2	98
[Jon]athan, s. Jonathan, b. Mar. 6, 1746/7	LR7	G
Joseph, s. Thomas, b. Dec. 24, 1696	LR2	98
Joseph, s. Samuel & [E]unice, b. Aug. 29, 1735	LR5	645
Joseph, of Berlin, m. Lovicia **BIRDSEYE**, of Farmington, May 9, 1823, by Noah Porter, V.D.M.	LR40	572
Julia, of Farmington, m. Norton **LEWIS**, of Berlin, Nov. 16, 1830, by Amzi Benedict	LR42	560
Ledia, w. James, d. Jan. 14, 1659	LR2	319
Lidya, d. Thomas, b. June 10, 1707	LR2	98
Lydia, d. Jonathan, b. May 24, 1744	LR7	G
Mary, d. Thomas, b. Dec. 25, 1691	LR2	98
Mary, 1st d. Thomas, d. Aug. 3, 1693	LR2	141
Mary, d. Thomas, b. June 10, 1702	LR2	98
Mary, m. Joseph **HART**, b. of Ffarmington, Dec. 6, 1722	LR2	100
Mary, w. Thomas, d. Nov. 9, 1723	LR2	66
Mary, wid. Joseph, Jr., d. Jan. 22, 1729/30	LR5	50
Mary, of Litchfield, m. Jesse **JUDD**, of Farmington, Oct. 29, 1765	LR11	594
Mehitibel, m. Simon **NEWEL**, b. of Ffarmington, Mar. 22, 1711	LR2	123
Mehetible, d. Jonathan & Hannah, b. July 15, 1738	LR6	1
Mahitabel, m. Thomas **HART**, Feb. 2, 1758	LR11	594
Rachel, m. Daniel **BARNES**, Nov. 9, 1744	LR7	46
Rebeckah, d. Thomas, b. Jan. 14, 1703/4	LR2	98

	Vol.	Page
BIRD, BURD (cont.)		
Ruth, m. John **NORTON**, b. of Farmington, Jan. 28, 1730/1	LR5	13
Sally, m. Benjamin F. **CLOYES**, Nov. 18, 1824, by Rev. Noah Porter	LR42	568
Samuel, m. Esther **WOODFORD**, b. of Ffarmington, Jan. 2, 1695/6	LR2	123
Samuel, s. Samuel, b. June 10, 1699	LR2	91
Samuel, s. Samuel, b. Aug. 20, 1747	LR8	3
Samuel, s. Samuel, b. Jan. 29, 1762	LR14	5
Sarah, wid. Thomas, d. Mar. 31, 1737	LR6	10
Sarah, wid. Nathaniel, d. Sept 21, 1750	LR7	540
Thomas, m. Mary **WOODFORD**, b. of Farmington, July 3, 1693	LR2	125
Thomas, d. Apr. 30, 1725	LR2	107
Thomas, s. Jonathan, b. Apr. 5, 1733	LR5	1
Thomas, s. Jonathan, d. Apr. 12, 1734	LR5	50
Zeruiah, d. Jonathan, b. Mar. 30, 1734	LR5	307
-----, m. [E]unice **WADSWORTH**, Feb. 13, 1729/30	LR5	13
BIRDSEYE, Lovicia, of Farmington, m. Joseph **BIRD**, of Berlin, May 9, 1823, by Noah Porter, V.D.M.	LR40	572
[BIRGE], [see under **BURGE**]		
BISHOP, Ann, d. Benjamin, b. Apr. 20, 1755	LR11	579
Ann, d. Benjamin, b. Apr. 21, 1755	LR9	6
Benjamin, s. Benjamin, b. Sept. 23, 1745	LR11	579
Benjamin, s. Benjamin, b. Oct. 28, 1750	LR8	3
Elizabeth, d. Benjamin, b. Mar. 31, 1753	LR8	3
Elizabeth, d. Benjamin, b. Mar. 31, 1753	LR11	579
Flora, m. Stephen **COLEGROVE**, b. of Farmington, Sept. 7, 1836, by Rev. Noah Porter	LR47	94
James P., of Watertown, m. Celestia O. **KETCHEL**, of Sandgate, Vt., Feb. 14, 1843, by Rev. Harvey P. Ketchel	LR47	109
Jeffrey, m. Dolly **WOODFORD**, b. of Farmington, May 18, 1822, by Bela Kellogg, V.D.M.	LR40	571
[Jo]seph, s. Benjamin, b. Sept. 18, 1743	LR7	G
Joseph, s. Benjamin, b. Sept. 18, 1743	LR11	579
Lucia E., of Farmington, m. James H. **MILLER**, of Bristol, Sept. 26, 1848, by Rev. Noah Porter	LR47	123
Mary, d. Benjamin, b. Oct. 8, 1750	LR11	579
Rebeckah, m. Josiah **ANDRUS**, Jan. 6, 1762	LR11	575
Samuel, s. Benjamin, b. May 6, 1757	LR11	579
Sarah, d. Benjamin, b. Sept. 25, 1748	LR11	579
Sarah, d. Benjamin, d. Feb. 24, 1766, ae 17 y. 6 m.	LR14	3
Sarah A., m. Alford **BISSELL**, b. of Farmington, May 16, 1827, by Rev. Bela Kellogg	LR42	565
Thomas, m. Sarah D. **HILLS**, Sept. 12, 1839, by Elisha C. Jones	LR47	101
Thomas Fitch, s. Benjamin, b .Oct. 20, 1763	LR11	587
Thomas Fitch, s. Benjamin, b. Oct. 20, 1763	LR15	C
William, [s. Benjamin], b. Sept. 23, 1745	LR7	G
BISSELL, BISEL, Alford, m. Sarah A. **BISHOP**, b. of Farmington, May 16, 1827, by Rev. Bela Kellogg	LR42	565

	Vol.	Page
BISSELL, BISEL (cont.)		
Lawrence B., of East Windsor, m. Sabra S.		
CARRINGTON, of Farmington, Oct. 7, 1833, by		
Rev. Noah Porter	LR42	A
Mary, d. Mary Stimson, b. July 17, 1749	LR8	3
Mary, d. Mary Stimson, d. Aug. 13, 1751	LR8	11
BLAKESLEE, BLAKESLEY, BLAKSLEE, BLAKELEY,		
Asahel C., of Bristol, m. Sarah J. **GAYLORD**, of		
Canistota, N.Y., Feb. 29, 1852, by Rev. P. G.		
Wightman, at his house	LR47	130
Charles, m. Viola **PALMER**, b. of Farmington, Aug. 5,		
1849, by Rev. Henry J. Fox	LR47	125
Ephraim, s. Baley, b. Aug. 21, 1770	LR17	430
Easther, m. Seth **GRIDLEY**, Feb. 12, 1772	LR17	442
Huldah, d. Rufus, b. Feb. 15, 1772	LR17	432
James, of Middletown, m. Alice W. **CONE**, of		
Farmington, Oct. 11, 1831, by Rev. Noah Porter	LR42	560
Margaret E., m. Luther **BAILEY**, Dec. 12, 1837, by Rev.		
David G. Parmelee	LR47	96
Merret, s. Daniel, b. June 2, 1759	LR15	C
Revel, s. Daniel, b. Aug. 5, 1762	LR15	C
Richard, m. Jane **PHILLIPS**, b. of Farmington, Aug. 13,		
1848, by Rev. Henry J. Fox	LR47	119
Rufus, m. Esther **BROWNSON**, Sept. 12, 1771	LR17	G
Rufus, d. June 22, 1773	LR17	445
BLINN, BLIN, Hanah, d. Ephraim, b. Nov. 24, 1752	LR11	579
Margaret, d. Ephraim, b. May 13, 1759	LR11	579
Martin, H., m. Mary E. **THORP**, Sept. 24, [1850], by		
Rev. Charles Kelsey	LR47	127
Silas, s. Ephraim, b. Nov. 14, 1756	LR11	579
BLOOD, Mary M., of Chatham, m. Prentiss **MORSE**, of		
Southbridge, Mass., Mar. 18, 1834, by Rev. Noah		
Porter	LR42	D
BOARDMAN, BORTMAN, BORMAN, Alphonso, of		
Bristol, m. Sarah Jane **STOW**, of Farmington, Apr.		
8, 1849, by William Wright	LR47	125
Charles, m. Nancy H. **HOLMES**, b. of Hartford, Nov. 2,		
1835, by Rev. Noah Porter	LR47	91
Ephraim, m. Mehitabel **COLE**, b. of Farmington, Oct. 15,		
1735	LR6	27
Olive, m. Theodora **LEE**, Dec. 10, 1768	LR17	442
Ruth, d. Ephraim & Mahitable, b. Aug. 19, 1737	LR6	1
Ruth, m. Hezekiah **WOODRUFF**, Jr., Oct. 15, 1761	LR11	575
Sarah, d. Ephraim & Mahitable, b. Oct. 18, 1735	LR6	1
Sary, d. Ephraim, d. Feb. 15, 1742	LR6	305
BODURTHA, Hannah, of Springfield, m. Jonathan **SMITH**, s.		
Jonathan, June 30, 1708	LR2	145
BODWELL, Elizabeth, of Farmington, m. John B. **LEWIS**, of		
Schulerville, N.Y., Feb. 2, 1848, by Noah Porter	LR47	122
BOLLES, Joshua W., of Colebrook, m. Anne **WOODWARD**,		
of Bristol, Jan. 11, 1826, by Rev. Noah Porter	LR42	569
BOOGE, BOOG, BOGE, A[a]ron Jurdson, s. Rev. Ebenezer,		
b. May 6, 1752	LR8	3

	Vol.	Page
BOOGE, BOOG, BOGE (cont.)		
Damaris Corintha, d. Ebenezer, b. Aug. 26, 1761	LR11	579
Jeffrey Amhurst, s. Ebenezer, b. Aug. 21, 1759	LR11	579
Oliver, s. Ebenezer, b. Apr. 13, 1757	LR11	579
Publius Virgilous, s. Rev. Ebenezer, b. Mar. 30, 1764	LR11	578
Rebeckah Wakly, d. Ebenezer, b. Dec. 29, 1753	LR9	6
Samuell Cook, s. Ebenezer, b. Aug. 7, 1755	LR9	6
BOOTH, Abi, d. Elisha, b. May 30, 1784	LR22	460
Abigail, d. Nathan, b. Oct. 3, 1748	LR7	G
Abigall, m. Joshua **WEBSTER**, Mar. 24, 1773	LR17	443
Amos, s. Robert, b. June 2, 1779	LR22	460
Anna, d. Robert, b. Sept. 16, 1718	LR2	83
Cynthia, of Farmington, m. Samuel **BYINGTON**, of		
Southwick, Mass., Oct. 17, 1838, by Rev. S. H.		
Clark	LR47	98
David, s. Robert, b. Feb. 23, 1759	LR11	579
Elisha, s. Robert, b. May 20, [ ]	LR5	1
Elisha, s. Elisha, b. Nov. 8, 1753	LR9	6
Elisha, m. Esther **HOLLISTER**, Dec. 6, 1754	LR11	576
Esther, d. Elisha, b. Sept. 1, 1755	LR9	6
Fanny, d. Nathan, Jr., b. Dec. 27, 1776	LR21	540
Hannah, d. Robert, b. July 22, 1716	LR2	96
Hannah, d. Elisha, b. Aug. 17, 1779	LR21	540
Huldah, d. Elisha, b. Oct. 28, 1760	LR11	579
James, s. Robert, b. May 25, 1723	LR4	374
Jeames, s. Nathan, b. Mar. [ ], 1748	LR7	J
James, m. Thankfull **WINCHELL**, Nov. 23, 1775	LR21	557
James, s. James, b. Sept. 11, 1776	LR21	540
Jane L., m. Ambrose A. **HULL**, b. of Farmington, Nov.		
17, 1850, by Rev. Charles Kelsey	LR47	128
Johnson, s. Robert, b. Feb. 26, 1777	LR22	460
Joseph, s. Nathan, b. Oct. 1, 1751	LR8	3
Lois, d. Elisha, b. Jan. 14, 1782	LR22	460
Lucy, d. Nathan, b. Mar. [ ], 1760	LR11	578
Lydia, of Farmington, m. Nelson E. **THATCHER**, of		
Burlington, Sept. 8, 1850, by Rev. Charles Kelsey	LR47	127
Marian, of Farmington, m. Daniel **BARROWS**, of		
Mansfield, Nov. 27, 1835, by Rev. Noah Porter	LR47	91
Mahitabel, d. Nathaniell, Jr., b. Nov. 21, 1774	LR17	432
Nancy, d. Elisha, b. Aug. 18, 1768	LR17	430
Nathan, s. Robert, b. Aug. 6, 1721	LR2	102
Nathan, s. Nathan, b. Mar. 1, 1749/50	LR7	E
Nathan, Jr., m. Fanne **SMITH**, June 24, 1773	LR17	432
Nathan, Jr., m. Fanna **SMITH**, June 24, 1773	LR17	442
Orrin L., of Avon, m. Catharine **ROLY**, of Farmington,		
Feb. 23, 1846, by Rev. S. H. Clark	LR47	116
Robert, s. Robert, b. Aug. 20, 1730	LR5	1
Robert, m. Ruth **KILLBORN**, May 9, 1757	LR11	576
Robert, s. Nathan, b. June 20, 1758	LR11	579
Sally, of Farmington, m. Luther **BARROWS**, of		
Mansfield, June 25, 1837, by Rev. S. H. Clark	LR47	95
Sarah, d. Elisha, b. July 25, 1770	LR17	430
Silvanus, s. Elisha, b. Feb. 10, 1763	LR11	578

	Vol.	Page
BOOTH (cont.)		
Thomas, s. Elisha, b. Sept. 6, 1757	LR11	579
Ziba, s. Robert, b. Jan. 17, 1775	LR22	460
[BOSWORTH], BOZWORTH, Sally, m. Rufus **GORHAM,**		
b. of Montgomery Mass., June 8, 1828, by Noadiah		
Woodruff, J.P.	LR42	564
BOWEN, Charlotte M., m. Timothy C. **LEWIS,** b. of		
Farmington, May 26, 1841, by Rev. Noah Porter	LR47	105
BRACE, [see also **BRACY**], Almira, of Farmington, m. Levi		
SNOW, of Ellington, Sept. 3, 1822, by Pierpoint		
Brockett	LR40	572
Truman, m. Roxana **THOMSON,** b. of Farmington, Nov.		
15, 1825, by Rev. Noah Porter	LR42	569
William, s. Mehitabel **LOVELAND,** b. May 10, 1744	LR8	3
BRACY, [see also **BRACE**], Anne, of Hartford, m. Samuel		
STANLEY, Jr., of Ffarmington, Sept. 1, 1727	LR4	423
BRADLEY, Highly, d. James, b. Feb. 28, 1775	LR17	432
Ira, s. James, b. Feb. 3, 1760	LR11	578
Ire, s. James, d. June 20, 1766, in the 7th y. of his age	LR14	3
Isaac, m. Clara **COWLES,** b. of Farmington, May 10,		
1848, by William Wright	LR47	119
Isaac B., m. Martha J. **COWLES,** b. of Farmington, Mar.		
4, 1835, by Rev. Noah Porter	LR47	89
Jemima, d. James, b. May 11, 1758	LR11	578
Levi, s. Philomon, b. July 19, 1778	LR22	460
Lewis B., of Farmington, m. Ursula **HUNTLEY,** of		
Harwinton, July 8, [1833], by Rev. Noah Porter	LR42	A
Lucy, d. Phelemon, b. Nov. 26, 1770	LR21	540
Nancy, m. Norman **PORTER,** b. of Farmington, Sept.		
23, 1828, by Rev. Noah Porter	LR42	564
Nathaniel, s. James, b. Nov. 16, 1755	LR11	578
Nathaniel, s. James, b. Nov. [ ], 1755	LR11	579
Philemon, m. Hannah **TALMAGE,** Dec. 20, 1774	LR21	557
Sarah, d. James, b. May 6, 1767	LR15	C
Volney, of Bristol, m. Rodah **LANE,** of Farmington, Jan.		
20, 1850, by William Wright	LR47	127
William K., of New Marlborough, Mass., m. Adaline		
GRISWOLD, of Weathersfield, Oct. 24, 1841, by		
Rev. Aaron S. Hill	LR47	105
BRAINARD, BRAYNARD, Prudence, m. John **PORTER,**		
Nov. 11, 1779	LR22	480
Sarah, m. Abraham **PIERSON,** Aug. 7, 1746	LR7	35
BRASON, William P., m. Salina B. **TUTTLE,** b. of Brimfield,		
Mass., Apr. 10, 1828, by Rev. Noah Porter	LR42	564
BRAY, Asa, m. Lydia **ANDRUS,** May 12, 1763	LR11	592
BRECK, Mehetabel, of Weathersfield, m. Ebenezer **SMITH,**		
Jr., Oct. 18, 1750	LR11	575
BRESOW, [see also **BRISTOLL & BRISTOL**], Mercy, m.		
Gershom **MILLER,** Oct. 20, 1763	LR11	592
BREWER, Lavinia Amanda, m. John **DUNCAN,** Apr. 1,		
1823, by Elisha Cushman	LR40	572
BRINSMADE, Horatio N., of Hartford, m. Maria S. **TINKER,**		
of Farmington, Sept. 29, 1825, by Rev. Noah Porter	LR42	569

	Vol.	Page
BRISTOLL, [see also BRESOW & BRISTOW], David, m.		
Lois HART, May 29, 1771	LR17	G
BRISTOW, [see also BRISTOLL & BRESOW], Elydya, m.		
John WINSTON, Mar. 12, 1752	LR8	10
BROCKWAY, Huldah, m. Alfred HULL, b. of Farmington,		
Oct. 14, 1822, by Noah Porter, V.D.M.	LR40	572
BRONING, Ezekial, illeg. s. John BRONING & Lowis		
DEMING, b. Oct. 5, 1748	LR7	G
BRONSON, BRUNSON, BROWNSON, Aaron, s. Samuel (s.		
of Richard), b. Nov. 10, 1712	LR2	232
Aaron, m. Abigail PORTTER, d. John, Oct. 26, 1737	LR6	27
Abel, s. Moses, b. Jan. 19, 1742/3	LR6	1
Abigail, d. Jonathan & Abigail, b. Feb. 18, 1738/9	LR6	1
Abigail, d. [Ephraim], b. June 21, 1742	LR6	1
Abigail, d. Aron, b. Jan. 10, 1749/50	LR8	3
Abigail, m. Timothy BROWNSON, Dec. 1, 1763	LR11	594
Abijah Peck, s. Ozias, b. Aug. 2, 1772	LR17	430
Abina, s. Titus, b. Jan. 12, 1774	LR21	540
Achsah, d. Asa, b .Jan. 22, 1767	LR15	C
Affia, d. Elijah, b. Mar. 15, 1756	LR9	6
Amacy, s. Stephen, b. Oct. 17, 1779	LR22	460
Amos, s. William. b. Sept. 5, 1718	LR2	83
Amos, s. William, d. May 30, 1723	LR2	61
Amos, s. Hezekiah, b. about July 4, 1728	LR4	395
Amos, s. Joseph, b. Oct. 16, 1744; d., Dec. 2, 1744	LR7	G
Amos, m. Mercy WINCHEL, June 13, 1748	LR7	35
Amos, d. Feb. 14, 1754	LR8	12
Ann, d. Jonathan & Abigail, b. Mar. 30, 1737	LR6	1
Ann, d. Hezekiah, b. Dec. 13, 1742/3	LR6	1
Anna, d. Samuel, [s.] of R[ichar]d, b. Nov. 28, 1709	LR2	112
Anna, d. William, b. Feb. 8, 1719/20	LR2	102
Anna, [d.] Hezekiah, b. May 20, 1738	LR6	1
Anne, d. Tellus,* b. May 3, 1761 *("Titus"?)	LR11	578
Asa, s. Timothy, b. Aug. 24, 1742	LR6	1
Asa, m. Mary WINCHELL, Aug. 22, 1765	LR12	513
Asa, d. Feb. 27, 1778, in the 45th y. of his age	LR22	482
Asahel, s. Charles, b. June 23, 1760	LR11	578
Asahel, s. Ozias, b. Dec. 17, 1769	LR17	430
Asenah, d. Titus, b. Nov, 3, 1771	LR17	430
Ashbil, s. Elisha, b. Nov 11, 1752	LR8	3
Barnabus, s. Moses, b. Dec. 10, 1744	LR7	G
Bela, s. Ben[jamin], b. Jan. 10, 1732/3	LR5	1
Benjamin, s. Samuel, of Rd., b. Apr. 4, 1697	LR2	112
Benjamin, m. Martha BARNS, b. of Ffarmington, Dec.15,		
1725	LR2	51
Benjamin, his s. [ ], b. [ ], 1729 & s. [ ],		
[ ], [ ], 1729	LR4	396
Benjamin, s. John, b. Aug. 19, 1763	LR11	578
Benoni, s. Charles, b. May 30, 1757	LR11	578
Candace, d. Charles, b Apr. 9, 1751	LR11	579
Caroline, d. Jesse, b. Feb. 21, 1768	LR15	C
Charles, s. Samuell, Jr., b. Sept. 24, 1723	LR2	87
Charles, m. Thankfull HART, Nov. 5, 1747	LR7	46

	Vol.	Page
BRONSON, BRUNSON, BROWNSON (cont.)		
Charles, m. Thankfull **HART**, Nov. 5, 1747	LR8	10
Charles, had d. [ ], b,. Aug. 6, 1748/9	LR7	G
Charles, m. Martha **BARRIT**, May 30, 1759	LR11	575
Daniel, s. Samuel, of Rd., b. Aug. 7, 1703	LR2	112
Daniel, of Ffarmington, m. Mary **PEET**, of Stratford,		
Apr. 2, 1725	LR4	423
Daniel, s. Daniel, b. Mar. 15, 1728/9	LR5	1
David, s. John, b. Aug. 9, 1704	LR2	109
David, m. Susannah **JUDD**, July 1, 1756	LR10	6
David, d. Oct. 30, 1771, in the 68th y. of his age	LR17	445
David, s. Jonathan, b. Dec. 8, 1772	LR17	430
Deborah, w. Timothy, d. Sept. 4, 1751	LR8	11
Dorcas, d. Moses, b. Aug. 14, 1746	LR7	G
Dorcas, w. Timothy, d. Apr. 30, 1747	LR7	36
Dorcas, d. Titus, b. Jan. 9, 1766	LR15	C
Ebenezer, his d. [ ], b. [ ], 1729	LR4	396
Ebenezer Allin, s. Timothy, b. May 18, 1754	LR9	6
Eldad, s. James & Hannah, b. July 30, 1740	LR7	E
Elidia, d. Charles, b. Nov. 5, 1754	LR11	578
Elijah, m. Abigail **WINCHEL**, Apr. 13, 1739	LR6	27
Elisha, s. Samuel, Jr., b. Apr. 9, 1718	LR2	83
Elisha, of Farmington, m. Sarah **HOLLISTER**, of		
Glastenbury, Sept. 16, 1737	LR6	27
Elizabeth, d. Samuel, b. Apr. 4, 1688	LR2	112
Elizabeth, m. Thomas **GRIDLEY**, s. Thomas, Aug. 3,		
1710	LR2	145
Elizabeth, d. Stephen, b. Apr. 21, 1782	LR22	460
Ephraim, s. Moses, b. Nov. 27, 1750	LR8	3
Esther, d. William, b. Apr. 2 ,1716	LR2	81
Esther, d. William, b. Apr. 3, 1716	LR2	96
Esther, m. James **BARET**, Dec. 20, 1753	LR9	12
Esther, m. Rufus **BLAKESLEY**, Sept. 12, 1771	LR17	G
Grace, m. Jacob **BARNES**, b. of Ffarmington, Mar. 19,		
1710/11	LR2	123
Hannah, d. Timothy, b. Oct. 3, 1730	LR5	1
Hannah, d. Moses, b. June 25, 174[ ]	LR6	1
Hannah, d. James, b. Jan. 18, 1754	LR9	6
Hezekiah, s. Samuel, of Rd., b. Oct. 23, 1699	LR2	112
Hezekiah, of Ffarmington, m. Abiah **BALDWIN**, of		
Durham, July 26, 1727	LR4	423
Hezekiah, s. Hezekiah, b. Feb. 6, 1732/3	LR5	1
Hezekiah, d. Sept. [ ], 1752	LR11	577
Hezekiah, d. Oct. 2, 1752	LR8	11
Hezekiah, d. Dec. [ ], 1752	LR8	12
Hezekiah, of Farmington, m. Abigail **DRINKWATTER**,		
of New Milford, Apr. 19, 1756	LR9	286
Hezekiah, m. Abigail **DRINKWATER**, Apr. 21, 1756	LR11	576
Huldah, d. Jonathan, b. Apr. 18, 1747	LR7	G
Huldah, d. Moses, b. Oct. 26, 1748	LR7	G
Ichabod, s. Michael, b. Mar. 19, 1735/6	LR5	1
Icabod, s. Mich[ae]l, d. Nov. 17, 1741	LR6	305
Isaac, s. Jonathan & Abigail, b. June 20, 1751	LR8	3

	Vol.	Page
BRONSON, BRUNSON, BROWNSON (cont.)		
Isaac, s. John, b. July 19, 1761	LR11	578
Isaac, s. Asa, b. Oct. 21, 1773	LR17	432
James, s. William, b. Mar. 12, 1708* *(Perhaps "1709")	LR2	109
James, s. William, d. Mar. 24, 1708	LR2	141
James, s. John, b. Nov. 29, 1713	LR2	99
James, m. Hannah **PECK**, b. of Farmington, Apr. 26, 1737	LR6	27
James, s. James, b. July 29, 1751	LR9	6
James, d. Mar. 28, 1775, in the 82nd y. of his age	LR17	445
Jemima, d. Elijah, d. May 8, 1759	LR11	574
Jemima, d. Elijah, b. May 24, 1759	LR11	578
Jerusha, d. Timothy, b. Nov. 19, 1736	LR6	1
Jerusha, m. Robert **WOODRUFF**, Feb. 17, 1757	LR11	575
Jesse, s. Aaron, b. June 20, 1738	LR6	1
Jesse, m. [ ], May 7, 1767	LR15	A
Job, s. Samuel, Jr., b. Dec. 5, 1732	LR5	1
Job, s. Samuel, 2nd & Abigail, b. Dec. 17, 1732	LR6	1
Job, m. Temperance **ROOT**, Oct. 8, 1752	LR8	10
Joel, s. John, b. Mar. 9, 1759	LR11	579
John, m. Rachel **BUCK**, Jan. [ ], 1697	LR1	4
John, s. John, b. Nov. 21, 1698	LR1	2
John, m. wid. Mary **CHATTERTON**, of New Haven, Apr. 17, 1709	LR2	145
John, s. John, d. June 15, 1716	LR2	62
John, s. William, b. May 2, 1723	LR2	88
John, s. William, d. May 3, 1723	LR2	61
John, s. Aaron, b. May 4, 1743	LR6	1
John, d. Aug. 9, 1749	LR8	12
John, m. Sarah **BARNES**, Mar. 30, 1758	LR1	576
Jonathan, s. John, b. May 14, 1706	LR2	109
Jonathan, of Farmington, m. Abigail **CLARK**, living between Farmington & Wallingford, May 17, 1732	LR5	300
Jonathan, s. Jonathan & Abigail, b. Dec. 24, 1740	LR6	1
Jonathan, his s. [ ], b. Jan. 20, 1743/4	LR7	H
Jonathan, d. Aug. 20, 1751	LR8	11
Jonathan, m. Susannah **JUDD**, Mar. 5, 1772	LR17	442
Joseph, s. John, b. June 15, 1708	LR2	109
Joseph, m. Ester **RUST**, Mar. 4, 1741	LR7	35
Joseph, his d. [ ], b. Mar. 15, 1742	LR7	H
Joseph, s. Job, b. Feb. 9, 1757	LR11	579
Josiah, s. Hezekiah, b. Sept. 18, 1726	LR4	382
Josiah, s. Micael, b. June 8, 1738	LR6	1
Josiah, m. Sarah **WINCHEL**, Nov. 12, 1747	LR7	35
Josiah, s. Josiah, b. Oct. 17, 1755	LR11	579
Levy, s. Benjamin, b .June 5, 1734	LR5	307
Levi, s. Elisha, b Sept. 15, 1746	LR7	G
Levi, s. Ozias, b. Jan. 23, 1766	LR17	430
Lois, d. Jonathan & Abigail, b. June 6, 1749	LR8	3
Lois, d. Ozias, b. Sept. 15, 1762	LR11	578
Louis, d. Stephen, b. Dec. 24, 1772	LR22	460
Luca, d. Hezekiah, b. Oct. 4, 1730	LR5	1

	Vol.	Page
BRONSON, BRUNSON, BROWNSON (cont.)		
Lucinda, m. W[illia]m M. **ROOT**, b. of Farmington, Sept.		
21, 1829, by Rev. Noah Porter	LR42	562
Luke, s. Elisha, b. Mar. 3, 1755	LR9	6
Lydia, d. James & Hannah, b. Aug., last, 1738	LR7	E
Mabel, s. Jonathan, b. Oct. 25, 1735	LR5	1
Marinda, of Berlin, m. Simeon **ROWLEY**, of		
Farmington, July 27, 1836, by Rev. Noah Porter	LR47	93
Martha, d. William, b. Oct. 18, 1711	LR2	97
Martha, d. Benjamin, b. July 20, 1738	LR6	1
Martha, m. John **KELLCEY**, b. of Farmington, Apr. 26,		
1739	LR6	27
Martin, s. Moses, b. May 24, 1738	LR6	1
Martin, s. Moses, d. June 28, 1758	LR11	577
Martin, s. Silas, b. Oct. 6, 1761	LR11	578
Mary, w. Hezekiah, d. Sept. 30, 1626* *("1726"		
overwritten in pencil)	LR2	147
Mary, d. John, b. Jan. 30, 1711/12	LR2	97
Mary, d. Daniel, b. Mar. 14, 1726/7	LR4	395
Mary, d. Hezekiah, b. May 9, 1735	LR5	1
Mary, d. Ephraim, b. Sept. 25, 1739	LR6	1
Mary, d. James & Hannah, b. Feb. 8, 1742/3	LR7	E
Mary, m. William **PARSONS**, Jr., Apr. 4, 1755	LR9	286
Mary, m. Adonijah **LEWIS**, July 31, 1760	LR11	592
Mary, d. Titus, b. May 13, 1764	LR15	C
Mary, d. Asa, b. Nov. 10, 1771	LR17	430
Mary, m. Ezekiel **UPSON**, Sept. 17, 1772	LR17	442
Matthew, s. Hezekiah, b. Mar. 25, 1725	LR2	65
Matthew, d. Apr. 3, 1742	LR6	305
Mathew, s. Josiah, b. Jan. 10, 1750/1	LR8	3
Mercy, d. Elisha & Abigail, b. Nov. 13, 1738	LR6	1
Micah, s. Samuel, [s,] of R[ichar]d, b. Sept. 17, 1707	LR2	112
Micah, s. Micah, b. Nov. 19, 1751	LR8	3
Michael, of Farmington, m. Elizabeth **SQUIER**, of		
Woodbury, May 8, 1735	LR5	539
Moses, s. William, b. May 2, 1710	LR2	109
Moses, of Farmington, m. Hannah **KELLEY**, of		
Weathersfield, Oct. 6, 1737	LR6	27
Nathaniel, s. Samuel, [s.] of R[ichar]d, b. Sept. 1, 1705	LR2	112
Nathaniel, s. Samuel (s. Richard), d. Jan. 11, 1712/13	LR2	141
Nathaniel, s. Timothy, b. Oct. 5, 1726	LR4	382
Noadiah, s. Elijah, b. Sept. 18, 1740	LR6	1
Ozias, s. Elisha, b. Sept. 3, 1742	LR6	1
Ozias, m. Abigail **PECK**, Oct. 23, 1762	LR11	592
Ozias, s. Ozias, b. Mar. 7, 1764	LR17	430
Phebe, d. Benjamin, b. Mar. 4, 1733/4	LR5	1
Phebe, d. Stephen, b. Mar. 23, 1776	LR22	460
Rachel, w. John, d. June 21, 1708	LR2	141
Rachel, d. John, b. July 6, 1710	LR2	109
Rachel, d. Eliah, b. Apr. 27, 1744	LR7	G
Rachel, m. Elisha **SQUIRE**, Apr. 11, 1767	LR15	A
Roger, s. Aaron, b. Mar. 24, 1746	LR7	G
Rozanne, d. James & Hannah, b. Apr. 29, 1748	LR7	E

	Vol.	Page
BRONSON, BRUNSON, BROWNSON (cont.)		
Ruth, d. John, b. Feb. 1, 1715/16	LR2	96
Ruth, d. Elijah, b. Oct. 26, 1760	LR11	578
Salmon, s. Ozias, b. Dec. 16, 1767	LR17	430
Samuel, of Ffarmington, s. Richard, m. Sarah **GIBBS**, of		
Windsor, May 4, 1687	LR2	145
Samuel, s. Samuel, [s.] of R[ichar]d, b. Dec. 30, 1692	LR2	112
Samuel, cooper, d. Feb. 19, 1724/5	LR2	66
Samuel, s. Elisha & Sarah, b. June 16, 1740	LR6	1
Samuell, d. Jan. 18, 1741/2	LR6	305
Samuel, d. Apr. 22, 1752	LR8	12
Samuel, d. Apr. 22, 1752	LR11	577
Samuel, s. Elijah, b. Oct. 31, 1752	LR8	3
Sarah, d. Samuel, [s.] of R[ichar]d, b. Mar. 5, 1694/5	LR2	112
Sarah, wid., of John, of Waterbury, d. Jan. 6, 1711/12	LR2	141
Sarah, m. Daniel **THOMSON**, b. of Ffarmington, Sept.		
21, 1727	LR4	423
Sarah, d. Elisha, b. July 21, 1738	LR6	1
Sary, w. Samuel, d. Oct. 27, 1740	LR6	305
Sary, d. Mich[ae]l, b. Dec. 17, 1742	LR6	1
Sarah, d. James & Hannah, b. Aug. 29, 1745	LR7	E
Sarah, d. Josiah, b. Oct. 13, 1753	LR11	579
Sarah, d. Daniel, b. Nov. 24, [ ]	LR5	1
Selah, s. Tellus,* b. Nov. 3, 1762 *("Titus"?)	LR11	578
Silas, s. Moses, b. Dec. 16, 1739	LR6	1
Silvester, s. Noadiah, b. June 7, 1772	LR17	432
Simeon, s. Job, b. Aug. 24, 1754	LR9	6
Stephen, s. Aaron, b. Feb. 18, 1740/1	LR6	1
Stephen, s. Hezekiah, b. Apr. 21, 1741	LR6	1
Stephen, s. Hezekiah, d. Jan. 1, 1741/2	LR6	305
Stephen, s. Hezekiah, b. Oct. 7, 1758	LR11	579
Stephen, m. Elizabeth **DUTTON**, Sept. 5, 1771	LR17	G
Stephen, s. Stephen, b. Dec. 27, 1784	LR22	460
Sible, d. Amos, b. Apr. 21, 1750	LR8	3
Sibel, d. Amos, d. Dec. 9, 1751	LR8	11
Sibble, d. Amos, b. Nov. 12, 1753	LR8	3
Sibbel, d. Noadiah, b. Mar. 29, 1775	LR17	432
Temperance, d. Asa, b. Feb. 6, 1776	LR17	432
Temperance, w. Job, d. May 19, 1778, in the 45th y. of		
her age	LR22	482
Thadeus, s. Daniel, b. Sept. 22, 1732	LR5	1
Thankfull, d. Elijah, b. Nov. 5, 1747	LR7	G
Thankfull, w. Charles, d. May 20, 1757	LR11	574
Thankfull, d. Charles, b. Feb. 12, 1762	LR11	578
Thankfull, d. Asa, b. Mar. 8, 1769	LR15	B
Timothy, s. Samuel, [s.] of R[ichar]d, b. Sept. 19, 1701	LR2	112
Timothy, of Farmington, m. Dorcas **HOPKINS**, of		
Hartford, July 19, 1725	LR2	52
Timothy, his s. [ ], b. [ ] 27, 1728	LR4	396
Timothy, s. Timothy, b. Sept. 19, 1732	LR5	1
Timothy, s. Timothy, d. Jan. 26, 1734/5	LR5	50
Timothy, s. Timothy 2nd, b. Dec. 11, 1738	LR6	1

	Vol.	Page
BRONSON, BRUNSON, BROWNSON (cont.)		
Timothy, of Farmington, m. Deborah **TAMAGE**, of New		
Haven, Jan. 14, 1747/8	LR7	35
Timothy, m. Susannah **ALLIN**, Dec. 2, 1752	LR8	10
Timothy, m. Abigail **BROWNSON**, Dec. 1, 1763	LR11	594
Titus, m. [ ] **WHEDON**, Mar. 20, 1761	LR11	592
Titus, s. Titus, b. July 17, 1768	LR15	B
Tryphene, d. Elijah, b. Mar. 25, 1746	LR7	G
William, m. Esther **BARNES**, Mar. 20, 1707	LR2	145
William, d. Aug. 20, 1761	LR11	593
[Z]adack, s. Jonathan, b. Aug. 7, 1745	LR7	G
Zenas, s. Timothy, b. Sept. 29, 1764	LR14	5
Ziba, s. Micahel, b. Mar. 21, 1739/40	LR6	1
Zuriah, had d. [ ]cas, b .May 3, 1745	LR7	G
---cas, d. Zuriah, b. May 3, 1745	LR7	G
BROOKS, Abraham, m. Deborah **HUNGERFORD**, Mar. 5,		
1767	LR15	A
Abraham, s. Abraham, b. Oct. 23, 1775	LR17	432
Azael, s. Benjamin, b. Dec. 11, 1754	LR9	6
Barnaby, s. Benjamin, b. June 15, 1749	LR7	E
Benjamin, s. Benjamin, b. Nov. 4, 17[ ]	LR7	E
Cornelius, s. Benjamin, b. May 11, 17[ ]	LR7	E
Syrus,* s. Abraham, b. Oct. 2, 1773 *("Cyrus")	LR17	432
Doboray, d. Abraham, b. Mar. 9, 1781	LR22	460
Jerusha, d. Stephen, d .Nov. 7, 1749	LR7	36
Jarusha, d. Abraham, b. Feb. 17, 1772	LR17	430
John, s. Benjamin, b. May 17, 1752	LR8	3
Ruben, s. Benjamin, b. Sept. 7, 1742	LR7	542
Stephen, s. Stephen, d. June 27, 1748	LR7	36
Stephen, s. Abraham, b .May 13, 1769	LR15	B
Vashty, d. Abraham, b. Sept. 20, 1767	LR15	C
BROWN, Allice, m. Noah **FULLER**, June 2, 1757	LR11	576
Chauncey, m. Julia M. **STRONG**, b. of Farmington, Aug.		
10, 1836, by Rev. Noah Porter	LR47	93
Ebenezer, s. Thomas & Mary, b. Oct. 11, 1760, in Great		
Nine Partners in Dutchess Cty,., in Crumbe Precenct	LR11	578
Elias, of Farmington, m. Nancy **HART**, of Berlin, Oct.		
20, 1825, by Rev. Stephen Crosby	LR42	569
Easther, of Arther Cull, m. Joseph **WOODRUFF**, s.		
Matth[e]w, Oct. 24, 1717	LR2	94
George W., of Bolton, m. Elizabeth R. **ORTON**, May 6,		
1850, by William Wright	LR47	127
Hannah, of New Haven, m. John **CROW**, Jr., of		
Farmington, Mar. 22, 1742	LR6	304
Hezekiah, of Ffarmington, m. Mary **DEMING**, of		
Weathersfield, June 8, 1723/4	LR2	60
John, m. Lois **DEMING**, b. of Farmignton, Mar. 6, 1746	LR7	35
John, m. Clarissa **HENDRICK**, b. of Farmington, May		
23, 1822, by Noah Porter, V.D.M.	LR40	571
Joseph, of Crum Elbow Precinct, Dutchess Cty., N.Y., m.		
Mary **RICHARDS**, of Farmington, Mar. 20, 1760	LR11	575
Lucinda, m. Samuel **SAMMADY**, b. of Farmington,		
Sept. 4, 1834, by Rev. Noah Porter	LR42	E

	Vol.	Page
BROWN (cont.)		
Mary S., m. Richard **ORVIS**, July 8, 1839, by Rev. Ezra		
S. Cook. Witnesses Ira W. Rowe & Richard Yale	LR47	100
Simeon, s. John, b. Sept. 6, 1746	LR7	G
Simeon, s. John, d. Apr. 19, 1747	LR7	36
William, m. Lucy J. **SMITH**, b. of Farmington, Sept. 1,		
1834, by Rev. Noah Porter	LR42	E
BUCK, Benjamin, m. Mercy **PARSONS**, b. of Ffarmington,		
Dec. 10, 1728	LR4	423
Daniel, of Weathersfield, now of Farmington, m.		
Elizabeth **PIRKINS**, of Norwich, June 11, 1722	LR2	60
Ebenezer, m. Mary **GRAHAM**, b. of Farmington, Apr.		
11, 1740	LR6	27
Ebenezer, s. Ebenezer, b. Feb. 12, 1742/3	LR6	1
Elizabeth, d. Daniel & Elizabeth, b. May 11, 1723	LR2	87
Esther, m. John **RUSS**, b. of Farmington, Nov. 25, 1736	LR6	27
[E]unice, d. Benjamin, b. Apr. 2, 1731	LR5	1
Lidia, m. Samuel **RICHARDS**, Dec. 8, 1747	LR8	10
Mary, d. Ebenezer, b. Nov. 20, 1740	LR7	E
Mercy, wid., m. Ebenezer **RICHARDS**, b. of		
Farmington, Dec. 6, 1736	LR6	27
Phebe, d. Ebenezer, b. Feb. 10, 1757	LR11	579
Rachel, m. John **BROWNSON**, Jan. [ ], 1697	LR1	4
Solomon, s. Benjamin, b. Aug. 13, 1729	LR5	1
Solomon, s. Benjamin, d. June 3, 1731	LR5	50
Solomon, s. Zephaniah, b Aug. 24, 1757	LR11	579
Stephen, Jr., m. Deborah **BARNES**, June 14, 1739	LR6	27
Stephen, d. Jan. 15, 1747/8	LR7	36
Stephen, m. Hanah **COUCH**, Jan. 16, 1749	LR9	286
Stephen, Jr. [	LR6	1
William, s. Ebenezer, b. Dec. 23, 1740	LR6	1
Zephaniah, m. Phebe **PERSONS**, Feb. 6, 1756	LR11	576
----sa, s. Stephen, b. Oct. 13, 1746	LR7	G
BUCKINGHAM, An[n], m. Thomas **ORTON**, May 9, 1698	LR1	4
Thomas, m. Mrs. Mary **HOOKER**, Aug. 10, 1703	LR1	4
[BUEL], BEWEL, BEAWEL, Anne, m. Noah **MILLER**,		
Apr. 9, 1760	LR11	575
Hephsibah, m. Sergt. Thomas **ORTON**, Feb. 18, 1741/2	LR6	304
Samuel, d. June [ ], 1755	LR11	577
BULL, Abiga[i]l, m. Ebenezer **LEE**, June 20, 1750	LR7	46
Amos, m. Lucy **SMITH**, Oct. 5, 1767	LR15	A
David, s. Thomas, b. June 4, 1687	LR1	2
David, of Ffarmington, m. Sarah **ASHLEY**, of Westfield,		
July 4, 1717	LR2	101
David, s. David, b. May 31, 1723	LR2	88
David, d. Jan. 17, 1762	LR11	574
Ebenezer, twin with John, s. John, decd., b. Aug. 17, 1705	LR1	7
Ebenezer, s. John, d. Nov. 9, 1705	LR1	2
Easther, d. [Thomas], b. Feb. 14, 1674	LR1	2
Esther, d. Thomas, d. Aug. 18, 1689, ae 15	LR1	2
Esther, w. Thomas, d. Apr. 17, 1691, ae 42	LR1	2
Esther, d. David, b .Jan. 3, [ ]	LR5	1

	Vol.	Page
BULL (cont.)		
Henry C., m. Mary E. **CAMERON**, b. of Farmington,		
Nov. 4, 1835, by Rev. Noah Porter	LR47	91
[Huldah*], d. Jonathan, b. Apr. 26, 1743 *(Supplied by		
Mrs. Bissell from Bible Record)	LR7	G
Huldah, m. Thomas **MATHER**, Mar. 12, 1764	LR11	592
John, s. Thomas, b. Feb. 1, 1670	LR1	2
John, m. Easther **ROYCE**, Nov. 23, 1698	LR1	4
John, s. Dea. Thomas, d. Apr. 19, 1705	LR1	2
John, twin with Ebenezer, s. John, decd., b. Aug. 17, 1705	LR1	7
Jonathan, s. Thomas, b. May 14, 1682	LR1	2
Jonathan, s. David, b. June 23, 1718	LR2	83
Jonathan, s. Moses & Mabell, b. Oct. 14, 1734	LR9	6
Jona[than], [s.] Jonathan, b. Dec. 3, 1744	LR7	G
Juanah, m. Timothy **PORTER**, Apr. 22, 1697	LR1	4
Katherine, d. Martin, b. May 28, 1772	LR17	430
Lucy, d. Jonathan, b Mar. 7, [ ]	LR7	E
Martin, m. Elizabeth [ ], Nov. 9, 1768	LR15	A
Mary, wid. Dr. Thomas, d. Jan. 10, 1726/7	LR4	396
Mary, d. David, b. May 2, 1736	LR5	692
Mary, m. William **LEWIS**, Dec. 7, 1758	LR11	592
Noah, s. David, b. Dec. 2, 1726	LR2	242
Samuell, s. Thomas, b. Aug. 8, 1676	LR1	2
Sarah, d. Thomas, b. Nov. 5, 1684	LR1	2
Sarah, m. Josiah **HART**, b. of Farmington, Jan. 7,		
1713/14	LR2	93
Sarah, d. David, b. Jan. 5, 1720/1	LR2	102
Sophia, d. Martin, b. Oct. 24, 1769	LR15	B
Susanah, d. Thomas, b. Nov. 2, 1679	LR1	2
Susannah, m. Amos **COWLES**, Nov. 13, 1755	LR9	286
Thankfull, m. Elijah **PORTER**, Sept. 21, 1748	LR7	46
Thomas, m. Easther **COWLES**, Apr. 29, 1669	LR1	4
Thomas, s. Thomas, b. Aug. 1, 1672	LR1	2
Thomas, s. Thomas, d. Aug. 15, 1689, ae 17	LR1	2
Thomas, m. Mary **LEWIS**, Jan. 13, 1691/2	LR1	5
Thomas, s. John, b. Oct. 22, 1699	LR1	2
Thomas, s. David, b. Mar. 15, 1728/9	LR4	396
BULLOCK, Cyrrel, of Rehobath, Mass., m. Matilda M.		
ROWE, of Farmington, Mar. 8, 1843, by S. W.		
Smith, Elder	LR47	110
[**BUNCE**], **BUNSE**, Sarah, m. William **WADSWORTH**, Jan.		
13, 1708/9	LR2	145
[**BUNNELL**], **BUNEL**, **BUNNEL**, Abel, s. Jesse, b. Apr. 29,		
1758	LR11	579
Amos, s. Joseph, b. May 9, 1761	LR11	578
Asa, s. Titus, b. May 24, 1776	LR21	540
Bela, s. Jesse, b. Aug. 27, 1765	LR15	C
Elizabeth S., of Farmington, m. Earl **PECK**, of		
Cabotville, Mass., June 10, 1844, by William		
Wright	LR47	113
Hezekiah, d. May 25, 1764	LR11	593
Jesse, m. Mehetable **ROYCE**, Apr. 19, 1757	LR11	576
Jesse, s. Jesse, b. June 19, 1763	LR11	578

	Vol.	Page
[BUNNELL], BUNEL, BUNNEL		
Hezekiah, d. May 25, 1764	LR11	593
Jesse, m. Mehetable **ROYCE**, Apr. 19, 1757	LR11	576
Jesse, s. Jesse, b. June 19, 1763	LR11	578
Joel, s. Joseph, b. Nov. 12, 1758	LR11	579
John M., of Canaan, m. Julia E. **LOVELAND**, of		
Farmington, Feb. 25, 1844, by William Wright	LR47	112
Levi, s. Jesse, b. Sept. 14, 1768	LR15	C
Marcus, m. Eliza **SMITH**, b. of Farmington, May 1,		
1831, by Rev. Noah Porter	LR42	560
Meriam, d. Joseph, b. Mar. 20, 1753	LR9	6
Nathaniel, m. Thankfull **SPENCER**, Sept. 8, 1755	LR9	286
Nathaniel, s. Nathaniel, b. May 9, 1758	LR11	579
Nathaniell, s. Nathaniell, decd., b. June 26, 1776	LR22	460
Oliver, s. Titus, b. Dec. 29, 1768	LR15	C
Rhoda, d. Ens. Titus, b. Aug. 2, 1778	LR22	460
Ruth, d. Jesse, b. Mar. 19, 1760	LR11	579
Solomon, Jr., m. Helen **WILMOT**, b. of Bristol, Sept. 19,		
1836, by Rev. Noah Porter	LR47	94
Susan M., of Southington, m. James **SWEET**, Jr., of		
Farmington, Dec. 10, 1843, by William Wright	LR47	112
Susannah, d. Nathaniel & Thankfull, b. Aug. 4, 1756	LR9	6
Susannah, of Burlington, m. Edward **PORTER**, of		
Farmington, Apr. 5, 1852, at the house of Chauncey		
Porter, by Rev. P. G. Wightman, of Plainville	LR47	131
Sibbel, d. Titus, b. June 26, 1771	LR17	430
Titus, s. Titus, b. July 19, 1769	LR15	B
William L., of Farmington, m. Phebe **DURAND**, of		
Sheffield, Mass., Dec. 12, 1842, by Rev. C. D.		
Cowles	LR47	109
BURD, [see under **BIRD**]		
BURDICK, Emmeline, of Burlington, m. James C.		
JOHNSON, of Farmington, Mar. 1, 1836, by Rev.		
Noah Porter	LR47	93
Mary, of Burlington, m. Almon **FULLER**, of		
Farmington, Oct. 28, 1840, by Rev. Aaron S. Hill	LR47	103
BURGE, Damaras, Mrs., m. John **NORTHAWAY**, July 14,		
1772	LR17	442
BURNHAM, BARNHAM, Abigail, d. William, b. Sept. 14,		
1713	LR2	95
Abigail, d. Elisha, b. June 7, 1756	LR11	578
Abigail, d. Elisha, b. June 7, 1756	LR15	B
Appleton, s. Rev. William, b. Apr. 28, 1724	LR4	395
Cloe, d. Elisha, b. Dec. 28, 1757	LR11	578
Cloe, d. Elisha, b. Dec. 28, 1757	LR15	B
Elisha, s. William, Jr., b. Jan. 14, 1729/30	LR5	307
Elisha, m. Jerusha **LEE**, Nov. 9, 1749	LR7	46
Hannah, d. William, b. Nov. 18, 1708	LR2	111
Hannah, m. Jeremiah **CURTISS**, b. of Farmington, Jan.		
7, 1730/1	LR5	13
Jerusha, d. Elisha, b. Mar. 27, 1752	LR11	578
Jerusha, d. Elisha, b. Mar. 27, 1752	LR15	B
Josiah, s. William, b. Apr. 28, 1716	LR2	84

	Vol.	Page
BURNHAM, BARNHAM (cont.)		
Josiah, s. Josiah, b. Aug. 12, 1743	LR6	1
Lucius, of New Hartford, m. Sarah A. **TODD**, of		
Mereden, Oct. 10, 1852, at the house of her father in		
Plainville, by Rev. P. G. Wightman, of Plainville	LR47	131
Lucy, d. William, b. May 22, 1711	LR2	98
Marah, m. Seth **HOOKER**, Sept. 4, 1755	LR9	286
Mary, d. Rev. William, b. Feb. 7, 1721/2	LR4	395
Rhoda, d. Appleton, b. Feb. 2, 1755	LR11	579
Rosalanda, d. Elisha, b. May 1, 1754	LR11	578
Rosalinda, d. Elisha, b. May 1, 1754	LR15	B
Ruth, d. W[illia]m, Jr. & Ruth, b. Sept. 15, 1739	LR6	1
Ruth, d. Josiah, b. Jan. 24, 1741	LR6	1
Ruth, d. Elisha, b. Dec. 5, 1766	LR15	B
Samuel, s. William, b. May 28, 1707, at Weathersfield; d.		
Jan. 22, 1707/8	LR2	141
Sarah, d. Rev. William, b. May 28, 1719	LR2	83
Sarah, d. Rev. William, d. Nov. 23, 1726	LR4	396
Sarah, d. W[illia]m, Jr., b. June 5, 1734	LR6	1
Sarah, d. Elisha, b. July 12, 1762	LR11	578
Sarah, d. Elisha, b. July 12, 1762	LR15	B
Silvia, d. Elisha, b. Jan. 7, 1760	LR11	578
Silvia, d. Elisha, b. Jan. 7, 1760	LR15	B
Silviah, d. Mar. 3, 1769, in the 9th y. of his age	LR15	M
William, Capt., d. Mar. 12, 1749	LR7	540
William, s. Elisha, b. Oct. 14, 1750	LR8	3
William, s. Elisha, b. Oct. 14, 1750	LR11	578
William, s. Elisha, b. Oct. 14, 1750	LR15	B
William, s. Elisha, d. Dec. 18, 1750	LR11	593
William, d. Dec. 18, 1750, in the 1st y. of his age	LR15	M
William, s. Elisha, d. Dec. 19, 1750	LR7	540
William, s. Elisha, b. Dec. 25, 1764	LR15	B
BURR, [see also **BARR**], Amos, m. Ann [　], Dec. 30, 1761	LR15	N
Amos, s. Amos, b. Apr. 17, 1764	LR15	B
Christian, d. Samuel, b. Oct. 5, 1753	LR14	5
Clarissa B., of Farmington, m. Caleb C. **SPENCER**, of		
Windsor, Jan. 23, 1822, by Rev. Augustus Bolles, of		
Wentonbury	LR40	571
Ebenezer, twin with Thankfull, s. John, b. July 9, 1712	LR5	1
Eleanor, d. Samuel, b. Mar. 22, 1755	LR14	5
Gideon, s. John, b. Nov. 16, 1715	LR5	1
John, Jr., m. Mary **ROOT**, of Ffarmington, Nov. 15, 1722	LR2	51
John, s. John, Jr., b. May 28, 1726	LR5	1
John, s. John, Jr., b. July 19, 1750	LR7	E
Lodima, d. Samuel, b. Sept. 13, 1764	LR14	5
Mary, d. Samuel, b. June 21, 1766	LR14	5
Mary, d. John, Jr., b .June 14, [　]	LR5	1
Mahetabel, m. Joseph **TWIST**, Sept. 3, 1751	LR8	10
Nodiah, m. Hannah **JELLETT**, Nov. 5, 1732	LR5	1
Noadiah, of Farmington, m. Hannah **JELETT**, of		
Hartford, Nov. 5, 173[ ]*　 *(In pencil "1730")	LR5	13
Obadiah, s. Noadiah, b. Apr. 29, 1732	LR5	1
Rosalinda, d. Samuel, b. Oct. 22, 1759	LR14	5

	Vol.	Page
BURR, [see also **BARR**], (cont.)		
Ruth, d. John, Jr., b. Oct. 26, [ ]	LR5	1
Salmon, s. John, Jr., b. Sept. 25, 1723	LR2	70
Samuel, m. Christian **CADWELL**, Dec. 27, 1752	LR12	513
Samuel, s. Samuel, b. Oct. 4, 1761	LR14	5
Sarah, d. Samuel, b. Oct. 6, 1757	LR14	5
Thankfull, twin with Ebenezer, d. John, b. July 9, 1712	LR5	1
Titus, s. Noadiah, b. Oct. 14, 1737	LR6	1
BURROWS, BURRUS, [see also **BARROWS**], Almyra Ann,		
m. Daniel **WHITEHOUSE**, Nov. 29, 1839, by Rev.		
Ezra S. Cook	LR47	101
Harriet E., of Farmington, m. Norman **HOUGH**, of		
Berlin, Apr. 9, 1834, by Rev. Noah Porter	LR42	E
Sarah A., m. Reuben L. **HILLS**, b. of Farmington, Jan.		
24, 1839, by Rev. Noah Porter	LR47	99
BUSHNELL, BUSHNAL, BUSHNEL, Abraham, s. Stephen,		
b. Dec. 27, 1744	LR11	579
Catherine, d. Stephen, b. Sept. 13, 1748	LR11	579
Stephen, s. Stephen, b. Sept. 15, 1743	LR11	579
Stephen, d. Sept. 10. 1748	LR11	577
Temperance, d. Stephen & Temperance, b. Oct. 4, 1747	LR8	3
Temperance, m. Samuel **BARNES**, June 2, 1751	LR8	10
BUTLER, Abby, of Burlington, m. Dwight **SPENCER**, of		
New Hartford, Sept. 1, 1850, by Rev. Peter Tatro,		
Jr., of Bristol	LR47	127
Charles, of New Britain, m. Fanny **HART**, of Plainville,		
Nov. 15, 1848, by William Wright	LR47	123
Frederick R., of Weathersfield, Rocky Hill Soc., m.		
Harriet L. **CUMMINGS**, of Goshen, Feb. 6, 1842,		
by Richard Woodruff	LR47	106
Hiram, of Mereden, m. Jane M. **WOODRUFF**, of		
Farmington, July 25, 1843, by Rev. Noah Porter	LR47	110
Horace M., of Westfield, Mass., m. Cornelia C.		
DORMAN, Nov. 15, 1846, by Rev. Noah Porter	LR47	118
John L., of Wilkesbarrie, Pa., m. Cornelia **RICHARDS**,		
of Farmington, Nov. 9, 1826, by Rev. Noah Porter	LR42	567
BUTTRICKS, Elizabeth, m. Cornielus **CORNWELL**, Jan. 9,		
1771	LR22	480
BYINGTON, Samuel, of Southwick, Mass., m. Cynthia		
BOOTH, of Farmington, Oct. 17, 1838, by Rev. S.		
H. Clark	LR47	98
Sarah, m. Nathan **BARNS**, Dec. 1, 1763	LR17	G
CABLE, Ann, of Burlington, m. James **ROBERTS**, of		
Hartford, Oct. 11, 1835, by Rev. Noah Porter	LR47	90
CADWELL, CADWEL, Christian, m. Samuel **BURR**, Dec.		
27, 1752	LR12	513
Clarinda, of Farmington, m. Humphrey **PHELPS**, of		
Barkhamsted, Nov. 4, 1824, by Rev. Augustus		
Bolles	LR42	568
James, s. James, b. Dec. 24, 1752	LR8	4
Lois, d. Moses, b. Jan. 12, 1729/30	LR5	2

	Vol.	Page

CADWELL, CADWEL (cont.)

Maria, of Farmington, m. Henry M. **CARTY,*** of
Martinsburgh, N.Y., Jan. 19, 1824, by Rev.
Augustus Bolles   *("**McCARTY**"?) — LR42 — 568

Mary, m. Noah **WOODRUFF**, Jan. 3, 1760 — LR11 — 575

Moses, s. Moses, b. Apr. 3, 1728 — LR5 — 2

Timothy, s. Moses, b. Aug. 18, 1731 — LR5 — 2

CADY, Annah, d. Aaron, b. July 7, 1750 — LR8 — 4

CAHOON, Frederick, m. Mary M. **CARPENTER**, b. of
Hartford, Apr. 30, 1839, by Rev. S. H. Clark — LR47 — 99

CAMERON, Emeline, of Farmington, m. John **WRIGHT**, of
Berlin, Sept. 22, 1829, by Rev. Noah Porter — LR42 — 562

Mary E., m. Henry C. **BULL**, b. of Farmington, Nov. 4,
1835, by Rev. Noah Porter — LR47 — 91

CAMP, Anna, m. Amos **LEE**, May 23, 1765 — LR11 — 594

Frances Cowles, of Farmington, m. William Henry
STARR, of New York, Mar. 2, 1836, by Rev. Noah
Porter — LR47 — 93

Isaac, s. Isaac, b. Apr. 5, 1775 — LR17 — 431

Mary, of Hartford, m. Thomas **LEE**, of Ffarmington,
Sept. 11, 1707 — LR2 — 125

CAMPBELL, Catharine, of Southwick, Mass., m. James S.
FREEMAN, of Granby, Mar. 11, 1846, by Rev.
Noah Porter — LR47 — 117

CAMPTON, Charity, of Farmington, m. Lloyd **ATKINS**, of
Bristol, Oct. 22, 1823, by Noah Porter, V.D.M. — LR40 — 572

CAPT, Lucy, d. Dea. John, m. Timothy **LEE**, Apr. 23, 1772 — LR17 — G

CAREY, Jane, m. Robert **GRAHAM**, Jan. 6, 1847, by Rev. B.
Creagh — LR47 — 119

CARLILE, Samuel, s. Azor & Margary, b. Feb. 6, 1758 — LR11 — 580

CARPINTER(?), David, d. Jan. 22, 1650 — LR2 — 320

Jane L., of Farmington, m. William C. **NASBURY**, of
Barrington, Mass., Oct. 30, 1844, by Rev. William
Wright — LR47 — 113

Mary M., m. Frederick **CAHOON**, b. of Hartford, Apr.
30, 1839, by Rev. S. H. Clark — LR47 — 99

CARRINGTON, CARINGTON, Anas, d. Jesse, b. June 24,
1774 — LR22 — 461

Anner, d. Lamuel, b. Feb. 11, 1773 — LR17 — 431

Aurelia, of Farmington, m. Chester **PENFIELD**, of
Berlin, June 12, 1820, by Noah Porter, V.D.M. — LR40 — 570

David,* d. Jan. 22, 1650   *(Perhaps "David
CARPINTER"(?)) — LR2 — 320

Hester, had d. Alma Smith, b. Aug. 6, 1780 — LR21 — 550

Huldah, d. Jesse, b. May 22, 1776 — LR22 — 461

Marvin, s. Jesse, b. July 23, 1781 — LR22 — 461

Meriam, d. Lamuel, b. Sept. 8, 1770 — LR17 — 431

Phebee, d. Timothy, b. Apr. 21, 1754 — LR9 — 5

Philena, d. Jesse, b. Dec. 2, 1778 — LR22 — 461

Sabra S., of Farmington, m. Lawrence B. **BISSELL**, of
East Windsor, Oct. 7, 1833, by Rev. Noah Porter — LR42 — A

Sarah, m. Aaron **PARSONS**, b. of Farmington, Sept. 10,
173[ ] — LR5 — 13

	Vol.	Page

CARRINGTON, CARINGTON (cont.)

Sophia, of Farmington, m. Owen **WINCHEL**, of Berlin,
Nov. 8, 1825, by Rev. Noah Porter — LR42 — 569

CARTER, CARTTER, Abell, m. Mercy **WEBSTER**, Apr.
17, 1777 — LR22 — 480

Anne, d. Abel, b. July 7, 1758 — LR11 — 580

Asanath, d. Abel, b. Apr. 18, 1755 — LR9 — 6

Asenath, m. Lamuel **CLARK**, Oct. 14, 1773 — LR17 — 443

C. Horanda, d. William, b. May 30, 1765 — LR14 — 5

Elizabeth, d. Jacob, b. Nov. [ ], 1750 — LR8 — 4

Isaac, s. Jacob, b. May 12, 1757 — LR11 — 580

Ithiel, s. Jacob, b. Aug. 1, 1753 — LR8 — 4

Ithael, s. Jacob, b. Aug. 1, 1753 — LR9 — 6

Jacob, s. Jacob, b. May 3, 1745 — LR8 — 4

Jerusha, d. Abell, b. Oct. 21, 1767 — LR15 — C

Jonathan, s. Jacob, b. May 20, 1751 — LR8 — 4

Levi, s. Jacob, b. Sept. 23, 1762 — LR11 — 581

Loyal W., of Leyden, N.Y., m. Lucy **ROSE**, of
Middlebury, Vt., Jan. 6, 1839, by Rev. S. H. Clark — LR47 — 99

Lucas H, of Wolcott, m. Jane **STANLEY**, of Farmington,
Sept. 11, 1833, by Rev. Noah Porter — LR42 — A

Mary, w. Abell, d. Apr. 5, 1776, in the 55th y. of her age — LR17 — 445

Ruth, d. Abel, b. Nov. 25, 1760 — LR11 — 581

Sarah, d .Jacob, b. Sept. 16, 1747 — LR8 — 4

Sarah, d. Abel, b. Sept. 18, 1763 — LR14 — 5

Stephen, s. Jacob, b. July 11, 1749 — LR8 — 4

William W., m. Clarissa **BARNES**, of Bristol, July 21,
1841, by Rev. Noah Porter — LR47 — 105

CARTY, Henry M.,* of Martinsburgh, N.Y., m. Maria
CADWELL, of Farmington, Jan. 19, 1824, by Rev.
Augustus Bolles   *("M'Carty") — LR42 — 568

CASE, Asahel, s. Solomon, b. Aug. 4, 1776 — LR21 — 541

Bette, d. John, b. Mar. 24, 1767 — LR15 — C

Candice, d. John, b. June 11, 1770 — LR15 — J

Caroline, m. Sedgwick **RICE**, Jan. 20, 1823, by Elisha
Cushman — LR40 — 572

Hanah, d. Ebenezer, b. July 7, 1765 — LR14 — 5

Solomon, d. Sept. 13, 1777 — LR21 — 558-9

CATLIN, Ellen B., of Farmington, m. David **GRIFFING**, of
New Haven, Sept. 22, 1845, by Rev. Noah Porter — LR47 — 115

Joel, of Augusta, Ga., m. Calista **HAWLEY**, of
Farmington, Aug. 31, 1820, by Ludovicus Robbins,
V.D.M. — LR40 — 570

John R., of Farmington, m. Eliza J. **GRANNIS**, of
Southington, Dec. 11, 1843, by William Wright — LR47 — 112

Thomas, m. Mary **ORVIS**, b. of Farmington, Mar. 1,
1843, by A. Benedict — LR47 — 109

CHALKER, William, of Hartford, m. Huldah **HILLS**, of
Plainville, Oct. 29, 1848, by William Wright — LR47 — 123

CHAMBERLIN, -----, of Lebanon, m. Samuel **GRIDLEY**, of
Kensington, Dec. 12, 1727 — LR4 — 423

CHAPIN, Charles A., of Canton, m. Cornelia H. **NEWELL**, of
Farmington, May 28, 1849, by Rev. Noah Porter — LR47 — 124

	Vol.	Page
CHAPMAN, Silence, m. Dea. Timothy **PORTTER**, Oct. 10, 1750	LR7	46
Timothy P., m. Rosmond **McCRAY**, b. of Ellington, Apr. 6, 1843, by Rev. Jesse Baker	LR47	109
CHATTERTON, Mary, wid. of New Haven, m. John **BROWNSON**, Apr. 17, 1709	LR2	145
CHEVERS, Mary, w. Dr. John, d. Aug. 28, 1750	LR7	540
CHEWER, Mary, m. William **LEWIS**, Nov. 22, 1671, in Boston	LR1	5
CHIDSEY, Alma, m. Harvey **WOODFORD**, b. of Avon, May 2, [1833], by Rev. Noah Porter	LR42	A
Edward C., of Farmington, m. Jane C. **GRANNIS**, of Southington, May 22, 1836, by Rev. Noah Porter	LR47	93
Harry, m. Mariah **HUMPHREYS**, b. of Farmington, Nov. 9, 1826, by James Humphreys, J.P.	LR42	567
John, m. Emily D. **SOPER**, b. of Farmington, Apr. 26, 1829, by Harry Bushnell	LR42	562
Lucy A., of Farmington, m. Martin **LUTHER**, of Simsbury, Mar. 19, 1845, by Rev. S. H. Clark	LR47	114
CHILDS, John, of Sandlake, N.Y., m. Sarah **FOWLER**, of Farmington, Feb. 8, 1826, by Rev. Bela Kellogg	LR42	569
Laura, m. Charles **PECK**, b. of Farmington, Sept. 3, 1826, by Rev. Noah Porter	LR42	567
CHISTISTER, David, m. Jemima **HOUGH**, b. of Farmington, Aug. 21, 1723	LR2	60
CHURCH, CURCH, Samuel, m. Marah **JONES**, Nov. 30, 1774	LR21	557
Samuel, s. Sam[ue]ll, b. Dec. 5, 1775	LR21	541
CHURCHILL, CHURCHEL, CHURCHIL,		
CHURCHWELL, Abiah, [child of William], b. Dec. 17, 1782	LR29	578
Asa, [s. William], b. July 12, 1780	LR29	578
David, s. William, b. Dec. 20, 1762	LR17	431
Elizabeth, d. Jesse, b. Mar. 29, 1755	LR9	5
Elizabeth, d. Jesse, b. Mar. 29, 1755	LR11	581
Giles, s. Jesse, b. Dec. 17, 1763	LR11	581
Jamima, d. William, b. Apr. 15, 1761	LR17	431
Jerusha, d. Jesse, b. Nov. 6, 1761	LR11	581
Jesse, m. Jerusha **GAYLORD**, Nov. 8, 1750	LR8	10
Jesse, s. Jesse, b. May 18, 1757	LR11	581
Jonathan, m. Lydia **SMITH**, Nov. [ ], 1746	LR7	35
Jonathan, s. Oliver, b. [ ] 30, 1747	LR7	H
Levi, s. Jesse, b. Dec. 18, 1759	LR11	581
Martha, d. Jesse, b. Oct. 2, 1751	LR9	5
Martha, d. Jesse, b. Oct. 5, 1751	LR11	581
Martha, d. Jesse, b. Oct. 8, 1751	LR8	4
Martha, d. William, b. Oct. 25, 1769	LR17	431
Mary, d. William, b. July 6, 1773	LR17	431
Mary, of Bristol, m. Lewis A. **MORSE**, of Farmington, Sept. 1, 1844, by Rev. William Wright	LR47	113
Phebe, d. William, b. Apr. 27, 1764	LR17	431
Ruth, d. William, b. Dec. 13, 1767	LR17	431
Samuel, s. Jesse, b. June 7, 1753	LR9	5

	Vol.	Page
CHURCHILL, CHURCHEL, CHURCHIL,		
CHURCHWELL (cont.)		
Samuel, s. Jesse, b. June 7, 1753	LR9	5
Samuel, s. Jesse, b. June 7, 1753	LR11	581
Samuel, s .William, b. Mar. 4, 1766	LR17	431
Samuel, [s. William], b. May 22, 1778	LR29	578
William, m. Ruth **TRYON**, Sept. 25, 1760	LR17	442
William, s. William, b. Dec. 26, 1771	LR17	431
-----, of Berlin, m. Emeline **CLEAVELAND**, of Canton,		
Oct. 30, 1831, by Rev. Quartus Stewart	LR42	559
CLANO, Nancy E., m. Sheldon **HILLS**, b. of Farmington,		
Aug. 5, 1849, by William Wright	LR47	127
CLAP[P], Temperance, Mrs., m. Timothy **PITKIN**, Aug. 13,		
1753	LR9	286
CLARK, Aaron, s. Enos, b. July 10, 1764	LR15	C
Abell, m. Abigal **JUDD**, Jan. 6, 1774	LR17	443
Abel, had s. [ ], b. Oct. 30, 1774	LR17	431
Abel, his s. [ ], d. Nov. 6, 1774	LR17	445
Abi, d. Hezekiah, b. Apr. 29, 1742	LR6	2
Abigail, living between Farmington & Wallingford, m.		
Jonathan **BROWNSON**, of Farmington, May 17,		
1732	LR5	300
Abigall, d. Simon, b. Sept. [ ], 1775	LR21	541
Abigail, d. [ ]	LR7	G
Abner, s. Abraham, Jr., b. Aug. 1, 1764	LR14	5
Abraham, Jr., m. Sarah **HUTSON**, Mar. 10, 1762	LR11	575
Abraham, s. Marvin, b. Sept. 5, 1780	LR22	461
Abram, s. Abraham, b. Apr. 2, 1740	LR6	2
Allen, s. Samuel, b .Nov. 26, 1774	LR21	541
Amanda, of Farmington, m. Chancey **IVES**, of Bristol,		
May 10, 1826, by Jonathan Cone, V.D.M.	LR42	569
Amos, m. Mercy **CLARK**, Mar. 22, 1751	LR7	46
Anna, d. Enos & Desire, b. Nov. 3, 1769	LR17	431
Anah, d. Ingham, b. Oct. 17, 1770	LR17	431
Asahel, s. Daniell, b. Mar. 13, 1773	LR22	461
Avura, s. Enos, Jr. & Elizabeth, b. June 7, 1769	LR17	431
Betsey, of Farmington, m. Garry H. **ROBERTS**, of		
Bristol, Jan. 24, 1837, by Rev. Noah Porter	LR47	95
Bildad, s. David, b. Dec. 7, 1756	LR15	C
Christian, d. David, b. Sept. 11, 1761	LR15	C
Christian, w. Nathan, d. July 30, 1766	LR14	3
Dan, b. Aug. 11, 1748	LR7	H
Daniel, s. Ruffus, b. Feb. 26, 1754	LR9	6
Daniel, s. Rubin, b. Mar. 19, 1769	LR11	581
Daniel, m. Huldah **WOODS**, June 11, 1772	LR22	480
Daniel, of Southington, m. Dimis A. **CULVER**, of		
Farmington, May 3, 1847, by William Wright	LR47	119
David, s. David, b. May 24, 1754	LR15	C
David, m. Lois **ANDRUS**, Nov. 18, 1756	LR11	576
Dorcas, d. Abraham, b. Sept. 30, 1766	LR14	5
Elizabeth, m. Thomas **GRIDLEY**, Sr., b. of Ffarmington,		
Dec. 25, 1679	LR2	257
Elizabeth, d. Abram, b. Nov. 4, 1743	LR6	2

	Vol.	Page
CLARK (cont.)		
Emogene H., m. William L. **COWLES**, Aug. 5, 1850, by		
William Wright	LR47	127
Enos, s. Enos, b. Feb. 7, 174[ ]	LR7	G
Enos, m. [E]unis **RUSIL**, Dec. 7, 1743/4	LR7	35
Enos, m. Desire **ROYS**, Dec. 11, 1760	LR11	575
Enos, Jr., m. Elizabeth [ ], May 21, 1767	LR15	A
Esther, m. Elihu **MOSS**, Feb. 22, 1758	LR11	575
Eunice, d. Enos, Jr., b. Mar. 15, 1768	LR15	C
Hannah, m. Joseph **WOODRUFF**, s. John, b. of		
Farmington, Dec. 17, 1722	LR2	257
Hanah, m. Abel **GRIDLEY**, Jan. 12, 1757	LR11	575
Henry, m. Antonette **STONE**, b. of Farmington, June 26,		
1847, by Rev. Noah Porter	LR47	121
Hezekiah, s. [ ]	LR7	G
Huldah, m. Daniel **ALLEN**, Mar. 31, 1755	LR10	6
Hulda, d. David, b .Mar. 13, 1759	LR15	C
Huldah, m. Eri **GILLET**, b. of Farmington, Dec. 30,		
1823, by Bela Kellogg	LR42	568
Ingham, m. Sarah **BEACH**, Oct. 28, 1767	LR17	443
Jemima, d. Marvin, b. Jan. 18, 1775	LR17	431
Jerusha, d. Rev. Samuel, b. Mar. 9, 1774	LR21	541
Jesse, s. Simon, b. Apr. 21, 1769	LR21	541
Joel, m. Lois **CLARK**, May 13, 1748	LR7	46
Joel, s. Rufus, b. Mar. 6, 1763	LR14	5
Joel, s. Ingham, b. Apr. 10, 1769	LR17	431
John, Sergt., d. Oct. 6, 1709	LR2	141
John, s. Matthew, b. Sept. 1, 1712	LR2	98
John, "ye aged", d. Nov. 22, 1712	LR2	141
John, m. Elizabeth **NEWEL**, Sept. 2, 1742	LR6	305
John, s. John, b. Mar. 18, 1754	LR9	6
John, s. John, d. Jan. 5, 1756	LR9	495
John, s .John (s. of John), b. June 24, 1761	LR11	581
John, 3rd, m. Bulah **TUBBS**, Sept. 23, 1773	LR17	442
Jonathan H., of Chester, Cty., of Hampden, Mass., m.		
Roxana **SPARROW**, of Tolland, Conn., Apr. 28,		
1839, by Rev. S. H. Clark	LR47	99
Joseph, s. Rufus, b. Mar. 19, 1756	LR11	580
Joseph, s. Rufus, d. June 2, 1777, in the 22nd y. of his age	LR22	482
Jude, s. [Dan---]	LR7	G
Lamint, d. Lucy, b. Dec. 27, 1772	LR17	431
Lamuel, m. Asenath **CARTER**, Oct. 14, 1773	LR17	443
Lois, m. Joel **CLARK**, May 13, 1748	LR7	46
Lois, d. Joel, b. Oct. 27, 1757	LR11	580
Lois, d. Capt. Joel & Lois, b. Oct. 27, 1757	LR11	580
Luanna, of Farmington, m. Ira S. **LOVELAND**, of		
Glastonbury, Mar. 2, 1835, by Rev. Noah Porter	LR47	88
Lucy, had d. Lamint, b. Dec. 27, 1772	LR17	431
Lidea, d. Abraham, Jr., b. Nov. 1, 1772	LR17	431
Lydia North, d. Simon, b. Feb. 28, 1773	LR21	541
Manly, s. Abell, b. Apr. 1, 1776	LR21	541
Martha, d. David, b. Feb. 27, 1746	LR8	4
Martha, d. Abraham, Jr., b. June 23, 1778	LR22	461

	Vol.	Page
CLARK (cont.)		
Marvin, s. John, b. Nov. 26, 1746	LR7	H
Marvin, m. Sarah **WOODRUFF**, Jan. 18, 1773	LR17	443
Mary, d. Matthew, b. Apr. 14, 1710	LR2	109
Mary, m. Stephen **SMITH**, b. of Farmington, Nov. 1, 1733	LR5	300
Mary, d. John, b. Feb. 23, 1745	LR7	H
Mary, m. Joseph **JUDD**, Jan. 18, 1752	LR8	10
Mary, d. Rubin, b. Dec. 12, 1760	LR11	581
Mary, d. Rufus, b. Feb. 27, 1773	LR22	461
Mary S., of Hartford, m. Charles T. **STEAL**, of Farmington, Nov. 27, 1845, by William Wright	LR47	116
Matilda, m. Charles A. **WARNER**, b. of Berlin, Dec. 12, 1836, by Rev. Noah Porter	LR47	95
Matthew, s. Matthew, b. May 8, 1708	LR1	4
Matthew, s. Matthew, d. Dec. 12, 1716	LR2	62
Matthew, 2nd, s. Matthew, b. Dec. 19, 1719	LR2	102
Matthew, Jr., m. Sarah **MERIL**, May 8, 1746	LR7	46
Matthew, Sergt., d. Sept. 24, 1751	LR8	11
Matthew, Sergt., d. Sept. 24, 1751	LR11	577
Matthew, s. Dan, b. Oct. 2, 1773	LR21	541
Mahetabel, d. Joel, b. Oct. 15, 1748	LR8	4
Mercy, d. John, b. Nov. 9, 1743	LR6	2
Mercy, d. John, b. Nov. 9, 1743	LR7	G
Mercy, m. Amos **CLARK**, Mar. 22, 1751	LR7	46
Meriam, d. Enos, b. Aug. 25, 1766	LR15	C
Meriam, d. [ ]	LR7	G
Moses, s. Joel, b. Apr. 21, 1753	LR9	5
Moses, s. Joel, b. Apr. 21, 1753	LR11	580
Moses, s. Enos, b. Oct. 22, 1761	LR11	581
Nancy, d. David, b .July 30, 1765	LR15	C
Orson, s. Marvin, b. Nov. 20, 1777	LR22	461
Patience, m. Oliver **PECK**, Feb. 24, 1757	LR11	576
Phebe, m. Daniel **LANKTON**, Mar. 31, 1755	LR10	6
Phebe, d. Rufus, b. Dec. 24, 1759	LR11	581
Phebe, d. Lemuel, b. Dec. 11, 1773	LR22	461
Rebeckah, d. Abram, b. Mar. 1, 1747	LR7	H
Reuben, s. Rufus, b. Apr. 1, 1775	LR22	461
Rhoda, d. Daniell, b. Jan. 25, 1775	LR22	461
Rufus, m. Mary **NEAL**, Mar. 22, 1753	LR9	286
Ruth, d. Matthew, b. Dec. 16, 1706	LR1	4
Ruth, d. Matthew, d. Jan. 3, 1706/7	LR1	3
Ruth, d. Matthew, b. May 14, 1716	LR2	81
Ruth, m. David **COLLVER**, b. of Farmington, Jan. 7, 1734/5	LR5	539
Ruth, d. John, b. Mar. 19, 1752	LR8	4
Ruth, d. John, b. Mar. 19, 1752	LR11	580
Ruth, m. Seth **STANLEY**, Jan. 6, 1774	LR17	442
Samuel, s. Hezekiah, b. July 13, 1747	LR7	H
Samuel, s. Rev. Samuel, b. May 17, 1770	LR21	541
Sarah, d. Simon, b. Mar. 12, 1771	LR21	541
Sarah, d. Abraham, Jr., b. Sept. 19, 1774	LR17	431
Seth, s. Rufus, b. Oct. 24, 1770	LR22	461

	Vol.	Page
CLARK (cont.)		
Silas, s. Silas, b. Aug. 10, 1743	LR6	2
Simon, d. Sept. 14, 1776, in the 33rd y. of his age	LR21	558-9
Thankfull, d. Joel, b. Dec. 15, 1750	LR8	4
Thankfull, d. Capt. Joel & Lois, b. Dec. 31, 1759	LR11	580
Thomas, s. Rev. Samuell, b. Mar. 21, 1776	LR21	541
Thomas, m. Olive **THORN**, Jan. 6, 1824, by Rev. Rufus Hawley	LR42	568
CLEVELAND, CLEAVELAND, Emeline, of Canton, m. [ ]**CHURCHILL**, of Berlin, Oct. 30, 1831, by Rev. Quartus Stewart	LR42	559
Lemuel, s. Johnson, b. Sept. 21, 1761	LR11	581
Lydya, d. Johnson, b Oct. 26, 1758	LR11	580
Solomon, s. Johnson, b. Sept. 17, 1756	LR11	580
Stephen, s. Johnson, b. Aug. 27, 1754	LR11	580
CLOUGH, Isaac S., of Waltham, Mass., m. Emeline E. **ROOT**, of Farmington, [ ]1, 1848, by Rev. J. Sykes	LR47	122
CLOYES, Benjamin F., m. Sally **BIRD**, Nov. 18, 1824, by Rev. Noah Porter	LR42	568
COE, Hanah, m. Thomas **HART**, Mar. 23, 1743	LR8	10
COFFIN, W[illia]m B., of Easton, N.Y., m. Lydia **WARNER**, of Farmington, July 12, [1833], by Rev. Noah Porter	LR42	A
COGSWELL, COGSWEL, COGGSWELL, Anna, d. Joseph, Jr., d. Oct. 31, 1736	LR6	10
Anna, d. Nathan, b. July 24, 1738	LR6	2
Anne, d. Joseph, Jr., b. Mar. 6, 1732/3	LR5	2
Asahel, s. Samuell, b .Apr. 16, 1741	LR6	2
David, s. Joseph, b. Mar. 26, 1725	LR2	65
David, m. Mary **WOODRUFF**, July 10, 1749	LR8	10
Deborah, d. Joseph, b. Apr. 23, 1731	LR5	2
Elizabeth, d. Joseph, Jr., b. Mar. 31, 1735	LR5	2
Elizabeth, m. Ebenezer **HULBERT**, Aug. 20, 1752	LR8	10
George L., of New Preston, m. Ellen R. **WHITTLESEY**, of Farmington, May 21, 1851, by Rev. Noah Porter	LR47	129
George Lyman, of New Preston, m. Ellen R. **WHITTLESEY**, of Farmington, May 21, 1851, by Rev. Noah Porter	LR47	130
Huldah, d. David, b. Sept. 22, 1751	LR8	4
Joseph, m. Anna **ORUIC**, b. of Farmington, Aug. 25, 1710	LR2	123
Joseph, s. Joseph, b. May 24, 1711	LR2	99
Joseph, m. [ ]	LR5	13
Levi, s. Samuel, b. Sept. 6, 1759	LR11	580
Lurana, d. Joseph, Jr., b. July 13, 1737	LR6	2
Martha, d. Joseph, b. Aug. 24, 1721	LR2	87
Mary, d. Joseph, b. May 21, 1728	LR4	395
Mary, d. Samuel, b. Apr. 1, 1739	LR6	2
Mary, m. Joseph **BARRIT**, Oct. 6, 1756	LR11	576
Nathan, s. Joseph, b. May 20, 1716	LR2	87
Nathan, m. Susanah **WARNER**, Nov. 24, 1737	LR6	27
Nathaniel, m. Bulah **SCOTT**, Sept. 11, 1760	LR11	575
Noah, s. David, b. Sept. 27, 1761	LR11	581

	Vol.	Page
COGSWELL, COGSWEL, COGGSWELL (cont.)		
Rubin, s. Samuel, b. Mar. 1, 1756	LR11	580
Rubin, s. Samuel, b. Mar. 7, 1757	LR11	580
Ruth, d. David, b. Dec. 6, 1749	LR8	4
Salmon, s. David, b. Mar. 18, 1768	LR15	J
Samuel, s. Joseph, b. May 23, 1713	LR2	99
Samuel, m. Mary **LANGTON**, b. of Farmington, Nov. 20, 1734	LR5	545
Samuel, his child b. Sept. 21, 1735 & another b. Jan. 15, 1736	LR6	2
Samuel, his two children, one d. Sept. 21, 1735, other d. Jan. 15, 1736	LR6	10
Samuel, s. Samuel, b. Sept. 17, 1754	LR11	580
Susannah, d. Joseph, b. Aug. 18, 1718	LR2	87
Susanah, m. Jedadiah **SMITH**, b. of Farmington, Jan. 1, 1740/1	LR6	304
----teman, s. Nathan, b. Mar. 20, 1743	LR6	2
COKER, Hannah, m. John **WELLS**, July 20, 1738	LR6	304
COLEGROVE, Stephen, m. Flora **BISHOP**, b. of Farmington, Sept. 7, 1836, by Rev. Noah Porter	LR47	94
COLEMAN, William, Jr., of Hartford, m. Lydia **KILLBORN**, of Farmington, Feb. 12, 1824, by Bela Kellogg	LR42	568
COLLINS, COLINS, Ann, d. John, b. Sept. 18, 1742	LR6	2
Anna, m. Eli **LEWIS**, Jan. 31, 1765	LR11	594
Asnah, d. John, b. Aug. 16, 1754	LR9	6
Elidia, twin with Mary, d. John, b. June 20, 1753	LR9	6
Lydia, m. Thomas **PARSONS**, Nov. 6, 1777	LR21	557
Mary, twin with Elidia, d. John, b. June 20, 1753	LR9	6
COLYER, Abigail, alias **MOOR**, d. Phebe **MOOR**, b. May 9, 1738	LR8	6
CONE, Alice W., of Farmington, m. James **BLAKESLEE**, of Middletown, Oct. 11, 1831, by Rev. Noah Porter	LR42	560
COOK, Abraham, m. Margary **JEALETT**, Oct. 4, 1742	LR6	305
Annah, d. Feb. 9, 1761	LR11	574
Azubah, d. Robert, b. Jan. 23, 1732/3	LR5	2
Azubah, m. Samuel **BENHAM**, Mar. 1, 1753	LR8	10
Daniel, of Bristol, m. Mary **EATON**, of Farmington, Nov. 3, 1845, by William Wright	LR47	116
Fanny, m. Lewis **MUNSON**, b. of Farmington, Mar. 23, 1831, by Rev. Noah Porter	LR42	560
John, s. Robert & Hannah, b. Aug. 28, 1730	LR5	2
John H., m. Ruby **HOTCHKISS**, Dec. 9, 1824, by Rev. Noah Porter	LR42	568
Jonathan Floyd, m. Fanny **POTMER**, Mar. 21, 1848, by Rev. Joel Grant, of Avon	LR47	122
Margaret, twin with Nathaniel, d. Robert, b. Sept. 25, 1725	LR6	2
Nathaniel, twin with Margaret, d. Robert, b. Sept. 25, 1725	LR6	2
Nathaniel, m. Martha **SCOTT**, Mar. 8, 1754	LR8	10
Rebeckah, d. Robert, b. Sept. 10, 1737	LR6	2

	Vol.	Page
COOK (cont.)		
Robert, m. Hannah **HUNN**, b. of Farmington, Nov. 19,		
1729	LR5	13
COOLE, [see under **COWLES**]		
COOPER, Abigail, m. Jabash **ROBARDS**, Feb. 2, 1744	LR8	10
CORNISH, Charles E., m. Mary N. **VINING**, b. of Simsbury,		
Sept. 16, 1829, by Smith Dayton, Elder	LR42	562
Mindwell, of Simsbury, m. Chancy **DERRIN**, of		
Farmington, Aug. 11, 1822, by W. Eli, V.D.M.	LR40	571
Virgil, of Hartford, m. Miranda **WILCOX**, of Granby,		
July 30, 1839, by Isaac Porter	LR47	100
CORNWELL, Chancey, s. Cornelius, b. June 4, 1781	LR22	461
Cornielus, m. Elizabeth **BUTTRICKS**, Jan. 9, 1771	LR22	480
Eli, s. Cornelius, b. Nov. 16, 1775	LR22	461
Elizabeth, d. Cornelius, b. Nov. 29, 1772	LR22	461
Rachel, d. Cornelius, b. Nov. 11, 1777	LR22	461
COTCH, [see also **COUCH**], John, of Simsbury, m. Lowey		
DAILEY, of Farmington, Nov. 5, 1823, by Rev.		
Stephen S. Nelson, of Canton & Northington	LR40	573
COTTON, Leonard, of Middletown, m. Mrs. Eliza D. **SMITH**,		
of Farmington, Apr. 22, 1841, by Rev. Aaron S. Hill	LR47	104
COUCH, [see also **COTCH**], Abigail, of Bristol, m. George		
STONE, of Harwinton, Jan. 3, 1827, by Rev.		
Rodney Rosseter, of Plymouth	LR42	567
Eliza, m. John R. **JONES**, of Berlin, Mar. 23, 1845, by R.		
Stanley	LR47	114
Hanah, m. Stephen **BUCK**, Jan. 16, 1749	LR9	286
COVEY, Elizabeth, m. Jonathan **DAVIS**, Oct. 13, 1777	LR22	480
COWLES, COAL, COALES, COLE, COOLE, COWL,		
COWLS, Abel Ward, s. William, b. [ ] 2, 1763	LR14	5
Abigail, d. Samuel, b. Jan. 13, 1663	LR1	2
Abigail, m. Thomas **PORTTER**, s. Robert, b. of		
Ffarmington, May [ ], 1678	LR2	145
Abigail, d. Isaac, b. Nov. 1, 1699	LR1	4
Abigail, d. Caleb, b. Sept. 11, 1713	LR4	374
Abigail, d. Stephen & Abigail, b. June 25, 1735	LR5	307
Abigail, w. Stephen, d. Oct. 20, 1736	LR6	10
Abigall, w. James, d. Feb. 27, 1772, in the 37th y. of her		
age	LR17	444
Abigall, d. Zebulon, b. Feb. 15, 1780	LR21	541
Addison, s. Ashbel, b. Feb. 17, 1770	LR17	431
Alma, d. Samuell & Bathia, b. Feb. 1, 1761	LR11	580
Alma, d. [ ], d. Nov. 27, 1775, in the 15th y. of her age	LR15	M
Ame, d. James & Abigail, b. Dec. 25, 1758	LR11	580
Amos, s. Lieut. Isaac, b. July 29, 1730	LR5	2
Amos, s. William, b. Nov. 4, 1750	LR8	4
Amos, m. Susannah **BULL**, Nov. 13, 1755	LR9	286
Ann, d. Oct. 21, 1736	LR6	10
Anna, d. John, Jr., b. Aug. 10, 1728	LR4	395
Anne, m. Ezekiel **WOODRUFF**, b. of Farmington, Feb.		
20, 1734/5	LR5	539
Anne, d. Ezekiel, b. July 18, 1761	LR11	580
Anne Catharine, d. Samuel & Mary, b. May 4, 1754	LR9	6

	Vol.	Page
COWLES, COAL, COALES, COLE, COOLE, COWL,		
COWLS (cont.)		
Anthony, s. Zebulon, b. Apr. 12, 1769	LR15	J
Asa, s. Timothy, b. Mar. 7, 1731/2	LR5	2
Asa, m. Eunice **HART**, May 9, 1755	LR9	286
Asa, s. Nathaniell, b. Feb. 10, 1757	LR11	580
Asahel, s. Samuel, Jr., b. July 18, 1728	LR4	395
Asahel,* s. Josiah & Jemimah, b. Sept. 29, 1740 *(In		
pencil "Ashbel")	LR6	2
Asahel, s. Zebulon, b Apr. 6, 1778	LR21	541
Asahel, s. Zebulon, d. Feb. 23, 1779, in the 1st y. of his		
age	LR22	482
Asaph, s. Elisha, b. Oct. 10, 1757	LR11	580
Ashbell, m. Rhoda **LEE**, Apr. 27, 1769	LR17	442
Augustus, of Farmington, m. Eliza **LANGDON**, of New		
Haven, Sept. 12, 1849, by Rev. Noah Porter	LR47	125
Benjamin, s. Nathaniel & Mary, b. Dec. 18, 1713	LR2	99
Bethiah, w. Samuell, d. July 19, 1766, in the 34th y. of		
her age	LR15	M
Caleb, m. Abigail **WOODFORD**, b. of Woodford, Aug.		
8, 1710	LR2	125
Caleb, s. Caleb, b. Nov. 18, 1719	LR4	374
Caleb, d. Nov. 15, 1725	LR2	148
Calvin, s. Josiah & Mary, b. Nov. 13, 1749	LR8	4
Carroline, s. James, b. Apr. 12, 1771	LR17	431
Caroline, of Farmington, m. John S. **MOORE**, of		
Dummerston, Vt., Oct. 31, 1824, by Rev. Joshua		
Williams	LR42	568
Caroline A., of Farmington, m. Isaac N. **LEE**, of Berlin,		
June 23, 1843, by Rev. Noah Porter	LR47	110
Catharine, m. Hezekiah W. **HAMLIN**, b. of Farmington,		
Apr. 11, 1849, by Rev. Noah Porter	LR47	124
Catharine L., of Farmington, m. Rev. Raymond H.		
SEELEY, of Bristol, Oct. 9, 1843, by Noah Porter,		
Int. Pub.	LR47	111
Charlotte L., of Farmington, m. Joseph D. **HULL**, of New		
Haven, Dec. 14, 1843, by Noah Porter, Int. Pub.	LR47	111
Chauncey D., m. Jane E. **BIDWELL**, b. of Farmington,		
Jan. 7, 1835, by Rev. Noah Porter	LR47	88
Clara, m. Isaac **BRADLEY**, b. of Farmington, May 10,		
1848, by William Wright	LR47	119
Cyprian, s. Enos (?), b. Feb. 6, 1769	LR17	431
Cyrian, s. Eneas, d. May 30, 1772	LR17	444
Daniel, s. Caleb, b. Dec. 14, 1717	LR4	374
Daniel, s. Nathaniell, b .Nov. 4, 1722	LR4	375
Daniel, Jr., m. [ ] **RODES**, Apr. 25, 1766	LR22	480
Daniel, twin with Esther, s. Daniell, Jr., b. Jan. 9, 1767	LR22	461
Diadama, d. James, b. Dec. 25, 1756	LR9	6
Diana, d. Zebulon, b. Feb. 23, 1766	LR15	J
Dinah, m. Jeames **NEWEL**, Nov. 23, 1742	LR6	305
Eli, s. Benjamin, b. June 29, 1739	LR6	2
Elias, s. James, b. Oct. 11, 1765	LR14	5
Elidia, d. Job & Elidia, b. Mar. 10, 1744	LR8	4

	Vol.	Page
COWLES, COAL, COALES, COLE, COOLE, COWL, COWLS (cont.)		
Elijah, m. Sarah HART, July 11, 1750	LR7	46
Elijah, s. Elijah, b. May 20, 1755	LR9	6
Elijah, s. Elijah, b. Dec. 5, 1775	LR22	461
Elijah, m. Mary D. LEWIS, Apr. 16, 1845, by Rev. Noah Porter	LR47	114
Elisha, s. Nathaniel, b. Apr. 7, 1718	LR2	84
Elisha, m. Keziah JUDD, Apr. 25, 1754	LR9	286
Elisha, d .Mar. 7, 1778, in the 60th y. of his age	LR21	560
Eliza E., of Farmington, m. Gad H. HART, of Hartford, Mar. 20, 1829, by Rev. George Phippen, of Canton & Northington	LR42	564
Elizabeth, d. Isaac, b. May 26, 1705	LR1	4
Elizabeth, m. Dr. Thomas THOMSON, b. of Ffarmington, Jan. 15, 1706/7	LR2	145
Elizabeth, m. Timothy HEART, b. of Ffarmington, Oct. 25, 1728	LR4	423
Elizabeth, d. John, b. Aug. 1, 1738	LR6	2
Elizabeth, d. Benjamin, b. July 29, 1740	LR6	2
Elizabeth, m. Stephen DOCHESTER, Oct. 29, 1754	LR8	10
Elizabeth, d. James, b. Aug. 13, 1768	LR15	J
Elizabeth, d. Daniell, b. June 3, 1769	LR22	461
Elizabeth, m. William WHEELER, b. of Farmington, Feb. 6, 1834, by Rev. Noah Porter	LR42	D
Emily, of Farmington, m. Rev. John RICHARDS, of Woodstock, Vt., June 16, 1828, by Rev. N. Porter	LR42	564
Eneas, s. Thomas, Jr. & Ruth, b. Mar. 8, 1740/1	LR6	2
Eneas, m. Esther BIRD, Oct. 3, 1765	LR11	594
Eneas, of Westfield, Mass., m. Celia M. MORSE, of Farmington, Feb. 10, 1830, by Rev. Noah Porter	LR42	561
Easther, m. Thomas BULL, Apr. 29, 1669	LR1	4
Esther, d. Caleb, b. Jan. 9, 1715/16	LR4	374
Easther, m. Thomas STANLEY, s. Thomas, b. of Ffarmington, Jan. 2, 1717/18	LR2	87
Esther, d. Samuel, m. Thomas STANLEY, 2nd, Jan. 2, 1717/18	LR4	271
Esther, d. Nathaniel, b. July 8, 1723	LR2	87
Esther, d. William, b. Nov. 1, 1746	LR7	H
Esther, m. Nathaniel WADSWORTH, May 16, 1754	LR9	286
Esther, twin with Daniel, d. Daniell, Jr., b. Jan. 9, 1767	LR22	461
Esther, d. Phinehas, b. Oct. 1, 1767	LR15	C
Esther, m. William CRAMPTON, b. of Farmington, May 17, 1827, by Rev. Noah Porter	LR42	565
Esther, of Farmington, m. Haynes LORD, of New York City, Oct. 24, 1837, by Rev. Noah Porter	LR47	96
[E]unic[e], d. Nathaniell, b. July 7, 1722	LR4	374
[E]unice, d. Thomas, b. Aug. 4, 1749	LR7	542
Eunice, d. Elijah, b. Nov. 15, 1765	LR15	J
Experience, m. Solomon HART, Mar. 8, 1749/50	LR7	46
Ezekiel, s. John, b. May 2, 1742	LR6	2
Ezekiel, s. Ezekiel, b. Sept. 14, 1757	LR8	4

	Vol.	Page
COWLES, COAL, COALES, COLE, COOLE, COWL,		
COWLS (cont.)		
Francis W., m. Mary L. **ROOT**, b. of Farmington, Sept.		
9, 1835, by Rev. Noah Porter	LR47	90
Gad, s. Elijah, b. Mar. 3, 1761	LR11	580
Gad, s. Elijah, b. Nov. 23, 1768	LR15	J
Gamaliel, s. Josiah, b. July 12, 1742	LR6	2
George, s. Capt. Josiah, b. July 29, 1761	LR11	581
George D., m. Charlotte **PHELPS**, b. of Farmington,		
Sept. 29, 1831, by Rev. Noah Porter	LR42	560
Gideon, s. Thomas, b. May 17, 1748	LR7	H
Gideon, s. Thomas, Jr., b. Sept. 14, [ ]	LR7	H
Gideon, s. Thomas, Jr., d. Nov. 16, 1743	LR7	36
Giles, s. Ezekiel & Martha, b. Sept. 5, 1754	LR9	6
Hannah, d. Samuell, b. Dec. 10, 1664	LR1	2
Hannah, d. Ben[jamin], b. Feb. 22, 1741/2	LR6	2
Hannah, [d. of] Caleb, m. Nathaniel **WINCHEL**, Jr., June		
8, 1746	LR7	35
Hannah, m. Nathaniel **WINCHEL**, Jr., June 9, 1746	LR7	46
Harriet E., of Farmington, m. Charles **THOMSON**, of		
New York, Nov. 10, 1841, by Rev. Noah Porter	LR47	106
Helen, m. George **SPAULDING**, Feb. 25, 1824, by		
Henry M. Mason	LR42	568
Hesther, d. Samuel, b. May 18, 1697	LR1	3
Hezekiah, s. Caleb, b. Sept. 15, 1711	LR2	97
Horace, m. Elizabeth **HURLBUT**, b. of Farmington, Nov.		
8, 1838, by Rev. Noah Porter	LR47	98
Horace, s. Samuel S., b. Aug. 16, 1844	LR47	447
Hulda, d. Elisha, b. June 18, 1756	LR11	580
Huldah, d. Elisha, d. Sept. 28, 1756	LR11	574
Huldah, d. Elisha, d. Sept. 28, 1756	LR11	577
Hulda, d. Elisha, b. June 8, 1759	LR11	580
Ira, s. Isaac, b .May 10, 1764	LR14	6
Ira, s. Stephen, b. Aug. 11, 1779	LR21	541
Issack, s. Samuell, b. Mar. 28, 1675	LR1	2
Isaac, m. Mary **ANDRUSS**, Jan. 2, 1694	LR1	4
Isaac, s. Isaac, b. Apr. 21, 1702	LR1	4
Isaac, of Ffarmington, m. Sarah **ANDRUS**, of New		
Haven, Nov. 1, 1709	LR2	145
Isaac, m. Elizabeth **SMITH**, b. of Ffarmington, Dec. 27,		
1716	LR2	94
Isaac, s. Lieut. Isaac, b. Jan. 12, 1726/7	LR4	382
Isaac, Ens. of Southington, d. Sept. 29, 1737	LR6	10
Isaac, s. Solomon, d. Aug. 20, 1755, in the 3rd y. of his		
age	LR9	495
Isaac, Capt. d. Feb. 7, 1756	LR8	12
Isaac, s. Solomon, b. July 29, 1756	LR9	6
James, s. Samuel, Jr., d. June 7, 1720	LR2	148
James, s. Samuel, Jr., b. Mar. 4, 1721/2* *(Written in		
pencil "Mar. 14, 1719/20"?)	LR4	374
James, s. Lieut. Isaac, b. Dec. 20, 1723	LR2	87
Jeames, s. Jeames, b. Jan. 24, 1750/1	LR8	4
James, m. Abigail **HOOKER**, Aug. 30, 1753	LR8	10

	Vol.	Page
COWLES, COAL, COALES, COLE, COOLE, COWL, COWLS (cont.)		
James, s. Elisha, b. Feb. 25, 1770	LR15	J
James, Lieut. m. Mary **LEWIS** (wid.), Nov. 15, 1773	LR17	443
James, of Farmington, m. Jane E. **LEWIS**, of Northumberland, N.Y., Feb. 22, 1838, by Rev. Noah Porter	LR47	97
James W., m. Amelia Ann **HILLS**, b. of Farmington, Oct. 9, 1838, by Rev. S. H. Clark	LR47	97
Jarud, s. William, b. Mar. 20, 1733/4	LR6	2
Jedadiah, s. Isaac, b. Aug. 23, 1713	LR2	99
Jedadiah, s. Isaac, d. Nov. 5, 1713	LR2	62
Jemima, d. Isaac, b. Sept. 26, 1707	LR2	109
Jemima, m. Ebenezer **LANGTON**, b. of Ffarmington, Nov. 30, 1727	LR4	423
Jemima, w. Josiah, d. Oct. 9, 1748* *(In pencil "1746") (Grave stone Oct. 19, 1746)	LR7	36
Jamima, d. Ashbel, b. Feb. 20, 1772	LR17	431
Jamima Dickason, d .Josiah, b. Oct. 1, 174[ ]	LR7	G
Jeremiah, s. James, b. Aug. 14, 1774	LR17	431
Jerusha, m. Eldad **LEWIS**, July 4, 1745	LR7	46
Jesse, s. Matthew, b. Oct. 16, 1739	LR6	2
Jesse, s. Phinehas, b. Sept. 14, 1765	LR14	5
Job, s. Nathaniel, b. Oct. 20, 1714	LR2	84
Job, m. Lydia **JUDD**, Sept. 4, 1741	LR8	10
John, s. Samuel, b. Jan. 28, 1670	LR1	2
John, 1st, d. Sept. 13 or 14, 1689. Certified by his d. Rachel **SMITH** & his son-in-law Ephraim Smith	LR5	50
John, of Ffarmington, m. Mehitabel **LOMMIS**, sometime of Windsor, June [ ], 1691	LR2	123
John, s. Samuel, b. Aug. 24, 1694	LR1	3
John, s. John, b. Mar. 9, 1696	LR2	91
John, d. Mar. [ ], 1707/8	LR2	141
John, s. Samuel, m. Mary **PORTTER**, d. Jno, July 12, 1721	LR2	101
John, s. Samuel, Jr., b. July 20, 1724	LR4	374
John, Jr., had twin s. [ ], b. about June 11, 1727. One was st. b., the other d. in a short time	LR4	395
John, s. John, b. Mar. 11, 1730/1	LR5	307
John, m. Elizabeth **WHAPLES**, Nov. 11, 1737	LR6	27
John, s. Nathaniel, b. Sept. 18, 174[ ]	LR7	G
John, s. John, b. May 27, 1740	LR6	2
John, d. Oct. 10, 1748	LR7	36
John, of Simsbury, m. Ruth **HUMASON**, of Farmington, Feb. 10, 1828, by James Cornish, J.P.	LR42	565
John Strong, d. Feb. 2, 1777, in the 72nd y. of his age	LR21	558-9
Jonathan, s. Elijah, b. Feb. 3, 1757	LR11	580
Jonathan Hart, s. Elijah & Sarah, b. July 7, 1751	LR8	4
Jonathan Hart, s. Elijah, d. July 23, 1751	LR8	11
Joseph, s. Nathaniell, b. Sept. 17, 1715	LR4	375
Josiah, s. Thomas & Martha, b. Nov. 20, 1716	LR2	81
Josiah, m. Jamimah **DICKASON**, b. of Farmington, Nov. 10,* 1739 *(In pencil "11th")	LR6	27

	Vol.	Page
COWLES, COAL, COAL ES, COLE, COOLE, COWL,		
COWLS (cont.)		
Josiah, m. Mary **SCOTT**, Nov. 23, 1748	LR7	35
Josiah, s. William, b. Apr. 13, 1753	LR9	6
Julia, of Farmington, m. Stephen **CROSBY**, of Spencer,		
Mass., Sept. 16, 1822, by Noah Porter, V.D.M.	LR40	572
Julia Ann, m. Thomas **COWLES**, b. of Farmington, Oct.		
9, 1833, by Rev. Noah Porter	LR42	A
Julius D., m. Mary **HULL**, b. of Farmington, Sept. 11,		
1842, by Rev. S. H. Clark	LR47	108
Keziah, w. Elisha, d. Dec. 29, 1760	LR11	574
Lemuel, s. Dan[ie]ll, b. Aug. 17, 1776	LR22	461
Lemuel W., m. Ann M. **HOLMES**, b. of (Unionville),		
Apr. 29, [1846], by Rev. Richard Woodruff	LR47	117
Levia, d .Phinehas, b. Apr. 26, 1785	LR22	461
Louisa Mary, of Farmington, m. William S. **COWLES**,		
of Rhinebeck, N.Y., Nov. 13, 1837, by Rev. Noah		
Porter	LR47	96
Lucius, s., m. Louisa **WHITMAN**, b. of Farmington,		
Sept. 20, 1848, by Rev. Noah Porter	LR47	123
Lucretia, d. Phinehas, b. Oct. 4, 1772	LR17	436
Lucy, d. Phinehas, b. Oct. 4, 1772	LR17	436
Lucy, d. Stephen, b. May 24, 1782	LR22	461
Lucy, [d. William] b. [ ]	LR7	H
Lydia, d. Nathaniel, b. Aug. 1, 1709	LR2	91
Lydia, m. Zebulon **CURTICE**, b. of Farmington, July 3,		
1735	LR6	27
Lydya, d. Stephen, b. Jan. 2, 1747/8	LR7	H
Lydia, d. Daniell, b. Jan. 27, 1771	LR22	461
Lydia, d. Stephen, b. Oct. 9, 1774	LR21	541
Lydia, d .Nov. 2, 1783, in the 79th y. of her age	LR22	482
Marcy, m. Ebenezer **GILBERT**, b. of Farmington, May		
1, 1735	LR6	27
Margaret, d. Timothy, b. Dec. 30, [ ]; d. Jan. 1, 1730/1	LR5	1
Mark, s. Eneas, b. Feb. 9, 1767	LR14	6
Martha, d. Thomas, b. Dec. 29, 1724	LR2	70
Martha, d. Thomas, d. Jan. 27, 1724/5	LR2	66
Martha, d. Solomon, b. June 29, 1751	LR8	4
Martha, d. Josiah, b. Aug. 23, 1751	LR8	4
Martha, wid., d. Oct. 15, 1768, in the 76th y. of her age	LR16	3
Martha, wid., d. Oct. 15, 1768, in the 76th y. of her age	LR15	M
Martha, d. Phinehas, b. Sept. 30, 1769	LR15	J
Martha, [of Farmington], m. Rev. Amzi **BENEDICT**, of		
Vernon, Oct. 5, 1824, by Rev. Noah Porter	LR42	568
Martha J., m. Isaac B. **BRADLEY**, b. of Farmington,		
Mar. 4, 1835, by Rev. Noah Porter	LR47	89
Mary, d. Isaac, b. Apr. 26, 1697	LR1	4
Mary, d. John, b. July 5, 1700	LR2	91
Mary, w. Isaac, d. July 19, 1708	LR1	3
Mary, wid. Samuell, m. Samuel **LEWIS**, Jr., b. of		
Ffarmington, Aug. 11, 1720	LR2	101
Mary, m. Daniel **ANDRUS**, s. Benjamin, b. of		
Ffarmington, Feb. 8, 1720/1	LR2	51

	Vol.	Page
COWLES, COAL, COALES, COLE, COOLE, COWL,		
COWLS (cont.)		
Mary, m. Daniel **ANDRUS**, b. of Ffarmington, Feb. 9,		
1720/1	LR2	100
Mary, d. John, s. Samuell, b. May 18, 1722	LR2	102
Mary, d. John, Jr., d. Sept. 16, 1722	LR2	107
Mary, m. Hezekiah **WINCHEL**, b. of Ffarmington, Feb.		
10, 1724/5	LR2	257
Mary, d. John, Jr., b. Sept.* 10, 1725 *(Written in		
pencil "Nov.?")	LR4	374
Mary, d. John, Jr., d. Nov. 28, 1725	LR2	107
Mary, d. Isaac, Jr. & Ruth, b. Dec. 14, 1729	LR5	2
Mary, d. Stephen, b. Feb. 18, 1731/2	LR5	2
Mary, d. Benjamin, b. Jan. 9, 1736/7	LR6	2
Mary, m. Timothy **WADSWORTH**, Sept. 20, 1750	LR7	46
Mary, d. Samuel, b. Sept. 12, 1755	LR11	580
Mary, m. Selah **HART**, Mar. 4, 1756	LR9	286
Mary, w. Samuel, d. May 10, 1756	LR11	577
Mary, d. Josiah, b. Oct. 2, 1757	LR11	580
Mary, d. Daniell, b. Nov. 9, 1779	LR22	461
Mary, d. Matthew, b. Jan. 4, [ ]	LR7	G
Mary A., d. Horace, decd., of Farmington, m. Aaron A.		
HARDY, of Pittsburgh, Pa., Nov. 1, 1848, by		
Joseph D. Hull	LR47	123
Matthew, s. John, b. Dec. 28, 1703	LR2	91
Matthew, of Kensington, in Torrington, m. Ruth		
HUBERT, of Middletown, Apr. 10, 1732	LR5	300
Matthew, s. Matthew & Ruth, b. Feb. 4, 1733/4	LR5	2
Matthew, m. Mary **NEWEL**, b. of Farmington, Jan. 3,		
1738/9	LR6	27
Matthew, Jr., m. Rhoda **SMITH**, Dec. 9, 1756	LR11	576
Matthew, s. Matthew, Jr., b. Nov. 13, 1760	LR11	580
Matthew, d. [ ] 30, 1761, in the 58th y. of his age	LR11	574
Mehetibel, d. John, b .July 5, 1708	LR2	91
Mehitabel, m. Ephraim **BORDMAN**, b. of Farmington,		
Oct. 15, 1735	LR6	27
Mercy, d. Samuel, Jr., b. Dec. 14, 1717	LR2	102
Mercy, d. Caleb, b. Feb. [ ], 1724/5	LR4	374
Mercy, d. Matthew, Jr., b. Sept. 6, 1757	LR11	580
Nancy, of Farmington, m. Thomas K. **FESSENDEN**, of		
Norwich, Oct. 23, 1839, by Rev. Noah Porter	LR47	101
Nathan, m. Anna **GALPIN**, Apr. 1, 1736	LR6	304
Nathan, s. Elisha, b. Dec. 19, 1760	LR11	580
Nathaniell, b. Feb. 11, 1672	LR1	2
Nathaniel, m. Phebe **WOODRUFF**, b. of Farmington,		
Feb. 11, 1696/7	LR2	93
Nathaniel, s. Nathaniel & Phebe, b. Apr. 28, 1698	LR2	99
Nathaniel, m. Elizabeth **WOODFORD**, b. of		
Ffarmington, June 11, 1707	LR2	123
Nathaniel, s. Nathaniel, b. Feb. 15, 1710/11	LR2	91
Nathaniel, m. Mary **ANDRUS**, b. of Farmington, Feb. 26,		
1712/13	LR2	93
Nathaniel, s. Nathaniel, b. Aug. 28, 1716	LR2	84

	Vol.	Page
COWLES, COAL, COALES, COLE, COOLE, COWL, COWLS (cont.)		
Nathaniel, Jr., m. Sarah **GRIDLEY**, b. of Ffarmington, Mar. 15, 1721/2	LR2	100
Nathaniel, s. Nathaniell, 2nd, decd. & Sarah, b. May 31, 1725	LR2	65
Nathaniell, 2nd, s. Nathaniell, Sr., decd., b. May 5, 1730	LR5	2
Nathaniel, m. Phebe **COLE**, Nov. 5, 1745	LR7	46
Nathaniel, s. Nathaniel, of Kensington, b. Dec. [ ], 174[ ]	LR7	H
Nathaniel, of Kensington, m. Sarah **STEEL**, May 15, 1748	LR7	46
Noah, s. John, b. Dec. 9, 1733	LR5	307
Oliver, s. Matthew, b. Jan. 17, 1752	LR8	4
Orpha, m. Ard **WOODRUFF**, b. of Southington, July 13, 1842, by Rev. C. D. Cowles	LR47	108
Parcy, d. Daniell, b. Apr. 16, 1774	LR22	461
Phebe, w. Nathan, d. Feb. 4, 1711/12	LR2	62
Phebe, d. Nathaniell, b. Aug. 12, 1718	LR4	375
Phebe, m. Nathaniel **COWLES**, Nov. 5, 1745	LR7	46
Phebe, d. Nathaniel, b. Mar. 9, 1748	LR7	H
Phinehas, s. Thomas & Martha, b. Mar. 5, 1729/30	LR5	2
Rachel, m. Ephraim **SMITH**, b. of Ffarmington, Apr. [ ], 1686	LR2	145
Rachel, d. Nathaniell & Elizabeth, b. Jan. 17, 1712/13	LR2	99
Rachel, m. Joseph **LANGTON**, Jr., b. of Farmington, Dec. 24, 1713	LR2	93
Rachel, d. John, Jr., b. Dec. 6,* 1723 *(Written in pencil "11th"?)	LR4	374
Rachel, w. Samuel, Jr., d. Oct. 4, 1743	LR7	36
Rachel, d. Elisha, b. Aug. 11, 1766	LR15	C
Rene, d. Enos, b .July 10, 1774	LR17	431
Rhoda, d. Job & Elidia, b. Aug. 2, 1750	LR8	4
Rhoda, d. Mathew, b. Nov. 16, 1760	LR15	C
Rosetty, twin with Statey, d. Dan[ie]ll, b. July 3, 1778	LR22	461
Rufus, s. Phinehas, b. Aug. 23, 1779	LR21	541
Russell, s. Stephen, b. Oct. 18, 1772	LR21	541
Ruth, d. Samuel, b. Nov. 11, 1688	LR1	3
Ruth, d. John, b. Mar. 16, 1705	LR2	91
Ruth, d. Isaac, Jr., b. Dec. 28, 1731	LR5	2
Ruth, w. Matthew, d. June 25, 1735	LR5	50
Ruth, 2nd, d. Isaac, Jr., b. Oct. 8, 1737	LR6	2
Ruth, d. Matthew, b. Oct. 18, 1742	LR6	2
Ruth, d. Job & Elidia, b. Jan. 16, 1746	LR8	4
Ruth, m. Samuel **UPTON**,* Apr. 5, 1759 *(In pencil "UPSON")	LR11	575
Samuel, s. Samuell, b. Mar. 17, 1661	LR1	2
Samuell, m. Abigall **STANDLY**, June 14, 1660	LR1	5
Samuell, s. Samuell, m. Rachel **PORTER**, May 12, 1685	LR1	4
Samuel, s. Samuel, b. May 16, 1692	LR1	3
Samuel, m. Mary **SMITH**, d. Jonathan, b. of Ffarmington, Mar. 17, 1707/8	LR2	145
Samuel, s. Samuel, b. Feb. 17, 1708/9	LR2	112

	Vol.	Page

**COWLES, COAL, COALES, COLE, COOLE, COWL,
COWLS** (cont.)

	Vol.	Page
Samuel, Jr., m. Sarah **WADSWORTH**, b. of Ffarmington, Nov. 28, 1716	LR2	94
Samuel, d. Apr. 17, 1718	LR2	62
Samuel, s. Nathaniel, b. Oct. 9, 1720	LR4	375
Samuel, s. Samuel, Jr., b. July 28, 1724	LR2	46
Samuel, s. Samuel, Jr., d. Sept. 17, 1724	LR2	148
Samuel, d. Oct. 14, 1748	LR7	36
Samuell, s. Thomas, b. Oct. 28, [ ]; d. Dec. 5, 1750	LR8	4
Samuel, m. Mrs. Mary **DEAN**, of Stratford, Apr. 5, 1753	LR9	286
Samuel, s. Josiah, b. Nov. 28, 1755	LR11	580
Samuel, m. Bathiah **BACON**, Nov. 27, 1759	LR11	575
Samuel, s. Samuel, b. Nov. 27, 1762	LR11	581
Samuel, s. Samuel, d. Jan. 15, 1763	LR11	593
Samuel, s. Zebulon, b. May 25, 1764	LR15	J
Samuel F., m. Rumah **FINNEY**, b. of Farmington, Sept. 5, 1827, by Rev. Noah Porter	LR42	565
Sarah, d. Samuell, b. Dec. 25, 1668	LR1	2
Sarah, m. Stephen **HART**, s. Stephen, b. of Ffarmington, Dec. 18, 1689	LR2	123
Sarah, d. John, b. Aug. 20, 1693	LR2	91
Sarah, w. Isaac, d. June 14, 1715	LR2	62
Sarah, d. Samuel, Jr., b. Oct. 7,* 1726 *(In pencil "Oct. 7")	LR4	374
Sarah, d. Samuel, Jr., d. Nov. 26, 1726	LR2	148
Sarah, d. Stephen, b. Sept. 15, 1730	LR5	2
Sarah, d. William, b. Apr. 3, 1737	LR6	2
Sarah, d. Nathaniel, b. July 28, 1750	LR8	4
Sarah, w. Elijah, d. July 12, 1751	LR8	11
Sarah, m. John **LEE**, May 7, 1752	LR8	10
Sarah, m. Elisha **HART**, July 14, 1753	LR8	10
Sarah, w. Asa, d. June 11, 1754	LR9	495
Sarah, d. Nathaniel, b. [ ],31, 1754	LR9	6
Sarah, m. John **THOMSON**, b. of Farmington, July 29, 1827, by Rev. Noah Porter	LR42	565
Sarah, d. [Thomas, Jr.], b. [ ]	LR7	H
Sarah G., m. George **ROBINSON**, Nov. 30, 1820, by Noah Porter, V.D.M.	LR40	570
Sarah Hart, d. Elijah, b. Jan. 18, 1759	LR15	J
Sarah Hart, d. Zebulon, b. July 13, 1775	LR21	541
Sarah Lason, d. Elijah, b. Oct. 10, 1782	LR22	461
Selah, s. Elisha, b. Mar. 6, 1755	LR9	6
Seth, s. Elijah, b. June 11, 1763	LR15	J
Seth, s. Mathew, b. Sept. 19, 1768	LR15	C
Seth, s. Mathew, b. Nov. 19, 1768	LR15	J
Silvia, d. Phinehas, b. Sept. 6, 1776	LR21	541
Solomon, m. Martha **SAYMORE**, Dec. 22, 1742	LR6	305
Statey, twin with Rosetty, d. Dan[ie]ll, b. July 3, 1778	LR22	461
Stephen, s. John, b. Oct. 3, 1698	LR2	91
Stephen, m. Abigail **HART**, b. of Ffarmington, June 11, 1729	LR5	13
Stephen, s. Stephen, b. Jan. 16, 1745	LR7	G

	Vol.	Page

COWLES, COAL, COALES, COLE, COOLE, COWL, COWLS (cont.)

	Vol.	Page
Stephen, of Farmington, m. Lidya **BENTON**, of Hartford, Apr. 26, 1745	LR7	35
Stephen, m. Lucy **DEMING**, Dec. 26, 1771	LR17	443
Stephen, d. Jan. 11, 1777, in the 79th y. of his age	LR21	560
Stephen, s. Stephen, b. Jan. 22, 1777	LR21	541
Susan, of Farmington, m. Augustus **WARD**, of Berlin, May 19, 1840, by Rev. Noah Porter	LR47	102
Susannah, d. Caleb, b. Oct. 22, 1721	LR4	374
Susanah, m. Solomon **WHITMAN**, b. of Farmington, Dec. 17, 1736	LR6	27
Susannah, d. James, b. Sept. 22, 1754	LR9	6
Sylvia, m. Albert **DUNHAM**, b. of Farmington, Feb. 24, 1825, by Rev. Noah Porter	LR42	568
Tennette, m. Austin F. **WILLIAMS**, b. of Farmington, Sept. 11, 1828, by Rev. Noah Porter	LR42	564
Thankfull, d. Nathaniel & Phebe, b. July 21, 1700	LR2	99
Thankfull, d. Benjamin, b. Feb. 23, 1737/8	LR5	2
Thankfull, d. Elisha, b. Jan. 21, 1760	LR11	580
Thankfull, d. Elisha, d. Feb. 6, 1760	LR11	574
Thankfull, d. Elisha, b. Apr. 19, 1768	LR15	C
Thomas, s. Samuel, b. Feb. 5, 1685* *(Written "1685/6")	LR1	3
Thomas, of Ffarmington, m. Martha **JUDD**, of Watterbury, Jan. 6, 1713/14	LR2	93
Thomas, his 1st child s. [ ], b. May 30, 1715; d. June 4, 1715	LR2	93
Thomas, his 1st child s. [ ], b. May 30, [ ]*; d. June 4, 1715 *(Written over "1715")	LR2	95
Thomas, had twin children b. June 24, 1727	LR4	395
Thomas, his twin children d. June 25, 1727	LR4	396
Thomas, Jr., m. Ruth **NEWEL**, b. of Farmington, Nov. 20, 1740	LR6	27
Thomas, of Farmington, m. Mary **WILLIAMS**, of Waterbury, June 20, 1744	LR7	35
Thomas, d. Mar. 11, 1750/1	LR8	11
Thomas, s. Josiah, b. Sept. 27, 1753	LR8	4
Thomas, s. Enos (?), b. Mar. 14, 1772	LR17	431
Thomas, m. Julia Ann **COWLES**, b. of Farmington, Oct. 9, 1833, by Rev. Noah Porter	LR42	A
Timothy, s. Samuell, b. Nov. 4, 1666	LR1	2
Timothy, s. Nathaniel & Phebe, b. Aug. 20, 1704	LR2	99
Timothy, s. Nathaniel, b. Feb. 19, 1752	LR8	4
Timothy, s. Asa, b. May 16, 1754	LR9	6
Timothy, of Farmington, m. Content **JONSON**, of Middletown, [ ]	LR5	13
Urene, d. Zebulon, b. Sept. 28, 1781	LR22	461
Ursula, d. Amos, b. Sept. 9, 1770	LR17	431
Walter H., of Farmington, m. Azuba **STEDMAN**, of Berlin, July 10, 1822, by W. Eli, V.D.M.	LR40	571
Wickliff, s. Capt. Josiah, b. Aug. 22, 1759	LR11	581
William, s. Ezekiel, b. Apr. 18, 1759	LR11	580

	Vol.	Page
COWLES, COAL, COALES, COLE, COOLE, COWL, COWLS (cont.)		
William, Jr., m. Laura HAMLIN, b. of Farmington, Aug. 30, 1848, by Rev. Noah Porter	LR47	122
William, had s. [ ]	LR7	H
William L., m. Emogene H. CLARK, Aug. 5, 1850, by William Wright	LR47	127
William S., of Rhinebeck, N.Y., m. Louisa Mary COWLES, of Farmington, Nov. 13, 1837, by Rev. Noah Porter	LR47	96
Zachariah, d. Thomas & Martha, b. Apr. 18, 1723	LR2	87
Zachariah, s. Thomas, d. Apr. 29, 1723	LR2	61
Zebulon, s. William, b. Mar. 20, 1733/4	LR6	2
Zenas, s. Capt. Solomon, b. Feb. 16, 1762	LR11	581
CRAMPTON, CHRAMTON, Adnah, s. Miles, b. Jan. 27, 1774	LR21	541
Jennet, m. Heman H. ORTON, b. of Farmington, Nov. 28, 1839, by Rev. Noah Porter	LR47	101
Julia, m. Ava HART, b. of Farmington, Nov. 6, 1827, by Rev. Noah Porter	LR42	565
Maria, m. Almyran YOUNG, Mar. 12, 1833, by Rev. David L. Parmelee	LR42	A
Mary, m. Eri LEWIS, b. of Farmington, Oct. 25, 1827, by Rev. Noah Porter	LR42	565
Stephen, s. Miles, b. May 13, 1776	LR21	541
William, m. Esther COWLES, b. of Farmington, May 17, 1827, by Rev. Noah Porter	LR42	565
CRANE, Asahel, s. Thomas & Ruth, b. Nov. 22, 1711	LR5	307
Russel, m. Martha GLADDING, b. of Farmington, Oct. 28, 1832, by Rev. Noah Porter	LR42	558
CRITTENDEN, CRETTENTON, CRITENTON, CRUTTENDEN, Hopestill, had s. Jemiah, b. Aug. 19, 1767	LR15	C
Jason, s. Abraham & Sarah, b. Mar. 30, 1761	LR11	580
Jemiah, s. Hopestill, b. Aug. 19, 1767	LR15	C
Levi, s. Abraham & Sarah, b. Nov. 28, 1758	LR11	580
Stephen, s. Abraham & Sarah, b. Apr. 15, 1755	LR11	580
CROSBY, David F., of Hawley, Mass., m. Lucy A. KINNEY, of Manchester, Aug. 2, 1838, by Rev. Noah Porter	LR47	97
Stephen, of Spencer, Mass., m. Julia COWLES, of Farmington, Sept. 16, 1822, by Noah Porter, V.D.M.	LR40	572
CROW, John, Jr., of Farmington, m. Hannah BROWN, of New Haven, Mar. 22, 1742	LR6	304
CULVER, COLLVER, David, m. Ruth CLARK, b. of Farmington, Jan. 7, 1734/5	LR5	539
Dimis A., of Farmington, m. Daniel CLARK, of Southington, May 3, 1847, by William Wright	LR47	119
Elizabeth, d. Samuel, b. Dec. 28, 1773	LR21	541
Mary, d. Andrew, b. Feb. 5, 1768	LR15	C
Philogus, s. Andrew, b. June 4, 1766	LR14	5
Polly C., of Bristol, m. Roswell LEWIS, of Farmington, Nov. 4, 1829, by Rev. Noah Porter	LR42	561
Ruth, d. Andrew, b. July 28, 1770	LR15	J
Samuel, m. Elizabeth SPENCER, Dec. 22, 1763	LR11	594

	Vol.	Page
CULVER, COLLVER (cont.)		
Shaler, d. Samuel, b. Apr. 13, 1766	LR14	5
Sylva, d. Samuell, b. Oct. 10, 1764	LR14	5
CUMMINGS, Harriet L, of Goshen, m. Frederick R.		
BUTLER, of Weathersfield, Rocky Hill Soc., Feb.		
6, 1842, by Richard Woodruff	LR47	106
CURTIS, CURTIC, CURTICE, CURTISS, CURTESS,		
CURTISE, Abigail, of Weathersfield, m. Isaac LEWIS, of		
Ffarmington, May 4, 1710	LR2	123
Abigail, of Stratford, m. Hezekiah HOOKER, of		
Ffarmington, Dec. 18, 1716	LR2	94
Abigail, of Newington, m. John WOODRUFF, of		
Kensington, s. John, b. of Farmington, Nov. 28,		
1734	LR5	539
Abigall, d. Solomon, b. Dec. 10, 1779	LR17	431
Abigail, d. Jeremiah, b. May [ ], [ ]	LR7	H
Adah, d. Enoch, b. Mar. 12, 1753	LR9	6
Azor, s. Azor & Margary, b. Oct. 22, 1750	LR8	4
Azubah Smith, d. Jesse, b. Apr. 6, 1776	LR21	541
Azubah Smith, d. Jesse, d. Nov. 24, 1777, in the 2nd y. of		
her age	LR22	482
Azubah Smith, d. Jesse, b. Oct. 2, 1778	LR22	461
Celestia, m. Loderic S. LEWIS, b. of Burlington, July 20,		
1842, by Rev. C. D. Cowles	LR47	108
Daniel, Jr., m. Mary ANDRUS, Feb. 4, 1773	LR17	442
David, Jr., m. Abigail WOODRUFF, b. of Farmington,		
Apr. 27, 1738	LR6	27
Deliverance, d Azor & Margary, b. [ ] 7, 1752	LR8	4
Eleazer, s. Daniel, b. Sept. 3, 1754	LR8	4
Elidia, d. Azor, b. Oct. 17, 1762	LR11	581
Elihu, s. Allen, b. Dec. 20, 1732	LR5	2
Eliza, m. Owen KANE, Mar. 17, 1828, by Rev. Noah		
Porter	LR42	565
Elizabeth, of Weathersfield, m. Joseph WOODRUFF, of		
Ffarmington, s. John, Apr. 15, 1708	LR2	101
Elizabeth, d. Zebulon & Lydia, b. June 4, 1737	LR6	2
Elizabeth, m. Josiah WILLCOX, Jan. 1, 1750/1	LR7	35
Elizabeth, d. Enoch & Rachel, b. Oct. 16, 1751	LR8	4
Elnathan, s. Thomas, b. Mar. 22, 1713	LR2	282
Emeline, of Farmington, m. Elbridge G. ATKINS, of		
Bristol, Feb. 6, 1833, by Rev. Henry Stanwood, of		
Bristol	LR42	558
Emily S., of Farmington, m. Sylvester FITTS, of East		
Windsor, Aug. 12, 1830, by Rev. Noah Porter	LR42	560
Esther, m. Gideon HILL, Dec. 7, 1769	LR21	557
[E]unie, d. David, b. Oct. 22, 1719	LR2	102
Eunice, d. Solomon, b. Apr. 16, 1778	LR17	431
Hannah, d. Jeremiah & Hannah, b. Sept. 1, 1735	LR5	306
Hannah, d. Allen, b. Nov. 12, 1735	LR5	2
Hannah, m. Job LEWIS, Nov. 13, 1755	LR11	576
Hannah, w. Jeremiah, d. Apr. 6, 1772, in the 64th y. of her		
age	LR17	444

	Vol.	Page

CURTIS, CURTIC, CURTICE, CURTISS, CURTESS, CURTISE (cont.)

	Vol.	Page
Harvey, m. Phebe **PERKINS**, b. of Farmington, Sept. 1, 1822, by Noah Porter, V.D.M.	LR40	571
Jeremiah, m. Hannah **BURNHAM**, b. of Farmington, Jan. 7, 1730/1	LR5	13
Jeremiah, s. Jeremiah, clerk, b. Nov. 7, 1752	LR8	4
Jeremiah, s. Jeremiah, d. Dec. 23, 1755	LR9	495
Jeremiah, s. John, b. Sept. 6, 1770	LR17	431
Jeremiah, of Southington, m. Rachel **GARNSEY**, of Westbury, May 4, 1774	LR17	442
Jesse, m. Martha **ROOT**, Dec. 2, 1772	LR17	442
John, s. Jeremiah & Hannah, b. Jan. 20, 1739/40	LR6	2
John, m. Mary [ ], Dec. 3, 1762	LR15	A
Levi, s. Solomon, b. Jan. 10, 1772	LR17	431
Lois, d. Thomas, b. Mar. 3, 1725/6	LR2	282
Lowis, m. Timothy **JUDD**, Nov. 9, 1744	LR7	46
Lois, d. Azor, b. Apr. 8, 1754	LR9	6
Lois, m. Dan **WINCHEL**, Oct. 9, 1755	LR11	576
Lois, d. Sylvanus, b. June 6, 1764	LR14	5
Lucas, s. John, b. June 17, 1766	LR15	C
Lucina, d. John, b. Sept. 11, 1763	LR15	C
Lucretia, m. Elnathan **STRONG**, Nov. 15, 1764	LR11	592
Luce, d. Jeremiah, b. [ ] 5, 174[ ]	LR7	G
Lucy, m. Elisha **ROOT**, Jan. 16, 1764	LR17	G
Lucy, d. Jesse, b. Mar. 21, 1774	LR17	431
Lucy, d. John, b. July 25, 1776	LR21	541
Lydia, d. Thomas, b. July 9, 1721	LR2	282
Lydia, m. Jeames **WOODRUFF**, Feb. 4, 1742	LR6	305
Lyman, of Plymouth, m. Lucy **GILLET**, of Farmington, Nov. 27, 1831, by Rev. Noah Porter	LR42	559
Marcus, s. Jesse, b. Nov. 13, 1781	LR22	461
Margaret, w. Samuel, d. Dec. 20, 1769, ae 24	LR15	M
Margary, d. Azor, b. Feb. 6, 1756	LR9	5
Martin, s. Allen, b. Mar. 14, 1729/30	LR5	2
Martain, s. Allen, d. Mar. 15, 1729/30	LR5	50
Mary, d. Thomas, b. July 9, 1716	LR2	282
Mary, d. Rev. Jeremiah, b. Aug. 20, 1742	LR6	2
Mercy, d. Thomas, b. Jan. 20, 1726/7	LR2	282
Otis, s. Sylvanus, b. May 24, 1766	LR14	6
Peter, m. Eliza F. **WADSWORTH**, Apr. 30, 1823, by Noah Porter, V.D.M.	LR40	572
Phineas, m. Catharine E. **PORTER**, b. of Bristol, Nov. 26, 1845, by Rev. Noah Porter	LR47	115
Polly, d. John, b. June 5, 1773	LR17	431
Polly, d. John, d. Aug. 22, 1777	LR21	560
Prudence, d. Thomas, b. Oct. 13, 1718	LR2	282
Rebeckah, m. Daniel **DEWEY**, b. of Farmington, Jan. 27, 1731/2	LR5	300
Roxy, b. May 6, 1767; m. Shubael **PORTER**, Jan. 9, 1786; d. [ ], 1812	LR47	A-B
Ruth, d. Abner, b. Apr. 29, 1784	LR22	461
Samuel, s. Jeremiah & Hannah, b. Nov. 15, 1737	LR6	2

	Vol.	Page
CURTIS, CURTIC, CURTICE, CURTISS, CURTESS, CURTISE (cont.)		
Samuel, m. Margaret [ ], May 13, 1766	LR15	A
Samuel, s. Samuel, b. Dec. 8, 1769	LR15	J
Samuel, s. Daniell, Jr., b. Dec. 16, 1773	LR17	431
Sarah, d. Rev. Jeremiah, b. Apr. 12, 1733	LR5	2
Sarah, m. Noah **GRIDLEY**, Aug. 15, 1751	LR7	46
Sarah, d. Solomon, b. Nov. 6, 1776	LR17	431
Seth, s. Allen, b. May 24, 1730/1	LR5	2
Seth, s. Allen, d. July 6, 1731	LR5	50
Simeon, m. Maria **HOSKINS**, b. of Farmington, Nov. 28, 1844, by Noah Porter	LR47	113
Solomon, m. Hannah **WOODRUFF**, Dec. 6, 1764	LR11	592
Solomon, m. Abigail **GILLET**, Feb. 18, 1766	LR17	443
Sibbel, d. Thomas, b. Oct. 23, 1708 (Sybil)	LR2	282
Sible, m. Ebenezer **NORTH**, b. of Farmington, Dec. 10, 1730	LR5	300
Sylvanus, m. Jemima **NORTON**, Oct. 22, 1762	LR11	594
Sylvester, of Burlington, m. Evelina A. **HORTON**, of Cheshire, Aug. 25, 1840, by Rev. Aaron S. Hill	LR47	103
Thomas, his 6th child b. June 6, 1715	LR2	282
Thomas, his 6th child d. June 8, 1726	LR2	66
Vasti, d. Azor, b. Jan. 1, 1765	LR14	5
Zebulon, s .Thomas, b. Jan. 16, 1710/11	LR2	282
Zebulon, m. Lydia **COLE**, b. of Farmington, July 3, 1735	LR6	27
CUSACK, John, of Ireland, m. Abigail **PAGE**, of Southington, Aug. 10, 1826, by Rev. David L. Ogden	LR42	564
DAILEY, Harriet, of Farmington, m. George N. **VIBBERTS**, of East Hartford, July 26, 1840, by Rev. Aaron S. Hill	LR47	103
Lowey, of Farmington, m. John **COTCH**, of Simsbury, Nov. 5, 1823, by Rev. Stephen S. Nelson, of Canton & Northington	LR40	573
DANIELS, Eliza, m. Martin **YEOMAN**, b. of Farmington, Sept. 15, 1822, by Amzi Benedict	LR40	572
DARREN,* Josiah, s. Dan, b Sept. 10, 1767 *(Perhaps "Darrow")	LR15	D
DARROW,*, Josiah, s. Dan, b. Sept. 10, 1767 *(Perhaps "Darren")	LR15	D
Maria, m. Edwin **TUCKER**, b. of Farmington, May 1, 1839, by Rev. Noah Porter	LR47	99
DART, Hiram, m. Emma **DICKINSON**, b. of Northington, Mar. 3, 1825, by Bela Kellogg	LR42	568
DAVIS, Experience, m. Hezekiah **WEST**, Nov. 20, 1777	LR22	480
James, s. John, b. Feb. 26, 1753	LR8	4
James, [s. John], b. Aug. 9 [ ]	LR7	K
Jared, s. Sam[ue]ll & Hannah **DAVIS**, alias **NORTON**, b. Dec. 1, 1777	LR22	462
John, m. Ruth **LEWIS**, Dec. 1, 1748	LR7	46
John, Jr., of Farmington, m. Naomi **KINYON**, of Hopkinton, R. I., Mar. 27, 1773	LR17	442
John, s. John, b. Mar. [ ]	LR7	K
Jonathan, m. Elizabeth **COVEY**, Oct. 13, 1777	LR22	480

	Vol.	Page
DAVIS (cont.)		
Thomas, m. Mary **WEST**, Nov. 20, 1777	LR22	480
DAY, Anna, of Farmington, m. Timothy **NORTH**, of Candor,		
N.Y., June 29, 1829, by Rev. Harry Bushnell	LR42	562
Erastus, s. Thomas Stanley, b. Oct. 1, 1775	LR17	432
Hannah, of Hartford, m. Thomas **BARNES**, s. Ebenezer,		
of Ffarmington, May 19, 1726	LR2	100
Julia, m. Oliver **TILLOTSON**, b. of Farmington, Jan. 12,		
1825, by Rev. Harry Bushnell	LR42	568
Thomas Stanley, m. Ruth **NEWEL**, Dec. 21, 1774	LR17	443
DAYTON, Chester, m. Julia Ann **PARSONS**, b. of		
Farmington, Oct. 16, 1838, by Rev. S. H. Clark	LR47	97
DEAN, Mary, Mrs. of Stratford, m. Samuel **COLE**, Apr. 5,		
1753	LR9	286
DEING(?), Sarah, m. Phinehas **WOODRUFF**, June 10, 1762	LR11	575
DEMING, DEMON, DEMAN, Abigail, d. Thomas, b. Aug.		
22, 1652	LR2	329
Almah, d. Eliakim, b. Apr. 24, 1750	LR8	4
Amme, s. Eliakim, b. Nov. 4, 1767	LR15	D
Ann, d. Moses, b. July 22, 1755	LR11	580
Anne, d. Jacob, b. July 4, 1716	LR2	102
Anne, m. Timothy **THOMSON**, b. of Farmington, Feb. 1,		
1738/9	LR6	27
Benjamin, s. Elisha & Mary, b. Sept. 18, 1758	LR11	580
Caroline, m. Romanta **HAWLEY**, b. of Farmington, May		
26, 1824, by Rev. Harry Bushnell	LR42	568
Catharine, d. Ebenezer, b. June 25, 1773	LR21	542
Dinah, w. Jacob, d. Oct. 3, 1751	LR8	11
Dolly, of Farmington, m. Norman **NERING**, of		
Burlington, June 12, 1823, by Erastus Clapp,		
V.D.M.	LR40	572
Ebenezer, d. Aug. 30, 1775, in the 40th y. of his age	LR21	558-9
Eliakim, m. Lucy **GRIDLEY**, Oct. 1, 1746	LR7	46
Eliakim, s. Eliakim, b. July 7, 1766	LR15	D
Elizabeth, of Weathersfield, m. Thomas **NORTON**, Sept.		
11, 1753	LR9	286
Elizabeth M., of Farmington, m. Edgar **FREEMAN**, of		
Hartford, Aug. 29, 1852, by Rev. Cephas Brainerd	LR47	131
Emily Maria, m. Alexander **POSEY**, b. of Farmington,		
Dec. 8, 1840, by Rev. Aaron S. Hill	LR47	103
[E]unice, m. Joseph **OLMSTEAD**, b. of Farmington,		
Aug. 11, 1737	LR6	27
Honour, m. Samuel **STEEL**, May 4, 1749	LR7	46
Ichabod, s. Ebenezer, b. Aug. 15, 1775	LR21	542
Jacob, s. Jacob, b. Dec. 13, 1713	LR2	102
Jacob, m. Abigail **JEROME**, Mar. 29, 1752	LR8	10
Jacob, s. Moses, b. Nov. 18, 1757	LR11	580
Jacob, d. Apr. 2, 1771	LR17	444
John, s. Thomas, b. Feb. 4, 1653	LR2	329
John, m. Catharine H. **WILLIAMS**, Sept. 1, 1846, by		
Noah Porter	LR47	118
Levi, of Berlin, m. Sarah B. **MERRIMAN**, of		
Farmington, May 26, 1842, by Rev. Noah Porter	LR47	108

	Vol.	Page
DEMING, DEMON, DEMAN (cont.)		
Lois, m. John **BROWN**, b. of Farmington, Mar. 6, 1746	LR7	35
Lowis, had illeg. s. Ezekiel **BRONING**, b. Oct. 5, 1748;		
f. John **BRONING**	LR7	G
Luca, d. Jacob, b. Mar. 18, 1717/18	LR2	102
Luca, d. Jacob, d. Aug. 8, 1719	LR2	61
Lucy, d. Eliakim, b. Dec. 8, 1747	LR8	4
Lucy, d .Moses, b. Sept. 12, 1750	LR8	4
Lucy, m. Samuel **NORTH**, Jr., Nov. 29, 1770	LR17	G
Lucy, m. Stephen **COLE**, Dec. 26, 1771	LR17	443
Mary, of Weathersfield, m. Hezekiah **BROWN**, of		
Ffarmington, June 8, 1723/4	LR2	60
Mary, d. Elisha, b. Apr. 27, 1753	LR9	7-8
Mary, d. Elisha, d. Aug. 8, 1755	LR9	495
Moses, s. Jacob, b. Sept. 8, 1720	LR2	102
Ruth, d. Elisha & Mary, b. Nov. 27, 1756	LR11	580
Samuel, m. Catharine M. **LEWIS**, b. of Farmington, Jan.		
18, 1821, by Noah Porter, V.D.M.	LR40	571
Sarah, d. Moses, b. May 12, 1754	LR8	4
Sarah, m. Lieut. John **ROW**, Feb. 15, 1759	LR11	576
Sarah, d. Eliakim, b. May 8, 1760	LR15	D
Selah, s. Eliakim, b. Nov. 15, 1762	LR15	D
Seth, s. Moses, b. [ ]	LR7	K
Ze[b]ulon, s. Zebulon, b. Feb. [ ]	LR7	K
----nia, d. Zebulon, b. Feb. 17, 1741	LR6	2
-----, s. [-----], st. b. Dec. 23, 1743	LR7	H
DENTON, Anne, d. Benjamin, b. Oct. 10, 1733/4	LR5	2
Benjamin, of Ffarmington, m. Rachel **WHEELER**, of		
Hartford, Dec. 1, 1724	LR2	52
Benjamin, s. Benjamin, b. Apr. 14, 1736	LR5	2
Hushah (?), s. Benj[amin], d. Jan. 7, 1736/7		
*("Thurston"?)	LR6	10
John, s. Benjamin, b. Apr. 21, 1727	LR4	395
Mary, d. Benjamin, b. Oct. 17, 1728	LR4	395
Rachel, d. Benjamin, b. Aug. 22, 1738	LR6	2
Sarah, d. Benjamin, b. Mar. 19, 1730/1	LR5	2
Thurston, s. Benjamin, b. Sept. 15, 1725	LR2	70
Thurston, see also Hushah (?) Denton		
DEPATUR, Martin, of Northford, m. Minerva		
BARRINGTON, Oct. 5, 1851, by Rev. Nathan E.		
Shailer	LR47	130
DERRIN, Chancy, of Farmington, m. Mindwell **CORNISH**,		
of Simsbury, Aug. 11, 1822, by W. Eli, V.D.M.	LR40	571
Diana, m. Orrin **WOODFORD**, b. of Farmington, Apr. 4,		
1830, by Rev. Harry Bushnell	LR42	561
DEWEY, Asahel, s. David, b. Oct. 24, 1768	LR15	D
Daniel, of Ffarmington, m. Catharen **BECKLEY**, of		
Weathersfield, Sept. 27, 1706	LR2	125
Daniel, s. Daniel, b. Aug. 24, 1707	LR2	232
Daniel, m. Rebeckah **CURTISS**, b. of Farmington, Jan.		
27, 1731/2	LR5	300
Daniel, s. David, b. May 6, 1771	LR17	432
David, s. Daniel, b. Mar. 16, 1732/3	LR5	2

	Vol.	Page
DEWEY (cont.)		
David, m. Esther **DUNHAM**, Feb. 12, 1755	LR11	576
Elishama, s. David, b. Apr. 6, 1774	LR17	432
Hanah, d. Daniel, b. Mar. 9, 1740	LR11	580
Josiah, s. Daniel, b. July 7, 1737	LR11	580
Josiah, s. Daniel, d. July 16, 1737	LR11	574
Josiah,* s. David, b. Jan. 6, 1756 *(Written "Josiah		
JEWEY")	LR11	580
Lucy, d. Daniel, b. Nov. 1, 1742	LR11	580
Lucy, d. Daniel, d. Oct. 22, 1748	LR11	574
Oliver, s. David, b. Oct. 3, 1766	LR15	D
Rhode, d. Daniel, b. Nov. 24, 1736	LR6	2
Rhoda, d. Daniel, d. Oct. 15, 1748	LR11	574
Rhoda, d. David, b. Feb. 14, 1758	LR11	580
Sarah, d. Daniel, b. Aug. 2, 1712	LR2	232
DeWITT, John Frederick, of Northford, m. Althia **MORE**, of		
Northfield, July 8, 1828, by Rev. Noah Porter	LR42	564
[DIBBELL], **DIBELL**, Aabraham, his w. [ ], joined church		
Apr. 20, 1663	LR2	327
DICKENSON, DICASON, DICKASON, DICKINSON,		
Clarissa, m. Noadiah **HART**, b. of Farmington,		
Sept. 12, 1826, by Rev. Bela Kellogg	LR42	567
Ebenezer, m. Mary **HART**, May 31, 1744	LR7	35
Ebenezer, d. Sept. 2, 1751	LR8	11
Ebenezer, d. Ebenezer, decd., b. Nov. 23, 1751	LR8	4
Ebenezer, m. Mabel **WHAPLES**, June 2, 1757	LR11	576
Elisha, s. Ebenezer, decd., d. June 15, 1753	LR8	12
Elizabeth, m. John **RICHARDS**, Dec. 26, 1776	LR21	557
Emma, m. Hiram **HART**, b. of Northington, Mar. 3,		
1825, by Bela Kellogg	LR42	568
Jamimah, m. Josiah **COWLES**, b. of Farmington, Nov.		
10,* 1739 *(In pencil "11th")	LR6	27
Mary, d. Ebenezer, b. Dec. 4, 1745	LR7	542
Samuel, m. Cornelia **SCOTT**, Oct. 17, 1849, by Noah		
Porter, Jr.	LR47	125
Sarah Omsted, d. W[illia]m, b. Mar. 3, 1767	LR15	D
Susan, m. Chauncey **ROWE**, b. of Farmington, Oct. 9,		
1839, by Rev. Noah Porter	LR47	101
Waitstill, s. Ebenezer, b .July 2, 1758	LR11	580
William, m. Mary **OLMSTEAD**, Apr. 4, 1765	LR15	A
DIX, Charlotte, m. Eli **SPERRY**, b. of Farmington, Nov. 3,		
1824, by Amasa Woodford, J.P.	LR42	568
Rebecka, m. Ezra **BELDING**, Sept. 30, 1745	LR7	35
Rebecca, of Farmington, m. William G. **McWARY**, of		
New Hartford, Mar. 8, 1836, by Rev. Noah Porter	LR47	93
DOAK, David, of Brooklyn, N.Y., m. Rebecca **McLINTOCK**,		
Dec. 15, 1845, by Rev. Noah Porter	LR47	116
DOCHESTER, Alexander, s. Stephen, b. June 8, 1760	LR11	580
Brillah, d. Stephen, b. Nov. 16, 1762	LR11	581
Charles, s. Stephen, b. Aug. 10, 1758	LR11	580
Elizabeth, d. Stephen, b. Dec. 25, 1768	LR15	D
Elizabeth, d. Stephen, d. Aug. 17, 1770	LR17	444
Elizabeth, d. Stephen, b. Aug. 28, 1771	LR17	432

	Vol.	Page
DOCHESTER (cont.)		
Stephen, m. Elizabeth **GOUL,*** Oct. 29, 1754		
*(**COLE**"?)	LR8	10
DONOLDS, Jonathan, of Canaan, m. Abigail H. **PORTER**, of		
Farmington, May 29, 1839, by Rev. Noah Porter	LR47	100
DOOLITTLE, Abigail H. G., of Farmington, m. Andrew L.		
WALLACE, of Berlin, Nov. 30, 1837, at the house		
of Amos Doolittle, by Rev. J. Goodwin	LR47	96
Sibbel E., m. Alfred **ROOT**, b. of Farmington, Nov. 18,		
1838, by Rev. Noah Porter	LR47	98
DORMAN, Alfred, of Farmington, m. Emily **TAYLOR**, of		
Glastonbury, Oct. 19, 1835, by Rev. Noah Porter	LR47	90
Annis M., of Farmington, m. Noadiah **BARBER**, of		
Avon, May 4, 1837, by Rev. Noah Porter	LR47	95
Catharine L., m. Selah **WESTCOTT**, Nov. 17, 1842, by		
Rev. C. D. Cowles	LR47	109
Cornelia C., m. Horace M. **BUTLER**, of Westfield, Mass,		
Nov. 15, 1846, by Rev. Noah Porter	LR47	118
Edward H., of Farmington, m. Laura A. **FRISBIE**, of		
Bristol, Nov. 26, 1843, by Rev. R. A. Chalker	LR47	112
Elizabeth M., of Farmington, m. James M. **FORBES**, of		
East Granville, Mass., July 14, 1847, by Noah Porter	LR47	121
Harriet J., of Farmington, m. William J. **HOTCHKISS**,		
of Burlington, Apr. 26, 1849, by Rev. Henry J. Fox	LR47	124
Julia A., of Farmington, m. Norton Z. **HOSKINS**, of		
Bloomfield, Dec. 23, 1849, by Rev. Noah Porter	LR47	126
Julius, m. Esther **ORR**, Mar. 1, 1848, by Rev. William		
McAlister	LR47	122
Sarah L., of Farmington, m. Horace B. **PALMER**, of		
Windsor, Dec. 2, 1849, by Rev. Noah Porter	LR47	126
DOUGLASS, Jennet, m. Bidwell **SWERES**, b. of Farmington,		
Nov. 10, 1829, by Rev. Noah Porter	LR42	561
DOWD, DOUD, Cloe, d. Ezra, b. Aug. 18, 1765	LR14	5
Jesse, s. Ezra, b. Nov. 5, 1762	LR11	581
Rachel, d. Ezra, b. July 28, 1772	LR17	432
Ruben, s. Ezra, b. Apr. 3, 1768	LR15	D
Ruama, d. Ezra, b. May 2, 1770	LR17	432
DRIGGS, Betty, d. Bartholomew, b. Dec. 28, 1781	LR22	464
Deolotus, 6th s. Bartholomew, b. Feb. 27, 1779	LR22	464
Eliot, 3rd s. Bartholomew, b. Aug. 6, 1772	LR22	464
George, 2nd s. Bartholomew, b. June 3, 1770	LR22	464
Griswould, 4th s. Bartholomew, b. Mar. 17, 1775	LR22	464
Seth, 1st s. Bartholomew, b. Oct. 8, 1768	LR22	464
Spencer, 5th s. Bartholomew, b. Apr. 27, 1777	LR22	464
DRINKWATER, DRINKWATTER, Abigail, of New		
Milford, m. Hezekiah **BROWNSON**, of		
Farmington, Apr. 19, 1756	LR9	286
Abigail, m. Hezekiah **BROWNSON**, Apr. 21, 1756	LR11	576
DUDLEY, Sarah, of Saybrook, m. Thomas **ROOT**, of		
Farmington, Feb. 15, 1726/7	LR2	258
DUNCAN, John, m. Lavinia Amanda **BREWER**, Apr. 1,		
1823, by Elisha Cushman	LR40	572

	Vol.	Page
DUNHAM, Albert, m. Sylvia **COWLES**, b. of Farmington, Feb. 24, 1825, by Rev. Noah Porter	LR42	568
Cornelius, s. Cornelius, b. Apr. 25, 1756 (Date conflicts with birth of Jemima)	LR14	5
Desire, m. Roswell **MOOR**, June 30, 1755	LR9	286
Esther, m. David **DEWEY**, Feb. 12, 1755	LR11	576
Hanah, m. David **MATHER**, June 3, 1757	LR11	576
Jane, m. George S. **WOODRUFF**, b. of Farmington, July 4, 1847, by William Wright	LR47	119
Jemima, d. Cornelius, b. Mar. 1, 1756 (Date conflicts with birth of Cornelius)	LR14	5
Marah, m. Amos **HART**, Nov. 23, 1758	LR11	592
Samuel s. Cornelius, b. July 26, 1768	LR14	5
Samuel C., of Farmington, m. Augusta **RECOR**, of New Britain, Aug. 29, 1847, by William Wright	LR47	121
DURAND, Phebe, of Sheffield, Mass., m. William. L.		7
BUNNEL, of Farmington, Dec. 12, 1842, by Rev. C. D. Cowles	LR47	109
DUTTON, Abigail, w. Benjamin, d. Sept. 13, 1758	LR11	577
Amasa, s. Joseph, b. June 9, 1768	LR15	D
Amos, s. Benjamin, b. [ ], 19, 1757	LR11	580
Benjamin, s. Benjamin, b. Jan. 28, 1754	LR8	4
Elizabeth, m. Stephen **BROWNSON**, Sept. 5, 1771	LR17	G
Elvira, m. Dennis **HART**, Feb. 1, 1825, by Rev. Noah Porter	LR42	568
Elydia, d. Joseph, b. Mar. 2, 1750/1	LR8	4
John, m. Abigail **WEBSTER**, Mar. 14, 1754	LR9	286
John, s. John, b. Aug. 25, 1758	LR11	581
Levi, s. John, b. Feb. 14, 1760	LR11	581
Lucy, d. Benjamin, b. Feb. 10, 1763	LR11	581
Luthaner, d. John, b. July 31, 1756	LR11	581
Marah, d. Joseph, b. Sept. 3, 1753	LR8	4
Martha, d. Benjamin, b. Dec. 20, 1767	LR15	D
Moses, s. Joseph, b. Mar. 20, 1763	LR11	581
Oliver, s. Samuel, b. June 25, 1759	LR9	7-8
Osee, d. John, b. Dec. 29, 1754	LR9	7-8
Samuell, m. Lois **HITCHCOCK**, Apr. 25, 1753	LR8	10
Samuel, s. Joseph, b. Apr. 9, 1766	LR15	D
Sarah, d. Joseph, b. June 16, 1757	LR11	580
Timothy, s. Benjamin, b. Feb. 7, 1761	LR11	580
Timothy, s. Benjamin, b. Feb. 7, 1761	LR11	581
EATON, Mary, of Farmington, m. Daniel **COOK**, of Bristol, Nov. 3, 1845, by William Wright	LR47	116
William, m. Lucinda **SHEPARD**, b. of Bristol, May 6, 1841, by Rev. Aaron S. Hill	LR47	104
EAVENS, [see under **EVANS**]		
EDGERTON, Elizabeth, m. Dr. Elisha **LORD**, Nov. 10, 1751	LR8	10
[ELLIS], ELIS, Jeremiah, of Litchfield, m. Aphia **WOODRUFF**, of Farmington, Jan. 3, 1827, by Rev. Harvey Bushnell	LR42	567
ELSWORTH, ELLSWORTH, Elizabeth, of Windsor, m. John **GRIDLEY**, of Ffarmington, May 30, 1711	LR2	125
Mary, m. James **NEWELL**, Mar. 1, 1759	LR11	576

	Vol.	Page
ELSWORTH, ELLSWORTH (cont.)		
Ollive, d. Olever, b. Aug. 24, 1767	LR15	D
Oliver, m. Mahitabel [ ], May 28, 1767	LR15	A
Sarah, of Hartford, m. John **GRIDLEY**, of Farmington,		
Aug. 16, 1756	LR9	286
ELTON, Cyprian, s. Ebenezer, b. Oct. 19, 1778	LR21	542
Ebenezer, m. Rhoda **HURLBURT** Feb. 2, 1764	LR15	A
Hannah, of Burlington, m. Daniel **WHEELER**, of		
Bristol, July 16, 1827, by Rev. Noah Porter	LR42	565
James, s. Ebenezer, & Rhoda, b. Aug. 22, 1770	LR21	542
Pamela, d. Ebenezer & Rhoda, b. Feb. 28, 1766	LR15	D
Phileana, d. Ebenezer & Rhoda, b. Oct. 15, 1764	LR15	D
Rhesa, s. Ebenezer, b. Oct. 13, 1775	LR21	542
Rhoda, d. Ebenezer, b. Feb. 24, 1773	LR21	542
ENO, Nancy, of Simsbury, m. Walter **FILLEY**, of		
Wentonbury, Dec. 30, 1824, by Rev. Harry		
Bushnell	LR42	568
ENOS, Mary, m. John **LANKTON**, Dec. 12, 1754	LR11	576
EVANS, EAVENS, Asahel, s. Ebenezer, b. Dec. 8, 1750	LR9	7-8
Dorothy, d. Ebenezer, b. May 15, 1747	LR9	7-8
Ebenezer, m. Mary **GRIDLEY**, d. Jno, b. of Farmington,		
Dec. 21, 1737	LR6	27
Ebenezer, s. Ebenezer, b. Sept. 19, 1743	LR9	7-8
Ebenezer, d. Dec. about middle, 1754	LR11	593
Mary, d. Ebenezer, b. Aug. 1, 1744	LR9	7-8
EVERS, Henry W., of Manlius, N.Y., m. Sarah G.		
TILLOTSON, of Farmington, Oct. 5, 1824, by		
Rev. Noah Porter	LR42	568
FAIRCHILD, Clarissa, of Farmington, m. Ogden C. **PRATT**,		
of Middletown, Nov. 24, 1831, by Rev. Noah Porter	LR42	559
Eliza, m. Alison **MORSE**, b. of Farmington, July 24,		
1834, by Rev. Noah Porter	LR42	E
Estus F., m. Cynthia **MILLER**, Feb. 4, 1823, by Horace		
Cowles, J.P.	LR40	572
FANNING, July Ann, m. Eli **HULL**, Nov. 14, 1846, by		
William Wright	LR47	118
FARNSWORTH, Samuel R., m. Mary A. **MORSE**, Nov. 17,		
1846, by William Wright	LR47	121
FARNUM, Henry, of New Haven, m. Ann Sophia		
WHITMAN, of Farmington, Dec. 1, 1839, by Rev.		
Noah Porter	LR47	102
FARR, Emory, m. Maria **SWEET**, b. of Farmington, Sept. 18,		
1838, by Rev. Noah Porter	LR47	97
FENN, FFENN, Alfred, of Plymouth, m. Sophronia		
LANGDON, of Farmington, [Mar. 30, 1830], by		
Rev. Noah Porter	LR42	561
Joel, of Wallingford, m. Mary **HAMLIN**, of Farmington,		
June 26, 1844, by Rev. Edward Savage, of Bristol	LR47	112
Susannah, of Milford, m. Samuel **WADSWORTH**, Jr., of		
Ffarmington, Aug. 15, 1728	LR4	423
FESSENDEN, Thomas K., of Norwich, m. Nancy **COWLES**,		
of Farmington, Oct. 23, 1839, by Rev. Noah Porter	LR47	101

	Vol.	Page
FIELDS, Sarah Ann, of Haddam, m. Charles **HOMER**, of		
Farmington, Jan. 7, 1838, by Adna Whiting, J.P.	LR47	97
FILLEY, Walter, of Wentonbury, m. Nancy **ENO**, of		
Simsbury, Dec. 30, 1824, by Rev. Harry Bushnell	LR42	568
FINNEY, Rumah, m. Samuel F. **COWLES**, b. of Farmington,		
Sept. 5, 1827, by Rev. Noah Porter	LR42	565
FISKE, Susan F., m. Loring **RUNSMEL**, b. of Hartford, Sept.		
14, 1830, by Rev. Noah Porter	LR42	560
FITTS, Sylvester, of East Windsor, m. Clarissa **WILCOX**, of		
Farmington, July 4, 1827, by Rev. Bela Kellogg	LR42	565
Sylvester, of East Windsor, m. Emily S. **CURTIS**, of		
Farmington, Aug. 12, 1830, by Rev. Noah Porter	LR42	560
FOOT, Emily, m. Lowrey **ROBBINS**, Oct. 19, 1835, by David		
G. Ogden	LR47	92
FORBES, FORBS, Catharine, m. Stephen **LEE**, Feb. 6, 1746	LR15	A
James M., of East Granville, Mass., m. Elizabeth M.		
DORMAN, of Farmington, July 14, 1847, by Noah		
Porter	LR47	121
Samuel G., m. Ellen E. **HAMLIN**, Apr. 8, 1828, by Rev.		
David L. Ogden	LR42	564
FORD, Anne, d. William, b. Mar. 31, 1760	LR11	581
Elizabeth, d. William, b. Feb. 12, 1754	LR11	581
John, s. William, b. Sept. 23, 1752	LR11	581
Joseph, s. William, b. Mar. 30, 1763	LR11	581
Mary, d. William, b. June 25, 1757	LR11	581
Thankfull, d. William, b. Mar. 4, 1750	LR11	581
Thankfull, d. William, b. June 3, 1750	LR8	4
William, d. Aug. 30, 1763	LR11	593
FORWOOD, Martha, wid. of Samuell, of Simsbury, m. Sergt.		
Thomas **LEE**, of Farmington, Apr. 17, 1739·	LR6	27
FOSTER, Mary, m. Eldad **PECK**, Feb. 9, 1764	LR11	594
FOWLER, Sarah, of Durham, m. Elisha **MILLER**, Oct. 18,		
1764	LR11	592
Sarah, of Farmington, m. John **CHILDS**, of Sandlake,		
N.Y., Feb. 8, 1826, by Rev. Bela Kellogg	LR42	569
Sophia, of Farmington, m. Silas **LYMAN**, of Vernon,		
Feb. 8, 1826, by Rev. Bela Kellogg	LR42	569
FOX, Betsey, of Manchester, m. Charles A. **GOSS**, of Canton,		
May 15, 1842, in Unionville, by Rev. Merrell		
Richardson	LR47	107
Chauncey M., of New Hartford, m. Elizabeth **OLIN**, of		
Farmington, Apr. 2, 1843, by Noah Porter	LR47	109
Elisha, s. Elisha, b. Mar. 4, 1766	LR22	463
Eunice, d. Elisha, b. May 26, 1772	LR22	463
Nelson, of Avon, m. Mary **McAULEY**, of Farmington,		
Mar. 29, 1846, in Avon, by Rev. Stephen Hubbell,		
of Avon	LR47	117
Prudence, d. Elisha, b. June 20, 1774	LR22	463
Silas, s. Elisha, b. July 27, 1776	LR22	463
Thomas, s. Elisha, b. Feb. 23, 1770	LR22	463
Timothy, s. Elisha, b. Jan. 25, 1764	LR22	463
Zenas, s. Elisha, b. Jan. 28, 1768	LR22	463

	Vol.	Page
FRANCIS, FRANCES, Blynn, of Newington, m. Lucy HART, of Farmington, Apr. 26, 1848, by Noah Porter	LR47	122
Elijah, m. Hannah [ ], Apr. 22, 1755	LR15	A
Elijah, s. Elijah, b. Jan. 6, 1760	LR15	E
Elizabeth, d. Elijah, b. Dec. 12, 1755	LR15	E
Hannah, d. Elijah, b. Nov. 20, 1765	LR15	E
James, s. Elijah, b. Oct. 11, 1757	LR15	E
Justus, s. Elijah, b. Jan. 29, 1762	LR15	E
Mary, of Weathersfield, d. James, of Newington Parish, m. Thomas STANLEY, 3rd, of Farmington, May 22, 1740	LR4	271
Orange, d. Elijah, b. Apr. 21, 1771	LR15	E
Orpha, m. Moses WOODRUFF, Oct. 4, 1824, by Rev. Harry Bushnell	LR42	568
Seale, s. Elijah, b. Apr. 5, 1768	LR15	E
Sylvee, d. Elijah, b. Dec. 12, 1763	LR15	E
Silva, d. Elijah, b. Dec. 12, 1763	LR15	E
FRANK, Bulah, d. Thankfull STEPHENS, b. June 27, 1778 or 1788	LR21	543
FRANKLIN, Emeline, of Berlin, m. John B. JONES, Sept. 22, 1825, by Rev. Noah Porter	LR42	569
FREEMAN, FREMAN, Abbey, of Colchester, m. William MASON, of Hartford, Oct. 9, 1831, by Rev. Noah Porter	LR42	560
Alanson, m. Fanny SUMMADY, b. of Farmington, Nov. 29, 1838, by Rev. Noah Porter	LR47	98
Anne Honeor, d. Israel, b. May 29, 1763	LR15	E
Augustus, m. Marietta H. GIBSON (colored), Dec. 28, 1846, by Rev. B. Creagh	LR47	118
Edgar, of Hartford, m. Elizabeth M. DEMING, of Farmington, Aug. 29, 1852, by Rev. Cephas Brainerd	LR47	131
James S., of Granby, m. Catharine CAMPBELL, of Southwick, Mass., Mar. 11, 1846, by Rev. Noah Porter	LR47	117
Martha, m. Samuell PORTER, Feb. 18, 1685	LR1	5
FRENCH, Marah, m. John RICHARDS, Apr. 14, 1752	LR8	10
FRISBIE, FRISBEE, Abel, s. Zebulon, b. Nov. last day, 1755	LR9	7-8
Anne, d. Zebulon, Jr., b. Dec. 22, 1772	LR21	543
Elizabeth, d. Zebulon, b. Sept. 24, 1747	LR9	7-8
Elizabeth, m. George NORTON, b. of Farmington, Dec. 20, 1820, by Bela Kellogg, V.D.M.	LR40	570
Frederick T., of Watertown, m. Caroline BAKER, of Farmington, Jan. 1, 1842, by Noah Porter	LR47	109
Gad, s. Zebulon, b. Apr. 14, 1778	LR21	543
Laura A., of Bristol, m. Edward H. DORMAN, of Farmington, Nov. 26, 1843, by Rev. R. A. Chalker	LR47	112
Levi, s. Zebulon, b. July [ ], 1753; d. Nov. 10, 1755	LR9	7-8
Levi, s. Zebulon, b. Jan. last day, 1759	LR11	581
Lole, d. Zebulon, b. Nov. 8, 1749	LR9	7-8
Lucy, d. Zebulon, b. Jan. 14, 1741/2	LR9	7-8

	Vol.	Page

FRISBIE, FRISBEE (cont.)

Lucy D., m. Samuel C. **MILLER**, b. of Southington, Dec.
16, 1850, by William Wright — LR47 — 128

Mary, d. Zebulon, b. Aug. 6, 1745 — LR9 — 7-8

Mary, d. Zebulon, d. Aug. 22, 1757 — LR11 — 577

Susana, d. Zebulon, Jr., b. Mar. 10, 1783 — LR21 — 543

W[illia]m, of Westport, N.Y., m. Mary **PECK**, of
Farmington, Sept. 10, 1829, by Rev. Noah Porter — LR42 — 562

Zebulon, s. Zebulon, b. May 2, 1752 — LR9 — 7-8

FROST, Abigaill, d. Timothy, b. Apr. 12, 1769 — LR15 — E

David, s. David, b. Mar. 1, 1767 — LR15 — E

Mary, d. David, b. Mar. 24, 1775 — LR21 — 543

Naomi Elizabeth, d. David, b. July 1, 1770 — LR15 — E

FULLER, Almon, of Farmington, m. Mary **BURDICK**, of
Burlington, Oct. 28, 1840, by Rev. Aaron S. Hill — LR47 — 103

Amelia, m. George C. **WARIEN**, b. of Farmington, Aug.
27, 1834, by Rev. Noah Porter — LR42 — E

Celia Ann, m. Noble P. **WIARD**, Oct. 6, 1845, by Rev. J.
Burton Beach — LR47 — 115

Gad, s. Noah, d. Dec. 2, 1776, in captivity in New York
City — LR21 — 558-9

James B., m. Emeline E. **HORSFORD**, May 7, 1851, by
Rev. G. M. Porter — LR47 — 128

Julia M., m. Royal **ANDRUS**, b. of Farmington, Dec. 3,
1840, by Rev. Aaron S. Hill — LR47 — 103

Martha, m. Ambrose **HART**, Aug. 20, 1755 — LR11 — 576

Nancy A., m. Oliver **LEWIS**, b. of Farmington, Nov. 14,
1838, by Rev. S. H. Clark — LR47 — 98

Noah, m. Allice **BROWN**, June 2, 1757 — LR11 — 576

Ruell, of Sherman, N.Y., m. Lois L. **ORVIS**, of
Farmington, Oct. 7, 1832, by Rev. Noah Porter — LR42 — 558

Seth, m. Jane **HOSFORD**, [May] 1, 1850, by Herman
Northrop, J.P. — LR47 — 126

GALPIN, Albert, of Weathersfield, m. Esther M.
WASHBURN, of Hartford, July 4, 1843, by Rev.
Horace Bushnell, of Hartford — LR47 — 110

Anna, m. Nathan **COLE**, Apr. 1, 1736 — LR6 — 304

Elizabeth, of Stratford, m. Isaac **NORTON**, of
Ffarmington, May 6, 1707 — LR2 — 145

Elizabeth, m. Joseph **HOPKINS**, s. Joseph, Apr. 25, 1733 — LR5 — 300

GARDNER, Betsey, d. John, b. Jan. 27, 1779 — LR21 — 543

John, m. Eunice **BIRD**, Jan. 3, 1776 — LR21 — 557

Margaret, of Penn., m. Ezra **PAGE**, of Windham, Mar.
19, 1827, by Rev. H. Bushnell — LR42 — 567

Mary, d. John, b. Feb. 23, 1777 — LR21 — 543

GARNSEY [GUERNSEY], Rachel, of Westbury, m.
Jeremiah **CURTISS**, of Southington, May 4, 1774 — LR17 — 442

Sarah, of Durham, m. Thomas **LEWIS**, Dec. 24, 1765 — LR11 — 594

GARRETT, GARRET, Anna, m. Samuel **NORTHAWAY**,
Oct. 5, 1746 — LR7 — 35

John, s. John Garrit & Elydya **WOODFORD**, b. July 21,
1751 — LR8 — 5

Susannah, m. William **WOODFORD**, Oct. 31, 1745 — LR7 — 35

	Vol.	Page
GAY, Almira, d. Fisher, b. Sept. 17, 1764	LR11	581
Erastus, s. Fisher, b. Nov. 20, 1768	LR15	E
Erastus, s. Fisher, d. Mar. 19, 1770	LR15	M
Erastus, s. Fisher, b. Sept. 21, 1772	LR17	433
Fisher, of Farmington, m. Ruth **HOOKER**, of Hartford, Sept. 1, 1773	LR17	442
Fisher, m. Harriet L. **WADSWORTH**, Oct. 5, 1824, by Rev. Noah Porter	LR42	568
Fisher, m. Lucy **THOMSON**, b. of Farmington, Sept. 28, 1830, by Rev. Noah Porter	LR42	560
Mary, m. Henry **ROOT**, b. of Farmington, Oct. 12, 1825, by Rev. Noah Porter	LR42	569
Phebe, d. Fisher, b. Aug. 17, 1766	LR14	6
Phebe, w. Fisher, d. Oct. 17, 1772, in the 37th y. of her age	LR17	444
Phebe, of Farmington, m. Thomas **MYGOTT**, Jr., of Canton, Sept. 29, 1823, by Noah Porter, V.D.M.	LR40	572
Seth, s. Fisher, b. June 8, 1763	LR11	581
Seth, s. Fisher, b .June 8, 1763; d. Oct. 18, 1763	LR14	6
GAYLORD, GAILORD, GAILER, Abigail, d. John, b. Mar. 11, 1750/1	LR8	5
Amasa, [s. Benjamin], b. July 22, 1748	LR7	H
Ambros, [s.] Justus, b. Nov. 26, 1755	LR9	7-8
Amos, s. Jno, b. Dec. 10, 1745	LR7	H
Amos, m. Lucy **SAGE**, Feb. 15, 1773	LR17	442
Amos, d. May 28, 1785, in the 39th y. of his age	LR22	482
Anne, m. Andrew **NORTON**, Sept. 15, 1750	LR8	10
Benjamin, s. [Benjamin], b. Mar. 19, 1743	LR7	H
Chaney, s. Joseph, b. Feb. 14, 1757	LR11	582
Cloe, d. Joseph, Jr., b. Mar. 15, 1758	LR11	581
Cloa, d. Joseph, Jr., b. Mar. 15, 1759	LR11	582
Syras, s. Joseph, Jr., b. Oct. 6, 1763	LR11	581
Cyrus, s. Joseph, b. Oct. 10, 1763	LR15	E
Edward, [s. Edward], b. Nov.6, 1743	LR7	H
Elijah, s. John, b. June 1, 1742	LR7	544
Elijah, of Farmington, m. Hannah **HULL**, of Wallingford, Oct. 13, 1763	LR11	592
Elizabeth, d. Jo[h]n, b. Mar. 2, 1744	LR7	544
Elizabeth, d. Joseph, b. Oct. 27, 1749	LR7	H
Enos, s. Benjamin, b. Apr. about 10, 1741	LR7	H
Eunice, d. Elijah, b. Oct. 19, 1764	LR14	6
Experience, d. Edward, b. Mar. 14, 1742	LR7	H
Giles, s. Samuel, b. July 16, 1749	LR7	H
Hannah, of Windsor, m. David **ORUIS**, of Ffarmington, Feb. 5, 1718/19	LR2	101
Hester, d. Samuel, b. July 10, 1752	LR8	5
Ira, s. Joseph, b. Jan. 15, 1768	LR15	E
Jerusha, m. Jesse **CHURCHWELL**, Nov. 8, 1750	LR8	10
Jesse, of Bristol, m. Lois **ALCOTT**, of Wolcott, [Jan. 14, 1830], by Erastus Scranton, V.D.M.	LR42	561
John, s. John, b. Jan. 9, 1752	LR8	5
John, s. Amos, b. Aug. 11, 1779	LR22	464
Jonathan, [s. Benjamin], b. Sept. 22, 1746	LR7	H

	Vol.	Page
GAYLORD, GAILORD, GAILER (cont.)		
Joseph, had d. [ ], b. Mar. 5, 1743	LR7	H
Lemens, s .Joseph, b. Dec. 16, 1765	LR15	E
Lucy, d. Amos, b. Sept. 5, 1776	LR22	464
Mamee, d .Justus, b. May 13, 1751	LR9	7-8
Minnie, d. Joseph, Jr., b. Dec. 29, 1760	LR11	581
Ozias, s. Benjamin, b. Sept. 11, 1753	LR9	7-8
Patty, of Bristol, m. Samuel **ORTON**, of Wolcott, Apr. 3, 1833, by Rev. Noah Porter	LR42	558
Phebe, d. Joseph, b. Oct. 8, 1771	LR17	433
Phebe, d. Amos, b. Oct. 1, 1781	LR22	464
Philip, s. Joseph, b. Aug. 21, 1778	LR21	543
Rebeckah, d. Joseph, b. May 7, 1741	LR7	H
Samuel, s. Samuell, b. Apr. 29, 1743	LR6	3
Sarah, m. John **WELLS**, Dec. [ ], 1735	LR6	304
Sarah J., of Canistota, N.Y., m. Asahel C. **BLAKESLEY**, of Bristol, Feb. 29, 1852, by Rev. P. G. Wightman, at his house	LR47	130
Sophronia, m. Alva L. **WOODEN**, b. of Bristol, May 4, 1831, by Rev. Noah Porter	LR42	560
Stephen, s. Amos, b. July 6, 1774	LR17	432
Stephen, s. Amos, decd. b. July 6, 1774	LR22	464
Susannah, d. Edward, b. Apr. 15, 1745	LR7	H
Sibbel, d. Justus, b. Oct. 27, 1754	LR9	7-8
Thankfull, d. Joseph, b. Sept. 6, 1741	LR6	2
Thankfull, d. Samuell, b. Sept. 6, 1741	LR6	3
Thankfull, d. Augur, b. Oct. 22, 1775	LR22	464
Timothy, s. Samuel, b. May 7, 1747	LR7	H
William, s. Joseph, b. Jan. 16, 1755	LR9	7-8
GIBBS, GIBS, Abigail, m. Josiah **BARNES**, July 5, 1684	LR1	5
Sarah, of Windsor, m. Samuel **BROWNSON**, of Ffarmington, s. Richard, May 4, 1687	LR2	145
GIBSON, Marietta H., m. Augustus **FREEMAN** (colored), Dec. 28, 1846, by Rev. B. Creagh	LR47	118
GILBERT, GILLBUT, GILLBARD, GILLBART, Abigail, d. Jonathan, b. May 28, 1743	LR7	J
Abigail, d. Seth, b. May 18, 1781	LR22	464
Anne E., of Farmington, m. Seth **WOODRUFF**, of Avon, Nov. 5, 1848, by Rev. Noah Porter	LR47	123
Chloe, d. Thomas, b. July 28, 1773	LR17	432
Daniel, [s. Jonathan], b. Nov. 18, 1749	LR7	1
Ebenezer, d. Aug. 11, 1730	LR6	10
Ebenezer, m. Marcy **COWLES**, b. of Farmington, May 1, 1735	LR6	27
Ebenezer, s. Moses, b. Jan. 15, 1741/2	LR6	3
Ebenezer, d. Oct. 1, 1750	LR8	11
Elidia, d. Ebenezer, b. Jan. 24, 1749/50	LR8	5
Esther, d. Moses, b. May 25, 1739	LR6	3
Esther, Mrs., d. Oct. 4, 1750	LR8	12
Hooker, s. Moses, b. June 5, 1751	LR8	5
Hooker, s. Moses, b. June 5, 1754	LR9	7-8
Jaurus D., of New Haven, m. Rosina A. **ROBERTS**, of Hartford, Oct. 2, 1821, by Noah Porter, V.D.M.	LR40	571

	Vol.	Page
GILBERT, GILLBUT, GILLBARD, GILLBART (cont.)		
John, s. Jonathan, b. Nov. 20, 1746	LR7	1
Jonathan, m. Geria* SMITH, June 24, 1742 *(In pencil "Keziah")	LR7	35
Lucy, d. Seth, b. June 25, 1779	LR21	543
Lydia, d. Thomas, b. Aug. 22, 1765	LR17	432
Mary, d. Thomas, b. May 1, 1761	LR17	432
Moses, m. Elizabeth HOOKER, b. of Farmington, Feb. 21, 1733/4	LR5	300
Moses, s. Moses, b. May 24, 1744	LR6	3
Ruth, d. Ebenezer, b. July 23, 1742	LR6	3
Sarah, d. Ebenezer & Mercy, b. May 11, 1737	LR6	3
Sarah Gridley, d. Moses, b. Oct. 7, 1740	LR6	3
Seth, s. [Jonathan], b. Oct. 22, 1752	LR7	1
Seth, s. Seth, b. Sept. 18, 1777	LR22	464
Thomas, s. Moses, b. Oct. 21, 1736	LR6	3
Thomas, m. Mary NORTH, Apr. 24, 1760	LR17	443
GILLET, GILLIT, GELET, JEALET, JELETT, JOLEET, JELET, Abigail, d. Zachariah, b. Jan. 2, 1741	LR7	J
Abigail, m. Solomon CURTIS, Feb. 18, 1766	LR17	443
Abner, m. Mary HIGINSON, b. of Farmington, Sept. 6, 1710	LR2	123
Amos, s. Noah, b. May 16, 1765	LR15	E
Benj[ami]n, s. Noah, b. Jan. 26, 1784	LR22	464
Betsey, d. Noah, b. Oct. 5, 1793	LR22	464
Caroline, of Farmington, m. Lyman HURLBUT, of Berlin, May 27, 1836, by Rev. Noah Porter	LR47	93
Edward, s. Noah, b. Aug. 19, 1788	LR22	464
Elidea, d. Noah, b. Aug. 2, 1752	LR9	7-8
Eliza, d. Abner, b. Feb. 4, 1716/17	LR5	4
Elizabeth, of Seffield, m. James ANDRUS, of Farmington, Dec. 9, 173[ ]	LR5	13
Eri, m. Huldah CLARK, b. of Farmington, Dec. 30, 1823, by Bela Kellogg	LR42	568
Francis, of Windsor, m. Eliza D. HOOKER, of Farmington, Sept. 10, 1834, by Rev. Noah Porter	LR42	E
Hannah, of Hartford, m. Noadiah BURR, of Farmington, Nov. 5, 173[ ]* *(In pencil "1730")	LR5	13
Hannah, m. Nodiah BURR, Nov. 5, 1732	LR5	1
Isaac, s. Noah, d. Feb. 4, 1748/9	LR7	36
Isaac, s. Noah, b .Jan. 3, 1749/50	LR7	F
Isaac, s. Noah, d. June 25, 1755	LR9	495
Isaac, s. J[ ], [ ]	LR7	F
Joel, s. [Zachariah], b. [ ], 1745	LR7	J
John, s. Zachariah, b. Dec. [ ], 1743	LR7	J
Laura, d. Noah, b. Aug. 21, 1790	LR22	464
Lucy, of Farmington, m. Lyman CURTIS, of Plymouth, Nov. 27, 1831, by Rev. Noah Porter	LR42	559
Lydia, b. Aug. 12, 1752 O.S., m. Gad HAWLEY, Feb. 8, 1776	LR47	W-Y
Lydia, m. Gad HAWLEY, Feb. 8, 1776	LR21	557
Margary, m. Abraham COOK, Oct. 4, 1742	LR6	305
Mary, d. Abner, b. Apr. 30, 1719	LR5	4

	Vol.	Page
GILLET, GILLIT, GELET, JEALET, JELETT, JOLEET, JELET (cont.)		
Mary Ann, m. Henry **ANDRUS**, b. of Farmington, Dec. 4, 1836, by Rev. Noah Porter	LR47	94
Noah, m. Elyidia **HART**, Dec. 15, 1748	LR7	46
Noah, had s. [ ], b. Jan. 29, 1748/9	LR7	F
Noah, s. Noah, b. Mar. 10, 1755	LR9	7-8
Obediah, s. Noah, b. May 6, 1763	LR11	581
Rubin, s. Samuel, b. Nov. 5, 1753	LR9	7-8
Richard, s. Noah, b. May 8, 1785	LR22	464
Ruby H., of Farmington, m. James M. **ORTON**, of Rome, N.Y., Oct. 25, 1837, by Rev. Noah Porter	LR47	96
Samuel, s. Abner, b. Sept. 27, 1730	LR5	4
Samuel, s. Noah, b. Oct. 17. 1786	LR22	464
Sarah, d. Abner, b. Apr. 12, 1715	LR5	4
Sarah, d. [Zachariah], b. [ ]	LR7	J
Sena, of Farmington, m. Joel **BARNES**, of Burlington, Jan. 10, 1822, by Noah Porter, V.D.M.	LR40	571
Serepta, m. Romeo **ANDRUS**, b. of Farmington, Jan. 1, 1824, by Bela Kellogg	LR42	568
Solomon, s. Abner, b. July 12, 1725	LR5	4
Tittus, s. Noah, b. Nov. 7, 1759	LR11	582
Titus, s. Noah, b. May 26, 1782	LR22	464
Zachariah, s. Abner, b. Mar. 31, 1721	LR5	4
GLADDING, GLADDEN, Charlotte, of Farmington, m. Goodrich E. **MOORE**, of Mass., Apr. 15, 1849, by Rev. Henry J. Fox	LR47	124
Lucy Maria, of Burlington, m. Henry **HART**, of Farmington, June 24, 1838, by Rev. S. H. Clark	LR47	97
Martha, m. Russel **CRANE**, b. of Farmington, Oct. 28, 1832, by Rev. Noah Porter	LR42	558
Phila, m. Samuel **WARREN**, Nov. [ ], 1847, by Egbert Cowles, J.P.	LR47	128
Stephen, of Farmington, m. Cynthia L. **POST**, of Batavia, N.Y., Aug. 3, 1845, by Rev. S. H. Clark	LR47	114
GLEASON, Asahel, m. Etna **JUDD**, b. of Farmington, May 12, 1825, by Rev. Harvey Bushnell	LR42	569
Cheaney, s. Isaac, b. Aug. 28, 1763	LR11	581
Dolly, d. Isaac, b. Dec. 12, 1769	LR17	E
Ebenezer Steel, s. Isaac, b. Dec. 6, 1757	LR15	E
Hiram N., m. Sarah **ROOT**, [Feb.] 3, 1825, by Rev. Noah Porter	LR42	568
Isaac, m. Mary **SMITH**, Oct. 18, 1759	LR11	592
Maria V., m. Montgomery **HUMPHREY**, b. of Farmington, Oct. 20, 1830, by Rev. Noah Porter	LR42	560
Polley, d. Isaac, b. Dec. 2, 1759	LR11	581
GOODHUE, GOODHEW, Julia Ann, of Avon, m. Samuel **MUNN**, of Saybrook, Sept. 10, 1837, by Rev. S. H. Clark	LR47	96
Julius of Avon, m. Jennet **GRANNIS**, of Southington, June 12, 1836, by Ephraim Lyman, V.D.M.	LR47	93
GOODMAN, Sarah, m. Elijah **GRIDLEY**, Nov. 1, 1789	LR22	480

	Vol.	Page
GOODRICH, Abigail, m. Elijah **HART**, b. of Farmington,		
Dec. 26, 1734	LR5	539
Abigail, d. Jedidiah, b. Oct. 30, 1753	LR9	7-8
Abigail, d. Jedediah, b. Oct. 30, 1753	LR11	582
Abigail, m. Isaac **LEE**, 3rd, May 12, 1773	LR17	443
Allen, s. Allen, b. Aug. 18, 1725	LR4	374
Allen, m. Hannah **SEAMOUR**, Dec. 10, 1729	LR5	13
Allin, m. Lydia **NORTH**, June 15, 1748	LR7	46
Ann, d. Zebulon, b. Nov. 23, 1746	LR11	582
Asa, s. Samuel, b. June 26, 1750	LR8	5
David, s. William, b. Nov. 1, 1719	LR2	102
David, s. Zebulon, b. Dec. 14, 1757	LR11	582
Elezier, s. Timothy, b. Dec. 15, 1752	LR11	582
Elijah, s. Zebulon, b. June 3, 1755	LR11	582
Elisha, m. Rebeckah **SEAMOUR**, b. of Farmington, Nov.		
21, 1734	LR5	545
Elizabeth, w. Allen, d. Aug. 25, 1726	LR2	148
Elizabeth, d. Zebulon, b. June 4, 1739	LR11	582
Hannah, d. Allen, b. Aug. 9, 1732	LR5	3
Hannah, m. Thomas **GRIDLEY**, Jr., Jan. 11, 1749/50	LR7	46
Huldah, d. [Allen], b. July 9, 1749	LR7	H
James, s. David, b. Feb. 23, 1784	LR22	464
John, s. Allin, b. Feb. 17, 1722/3	LR2	88
John, s. Allen, b. Mar. 17, 1736/7	LR6	3
Josiah, m. Mariah **HUMPHREY**, b. of Farmington, Nov.		
29, 1826, by Rev. Harry Bushnell	LR42	567
Lemuel, s. Allen, b. Oct. 9, 1746	LR7	H
Lydia, d. Allen, b. Nov. 20, 1748	LR7	H
Mary, m. Samuel **SMITH**, Dec. 6, 1759	LR11	575
Mather, s. Samuel, b. Nov. 16, 1756	LR11	582
Melesent, d. Zebulon, b. Jan. 24, 1752	LR11	582
Mercy, d. Jedediah, b. Jan. 1, 1750/1	LR8	5
Phebe, d. Zebulon, b. July 9, 1741	LR11	582
Rhoda, d. Samuell, b. Jan. 28, 1760	LR11	582
Salmon, s. John & Hannah, b. Oct. 17, 1757	LR11	582
Samuel, s. Samuel, b. Dec. 17, 1747	LR7	H
Samuel, s. Samuel, d. Dec. 6, 1750	LR8	11
Sarah, d. Samuel, b. July 6, 1753	LR9	7-8
Sarah, d. Zebulon, Jr., b. June 13, 1770	LR15	E
Seth, s. John & Hannah, b. Feb. 13, 1760	LR11	582
Seth, s. Zebulon, Jr., b. Oct. 7, 1771	LR17	433
Thomas, s. Jedediah, b. June 20, 1762	LR11	582
Timothy, m. Sarah **MESENGTEER**, Sept. 29, 1748	LR7	35
Timothy, s. Timothy, decd. & Sarah, b. Sept. 24, 1756	LR11	582
Timothy, s. Zebulon, Jr., b. Feb. 10, 1773	LR17	433
Zebulon, s. Zebulon, b. June 11, 1744	LR11	582
Zebulon, Jr., m. Honor **WHAPLES**, Oct. 4, 1769	LR17	442
Zenas, s. John, b. Nov. 6, 1763	LR11	581
GOODWIN [E]unice, m. Samuel **LEE**, b. of Ffarmington,		
Dec. 4, 1717	LR2	100
Hezekiah, of Salisbury, m. Fanny **LOWREY**, of		
Farmington, Apr. 4, 1830, by Rev. Noah Porter	LR42	561

	Vol.	Page
GOODRICH (cont.)		
Roxy, m. Amon **ANDRUS**, May 2, 1827, by Rev. Harry		
Bushnell	LR42	555
Susannah, Mrs., d. May 17, 1676	LR2	141
William, d. Mar. 11, 1673	LR2	141
GORDON, Johnson, m. Belinda **HILLS**, Jan. 13, 1824, by		
Rev. Noah Porter	LR42	568
Sylvia, m. William **KELLEY**, b. of Farmington, Jan. 26,		
1834, by Rev. L. C. Cheney	LR42	A
Thomas, of Philadelphia, m. Sylvia **LIVINGSTON**, of		
Farmington, Sept. 20, 1829, by Rev. Noah Porter	LR42	562
GORHAM, Rufus, m. Sally **BOSWORTH**, b. of		
Montgomery, Mass., June 8, 1828, by Noadiah		
Woodruff, J.P.	LR42	564
GOSS, Charles A., of Canton, m. Betsey **FOX**, of Manchester,		
May 15, 1842, in Unionville, by Rev. Merrell		
Richardson	LR47	107
GOUL,* Elizabeth, m. Stephen **DOCHESTER**, Oct. 29, 1754		
*(**COLE**"?)	LR8	10
GOULD, Huldah, m. John **HART**, Jr., Jan. 30, 1749	LR7	35
GRAHAM, Mary, m. Ebenezer **BUCK**, b. of Farmington, Apr.		
11, 1740	LR6	27
Robert, m. Jane **CAREY**, Jan. 6, 1847, by Rev. B. Creagh	LR47	119
GRANNIS, Charles S., m. Mary Ann **OLIN**, b. of Farmington,		
Feb. 13, 1842, by Rev. Aaron S. Hill	LR47	106
Eliza J., of Southington, m. John R. **CATLIN**, of		
Farmington, Dec. 11, 1843, by William Wright	LR47	112
Jane C., of Southington, m. Edward C. **CHIDSEY**, of		
Farmington, May 22, 1836, by Rev. Noah Porter	LR47	93
Jennet, of Southington, m. Julius **GOODHUE**, of Avon,		
June 12, 1836, by Ephraim Lyman, V.D.M.	LR47	93
Rhoda, m. Edward **HART**, b. of Southington, May 14,		
1835, by Rev. Noah Porter	LR47	89
GRANT, Alfred S., of Bristol, m. Julia **WOODRUFF**, of		
Farmington, Dec. 16, 1840, by Rev. Noah Porter	LR47	104
Elizabeth, Jr., of East Windsor, m. Isaac **LEE**, of		
Farmington, Dec. 30, 1772	LR17	442
GRAVES, Abner, m. wid. **JUDD**, Apr. 21, 1743	LR6	305
Asahel, s. Abner, b. Aug. 23, 1746	LR7	H
Bela, s. Abner, b. Sept. 23, 1751	LR11	582
Ezekiel, s. Abner, b. Sept. 13, 1753	LR11	582
Silvanus, s. Abner, b. Aug. 25, 1756	LR11	582
GREEN, Huldah, m. Velina Heart **HART**, Dec. 3, 1782	LR22	480
Julia Ann, m. Jacob W. **WILLIAMS**, b. of Farmington,		
Nov. 12, 1843, by Noah Porter, Int. Pub.	LR47	111
GREENFIELD, Clarissa, m. William H. **HORTON**, b. of		
Middletown, Aug. 25, 1828, by Rev. Noah Porter	LR42	564
GRIDLEY, GRIDLEE, Abel, s. Joseph & Hannah, b. Sept.		
28, 1720	LR5	3
Abel, s. Clement, b. July 16, 1756	LR11	582
Abel, m. Hanah **CLARK**, Jan. 12, 1757	LR11	575
Abel, s. Abel, b. Feb. 11, 1764	LR11	581
Abel, s. Abel, d. Jan. 18, 1766, in the 3rd y. of his age	LR14	3

	Vol.	Page
GRIDLEY, GRIDLEE (cont.)		
Abigail, d. Thomas, s. Thomas, b. Feb. 11, 1717/18	LR2	84
Abigail, w. Samuel, d. Jan. 3, 1724/5	LR2	66
Abigail, d. James, b. Sept 27, 1727	LR4	395
Abigail, d. Samuel (s. of Thomas), b. Apr. 20, 1730	LR5	3
Abigail, m. Stephen HART, Jr., Sept. 13, 1750	LR7	46
Abigail, d. Andrew, b Sept. 15, 1752	LR8	5
Abigail, d. Hezekiah, Jr., b. Nov. 1, 1759	LR11	582
Abraham, s. Jonathan, b. Feb. 23, 1720/1	LR2	102
Abraham, s. Jonathan, Jr., b. May 10, 1753	LR9	7-8
Abraham, m. Phebe [ ], July 7, 1768	LR15	A
Abram, s. Jonathan, d .Nov. 12, 1736	LR6	10
Abram, s. Samuel, b. May 16, 1742	LR6	3
Amos, s. John [s. Samuel], b. Apr. 19, 1726	LR4	375
Andru, s. John, s. Samuel, b. July 14, 1723	LR2	88
Andrew, m. Marah PERSONS, Oct. 10, 1749	LR7	46
Ann, m. Amos HART, July 20, 1749	LR7	46
Ann, d. Abell, b. Feb. 16, 1760	LR14	6
Ann, d. Abel, d. Apr. 4, 1760, ae 7 w.	LR14	3
Anna, d. Joseph, b. May 22, 1727	LR4	395
Anah, s .Seth, b. June 25, 1782	LR22	464
Anne, d. Ebenezer, b. Dec. 1, 1758	LR11	582
Ard, s. Joseph, b. Nov. 6, 1768	LR15	E
Asahel, s. Hezekiah, Jr., b. Oct. 13, 1757	LR11	582
Asahel, s. Joseph, b. May 22, 1764	LR15	E
Asaell, s. Clement, b. Mar. 30, 1765	LR14	6
Azubah, d. Ebenezer, b. Feb. 8, 1748/9	LR7	H
Chancey, s. Hezekiah, Jr., b. Feb. 20, 1774	LR17	433
Chester, s. Roger, b. Mar. 26, 1776	LR21	543
Chester, s. Roger, d. Sept. 12, 1777, in the 7th m. of his		
age	LR21	560
Chester, s. Roger & Sarah, b. Dec. 22, 1778	LR22	464
Cloe, d. Luke, b. Apr. 25, 1769	LR17	433
Clarinda, d. Elisha, b. Apr. 29, 1779	LR22	464
Clement, s. Samuel (s. of Thomas), b. May 7, 1732	LR5	3
Clemmon, m. Sarah HUBBARD, Dec. 25, 1755	LR11	576
Curtiss, s. Elisha, b. July 6, 1774	LR22	464
Daniel, s. Samuel, Sr., b Dec. 1, 1711	LR2	97
Daniel, m. Mary WOODRUFF, b. of Farmington ,Feb.		
14, 1732/3	LR5	300
David, s. James, Jr., b. Jan. 18, 1756	LR9	7-8
Dena, d. Ebenezer, b. Mar. 15, 1769	LR15	E
Dolly, d. Seth, b. June 30, 1784	LR22	464
Ebenezer, s. Thomas, Jr., b. Dec. 16, 1712	LR2	98
Ebenezer, m. Azubah ORUIS, June 20, 1744	LR7	35
Ebenezer, had d. [ ], b. Nov. 1, 1746	LR7	H
Ebenezer, s. Ebenezer, b. July 8, 1764	LR11	581
Ebenezer, s. Seth, b. July 2, 1780	LR22	464
Ebenezer, s. Ebenezer, d. Mar. 29, 17[ ], in the 5th y. of		
his age	LR15	M
Eli, s. Abell, b. Nov. 23, 1761	LR14	6
Elihu, s. Hezekiah, Jr., b. Nov. 6, 1755	LR11	582
Elijah, s. Clement, b. Mar. 18, 1760	LR11	581

	Vol.	Page
GRIDLEY, GRIDLEE (cont.)		
Elijah, s. Thomas, Jr., b. Mar. 27, 1760	LR11	582
Elijah, s. Elnathan, b. Sept. 21, 1761	LR11	582
Elijah, m. Sarah **GOODMAN**, Nov. 1, 1789	LR22	480
Elijah, m. Hannah **WHETTESEY**, Nov. 26, 1793	LR29	576
Elijah O., m. Antonette **JOHNSON**, b. of Farmington, Mar. 5, 1833, by Rev. Noah Porter	LR42	558
Elisha, s. Joseph, b. June 2, 1715	LR2	81
Elisha, s. Joseph & Hannah, d. Feb. 26, 1734/5	LR6	10
Elisha, s. Hezekiah & Sarah, b. Dec. 15, 1736	LR6	3
Elisha, s. Noah, b. Sept. 16, 1752	LR8	5
Elisha, s. Luke, b. May 17, 1765	LR14	6
Elizabeth, d. Thomas, Sr., b. Oct. [ ], 1693	LR4	382
Elizabeth, w. Thomas, Sr., d. Apr. [ ], 1696	LR2	147
Elizabeth, m. Benjamin **ANDRUS**, Jr., b. of Farmington, Dec. 6, 1711	LR2	125
Elizabeth, d. Thomas, Jr., b. Sept. 29, 1715	LR2	95
Elizabeth, d. John, s. Thomas, b. Apr. 1, 1716	LR2	96
Elizabeth, d. Thomas, Jr., m. Charles **ORUIS**, b. of Farmington, Oct. 2, 1734	LR5	300
Elizabeth, m. Samuel **HAWLEY**, b. of Farmington, Dec. 7, 1736	LR6	27
Elizabeth, d. Ebenezer, b. May 17, 1751	LR8	5
Elizabeth, w. John, d. June 10, 1756	LR9	495
Elnathan, s. Thomas, b. Mar. 30, 1727	LR4	395
Elnathan, m. Sarah **PRATT**, Feb. 27, 1753	LR8	10
Esther, m. John **HART**, Jr., b. of Farmington, Mar. 20, 1706	LR2	125
Esther, m. Hawkins **HART**, b. of Farmington, Apr. 5, 1738	LR6	27
Esther, d. Seth, b. May 31, 1774	LR17	433
Eunis, d. Samuel (s. Thomas), b. Oct. 14, 1744	LR7	J
Giles, s. Thomas, b. Dec. 10, 1769	LR15	E
Hannah, d. Joseph, b. Feb. 19, 1713/14	LR2	81
Hannah, d. Thomas, [blacksmith], b. Nov. 11, 1723	LR2	87
Hannah, w. Thomas, blacksmith, d. Nov. 19, 1733	LR5	50
Hannah, m. Nathaniel **WADSWORTH**, Jr., June 12, 1746	LR7	46
Hannah, d. Elnathan, b. Feb. 14, 1756	LR9	7-8
Hannah, w. Thomas, d. Nov. 12, 17[ ]	LR15	M
Hannah Ann, d. Abell, b. Mar. 2, 1771	LR17	433
Hesther, d. Thomas [blacksmith], b. Mar. 17, 1705/6	LR1	3
Hezekiah, s. Samuell, Sr., b. Aug. [ ], 1701	LR2	109
Hezekiah, m. Sarah **NEWEL**, b. of Farmington, [ ] 5, 1731	LR5	13
Hezekiah, s. Hezekiah, b. Jan. 30, 1732/3	LR5	3
Hezekiah, Jr., m. Abigail **PECK**, Dec. 13, 1754	LR11	592
Hezekiah, s. Hezekiah, Jr., b. Dec. 24, 1765	LR17	433
Hezekiah, d. July 21, 1776, in the 73rd y. of his age	LR21	558-9
Hooker Thomas, s. Thomas, b. Jan. 31, 1775	LR21	543
Huldah, m. Benjamin **NICHOLS**, Jan. 2, 1754	LR11	575
Huldah, d. Elnathan, b. Nov. 14, 1763	LR11	581
Isaac, s. Jonathan, b. Jan. 9, 1715/16	LR2	95

	Vol.	Page
GRIDLEY, GRIDLEE (cont.)		
Isaac, s. Jonathan, d. Dec. 6, 1736	LR6	10
Isaac, s. Jonathan, Jr., b. [ ] 2, 1751	LR9	7-8
Isaac, s. Samuel, Jr., b. July 7, 1754	LR11	582
Jabez, s. Clement, b. Aug. 16, 1769	LR15	E
James, m. Susannah **SMITH**, Nov. 26, 1719	LR2	101
James, s. James, b. Dec. 7, 1725	LR2	70
James, Jr., m. Sibble **NORTH**, Dec. 3, 1750	LR7	46
James, s. James, b. Jan. 12, 1765	LR11	581
Jerusha, d. Samuel, Jr., b. Feb. 6, 1711/12	LR2	97
Jerusha, m. Nehemiah **LEWIS**, Nov. 21, 1728	LR4	423
Job, s. Samuel (s. of Thomas), b. Feb. 4, 1746/7	LR7	H
Job, m. Sible [ ], May 10, 1768	LR15	A
Johannah, d. Thomas, blacksmith, b. Sept. 10, 1708	LR1	2
Joannah, d. Thomas, blacksmith, m. John **THOMSON**,		
Jr., b. of Farmington, June 7, 1731	LR5	13
John, s. Thomas, Sr., b. Oct. [ ], 1684	LR4	382
John, of Ffarmington, s. Thomas, m. Elizabeth		
ELSWORTH, of Windsor, May 30, 1711	LR2	125
John, s. Samuell, of Farmington, m. Dorothy **BENTON**,		
of Hartford, May 3, 1716	LR2	94
John, s. John, s. of Samuell, b. Mar. 10, 1720/1	LR2	102
John, of Kensington, d. Dec. 17, 1739	LR6	10
John, of Farmington, m. Sarah **ELLSWORTH**, of		
Hartford, Aug. 16, 1756	LR9	286
Jonathan, s. Thomas, Sr., b. Oct. [ ], 1690	LR4	382
Jonathan, of Ffarmington, m. Mary **PINNEY**, of		
Windsor, Nov. 17, 1714	LR2	93
Jonathan, s. Jonathan, b. Dec. 12, 1726	LR4	375
Jonathan, Jr., m. Martha **ADAMS**, Oct. 18, 1750	LR7	46
Joseph, s. Joseph, b. Oct. 30, 1716	LR2	81
Josiah, s. John, s. Thomas, b. Apr. 10, 1712	LR2	97
Josiah, s. John (s. Thomas), d. May 13, 1717	LR2	62
Josiah, s. John (s. of Thomas), b. Apr. 20, 1724	LR2	46
Judah, s. James, Jr., b. Jan. 14, 1750/1	LR8	5
Lemen, s. Joseph, b. Feb. 14, 1770	LR17	433
Levina, d. Abraham, b. Feb. 26, 1771	LR17	433
Lott, s. Luke, b. Apr. 2, 1774	LR17	433
Lovisanah, d. Samuell, Jr., b. Apr. 18, 1758	LR11	582
Luca, d. Joseph & Hannah, b. Dec. 30, 1723	LR2	46
Lucy, m. Eliakim **DEMING**, Oct. 1, 1746	LR7	46
Luke, s. Hezekiah, b. July 31, 1734	LR5	3
Luke, m. Mary **HART**, June 25, 1761	LR11	594
Luke, s. Luke & Almira, b. Nov. 22, 1776	LR21	543
Lydia, d. James, b. July 1, 1723	LR2	88
Lydia, m. Samuel **HART**, s. Stephen, b. of Farmington,		
Aug. [ ], 1745	LR7	35
Lidia, d. Clement, b. Aug. 16, 1769	LR15	E
Martha, d. John, s. Thomas, b. Sept. 9, 1718	LR2	83
Martha, d. Ebenezer, b. Apr. 10, 1756	LR9	7-8
Matha, m. Reuben **WRIGHT**, Mar. 12, 1780	LR21	557
Mary, d. Thomas, Sr., b. Jan. [ ], 1688/9	LR4	382
Mary, d. Samuell, b. Aug. 17, 1708	LR1	2

	Vol.	Page
GRIDLEY, GRIDLEE (cont.)		
Mary, m. William **JUDD**, s. Philip, Dec. 23, 1709	LR2	145
Mary, m. Sergt. John **WADSWORTH**, b. of		
Ffarmington, Sept. 2, 1714	LR2	93
Mary, d. John (s. of Samuell), b. May 9, 1717	LR2	81
Mary, d. John, s. Thomas, b. Nov. 9, 1721	LR2	102
Mary, m. Nathan **LEWIS**, b. of Farmington, July 28,		
1730	LR5	13
Mary, d. Samuel, b .May 22, 1733	LR5	3
Mary, d. Jno, m. Ebenezer **EAVENS**, b. of Farmington,		
Dec. 21, 1737	LR6	27
Mary, d. Samuell (s. Thomas), d. Mar. 7, 1737/8	LR6	10
Mary, d. Samuell (s. Thomas), b. June 17, 1739	LR6	3
Mary, m. Abel **HAWLEY**, Aug. 19, 1742	LR6	305
Mary, d. Elnathan, b. Apr. 21, 1754	LR9	7-8
Mary, w. Andrew, d. May 6, 1759	LR11	577
Mary, d. Luke, b. Apr. 17, 1762	LR14	6
Mary, m. Noah **ROOT**, June 10, 1762	LR9	12
Mary, d. Hezekiah, d. Jan. 14, 1775	LR17	445
Matthew, s. Thomas, Jr., b. Sept. 9, 1711	LR2	97
Matthew, s. Thomas, Jr., d. Oct. 3, 1711	LR2	141
Matthew, s. Thomas, Jr., b. Dec. 2, 1720	LR2	102
Mercy, d. John, s. Samuell, b. Apr. 2, 1719	LR2	83
Mercy, m. Asahel **BARNES**, May 3, 1769	LR17	G
Mercy, m. Joseph **BARKER**, Feb. 16, 1773	LR17	443
Mercy, b. Aug. 27, 1807; m. Horace **THOMSON**, Dec.		
10, 1828	LR22	476
Naoma, d. Elnathan, b. Oct. 13, 1771	LR17	433
Nathaniell, s. Samuell, Sr., b. Oct. [ ], 1699	LR2	109
Noadiah, s. Andrew, b. May 27, 1750	LR8	5
Noah, s. Samuell (s. of Thomas), b. Oct. 31, 1736	LR6	3
Noah, m. Sarah **CURTIS**, Aug. 15, 1751	LR7	46
Obid, s. James, Jr., b. Apr. 28, 1760	LR11	582
Oliver, s. John, b. Sept. 2, 1751	LR8	5
Oliver, s. James, b. Nov. 27, 1767	LR15	E
Oliver, s. Seth, b. July 8, 1786	LR22	464
Phebe, m. Josiah **LEWIS**, b. of Farmington, July 6, 1737	LR6	27
Phebe, d. Abell, b. Mar. 7, 1769	LR17	433
Polly, d. Elisha, b. Mar. 23, 1776	LR22	464
Rachel, d. Ebenezer, b. Nov. 10, 1753	LR8	5
Rachell, d. Luke, b. Oct. 17, 1771	LR17	433
Rebeckah, d. Samuel, b. Oct. 29, 1728	LR4	395
Rebeckah, d. Timothy, b. Aug. 30, 1738	LR6	3
Rebeckah, m. Elijah **ANDRUS**, 2nd, Mar. 2, 1775	LR21	557
Reuben, s. Job, b. Apr. 14, 1770	LR17	433
Reuel, s. Abell, b. Dec. 1, 1765	LR14	6
Rhoda, d. Timothy, b. June 9, 1767	LR17	433
Rhoda, d. Hezekiah, Jr., b. Dec. 1, 1769	LR17	433
Roger, m. Sarah **THOMSON**, June 1, 1775	LR21	557
Root, m. Betsey **LEWIS**, June 30, 1824, by Rev. Noah		
Porter	LR42	568
Rosete, d. Job, b. Oct. 21, 1771	LR17	433
Ruth, d. Thomas (blacksmith), b. Mar. 1, 1720/1	LR2	102

	Vol.	Page
GRIDLEY, GRIDLEE (cont.)		
Ruth, w. Jonathan, d. Nov. 1, 1748	LR7	36
Ruth, m. Abell THOMSON, Dec. 7, 1775	LR21	557
Ruth, m. Abel THOMSON, Dec. 7, 1775; d. Jan. 11, 1793	LR22	476
Samuel, s. Thomas, b. Mar. [ ], 1686/7	LR4	382
Samuel, of Ffarmington, m. Mary HUMPHRIES, sometime of Simsbury, Dec. 1, 1698	LR2	145
Samuel, s. Samuel, b. Ruth LEWIS, June 8, 1710	LR2	145
Samuel, s. Thomas (blacksmith), b. June 26, 1714	LR2	99
Samuel, s. Thomas, m. Abigail HOUGH, b. of Farmington, Aug. 21, 1723	LR2	60
Samuel, s. Samuell (s. of Thomas), b. Dec. 20, 1724	LR2	46
Samuel, of Kensington, m. [ ] CHAMBERLIN, of Lebanon, Dec. 12, 1727	LR4	423
Samuel, m. Sarah WADSWORTH, Feb. 14, 1744/5	LR7	35
Samuel, d. Feb. 26, 1764	LR11	593
Samuel, s. Elnathan, b. Oct. 19, 1766	LR15	E
Samuel, s. Elnathan, d. Jan. 23, 1769	LR15	M
Sarah, d. Joseph, b. Sept. 1, 1718	LR2	102
Sarah, m. Nathaniel COWLES, Jr., b. of Farmington, Mar. 15, 1721/2	LR2	100
Sarah, d. Hezekiah, b. Feb. 24, 1738/9	LR6	3
Sarah, d. James, Jr., b. June 18, 1752	LR8	5
Sarah, d. James, Jr., d. Sept. 18, 1753	LR8	12
Sarah, d. Clement, b. Jan. 10, 1758	LR11	582
Sarah, d. Elnathan, b. Mar. 7, 1759	LR11	582
Sarah, m. Jacob BARTHOLOMEW, Sept. 10, 1761	LR11	575
Sarah, wid., m. Thomas STANLEY, Feb. 28, 1765	LR11	594
Sarah, m. Nathaniell LEWIS, Feb. 15, 1769	LR17	443
Sarah Goodman, d. Elijah, b. Aug. 25, 1790	LR22	464
Selah, s. Thomas, Jr., b. Aug. 31, 1757	LR11	582
Selah, s. Timothy, b. June 3, 1770	LR17	433
Selah, m. Sarah RUSSELL, Jan. 1, 1779	LR22	480
Seth, m. Easther BLAKESLEY, Feb. 12, 1772	LR17	442
Seth, s. Seth, b. Dec. 1, 1777	LR22	464
Silas, s. Abell, b. Nov. 7, 1757	LR14	6
Simeon, s. Job, b. Sept. 28, 1769	LR17	433
Stephen, s. James, Jr., b. Dec. 16, 1757	LR11	582
Susannah, d. James, b. Sept. 5, 1720	LR2	102
Susannah, d. James, d. Sept. 5, 1720	LR2	62
Susannah, d. James, b. July 25, 1721	LR2	102
Susannah, m. Solomon THOMSON, Dec. 26, 1745	LR7	35
Sibel, d. James, Jr., b. Sept. 23, 1762	LR11	582
Sylvester, s. Abraham, b. Apr. 17, 1767	LR15	E
Silve, d. Timothy, b. Dec. 5, 1768	LR17	433
Thomas, Sr., m. Elizabeth CLARK, b. of Ffarmington, Dec. 25, 1679	LR2	257
Thomas, Sr., his 1st child, b. June [ ], 1681	LR4	382
Thomas, Sr., his 1st child, d. June [ ], 1681	LR2	147
Thomas, his 2nd child, b. Sept. 9, 1682	LR4	382
Thomas, Sr., his 2nd child d. Sept. [ ], 1682	LR2	147
Thomas, Sr., his last child, d. Mar. [ ], 1695/6	LR2	147

	Vol.	Page
GRIDLEY, GRIDLEE (cont.)		
Thomas, s. Thomas, Sr., b. June [ ], 1683	LR4	382
Thomas, Sr., his last child b. Mar. [ ], 1696/7	LR4	382
Thomas, m. Hanah **WILCOKSON**, of Stratford, Oct. 31, 1704	LR1	4
Thomas, s. Thomas, b. Elizabeth **BROWNSON**, Aug. 3, 1710	LR2	145
Thomas, s. Thomas, [blacksmith], b. Oct. 1, 1725	LR2	65
Thomas, s. Thomas, (blacksmith), Oct. 14, 1725	LR2	66
Thomas, s. Thomas, Jr., b. Nov. 18, 1727	LR4	395
Thomas, blacksmith, m. Sarah **ROOT**, b. of Farmington, Dec. 5, 1734	LR5	539
Thomas, Jr., m. Hannah **GOODRICH**, Jan. 11, 1749/50	LR7	46
Thomas, s. Thomas, d. Jan. 22, 1754	LR8	12
Thomas, d. Nov. 18, 1758	LR11	577
Thomas, s. Ebenezer, b. Apr. 19, 1761	LR11	582
Thomas, m. Mary [ ], June 23, 1768	LR15	N
Timothy, s. Thomas, [blacksmith], b. Dec. 25, 1711	LR2	98
Timothy, m. Esther **PORTTER**, b. of Farmington, Apr. 5, 1737	LR6	27
Timothy, d. Oct. 14, 1764	LR17	444
Timothy, m. Rhoda **WOODRUFF**, May 8, 1766	LR17	G
Zeanus, s. Seth, b. Sept. 6, 1772	LR17	433
Zeanos, s. Seth, d. May 26, 1778, in the 6th y. of his age	LR22	482
Zephanias, s. James, b. Feb. 19, 1732/3	LR5	3
Zephaniah, s. James, d. Mar. 20, 1732/3	LR5	50
Zephaniah, s. James, Jr., b. Apr. 6, 1754	LR9	7-8
Zephaniah, s. James, d. Jan. 7, 1756	LR9	495
GRIFFIN, GRIFFEN, GRIFFING, David, s. John & Elizabeth, b. Aug. 4, 1748	LR7	H
David, of New Haven, m. Ellen B. **CATLIN**, of Farmington, Sept. 22, 1845, by Rev. Noah Porter	LR47	115
Peter, of Mereden, m. Sybel **JACKSON**, of Farmington, June 4, 1820, by Noah Porter, V.D.M.	LR40	570
GRIMES, Sarah, m. Elijah **SMITH**, Apr. 6, 1752	LR8	10
Sarah J., of Simsbury, m. Wells **WEBSTER**, of Windsor, Oct. 12, 1835, by Rev. Noah Porter	LR47	90
William, of Simsbury, m. Catharine J. **HART**, of Farmington, Mar. 1, 1835, by Rev. Noah Porter	LR47	88
GRISWOLD, GRISWOULD, Adaline, of Weathersfield, m. William K. **BRADLEY**, of New Marlborough, Mass., Oct. 24, 1841, by Rev. Aaron S. Hill	LR47	105
Anna, d. David & Severance, b. Feb. 22, 1715/16*		
*(Written "1711/6" in original)	LR2	88
Annah, d. Gideon, b. Apr. 3, 1760	LR21	543
Ashbel, s. Jonathan, b. Sept. 8, 1733	LR5	3
Ashbel, s. Gideon, b. May 13, 1757	LR11	582
Cable, d. David, b. Sept. 17, 1726	LR2	242
Eliakim, s. David & Leucranee, b. July 17, 1722	LR2	88
Eliakim, s. David & Severance, d. Nov. 21, 1723	LR2	61
Elijah, s. David & Leucranee, b. May 20, 1719	LR2	88
Gideon, s. David & Leucranee, b. Oct. 2, 1717	LR2	88
Gideon, his s. [ ], b. Jan. 15, 1754	LR9	7-8

	Vol.	Page
GRISWOLD, GRISWOULD (cont.)		
Hannah, d. David, b. Nov. 2, 1724	LR2	46
Jonathan, m. Mary **WILLARD**, Feb. 23, 1725/6	LR2	100
Jonathan, s. Jonathan, b. Apr. 25, 1731	LR5	3
Jonathan, m. Experience **WARREN**, Oct. 6, 1748	LR7	46
Jonathan, m. Experience **WARREN**, Oct. 6, 1748	LR9	286
Lydia, d. Gideon, b. Nov. 24, 1765	LR21	543
Lydia W., m. Sidney **HART**, Jr., Sept. 3, 1839, by Rev. Ezra S. Cook. Witnesses William H. Grimes & Sidney Hart	LR47	100
Mary, d. David & Leucranee, b. Feb. 15, 1720/1	LR2	88
Mary, d. Jonathan, b. Nov. 27, 1726	LR4	382
Mary, w. Jonathan, d. Apr. 30, 1741	LR6	305
Mary E., m. Romulus **ANDRUS**, b. of Farmington, Sept. 24, 1837, by Rev. S. H. Clark	LR47	96
Rhody, d. Jonathan, b. Apr. 4, 1733	LR5	3
Rhody, d. Jonathan, d. Aug. 23, 1733	LR5	50
[GUERNSEY], [see under **GARNSEY**]		
HADSELL, Ira, m. Betsey **BIRD**, b. of Farmington, May 9, 1825, by Rev. Noah Porter	LR42	568
Julia, of Torrington, m. Truman **ALDERMAN**, of Burlington, Dec. 27, 1820, by Ludovicus Robbins, V.D.M.	LR40	571
Olive, of Farmington, m. David **PORTER**, of Weathersfield, Oct. 12, 1824, by Rev. Harry Bushnell	LR42	568
Samuel, of Burlington, m. Charlotte **WOLCOTT**, of Farmington, Nov. 2, 1827, by Harvey Bushnell	LR42	565
HALE, George M., of Burlington, m. Dolly **HART**, of Farmington, Apr. 5, 1841, by Rev. Noah Porter	LR47	104
HALL, [see also **HALE & HULL**], Elizabeth, m. [ ]uel **LEE**, Sept. 4, 1771	LR17	G
Mary, of Wallingford, m. Col. Isaac **LEE**, of Farmington, Oct. 9, 1783	LR22	480
Mary Ann, of Plymouth, m. James H. **WOODRUFF**, of Watertown, Jan. 12, 1835, by Rev. Noah Porter	LR47	88
HAMLIN, HAMBLIN, Abigail, of Farmington, m. Chauncey H. **ATWOOD**, of Woodbury, Dec. 24, 1845, by Rev. S. H. Clark	LR47	117
Angeline M., of Farmington, m. Cyrenus **SMITH**, of Chatham, Sept. 6, 1844, by William Wright	LR47	113
Charles F., of Farmington, m. Maria **BARTHOLOMEW**, of Harwinton, Oct. 26, 1835, by Rev. Noah Porter	LR47	90
Ellen, E., m. Samuel G. **FORBES**, Apr. 8, 1828, by Rev. David L. Ogden	LR42	564
Hezekiah W., m. Catharine **COWLES**, b. of Farmington, Apr. 11, 1849, by Rev. Noah Porter	LR47	124
James, m. Harriet **HILLS**, Oct. 16, 1824, by Rev. Noah Porter	LR42	568
Laura, m. William **COWLES**, Jr., b. of Farmington, Aug. 30, 1848, by Rev. Noah Porter	LR47	122
Lucy, m. Daniel **MILLER**, Apr. 19, 1774	LR17	443

	Vol.	Page
HAMLIN, HAMBLIN (cont.)		
Mark, s. Ebenezer, b. Feb. 25, 1765	LR15	F
Mary, of Farmington, m. Joel **FENN**, of Wallingford,		
June 26, 1844, by Rev. Edward Savage, of Bristol	LR47	112
Mehitabel, of Middletown, m. Samuel **HOOKER**, of		
Ffarmington, s. Rev. Samuel, June latter end, 1687	LR2	145
Rozabello, d. Ebenezer, b. June 13, 1767	LR15	F
Thankfull, m. Jacob **ROYSE**, Oct. 10, 1753	LR11	576
HAMOND, Lettes, m. Esther **BIRD**, b. of Farmington, Apr. 8,		
1834, by Rev. Noah Porter	LR42	E
HANCOX, Amy, d. Daniel, b. Mar. 25, 1724	LR5	8
Daniel, s. Thomas, b. Jan. 1, 1694/5	LR2	232
Daniel, m. Rachel **PORTTER**, b. of Ffarmington, June 4,		
1724, by William Wadsworth, J.P.	LR2	258
John, s. Thomas, b. Aug. 1, 1688	LR2	232
Jonathan, s. Daniel, .b. Mar. 11, 1730/1	LR5	8
Mary, d. Daniel, b. Jan. 17, 1732/3	LR5	306
Mehitabel, d. Thomas, b. Dec. 4, 1698	LR2	232
Rachel, d. Thomas, b. Feb. 7, 1692/3	LR2	232
Rede,* d. Daniel, b. June 10, 1727 *(Written in pencil,		
"Perle")	LR5	8
Thomas, of Farmington, m. Rachel **LENERD**, of		
Springfield, Mar. 17, 1684/5	LR2	125
Thomas, s. Thomas, b. Mar. 13, 1685/6	LR2	232
Thomas, Sr., d. July 11, 1734	LR5	50
William, s. Thomas, b. Mar. 2,* 1690/1 *(Perhaps		
"Mar. 1")	LR2	232
HANLEY, [see also **STANLEY**], Thomas, s. John, m. Hanah		
HART, d. Nathaniel, Mar. 21, 1754	LR9	286
HANNISON, Mirryam, of Hartford, m. Roger **ORUIC**, of		
Ffarmington, Dec. 15, 1692	LR2	123
HARAS, Hanah, of Toland, m. Eleazer **NASH**, of Farmington,		
May 19, 1741	LR6	304
[HARD], [see under **HURD**]		
HARDY, Aaron A., of Pittsburgh, Pa., m. Mary A. **COWLES**,		
d. Horace, decd., of Farmington, Nov. 1, 1848, by		
Joseph D. Hull	LR47	123
HARRISON, Aaron, s. Capt. Aaron, b. Jan. 29, 1770	LR15	J
Amanda, of Waterbury, m. John B. **TERRY**, of		
Plymouth, June 16, 1828, by Rev. Noah Porter	LR42	564
Hephsibah, d. Daniel, b. Jan. 14, 1775	LR21	544
Horace, s. Daniel, b. Feb. 23, 1777	LR21	544
Jared, m. Hannah **WEBSTER**, Dec. 27, 1769	LR15	N
John, s. Aaron, d. Nov. 10, 1776	LR21	558-9
Lydiah, d. Capt. Aaron, b. Apr. 18, 1767	LR15	J
HARSINGTON, [see under **HOISINGTON**]		
HART, HEART, HARTT, Aaron, s. Elijah, Jr., b. Oct. 16,		
1761	LR11	582
Abel, s. Ebenezer, Jr. & Martha, b. Jan. 11, 1747	LR11	583
Abel, s. Thomas, b. Sept. 5, 1756	LR11	583
Abi, d. Abross, b. July 8, 1764	LR14	7
Abigail, d. Stephen, b. Feb. 28, 1701/2	LR2	91
Abigail, d. Nathaniel, b. July 21, 1723	LR2	87

	Vol.	Page
HART, HEART, HARTT (cont.)		
Abigail, m. Stephen **COLE**, of Ffarmington, June 11, 1729	LR5	13
Abigail, d. Timothy, b. Aug. 28, 1737	LR6	3
Abigail, d. Stephen, Jr., b. Mar. 18, 1751	LR11	583
Abigail, m. Elisha **NEWELL**, Mar. 13, 1755	LR9	286
Abigail, w. Daniel, d. Dec. 7, 1760	LR11	574
Abigail, d. Thomas, b. Oct. 27, 1761	LR14	7
Abigail, d. Hezekiah, b. Aug. 14, 1762	LR11	584
Abigail, d. Eldad, b. Aug. 2, 1763	LR11	584
Abigail, d. Eldad, b. Aug. 2, 1763	LR14	7
Abigail, w. Zachariah, d. July 12, 1765	LR14	3
Abigail, d. Zachariah, b. May 21, 1768	LR15	F
Abigail, d. Samuel, (s. Thomas), b. Feb. 20, [ ]	LR7	J
Abijah, s. Thomas, b. Apr. 7, 1764	LR14	7
Adeline, m. Norman **HART**, b. of Farmington, Oct. 11, 1826, by Rev. Harry Bushnell	LR42	567
Amanda, of Farmington, m. Elisha **WHAPLES**, of Weathersfield, Oct. 11, 1825, by Rev. Harry Bushnell	LR42	567
Amasa, s. Thomas, [s. of Hawkins], b. June 19, 1754	LR9	9
Ambrus, s. Joseph, b. Aug. 25, 1732	LR5	8
Ambrose, m. Martha **FULLER**, Aug. 20, 1755	LR11	576
Ambros, s. Simeon, b. Mar. 28, 1759	LR11	582
Amos, s. Thomas & grandson of Sergt. Thomas, b. Feb. 20, 1721/2	LR2	102
Amos, m. Ann **GRIDLEY**, July 20, 1749	LR7	46
Amos, s. Amos, b. Mar. 16, 1755	LR9	9
Amos, m. Marah **DUNHAM**, Nov. 23, 1758	LR11	592
Ame, d. John, b. Aug. 28, 1753	LR8	5
Ann, d. Joseph, Jr., b. July 21, 1756	LR9	9
Anna, d. Stephen, b. Aug. 18, 1695	LR2	91
Anna, m. Samuel **PORTTER**, b. of Ffarmington, Dec. 23, 1714	LR2	93
Anna, d. Thomas & Anna, b. Nov. 11, 1724	LR2	46
Annah, d. Samuel & Elizabeth, b. Jan. 31, 1730/1	LR5	4
Anna, m. Thomas **HOLLISTER**, Oct. 15, 1747	LR7	46
Annah, d. Amos, d. Jan. 8, 1754	LR8	12
Anner, d. Eldad, b. Apr. 17, 1765	LR14	7
Anne, m. Samuel **JUDD**, Apr. 20, 1710	LR2	145
Anne, d. Samuel & Mary, b. Sept. 25, 1724	LR2	46
Anne, d. Judah, b. May 22, 1739	LR6	3
Anne, d. Judah, Jr., b. Mar. 17, 1780	LR21	544
Anthony, s. Samuell (s. Thomas), b. Jan. 25, 1750/1	LR8	5
Arena, d. Eldad, b. Jan. 25, 1771	LR17	435
Asa, s. David, b. Jan. 4, 1759	LR11	583
Asahel, s. Samuel & Mary, b. May 10, 1726	LR2	69
Asahel, s. Samuell & Mary, d. Oct. 6, 1736	LR5	500
Asahel, s. Joseph, Jr., b. May 12, 1754	LR9	9
Asahell, m. Anne **KILLBORN**, b. of Farmington, Nov. 5, 1778	LR22	480
Astath, d. Ambrose, b. Apr. 4, 1756	LR11	583

	Vol.	Page
HART, HEART, HARTT (cont.)		
Ava, m. Julia **CRAMPTON**, b. of Farmington, Nov. 6,		
1827, by Rev. Noah Porter	LR42	565
Azubah, d. Eldad, b. Feb. 12, 1762	LR11	584
Azuba, d. Eldad, b. Feb. 12, 1762	LR14	7
Azuba, d. Joseph, Jr., b. Sept. 28, 1765	LR14	7
Barbara, d. Thomas (s. of Hawkins), b. May 24, 1758	LR11	583
Benjamin, s. Hawkins, b. Jan. 4, 1750/1	LR8	5
Benjamin, s. Elijah, b. Oct. [ ]	LR7	J
Bethuel, s .Joseph, Jr., b. Dec. [ ], [ ]	LR11	584
Betse, d. Ebenezer, Jr., b. Feb. 21, 1771	LR17	343
Betsey, of Farmington, m. Andrew J. **PAYNE**, of Avon,		
Oct. 17, 1838, by Rev. S. H. Clark	LR47	98
Bloss, s. Simeon, b. Mar. 10, 1761	LR11	582
Calvin, s. Thomas, b. Sept. 23, 1767	LR15	F
Carline, d. Zachariah, b. Oct. 12, 1762	LR14	7
Catharine J., of Farmington, m. William **GRIMES**, of		
Simsbury, Mar 1, 1835, by Rev. Noah Porter	LR47	88
Charlotte, of Farmington, m. Charles **WILCOX**, of		
Harwinton, Oct. 14, 1845, by William Wright	LR47	116
Chastinah, d. Stephen, Jr., b. Oct. 22, 1773	LR21	544
Clarissa, of Farmington, m. David E. **STODDARD**, of		
Avon, Nov. 16, 1846, by Noah Porter	LR47	118
Cyrian, s. Noadiah, b. May 23, 1772	LR21	544
Dan, s. Noah, b. July 6, 1762	LR11	582
Daniel, s. Stephen, b. Mar. 21, 1708	LR2	91
Daniel, s. Hezekiah, b. [ ], 1724	LR4	374
Daniel, m. Abigail **THOMSON**, b. of Farmington, July		
18, 1734	LR5	300
Daniel, had child, b. Mar. 5, 1735/6	LR6	3
Daniel, had child, d. Mar. 5, 1739/40, soon after birth	LR6	10
Daniel, s. Hezekiah, b. Oct. 10, 1763	LR11	584
Daniel, s. Hezekiah, b. Oct. 10, 1763	LR17	434
Daniel, s. Eldad, b. Mar. 6, 1775	LR17	435
David, s. Stephen, Jr., b. June 28, 1734	LR5	8
David, s. Hawkins, b. July 22, 1745	LR7	1
David, m. Elizabeth **PORTTER**, Feb. 9, 1758	LR11	576
Dennis, m. Elvira **DUTTON**, Feb. 1, 1825, by Noah		
Porter	LR42	568
Dinah, d. Lieut. Thomas & Anne, b. Feb. 12, 1733/4	LR5	307
Dinah, d. Capt. Thomas, d. Aug. 10, 1738	LR6	10
Dina, d. Joseph & Mary, b. Nov. 9, 1738	LR6	3
Dinah, d. Capt. Thomas, b. Oct. 10, 1742	LR6	3
Dinah, m. Appleton **WOODRUFF**, Mar. 27, 1758	LR11	576
Dolly, of Farmington, m. George M. **HALE**, of		
Burlington, Apr. 5, 1841, by Rev. Noah Porter	LR47	104
Dorcas, d. Joseph, Jr., d. June 2, 1750	LR7	540
Dorcas, d. Medad, b. Jan. 14, 1756	LR9	9
Ebenezer, s. Thomas, b. Apr. 13, 1705	LR1	3
Ebenezer, s. Isaac, b. Nov. 27, 1722	LR2	34
Ebenezer, m. Elizabeth **LARRANCE**, June 9, 1741	LR6	305
Ebenezer, s. Ebenezer, b. July 27, 1742	LR6	3
Ebenezer, s. Ebenezer, Jr. & Martha, b. Jan. 5, 1750	LR11	583

	Vol.	Page
HART, HEART, HARTT (cont.)		
Ebenezer, Jr., d. Nov. 28, 1753	LR11	577
Ebenezer, s. Stephen, 3rd, b. Feb. 8, 1768	LR15	J
Ebenezer, Jr., m. Lidia **BENTON**, Apr. 5, 1770	LR17	G
Edward, of Sourthington, m. Rhoda **GRANNIS**,of		
Southington, May 14, 1835, by Rev. Noah Porter	LR47	89
Eeter,* twin with Lowis, d. Judah, b. Apr. 4, 1742		
*("Esther"?)	LR6	3
Eldad, s. Daniel & Abigail, b. June 6, 1735	LR5	307
Eldad, s. Daniel, d. May 17, 1736	LR5	50
Eldad, s. Daniel, b. Mar. 22, 1736/7	LR6	3
Eldad, m. Achael **STEVENS**, July 8, 1761	LR11	592
Eldad, d. Sept. 22, 1776, in the 40th y. of his age	LR21	558-9
Eldad, s. Eldad, decd., b. Feb. 16, 1777	LR21	544
Elias, s. Judah & Anne, b. Feb. 25, 1735/6	LR6	3
Elias, of Farmington, m. Hope **WHAPLES**, of		
Weathersfield, Oct. 17, 1753	LR9	286
Elyidia, m. Noah **JELET**, Dec. 15, 1748	LR7	46
Elijah, s. Thomas, of Thomas, b. Feb. 1, 1706/7	LR1	3
Elijah, m. Abigail **GOODRICH**, b. of Farmington, Dec.		
26, 1734	LR5	539
Elijah, s. Elijah, b. Sept. 26, 1735	LR5	8
Elijah, s. Thomas, b. Nov. 16, 1752	LR11	583
Elijah, had negro Abed Metick, s. Phebe, b. Jan. 11, 1756	LR9	9
Elijah, s. Elijah, Jr., b. May 7, 1759	LR11	583
Elisha, s. Thomas, Jr., b. June 18, 1711	LR2	97
Elisha, s. Timothy, b. Apr. 28, 1731	LR5	4
Elisha, s. Ebenezer, b. Mar. 4, 1751	LR8	5
Elisha, m. Sarah **COLE**, July 14, 1753	LR8	10
Elisha, d. Feb. 29, 1768, ae 37	LR15	M
Elizabeth, d. Sergt. Thomas, of Farmington, m. Silvanus		
WOODRUFF, of Farmington, May 27, 17[ ]	LR5	13
Elizabeth, d. Ens. Isaac, b. [ ], 1726	LR4	374
Elizabeth, d. Ens. Isaac, d. Jan. 24, 1726/7	LR4	396
Elizabeth, d. William, b. Apr. 2, 1731	LR7	1
Elizabeth, d. Samuel (s. of Ch[arle]s), b. Sept. 25, 1732	LR5	306
Elizabeth, w. Timothy, d. Nov. 29, 1740	LR6	10
Elizabeth, wid. Thomas, d. Mar. 18, 1743	LR6	305
Elizabeth, d. Ebenezer, b. May 20, 1746	LR7	1
Elizabeth, d. Ebenezer, Jr., & Martha, b. Sept. 14, 1752	LR11	583
Elizabeth, m. Gideon **HART**, Nov. 15, 1759	LR11	575
Elizabeth, d. Gideon, b. May 10, 1762	LR11	584
Elizabeth, d. Elisha, b. May 31, 1766	LR15	J
Elizabeth, d. Ebenezer, d. Nov. 4, 1766	LR14	3
Elizabeth, d. Oliver, b. Dec. 19, 1769	LR15	J
Elnathan, s. James, b. Sept. 10, 1735	LR5	306
Emeline G., m. Amariah **WADSWORTH**, b. of		
Farmington, Apr. 26, 1826, by Rev. Harry Bushnell	LR42	569
Enos J., of Bristol, m. Helen E. **BELDEN**, of Farmington,		
June 7, 1849, by Rev. Noah Porter	LR47	125
Esther, d. John, Jr., b. Sept. 19 ,1707	LR2	98
Esther, m. Nathaniel **NEWEL**, b. of Ffarmington, June		
29, 1727	LR4	423

	Vol.	Page
HART, HEART, HARTT (cont.)		
Ester, w. John, d. July 10, 1743, in the 57th y. of her age	LR6	305
Esther, d. Thomas & Hannah, b. Nov. 16, 1751	LR8	5
Esther, d. Solomon, b. Mar. 26, 1752	LR9	9
Esther, d. Samuel, [s. of Stephen], b. Aug. 17, 1757	LR11	583
Esther, d. Benjamin, b. Nov. 8, 1776	LR21	544
E[u]nis, d. Jeames, b. Aug. 9, 1746	LR7	544
Eunice, m. Asa **COWLES**, May 9, 1755	LR9	286
Eunice, d. Stephen, Jr., b. Feb. 22, 1757	LR11	583
Eunice, d. Stephen, Jr., b. Feb. 22, 1757	LR11	583
Eunice, m. Eli **NORTH**, Oct. 3, 1765	LR11	594
Ezra, s. Joseph, Jr., b. Oct. 5, 1768	LR15	F
Fanny, of Plainville, m. Charles **BUTLER**, of New		
Britain, Nov. 15, 1848, by William Wright	LR47	123
Gad, s. Stephen, Jr., b. Mar. 24, 1759	LR11	583
Gad H., of Hartford, m. Eliza E. **COWLES**, of		
Farmington, Mar. 20, 1829, by Rev. George		
Phippen, of Canton & Northington	LR42	564
George, m. Esther **HAWLEY**, b. of Farmington, Apr. 3,		
1827, by Rev. Noah Porter	LR42	565
Gideon, s. Joseph, b. Sept. 11, 1730	LR5	4
Gideon, s. Nathaniel, b. Nov. 1, 1759	LR11	583
Gideon, m. Elizabeth **HART**, Nov. 15, 1759	LR11	575
Gideon, s. Nathaniell & Marthay, b. Nov. 23, 1759	LR11	583
Gideon W., of Avon, m. Mary S. **PARCELLS**, of New		
Fairfield, Dec. 10, 1844, by Rev. S. H. Clark	LR47	113
Gilbert, s. Thomas, b. May 24, 1762	LR15	F
Hannah, d. Thomas, s. Capt. Thomas, b. Feb. 1, 1708/9	LR2	109
Hannah, d. Dea. Ebenezer, m. Joseph **PORTTER**, July		
11, 1728	LR4	423
Hannah, d. Nathaniell & Abigail, b. Aug. 11, 1729	LR5	4
Hannah, w. Lieut. John, d. Feb. 8, 1737/8	LR6	10
Hanah, d. Jeames, b. Sept. 9, 1744	LR6	3
Hannah, d. Thomas, b. Oct. 25, 1747	LR8	5
Hannah, d. Amos, b. Jan. 5, 1751	LR8	5
Hannah, d. Joseph, Jr., b. Feb. 23, 1752	LR8	5
Hannah, d. Joseph, Jr., d. June 28, 1753	LR8	12
Hanah, d. Nathaniel, m. Thomas **HANLEY**, s. John, Mar.		
21, 1754	LR9	286
Hannah, d. Hezekiah, b. Oct. 3, 1765	LR17	434
Hannah, m. Obadiah **ANDRUS**, Oct. 3, 1765	LR11	594
Hawkins, s. Hawkins & Susanah, b. Mar. 8, 1731/2	LR5	4
Hawkins, s. Hawkins, Jr., d. Apr. 4, 1732	LR5	50
Hawkins, s. Hawkins & Susanah, b. Jan. 30, 1736/7	LR6	3
Hawkins, m. Esther **GRIDLEY**, b. of Farmington, Apr. 5,		
1738	LR6	27
Hawkins, m. Huldah **WOODRUFF**, Apr. 17, 1758	LR11	575
Henry, of Farmington, m. Jane **TAYLOR**, of		
Glastonbury, Dec. 7, 1834, by Rev. Noah Porter	LR47	88
Henry, of Farmington, m. Lucy Maria **GLADDEN**, of		
Burlington, June 24, 1838, by Rev. S. H. Clark	LR47	97
Henry J., m. Sophia **PECK**, b. of Southington, Aug. 25,		
1842, by [ ]	LR47	108

	Vol.	Page
HART, HEART, HARTT (cont.)		
Hephzibah, d. Hezekiah, b. Apr. 16, 1732	LR5	645
Hezekiah, s .Hezekiah, b. Dec. 11, 1714	LR2	95
Hezekiah, s. Hezekiah, b. [ ], 1714	LR4	374
Hezekiah (?) s. Isaac (?), b. [ ], 1729 (Perhaps		
"----Hart, s. Hezekiah, [s.] Isaac". Entry illegible)	LR4	396
Hezekiah, s. Hezekiah, d. Mar. 29, 1730	LR5	645
Hezekiah, s. Hezekiah, b. June 7, 1730	LR5	645
Hezekiah, m. Abigail **ADKINS**, Jan. 10, 1757	LR11	575
Hezekiah, s. Hezekiah, b. May 25, 1759	LR11	582
Hiram, m. Mary **ROBINS**, b. of Farmington, May 22,		
1827, by Rev. Harvey Bushnell	LR42	565
Huldah, d. Samuel & Mary, b. Nov. 2, 1731	LR5	4
Huldah, d. Stephen, Jr., b. Dec. 27, 1752	LR8	5
Huldah, d. Gideon, b. Sept. 29, 1760	LR11	582
Isaac, Sergt., m. Elizabeth **WHEPLES** Nov. 24, 1721	LR2	60
Isaac,* s. Hezekiah, b. [ ], 1729 *(Perhaps "-----		
Hart, s. Hezekiah, [s.] Isaac". Entry illegible.)	LR4	396
Isaiah, s. David, b. Sept. 22, 1761	LR11	582
Ithurell, s. Thomas, b. Nov. 15, 1759	LR15	F
Jabez, s. Hezekiah, b. Oct. 3, 1765	LR17	434
Jacob, s. Elias, b. May 2, 1754	LR9	9
James, s. Thomas, b. Dec. 14, 1707	LR2	91
James, m. Thankful **NORTH**, b. of Farmington, Oct. 10,		
1734	LR5	545
Jane Nash, w. Amos, d. Mar. 27, 1755	LR9	495
Jason, s. Thomas, b. May 13, 1757	LR11	583
Job, s. Capt. Isaac, b. Jan. 31, 1731/2	LR5	8
Joel, s. Amos, b. May 28, 1753	LR8	5
Joel, s. Noah, b. Sept. 2, 1754	LR9	9
Joel, m. Huldah **WOODRUFF**, Mar. 15, 1781	LR22	480
John, s. Stephen, of Ffarmington, m. Hannah **TREET**,		
wid., sometime of Weathersfield, Apr. 12, 1694	LR2	123
John, s. William, b. July 26, [17]; d. [ ], 17[ ]	LR7	1
John, Jr., m. Esther **GRIDLEY**, b. of Farmington, Mar.		
20, 1706	LR2	125
John, s. John, Jr., b. Oct. 11, 1714	LR2	95
John, Capt. d. Nov. 11, 1714	LR2	62
John, s. Capt. Thomas & Anne, b. Dec. 9, 1731	LR5	4
John, s. Judah, b. Jan. 20, 1743	LR6	3
John, m. Hannah **HULL**, 2nd, Jan. 11, 1743/4	LR7	35
John, Jr., m. Huldah **GOULD**, Jan. 30, 1749	LR7	35
John, s. John, Jr., b. Nov. 19, 1751	LR8	5
John, s. Lieut. Ebenezer, b. Mar. 11, 1753	LR8	5
John, Dea., d. Oct. 7, 1753	LR8	12
John, s. Thomas, m. Desire **PALMER**, Apr. 10, 1755	LR10	6
Jonathan, s. Josiah, b. Feb. 7, 1725/6	LR2	242
Jonathan, s. Capt. Josiah & Sarah, d. Sept. 23, 1736	LR5	500
Jonathan, s. Thomas, b. Mar. 22, 1746	LR8	5
Jonathan, s. Ebenezer, [ ]	LR7	1
Joseph, m. Mary **BIRD**, b. of Ffarmington, Dec. 6, 1722	LR2	100
Joseph, s. Joseph, b. Oct. 1, 1723	LR4	374
Joseph, Jr., m. Ann **BARNS**, June 29, 1749	LR7	46

	Vol.	Page
HART, HEART, HARTT (cont.)		
Joseph, s. Joseph, Jr., b. July 29, 1759	LR11	583
Joseph, s. Zachariah, b. Oct. 14, 1760	LR14	7
Joseph, d. Nov. 9, 1760	LR14	3
Joseph, of Farmington, m. Tryphenia **RICE**, of		
Barkhamsted, July 26, 1826, by Harry Bushnell	LR42	569
Josiah, m. Sarah **BULL**, b. of Farminigton, Jan. 7,		
1713/14	LR2	93
Josiah, s. Josiah, d. Jan. 28, 1721/2	LR2	61
Josiah, s. Josiah, b. Jan. 24, 1721/2	LR2	102
Josiah, s. Hawkins, b. June 30, 1740	LR6	3
Josiah, s. Eluah, b. Apr. 28, 1742	LR6	3
Josiah, Capt., d. Jan. 28, 1758	LR11	577
Judah, s. John, Jr., b. Oct. 25, 1709	LR2	98
Judah, m. Anne **NORTON**, b. of Farmington, Feb. 20,		
1734/5	LR5	545
Judah, s. Judah, b. Sept. 5, 1737	LR6	3
Judah, s. Elijah, b. Dec. 2, 1739	LR6	3
Judah, s. Judah, d. Nov, 3, 1745	LR7	36
Judah, s. Judah, Jr., b. Dec. 16, 1777	LR21	544
Julia, m. Edwin **SWEET**, b. of Farmington, Oct. 12,		
1823, by Noah Porter, V.D.M.	LR40	572
Keziah, d. Timothy, b. Oct. 25, 1735	LR6	3
Keziah, d. Timothy, d. Apr. 29, 1739	LR6	10
Caziah, d. Timothy, b. May 6, 1740	LR6	3
Coziah, d. Timothy, d. Dec. 23, 1740	LR6	10
Lavinia, d. David., Oct. 13, 1764	LR11	582
Leffort, m. Nancy **WOODFORD**, b. of Farmington, Sept.		
12, 1826, by Rev. Bela Kellogg	LR42	567
Lemuel Stevens, s. Eldad, b. Mar. 15, 1767	LR14	7
Levy, s. Capt. Thomas & Anna, b. Mar. 30, 1738	LR6	3
Levi, s. Simeon, b. Mar. 22, 1758	LR11	582
Levi, s. Simeon, d. Apr. 14, 1758	LR11	574
Levi, s. Noah, b. Aug. 12, 1770	LR17	434
Lewis, m. Julia Ann **ROOT**, b. of Farmington, Apr. 10,		
1842, by Rev. Aaron S. Hill	LR47	107
Linda, d. Eldad, b. Jan. 25, 1773	LR17	435
Linn, s. Elnathan, b. Sept. 30, 1761	LR14	7
Lois, d. Matthew & Sarah, b. May 13, 1730	LR5	4
Lois, d. Nathaniell & Sarah, d. Oct. 11, 1736	LR5	500
Lowis, twin with Eeter,* d. Judah, s. b. Apr. 4, 1742		
*("Esther"?)	LR6	3
Lois, m. Bethuel **NORTON**, Oct. 31, 1765	LR11	594
Lois, m. David **BRISTOLL**, May 29, 1771	LR17	G
Louie, s. Capt. [ ], d. Sept. 10. 1743	LR6	305
Luca, d. Hezekiah, b. [ ], 1720	LR4	374
Lucy, d. James, b. Oct. 5, 1740	LR6	3
Lucy, d. Hezekiah, b. Aug. 10, 1761	LR11	582
Lucy, d. Reuben, b. May 8, 1764	LR14	7
Lucy, d. Ruben, d. June 6, 1764	LR14	3
Lucy, of Berlin, m. Isaac **STEARNS**, of Lanesborough,		
Mass., Sept. 19, 1831, by Rev. Noah Porter	LR42	560

	Vol.	Page
HART, HEART, HARTT (cont.)		
Lucy, of Farmington, m. Blynn **FRANCIS**, of		
Newington, Apr. 26, 1848, by Noah Porter	LR47	122
Lucy Ann, m. Simeon **STEDMAN**, b. of Farmington,		
Mar. 2, 1845, by Rev. S. H. Clark	LR47	113
Luke, s. Hawkins, b. Jan. 8, 1738/9	LR6	3
Lydia, d. Joseph, b. Aug. 8, 1728	LR5	4
Lydia, d. Samuel, b. Feb. 23, 1746	LR7	1
Lydia, of Farmington, m. Julius **JONES**, of Harwinton,		
Dec. 4, 1821, by L. Robbins, V.D.M.	LR42	571
Marah, d. Thomas & Hannah, b. Nov. 23, 1743	LR8	5
Margaret, of Ffarmington, m. Asahel **STRONG**, of		
Northampton, June 11, 1689	LR2	257
Martha, d. Hezekiah, b. [ ]. 1717	LR4	374
Martha, d. Samuell, b. July 31, 1739	LR6	3
Martha, m. Daniel **OWEN**, Feb. 4, 1759	LR11	576
Martin, s. Elisha, b. Oct. 3, 1758	LR11	583
Mary, m. Samuell **NEWELL**, Dec. 20, 1683	LR1	5
Mary, d. Thomas, b. Sept. 29, 1703	LR1	3
Mary, d. Sergt. Thomas, b. Sept. 7, 1714	LR2	95
Mary, d. Sergt. Thomas, d. Sept. 18, 1716	LR2	62
Mary, d. John (s. of Capt. John), b. Mar. 9, 1716/17	LR2	81
Mary, d. Steven, (s. of Thomas), b. Jan. 5, 1723/4	LR2	46
Mary, d. Matthew & Sarah, b. July 1, 1728	LR4	395
Mary, d. Dea. Ebenezer, m. John **HOOKER**, Jr., July 4,		
1728	LR4	423
Mary, d. Samuel, b. Apr. 26, 1730	LR5	4
Mary, d. Joseph & Mary, b. Sept. 11, 1736	LR6	3
Mary, d. Dea. Jno, m. Timothy **ROOT**, b. of Farmington,		
Dec. 6, 1739	LR6	27
Mary, d. William, b. Sept. 13, 174[ ]; d. same day	LR7	1
Mary, of Wallingford, m. Ebenezer, **HAWLEY**, of		
Farmington, July 1, 1741	LR6	304
Mary, m. Ebenezer **DICASON**, May 31, 1744	LR7	35
Mary, d. Elijah, b. Dec. 26, 1744	LR7	544
Mary, d. Noah, b. May 20, 1748	LR11	583
Mary, m. Amos **PECK**, July 26, 1750	LR7	46
Mary, m. Dr. Joseph **WELLS**, Jan. 17, 1754	LR9	286
Mary, d. Stephen, Jr., b. Feb. 20, 1755	LR11	583
Mary, m. Obadiah **OWEN**, Nov. 27, 1760	LR11	575
Mary, m. Luke **GRIDLEY**, June 25, 1761	LR11	594
Mary, d. Stephen, b. June 25, 1770	LR17	434
Matthew, m. Sarah **HOOKER**, b. of Farmington, Jan. 7,		
1724/5	LR2	52
Matthew, s. Matthew & Sarah, b. Jan. 23, 1736/7	LR6	3
Matthew, m. Elizabeth **HOPKINS**, Nov. 15, 1759	LR11	575
Matthew, s. Matthew & Elizabeth, b. Aug. 12, 1760	LR11	583
Medad, s. Joseph, b. July 27, 1734	LR5	8
Medad, m. Phebe **MILLER**, Nov. 18, 1754	LR9	286
Mercy, d. Josiah, b. Aug. 28, 1719	LR2	83
Mercy, d. Dea.* Thomas, b. Jan. 18, 1723/4 *(Perhaps		
"Doc")	LR2	87

	Vol.	Page
HART, HEART, HARTT (cont.)		
Mercy, d. Dr. * Thomas, d. Nov. 8, 1726 *(Perhaps		
"Deac")	LR2	66
Mercy, d. Capt. Isaac, b. Apr. 4, 1729	LR5	4
Mercy, d. Sameull (s. of T[homas]), b. Jan. 10, 1736/7	LR6	3
Mercy, m. Roger **HOOKER**, b. of Farmington, Jan. 29,		
1739/40	LR6	27
Mercy, d. Stephen, Jr., b. Feb. 20, 1755	LR11	583
Munson, s. Samuel (s. Stephen), b. Mar. 2, 1750/1	LR8	5
Nancy, d. Joseph, b. Oct. 28, 1726	LR4	374
Nancy, of Berlin, m. Elias **BROWN**, of Farmington, Oct.		
20, 1825, by Rev. Stephen Crosby	LR42	569
Nathaniel, m. Abigail **HOOKER**, Dec. 3, 1719	LR2	101
Nathaniel, s. Nathaniel & Abigail, b. June 24, 1728	LR4	395
Nathaniel, s. Nathaniel, d. June 24, 1728	LR4	396
Nathaniell, s. Nathaniell & Abigail, b. Mar. 17, 1734/5	LR5	306
Nathaniell, d. Oct. 3, 1736	LR5	500
Nathaniel, Ens., d. Oct. 24, 1758, in the 64th y. of his age	LR11	577
Nathaniel, m. Martha **NORTON**, Nov. 23, 1758	LR11	576
Nathaniel, s. Nathaniel, b. May 2, 1765	LR14	7
Noadiah, s. Nathaniell & Abigail, b. July 30, 1737	LR6	3
Noadiah, m. Lucy **HURLBUT**, Nov. 20, 1761	LR11	575
Noadiah, m. Clarissa **DICKENSON**, b. of Farmington,		
Sept. 12, 1826, by Rev. Bela Kellogg	LR42	567
Noah, m. Sarah **MILLER**, May 31, 1753	LR9	286
Noah, d. Mar. 21, 1777, in the 51st y. of his age	LR22	482
Norman, m. Adeline **HART**, b. of Farmington, Oct. 11,		
1826, by Rev. Harry Bushnell	LR42	567
Olive, d. Zachariah, b. June 24, 1759	LR11	583
Oliver, s. Matthew & Sarah, b. July 16, 1733	LR5	307
Oliver, s. Mathew, b. Aug. 10, 1774	LR17	435
Ozias, s. Eldad, b. Jan. 25, 1769	LR17	435
Percy, d. Noadiah, b. Aug. 11, 1774	LR21	544
Rebeckah, d. Hezekiah, b. Aug. 27, 1711	LR2	97
Rubin, m. Rhoda **PECK**, Dec. 27, 1759	LR11	575
Rubin, s. Elisha, b. May 31, 1763	LR11	584
Ruben, s. Elisha, b. May 13, 1763	LR15	J
Ruba, d. Joel, b. Feb. 23, 1786	LR22	465
Richard, of Hartford, m. Mary **JONES**, of Farmington,		
Dec. 23, 1849, by Rev. Noah Porter	LR47	126
Roger, s. Judah, b. May 10, 1745	LR7	1
Rosannah, m. Joseph **YEOMANS**, b. of Farmington, Jan.		
18, 1826, by Rev. Harvey Bushnell	LR42	569
Rose, d. Elias, b. Jan. 8, 1756	LR9	9
Roswell, s. Ruben, b. Aug. 22, 1768	LR15	F
Ruth, d. Thomas, Jr., s. of Capt. [ ], b. Aug. 14, 1713	LR2	99
Ruth, d. Josiah, b. May 13, 1717	LR2	81
Ruth, d. Josiah, d. May 20, 1717	LR2	62
Ruth, w. Capt. Thomas, d. Oct. 9, 1724	LR2	66
Ruth, d. Joseph, b. Dec. [ ], 1724	LR4	374
Ruth, d. Matthew & Sarah, b. Jan. 1, 1725/6	LR2	69
Ruth, d. Hezekiah, b. [ ], 1725	LR4	374

	Vol.	Page
HART, HEART, HARTT (cont.)		
Ruth, m. William **WADSWORTH**, Jr., b. of Farmington, May 15, 1740	LR6	27
Ruth, d. Thomas & Hannah, b. Mar. 1, 1744	LR8	5
Ruth, m. Barnabus **THOMSON**, June 16, 1748	LR7	46
Ruth, d. Judah, b. Jan. 19, 1748/9	LR7	L
Ruth, d. Solomon, b. Dec. 31, 1750	LR8	5
Ruth, d. Thomas, b. Nov. 10, 1759	LR14	7
Ruth, m. Dan **HILLS**, June 2, 1768	LR15	A
Sabree, d. Ambros, b. Sept. 11, 1772	LR17	435
Salmon, s. Nathaniel, b. July 9, 1763	LR14	7
Salmon, s. Judah, Jr., b. May 20, 1775	LR21	544
Samuel, s. Stephen, Jr., b. Dec. 2, 1721	LR2	102
Samuel, m. Mary **HOOKER**, b. of Ffarmington, Dec. 25, 1723	LR2	60
Samuel, s. Thomas, m. Elizabeth **THOMSON**, Feb. 25, 1729/30	LR5	13
Samuel, s. Lieut. Samuel & Mary, b. Jan. 20, 1737/8	LR6	3
Samuel, s. Samuel (s. of Thomas), b. Dec. 14, 1741; d. Jan. 15, 1741/2	LR6	2
Samuel, s. Stephen, m. Lydia **GRIDLEY**, b. of Farmington, Aug. [ ], 1745	LR7	35
Samuel, s. Rubin, b. Aug. 31, 1761	LR11	582
Sarah, d. Stephen, b. Oct. 16, 1692	LR2	91
Sarah, m. Ebenezer **STEEL**, Feb. 15, 1704/5	LR2	145
Sarah, d. Dr. John, b. June 19, 1719	LR2	102
Sarah, d. Nathaniel, b. Nov. 13, 1720	LR2	102
Sarah, d. Stephen, m. Ephraim **SMITH**, Jr., Jan. 19, 1720/1	LR2	101
Sarah, d. Josiah & Sarah, b. Apr. 17, 1723	LR2	87
Sarah, d. Hawkins, Jr., b. May 1, 1733	LR5	307
Sarah, d. Hawkins, Jr., b. Dec. 26, 1734 (Conflicts with birth of "Susannah")	LR5	307
Sarah, w. Capt. Josiah, d. July 1, 1737	LR6	10
Sarah, d. Timothy & Elizabeth, b. Mar. 25, 1739	LR6	3
Sarah, d. Timothy, d. Apr. 15, 1739	LR6	10
Sarah, d. Dea. Jno, m. Stephen **ROOT**, June 19, 1740	LR6	27
Sarah, d. Joseph, b. Oct. 3, 1741	LR6	3
Sarah, d. Joseph, d. Oct. 25, 1741	LR6	10
Sarah, d. Daniel, b. May 18, 1742	LR6	3
Sarah, d. Hawkins, b. Nov. 27, 1742	LR6	3
Sarah, d. Hawkins, d. Dec. 1, 1742	LR6	305
Sarah, d. Jeames, b. July 15, 1743	LR6	3
Sarah, of Farmington, m. Dr. Jonathan **MARSH**, of Norwich, Nov. 5, 1747	LR7	46
Sarah, m. Elijah **COWLES**, July 11, 1750	LR7	46
Sarah, w. Thomas, Jr., d. Nov. 16, 1750	LR7	540
Sarah, d. Elisha, b. Feb. 25, 1754	LR9	9
Sarah, d. Elisha, b. June 3, 1754	LR9	9
Sarah, d. Matthew, b. Sept. 19, 1766	LR14	7
Sarah, d. Reuben, b. Oct. 18, 1766	LR14	7
Sarah, d. Elisha, b. Sept. 6, 1768	LR15	J
Sarah, d .Judah, Jr., b. Nov. 7, 1770	LR21	544

	Vol.	Page
HART, HEART, HARTT (cont.)		
Sarah, w. Noah, d. Oct. 18, 1776, in the 51st y. of her age	LR22	482
Sarah, d. Joel, b. Feb. 13, 1782	LR22	465
Sarah, of Farmington, m. Timothy **SMITH**, of New		
Haven, June 1, 1850, by William Wright	LR47	127
Selah, s. Nathaniel & Abigail, b. May 23, 1732	LR5	307
Selah, m. Mary **COLE**, Mar. 4, 1756	LR9	286
Selah, s. Noah, b. July 1, 1760	LR11	582
Selah, s. Nathaniel, b. Jan. 30, 1767	LR14	7
Senie, d. Gad, b. Feb. 4, 1784	LR22	465
Seth, s. Noah, b. May 23, 1756	LR11	583
Seth, s. Nathaniel, b. Aug. 19, 1761	LR11	582
Seth, s. Matthew, b. June 25, 1763	LR11	584
Seth, s. Thomas, b. Apr. 19, 1765	LR15	F
Sidney, Jr., m. Lydia W. **GRISWOLD**, Sept. 3, 1839, by		
Rev. Ezra S. Cook. Witnesses William H. Grimes,		
Sidney Hart	LR47	100
Simeon, s. Capt. Thomas & Anne, b. Dec. 28, 1735	LR5	645
Simeon, m. Sarah **HOPER**, Sept. 14, 1755	LR11	575
Simeon, Jr., m. Abigail M. **ANDRUS**, Dec. 9, 1824, by		
Rev. Noah Porter	LR42	568
Solomon, s. Dr.* John, b. Oct. 1, 1724 *(Perhaps		
"Deacon")	LR2	46
Solomon, m. Experience **COLE**, Mar. 8, 1749/50	LR7	46
Stephen, s. John, bp. July 19, 1657	LR2	328
Stephen, s. Stephen, m. Sarah **COWLES**, b. of		
Ffarmington, Dec. 18, 1689	LR2	123
Stephen, s. Thomas, b. July 30, 1693	LR2	91
Stephen, s. Stephen, b. Mar. 7, 1697/8	LR2	91
Stephen, s. Thomas, m. [E]unice **MUNSON**, Dec. 29,		
1720	LR2	101
Stephen, Jr., s. Stephen, d. May 9, 1725	LR2	66
Stephen, s. Stephen (s. Thomas), b. July 21, 1725	LR2	65
Stephen, s. Timothy & Elizabeth, b. Aug. 11, 1729	LR5	4
Stephen, s. Sergt. Stephen, d. Aug. 18, 1733	LR5	50
Stephen, s. Timothy, d. Nov. 9, 1740	LR6	10
Stephen, s. Daniel, b Dec. 8, 1744	LR7	1
Stephen, Jr., m. Abigail **GRIDLEY**, Sept. 13, 1750	LR7	46
Stephen, 3rd., m. Rhodah [ ], Oct. 6, 1767	LR15	N
Stephen, s. Stephen, Jr., b. Oct. 21, 1775	LR21	544
Stephen Hurlbut, s. Noadiah, b. Sept. 20, 1765; d. Sept.		
15, 1766	LR21	544
Stephen, Hurlburt, s. Noadiah, d. Sept. 15, 1766	LR21	558-9
Stephen Hurlbut, 2nd, s. Noadiah, b. Nov. 1, 1767	LR21	544
Susannah, d. Hawkins, Jr., b. Dec. 31, 1734, (Conflicts		
with birth of "Sarah")	LR5	307
Susanah, w. Hawkins, d. Feb. 23, 1736/7	LR6	10
Susanah, d. Hawkins, d. Dec. 3, 1742	LR6	305
Susannah, d. Hawkins, b. Jan. 12, 1747/8	LR7	1
Susannah, d. William, d. Dec. 13, 1748/9	LR7	36
Susannah, d. Medad, b. June 12, 1756	LR11	583
Susanah, d. Samuel (s. Stephen), b. Oct. 24, [ ]	LR7	J
Susanah, d. William b. Nov. 30, [ ]	LR7	J

	Vol.	Page
HART, HEART, HARTT (cont.)		
Sibil, d. Abross, b. Oct. 14, 1766	LR14	7
Sybel, m. Abel **THOMSON**, Nov. 14, 1793; d. May 2, 1822	LR22	476
Thankfull, d. Nathaniel, b. July 4, 1728 (Perhaps "1725")	LR2	65
Thankfull, m. Charles **BROWNSON**, Nov, 5, 1747	LR7	46
Thankfull, m. Charles **BRONSON**, Nov. 5, 1747	LR8	10
Thankfull, m. Charles **BROWNSON**, Nov. 5, 1747	LR8	10
Thankfull, w. James, d. Oct. 6, 1772, in the 65th y. of her age	LR17	444
Thomas, s. Stephen, m. Elizabeth **JUDD**, b. of Ffarmington, Dec. 19, 1689	LR2	123
Thomas, s. Thomas, b. June 5, 1692	LR2	91
Thomas, 2nd, s. Thomas, b. Nov. 3, 1695	LR2	91
Thomas, s. Capt. [ ], m. Mary **THOMSON**, Dec. 17, 1702	LR1	4
Thomas, s. Josiah, b. Nov, 7, 1714	LR2	95
Thomas, s. Sergt. Thomas, m. Anna **STANLEY**, Mar. 16, 1720/1	LR2	101
Thomas, Capt., d. Aug. 27, 1726	LR2	66
Thomas, Sergt., d. Mar. 23, 1727/8	LR4	396
Thomas, s. Elijah, b. Jan. 17, 1737	LR6	3
Thomas, m. Hanah **COE**, Mar. 23, 1743	LR8	10
Thomas, s. Thomas, b. Nov. 10, 1749	LR8	5
Thomas, Jr., m. Sarah **THOMAS**, Aug. 21, 1750	LR7	35
Thomas, Jr., d. Oct. 21, 1754	LR9	495
Thomas, s. Ebenezer, b. Dec. 1, 1754	LR9	9
Thomas, s. Thomas, b. Jan. 4, 1755	LR11	583
Thomas, m. Mahitabel **BURD**, Feb. 2, 1758	LR11	594
Timothy, s. Stephen, b. Aug. 31, 1705	LR2	91
Timothy, m. Elizabeth **COWLES**, b. of Ffarmington, Oct. 25, 1728	LR4	423
Timothy, s. Timothy, b. Sept. 1, 1733	LR5	306
Timothy, Sergt., d. Oct. 3, 1748, ae 44	LR7	36
Timothy, d. May 23, 1760	LR11	574
Timothy, s. Elisha, b. Apr. 7, 1761	LR11	583
Timothy, s. Reuben, b. July 15, 1770	LR17	434
Titus, s. Solomon, b .Jan. 24, 1754	LR9	9
Velina Heart, m. Huldah **GREEN**, Dec. 3, 1782	LR22	480
William, s. Thomas, b. Aug. 20, 1710	LR2	91
William, m. Elizabeth **WOODRUFF**, b. of Farmington, Feb. 2, 1737/8	LR6	27
William, s. William, b. Oct. 11, 174[ ]	LR7	1
William, m. Abigail [ ], Oct. 18, 1768	LR15	A
Zachariah, s. Hezekiah, b. Jan. 5, 1733/4	LR5	645
Zachariah, m. Abigail **BECKLEY**, Mar. [ ], 1758	LR11	576
Zachariah, s. Zachariah, b. Sept. 11, 1761	LR14	7
Zachariah, s. Zachariah, d. Jan. 8, 1762	LR14	3
Zachariah, 2nd, s. Zachariah, b. May 26, 1764	LR14	7
Zachariah, s. Zachariah, d. Nov. 17, 1764	LR14	3
Zenas, s. David, b. Aug. 30, 1767	LR15	F

	Vol.	Page
HART, HEART, HARTT (cont.)		
-----, s. Hezekiah, [s.] Isaac, b. [ ], 1729 (Entry		
illegible.)	LR4	396
-----ea, d. Joseph, b. May 17, 1750	LR7	K
HATCH, Mary D., m. Alpheas **PORTER**, b. of Farmington,		
Nov. 13, 1850, by Rev. Noah Porter	LR47	129
HATTEN, Hannah, d. Thomas, b. Mar. 31, 1755	LR9	6
HAWKENS, Sary, d. Antony, bp. June [ ], 1657	LR2	328
HAWLEY, Abel, s. Ens. Joseph, b. Oct. 20, 1716	LR2	81
Abel, m. Mary **GRIDLEY**, Aug. 18, 1742	LR6	305
Abel, s. Abel, b. Oct. 5, 1750	LR8	5
Abel, m. Abigail **ROYCE**, Nov. 13, 1754	LR9	286
Abell, m. Elizabeth **PECK**, Dec. 16, 1772	LR17	442
Abigail, d. Timothy, b. Feb. 17, 1732/3	LR5	307
Abigail, d. Timothy, d. Sept. 15, 1741	LR6	10
Abigaile, d. Timothy, b. Nov. 15, 1743	LR6	3
Almira, d. Joseph, b. Dec. 29, 1781	LR22	465
Amon, s. Gad, b. July 12, 1785	LR22	465
Amon, [s. Gad & Lydia], b. July 12, 1785	LR47	W-Y
Amon, b. [ ]; m. Flora **THOMPSON**, Oct. 27,		
1814	LR47	W-Y
Asa, s. Ebenezer, b. Aug. 28, 1743	LR6	3
Asa, d. July 3, 1768, in the 26th y. of his age	LR15	M
Asa, s. Ebenezer, b. Apr. 19, 1776	LR21	544
Benjamin, s. Ebenezer, b. June 26, 1745	LR6	3
Benjamin, s. Benjamin, decd., b. Mar. 26, 1770	LR17	434
Benjamin, d. Jan. 13, 1771	LR17	444
Benjamin, m. Lidia **ORVIS**, June 21, 1773	LR17	G
Benjamin, s. Ebenezer, b. May 17, 1779	LR22	465
Calista, of Farmington, m. Joel **CATLIN**, of Augusta,		
Ga., Aug. 31, 1820, by Ludovicus Robbins, V.D.M.	LR40	570
Charles, s. Joseph, Jr., b. Jan. 4, 1742	LR6	3
Charles, s. Joseph, Jr., d. May 4, 1742	LR6	305
Charles A., [s. Amon & Flora], b. Apr. 24, 1826; d.		
[ ], 1844	LR47	W-Y
Chancey, s. Gad, b. Oct. 30, 1779	LR21	544
Chauncey, [s. Gad & Lydia], b. Oct. 30, 1779	LR47	W-Y
David, s. Jos., Jr., b. July 27, 1737	LR6	3
Deborah, d. Timothy, b. Nov. 3, 1746	LR7	1
Desire (?), see under Lesiah		
Ebenezer, s. Joseph, b. Dec. 10, 1713	LR2	99
Ebenezer, of Farmington, m. Mary **HART**, of		
Wallingford, July 1, 1741	LR6	304
Ebenezer, twin with Mary, s. Ebenezer, b. Feb. 11, 1746/7	LR6	3
Ebenezer, m. Keziah **ROOT**, Oct. 19, 1757	LR11	575
Ebenezer, d. Mar. 3, 1769 in the 56th y. of his age	LR15	M
Ebenezer, m. Mahetebel **RICH**, Nov. 29, 1769	LR15	A
Ebenezer **ROYCE**, s. Abel, b. Apr. 11, 1760	LR11	583
Edward N., [s. Joseph & Hannah], b. June 4, 1824	LR47	W-Y
Elidia, d. Samuell, d. Jan. 13, 1753	LR8	12
Elidia, d. Samuel, b. Mar. 22, 1755	LR11	583
Elijah, twin with Elisata, s. Samuel, b. Oct. 22, 1748	LR7	L
Elisata, twin with Elijah, s. Samuel, b. Oct. 22, 1748	LR7	L

	Vol.	Page

HAWLEY (cont.)

	Vol.	Page
Elisha, s. Abel, b. Mar. 26, 1744	LR8	5
Elizabeth, m. John **NEWEL**, b. of Ffarmington, Sept. 24, 1719	LR2	101
Elizabeth, d. Joseph, Jr., b. May 2, 1736	LR6	3
Elizabeth, d. Joseph, Jr., d. Jan. 28, 1739/40	LR6	10
Elizabeth, d. Samuell, b. Jan. 10, 1741/2; d. [ ] 21, 1741/2	LR6	3
Elizabeth, d. Samuell, b. June 20, 1743	LR6	3
Elizabeth, d. Abell, b. May 9, 1774	LR17	435
Elizabeth W., [d. Joseph & Hannah], b. Jan. 11, 1817	LR47	W-Y
Emily C., [d. Joseph & Hannah], b. May 29, 1818	LR47	W-Y
Ester, d. Ebenezer, b. Sept. 14, 1748	LR6	3
Esther, d. Ebenezer, b. May 10, 1772	LR17	434
Esther, m. George **HART**, b. of Farmington, Apr. 3, 1827, by Rev. Noah Porter	LR42	565
Ezekiel, s. Abel, b. Oct. 14, 1752	LR8	5
Gad, b. Sept. 9, 1746, O.S., m. Lydia **GILLET**, Feb. 8, 1776	LR47	W-Y
Gad, m. Lydia **GILLET**, Feb. 8, 1776	LR21	557
George Washington, s. Rev. Rufus, b. Jan. 26, 1777	LR21	544
Hannah, d. Joseph, b. Aug. 25, 1707	LR1	2
Harriet S., [d. Amon & Flora], b. Apr. 11, 1824	LR47	W-Y
Harriet S., of Farmington, m Charles **RAMSEY**, of Springfield, Mass., Apr. 20, 1846, by Rev. Noah Porter	LR47	117
Henry D., [s. Amon & Flora], b. May 25, 1828	LR47	W-Y
Jame[s], s. Ebenezer & Keziah, b. Oct. 8, 1758 (In Arnold Copy "sic" is written after "Keziah")	LR11	583
Jehiel, s. Joseph, b. Feb. 13, 1711/12	LR2	97
Jesse, s. Timothy, b. June 12, 1738	LR6	3
Jesse Dudley, s. Rev. Rufus, b. Dec. 7, 1774	LR21	544
John, s. Samuel, b. Oct. 20, 1737	LR6	3
Joseph, his s. [ ], b. Mar. 25, 1702	LR1	2
Joseph, s. Joseph, 2nd, b. July 7, 1732	LR5	307
Joseph, Capt., d. Nov. 20, 1753	LR8	12
Joseph, d. Aug. 8, 1779, in the 78th y. of his age	LR22	482
Joseph, m. Elizabeth **WEBSTER**, Jan. 21, 1781	LR22	480
Joseph, s. Joseph, b. Oct. 24, 1785	LR22	465
Joseph, b. Oct. 24, 1785; m. Hannah **ROOT**, Feb. 16, 1816	LR47	W-Y
Lesiah,* d. Abel, b. Apr. 23, 1748 *("Desire"?)	LR8	5
Levi, s. Joseph, b. Oct. 15, 1783	LR22	465
Lucinda, d. Ebenezer, b. Dec. 15, 1770	LR17	434
Lucy A., m. Charles **RICHARDS**, b. of Farmington, Mar. 1, 1849, by Rev. D. M. Seward, of West Hartford	LR47	125
Lucy Ann, [d. Amon & Flora], b. Aug. 23, 1823	LR47	W-Y
Lydia, d. Samuell, b. Sept. 15, 1739	LR6	3
Mariette L., [d. Amon & Flora], b. Feb. 23, 1817; d. Feb. 4, 1819	LR47	W-Y
Martha, m. Charles **RICHARDS**, b. of Farmington, Dec. 2, 1840, by Rev. Noah Porter	LR47	103
Mary, d. Joseph, Jr., b. Feb. 8, 1730/1	LR5	4

	Vol.	Page
HAWLEY (cont.)		
Mary, twin with Ebenezer, d. Ebenezer, b. Feb. 11, 1746/7	LR6	3
Mary, w. Abel, d. Sept. 4, 1753, in the 32nd y. of her age	LR8	12
Mary, d. Abel, b. Aug. [ ], 1755	LR9	9
Mary, m. Heman **WATSON**, Feb. 14, 1770	LR17	G
Mary Ann, [d. Amon & Flora], b. Jan. 23, 1819; d. Feb. 19, 1819	LR47	W-Y
Mary Hart, d. Ebenezer, b. Mar. 11, 1774	LR17	435
Naomi, m. Roger S. **NEWELL**, b. of Farmington, Aug. 1, 1821, by Rev. Jonathan Cone	LR40	571
Orastus Kent, s. Rev. Rufus, b. Sept. 16, 1778	LR21	544
Ruben, s. Stephen, b. July 4, 1743	LR7	544
Rhoda, d. Samuel, b. July 29, 1751	LR8	5
Romanta, m. Caroline **DEMING**, b. of Farmington, May 26, 1824, by Rev. Harry Bushnell	LR42	568
Roxana, d. Gad, b. Oct. 29, 1776	LR21	544
Roxana, [d. Gad & Lydia], b. Oct. 29, 1777; d. Oct. 23, 1807	LR47	W-Y
Ruffus, s. Timothy & Rachel, b. Feb. 21, 1741	LR6	3
Rufus, Rev., m. Deborah **KENT**, Sept. 25, 1770	LR17	443
Rufus Forward, s. Rev. Rufus, b. Apr. 27, 1773	LR17	435
Ruth, d. Abel, b. Mar. 12, 1747	LR8	5
Samuel, s. Joseph, b. Aug. 29, 1709	LR2	109
Samuel, m. Elizabeth **GRIDLEY**, b. of Farmington, Dec. 7, 1736	LR6	27
Samuel, s. Samuel, b. Dec. 15, 1745	LR7	1
Samuel C., [s. Joseph & Hannah], b. Mar. 17, 1820	LR47	W-Y
Sarah, w. Timothy, d. Mar. 4, 1732/3	LR5	50
Sarah, d. Ebenezer, b. May 29, 1742	LR6	3
Selah, d. Gad, b. Feb. 20, 1781	LR21	544
Thomas, s. Timothy, b. July 27, 1731	LR5	4
Timothy, s. Joseph, b. Nov. 25, 1704	LR1	2
Timothy, m. Sarah **THOMSON**, b. of Farmington, Oct. 15, 1730	LR5	13
Timothy, of Farmington, m. Rachel **SHERWOOD**, of Simsbury, Jan. 5, 1736/7	LR6	27
Timothy Rugells, s. Rev. Rufus, b. June 29, 1771	LR17	435
Ursula, [d. Gad & Lydia], b. Feb. 20, 1781; d. Aug. 19, 1803	LR47	W-Y
[HAYDEN], [see under **HAYTON**]		
HAYES, Maudlin, wid., of Farmington, m. Dennis **HOOGINS**, formerly of Ireland, May 3, 1716	LR2	94
HAYTON, Charles, m. Roseanah **MANGER**, Mar. [ ], 1783	LR22	480
Polly, d. Charles, b. Dec. 26, 1783	LR22	465
HAZARD, Mary A., m. Zopher **BEACH**, Aug. 18, 1845, by Rev. John R. Keep	LR47	114
HEARD, [see under **HURD**]		
HECOX, Elizabeth, m. John **NORTON**, s. Thom[a]s, Dec. 9, 1724	LR2	52
HEFFORD, HEAFORD, HEAFORT, Ire, s. Joseph, b. Nov. 10, 1762	LR11	584
John, d. Oct. 16, 1742	LR7	36

	Vol.	Page
HEFFORD, HEAFORD, HEAFORT (cont.)		
John, s. John, decd., b. Apr. 17, 1743	LR7	J
Joseph, m. Elidia **BARTHOLOMEW**, Apr. 29, 1761	LR11	592
HENDRICK, Clarissa, m. John **BROWN**, b. of Farmington,		
May 23, 1822, by Noah Porter, V.D.M.	LR40	571
Henery, s. William, b. Aug. 9, 1770	LR17	434
Irene, of Canton, m. David **WILLIAMS**, of Granby, Jan.		
3, 1826, by Rev. Noah Porter	LR42	569
Joel, s. William, decd., b. Oct. 19, 1772	LR17	435
William, s. William, b. Feb. 26, 1775	LR17	435
William, d. Mar. 14, 1775	LR17	445
HENRY, HENERY, Phebe, d. Peter, negro, b. Mar. 24, 1743/4	LR8	5
Phebe, m. Ashbel [ ], negro, Mar. 1, 1750/1	LR7	35
HENSDEL, [see under **HINSDALE**]		
HESSINGTON, [see under **HOISINGTON**]		
HIBBARD, Mary, of Middletown, m. Isaac **LEE**, of		
Farmington, Dec. 8, 1713	LR5	13
[HIGBY], HIGHBY, m. Samuel **SMITH**, June 3, 1752	LR9	286
HIGGARSON, [see also **HIGGINSON**], Isaac, s. Marah		
POTTERS, b. June 20, 1768	LR15	F
[HIGGINSON], HIGINSON, [see also **HIGGARSON**],		
Mary, m. Abner **JOLEET**, b. of Farmington, Sept.		
6, 1710	LR2	123
HILLS, HILL, Abigail, d. Joseph, b. July 19, 1725	LR5	4
Abigail, wid. Joseph, d. Sept. 23, 1751	LR8	11
Abigail, m. Moses **PERSONS**, Mar. 23, 1758	LR11	576
Abraham, s. Joseph, b. Mar. 28, 1711	LR5	4
Abram, of Farmington, m. Elizabeth **HOGKIS**, of		
Wallingford, July 3, 1734	LR6	27
Abram, s. Abram, b. Feb. 5, 1745/6	LR7	1
Amelia Ann., m. James W. **COWLES**, b. of Farmington,		
Oct. 9, 1838, by Rev. S. H. Clark	LR47	97
Asahel, s. Moses, b. Mar. [ ]	LR7	J
Asahel, s. Moses, d. Sept. 18, 1751	LR8	11
Azell, m. Huldah **HUNGERFORD**, May 16, 1776	LR21	557
Belinda, m. Johnson **GORDON**, Jan. 13, 1824, by Rev.		
Noah Porter	LR42	568
Charlotte, of Farmington, m. Jeremiah **NEAL**, of		
Southington, Oct. 11, 1827, by Rev. Irenus Atkins	LR42	565
Dan, m. Hannah **MATTHEWS**, Dec. 20, 1757	LR11	575
Dan, m. Ruth **HART**, June 2, 1768	LR15	A
David, s. Joseph, b. Sept. 15, 1716	LR5	4
Diademe, d .Luke, b. Mar. 28, 1763	LR14	7
Ebenezer, s. Luck, b. Mar. about 20, 1656	LR2	328
Eliza, of Farmington, m. Amon **WOODRUFF**, of		
Southington, Feb. 9, 1837, by Rev. Noah Porter	LR47	95
Elizabeth, d. Abraham, b. Nov. 3, 1747	LR7	E
Erastus, s. Luke, b. Nov. 11, 1760	LR11	582
Esther, d. Gideon, b. Feb. 5, 1775	LR21	544
Francis, of Farmington, m. Jared H. **TRASK**, of Camden,		
N.Y., Sept. 22, 1829, by Rev. Noah Porter	LR42	562
Franklin, m. Huldah C. **PARMELEE**, b. of Farmington,		
June 2, 1840, by Rev. Noah Porter	LR47	102

	Vol.	Page
HILLS, HILL (cont.)		
Gaius, s. Dan, b. Apr. 24, 1759	LR11	583
Gideon, s. Joseph, b. June 4, 1714	LR5	4
Gideon, m. Esther **CURTIS**, Dec. 7, 1769	LR21	557
Gideon, s. [Abraham], b. Feb. 18, [ ]	LR7	J
Hannah, w. Dan, d. Feb. 13, 1766	LR14	3
Harriet, m. James **HAMLIN**, Oct. 16, 1824, by Rev.		
Noah Porter	LR42	568
Henry, m. Celestia **LEE**, b. of Farmington, Mar. 26,		
1833, by Rev. Noah Porter	LR42	558
Higason, m. Lina **MILLERS**, Mar. 10, 1769	LR15	N
Huldah, of Plainville, m. William **CHALKER**, of		
Hartford, Oct. 29, 1848, by William Wright	LR47	123
James, s. Joseph, b. Jan. 2, 1712/13	LR5	4
Jennette E., of Farmington, m. Emner S. **McINTIRE**, of		
Bristol, Feb. 3, 1850, by William Wright	LR47	127
Jesse, m. Sophia **ANDRUS**, b. of Farmington, Mar. 27,		
1822, by Noah Porter, V.D.M.	LR40	571
John, m. Mary A. **WHITMAN**, Aug. 5, 1846, by Noah		
Porter	LR47	117
John W., of East Hartford, m. Fidelia J. **ROWLEY**, of		
Farmington, Aug. 6, 1837, by Rev. S. H. Clark	LR47	95
Jonathan, s. Joseph, b. Feb. 19, 1720/1	LR5	4
Joseph, s. Joseph, b. Jan. 16, 1708/9	LR5	4
Joseph, d. Apr. 29, 1751	LR8	11
Joseph, s. Higenson, b. Jan. 19, 1770	LR15	J
Joseph, d. Aug. 19, 1771	LR17	444
Josiah, s. Abraham, b. Sept. 15, 1750	LR11	583
Julia, of Farmington, m. Leonard A. **WHEELER**, of		
Spencer of Tioga Cty., N.Y., June 30, 1842, by Rev.		
C. D. Cowles	LR47	107
Lucien W., m. Mrs. Eunice **WEBSTER**, b. of		
Farmington, May 1, 1842, by Rev. Aaron S. Hill	LR47	107
Lusina, d. Luke, b. July 25, 1765	LR14	7
Mary Ann, of Farmington, m. Henry **BATES**, of		
Southington, Nov. 2, 1847, by Rev. Noah Porter	LR47	121
Mary Ann, m. Samuel D. **HILLS**, b. of Farmington,		
[, 1838 (?)], by Rev. S. H. Clark	LR47	98
Mercy, d. Abram, b. Apr. 7, 1736	LR6	3
Mercy, m. John **PERSONS**, Jr., Oct. 27, 1757	LR11	576
Moses, s. Joseph, b. June 20, 1723	LR5	4
Moses, m. Mercy **LANGTON**, Jan. 6, 1747/8	LR7	35
Polle, d. Gideon, b. Sept 13, 1776	LR21	544
Rachel, of Farmington, m. Hopkins **STEVERY**, of		
Waterbury, Apr. 11, 1826, by Rev. Noah Porter	LR42	569
Reuben L., m. Sarah A. **BURROWS**, b. of Farmington,		
Jan. 24, 1839, by Rev. Noah Porter	LR47	99
Rhoda, d. Abraham, b. Feb. 16, 1757	LR11	583
Ruth, d. Gideon, b. Oct. 3, 1773	LR21	544
Sabrinah, d. Gideon, b. Oct. 25, 1770	LR21	544
Salmon, s. Moses, b. Dec. 5, 1750	LR8	5
Salmon, s. Moses, d. Sept. 15, 1751	LR8	11

	Vol.	Page

HILLS, HILL (cont.)

Samuel D., m. Mary Ann **HILLS**, b. of Farmington,
[, 1838 (?)], by Rev. S. H. Clark — LR47 — 98

Sarah, d. Abraham, b. May 3, 1739 — LR7 — J

Sarah D., m. Thomas **BISHOP**, Sept. 12, 1839, by Elisha
C. Jones — LR47 — 101

Sheldon, m. Nancy E. **CLANO**, b. of Farmington, Aug. 5,
1849, by William Wright — LR47 — 127

Solomon, s. Higason, b. June 28, 1772 — LR17 — 434

William, s. Joseph, b. Jan. 20, 1726/7 — LR5 — 4

William, of Farmington, m. Charlotte **PURDY**, of
Plymouth, Feb. 25, 1833, by Rev. Noah Porter — LR42 — 558

HINMAN, Diana, of Farmington, m. Hector **BARBER**, of
Harwinton, May 27, 1850, by Rev. Noah Porter — LR47 — 129

Eleanor, of Bristol, m. Lorenzo **SMITH**, of Farmington,
Apr. 7, 1830, by Rev. Noah Porter — LR42 — 561

Eunice, of Farmington, m. Charles **PECK**, of Burlington,
Nov. 24, 1825, by Rev. Noah Porter — LR42 — 569

Mary Ann, of Farmington, m. William C. **SCOVILLE**, of
Harwinton, Jan. 1, 1840, by Rev. Noah Porter — LR47 — 102

HINSDALE, HENSDEL, Charles, m. Elizabeth C.
STEDMAN, b. of Hartford, Nov. 2, 1845, by Rev.
S. H. Clark — LR47 — 115

Elida, m. Thomas **ROOT**, Jr., Apr. 3, 1755 — LR8 — 10

HITCHCOCK, HITCHCOX, Caleb, s. Samuel & Tamer, b.
May 14, 1760 — LR11 — 584

Catharine, m. Ezekiel **THOMSON**, Sept. 2, 1746 — LR7 — 35

Elida, m .James **BECKWITH**, 3rd, May 28, 1752 — LR8 — 10

Elizabeth, d. Samuel & Tamer, b. Dec. 29, 1763 — LR11 — 584

Hannah, d. David, b. Aug. 4, 1768 — LR15 — F

Harriet M., m. Harry **TOLLES**, b. of Southington, Aug.
13, 1844, by Rev. William Wright — LR47 — 113

Lois, m. Samuell **DUTTON**, Apr. 25, 1753 — LR8 — 10

Phebee, d. David, b. Nov. 27, 1766 — LR15 — F

Samuell, s. Samuell & Tamer, b. Feb. 27, 1757 — LR11 — 583

**HOISINGTON, HARSINGTON, HESSINGTON,
HORSINGTON, HOSINGTON**, Asahel, s. John & Sarah, b.
Nov. 30, 1738 — LR6 — 3

Asahel, s. John, d. Feb. 6, 1745 — LR7 — 36

Asahel 2nd, s. John, b. Dec. 3, 1749/50 [sic] — LR7 — K

Ebenezer, m. Elizabeth **MILLER**, July 5, 1751 — LR7 — 46

Ebenezer, s. Ebenezer, b. Sept. 23, 1752 — LR8 — 5

Elias, s. Ebenezer, b. Jan. 10, 1758 — LR11 — 583

Elisha, s. John, b. Nov. 8, 1719 — LR5 — 645

Elish[a], m. Hannah **BARR**, Dec. 22, 1742 — LR6 — 305

Elizabeth, d. John, b. June 20, 1717 — LR5 — 645

Elizabeth, d. May 21, 1740 — LR6 — 10

Elizabeth, d. James, b. Aug. 14, 1764 — LR14 — 7

Hannah, d. Ebenezer, b. Sept. 19, 1759 — LR11 — 583

James, s. John, b. Dec. 10, 1721 — LR5 — 645

James, m. Elizabeth **RICHARDS**, Dec. 24, 1750 — LR7 — 46

James, s. James, b. Jan. 2, 1757 — LR11 — 583

Joab, s. John, b. Sept. 19, 1736 — LR6 — 3

	Vol.	Page
HOISINGTON, HARSINGTON, HESSINGTON,		
HORSINGTON, HOSINGTON (cont.)		
Job, s. James, b. Aug. 10, 1762	LR11	584
John, s. John, b. Nov. 5, 1713	LR5	645
John, of Farmington, m. Sarah **TEMPLER**, of		
Wallingford, Nov. 3, 1735	LR5	539
Lucy, d. James, b. June 9, 1760	LR11	583
Lidia, d. James, b. Sept. 27, 1769	LR15	D
Nathaniell, s. John, b. Feb. 18, 1726/7	LR5	645
Noah, d. Nov. 20, 1728	LR5	50
Rhoda, d. John, b. Dec. 19, 1741	LR6	3
Rhoda, d. Ebenezer, b. Dec. 12, 1755	LR11	583
Rhoda, d. Ebenezer, b. Jan. 7, 1756	LR9	9
Samuel, s. Hannah Norton, b. Mar. 6, 1775	LR22	465
Samuel, s. Hannah Norton, d. Sept. 17, 1776, in the 2nd y.		
of his age	LR22	482
Sarah, d. John, b. Apr. 6, 1715	LR5	645
Sary, m. George **WELLTON**, Nov. 23, 1738	LR6	305
Sarah, w. John, d. Dec. 11, 1749/50	LR7	540
Sarah, d. James, b. Apr. 18, 1752	LR8	5
Sibel, d. John, [ ] [ ], 1745	LR7	1
Thankfull, d. John, b. Sept. 11, 1724	LR5	645
[HOLCOMB], HOLCOM, Margaret, of Simsbury, m.		
Nathaniel **NORTH**, June 10, 1708	LR2	94
Thankfull, m. Joseph **BARNES**, Jr., b. of Ffarmington,		
May 12, 1720	LR2	60
HOLLEY, Bettey, d. John, b. Oct. 28, 1786	LR22	465
HOLLISTER, HOLESTER, HOLISTER, Abel, s. Ephraim		
& Anne, b. Feb. 10, 1761	LR11	584
Abigail, m. Ebenezer **SEAYMOR**, Dec. 29, 1709	LR2	123
Anne, d. Stephen, b. June 28, 1758	LR11	583
Elijah, m. Mehetabel **JUDD**, Oct. 1, 1752	LR8	10
Elijah, had s. [ ], b. Feb. 2, 1756	LR11	583
Elisha, s. Samuell, b. Feb. 25, 1734/5	LR5	307
Ephraim, m. Rachel **PORTTER**, May 3, 1746	LR7	35
Ephraim, s. Ephraim, b. Oct. 23, 1748	LR8	5
Esther, d. Gershom, b. May 26, 1733	LR5	307
Esther, m. Elisha **BOOTH**, Dec. 6, 1754	LR11	576
[E]unice, of Weathersfield, m. Jonathan **SEAMOR**, of		
Ffarmington, Dec. 23, 1714	LR2	94
Gershom, s. Gershom, b. Apr. 6, 1742	LR6	3
Gershom, s. Samuel, b. May 26, 1748	LR6	3
Gideon, s. Gershom, b. [ ]	LR7	1
Joseph, of Farmington, m. Levicy **WATERS**, of Hartford,		
July 3, 1820, by Noah Porter, V.D.M.	LR40	570
Lotte, d. Stephen, b. June 21, 1766	LR17	434
Mary, d. Samuel, b. Sept. 27, 1736	LR6	3
Rhoda, d. Stephen, b. May 10, 1756	LR11	583
Rhoda, d. Ephraim & Anne, b. May 6, 1764	LR11	584
Samuel, s. Samuell, b. May 21, 1738	LR6	3
Samuel, s. Ephraim, b. Oct. 30, 1746	LR8	5
Sarah, of Glastonbury, m. Benjamin **JUDD**, Jr., of		
Ffarmington, Nov. 9, 1727	LR4	423

	Vol.	Page
HOLLISTER, HOLESTER, HOLISTER (cont.)		
Sarah, of Glastonbury, m. Elisha **BROWNSON**, of		
Farmington, Sept. 16, 1737	LR6	27
Stephen, s. Gershom, b. Aug. 6, 1729	LR5	4
Stephen, had d. [ ], b. July 5, 1754	LR9	9
Stephen, s. Stephen, b. Jan. 1, 1769	LR17	434
Thomas, s. Gideon, b. May 5, 1726	LR4	382
Thomas, m. Anna **HART**, Oct. 15, 1747	LR7	46
Thomas, had s., [A----], b. July 23, 1748	LR7	J
Thomas, d. Sept. 27, 1748	LR7	540
Thomas, s. Stephen, b. Sept. 10, 1762	LR14	7
HOLMES, Ann M., m. Lemuel W. **COWLES**, b. of		
(Unionville), Apr. 29, [1846], by Rev. Richard		
Woodruff	LR47	117
Nancy H., m. Charles **BOARDMAN**, b. of Hartford,		
Nov. 2, 1835, by Rev. Noah Porter	LR47	91
HOLT, Josiah, Dr., of Farmington, m. Keziah **ADAMS**, of		
Mass. Bay, May 28, 1777	LR22	480
HOLTON, Mindwell, d. Thomas, b. Dec. 27, 1746	LR7	J
HOMER, Caroline, m. Sherman B. **NAMAAN**, b. of		
Farmington, Mar. 19, 1840, by Elisha C. Jones	LR47	102
Charles, of Farmington, m. Sarah Ann **FIELDS**, of		
Haddam, Jan. 7, 1838, by Adna Whiting, J.P.	LR47	97
Nehemiah L., of Farmington, m. Elizabeth **LOOMIS**, of		
Haddam, Dec. 31, 1841, by Rev. C. D. Cowles	LR47	106
HOOGINS, Dennis, formerly of Ireland, m. Maudlin **HAYES**,		
wid., of Farmington, May 3, 1716	LR2	94
HOOKER, Abigall, d. John, b. May 25, 1691; d. Sept. 30,		
1692	LR1	5
Abigail, d. John, b. Jan. 14, 1697/8	LR1	5
Abigail, m. Nathaniel **HART**, Dec. 3, 1719	LR2	101
Abigail, d. Hezekiah, b. Sept. 25, 1724	LR2	46
Abigail, d. Joseph & Sarah, b. Feb. 5, 1735/6	LR5	645
Abigaile, w. John, d. Feb. 21, 1742/3, in the 74th y. of her		
age	LR7	36
Abigail, w. Jo[hn?], d. Feb. 21, 1742/3	LR6	305
Abigail, m. James **COWLES**, Aug. 30, 1753	LR8	10
Aliss, d. Nathaniell, b .Nov. 12, 1701	LR1	2
Andrew, s. Samuel, Jr., b. Mar. [ ], 1712/13	LR4	374
Andrew, m. Mary **LEE**, b. of Farmington, May 22, 1735	LR5	539
Ann, d. Samuel, Jr. & Sarah, b. Sept. 23, 1756	LR11	583
Anna, d. Lieut. Joseph, b. Dec. 4, [ ]	LR7	J
Anne, w. William, d. Dec. 12, 1727	LR4	396
Anne, d. Samuel, Jr. & Mercy, b. Aug. 27, 1728	LR5	4
Anne, d. William, b. Mar. 6, 1731/2	LR5	4
Anne, d. Samuel, d. Oct. 31, 1732	LR5	50
Anne, d. William, d. June 7, 1735	LR6	10
Anne, m. Thomas **SMITH**, Dec. 31, 1767	LR15	A
Asahel, s. Hezekiah, b. [ ] 13, 1736	LR6	3
Ashbel, s. John, Jr., b. Apr. 18, 1737	LR6	3
Daniel, s. Sam[ue]ll, b. Mar. 25, 1678/9	LR1	2
Daniel, [s. Rev. Samuel & Mary, (d. Capt. Thomas		
WILLETT], b. Mar. 25, 1678/9	LR3	553

	Vol.	Page
HOOKER (cont.)		
Eliza D., of Farmington, m. Francis **GILLET**, of		
Windsor, Sept. 10, 1834, by Rev. Noah Porter	LR42	E
Elizabeth, d. Samuel, Jr., b. [ ], 1714	LR4	374
Elizabeth, m. Moses **GILBERT**, b. of Farmington, Feb.		
21, 1733/4	LR5	300
Elnah, s. John, b. Apr. 13, 1746	LR7	1
Elnathan, m. Amey **NEWEL**, Dec. 13, 1781	LR22	480
Esther, d. Samuel, b. July 30, 1731	LR5	4
Ester, d. Samuel, Jr., b. Aug. 1, 1759	LR15	F
[E]unice, d. Hezekiah, b. Oct. 30, 1734	LR5	307
Gils, s. Samuel, b. Oct. 4, 1690	LR2	112
Giles, s. Andrew, b. Oct. 5, 1746	LR11	583
Hezekiah, s. Sam[ue]ll, b. Nov. 7, 1675	LR1	2
Hezekiah, [s. Rev. Samuel & Mary (d. Capt. Thomas		
WILLETT)], b. Nov. 7, 1675; d. [ ], 1686	LR3	553
Hezekiah, s. John, b. Oct. 14, 1688	LR1	5
Hezekiah, of Ffarmington, m. Abigail **CURTISS**, of		
Stratford, Dec. 18, 1716	LR2	94
Hezekiah, s. Hezekiah, b. Oct. 30, 1717	LR2	102
James, s. Samuell, b. Oct. 27, 1666	LR1	2
James, [s. Rev. Samuel & Mary (d. Capt. Thomas		
WILLETT)], b. Oct. 27, 1666	LR3	553
James, s. Hezekiah, b. Jan. 13, 1719/20	LR2	102
Jesse, s. Hezekiah, b. Apr. 27, 1732	LR5	4
Jo[ ], had d. [ ]	LR7	1
John, s. Samuell, b. Feb. 20, 1664/5	LR1	2
John, [s. Rev. Samuel & Mary (d. Capt. Thomas		
WILLETT)], b. Feb. 20, 1664/5	LR3	553
John, m. Abigall **STANLEY**, Nov. 24, 1687	LR1	5
John, s. John, b. Nov. 17, 1693; d. Dec. 26, 1693	LR1	5
John, s. John, b. Mar. 6, 1694/5	LR1	5
John, Jr., m. Mary **HEART**, d. Dea. Ebenezer, July 4,		
1728	LR4	423
John, s .John, Jr. & Mary, b. Mar. 19, 1728/9	LR4	396
John, d. Feb. 21, 1745/6, ae 82	LR7	36
John, d. Aug. 3, 1766	LR14	3
Joseph, s. John, b. Feb. 15, 1704/5	LR1	5
Joseph, m. Sarah **LEWIS**, b. of Farmington, Jan. 23,		
1734/5	LR5	545
Joseph, d. Dec. 19, 1764, in the 60th y. of his age	LR14	3
Joseph, s. Joseph, b. Mar. [ ]	LR7	J
Josiah, s. Hezekiah, b. Apr. 2, 1722	LR5	307
Lydia, w. William, d. June 1, 1723	LR2	61
Lydia, d. William, b. Apr. 13, 1725	LR2	65
Lydia, d. William, d. Oct. 27, 1736	LR6	10
Lidia, d. Samuell, Jr., b. Dec. 22, 1764	LR15	F
Margaret, [d. Samuel, Jr.], b. [ ], 1719	LR4	374
Martha, d. Giles, b. Aug. 8, 1734	LR5	307
Martha, w. Lieut. Giles, d. May 22, 1760	LR11	574
Martin, [s. Andrew], b. Apr. 16, 1734	LR6	3
Martin, s. Andrew, d. June 10, 1757	LR11	577
Mary, d. Sam[ue]ll, b. July 3, 1673	LR1	2

	Vol.	Page
HOOKER (cont.)		
Mary, m. Jeames **PARPOINT**, July 26, 1698	LR1	4
Mary, d. Nathaniell, b Dec. 31, 1699	LR1	2
Mary, d. John, b. June 11, 1780 (?)	LR1	5
Mary, Mrs., m. Thomas **BUCKINGHAM**, Aug. 10, 1703	LR1	4
Mary [d. Rev. Samuel & Mary (d. Capt. Thomas **WILLETT**)], b. July 3, 1713* *(Should be "1675")	LR3	553
Mary, m. Samuel **HART**, b. of Ffarmington, Dec. 25, 1723, by ( )	LR2	60
Mary, d. Hezekiah, b. Jan. 8, 1726/7	LR4	395
Mary, [d.] Andrew, b. May 18, 1731	LR6	3
Mehitabel, d. Samuel, b Sept. 30, 1706	LR2	112
Mehetabel, d. Samuel, Jr., b. [ ], 1722	LR4	374
Mercy, d. Joseph & Sarah, b. Jan. 17, 1741/2	LR6	3
Mercy, w. Roger, d. Aug. 27, 1745, ae 26 y. wanting 2 d.	LR7	36
Mercy, w. Samuel, d. Feb. 4, 1750/1	LR8	11
Nathan[ie]ll, s. Sam[ue]ll, b. Dec. 28, 1671	LR1	2
Nathaniel, [s. Rev. Samuel & Mary (d. Capt. Thomas **WILLETT**)], b. Dec. 28, 1671; d. July 21, 1711	LR3	553
Nathaniell, m. Mary **STANLY**, Dec. 23, 1698	LR1	4
Noadiah, s. Joseph & Sarah, b. Aug. 29, 1737	LR6	3
Rawlen, s. Andrew, b. Feb. 8, 1757	LR11	583
Richard, s. Samuel, b. Oct. [ ], 1700	LR2	112
Richard, s. William,* b. Dec. 2, 1727 *(In pencil "William")	LR4	395
Richard, s. William, d. Jan. 27, 1727/8	LR4	396
Roger, s. Samuel, b. Aug. [ ], 1698	LR2	112
Roger, s. Sam[ue]ll, b. Sept. 14, 1668	LR1	2
Roger, [s. Rev. Samuel & Mary (d. Capt. Thomas **WILLETT**)], b. Sept. 14, 1668; d. [ ], 1698	LR3	553
Roger, s. Sergt. Samuell, d. Aug. 10, 1703	LR2	141
Roger, s. John, b. Sept. 7, 1710	LR1	5
Roger, s William, b. May 20, 1723	LR2	87
Roger, m. Mercy **HART**, b. of Farmington, Jan. 29, 1739/40	LR6	27
Roger, s. William, d. Oct. 15, 1750	LR7	540
Roger, s. Roger, b. June 9, 1751	LR8	5
Ruth, d. John, b. Apr. 16, 1708	LR1	5
Ruth, m. Asahel **STRONG**, Jr., b. of Ffarmington, June 8, 173[ ]	LR5	13
Ruth, of Hartford, m. Fisher **GAY**, of Farmington, Sept. 1, 1773	LR17	442
Samuell, s. Samuell, b. May 29, 1661	LR1	2
Samuel, [s. Rev. Samuel & Mary (d. Capt. Thomas **WILLETT**)], b. May 29, 1661	LR3	553
Samuel, of Ffarmington, s. Rev. Samuell, m. Mehitibel **HAMLIN**, of Middletown, June latter end, 1687	LR2	145
Samuel, s. Samuel, b. Apr. 6, 1688	LR2	112
Samuel, Rev., 2nd minister in Farmington, d. Nov. 6, 1697	LR1	2
Samuel, Rev., d. Nov. 6, 1697	LR1	2
Samuel, Rev., d. Nov. 6, 1697	LR2	141

	Vol.	Page
HOOKER (cont.)		
Samuel, Jr., of Ffarmington, m. Mercy **LEET**, of Guilford, Jan. 9, 1710/11	LR2	257
Samuel, s. Samuel, Jr., b. [ ], 1726	LR4	374
Samuel, Jr., m. Sarah **NORTON**, Sept. 23, 1756	LR11	576
Sarah, d. Samuell, b. May 5, 1681	LR1	2
Sarah, [d. Rev. Samuel & Mary (d. Capt. Thomas **WILLETT**)], b. May 5, 1681	LR3	553
Sarah, d. John, b. Sept. 11, 1702	LR1	5
Sarah, d. Nathaniel, b. Nov. 7, 1704	LR1	3
Sarah, m. Matthew **HART**, b. of Farmington, Jan. 7, 1724/5	LR2	52
Sarah, d. Hezekiah, now of Woodbury, b. May 30, 1739	LR6	3
Sarah, d. Roger & Mercy, d. Apr. 19, 1741	LR6	10
Sarah, d. Roger, b. Sept. 16, 1743	LR6	3
Sarah, d. Roger & Mercy, b. Dec. 16, 1743	LR6	3
Sarah, d. Samuell, Jr., b. Apr. 11, 1763	LR15	F
Sarah, d. Noahdiah, b. Nov. 16, 1767	LR15	F
Seth, s. John, Jr. & Mary, b. Dec. 8, 1731	LR5	4
Seth, m. Marah **BURNHAM**, Sept. 4, 1755	LR9	286
Seth, s. John, d. Dec. 10, 1758	LR11	577
Sibbel, d. Samuel, Jr., b. [ ], 1724	LR4	374
Sibel, m. Solomon **WINCHEL**, Aug. 23, 1753	LR9	286
Thomas, s Sam[ue]ll, b. June 10, 1659	LR1	2
Thomas [s. Rev. Samuel & Mary (d. Capt. Thomas **WILLETT**)], b. June 10, 1659	LR3	553
Thomas, s. Samuel, b. Feb. 1, 1692/3	LR2	112
Thomas, s. Samuel, 3rd, b. Aug. 16, 1734	LR5	307
Thomas, s. Andrew, b. Aug. 30, 1743	LR11	583
William, s. Samuel, b .May 11, 1663	LR1	2
William, [s. Rev. Samuel & Mary (d. Capt. Thomas **WILLETT**)], b. May 11, 1773; d. [ ], 1689	LR3	553
William, s. Samuel, b. Feb. 16, 1694/5	LR2	112
William, m. Lidya **WOODFORD**, Feb. 15, 1721/2	LR2	100
William, of Ffarmington, m. Anna **STEEL**, of Weathersfield, July 16, 1724	LR2	52
William, s. Hezekiah, b. June 20, 1729	LR4	396
William, of Farmington, m. Abigail **PHELPS**, of Hartford, May 20, 1731	LR5	13
William, s. William, b. Jan. 10, 1733/4	LR5	8
William, Jr., d. Aug. 31, 1755	LR8	12
William, s. Seth & Deborah, b. Sept. 15, 1756	LR9	9
HOPER, Sarah, m. Simeon **HART**, Sept. 14, 1755	LR11	575
HOPKINS, Ann, d. Joseph, b. Feb. 19, 1742/3	LR6	3
Birzavith, s. Caleb, b. Aug. 16, 1766	LR14	7
Caleb, s. Joseph, b. June 23, 1737	LR6	3
Caleb, m. Mabel **SCOVEL**, Feb. 21, 1765	LR11	594
Caleb, s. Caleb, b. Dec. 27, 1770	LR17	434
Charlotte, d. Jos., Jr., b. Dec. 29, 1764	LR15	F
Dorcas, of Hartford, m. Timothy **BROWNSON**, of Ffarmington, July 19, 1725	LR2	52
Dorcas, m. [ ] **WIARD**, June 20, 1770	LR17	G

	Vol.	Page
HOPKINS (cont.)		
Dorcas, [d. Joseph], b. Dec. [ ]	LR7	J
Elizabeth, d. Joseph, b. Nov. 29, 1740	LR6	3
Elizabeth, m. Matthew **HART**, Nov. 15, 1759	LR11	575
Horace, s. Caleb, b. Nov. 4, 1780	LR21	544
Horace, s. Caleb, d. May 26, 1781	LR21	560
Joseph, s. Joseph, m. Elizabeth **GALPIN**, Apr. 25, 1733	LR5	300
Joseph, s. Joseph & Elizabeth, d. Dec. 25, 1733	LR5	6
Joseph, Jr., m. Anne **SMITH**, Apr. 15, 1760	LR11	575
Joseph, s. Jos. Jr., b. Mar. 26, 1767	LR15	F
Joseph, s. Caleb, b. Dec. 18, 1768	LR15	F
Lebbeus, s. Caleb, b. Dec. 1, 1775	LR21	544
Noah, s. Joseph, Jr., b. Dec. 14, 1762	LR15	F
Ruth, of Farmington or Hartford, m. Daniel **THOMSON**, of Ffarmington, June 28, 1729	LR5	13
Ruth, d. Joseph, b. Mar. 25, 1736	LR5	2
Ruth, m. Samuel **PECK**, Mar. [ ], 1757	LR11	576
Ruth, d. Caleb, b Sept. 30, 1773	LR17	435
Sarah, d. Joseph, b. [ ]	LR7	J
William, s. Caleb, b. Dec. 14, 1777	LR21	544
HORSINGTON, [see under **HOISINGTON**]		
HORTON, Evelina A., of Cheshire, m. Sylvester **CURTISS**, of Burlington, Aug. 25, 1840, by Rev. Aaron S. Hill	LR47	103
Roxanna, of Cheshire, m. Rodney **BARNS**, of Burlington, Feb. 27, 1842, by Rev. C. D. Cowles	LR47	106
William H., m. Clarissa **GREENFIELD**, b. of Middletown, Aug. 25, 1828, by Rev. Noah Porter	LR42	564
HOSFORD, HORSFORD, Damares C., m. Dr. Julius **WILLARD**, b. of Farmington, May w, 1837, by Rev. H. Bushnell	LR42	567
Elisha, s. John, b. July 8, 1751	LR8	5
Emeline E., m. James B. **FULLER**, May 7, 1851, by Rev. G. M. Porter	LR47	128
Jane, m. Seth **FULLER**, [May] 1, 1850, by Herman Northrop, J.P.	LR47	126
Lurene, m. Oliver **NEWELL**, Mar. 29, 1764	LR11	592
Martha, d. John, b. Sept. 8, 1754	LR9	9
HOSKINS, Maria, m. Simeon **CURTIS**, b. of Farmington, Nov. 28, 1844, by Noah Porter	LR47	113
Norton Z., of Bloomfield, m. Julia A. **DORMAN**, of Farmington, Dec. 23, 1849, by Rev. Noah Porter	LR47	126
HOSMER, Elezer, s. Elezer, b. Nov. 10, 1755	LR11	583
Frederick, s. Dr. Timothy, b. Oct. 31, 1772	LR17	434
John, s. Ebenezer, b. Feb. 25, 1758	LR11	583
Robert, s. Elezer, b. Dec. 15, 1751	LR11	583
HOTCHKISS, HODGKISS, HODGKIS, HOGKIS, HOGSKISS, Ann, of Farmington, m. Seth **LANGDON**, of Farmington, this day [Apr. 7, 1830], by Rev. Noah Porter	LR42	561
Candace N., of Farmington, m. Ebenezer H. **WHITNEY**, of Hampton, N.Y., Nov. 20, 1823, by Noah Porter, V.D.M.	LR40	573

	Vol.	Page
HOTCHKISS, HODGKISS, HODGKIS, HOGKIS,		
HOGSKISS (cont.)		
Elizabeth, of Wallingford, m. Abram **HILLS**, of		
Farmington, July 3, 1734	LR6	27
Josiah, s. Ladwick, b. Nov. 7, 1757	LR11	583
Lemuel, s. Ladwick, b. May 8, 1744	LR7	L
Lemuel, s. Lodock, b. [ ]	LR7	1
Lucien, of Bristol, m. Juliet **BARNES**, of Burlington,		
Aug. 21, 1836, by N. Porter	LR47	94
Marah, d. Joseph, b. June 24, 1750	LR8	5
Mary, d. Laddock, b. July 21, 1747	LR7	1
Ruby, m. John H. **COOK**, Dec. 9, 1824, by Rev. Noah		
Porter	LR42	568
Shelton, of Bristol, m. Emeline **LEWIS**, of Farmington,		
Mar. 29, 1835, by Rev. Noah Porter	LR47	89
William, J., of Burlington, m. Harriet J. **DORMAN**, of		
Farmington, Apr. 26, 1849, by Rev. Henry J. Fox	LR47	124
Zadock, m. Mary **NORTH**, Dec. 22, 1743	LR6	305
Zadock, s. Zadock, b. May 25, 1752	LR8	5
HOTTEN, [see also **HUDSON**], Hanah, d. Thomas, .b Mar.		
31, 1755	LR9	9
HOUGH, Abigail, m. Samuel **GRIDLEY**, s. Thomas, b. of		
Farmington, Aug. 21, 1723	LR2	60
Jemima, m. David **CHISTISTER**, b. of Farmington,		
Aug. 21, 1723	LR2	60
Norman, of Berlin, m. Harriet E. **BURROWS**, of		
Farmington, Apr. 9, 1834, by Rev. Noah Porter	LR42	E
Samuell, m. Susana **WROTHAM**, Nov. 25, 1679	LR1	5
Susanah, of Saybrook, m. Joseph **ANDRUS**, of		
Farmington, Feb. 10, 1707/8	LR2	93
HOWARD, Nelson, m. Mary **SMITH**, b. of Farmington, Sept.		
5, 1842, by Noah Porter, V.D.M.	LR47	108
HOWE, Maria, of Farmington, m. Mannah **ALDERMAN**, of		
Burlington, June 2, 1847, by William Wright	LR47	119
Samuel, of Plymouth, m. Mary Ann **HUNT**, of		
Farmington, Nov. 29, 1840, by Rev. Aaron S. Hill	LR47	103
HUBBARD, HUBBERT, HUBERT, Abigail, d. George, b.		
Jan. 16, 1711/12	LR2	232
Annah, d. Ebenezer, b. Aug. 19, 1753	LR9	9
Ebenezer, s. Elnathan, b. Dec. 20, 1766	LR15	J
Elizabeth, d. Selah, b. Sept. 20, 1765	LR17	434
Esther, d. Selah, b. Oct. 29, 1767	LR17	434
George, m. Mercy **SEAYMOR**, b. of Farmington, Feb.		
[ ], 1710/11	LR2	123
Lois, d. Selah, b. Sept. 27, 1770	LR17	434
Luther, s. Elnathan, b. Jan. 20, 1768	LR15	J
Mary, m. Isaac **LEE**, Dec. 8, 1713	LR2	257
Mercy, d. Selah, b. Nov. 1, 1771	LR17	434
Ruth, of Middletown, m. Matthew **COLE**, of Kensington,		
in Torrington, Apr. 10, 1732	LR5	300
Sarah, wid., m. Lieut. Samuell **ANDRUSS**, Mar. 18, 1742	LR6	305
Sarah, m. Timothy **ANDRUS**, June 16, 1749	LR8	10
Sarah, m. Clemmon **GRIDLEY**, Dec. 25, 1755	LR11	576

	Vol.	Page
HUBBARD, HUBBERT, HUBERT (cont.)		
Sarah, d. Selah, b. June 6, 1763	LR17	434
Selah, s. Selah, b. Jan. 15, 1762	LR17	434
Thankfull, of Middletown, m. Joseph **SMITH**, Jr., of		
Farmington, Mar. 2, 1737/8	LR6	27
HUBBELL, Joseph, of Wolcott, Vt., m. Ursula **TUBBS**, of		
Farmington ,Oct. 3, 1826, by Stephen Crosby	LR42	567
HUBERT [see under **HUBBARD**]		
HUDSON, HUTSON, HUTTSON [see also **HOTTEN**], Ann,		
[d. Thomas], b. Apr. 12, 1746	LR7	1
Daniel, [s. Thomas], b. Dec. 10, 174[ ]	LR7	1
Daniel, [s. Thomas], b. Dec. 14, 1741; d. Dec. [ ], 1741	LR7	1
Jonah, [s. Thomas], b. Feb. 3, 1739	LR7	1
Lott, s. Thomas, b. Jan. 16, 173[ ]	LR7	1
Margret, [d. Thomas], b. June 13, 1738	LR7	1
Mary, [d. Thomas], b .July 27, 1747	LR7	1
Phebe, [d. Thomas], b. Sept. 10, 1744	LR7	1
Sarah, m. Abraham **CLARK**, Jr., Mar. 10, 1762	LR11	575
Thomas, m. Margret **NEALE**, Mar. 29, 1736	LR7	35
HUGG, Agnes, wid., m Benjamin **SMITH**, Nov. 5, 1740	LR6	304
HULL, [see also **HALL**], Alfred, m. Huldah **BROCKWAY**,		
b. of Farmington, Oct. 14, 1822, by Noah Porter,		
V.D.M.	LR40	572
Ambrose A., m. Jane L. **BOOTH**, b. of Farmington, Nov.		
17, 1850, by Rev. Charles Kelsey	LR47	128
Eli, m. July Ann **FANNING**, Nov. 14, 1846, by William		
Wright	LR47	118
Fanny, see Fanny **HURD**	LR42	565
Fanny, m. Joseph **HEARD**, Feb. 9, 1824, by Rev. Noah		
Porter	LR42	568
Hannah, 2nd, m. John **HART**, Jan. 11, 1743/4	LR7	35
Hannah, of Wallingford, m. Elijah **GAYLORD**, of		
Farmington, Oct. 13, 1763	LR11	592
Joseph D., of New Haven, m. Charlotte L. **COWLES**, of		
Farmington, Dec. 14, 1843, by Noah Porter, Int.		
Pub.	LR47	111
Martha, m. Abial **ROBARDS**, Aug. 14, 1750	LR7	35
Martha, m. Abial **ROBARDS**, Aug. 14, 1750	LR8	8
Mary, m. Julius D. **COWLES**, b. of Farmington, Sept.		
11, 1842, by Rev. S. H. Clark	LR47	108
HULLBARD, [see under **HURLBURT**]		
HUMASON, Ruth, of Farmington, m. John **COWLES**, of		
Simsbury, Feb. 10, 1828, by James Cornish, J.P.	LR42	565
Ursula, m. Benjamin **JONES**, Apr. 18, 1827, by Rev.		
H. Bushnell	LR42	565
HUMPHREY, HUMPHRIES, HUMPHREYS, Abigail,		
some time of Simsbury, m. Dr. Samuel **PORTTER**,		
of Ffarmington, [ ], 1702	LR2	123
Amanda, m. Charles **UPSON**, b. of Burlington, Mar. 22,		
1832, by Rev. Noah Porter	LR42	559
Cynthia, m. Eli **ALDERMAN**, Sept. 3, 1823, by Rev.		
Stephen S. Nelson	LR40	572

	Vol.	Page
HUMPHREY, HUMPHRIES, HUMPHREYS (cont.)		
Henry, of Canton, m. Lucy **ALFORD**, of Farmington, Northington Soc., Feb. 27, 1828, by Rev. Isaac Kimball	LR42	565
Mariah, m. Josiah **GOODRICH**, b. of Farmington, Nov. 29, 1826, by Rev. Harry Bushnell	LR42	567
Mariah, m. Harry **CHIDSEY**, b. of Farmington, Nov. 9, 1826, by James Humphreys, J.P.	LR42	567
Mary, sometime of Simsbury, m. Samuel **GRIDLEY**, of Ffarmington, Dec. 1, 1698	LR2	145
Montgomery, m. Maria V. **GLEASON**, b. of Farmington, Oct. 20, 1830 by Rev. Noah Porter	LR42	560
HUNGERFORD, Deborah, m. Abraham **BROOKS**, Mar. 5, 1767	LR15	A
Harvey, s. Oliver, b. Dec. 12, 1773	LR17	435
Huldah, m. Azell **HILLS**, May 16, 1776	LR21	557
Jemima, d. Mathew, b. Oct. 1, 1763	LR15	J
Joseph, s. Mathew, b. Nov. 22, 1760	LR15	J
Luanna, d. Oliver, b. Apr. 16, 1768	LR17	435
Lucretia, of Harwinton, m. Jonathan **BELDEN**, of Berlin, Nov. 23, 1825, by Rev. Noah Porter	LR42	569
Margaret, d. Mathew, b. May 11, 1775	LR21	544
Matthew, m. Rachel **SPENCER**, Feb. 26, 1756	LR11	576
Mathew, s. Mathew, b. Oct. 20, 1768	LR15	J
Oliver, m. Lucy **STOW**, Dec. 24, 1767	LR17	443
Rachel, d. Mathew, b. Oct. 10, 1758	LR15	J
Sarah, d. Matthew, b. June 3, 1757	LR11	583
Susanna, d. Nathaniell, b. July 7, 1772	LR21	544
Tertius, s. Mathew, b. Oct. 16, 1765	LR15	J
HUNN, HUN, Deborah, d. Nathaniel & Martha, b. July 2, 1711	LR2	87
Hannah, d. Nathaniel & Martha, b. Oct. 4, 1705	LR2	87
Hannah, m. Robert **COOK**, b. of Farmington, Nov. 19, 1729	LR5	13
Martha, wid. Nathaniell, m. John **ROOT**, s. John, b. of Ffarmington, Dec. 9, 1714	LR2	93
Nathaniel, s. Nathaniel & Martha, b. Sept. 10, 1708	LR2	87
Rebeckah, of Weathersfield, m. William **SMITH**, of Ffarmington, July 22, 1725, by David Goodrich, J.P.	LR2	51
Rebeckah, of Weathersfield, m. William **SMITH**, of Farmington, July 22, 1725	LR6	27
Thankfull, m. Timothy **ANDRUS**, Sept. 9, 1756	LR8	10
HUNT, Hiram, m. Sarah **WOODFORD**, b. of Farmington, Apr. 25, 1821, by Noah Porter, V.D.M.	LR40	571
Mary Ann, of Farmington, m. Samuel **HOWE**, of Plymouth, Nov. 29, 1840, by Rev. Aaron S. Hill	LR47	103
HUNTLEY, Jannet, m. Henry **LAWRENCE**, of Mereden, Nov. 28, [1833], by Rev. Noah Porter	LR42	A
Ursula, of Harwinton, m. Lewis B. **BRADLEY**, of Farmington, July 8, [1833], by Rev. Noah Porter	LR42	A
HURD, HEARD, Asaph, m. Lurina **RICHARDS**, b. of Farmington, Feb. 6, 1828, by Amasa Woodford, J.P.	LR42	564
Fanny [Hull], of Farmington, m. John **HURD**, of Killingworth, June 2, 1827, by Rev. Noah Porter	LR42	565

	Vol.	Page

HURD, HEARD (cont.)

John, of Killingwroth, m. Fanny **HURD** [**HULL**], of
    Farmington, June 2, 1827, by Rev. Noah Porter   LR42   565
Joseph, m Fanny **HULL**, Feb. 9, 1824, by Rev. Noah
    Porter   LR42   568
Wilson, m. Caltha **WOODRUFF**, b. of Farmington, Dec.
    31, 1829, by George Norton, J.P.   LR42   561

HURLBURT, HOLBERT, HOLLIBUT, HULLBARD,
HULBERT, HURLBUT, Alvin B., m. Abigail **SWEET**, b. of
    Farmington, Nov. 7, 1823, by Noah Porter, V.D.M.   LR40   573
Ann, d. Jonathan, b. Dec. 16, 1732   LR5   307
Ebenezer, m. Elizabeth **COGSWELL**, Aug. 20, 1752   LR8   10
Elizabeth, d. Dr. Josiah, b. Jan. 17, 1748   LR8   5
Elizabeth, m. Horace **COWLES**, b. of Farmington, Nov.
    8, 1838, by Rev. Noah Porter   LR47   98
Hannah, d. Jonathan, b. Jan. 18, 1730/1   LR5   4
Hannah, b. Apr. 10, 1777; m. John Selden, [   ]   LR47   W-Y
Hart, s .Jonathan, b. July 13, 1728   LR4   395
Jonathan, s. Jonathan, b. Apr. 1, 1702 (living with John
    Hart)   LR2   91
Jonathan, m. Sarah **ORTON**, b. of Ffarmington, July 6,
    1727   LR2   258
Jonathan, s. Jonathan, b. June 11, 1735   LR5   2
Lucy, m. Noadiah **HART**, Nov. 20, 1761   LR11   575
Lyman, m .Lucy **WARREN**, b. of Farmington, May 5,
    1828, by Noadiah Woodruff, J.P.   LR42   564
Lyman, of Berlin, m. Caroline **GILLET**, of Farmington,
    May 27, 1836, by Rev. Noah Porter   LR47   93
Ozias, s. Jonathan, b. Apr. 29, 1741   LR6   3
Rhoda, m. Ebenezer **ELTON**, Feb. 2, 1764   LR15   A
Sarah, d. Jonathan, b. Sept. 24, 1736   LR6   3
Sarah, d. Jonathan, d. Feb. last day, 1744/5   LR7   36
Sumbitt, d. Jeames, b. Sept. 5, 1746   LR7   544

HUTSON, [see under **HUDSON**]

INGERSOLL, Rhoda Ann, of Farmington, m. Samuel A.
    BARNUM, of Lee, Mass, Sept. 18, 1836, by Rev.
    Noah Porter   LR47   94
Sarah, m. Seth **LEE**, Sept. 3, 1767   LR15   A

INGRAHAM, Jerusha, d. Nathaniell, b. Feb. [ ], 1770   LR15   F
Jerusha, d. Nathaniell, d. Aug. 13, 1771   LR17   444
John, s. Nathaniell, b. Sept. 29, 1766   LR15   F
Nathaniel, m. Mary **ALLYN**, Nov. 18, 1765   LR15   N
Sarah, d. Nathaniell, b. Feb. 7, 1768   LR15   F

IVES, Chancey, of Bristol, m. Amanda **CLARK**, of
    Farmington, May 10, 1826, by Jonathan Cone,
    V.D.M.   LR42   569
William A., m. Julia **ROOT**, Nov. 21, 1832, by Rev.
    David L. Parmelee   LR42   558

JACKSON, Joseph, of Simsbury, m. Emmett **WILLIAMS**, of
    Farmington, July 27, 1837, by Rev. S. H. Clark   LR47   95
Joseph, m. Margaret **MURRAY**, b. of Farmington, Jan.
    18, 1844, by Rev. Richard Woodruff   LR47   112

	Vol.	Page
JACKSON (cont.)		
Sybel, of Farmington, m. Peter **GRIFFEN**, of Mereden,		
June 4, 1820, by Noah Porter, V.D.M.	LR40	570
Sybel, of Farmington, m. Charles **PETERSON**, of New		
Haven, Jan. 31, 1831, by Rev. Noah Porter	LR42	560
JACKWAY, William R., m. Lucy **SHEPERD**, b. of		
Farmington, Oct. 11, 1827, by Rev. Noah Porter	LR42	565
JEALET, [see under **GILLET**]		
JELETT, [see under **GILLET**]		
JEROME, JEAROM, Abigail, m. Jacob **DEMING**, Mar. 29,		
1752	LR8	10
Abigail, m. Josiah **LEWIS**, Jr., May 8, 1766	LR15	A
Andrew, s. Andrew, b. Jan. 15, 1771	LR21	545
Andrew, d. May 26, 1778, in the 37th y. of his age	LR21	560
Chloe, d. Andrew, b. Dec. 25, 1768	LR21	545
Ester, d. Will[ia]m, b. [ ], 174[ ]	LR7	J
Lucy, d. Andrew, b. Feb. 6, 1773	LR21	545
Lyman, s. Andrew, b. Aug. 29, 1766	LR21	545
Mary, m. Joseph **SPENCER**, Oct. 12, 1758	LR11	576
Mary J., of Bristol, m. Frederick A. **MO[O]RE**, Aug. 2,		
1841, by Rev. Noah Porter	LR47	105
Roseanna, d. Andrew, b. May 16, 1775	LR21	545
Sarah, m. Abel **YALE**, July 20, 1759	LR11	575
Temperance, m. Nathaniel **STONE**, Apr. 30, 1772	LR17	443
JEWEY, [see under **DEWEY**]		
JOHNSON, JONSON, Antonette, m. Elijah O. **GRIDLEY**, b.		
of Farmington, Mar. 5, 1833, by Rev. Noah Porter	LR42	558
Asa, m. Hannah **TUTTLE**, May, 12, 1763	LR11	594
Azariah, s. Daniell, b. Apr. 22, 1772	LR17	434
Betta, d. Daniell, b. Aug. 10, 1765	LR11	584
Content, of Middletown, m. Timothy **COWLES**, of		
Farmington, [ ]	LR5	13
Daniel, s. Daniel, b. Feb. 2, 1760	LR11	584
Hannah, d. Daniel, b. July 28, 1762	LR11	584
Hannah, d. Asa, b. Jan. 10, 1764	LR11	584
Isaac, s. Zadock, b. Aug. 19, 1762	LR11	584
James C., of Farmington, m. Emmeline **BURDICK**, of		
Burlington, Mar. 1, 1836, by Rev. Noah Porter	LR47	93
Joanna, d. Daniell, m. Seth **LEE**, of Farmington, s. of		
Jared, Sept. 9, 1771, by Rev. Simeon Warterman	LR17	G
Joel, s. Daniel, b. Nov. 18, 1768	LR22	466
Mary E., of N.Y., m. Edward **STEPHENS**, of		
Kensington, Oct. 15, 1848, by William Wright	LR47	123
Rosilla, of Bristol, m .Henry **MILLER**, of Mereden, May		
11, 1830, by Rev. Irenus Atkins, of Southington	LR42	562
Stephen, m. Ruth **SMITH**, [ ], 1779	LR22	480
JOLEET, [see under **GILLET**]		
JONES, JOANE, Ann, m. Amzi **ROOT**, Aug. 10, 1821,		
by Noah Porter, V.D.M.	LR40	571
Belinda D., m. Augustus B. **WOODRUFF**, b. of		
Farmington, Sept. 11, 1831, by Rev. Noah Porter	LR42	560
Benjamin, m. Ursula **HUMASON**, Apr. 18, 1827, by		
Rev. H. Bushnell	LR42	565

	Vol.	Page

JONES, JOANE (cont.)

John B., m. Emeline **FRANKLIN**, of Berlin, Sept. 22,
1825, by Rev. Noah Porter — LR42 — 569

John R., of Berlin, m. Eliza **COUCH**, Mar. 23, 1845, by
R. Stanley — LR47 — 114

Julius, of Harwinton, m. Lydia **HART**, of Farmington,
Dec. 4, 1821, by L. Robbins, V.D.M. — LR40 — 571

Marah, m. Samuel **CHURCH**, Nov. 30, 1774 — LR21 — 557

Mary, m. Thomas **BARNES**, b. of Ffarmington, June [ ],
1690 — LR2 — 145

Mary, of Farmington, m Richard **HART**, of Hartford,
Dec. 23, 1849, by Rev. Noah Porter — LR47 — 126

Resin G., of Farmington, m. Jerusha **MATHER**, of
Berlin, May 15, 1827, by Rev. Noah Porter — LR42 — 565

Samuel, of Springfield, m. Martha **WILLIAMS**, of
Farmington, Mar. 30, 1842, by Rev. Aaron S. Hill — LR47 — 107

Timothy S., of Plymouth, m. Elizabeth A. **LANKIN**, of
Bristol, Sept. 19, 1836, by Rev. Noah Porter — LR47 — 94

JUDD, Abigail, d. Benjamin, b. Sept. 5, 1703 — LR2 — 92

Abigail, [d. Benjamin & Susanah], b. Sept. 5, 1703 — LR3 — 553

Abigail, w. Matthew, d. Oct. 28, 1733 — LR5 — 50

Abigail, wid. Samuel, m. John **NORTH**, s. Samuell, b. of
Farmington, Mar. 20, 1733/4 — LR5 — 300

Abigail, d. Matthew, d. Mar. 5, 1744 — LR7 — 36

Abigail, m. George **KILLBORN**, May 20, 1746 — LR7 — 35

Abigaile, m. George **KILBORN**, May 20, 1746 — LR7 — 35

Abigail, d. [Mathew & Ester], b. Jan. [ ], 1748 — LR7 — F

Abigail, d. [Mathew & Ester], "who is decd.", b. May 8,
1748 — LR7 — F

Abigail, d. James (s. Benjamin), b. June 5, 1752 — LR8 — 5

Abigail, d. James (s. of Benjamin), b. June 5, 1752 — LR8 — 5

Abigal, m. Abell **CLARK**, Jan. 6, 1774 — LR17 — 443

Abortioa, d. William & Elizabeth, b. Oct. 10, 1767; d.
Oct. 22, 1767 — LR15 — F

Elexander, s. John, b. Feb. 21, 1766   (Alexander) — LR14 — 7

Alvin, s. John, Jr., b. June 24, 1774 — LR21 — 545

Alvin, s. John, Jr., d. Nov. 7, 1776, in the 3rd y. of his age — LR21 — 560

Amos, s. Anthony, b. Apr. 5, 1708 — LR2 — 97

Amos, s. Dea. Anthony, m. Keziah **JUDD**, d. Sergt.
Benjamin, b. of Ffarmington, June 12, 1729 — LR5 — 4

Amos, d. Dec. 18, 1762 — LR11 — 593

Ann, d. Samuel, b. Oct. 15, 1712 — LR2 — 98

Anna, w. Samuel, d. June 22, 1719 — LR2 — 61

Anna, d. James, d. Oct. 31, 1775, in the 12th y. of her age — LR17 — 445

Anna, d. John, Jr., b. July 17, 1776 — LR21 — 545

Anna, d. John, Jr., d. Oct. 1, 1777, in the 2nd y. of her
age — LR21 — 560

Anne, m. Ebenezer **MOODEY**, b. of Farmington, Oct.
14, 1731 — LR5 — 13

Anne, d. Elnathan, b. May 15, 1763 — LR11 — 584

Anne, d. James [s. of Benjamin], b. Mar. 19, 1764 — LR14 — 7

Anthony, m. Susanah **WOODFORD**, b. of Ffarmington,
June 26, 1707 — LR2 — 125

	Vol.	Page
JUDD (cont.)		
Anthony, s. Phenias, b. Aug. 1, 1752	LR8	5
Asahel, s. James [s. of Benjamin], b. May 24, 1759	LR11	584
Asahel, s. James, d. Oct. 13, 1777, in the 19th y. of his age	LR17	445
Asaph, s. Joseph, b. Feb. 18, 1720/1	LR2	102
Asaph, s. Joseph, d. July 31, 1727	LR4	396
Asaph, s. Joseph, b. Aug. 12, 1728	LR4	395
Bathsheba, d. Benjamin, b. Aug. 20, 1707	LR2	92
Bathsheba, [d. Benjamin & Susanah], b. Aug. 20, 1707	LR3	553
Bela, s. John, Jr., b. Aug. 4, 1770	LR21	545
Benjamin, of Ffarmington, m. Susanah **NORTH**, of Weathersfield, Jan. 18, 1693/4	LR2	123
Benjamin, of Ffarmington, m. Susanah **NORTH**, of Weathersfield, Jan. 18, 1693/4	LR3	553
Benjamin, s. Benjamin, b. Mar. 2, 1696/7	LR2	92
Benjamin, [s. Benjamin & Susanah], b. Mar. 2, 1696/7	LR3	553
Benjamin, Jr., of Ffarmington, m. Sarah **HOLLISTER**, of Glastenbury, Nov. 9, 1727	LR4	423
Benjamin, d. Mar. 9, 1764	LR11	593
Calvin, s. Jonah, b. Sept. 20, 17[ ]	LR7	F
Calvin, s .Jonah, d. Sept. 23, 1751	LR8	11
Catheren, d. Benjamin, b. Oct. 26, 1711	LR2	98
Catharen, [d. Benjamin & Susanah], b. Oct. 26, 1711	LR3	553
Clarasa, d. Jesse, b. July 9, 1760	LR17	434
Daniel, of Ffarmington, m. Mercy **MITCHELL**, of Woodbery, Dec. 4, 1705	LR1	4
Daniel, s. Daniel, b. Nov. 22, 1721	LR4	374
Daniel, s. Daniel, d. Feb. 9, 1721/2	LR2	66
Daniel, s. Mathew & Ester, b. July 27, 1742	LR7	F
Daniel, s. James [s. of Benjamin], b. Aug. 14, 1761	LR11	584
David, s. Anthony, b. Oct. [ ], 1719	LR4	374
David, s. Dea. Anthony, d. Mar. 15, 1732/3	LR5	50
David, s. Amos, b. Apr. 30, 1735	LR6	4
Eleazer, s. Heman, b. Jan. 11, 1770	LR17	434
Elidia, d. James (s. of Benjamin), b. Oct. 6, 1754	LR9	9
Elizabeth, m. Samuell **LEWIS***, Dec. 27, 1653 *("**LOMES**")	LR2	331
Elizabeth, d. Benjamin, b. Aug. 21, 1668	LR1	2
Elizabeth, m. Thomas **HART**, s. Stephen, b. of Farmington, Dec. 19, 1689	LR2	123
Elizabeth, d. William, b. Sept. 19, 1710	LR2	109
Elizabeth, m. Thomas **THOMSON**, s. Thomas, May 25, 1721	LR2	101
Elizabeth, d. Ithiel, d. Mar. 3, 1742	LR6	305
Elizabeth, d. Hezekiah, b. Jan. 5, 1745/6	LR7	544
Elizabeth, twin with Mary, d. Simeon, b. Oct. 11, 1754	LR9	9
Elizabeth, a twin d. Simeon, d. Oct. 21, 1754	LR9	495
Elizabeth, w. Simeon, d. Sept. 22, 1757	LR11	577
Elizabeth, d. Simeon, b. Dec. 9, 1760	LR14	7
Elnathan, m. Lois **THORP**, Mar. 2, 1758	LR11	576
Emanuel, s. Simeon, b. Jan. 22, 1757	LR11	584
Enoch, s. Jeames, b. Sept. 14, 1743	LR6	4

	Vol.	Page
JUDD (cont.)		
Epaphras, s. Joseph, b. Sept. 19, 1723	LR2	87
Epheprass, s. Simeon, b. Aug. 10, 1752	LR8	5
Ephraim, s. Joseph, d. Aug. 17, 1727	LR4	396
Esther, d. Daniel, b. Sept. 24, 1716	LR2	83
Ester, d. Simeon, b. Nov. 8, 174[ ]	LR7	1
Etna, m. Asahel **GLEASON**, b. of Farmington, May 12, 1825, by Rev. Harvey Bushnell	LR42	569
Eunice, d. William, [s.], of Phill[ip], of Farmington, b. Jan. 23, 1712/13	LR2	232
[E]unice, d. William, b. Feb. 11, 1732/3	LR5	4
Eunis, d. Joseph, Jr., b. Dec. 17, 1745	LR7	J
Eunice, d. Nathaniell, b. Nov. 6, 1755	LR15	F
Eunice, d. Nathaniell, b. Sept. 1, 1758	LR15	F
Gideon, s. Anthony, b. Feb. 5, 1722/3	LR4	374
Gideon, s. Anthony, d. July [ ], 1724	LR2	148
Hannah, w. Joseph, d. Apr. 8, 1707	LR2	141
Hannah, d. Joseph, Jr. & Ruth, b. Nov. 15, 1735	LR5	4
Hannah, m. Daniel **UPTON**, [ ], 1751	LR9	286
Heman, s. [Mathew & Ester?], b. Apr. 7, 1745	LR7	F
Hezekiah, [s. Benjamin & Susanah], b. June 19, 1722; d. Sept. 9, 1727	LR3	553
Hezekiah, s. Amos, b. Oct. 12, 1737	LR6	4
Ichabod, s. Ithael, b. Aug. 1, 1738	LR6	4
Ichabod, s. Ithiel, d. Jan. 28, 1742	LR6	305
Isaac, s. Noah, b. May 26, 1757	LR11	584
Itheil, s. Dr. Anthony, b. Dec. 8, 1710	LR6	4
Ithiel, of Wallingford, now of Farmington, m. Mary **JUDD**, of Glastenbury, July 7, 1737	LR6	27
Ithiel, d. Feb. 24, 1742	LR6	305
James, s. Daniel, b. Aug. 27, 1713	LR2	83
James, s. Benjamin, b. Jan. 20, 1715/16	LR2	95
James, [s. Benjamin & Susanah], b. Jan. 20, 1715/16	LR3	553
James, m. [E]unice **THOMSON**, b. of Farmington, Jan. 29, 1740/1	LR6	304
James, m. Hannah **ANDRUS**, July 27, 1749	LR7	35
James, s. James, b. Sept. 4, 1750	LR8	5
James, s. James, b. Apr. 22, 1755	LR9	9
James, s. James, d. July 13, 1755	LR8	12
James, s. James, d. July 13, 1755	LR11	577
James, 2nd, s. James, b. Aug. 17, 1756	LR9	9
James, s. James, b. Aug. 17, 1756	LR11	584
James, s. James [s. Benjamin], b. Jan. 27, 1757	LR11	584
James, of New Britain, d. Feb. 15, 1783, in the 66th y. of his age	LR22	482
Jemimah, d. Daniel, b. Sept. 22, 1710	LR2	83
Jemimah, d. Daniel, d. July 19, 1712	LR2	62
Jerusha, d. Daniel, b. May 22, 1708	LR2	83
Jerusha, d. Daniel, d. Jan. 24, 1712/13	LR2	62
Jesse, s. William, b. Aug. 3, 1739	LR6	4
Jesse, of Farmington, m. Mary **BIRD**, of Litchfield, Oct. 29, 1765	LR11	594
Jesse, Jr., s. Jesse, b. Sept. 16, 1773	LR17	434

	Vol.	Page
JUDD (cont.)		
Joanna, d. Benjamin, b. Oct. 16, 1709	LR2	92
Joannah, [d. Benjamin & Susannah], b. Oct. 16, 1709	LR3	553
Job, s. Phenehas, b. Oct. 21, 1757	LR11	584
John, s. Anthony, b. Apr. [ ], 1718	LR4	374
John, s. William b. Jan. 1, 1725/6	LR2	34
John, m. Hannah **LEWIS**, Jan. 16, 1755	LR9	9
John, Jr., m. [ ], Nov. 23, 1769	LR21	557
John, s. John, Jr., b. May 8, 1772	LR21	545
Jonah, s. Joseph, b. Sept. 30, 1714	LR2	95
Jonah, m. Jemima **MILLER**, Nov. 18, 1748	LR7	46
Joseph, of Ffarmington, m. Hannah **BIDDEL**, of		
Hartford, Apr. 11, 1706	LR2	145
Joseph, s. Joseph, b. Apr. 1, 1707	LR2	111
Joseph, of Farmington, m. Sarah **WINCHEL**, of		
Windsor, June 3, 1713	LR2	125
Joseph, Jr., m. Ruth **THOMPSON**, b. of Farmington,		
Dec. 25, 1734	LR5	539
Joseph, m. Mary **CLARK**, Jan. 18, 1752	LR8	10
Joseph, d. Apr. 11, 1757	LR11	577
Jotham, s. Elnathan, b. Jan. 4, 1773	LR17	434
Keziah, d. Benjamin, b .Sept. 14, 1705	LR2	92
Keziah, [d. Benjamin & Susanah], b. Sept. 14, 1705	LR3	553
Keziah, d. Sergt. Benjamin, m. Amos **JUDD**, s. Dea.		
Anthony, b. of Ffarmington, June 12, 1729	LR5	4
Keziah, d. Amos [& Keziah], b. Sept. 9, 1730	LR5	4
Keziah, d. James & [E]unice, b. Sept. 3, 1741	LR6	4
Keziah, m. Elisha **COLE**, Apr. 25, 1754	LR9	286
Lemuel, s. Jeames, b. Mar. 13, 1744	LR7	1
Lois, d. William, b. Jan. 2, 1723/4	LR2	87
Lois, d. Ithael, b. July 3, 1741	LR6	4
Lois, m. Hezekiah **WADSWORTH**, Dec. 13, 1744	LR7	35
Lois, d. Timothy, b. Jan. 13, 1749	LR7	F
Lois, d. Elnathan, b. Jan. 29, 1769	LR15	F
Lucy, d. John & Hannah, b. Oct. 29, 1759	LR9	9
Lydia, d. Anthony, b. June 5, 1713	LR4	374
Lydia, m. Job **COLE**, Sept. 4, 1741	LR8	10
Lydia, d. John, Jr., b. Jan. 7, 1779	LR21	545
Mable, [w. Uriah], d. Aug. 25, 1745	LR7	46
Marah, wid., m. Lieut. Samuel **LANKTON**, Nov. 23,		
1752	LR8	10
Marah, m. Gad **STANLEY**, Oct. 29, 1767	LR15	A
Martha, of Watterbury, m. Thomas **COWLES**, of		
Ffarmington, Jan. 6, 1713/14	LR2	93
Martha, d. Joseph, b. Jan. 31, 1763	LR11	584
Mary, d .Benjamin, b. Feb. 6, 1701/2	LR2	92
Mary, [d. Benjamin & Susanah], b .Feb. 6, 1701/2	LR3	553
Mary, wid. Sergt. William, d. Oct. 22, 1718	LR2	61
Mary, d. Daniel, b. June 27, 1720	LR4	374
Mary, of Glastenbury, m. Ithiel **JUDD**, of Wallingford,		
now of Farmington, July 7, 1737	LR6	27
Mary, d. John, b. Sept. 8, 1748	LR7	F
Mary, d. James, b. July 4, 1753	LR9	9

	Vol.	Page
JUDD (cont.)		
Mary, d. James, b. July 4, 1753	LR11	584
Mary, twin with Elizabeth, d. Simeon, b. Oct. 11, 1754	LR9	9
Mary, 2nd, d. Jesse, b. Sept. 21, 1775	LR17	434
Matthew, s. Daniel & Marcy, b. Aug. 31, 1706	LR2	83
Matthew, m. Abigail **PHELPS**, b. of Farmington, June 28, 1733	LR5	300
Matthew & Abigail, had child, s. b. Oct. 24, 1733	LR5	4
Mehetabel, d. Benjamin, Jr., b. Oct. 6, 1732	LR5	4
Mehetabel, m. Elijah **HOLLISTER**, Oct. 1, 1752	LR8	10
Nancy, d. Jesse, b. Nov. 21, 1767	LR15	F
Nathan, s. Benjamin, b. Aug. 15, 1719	LR2	83
Nathan, [s. Benjamin & Susanah], b. Aug. 24, 1719	LR3	553
Nathan, m. Thankfull **WRIGHT**, Feb. 3, 1742	LR6	305
Nathan, d. Sept. 1, 1764	LR11	593
Nathaniell, s. Nathaniell, b. Aug. 12, 1760	LR15	F
Orren, s. Jesse, b. July 21, 1771	LR17	434
Phebe, d. Joseph, Jr., b. Feb. 14, 1753	LR9	9
Philip, s. Anthony, b. Feb. [ ], 1714/15	LR4	374
Phineas, s. Phineas, b. Dec. 13, 1750	LR8	5
Polly, d. Heman, b. Oct. 9, 1767	LR17	434
Rachel, d. Daniel, b. Apr. 22, 1723	LR4	374
Ruben, s. Joseph, b. Sept. 16, 1716	LR2	81
Rubin, s. Simeon, b. Aug. 9, 1750	LR8	5
Rhoda, m. Jared **LEE**, b. of Farmington, June 1, 1735	LR5	539
Rhoda, d. James, b. Apr. 1, 1748	LR8	5
Rhodah, m. James **NORTH**, Sept. 29, 1774	LR21	557
Roda, d. Jeames, b. Apr. [ ]	LR7	J
Rosine, d .John & Hannah, b. Jan. 18, 1758	LR9	9
Runah, s. Timothy, b. Dec. [ ]	LR7	J
Ruth, of Watterbury, m. James **SMITH**, of Ffarmington, Apr. 26, 1727	LR2	258
Ruth, d. William, b. Nov. 5, 1728	LR4	395
Ruth, d. Joseph, Jr., b. Apr. 24, 1730	LR6	4
Ruth, d. Amos, b. Mar. 12, 1731/2	LR5	4
Ruth, w. Joseph, of Southington, d. July 12, 1750	LR8	12
Ruth, d. Phinehas, b. Mar. last day, 1754	LR9	9
Ruth, d. Phenehas, b. Mar. 31, 1754	LR11	584
Ruth, m. Nathaniell **MESENGER**, Apr. 8, 1759	LR11	575
Ruth, d. Elnathan, b. Feb. 1, 1776	LR21	545
Salmon, s. John & Hannah, b. Apr. 17, 1762	LR9	9
Salmon, s. John & Hannah, d. May 13, 1762	LR11	593
Samuel, m. Anne **HART**, Apr. 20, 1710	LR2	145
Samuel, Sergt., of Ffarmington, m. Abigail **PHELPS**, of Westfield, (wid.), May 27, 1725	LR2	52
Samuel, s. James, d. Jan. 20, 1752	LR8	11
Samuel, s. John & Hannah, b. Nov. 23, 1755	LR9	9
Samuell, s. John & Hannah, d. Jan. 9, 1758	LR11	593
Samuel, s. Jesse, b. Sept. 25, 1777	LR17	434
Sarah, m. James **WILLIAMS**, Jr., Dec. 29, 1725	LR2	52
Sarah, d. Sergt. Samuel, b. Sept. 21, 1726	LR2	282
Sarah, d. Benjamin, Jr., b. Nov. 1, 1729	LR5	4
Sarah, m. Zebulon **WOODRUFF**, Oct. 25, 1744	LR7	46

	Vol.	Page
JUDD (cont.)		
Sarah, d. Elnathan, b. Aug. 10, 1760	LR11	584
Sarah, d. John & Hannah, b. Aug. 26, 1763	LR9	9
Sarah, d. James, b. Feb. 19, 1768	LR15	F
Seth, s. John (s. of Anthony), b. Apr. 8, 1751	LR8	5
Seth, s. Seth, decd., b. Sept. 27, 1777	LR21	545
Simmeon, s. Joseph, b. Jan. 6, 1718/9	LR2	83
Simeon, m. Elizabeth **NORTON**, Jan. 29, 1746	LR7	35
Simeon, s. Simeon, b. July 9, 1748	LR8	5
Susannah, d. Benjamin, b. Aug. 12, 1699	LR2	92
Susannah, [d. Benjamin & Susanah], b Aug. 12, 1699	LR3	553
Susannah, d. Dr. Anthony, b. [ ], 1726	LR4	374
Susannah, d. Phenehas, b. Feb. 7, 1756	LR11	584
Susannah, m. David **BROWNSON**, July 1, 1756	LR10	6
Susanah, d. Apr. 23, 1764	LR11	593
Susannah, m. Jonathan **BROWNSON**, Mar. 5, 1772	LR17	442
Thankfull, d. Aug. 25, 1764	LR11	593
Thomas, s. Thomas, b. Oct. 16, 1726	LR2	242
Timothy, s. William & Mary, b. Dec. 28, 1713	LR2	99
Timothy, s. Timothy, b. Sept. 21, 1744	LR7	1
Timothy, m. Lowis **CURTIS**, Nov. 9, 1744	LR7	46
Uriah, s. Benjamin & Susannah, b. Dec. 28, 1713	LR2	99
Uriah, [child of Benjamin & Susannah], b. Dec. 28, 1713	LR3	553
Uriah, m. Mable **BIDWELL**, Dec. 20, 1744	LR7	46
Uriah, m. Mercy **SEAMOUR**, Feb. 19, 1747	LR7	46
William, m. Mary **STEEL**, Mar. 31, 1657	LR2	331
William, s. Philip, m. Mary **GRIDLEY**, Dec. 23, 1709	LR2	145
William, s. Thomas, m. Mary **ROOT**, d. Stephen, b. of		
Farmington, Jan. 21, 1712/13	LR2	125
William, m. Ruth **LEE**, Mar. 14, 1722/3	LR2	60
William, s. William, b. July 20, 1743	LR6	4
William Samuel, s. William & Elizabeth, b. Jan. 10, 1766	LR15	F
-----, wid., m. Abner **GRAVES**, Apr. 21, 1743	LR6	305
----an, m. Anna [ ], Nov. 15, 1767	LR17	G
JUDSON, JUDDSON, Abi, d. Peter, b. Nov. 14, 1766	LR21	545
Elizabeth, d. Peter, b. July 15, 1758	LR11	584
Hannah, of Woodbury, m. Samuel **WADSWORTH**, of		
Ffarmington, June 12, 1689	LR2	125
Ira, s. Peter, b. July 25, 1760	LR11	584
Ira, d. Oct. 16, 1776, in the 17th y. of his age	LR21	558-9
Joshua, s. Peter, b. Feb. 22, 1756	LR11	584
Martha, d. Peter, b. June 18, 1753	LR11	584
Mary, of Woodbury, m. James **THOMSON**, of		
Farmington, Apr. 12, 1739	LR6	27
KANE, Owen, m. Eliza **CURTIS**, Mar. 17, 1828, by Rev.		
Noah Porter	LR42	565
KEEP, John R., of Franklin, N.Y., m. Rebecca Ann **PORTER**,		
of Farmington, Aug. 31, 1842, by Rev. Noah Porter	LR47	108
KELLEY, Hannah, of Weathersfield, m. Moses		
BROWNSON, of Farmington, Oct. 6, 1737	LR6	27
Hannah, d. James, b. July 9, 1740	LR6	4
William, m. Sylvia **GORDON**, b. of Farmington, Jan. 26,		
1834, by Rev. L. C. Cheney	LR42	A

	Vol.	Page
KELLOGG, KELODG, Alfred, Dr., m. Cordelia		
KELLOGG, b. of Farmington, Sept. 2, 1824, by		
Bela Kellogg	LR42	568
Chester M., of New Britain, m. Julia E. **PECK**, of		
Farmington, May 12, 1851, by Rev. Samuel		
Rockwell, of New Britain	LR47	128
Cordelia, m. Dr. Alfred **KELLOGG**, b. of Farmington,		
Sept. 2, 1824, by Bela Kellogg	LR42	568
Elizabeth, d. Joseph, b. Mar. 3, 1651	LR2	330
Joseph, s. Joseph, b. Aug. 11, 1653	LR2	330
Lois, w. Seth, d. Aug. 20, 1766	LR14	3
Rachel, of Weathersfield, m. Nathan **LEWIS**, Jr., of		
Farmington, Feb. 27. 1733/4	LR5	300
Sarah, of Hartford, m. Moses **PECK**, of Middletown,		
Aug. 14, 1732	LR5	300
KELSEY, KELLSEY, KELLSE, KELLCEY, Amos, s. John,		
b. Apr. 11, 1743	LR6	4
Amos, s. Amos, b. May 6, 1776	LR22	466
Comfort, m. Benjamin **STEPHENS**, Oct. 20, 1740	LR6	304
Ephraim, s. Jeames, b. Feb. 25, 1742/3	LR6	4
Isaac, s. Amos, b. May 17, 1778	LR22	466
Jeames, s. Jeames, b. Dec. 26, 1744	LR7	1
John, m. Martha **BROWNSON**, b. of Farmington, Apr.		
26, 1739	LR6	27
Silvah, d. Amos, b. July 19, 1774	LR22	466
----el, s. [Jeames], b. Mar. 26, 1747	LR7	1
KENT, Deborah, m. Rev. Rufus **HAWLEY**, Sept. 25, 1770	LR17	443
[KENYON], KINYON, Naomi, of Hopkinton, R.I., m. John		
DAVIS, Jr., of Farmington, Mar. 27, 1773	LR17	442
KETCHEL, Celestia O., of Sandgate, Vt., m. James P.		
BISHOP, of Watertown, Feb. 14, 1843, by Rev.		
Harvey P. Ketchel	LR47	109
KILBORN, KILLBORN, KILLBOURNE, Anna, d. Josiah,		
b. Dec. 24, 1759	LR17	438
Anne, m. Asahell **HART**, b. of Farmington, Nov. 5, 1778	LR22	480
Benjamin, m. Esther [ ], Apr. 25, 1770	LR15	N
Clarissa, d. Richard, b. Nov. 2, 1764	LR14	8
Elizabeth, d. Joshua, b. Sept. 24, 1765	LR15	G
Elizabeth, m. Jedediah **NORTON**, Jr., Nov. 7, 1771	LR17	G
Eunice, d. Josiah, b. July 7, 1762	LR17	438
Fanny, of Farmington, m. David **LEE**, of Barkhamsted,		
Nov. 4, 1824, by Rev. Harry Bushnell	LR42	568
George, m. Abigaile **JUDD**, May 20, 1746	LR7	35
George, had child, b. Dec. 13, 1749	LR7	1
George, d. Mar. 24, 1763	LR11	593
George, of Litchfield, now of Unionville, m. Betsey		
WRIGHT, of Hartland, July 4, 1839, by John		
Bartlett	LR47	100
Hopey, m. Timothy **WADSWORTH**, Nov. 16, 1753	LR11	576
James, s. Josiah, b. Oct. 19, 1770	LR17	438
John, s. Josiah, b. Apr. 23, 1733	LR5	5
Joshua, m. Mahitable **MATHER**, July 14, 1763	LR11	592
Josiah, s. Josiah, b. July 29, 1730	LR5	5

	Vol.	Page
KILBORN, KILLBORN, KILLBOURNE (cont.)		
Josiah, m. Anna **NEAL**, May 3, 1754	LR9	286
Josiah, d. Dec. 15, 1754	LR9	495
Josiah, s. Josiah, b. Feb. 15, 1756	LR17	438
Lemuel, s. Josiah, b. Oct. 7, 1764	LR17	438
Lydia, of Farmington, m. William **COLEMAN**, Jr., of		
Hartford, Feb. 12, 1824, by Bela Kellogg	LR42	568
Mahitabel, d. Joshua, b. Apr. 23, 1764	LR15	G
Mercy, d. Richard, b. Sept. 28, 1766	LR14	8
Richard, s. Josiah, b. Sept. 2, 1735	LR5	5
Richard, m. Mercy [ ], Dec. 8, 1763	LR14	8
Ruth, d. Josiah & Ruth, b. June 29, 1740	LR6	4
Ruth, m. Robert **BOOTH**, May 9, 1757	LR11	576
Sarah, m. Jeames **NAUGHTON**, Nov. 30, 1743	LR7	46
Truna, d. Josiah, b. Oct. 26, 1766	LR17	438
William, s. Josiah, b. Jan. 11, 1758	LR17	438
Zeuba, d. Josiah, b. Nov. 16, 1772	LR17	438
---rgaut, d .George, b. Feb. 29, 1730/1* *("1740/1"?)	LR7	1
-------n, s. [George], b. Nov. 20, 1735* *("1745"?)	LR7	1
KING, Juliaanna, b. Feb. 18, 1798; m. Samuel **ALLEN**, Jan. 2,		
1817	LR47	W-Y
KINNEY, Lucy A., of Manchester, m. David F. **CROSBY**, of		
Hawley, Mass., Aug. 2, 1838, by Rev. Noah Porter	LR47	97
KNOWLES, John S., m. Elizabeth M. **MILLER**, Sept. 4,		
1839, by Rev. Ezra S. Cook. Witnesses Henry		
Cadwell & Ira Rowe	LR47	100
LANE, Emma Ann, m. James H. **WHITING**, b. of		
Farmington, May 21, 1849, by William Wright	LR47	125
John, s. Allan, b. Jan. 4, 1783	LR22	467
Rodah, of Farmington, m. Volney **BRADLEY**, of Bristol,		
Jan. 20, 1850, by William Wright	LR47	127
LANGDON, LANGTON, LANKTON, LANGHTON		
LANCKTON, LANTION, LANDON, [see also **LANKIN**],		
Abigail, d. Joseph, b June 18, 1780	LR22	467
Abigail Hooker, d. Joseph, b. Aug. 3, 1772	LR22	467
Abigail Hooker, d. Feb. 20, 1775	LR22	482
Almira, m. Ezekiel **PORTER**, Feb. 25, 1824, by Rev.		
Noah Porter	LR42	568
Amon, s. Joseph & Ruth, b. Dec. 23, 1763	LR11	584
Amon, s. Joseph, b. Dec. 23, 1763	LR22	467
Asa, s. John, b. Sept. 14, 1755	LR11	585
Asa, s. John, d. Dec. 11, 1755	LR11	577
Asahel, s. Giles, b. Mar. 30, 1765	LR17	435
Azel, s .Jonathan, b. Sept. 14, 17[ ]	LR17	F
Azell, s. Jonathan, d. July 14, 1777, in the 8th y. of his		
age	LR21	558-9
Chancy, s. Ebenezer, b. Nov. 8, 1763	LR11	585
Daniel, s. Joseph, Jr., b. Dec. 24, 1728	LR5	5
Daniel, m. Phebe **CLARK**, Mar. 31, 1755	LR10	6
Ebenezer, s. Joseph, 1st, b. July 17, 1701	LR4	382
Ebenezer, m. Jemima **COWLES**, b. of Ffarmington, Nov.		
30, 1727	LR4	423
Ebenezer, s. Ebenezer & Jemimah, b. May 22, 1738	LR6	4

	Vol.	Page
LANGDON, LANGTON, LANKTON, LANGHTON,		
LANCKTON, LANTION, LANDON (cont.)		
Edmond, s .Joseph, b. Feb. 20, 1785	LR22	467
Edward, m. Emily **ROOT**, b. of Farmington, June 10,		
1834, by Rev. Noah Porter	LR42	E
Eliza, of New Haven, m. Augustus **COWLES**, of		
Farmington, Sept. 12, 1849, by Rev. Noah Porter	LR47	125
Elizabeth, d. Samuel, b. Nov. 12, 1732	LR5	5
Elizabeth, w. Lieut. Samuell, d. Oct. 11, 1750	LR7	540
Elizabeth, w Jona[than], d. July 23, 1777, in the 41st y. of		
her age	LR21	558-9
Easther, d. Ebenezer & Jemimah, b. Nov. 19, 1730	LR5	5
Giles, s. Joseph, Jr., b. July 22, 1720	LR2	65
Giles, m. Ruth **ANDRUSS**, Nov. 4, 1751	LR7	46
Giles, s. Giles, b. May 24, 1763	LR11	585
Giles, s. Giles, b. May 24, 1763	LR17	435
Hanah, s. Thomas, b. Nov. 10, 1743	LR6	4
Huldah, d. Jonathan, b. Nov. 18, 1762	LR11	584
Ire, s. Ebenezer, b. Dec. 4, 1761	LR11	584
Isaac Lomis, s. Joseph, b. July 10, 1766	LR14	8
Jabez, s. Jonathan, b. Mar. 6, 1777	LR21	546
James, s. Joseph, b .Mar. 3, 1783	LR22	467
Jemimah, d. Ebenezer, b. Oct. 29, 1734	LR5	307
Joel, s. Joseph, b. Nov. 24, 1765	LR14	8
Joel, s. Joseph, b. Nov. 24, 1765	LR22	467
Joel, s. Joseph, Jr., b. July 19, 1768	LR17	436
John, s. Joseph, 1st, b. Apr. 3, 1691	LR4	382
John, m. Sarah **LEE**, b. of Ffarmington, Jan. 18, 1721/2	LR2	100
John, m. Mary **ENOS**, Dec. 12, 1754	LR11	576
Jonathan, s. Samuel, b. Feb. 9, 1724/5	LR4	375
Joseph, s .John, bp. Mar. 18, 1659	LR2	327
Joseph, 1st, m. Susannah **ROOT**, b. of Ffarmington, Oct.		
[ ], 1683	LR2	257
Joseph, s. Joseph, 1st, b .Mar. [ ], 1688	LR4	382
Joseph, Jr., m. Rachel **COWLES**, b. of Farmington, Dec.		
24, 1713	LR2	93
Joseph, 1st, of Ffarmington, m. Mary **ROYCE**, of		
Wallingford, Oct. 18, 1714	LR2	257
Joseph, s. Joseph, Jr., b. Aug. 7, 1718	LR2	65
Joseph, s. Ebenezer & Jemimah, b. Dec. 12, 1740	LR6	4
Joseph, d. Apr. 8, 1749	LR7	36
Levi, s. Giles, b. Dec. 31, 1754	LR9	10-11
Lintha, d. Jonathan, b. May 14, 1765	LR11	584
Lucy, d. Giles, b. Apr. 2, 1767	LR17	435
Lucy, or Nancy, d. Joseph, b. Nov. 20, 1770	LR22	467
Lucy, d. Joseph, b. July 23, 1789	LR22	467
Mary, twin with Mercy, d. Joseph, 1st, b. Apr. [ ], 1704	LR4	382
Mary, twin with Mercy, d. Joseph, 1st, d. [ ],		
1704* *(Perhaps "1707")	LR2	148
Mary, d. Joseph, Jr., b. Nov. 13, 1716	LR2	65
Mary, d. Ebenezer, b. Feb. 22, 1733	LR5	5
Mary, m. Samuel **GOGGSWELL**, b. of Farmington,		
Nov. 20, 1734	LR5	545

	Vol.	Page
LANGDON, LANGTON, LANKTON, LANGHTON,		
LANCKTON, LANTION, LANDON (cont.)		
Mary, w. Samuel, d. July 9, 1765	LR11	593
Mercy, twin with Mary, d. Joseph, 1st, d. [ ],		
1704* *(Perhaps "1707")	LR2	148
Mercy, twin with Mary, d. Joseph, 1st, b .Apr. [ ], 1704	LR4	382
Mercy, m. Moses **HILLS**, Jan. 6, 1747/8	LR7	35
Nancy, see Lucy **LANCKTON**	LR22	467
Noah, s. Ebenezer, b. Aug. 10, 1728	LR4	395
Ozias, m. Loisa **WATERS**, Feb. 18, 1824, by Rev. Noah		
Porter	LR42	568
Patience, d. Giles, b. Oct. 2, 1756	LR11	585
Rachel, d. Joseph, Jr., b. Feb. 11, 1724/5	LR2	65
Rachel, m. Daniel **SLOPER**, Jan. 9, 1752	LR8	10
Reuben, s. Joseph, b. Oct. 18, 1777	LR22	467
Ruth, d. Giles, b. Aug. 31, 1758	LR11	585
Samuel, s. Joseph, 1st, b. Dec. [ ], 1694	LR4	382
Samuel, m. Elizabeth **LEE**, Dec. 28, 1721	LR2	60
Samuel, s. Samuell, b. Oct. 23, 1723	LR2	46
Samuel, his child, b. June 20, 1735; d. same day	LR5	49
Samuel, Lieut., m. wid. Marah **JUDD**, Nov. 23, 1752	LR8	10
Samuel, s. Jonathan, b. Apr. 21, 1773	LR17	436
Samuell, s. Joseph, b June 18, 1775	LR22	467
Samuell, s. Jonathan, d. July 11, 1777, in the 5th y. of his		
age	LR21	558-9
Samuel, d. Sept. 13, 1778, in the 84th y. of his age	LR21	560
Sarah, d. Joseph, 1st, b. Apr. 29, 1685	LR4	382
Sarah, m. Jonathan **WOODRUFF**, b. of Ffarmington,		
July 10, 1711	LR2	125
Sarah, d. Samuel, b. May 25, 1730	LR5	5
Sarah, d. Noah, b. Apr. 8, 1753	LR8	6
Sarah, d. John, b. Dec. 9, 1756	LR11	585
Seth, of Farmington, m. Ann **HOTCHKISS**, of		
Farmington, this day, [Apr. 7, 1830], by Rev. Noah		
Porter	LR42	561
Solomon, s. Ebenezer, b. July 25, 1749	LR8	6
Sophronia, of Farmington, m. Alfred **FENN**, of		
Plymouth, [Mar. 30, 1830], by Rev. Noah Porter	LR42	561
Susanah, d. Joseph, 1st, b. Oct. [ ], 1696	LR4	382
Susannah, w. Joseph, 1st, d. Dec. 5, 1712	LR2	148
Susanah, d. Ebenezer, b. June 28, 1753	LR8	6
Susanna, d. Joseph, b. June 20, 1768	LR22	467
Sylvester, s. Joseph, b. Mar. 10, 1787	LR22	467
Thomas, s. Joseph, 1st, b. Sept. [ ], 1707	LR4	382
Thomas, s. Joseph, 1st, d. [ ], 1707	LR2	148
Thomas, s. Joseph, Jr., b. Jan. 6, 1713/14	LR2	65
Thomas, s. Joseph, Jr., b. Jan. 6, 1714/15	LR2	95
Thomas, m. Abigail **RICHARDS**, Dec. 9, 1742	LR6	305
Thomas, s. Thomas, b. June 26, 1748	LR7	L
Thomas, s. Thomas, d. Aug. 28, 1750	LR7	540
Thomas, s. Jos[eph], Jr., b. Oct. 31, 1772	LR17	436
Timothy, s. John, b. Dec. 4, 1758	LR11	585

	Vol.	Page
LANGDON, LANGTON, LANKTON, LANGHTON, LANCKTON, LANTION, LANDON (cont.)		
----sanal,* d. Samuel & Elizabeth, b. Jan. 4, 1736/7 *(In pencil "Susannah"?)	LR6	4
LANKIN, [see also **LANGDON**], Elizabeth A., of Bristol, m. Timothy S. **JONES**, of Plymouth, Sept. 19, 1836, by Rev. Noah Porter	LR47	94
LATHROP, Hannah, of Wallingford, m. Samuel **THOMSON**, of Ffarmington, Feb. 17, 1706/7	LR2	125
LAWRENCE, LARRANCE, Eliza, m. James **SOUTHERGILL**, [ ], by Rev. William McAlister	LR47	122
Elizabeth, m. Ebenezer **HART**, June 9, 1741	LR6	305
Henry, of Mereden, m. Jannet **HUNTLEY**, Nov. 28, [1833], by Rev. Noah Porter	LR42	A
LEAMING, Anne, m. Joseph **ROBBARD**, Jan. 6, 1773	LR17	442
LECOUR (?), Martha, see under Martha **SECOUR**		
LEE, Abigail, d. Seth & Joanna, b. Oct. 4, 1778	LR21	546
Almera, d. Isaac, Jr., b. July 17, 1780	LR21	546
Amanda, d. William, b. July 24, 1778	LR21	546
Amos, s. Jared, b. July 19, 1738	LR14	8
Amos, m. Anna **CAMP**, May 23, 1765	LR11	594
Anna, d. Stephen, b. Jan. 22, 1756	LR15	1
Anna, d. Seth, b. Dec. 4, 1773	LR17	436
Asahel, s. Isaac, b. Apr. 22, 1759	LR11	585
Ashbell, s. Stephen, b. Jan. 28, 1747	LR15	1
Celestia, m. Henry **HILLS**, b. of Farmington, Mar. 26, 1833, by Rev. Noah Porter	LR42	558
Charles Johnson, s. Seth & Joanna, b. Sept. 1, 1772	LR17	436
Cloe, d. Isaac, b. Jan. 25, 1745	LR7	L
Cole, d. Stephen, b. Nov. 25, 1751	LR15	1
David, of Barkhamsted, m. Fanny **KILLBORN**, of Farmington, Nov. 4, 1824, by Rev. Harry Bushnell	LR42	568
Ebenezer, s. Stephen, b. Sept. 14, 1706	LR2	97
Ebenezer, s. Stephen, d. Aug. 28, 1725	LR2	148
Ebenezer, m. Abigal **BULL**, June 20, 1750	LR7	46
Ebenezer, s. Ebenezer, b. June 7, 1757	LR11	585
Elidya, m. Daniel **NORTH**, Mar. 15, 1750	LR8	10
Elisha Bordman, s. Theodora, b. Jan. 21, 1773	LR17	436
Elizabeth, d. Stephen, b. July 12, 1694	LR2	97
Elizabeth, d. John, b. Mar. 6, 1700	LR1	3
Elizabeth, d. Jonathan, b. July 15, 1716	LR2	282
Elizabeth, m. Samuel **LANGTON**, Dec. 28, 1721	LR2	60
Elizabeth, d. Ebenezer, b. Nov. 28, 1755	LR11	585
Elizabeth, d. William, b. Apr. 22, 1774	LR17	436
Erastus, of Farmington, m. Julia **TAYLOR**, of Burlington, Mar. 6, 1825, by Rev. Noah Porter	LR42	568
[E]unice, d. Jonathan, b. May 24, 173[ ]	LR5	5
Eunis, d. John, b. Jan. 6, 1744	LR7	L
George, s. Dr. Seth, b. June 6, 1784	LR22	467
Hannah, d. Stephen, b. Oct. 15, 1708	LR2	97
Hizekyah, s. John, b. June 6, 1697	LR1	3

	Vol.	Page
LEE (cont.)		
Hezekiah, m. [ ] **PORTER**, b. of Ffarmington,		
[ ], 1728	LR4	423
Isaac, s. Stephen, b. Sept. 5, 1691	LR2	97
Isaac, of Farmington, m. Mary **HIBBARD**, of		
Middletown, Dec. 8, 1713	LR5	13
Isaac, m. Mary **HUBBERT**, Dec. 8, 1713	LR2	257
Isaac, s. Isaac, b. Jan. 17, 1716/17	LR4	374
Isaac, s. Isaac, b. Jan. 17, 1716/17	LR5	5
Isaac, Jr., of Farmington, m. Tabitha **NORTON**, of		
Weathersfield or Middletown, July 10, 1740	LR6	27
Isaac, of Farmington, m Elizabeth **GRANT**, Jr. of East		
Windsor, Dec. 30, 1772	LR17	442
Isaac, 3rd, m. Abigall **GOODRICH**, May 12, 1773	LR17	443
Isaac, s. Isaac, 3rd, b. Apr. 13, 1775	LR17	435
Isaac, Col. of Farmington, m. Mary **HALL**, of		
Wallingford, Oct. 9, 1783	LR22	480
Isaac N., of Berlin, m. Caroline A. **COWLES**, of		
Farmington, June 23, 1843, by Rev. Noah Porter	LR47	110
Jeames, s. John, b. Sept. 30, 1742	LR7	L
James, m. Lucy **BARNS**, June 13, 1765	LR17	442
James, s. James, b. Dec. 10, 1770	LR17	435
Jarad, m. Rhoda **JUDD**, b. of Farmington, June 1, 1735	LR5	539
Jared, s. Amos & Anna, b. Dec. 31, 1767	LR15	G
Jerusha, d. Isaac, b. Mar. 18, 1724/5	LR4	374
Jerusha, d. Isaac, b. Mar. 18, 1725/6	LR5	5
Jerusha, 1st, d. Isaac, d. Jan. 19, 1726	LR5	50
Jerusha, 2nd, d. Isaac, b. Feb. 15, 173[ ]	LR5	5
Jerusha, m. Elisha **BURNHAM**, Nov. 9, 1749	LR7	46
John, m. Elizabeth **LUMMIS**, Dec. 27, 1682	LR1	4
John, s. John, b. Dec. 7, 1683	LR1	3
John, twin with Thomas, s. Thomas, b. Dec. 7, 1716	LR2	81
John, d. Apr. 24, 1723	LR2	61
John, s. Jonathan, b. Apr. 22, 1725	LR2	282
John, m. Lydia **PORTER**, b. of Ffarmington, Jan. 6,		
1741/2	LR6	304
John, d. Dec. 1, 1746	LR8	11
John, m. Sarah **COLE**, May 7, 1752	LR8	10
John, s. John, b. Apr. 25, 1763	LR11	585
John, s. James, b. May 26, 1766	LR17	435
Jonathan, s. John, b. Mar. 20, 1686	LR1	3
Jonathan, m. Mary **ROOT**, b. of Farmington, June 4,		
1713	LR2	125
Jonathan, s. John, b. Oct. 19, 1753	LR9	10-11
Jonathan, s. Jonathan, Jr., d. Nov. 6, 1754	LR9	495
Jonathan, 2nd, s. John, b. Oct 13, 1755	LR9	10-11
Jonathan, Dea., d. Jan. 16, 1758	LR11	577
Joseph, s. Thomas, b. Sept. 9, 1713	LR2	95
Joseph, m. Bette **STANDLEY** Feb. 1, 1743/4	LR7	35
Josiah, s. Stephen, b. Aug. 13, 1711	LR2	97
Josiah, of Farmington, m. Hannah **WARREN**, of		
Glastenbury, Nov. 3, 1737	LR6	27

	Vol.	Page
LEE (cont.)		
Julia A., of Farmington, m. Joseph L. **WOOD**, of		
Burlington, Sept. 3, 1843, by Noah Porter, Int. Pub.	LR47	111
Lemira, d. Amos, b. May 15, 1766	LR14	8
Liveras, s. Ebenezer, b. Apr. 9, 1754	LR9	10-11
Lois, d. Jared, b. Apr. 28, 1747	LR14	8
Lois, m. [ ]hel **LEWIS**, Feb. 1, 1769	LR17	G
Lois, d .Timothy & Lucy, b. Aug. 31, 1773	LR17	436
Lucy, d. Jonathan, b. Jan. 10, 1719/20	LR2	282
Lucy, d. Timothy & Lucy, b. Nov. 18, 1776	LR21	546
Lucy, d. Nov. 25, 1776	LR21	558-9
Lucy, d. James, b. Nov. 6, 1780	LR21	546
Lydia, d. Thomas, b. June 22, 1708	LR2	97
Lydia, m. Samuel **NORTON**, b. of Farmington, Feb. 2,		
1737/8	LR6	27
Mabell, d. Stephen, b. Feb. 19, 1750	LR15	1
Mable, of Farmington, m. Daniel **LUDINGTON**, Jr., of		
Wallingford, Apr. 26, 1773	LR17	442
Martha, d. Stephen, b. Feb. 17, 1701/2	LR2	97
Marther, d. Stephen, b. Mar. 28, 1754	LR15	1
Martin, s. Timothy, b. Oct. 10, 1778	LR22	467
Mary, d. John, b. Mar. 15, 1689/90	LR1	3
Mary, d. Stephen, b. Sept. [ ], 1704	LR2	97
Mary, d. Thomas, b. Oct. 2, 1709	LR2	97
Mary, m. Thomas **NEWEL**, b. of Farmington, July 9,		
1713	LR2	93
Mary, d. Jonathan, b. Oct. 4, 1714	LR2	282
Mary, d. Isaac, b. Aug. 10, 1718	LR5	5
Mary, d. Isaac, b. Aug. [ ], 1718	LR4	374
Mary, d. Isaac, d. Sept. 29, 1731	LR5	50
Mary, m. Andrew **HOOKER**, b. of Farmington, May 22,		
1735	LR5	539
Mary, w. Dea. Jonathan, d. Sept. 14, 1760	LR14	3
Mary Jane, m. Franklin **WARREN**, b. of Farmington,		
Oct. 6 [probably 1852], by Rev. Cephas Brainerd	LR47	131
Moses, s. Ebenezer, b. Feb. 4, 1750/1	LR8	6
Nanse, d. William, b. Aug. 30, 1776	LR21	546
Noah, s. Jared, b. Mar. 26, 1743; d. Mar. 29, 1743	LR6	4
Noah, s. Seth & Joanna, b. June 12, 1776	LR21	546
Orin, s. John, b. Oct. 9, 1760	LR11	585
Pauline, of Farmington, m. Charles F. **TOMPKINS**, of		
Bristol, Nov. 9, 1845, by Rev. S. H. Clark	LR47	115
Roday, d. Jared, b. Mar. 11, 1744	LR7	L
Rhoda, d. Jared, b. Mar. 11, 1744	LR14	8
Rhoda, m. Ashbell **COWLES**, Apr. 27, 1769	LR17	442
Rhoda, w. Jared, d. Feb. 12, 1771, in the 63rd y. of her		
age	LR17	444
Rhoda, d. Dr. Seth, b. Apr. 4, 1782	LR22	467
Riverias, s. Ebenezer, b. Apr. 9, 1754	LR11	585
Ruth, d. John, b. Jan. 14, 1703	LR1	3
Ruth, d. Jonathan, b. Aug. 3, 1722	LR2	282
Ruth, m. William **JUDD**, May. 14, 1722/3	LR2	60
Samuel, s. John, b. Mar. 23, 1694	LR1	3

	Vol.	Page
LEE (cont.)		
Samuel, m. [E]unice **GOODWIN**, b. of Ffarmington, Dec. 4, 1717	LR2	100
Samuel, s .John, b. Oct. 2, 1757	LR11	585
Samuel, s. Seth & Joanna, b. Jan. 18, 1775	LR17	436
Sarah, d. Stephen, b. Nov. 8, 1696	LR2	97
Sarah, m. John **LANGTON**, b. of Ffarmington, Jan. 18, 1721/2	LR2	100
Sarah, d. Hezekiah & Sarah, b. Oct. 27, 1729	LR5	5
Sarah, d. Stephen, b. Aug. 22, 1758	LR15	1
Sary, d. John, b. Aug. 13, 1767	LR15	G
Sarah, d. Seth & Sarah, b. Feb. 25, 1769	LR15	G
Sarah, w. Seth, d. July 15, 1770, in the 29th y. of her age	LR15	M
Sarah Ingersoll,* d. Seth, M. A. & Sarah, b. Feb. 25, 1769 *(On Oct 24, 1772, "Ingersoll" the maiden name of mother was added. This being done after the mother's death)	LR17	435
Seth, s. Jarad, b. Mar. 31, 1736	LR6	4
Seth, m. Sarah **INGERSOLL**, Sept. 3, 1767	LR15	A
Seth, of Farmington, s. Jared, m. Joanna **JOHNSON**, d. Daniell, Sept. 9, 1771, by Rev. Simeon Warterman	LR17	G
Seth, s. Dr. Seth, b. Jan. 26, 1780	LR22	467
Stephen, of Ffarmington, m. Elizabeth **ROYCE**, of Wallingford, Oct. 1, 1690	LR2	125
Stephen, his 2nd child, b. Apr. 18, 1693; d. same day	LR2	97
Stephen, s. Stephen, b. Apr. 18, 1700	LR2	97
Stephen, s. Stephen, d. Sept. 13, 1718	LR2	148
Stephen, s. Isaac, b. Mar. 18, 1722/3	LR4	374
Stephen, s. Isaac, b. Mar. 16, 1723/4	LR5	5
Stephen, m. Catharine **FURBS**, Feb. 6, 1746	LR15	A
Thankfull, d. Isaac, b. Nov. 9, 1726	LR4	374
Thankfull, d. Isaac, b. Nov. 9, 1729	LR5	5
Theodore, s. Isaac, Jr., b. May 20, 1741	LR6	4
Theodora, m. Olive **BORDMAN**, Dec. 10, 1768	LR17	442
Theodora, had s. Elisha **BARDMAN**, b. Jan. 21, 1773	LR17	436
Thomas, of Ffarmington, m. Mary **CAMP**, of Hartford, Sept. 11, 1707	LR2	125
Thomas, twin with John, s. Thomas, b. Dec. 7, 1716	LR2	81
Thomas, Sergt., of Farmington, m. Martha **FORWOOD**, wid. of Samuell, of Simsbury, Apr. 17, 1739	LR6	27
Thomas, s. Isaac, 3rd, b. Nov. 28, 1776	LR21	546
Thomas, m. Theodosia **THOMSON**, June 7, 1780, by [ ]	LR47	99
Timothy, s. Isaac, b. Nov. 8, 1713	LR5	5
Timothy, s. Isaac, b. Nov. 8, 1714	LR4	374
Timothy, s. Isaac, d. Feb. 14, 1731	LR5	50
Timothy, s. Jared, b. Nov. 26, 1740	LR14	8
Timothy, s. Stephen, b. Oct. 10, 1748	LR15	1
Timothy, s. Jared, m. Lucy **CAPT**, d. Dea. John, Apr. 23, 1772	LR17	G
Timothy, s. Seth, b. June 11, 1789	LR22	467
William, s. William, b. Dec. 24, 1781	LR21	546
----nel, m. Elizabeth **HALL**, Sept. 4, 1771	LR17	G

	Vol.	Page
LEET[E], Asa, s. Asa & Hannah, b. Mar. 22, 1759	LR11	585
Asa, s. Asa, b. Apr. 21,1763	LR11	585
Hannah, d. Asa, b. July 4, 1761	LR11	585
Mercy, of Gilford, m. Samuel **HOOKER**, Jr., of		
Ffarmington, Jan. 9, 1710/11	LR2	257
LENSAAS (?), Robert, s. Robert, b. Mar. 22, 1757	LR11	585
Seth, s. Robert, b. Nov. 19, 1755	LR11	585
[LEONARD], LENERD, Rachel, of Springfield, m. Thomas		
HANCOX, of Farmington, Mar. 17, 1684/5	LR2	125
LEWIS, Abel, s. Josiah, b. Sept. 17, 1749	LR8	6
Abigall, d. William, b. Sept. 19, 1678	LR1	2
Abigell, m. William **WADSWORTH**, Dec. 10, 1696	LR1	5
Abigel, d. Nathaniell, b. Nov. 15, 1701	LR1	2
Abigail, w. Ens. Nathaniel, d. Apr. 11, 1723	LR2	61
Abigail, d. Isaac, b. Apr. [ ], 1725	LR4	374
Abigail, w. Sergt. Isaac, d. Aug. [ ], 1727	LR4	396
Abigail, d. Daniel, b. June 8, 1731	LR5	5
Abigail, m. James **WADSWORTH**, Nov. 2, 1749	LR7	35
Abisha, s. Benjamin, b. May 15, 1766	LR14	8
Adonijah, s. Jonathan [& Elizabeth], b. July 12, 1722	LR2	104
Adonijah, m. Mary **BROWNSON**, July 31, 1760	LR11	592
Almira, d. Josiah, Jr., b. Feb. 22, 1772	LR17	435
Ann, m. John **STOUGHTON**, July 29, 1762	LR17	442
Anna, d. Eli, b. Feb. 16, 1769	LR15	1
Appleton, s. Nathaniell, b. Aug. 18, 1774	LR17	441
Asahel, s. Nathan, b. Feb. 25, 1744/5	LR7	L
Asahel, s. Ethan, b. Aug. 27, 1757	LR11	585
Asahel, had s. [ ], b. Jan. 13, 1770; d. Feb. 6, 1770	LR17	435
Benjamin, s. Benjamin, b. Apr. 18, 1764	LR11	584
Betsey, m. Root **GRIDLEY**, June 30, 1824, by Rev.		
Noah Porter	LR42	568
Catharine M., m. Samuel **DEMING**, b. of Farmington,		
Jan. 18, 1821, by Noah Porter, V.D.M.	LR40	571
Charles, s. Sergt. Isaac, d. [Dec.] 27, 1727	LR4	396
Charles, s. Nathaniel, b. Jan. 22, 1734	LR6	1
Charles, s. Nathaniel, Jr. & Rachel, b. Jan. 6, 1734/5	LR6	4
Charles, of Wolcott, m. Emeline M. **BARTHOLOMEW**,		
of Farmington, Oct. 30, 1827, by Rev. Noah Porter	LR42	565
Chauncey S., of Southington, m. Lucinda **PHINNEY**, of		
Farmington, Mar. 9, 1829, by Rev. Noah Porter	LR42	562
Daniell, s. William, b. July 16, 1681	LR1	2
Daniel, s. William, b. Dec. 10, 1691	LR4	395
Daniel, of Ffarmington, m. Mary **STRONG**, of		
Ffarmington, May 1, 1718	LR2	101
Daniel, s. Daniel, b. Sept. 24, 1721	LR2	102
Daniel, his d. [ ], b. Jan. [ ], 1727/8	LR4	396
Daniel, m. Keziah **WRIGHT**, Oct. 12, 1753	LR8	10
David, s. Josiah, b. Oct. 7, 1751	LR8	6
David, s. Josiah, d. June 9, 1752	LR8	12
Dorcas, s. Benjamin, b. Dec. 24, 1757	LR11	585
Ebenezer, s. Lelmuel, b. June 6, 1769	LR15	G
Eldad, s. Isaac, b. Feb. 11, 1710/11	LR2	99
Eldad, m. Sarah **WIARD**, Mar. 10, 1737	LR7	46

	Vol.	Page
LEWIS (cont.)		
Eldad, m. Jerusha **COWLES**, July 4, 1745	LR7	46
Eldad, Capt., m. wid. Sarah **ROOT**, Apr. 11, 1754	LR10	6
Eldad, s. Capt. Eldad & Sarah, b. Feb. 7, 1755	LR9	10-11
Eli, s. Josiah, b. Apr. 15, 1743	LR8	6
Elim, m. Anna **COLLINS**, Jan. 31, 1765	LR11	594
Eli, s. Eli, b. Apr. 20, 1773	LR17	436
Elias, s. Nehemiah & Experience, b. Aug. 9, 1750	LR8	6
Elias, s. Nehemiah, d. Feb. 20, 1750/1	LR8	11
Elias, s. William, b. Apr. 1, 1762	LR11	585
Elijah, s. Phineas, b. Mar. 21, 1750/1	LR8	6
Elisha, s. Nathaniell, b. Dec. 3, 1705	LR1	4
Elisha, s. Nathaniell, d. Apr. 28, 1708	LR1	7
Elisha, s. Nathaniel, b. July 23, 1710	LR2	109
Elisha, m. Ruth **WADSWORTH**, b. of Farmington, Apr. 18, 1739	LR6	27
Elisha, s. Thomas, b. Jan. 4, 1768	LR15	G
Elisha Slater, s. Elisha, b. Sept. 10, 1771	LR17	436
Elizabeth, d. William, b. Oct. 20, 1672	LR1	2
Elizabeth, d. Daniel, b. May 23, 1719	LR2	83
Elizabeth, d. Petres, d. Jan. 29, 1747/8	LR7	36
Elizabeth, d. Josiah, Jr., b. [ ] 3, 1767	LR15	G
Emeline, of Farmington, m. Shelton **HOTCHKISS**, of Bristol, Mar. 29, 1835, by Rev. Noah Porter	LR47	89
Enos, s. Samuel, Jr., b. Sept. 1, 1758	LR11	585
Eri, m. Mary **CRAMPTON**, b. of Farmington, Oct. 25, 1827, by Rev. Noah Porter	LR42	565
Easther, d. Nehemiah, b. July 27, 173[ ]	LR5	5
Ethan, s. Daniel, b. July 27, 1724	LR2	34
Ethan, m. Sible **PARMELE**, June 18, 1746	LR7	35
Ezekiell, s. William, b. Nov. 7, 1674	LR1	2
Ezekiel, s. Nathaniel, b. Nov. 19, 1718	LR2	83
Ezekiel, m. Hannah **SMITH**, b. of Farmington, Dec. 14, 1733	LR5	300
Ezekiel, 2nd, s. Ezekiel, b. Jan. 10, 1747	LR8	6
Ezekiel, of Farmington, m. Sarah **WRIGHT**, of Hatfield, July 27, 1747	LR7	35
Ezekiel, d. Dec. 27, 1757	LR8	13
Ezekiel, m. wid. Annah **PORTTER**, Mar. 9, 1758	LR11	576
Ezekiel, s. Thomas, b. Dec. 30, 1769	LR15	G
Gideon, s. Isaac, b. June 3, 1720/1	LR4	374
Hannah, d. Samuel, Jr., b. Sept 23, 1724	LR2	46
Hannah, had d. Patience, b. Apr. 7, 1752	LR8	6
Hannah, d. Apr. 14, 1752	LR8	11
Hannah, d. Nathan, b. [ ], 1753	LR9	10-11
Hannah, m. John **JUDD**, Jan. 16, 1755	LR9	9
Hannah, d. Samuel, Jr. & Ruth, b. Aug. 19, 1757	LR11	585
Harriet, of Farmington, m. Roswell **PHILIPS**, of Burlington, Nov. 1, 1824, by Rev. Noah Porter	LR42	568
Helena, d. Eli, b. May 16, 1771	LR17	435
Henry, m. Nancy **WOODRUFF**, Aug. 25, 1841, by Rev. Aaron S. Hill	LR47	105
Hester, d. Samuell, b. Nov. 8, 1708; d. Dec. 5, 1708	LR1	3

	Vol.	Page
LEWIS (cont.)		
Hewillia, d. Aug. 18, 1690	LR1	2
Isaac, s. William, b. Apr. 26, 1685	LR4	395
Isaac, of Ffarmington, m. Abibail **CURTIC**, of		
Weathersfield, May 4, 1710	LR2	123
Isaac, s. Isaac, b. Sept. 11, 1719	LR4	374
Isaac, Sergt. his s. [ ], b. [ ]12, 1728/9	LR4	396
James, s. William, b. about July 10, 1667	LR1	2
Jane E., of Northumberland, N.Y., m. James **COWLES**,		
of Farmington, Feb. 22, 1838, by Rev. Noah Porter	LR47	97
Jane T., of Farmington, m. William L. **THOMPSON**, of		
Hartford, Jan. 8, 1850, by Rev. Noah Porter	LR47	126
Jerusha, w. Capt. Eldad, d. Nov. 4, 1752	LR9	495
Jerusha, d .[Nehemiah], b. Jan. 15, [ ]	LR7	L
Job, s. Sergt. Samuel, b. June 18, 1713	LR2	99
Job, s. Sergt. Samuel, d. Aug. 4, 1713	LR2	142
Job, s. Nathan, b. Apr. 20, 1731	LR5	5
Job, m. Hannah **CURTICE**, Nov. 13, 1755	LR11	576
John, s. William, b. about May 15, 1665	LR1	2
John, s. Samuel, b. Sept. 28, 1703	LR1	3
John, s. Isaac, b. Oct. 2, 1722	LR4	374
John, of Farmington, m. Rachel **RICHASON**, of		
Wallingford, Dec. 2, 1736	LR6	27
John, of Farmington, m. Thankfull **BENNUM**, of		
Wallingford, Nov. 1, 1739	LR6	27
John, s. John, b. Oct. 25, 1743	LR6	4
John B., of Schulerville, N.Y., m. Elizabeth **BODWELL**,		
of Farmington, Feb. 2, 1848, by Noah Porter	LR47	122
Jonathan, s. William, b. June 2, 1697	LR4	395
Jonathan, m. Elizabeth **NEWEL**, b. of Ffarmington, Jan.		
28, 1719/20	LR2	104
Jonathan, s. Jonathan [& Elizabeth], b. Apr. 17, 1725	LR2	104
Jonathan, s. William, d. Sept. 29, 1727	LR4	396
Joseph, s. William, b. Mar. 15, 1679	LR1	2
Josiah, s. Samuel, b. Dec. 31, 1709	LR2	109
Josiah, m. Phebe **GRIDLEY**, b. of Farmington, July 6,		
1737	LR6	27
Josiah, s. Josiah, b. Nov. 1, 1739	LR6	4
Josiah, s. Josiah, b. Nov. 1, 1739	LR8	6
Josiah, Jr., m. Abigail **JEROME**, May 8, 1766	LR15	A
Josiah, s. Josiah, Jr., b. Oct. 30, 1769	LR17	435
Judah, s. Ezekiel, b. Mar. 30, 1752	LR8	6
Judith, d. Elisha, b. Aug. 22, 1765	LR15	G
Julian, of Berlin, m. Philo **ROWLEY**, of Farmington,		
[Feb.] 11, [1830], by Rev. Noah Porter	LR42	561
Lemuel, of Wolcott, m. Eliza C. **TUBBS**, of Farmington,		
Nov. 24, 1827, by Rev. Noah Porter	LR42	565
Loderic S., m. Celestia **CURTISS**, b. of Burlington, July		
20, 1842, by Rev. C. D. Cowles	LR47	108
Lory, s. Capt. Eldad & Sarah, b. May 8, 1757	LR11	585
Lucina, d .William, b. Feb. 23, 1760	LR11	585
Lucy, d. Benjamin, b. July 21, 1760	LR11	585
Lucy, d. Adonijah, b. Dec. 18, 1761	LR11	585

	Vol.	Page
LEWIS (cont.)		
Lucy, d. Eli, b. Mar. 3, 1775	LR17	441
Lidia, d. Eli, b. Oct. 29, 1765	LR15	G
Mark, s. Timothy, b. Nov. 6, 1769	LR17	435
Mark, m. Lura **NORTH**, b. of Farmington, May 4, 1835,		
by Rev. Noah Porter	LR47	89
Marshal, s. Elisha, b. Oct. 3, 1767	LR15	G
Martha, d. Lemuel, b. July 18, 1767	LR15	G
Martha, of Farmington, m. Robert A. **MORRIS**, of		
Ellington, June 17, 1845, by Rev. Noah Porter	LR47	114
Martin, s. Eli, b. Apr. 16, 1767	LR15	G
Mary, m. Thomas **BULL**, Jan. 13, 1691	LR1	5
Mary, d. William, b. Mar. 31, 1699/1700	LR4	395
Mary, d. Nathaniel, b. Dec. 18, 1714	LR2	95
Mary, d. Daniel, d. Sept. 5, 1736	LR5	50
Mary, d. John, b. Aug. 6, 1740	LR6	4
Mary, d. John, d. Sept. 2, 1740	LR6	10
Mary ,m. James **THOMSON**, b. of Farmington, Oct. 30,		
1741	LR6	304
Mary, d. Nathan, b. Dec. 31, 1743	LR7	L
Mary, wid. Sergt. Samuell, d. Feb. 16, 1744/5	LR7	36
Mary, w. Daniel, d. Apr. 9, 1751	LR8	11
Mary, wid., m. Lieut. James **COWLES**, Nov. 15, 1773	LR17	443
Mary, d. [Nehemiah], b. Aug. 30, [ ]	LR7	L
Mary D., m. Elijah **COWLES**, Apr. 16, 1845, by Rev.		
Noah Porter	LR47	114
Meedad, s. Isaac, b. Sept. 8, 1712	LR2	99
Mercy, d. Nathaniel, b. Apr. 16, 1717	LR2	81
Mercy, d. Nathaniel, d. Aug. 2, 1718	LR2	62
Mercy, m. Noah **PORTER**, May 10, 1764	LR11	592
Merrel, s. Lemuel, b. Mar. 1, 1765	LR15	G
Naomi, d. Bela, b. May 10, 1754	LR9	10-11
Nathan, s. Samuel, b. Jan. 23, 1706/7	LR1	3
Nathan, m. Mary **GRIDLEY**, b. of Farmington, July 28,		
1730	LR5	13
Nathan, Jr., of Farmington, m. Rachel **KELLOGG**, of		
Weathersfield, Feb. 27, 1733/4	LR5	300
Nathan, s. Nathan, b. Dec. 15, 1734	LR5	5
Nathan, m. Susan **WOODFORD**, b. of Farmington, Nov.		
11, 1829, by Rev. Noah Porter	LR42	561
Nathaniell, s. William, b. Oct. 1, 1676	LR1	2
Nathaniell, m. Abigell **ASHLEY**, Nov. 25, 1699	LR1	4
Nathaniell, s. Nathaniell, b. Jan. 1, 1703/4	LR1	2
Nathaniel, Ens. of Ffarmington, m. Thankfull **LYMAN**,		
of Northampton, July 4, 1726	LR2	100
Nathaniel, s. Nathan, b. Dec. [ ], 1747	LR9	10-11
Nathaniell, m. Sarah **GRIDLEY**, Feb. 15, 1769	LR17	443
Nehemyah, s. Samuel, b. May 3, 1705	LR1	3
Nehemiah, m. Jerusha **GRIDLEY**, Nov. 21, 1728	LR4	423
Nehemiah, Sergt., m. Phebe **WONG** (?), Sept. 19, 1749	LR7	35
Nehemiah, s. Nehemiah, b. Dec. 13, [ ]	LR7	L
Noadiah, s. Nathaniell, b. Apr. 27, 1708	LR1	7
Noadiah, d. Nov. 4, 1736	LR6	10

	Vol.	Page
LEWIS (cont.)		
Noadiah, s. Noadiah, b. Nov. 24, 1736	LR6	1
Nodiah, s. Nodiah, b. Nov. 24, 1736	LR6	4
Norton, of Berlin, m. Julia **BIRD**, of Farmington, Nov.		
16, 1830, by Amzi Benedict	LR42	560
Olive, d. Ens. Nehemiah, b. June 20, 1754	LR9	10-11
Oliver, b. Nov. 23, 1736	LR6	1
Oliver, s. Job & Hannah, b. Apr. 24, 1757	LR11	585
Oliver, m. Nancy A. **FULLER**, b. of Farmington, Nov.		
14, 1838, by Rev. S. H. Clark	LR47	98
Patience, d. Hannah, b. Apr. 7, 1752	LR8	6
Phebe, d. William, b. Sept. 3, 1694	LR4	395
Phebe, d. William, d. [ ] 11, 1712	LR2	141
Phebe, d. William; d. Apr. 11, 1713	LR4	396
Phebe, d. Isaac, b. Oct. 16, 1715	LR4	374
Phebe, d. Isaac, d. Sept. 27, 1719	LR2	148
Phebe, d. Jonathan [& Elizabeth], b. Dec. 5, 1720	LR2	104
Phebe, d. Jonathan, d. Jan. 17, 1724/5	LR2	66
Phebe, d. Daniel & Mary, b. Dec. 14, 1735	LR5	645
Philener, d. Elisha, b. Nov. 27, 1763	LR15	G
Phineas, s. Nathaniel, b. Apr. 11, 1722	LR2	102
Phineas, m. Sarah **NORTON**, Nov. 27, 1746	LR7	35
Prudence, m. Elias **WILLCOX**, Apr. 9, 1777	LR22	480
Rachal, d. John, b. June 27, 1738	LR6	4
Rachel, w. John, d. July 6, 1738	LR6	10
Rachel, d. John, d. Sept. 22, 1738	LR6	10
Rebeckah, d. Josiah, b. Mar. 18, 1741	LR8	6
Reuben, s. Nathaniell, b. Aug. 16, 1772	LR17	441
Rhoda, d. Nathan, b. Mar. 20, 1733	LR5	5
Rhoda, m. John **WEBSTER**, Nov. 3, 1755	LR9	286
Rhoda, d. Eli, b. Dec. 19, 1776	LR21	546
Rhoda, of Farmington, m. Miles **THORP**, of Bristol,		
Mar. 31, 1828, by Rev. Noah Porter	LR42	564
Roger, s. Josiah, b. July 17, 1738	LR6	4
Roger, d. Dec. 26, 1756	LR8	12
Roswell, of Farmington, m. Polly C. **CULVER**, of		
Bristol, Nov. 4, 1829, by Rev. Noah Porter	LR42	561
Royce, s. Josiah, b. Jan. 23, 1745	LR8	6
Ruth, d. William, b. Sept. 12, 1679	LR4	395
Ruth, m. Samuel **GRIDLEY**, s. Samuel, June 8, 1710	LR2	145
Ruth, d. Nehemiah & Jerusha, b. Sept. 1, 1729	LR5	5
Ruth, m. John **DAVIS**, Dec. 1, 1748	LR7	46
Ruth, d. Bela, b. Feb. 3, 1752	LR8	6
Sabra, d. Elisha, b. Dec. 16, 1769	LR17	435
Samuell,* m. Elizabeth **JUDD**, Dec. 27, 1653		
*("Samuel **LOMES**")	LR2	331
Samuel, s. Samuel, decd., supposed to have been b. May		
24, 1692; bp. May 29, 1692	LR5	5
Samuel, Jr., m. Mary **COLE**, wid. Samuell, b. of		
Ffarmington, Aug. 11, 1720	LR2	101
Samuel, s. Samuel, Jr., b. Aug. 16, 1721	LR2	102
Samuel, Sergt., d. Nov. 28, 1725	LR2	148
Samuel, s. John, b. July last day, 1746	LR7	L

	Vol.	Page
LEWIS (cont.)		
Samuel, s. John, of Southington, d. Apr. 3, 1747	LR7	36
Samuel, s. Josiah, b. Apr. 26, 1747	LR8	6
Samuel, Jr., m. Ruth **YALE**, Aug. 12, 1756	LR11	576
Samuel, s. Samuel, b. Sept. 20, 1762	LR11	585
Samuel, m. [ ], Oct. 10, 1762	LR15	A
Samuel Hart, s. Benjamin, b. Oct. 2, 1755	LR9	10-11
Sarah, d. William, b. Apr. 15, 1682	LR4	395
Sarah, m. Samuell **SMITH**, s. Jonathan, Aug. 15, 1706	LR1	4
Sarah, d. Nathaniel, b. May 8, 1712	LR2	98
Sarah, d. William, d. Aug. 19, 1725	LR4	396
Sarah, d. Daniel, b. Dec. 2, 1726	LR2	242
Sarah, m. Joseph **HOOKER**, b. of Farmington, Jan. 23, 1734/5	LR5	545
Sarah, w. Eldad, d. Aug. 10, 1742	LR7	36
Sarah, w. Ezekiel, d. Nov. 9, 1752	LR8	11
Sarah, d. Phinehas, b. Sept. 17, 1759	LR11	584
Sarah, d. Roger, b. Jan. 17, 1771	LR17	435
Sarah, w. Royce, d. Mar. 6, 1772, in the 23rd y. of her age	LR17	444
Sarah, d. Royce, d. Apr. 19, 1772	LR17	444
Sarah, d. Thomas, b. Aug. 28, 1774	LR17	436
Sarah, d. John, b. Mar. 5, 1751	LR8	6
Seth, s. Daniel, b. Nov. 14, 1733	LR5	5
Seth, s. Daniel, d. Nov. 15, 1750	LR7	540
Seth, s. Ethan, b. Mar. 5, 1751	LR8	6
Seth, s. Ethan, d. Sept. 20, 1757	LR11	577
Seth, s. Job, b. June 24, 1759	LR11	585
Sibbel, d. Elisha, b. Mar. 29, 1762	LR15	G
Silas, s. Elisha, Jr. & Tamer, b. Dec. 7, 1758	LR11	585
Susannah, d. Elisha, b. Aug. 19, 1760	LR15	G
Silvey, d. Nathaniel, b. Feb. 15, 1769	LR17	441
Tamer, d. Elisha, Jr., d. Mar. 14, 1759	LR11	577
Thankful, d. John, b. Nov. 25, 1743	LR6	7
Thomas, s. Eli & Ruth, b. Aug. 7, 1740	LR6	4
Thomas, m. Sarah **GARNSEY**, of Durham, Dec. 24, 1765	LR11	594
Thomas, s. William, b. July 20, 1768	LR15	G
Timothy, s. Nathan, b. Apr. 18, 1740	LR7	L
Timothy C., m. Charlotte M. **BOWEN**, b. of Farmington, May 26, 1841, by Rev. Noah Porter	LR47	105
Wadsworth Daniel, s. Thomas, b. Nov. 25, 1766	LR14	8
William, m. Mary **CHEVER**, Nov. 22, 1671, in Boston	LR1	5
William his d. [ ], d. [ ], 1674; his s. [ ], d. Aug. [ ], 1679; another s. [ ], d. Mar. [ ], 1681/2	LR1	2
William, s. William, b. Aug. 31, 1687	LR4	395
William, s. William, d. Jan. 17, 1712/13	LR2	141
William, s. Isaac, b. Dec. 24, 1713	LR2	99
William, s. William, d. Jan. 14, 1713/14	LR4	396
William, s. Nehemiah & Jerusha, b. Dec. 7, 1734	LR5	306
William, s. Daniel, d. Feb. 21, 1749/50	LR7	540
William, m. Mary **BULL**, Dec. 7, 1758	LR11	592
William, m. Hannah [ ], Oct. 1, 1767	LR15	A
Will[iam], s. Nehemiah, b. Dec. 7, [ ]	LR7	L
William, s. Daniel, b. [ ]	LR6	4

	Vol.	Page
LEWIS (cont.)		
----hel, m. Lois **LEE**, Feb. 1, 1769	LR17	G
---than, Jr., m. Jemima [ ], Dec. 15, 1769	LR17	G
----Sr., d. Aug. 2, 1683	LR1	2
LITTLE, Anne, d. Edward, b. Jan. 8, 1757	LR9	10-11
LIVINGSTON, Sylvia, of Farmington, m. Thomas		
GORDON, of Philadelphia, Sept. 20, 1829, by Rev.		
Noah Porter	LR42	562
LOOMIS, LUMMIS, LOMIS, LOMMIS, Caroline M., of		
New Hartford, m. William H. **LOOMIS**, of		
Torringford, Nov. 17, 1845, by Rev. Noah Porter	LR47	115
Elizabeth, m. John **LEE**, Dec. 27, 1682	LR1	4
Elizabeth, of Haddam, m. Nehemiah L. **HOMER**, of		
Farmington, Dec. 31, 1841, by Rev. C. D. Cowles	LR47	106
Harriet, m. George **WOODRUFF**, b. of Farmington,		
Mar. 13, 1845, by Noah Porter	LR47	113
Johanah, m. Joseph **SMITH**, Nov. 10, 1691	LR1	6
Mehitibel, sometime of Windsor, m. John **COLE**, of		
Ffarmington, June [ ], 1691	LR2	123
Rebeckah, m. Thomas **WOODRUFF**, June 26, 1748	LR7	46
Samuel,* m. Elizabeth **JUDD**, Dec. 27, 1653 *(Arnold		
Copy has "Samuel **LEWIS**")	LR2	331
Samuel K., m. Julia **ROBINSON**, b. of Farmington, Nov.		
16, 1826, by Rev. Noah Porter	LR42	567
William H., of Torringford, m. Caroline M. **LOOMIS**, of		
New Hartford, Nov. 17, 1845, by Rev. Noah Porter	LR47	115
LORD, Chancey, s. Dr. Elisha, b. Feb. 22, 1753	LR8	6
Elisha, Dr., m. Elizabeth **EDGERTON**, Nov. 10, 1751	LR8	10
Haynes, of New York City, m. Esther **COWLES**, of		
Farmington ,Oct. 24, 1837, by Rev. Noah Porter	LR47	96
Salle, d. Dr. Elisha, b. Nov. 24, 1757	LR11	585
Simeon, d. Sept. 7, 1753	LR8	12
LOVELAND, Ira S., of Glastonbury, m. Luanna **CLARK**, of		
Farmington, Mar. 2, 1835, by Rev. Noah Porter	LR47	88
Julia E., of Farmington, m. John M. **BUNNEL**, of		
Canaan, Feb. 25, 1844, by William Wright	LR47	112
Mehitabel, had s. William Brase,* b. May 10, 1744		
*("Brace"?)	LR8	3
Mehetable, had d. Abigail **PORTER**, b. Nov. 8, 1749	LR8	7
Sally, m. Giles **STILLMAN**, Nov. 27, 1822	LR47	W-Y
Stephen L., of Farmington, m. Maria **TODD**, of		
Plymouth, Sept. 5, 1847, by William Wright	LR47	121
LOWREY, LOWREE, Fanny, of Farmington, m. Hezekiah		
GOODWIN, of Salisbury, Apr. 4, 1830,by Rev.		
Noah Porter	LR42	561
George, s. John, b. Jan. 29, 1761	LR11	585
James, s. John, b. Mar. 30, 1759	LR11	585
John, m. Elidia **SCOTT**, Apr. 5, 1758	LR11	575
LUCAS, Henry, m. Sophia **NOBLE**, b. of Bristol, Apr. 17,		
1845, by William Wright	LR47	114
LUDDINGTON, Anne, d. Collins, b. Mar. 20, 1781	LR23	467
Collen, m. Sarah **SMITH**, Feb. 9, 1775	LR21	557

	Vol.	Page
LUDDINGTON (cont.)		
Daniel, Jr., of Wallingford, m. Mable **LEE**, of		
Farmington, Apr. 26, 1773	LR17	442
Salla, d. Callington, b. Feb. 5, 1777	LR21	546
LUMM, Hannah, of Woodbury, m. Nehemyah **PORTTER**, of		
Ffarmington, Jan. 21, 1686/7	LR2	125
LUSK, Bella, s. Andrew, b. Mar. 23, 1766	LR15	G
Margaret, m. [ ] **NORTH**, Mar. 8, 1770	LR17	G
Selah, s. Andrew, b. Mar. 25, 1764	LR15	G
LUTHER, Martin, of Simsbury, m. Lucy A. **CHIDSEY**, of		
Farmington, Mar. 19, 1845, by Rev. S. H. Clark	LR47	114
LYMAN, Silas, of Vernon, m. Sophia **FOWLER**, of		
Farmington, Feb. 8, 1826, by Rev. Bela Kellogg	LR42	569
Thankfull, of Northampton, m. Nathaniel **LEWIS** (Ens.),		
of Ffarmington, July 4, 1726	LR2	100
McAULEY, Mary, of Farmington, m. Nelson **FOX**, of Avon,		
Mar. 29, 1846, in Avon, by Rev. Stephen Hubbell,		
of Avon	LR47	117
M'CARTY,* Henry, of Martinsburgh, N.Y., m. Maria		
CADWELL, of Farmington, Jan. 19, 1824, by Rev.		
Augustus Bolles *(Perhaps "Henry M. **CARTY**")	LR42	568
McCLINTOCK, McLINTOCK, Ann, m. John		
THOMPSON, b. of Farmington, Nov. 15, 1849, by		
Rev. Noah Porter	LR47	126
Rebecca, m. David **DOAK**, of Brooklyn, N.Y., Dec. 15,		
1845, by Rev. Noah Porter	LR47	116
McCRAY, Rosmond, m. Timothy P. **CHAPMAN**, b. of		
Ellington, Apr. 6, 1843, by Rev. Jesse Baker	LR47	109
McDONALD, James, m. Catharine **REED**, b. of Hartford,		
Dec. 6, 1835, by Rev. Noah Porter	LR47	91
[McEWEN], **MACUN**, Elizabeth, of Stratford, m. Thomas		
NORTON, Jr., of Farmington, Nov. 17, 1724	LR2	257
Sarah, of Stratford, m. Hezekiah **WOODRUFF**, of		
Farmington, Dec. 3, 1730	LR5	13
McINTIRE, Emner S., of Bristol, m. Jennette E. **HILLS**, of		
Farmington, Feb. 3, 1850, by William Wright	LR47	127
McWARY, William G., of New Hartford, m. Rebecca **DIX**, of		
Farmington, Mar. 8, 1836, by Rev. Noah Porter	LR47	93
MANGER, Roseanah, m. Charles **HAYTON**, Mar. [ ], 1783	LR22	480
MARSH, Jonathan, Dr., of Norwich, m. Sarah **HART**, of		
Farmington, Nov. 5, 1747	LR7	46
Luke, s. Eleazer & Hannah, b. Nov. 5, 1741	LR6	5
Sarah, m. Thomas **NORTON**, July 8, 1762	LR11	594
Timothy, m. Sarah **ANDRUS**, Oct. 27, 1765	LR11	594
MARSHALL, MARSHAL, Oliver, s. Seth, b. Oct. 31, 1756	LR11	585
Preserved, s. Seth & Sarah, b. July 10, 1761	LR47	119
Roxy Emeline, of Windsor, m. Russell **WELLS**, of		
Farmington, Nov. 17, 1822, by Amasa Woodford,		
J.P.	LR40	572
Samuel, m. Mary **WELCH**, Dec. 22, 1848, by Rev.		
Henry J. Fox	LR47	124
Sarah, d. Seth, b. Jan. 19, 1750/1	LR8	6
Seth, m. Sarah **BARBER**, Jan. 19, 1749/50	LR7	35

	Vol.	Page
MARSHALL, MARSHAL (cont.)		
Seth, s. Seth, b. Dec. 1, 1754	LR9	10-11
Seth, had d. [ ], b. Feb. 11, 1759	LR11	585
MASON, William, of Hartford, m. Abbey **FREEMAN**, of		
Colchester, Oct. 9, 1831, by Rev. Noah Porter	LR42	560
MATHER, MARTHA, MARTHER, Anna, d. Joseph, b.		
Sept. 15, 1740	LR7	J
Betty, d. David, b. Nov. 20, 1767	LR21	547
Billey, s. Thomas, b. July 21, 1764	LR14	9
Bille, s. Dr. Thomas, dec., (?), b. July 21, 1764	LR15	H
Cotton, s. Joshua & Hannah, b. Sept. 19, 1737	LR6	5
Cotton, s. David, b. Sept. 2, 1771	LR21	547
Cotton, s. David, b. Aug. 23, 1764; d. Sept. 7, 1777	LR21	547
David, s. Joshua & Hannah, b. Oct. 7, 1738	LR6	5
David, m. Hanah **DUNHAM**, June 3, 1757	LR11	576
Elenor, d. Joshua, b. Sept. 27, 174[ ]	LR7	J
Elener, d. David, b. Mar. 14, 1758	LR11	585
Elisha, s. Joshua, b. Apr. 19, 1749	LR7	E
Hannah, d. Joshua, b. Jan. 25, 1745	LR7	J
Hannah, d. David, b. Aug. 10, 1769	LR21	547
Hannah, w. Joseph, d. Apr. 8, 1777	LR21	558-9
Hitte, [d. Joseph], b. Apr. [ ], 1742	LR7	J
Huldah, m. Samuel **SMITH**, Feb. 25, 1771	LR17	G
Jerusha, of Berlin, m. Resin G. **JONES**, of Farmington,		
May 15, 1827, by Rev. Noah Porter	LR42	565
Joshua, d. May 16, 1777	LR21	558-9
Leoe, d. Dr. Thomas, decd (?), b. Feb. 21, 1767	LR15	H
Lydia, [d. Joseph], b. Jan. 17, 1744	LR7	J
Mahitable, m. Joshua **KILLBORN**, July 14, 1763	LR11	592
Pernellepee, d. Joseph, b. May 27, 174[ ]	LR7	J
Phebe, d. [Joseph], b. Jan. 6, 1748	LR7	J
Pierce, s. David, b. Jan. 22, 1760	LR11	585
Rhoda, d. David, b. Oct. 27, 1776	LR21	547
Sarah, d. Joseph, b. Jan. 18, 1738/9	LR6	5
Thomas, s. Joshua, b. Sept. 7, 1741	LR6	5
Thomas, m. Huldah **BULL**, Mar. 12, 1764	LR11	592
Thomas, Dr., d. Aug. 10, 1766	LR14	3
Thomas, s. David, b. Dec. 10, 1773; d. Dec. 11, 1773	LR21	547
MATTHEWS, MATHEWS, Abiah, s. Benjamin, b .Apr. 8,		
1750	LR8	6
Amos, s. Abner, b. [ ] 27, 1754	LR9	10-11
Amos, s. Abner, b. Nov. 17, 1755	LR11	585
Benjamin, had d. [ ], b. June 21, 1752	LR8	6
Caleb, Jr., m. Annah [ ], Jan. 1, 1766	LR15	A
Caleb, s. Caleb, Jr., b. Oct. 16, 1767	LR15	H
Charlotte, d. Abell, b. Oct. 6, 1784	LR22	468
David, s. Abner, b. Oct. 27, 1744	LR7	N
Ebenezer, s. Abner, b. May 28, 1759	LR11	585
Elizabeth, d. Nathaniel, b. Mar. 8, 1752	LR8	6
Etheldred, d. Capt. Caleb, b. May 17, 1748	LR7	J
Etheldred, d. Capt. Caleb, b. Jan. 11, 1754	LR9	10-11
Hannah, m. Dan **HILLS**, Dec. 20, 1757	LR11	575

	Vol.	Page
MATTHEWS, MATHEWS (cont.)		
Harry P., of Southington, m. Harriet S. **THOMSON**, of		
Farmington, Jan. 30, 1832, by Rev. Irenus Atkins, of		
Southington	LR42	559
Heman, s. John, b. Sept. 21, 1770	LR17	436
John, [s. Capt. Caleb (?)], b. Apr. 24, 1750	LR7	J
John, m. Cloe **ROYS**, Nov. 30, 1769	LR17	G
John, s. John, b. May 31, 1781	LR22	468
Levi, s. Abner, Jr., b. Aug. 10, 1769	LR15	H
Lois, d. Abner, Jr., b. Dec. 14, 1767	LR15	H
Lucretia, d. Abner, Jr., b. Apr. 14, 1762	LR15	H
Mamre, d. Abner, Jr., b. July 14, 1760	LR15	H
Manne, d. Caleb, b. Feb. 19, 1745/6	LR7	J
Nancy, d. Caleb, Jr., b. June 21, 1771	LR17	436
Obadiah, s. Abner & Lois, b. Feb. 15, 1746/7	LR7	J
Olive, d. John, b. Jan. 3, 1776	LR17	436
Phebe, d. Nathaniel, Jr., b. Jan. 5, 1749/50	LR7	J
Phebe, d. John, b. May 29, 1778	LR21	547
Rhoda, d. John, b. May 21, 1773	LR17	436
Sarah, d. Abner, Jr., b. Mar. 2, 1764	LR15	H
Simeon, s. Caleb, Jr., b. May 20, 1769	LR15	H
Thomas, s. Abner, Jr., b. June 14, 1766	LR15	H
William, s. Abner, b. Apr. 17, 1757	LR11	585
MAYNARD, Eli, of Ellington, m. Harriet A. **SQUIERS**, of		
Hartford, Apr. 10, 1839, by Rev. Noah Porter	LR47	99
MEIGS, Angelica Y., m. Henry S. **NORTH**, b. of		
Middletown, Sept. 5, 1831, by Rev. Noah Porter	LR42	560
MERCHANT, Harvey, of Plainville, m. Catharine **WHITE**, of		
Bolton, Dec. 3, 1848,by William Wright	LR47	124
MERIAM, Ruth, of Wallingford, m. John **NEWELL**, Jr., of		
Farmington, May 22, 1760	LR11	575
MERRIMAN, MERIMAN, Abraham, s. Benjamin, b. Oct.		
17, 1747	LR9	10-11
Caleb, s. John, b. June 8, 1768	LR15	H
Jemima, d. John, b. June 30, 1764	LR15	H
John, s. John, b. Feb. 8, 1758	LR15	H
Mansfield, s. John, Jr., b. May 3, 1752	LR8	6
Mary, d. Mansfield, b. Jan. 5, 1775	LR22	468
Sarah B., of Farmington, m. Levi **DEMING**, of Berlin,		
May 26, 1842, by Rev. Noah Porter	LR47	108
[MERRILL], MERREL, MERRELLS, MERROL [see also		
MORIL], Abigail, of Hartford, m. John **SMITH**,		
weaver, of Farmington, Jan. 18, 1733/4	LR6	27
Allin, s. Allin, b. Apr. 3, 1768	LR17	436
Allin, d. July 11, 1771	LR17	444
Allison D., of Castleton, Vt, m. Dolly **PORTER**, of		
Farmington, Aug. 12, 1823, by Noah Porter, V.D.M.	LR40	572
Catharine H., of Unionville, m. Samuel **RUSSEL**, of		
Burlington, Apr. 27, 1842, by R. Woodruff	LR47	107
Daniel, of Canton, m. Lydia **RICHARDS**, of Bristol,		
Mar. 30, 1830, by Rev. Noah Porter	LR42	561
Margaret, of Hartford, m. Samuel **NASH**, of Farmington		
Jan. 24, 1733/4	LR5	300

	Vol.	Page
[MERRILL], MERREL, MERRELLS, MERROL (cont.)		
Mary, m. John THOMSON, Jr., Apr. 29, 1773	LR17	443
Seth, s. Allin, b. Oct. 4, 1766	LR17	436
MESSENGER, Nathaniel, m. Sarah SMITH, b. of Hartford,		
Jan. 1, 1729/30	LR5	300
Nathaniel, m. Sarah SMITH, b. of Hartford, Jan. 1,		
1729/30	LR5	307
Nathaniell, m. Ruth JUDD, Apr. 8, 1759	LR11	575
Nathaniel, s. Nathaniell, b. Mar. 16, 1787* *(In pencil		
"1737")	LR5	5
Ruth, d. Nathaniel, b. Jan. 8, 1760	LR11	585
Sarah, d. Nathaniell, b. Nov. 4, 1730	LR5	5
Sarah, m. Timothy GOODRICH, Sept. 29, 1748	LR7	35
MEZUZAN, Orian, s. Mark, b. Sept. 28, 1773	LR17	436
MIGALE, [see under MITCHELL]		
MILES, Beede, d. James, b. Mar. 7, 1772	LR17	436
Esther, d. John, b. Sept. 17, 1757	LR11	585
Eunice, d. John, b. July 26, 1751	LR8	7
Mary, m. David ANDRUS, Dec. 27, 1749	LR7	46
Rus[e]el[l], s. John, b. Mar. 16, 1756	LR11	585
MILLER, MILLERS, Allen W., m. Frances W. STANLEY,		
b. of Farmington, May 29, 1823, by Noah Porter,		
V.D.M.	LR40	572
Amelia F., m. William G. ROWE, Sept. 19, 1832, by		
Rev. Noah Porter	LR42	559
Anne, d. Joseph, b. Sept. 30, 1772	LR21	547
Clarinda, [d. Elisha & 2nd w. Wid. Abigail		
(ABERNATHA) BUNNEL,] b. Nov. 24, 1790	LR29	578
Cynthia, m. Estus F. FAIRCHILD, Feb. 4, 1823, by		
Horace Cowles, J.P.	LR40	572
Cyrus, s. Jonathan, Jr., b. Feb. 17, 1770	LR17	433
Daniel, s. wid. Martha Owen, b Apr. 21, 1764	LR11	585
Daniel, m. Lucy HAMBLIN, Apr. 19, 1774	LR17	443
Daniel, [s. Elisha & 2nd w. Wid. Abigail		
(ABERNATHA) BUNNEL], b. Oct. 17, 1787	LR29	578
Edward, m. Almira WOODFORD, b. of Farmington,		
Sept 12, 1826, by Rev. Bela Kellogg	LR42	567
Elener, d. Rubin, b. July [ ], 1763	LR11	585
Elijah, s. Jonathan, Jr., b. June 13, 1765	LR17	433
Elijah T., m. Ruth TILLOTSON, b. of Farmington, Sept.		
16, 1824, by Rev. Harry Bushnell	LR42	568
Elisha, m. Sarah FOWLER, of Durham, Oct. 18, 1764	LR11	592
Elisha, s. Elisha, b. July 5, 1777	LR22	468
Elisha, Jr., [s. Elisha & 2nd w. Wid. Abigail		
(ABERNATHA) BUNNEL], b. July 5, 1779	LR29	578
Elizabeth, m. Ebenezer HORSINGTON, July 5, 1751	LR7	46
Elizabeth M., m. John S. KNOWLES, Sept. 4, 1839, by		
Rev. Ezra S. Cook. Witnesses Henry Cadwell & Ira		
Rowe	LR47	100
Eunice, d. Joseph, b. Jan. 17, 1769	LR21	547
Eunice, d. Capt. Jonathan, d. Sept. 29, 1771	LR17	445
Ezra, s. Jonathan, Jr., b. Aug. 10, 1773	LR17	433
George Frederick, s. Jonathan, Jr., b. Apr. 20, 1767	LR17	433

	Vol.	Page
MILLER, MILLERS (cont.)		
Gershom, m. Mercy **BRESOW**, Oct. 20, 1763	LR11	592
Hannah, d. Noah, b. Nov. 26, 1764	LR14	9
Harriet, [d. Elisha & 2nd w. Wid. Abigail		
(**ABERNATHA**) **BUNNEL**], b. June 14, 1785	LR29	578
Henry, of Mereden, m. Rosilla **JOHNSON**, of Bristol,		
May 11, 1830, by Rev. Irenus Atkins, of		
Southington	LR42	562
James H., m. Matilda **WOODRUFF**, b. of Farmington,		
Sept. 24, 1828, by Rev. Noah Porter	LR42	564
James H., of Bristol, m. Lucia E. **BISHOP**, of		
Farmington, Sept. 26, 1848, by Rev. Noah Porter	LR47	123
Jemima, m. Jonah **JUDD**, Nov. 18, 1748	LR7	46
John, s. Elisha, b. Mar. 12, 1781	LR22	468
John, [s. Elisha & 2nd w. Wid. Abigail (**ABERNATHA**)		
BUNNEL], b. Mar. 12, 1781	LR29	578
Jonathan, Jr., m. Sarah **NORTH**, Sept. 24, 1761	LR11	575
Jonathan Allen, s. Jonathan, Jr. & Sarah (**WOODRUFF**		
North, wid. of Jos. North), b. July 21, 1762	LR17	433
Joseph, s. Joseph, b. May 11, 1775	LR21	547
Julia C., b. Dec. 25, 1797; m. Ira **ROWE**, Sept. 18, 1814	LR47	W-Y
Lina, m. Higason **HILLS**, Mar. 10, 1769	LR15	N
Lydia, d. Jonathan, Jr., b. Oct. 3, 1771	LR17	433
Mary, m. Jedediah **NORTON**, Jr., Jan. 8, 1767	LR17	G
Matilda W., of Farmington, m. William **TALCOTT**, of		
Coventry, Nov. 30, 1846, by Rev. Noah Porter	LR47	118
Merriam, m. Timothy **BARNES**, Mar. 19, 1760	LR11	575
Noah, m. Anne **BEAWEL**, Apr. 9, 1760	LR11	575
Noah, s. Noah, b. July 30, 1762	LR14	9
Olive, d. Rubin, b. Apr. 14, 1761	LR11	585
Phebe, m. Medad **HART**, Nov. 18, 1754	LR9	286
Rebecka Clark, d. Jonathan, Jr., b. Feb. 13, 1764	LR17	433
Rubin, m. Sarah **MILLER**, Jan. 15, 1757	LR11	576
Samuel C., m. Lucy D. **FRISBIE**, b. of Southington, Dec.		
16, 1850, by William Wright	LR47	128
Sarah, d. Abraham, b. Nov. 26, 1749	LR7	J
Sarah, m. Noah **HART**, May 31, 1753	LR9	286
Sarah, m. Rubin **MILLER**, Jan. 15, 1757	LR11	576
Sarah, d. Rubin, b. Feb. 21, 1759	LR11	585
Sarah, w. Elisha, d. Mar. 13, 1772	LR17	445
Sarah, w. Capt. Jonathan, d. Mar. 15, 1772	LR17	445
Selah, m. Emeline M. **THOMSON**, July 15, 1824, by		
Rev. Noah Porter	LR42	568
Selah Fowler, d. Elisha, b. June 5, 1770	LR17	436
William, s. Capt. Jonathan, d. Jan. 1, 1775	LR17	445
William, see book shelves for indexed copy of data found		
on pages 333-338, LR2, under title of "History of		
Miller Family" by Elbert H. T. Miller		
William Fowler, s. Elisha, b. May 24, 1768	LR15	H
MILLS, Catharine, of Wallingford, m. Ezekiel **SCOTT**, of		
Farmington, June 23, 1763	LR11	492
Mary, of Simsbury, m. Aaron **WOODRUFF**, Aug. 5,		
1743	LR6	305

	Vol.	Page
MINOR, Hannah, m. Ichabod TALMAGE, Mar. 9, 1774	LR17	443
MITCHELL, MITCHEL, MIGALE, Clarissa A., of		
Farmington, m. Walter B. SWEETLAND, of		
Hartford, May 22, 1828, by Rev. Noah Porter	LR42	564
Mary, d. Joel, b. Sept. 2, 1743	LR7	K
Medad, s. Samuel & Abigail, b. Aug. 18, 1751	LR8	6
Mercy, of Woodbery, m. Daniel JUDD, of Ffarmington,		
Dec. 4, 1705	LR1	4
Rachel, m. Hezekiah WINCHEL, Jan. 10, 1758	LR11	576
MIX, Julian, m. John SMITH, b. of Farmington, Oct. 9, 1831,		
by Rev. Noah Porter	LR42	560
Sarah, m. John STANLEY, May 11, 1743	LR7	46
[MONROE], MANROSS, Timothy, s. Samuel, b. Feb. 3, 1752	LR8	6
MOODEY, MOODY, Anna, wid., m. David PORTER, July		
26, 1744	LR7	46
Ebenezer, m. Anne JUDD, b. of Farmington, Oct. 14,		
1731	LR5	13
Eliza, of Burlington, m. Milo SWEET, of Farmington,		
Sept. 28, 1823, by Noah Porter, V.D.M.	LR40	572
Rene, d. Ebenezer & Anne, b. July 6, 1732	LR5	5
Samuel, s. Ebenezer & Anne, b. Mar. 17, 1734	LR5	5
Thankfull, m. Nehemiah STREET, Apr. 16, 1772	LR17	443
Zimri, s. Eben[eze]r & Anne, b. Dec. 22, 1736	LR6	5
MOORE, MOOR, MORE, Abigail, alias Colyer, d. Phebe		
Moor, b. May 9, 1738	LR8	6
Abigaill, d. Roswell & Desire, b. June 6, 1769	LR17	436
Althia, of Northfield, m. John Frederick DeWITT, of		
Northford, July 8, 1828, by Rev. Noah Porter	LR42	564
Ebenezer, s. Roswell, b. Feb. 1, 1764	LR14	9
Frederick A., m. Mary J. JEROME, of Bristol, Aug. 2,		
1841, by Rev. Noah Porter	LR47	105
Goodrich E., of Mass., m. Charlotte GLADDING, of		
Farmington, Apr. 15, 1849, by Rev. Henry J. Fox	LR47	124
John S., of Dummerston, Vt., m. Caroline COWLES, of		
Farmington, Oct. 31, 1824, by Rev. Joshua Williams	LR42	568
Lemuel, s. Phebe Moore, b. July 22, 1740	LR8	6
Martha, m. Josiah ROOT, Dec. 14, 1760	LR11	575
Oliver, s. Roswell, b. June 7, 1757	LR11	585
Phebe, had d. Abigail Colyer alias Moor, b. May 9, 1738		
& s. Lemuel More, b. July 22, 1740	LR8	6
Roswell, m. Desire DUNHAM, June 30, 1755	LR9	286
Roswell, s. Roswell & Desire, b. June 28, 1761	LR11	585
Ruth (?), w. Isak, d. May 26, 1691	LR1	2
MORIL, [see also MERRILL], Sarah, m. Matthew CLARK,		
Jr., May 8, 1746	LR7	46
MORRIS, Robert A., of Ellington, m. Martha LEWIS, of		
Farmington, June 17, 1845, by Rev. Noah Porter	LR47	114
MORSE, [see also MOSS], Alison, m. Eliza FAIRCHILD, b.		
of Farmington, July 24, 1834, by Rev. Noah Porter	LR42	E
Celia M., of Farmington, m. Eneas COWLES, of		
Westfield, Mass., Feb. 10, 1830, by Rev. Noah		
Porter	LR42	561
Chauncy, Jr., [s. Chauncy & Eunice], b. Sept. 1, 1830	LR47	W-Y

	Vol.	Page
MORSE (cont.)		
Chauncy & Eunice, had s. [ ], b. Oct. 2, 1835, ae 3 m. 14 d.	LR47	W-Y
Edward, m. Roxy **ROOT**, b. of Farmington, Aug. 22, 1820, by Noah Porter, V.D.M.	LR40	570
Edward Fenn, [s. Chauncy & Eunice], b. Aug. 17, 1827	LR47	W-Y
Francis Brainard, [child of Chauncy & Eunice], b. Sept 12, 1838	LR47	W-Y
Hiram Whitcomb, [s. Chauncy & Eunice], b. Feb. 17, 1829	LR47	W-Y
Lemuel, s. John & Elidea, b. Aug. 19, 1748	LR8	6
Lewis A., of Farmington, m. Mary **CHURCHILL**, of Bristol, Sept. 1, 1844, by Rev. William Wright	LR47	113
Maria Adaline, [d. Chauncy & Eunice], b .Mar. 9, 1833	LR47	W-Y
Martha E., of Plainville, m. Charles H. **WRIGHT**, of Milledgeville, Ga., Oct. 2, 1843, by Rev. William Wright	LR47	111
Mary A., m. Samuel R. **FARNSWORTH**, Nov. 17, 1846, by William Wright	LR47	121
Mary Adeline, [d. Chauncy & Eunice], b. Nov. 17, 1825	LR47	W-Y
Prentiss, of Southbridge, Mass., m. Mary M. **BLOOD**, of Chatham, Mar. 18, 1834, by Rev. Noah Porter	LR42	D
Richard Henry, [s. Chauncy & Eunice], b. Oct. 14, 1834	LR47	W-Y
MORTON, William T. G., of Boston, m. Elizabeth **WHITMAN**, of Farmington, May [ ], 1844, by Rev. Noah Porter	LR47	112
MOSES, Benony, m. Phebe **WOODRUFF**, b. of Farmington, Jan. 3, 1736/7	LR6	27
Elizabeth, m. Joseph A. **ROOT**, b. of Canton, Nov. 1, 1846, by Rev. Noah Porter	LR47	118
Phebe, d. Benony, b. July 9, 1737	LR6	5
Phebe, w. Benony, d. July 20, 1737	LR6	10
MOSS, [see also **MORSE**], Diantha, d. Elihu, b. Apr. 15, 1772	LR17	436
Ebairy (?), d. Elihu, b. Apr. 11, 1765	LR17	436
Elihu, m. Esther **CLARK**, Feb. 22, 1758	LR11	575
Elihu, s. Elihu, b. Mar. 8, 1767	LR17	436
Esther, d. Elihu, b. Feb. 22, 1761	LR17	436
Eunice, d. Elihu, b. Feb. 23, 1763	LR17	436
Job, s. Elihu, b. Jan. 5, 1771; d. same day	LR17	436
John, d. Oct. 29, 1750	LR7	540
Justus, s. Elihu, b. Dec. 28, 1768	LR17	436
Mary, d. Dec. 26, 1768, in the 33rd y. of her age	LR15	M
Mary Hart, d. Timothy, b. Dec. 26, 1768	LR15	H
Thankful, d. Elihu, b. Aug. 14, 1759	LR11	585
MUNGER, Levi, s. Levi, b. June 17, 1777	LR22	468
MUNN, Julia, m. Anvie **ROOT**, Oct. 7, 1850, by Rev. Charles Kelsey	LR47	127
Gaziah,* of Windsor, m. James **WOODRUFF**, of Farmington, Nov. 19, 1735 *("Keziah"?)	LR5	539
Samuel, of Saybrook, m. Julia Ann **GOODHEW**, of Avon, Sept. 10, 1837, by Rev. S. H. Clark	LR47	96
Steven B., m. Louisa M. **PERKINS**, b. of Southington, Apr. 12, 1846, by Rev. S. H. Clark	LR47	117

	Vol.	Page
MUNSON, Abigail, d. Moses, b. Mar. 9, 1771	LR21	547
Anne, d. Moses, b. Mar. 31, 1773	LR21	547
[E]unice, m. Stephen **HART**, s. Thomas, Dec. 29, 1720	LR2	101
Hannah, d. Jan. 3, 1767, ae 87 y.	LR14	3
Jemima, m. Eleazer **WILLCOX**, Mar. 16, 1790	LR22	480
Levina, d. Moses, b. Mar. 14, 1769	LR21	547
Lewis, m. Fanny **COOK**, b. of Farmington , Mar. 23, 1831, by Rev. Noah Porter	LR42	560
Lucius, of Litchfield, m. Sally **ORVIS**, of Farmington, Apr. 11, 1832, by Rev. Noah Porter	LR42	559
Moses, s. Moses, b. Aug. 3, 1767	LR21	547
Obadiah, s. Obadiah, b. Apr. 7, 1769	LR17	436
Rebeckah, of New Haven, m. Charles **NORTON**, of Farmington, Aug. 9, 1738	LR6	27
Sarah, d. Obadiah, b. Apr. 7, 1767	LR15	H
Sarah, d. Moses, b. Sept. 18, 1775	LR21	547
Walter, s. Obadiah, b. May 6, 1771	LR17	436
MURRAY, Almira, m. Montgomery **WICKS**, b. of Farmington, Nov. 15, 1838, by Rev. S. H. Clark	LR47	98
Margaret, m. Joseph **JACKSON**, b. of Farmington, Jan. 18, 1844, by Rev. Richard Woodruff	LR47	112
MYGATT, Henry, m. Sarah **WOODRUFF**, b. of Farmington, June 23, 1830, by Rev. Noah Porter	LR42	561
Thomas, Jr., of Canton, m. Phebe **GAY**, of Farmington, Sept. 29, 1823, by Noah Porter, V.D.M.	LR40	572
NAMAAN, Sherman B., m. Caroline **HOMER**, of Farmington, Mar. 19, 1840, by Elisha C. Jones	LR47	102
NASBURY, William C., of Barrington, Mass., m. Jane L. **CARPENTER**, of Farmington, Oct. 30, 1844, by Rev. William Wright	LR47	113
NASH, Eleazer, of Farmington, m .Hanah **HARAS**, of Toland, May 19, 1741	LR6	304
Henry, m. Julian **SMITH**, July 13, 1834, by Rev. Noah Porter	LR42	307
Huldah, d. Samuel, b. Jan. 2, 1734/5	LR5	307
Jerusha, d. Samuel, b. Oct. 5, 1736	LR6	5
Josiah, s. Samuel, b. Mar. 6, 1740/1	LR6	5
Samuel, now of Farmington, m. Margaret **MERROL**, of Hartford, Jan. 24, 1733/4	LR5	300
Samuel, s. Samuel, b. July 25, 1738	LR6	5
NEA----, William, m. [ ], b. of Farmington, [ ], 1728	LR4	423
NEAL, NEALE, Aaron, s. William, b. Mar. 24, 17[ ]	LR5	5
Abel, s. Edward, b Feb. 17, [ ]	LR7	K
Anna, m. Josiah **KILLBORN**, May 3, 1754	LR9	286
Anne, d. William, b. July 27, 1734	LR5	6
David, m. Mary [ ], Oct. 31, 1769	LR17	G
Edward, s. Edward, b. Oct. 22, 1713	LR2	282
Eunice, m. Ezekiel **WRIGHT**, Jan. 26, 1761	LR11	575
Jeremiah, of Southington, m. Charlotte **HILLS**, of Farmington, Oct. 11, 1827, by Rev. Irenus Atkins	LR42	565
John, s. Edward, b. Oct. 28, 1719	LR2	282
Joseph, s. David, b. June 24, 1770	LR15	N

	Vol.	Page
NEALN, NEALE (cont.)		
Margaret, d. Edward, b. June 5, 1709	LR2	282
Margrat, m. Thomas **HUTTSON**, Mar. 29, 1736	LR7	35
Mary, d. Samuell, b. June 8, 1734	LR6	5
Mary, m. Ruffus **CLARK**, Mar. 22, 1753	LR9	286
Noah, s. [Edward], b. Mar. 10, [ ]	LR7	K
Ruth, d. Samuell, b. May 13, 1738	LR6	5
Samuel, s. Edward, b. Dec. 20, 1706	LR2	282
Samuel, of Farmington, m. Elizabeth **STRICKLAND**, of		
Hartford, May 11, 1735	LR5	300
Samuel, s. Samuell, b. July 23, 1736	LR6	5
Sarah, d. Edward, b. July 3, 1722	LR2	282
Thomas, s. Edward, b. Nov. 5, 1716	LR2	282
William ,s. Edward, b. Apr. 15, 1705	LR2	282
William, s. William, b. Sept. 26, 1730	LR5	5
William, [ ]	LR5	13
NERING, Norman, of Burlington, m. Dolly **DEMING**, of		
Farmington, June 12, 1823, by Erastus Clapp,		
V.D.M.	LR40	572
NEVERS, Olive, illeg. d. Samuel Neavers & Mary		
PARMELEE, b. Sept. 10, 1758	LR11	586
NEWELL, NEWEL, NUELL, Abel, s. Nathaniel & Esther, b.		
Aug. 15, 1730	LR5	5
Amey, m. Elnathan **HOOKER**, Dec. 13, 1781	LR22	480
Anne, d. Samuell & Mary, b. Aug. 8, 1756	LR11	586
Asahel, s. Samuel, Jr., b. May 5, 1725	LR4	395
Asahell, s. John, Jr., b. Jan. 28, 1766	LR14	9
Ashble, s. Isaac, b. July 7, 1759	LR11	586
Chancey, s. Oliver, b. Feb. 15, 1765	LR11	586
Cloah, d. Nathan, b. Mar. 22, 1753	LR11	586
Cornelia H., of Farmington, m. Charles A. **CHAPIN**, of		
Canton, May 28, 1849, by Rev. Noah Porter	LR47	124
Daniel, s. Samuell, b. Apr. 18, 1700	LR1	4
Daniel, s. Thomas, s. of Samuell, b. Feb. 20, 1719/20	LR2	102
Daniel, m. Ruth **PORTTER**, Oct. 31, 1721	LR2	101
Daniel, m. Susannah **PORTER**, Feb. 13, 1753	LR8	10
David, s. Samuel, Jr., b. Nov. 28, 1716	LR2	81
David, s. Samuel, Jr., b. May 1, 1736	LR5	6
David, m. Sarah [ ], Dec. 10, 1761	LR14	10
David, s. David, b. Oct. 13, 1765	LR14	10
Diadema, d. Elihu, b. Sept. 12, 1760	LR11	586
Edmond, s. Elisha, b. Apr. 11, 1772	LR17	437
Elidiah, m. Timothy **STANLEY**, May 5, 1757	LR11	576
Elihu, s. Thomas (s. of Samuell), b. July 14, 1730	LR5	5
Elisha, s. Nathaniel, b. Dec. 6, 1710	LR5	5
Elisha, m. Abigail **HART**, Mar. 13, 1755	LR9	286
Elizabeth, d. Thomas, b. Nov. 29, 1694	LR2	91
Elizabeth, m. Jonathan **LEWIS**, b. of Ffarmington, Jan.		
28, 1719/20	LR2	104
Elizabeth, d. John, b. Jan. 29, 1720/1	LR2	102
Elizabeth, wid., d. Jan. 8, 1739/40	LR6	10
Elizabeth, m. John **CLARK**, Sept. 2, 1742	LR6	305
Esther, wid. Nathaniel, d. Oct. 3, 1762	LR11	574

	Vol.	Page
NEWELL, NEWEL, NUELL (cont.)		
[E]unie, d. Thomas, s. of Samuell, b. Mar. 25, 1722	LR2	102
Eunice, d. Thomas, Jr., b. June 14, 1753	LR8	7
Eunice, d. Sept. 19, 1777, in the 25th y. of her age	LR21	558-9
Hannah, d. Asahael, b. Nov. last day, 1753	LR9	10-11
Harriet A., m. Abner **WHITTLESEY**, b. of Farmington,		
May 24, 1848, by Noah Porter	LR47	122
Hesther, d. Thomas, b. Sept. 12, 1705	LR2	91
Isaac, s. Samuel, Jr., b. Aug. 17, 1711	LR2	232
Isaac, m. Rachel **PUMMARY**, of Northampton, May 15,		
1741	LR6	304
Isaac, s. Isaac, b. Jan. 31, 1753	LR9	10-11
James, s. Simon, b. Mar. 2, 1716/17	LR2	81
James, m. Jerusha **SAYMOUR**, Nov. 19, 1739	LR6	27
James, s. James & Jerusha, b. Jan. 16, 1739/40	LR6	5
Jeames, m. Dinah **COLE**, Nov. 23, 1742	LR6	305
James, his s. [ ], d. Feb. 20, 1749/50, ae 11 d.	LR7	540
James, m. Mary **ELSWORTH**, Mar. 1, 1759	LR11	576
James, d. Mar. 24, 1749/50	LR7	540
James, s. Thomas, 2nd, b. Feb. 13, 1772	LR21	548
Jerusha, d. Jeames, b. Feb. 4, 1741/2	LR6	5
Jerusha, w. Jeames, d. Feb. 10, 1741/2	LR6	305
John, s. Samuell, b. Jan. 17, 1692	LR1	2
John, m. Elizabeth **HAWLEY**, b. of Ffarmington, Sept.		
24, 1719	LR2	101
John, s. Ens. John, b. Dec. 16, 1733	LR5	6
John, s. Josiah, b. Apr. 7, 1747	LR9	10-11
John, s. Josiah, d. Aug. 26, 1750	LR8	12
John, 2nd, s. Josiah, b. Jan. 18, 1753	LR9	10-11
John, Jr., of Farmington, m. Ruth **MERIAM**, of		
Wallingford, May 22, 1760	LR11	575
John, s. John, Jr., b. Aug. 7, 1767	LR15	N
John, s. Josiah, b. Apr. 7, [ ]	LR7	L
Joseph, s. Thomas, b. Nov. 1, 1689	LR2	91
Josiah, s. Samuel, Jr., b. Aug. 17, 1722	LR2	88
Josiah, m. Mary **UPSON**, Feb. 18, 1745/6	LR7	35
Josiah, s. Josiah, b. May 13, 1749	LR9	10-11
Liverias, s. Thomas, b. Sept. 4, 1751	LR8	7
Lois, d. John, b. May 11, 1731	LR5	5
Lott, s. Samuel, b. Mar. 15, 1754	LR9	10-11
Lott, s. Rev. Samuel & Mary, b. Mar. 15, 1754	LR11	586
Lucina, d. John, Jr., b. Sept. 26, 1770	LR17	437
Lucy, d. Thomas (of Samuel), b. Jan. 25, 1724/5	LR2	65
Lucy, d. Nathan, b. Dec. 22, 1761	LR11	586
Lucy, d. Thomas, b. Jan. 23, 1773	LR17	437
Lucy, m. Edmond **STEELE**, Oct. 10, 1830, by David L.		
Ogden	LR42	560
Lowrana, d. Thomas, b. Jan. 13, 1769	LR15	N
Lurana, w. Thomas, d. July 4, 1786, in the 54th y. of her		
age	LR22	482
Lydia, d. Capt. John, b. May 20, 1738	LR6	5
Manna, s. John, Jr., b. Jan. 24, 1773	LR17	437
Martha, d. John, b. Feb. 23, 1725/6	LR2	242

	Vol.	Page
NEWELL, NEWEL, NUELL (cont.)		
Martha, m. John **WYARD**, Mar. 1, 1744	LR7	35
Mary, d. Samuell, b. Dec. 23, 1697	LR1	2
Mary, d. Thomas, s. Samuell, b. Nov. 7, 1715	LR2	95
Mary, m. John **STEEL**, Jr., b. of Ffarmington, Dec. 27, 1716	LR2	94
Mary, d. Samuel, Jr., b. July 2, 1731	LR5	5
Mary, m. Matthew **COLE**, b. of Farmington ,Jan. 3, 1738/9	LR6	27
Mary, d. Nathan, b. Oct. 1, 1750	LR8	7
Mary, d. Rev. Samuel & Mary, b. Oct. 30, 1750	LR11	586
Mary, d. Samuel & Mary, b. Nov. 30, 1750	LR8	7
Mary, m. Asa **UPSON**, Jan. 17, 1750/1	LR7	35
Mary, w. Ens. Samuell, d. Apr. 28, 1752	LR8	11
Mehetabel, w. Simon, d. Oct. 27, 1732	LR5	50
Mahetibel, d. Jeames, b. July 15, 1743	LR6	5
Mercy. d. Simon, d. Feb. 21, 1736/7	LR6	10
Mercy, d. Isaac, b .Nov. 16, 1742	LR6	5
Miranda, d. John, Jr., b. Apr. 7, 1769	LR15	N
Nathan, s. Thomas, Jr., b. May 6, 1714	LR2	99
Nathan, s. Nathan, b. Feb. 22, 1745/6	LR7	K
Nathan, s. Nathan, b. Feb. [ ]	LR7	K
Nathaniell, s. Samuel, b. Feb. 20, 1703/4	LR1	4
Nathaniel, m. Esther **HART**, b. of Ffarmington, June 29, 1727	LR4	423
Nathaniel, s. Nathaniel, b. July 30, 1728	LR4	395
Nathaniel, Dea., d. Aug. 31, 1753	LR8	12
Nathaniel, s. Nathaniel, d. Feb. 8, 1755	LR8	12
Norman, s. Thomas, Jr., b. Aug. 28, 1760	LR11	586
Oliver, s. Capt. John, b. Feb. 9, 1741	LR6	5
Oliver, m. Lurene **HORSFORD**, Mar. 29, 1764	LR11	592
Pomeroy, s. Isaac, b. Apr. 2, [ ]	LR7	K
Quartus, s. Isaac, b. Aug. 11, 1761	LR11	586
Rebecca, of Farmington, m. Enos **TOMPKINS**, of New York, June 6, 1824, by Rev. Harry Bushnell	LR42	568
Reverius, s. Thomas, d. Dec. 21, 1752	LR8	12
Riverias, s. Thomas, Jr., b. May 18, 1755	LR9	10-11
Roger S., m. Naomi **HAWLEY**, b. of Farmington, Aug. 1, 1821, by Rev. Jonathan Cone	LR40	571
Ruth, d. John, b. Oct. 10, 1722	LR2	87
Ruth, d. John, b. Nov. 1, 1723	LR2	88
Ruth, m. Thomas **COWLES**, Jr., b. of Farmington, Nov. 20, 1740	LR6	27
Ruth, d. Nathan, b. Sept. 6, 1759	LR11	586
Ruth, m. Thomas Stanley **DAY**, Dec. 21, 1774	LR17	443
Samuell, m. Mary **HART**, Dec. 20, 1683	LR1	5
Samuel, s. Samuell, b. Feb. 19, 1686	LR1	2
Samuel, Jr., of Ffarmington, m. Sarah **NORTON**, b. of Farmington, Aug. 8, 1710	LR2	125
Samuel, s. Samuel, Jr., b. Mar. 1, 1713/14	LR2	81
Samuel, s. Samuel, Jr., b. Mar. 1, 1713/14	LR2	96
Samuel, s. Jeames, b. Aug. 7, 1747	LR7	K
Samuel, Rev., m. Mrs. Mary **ROOT**, May 4, 1749	LR7	35

	Vol.	Page
NEWELL, NEWEL, NUELL (cont.)		
Samuel, s. Rev. Samuel, b. June 27, 1752	LR8	7
Samuell, s. Rev. Samuel & Mary, b. June 27, 1752	LR11	586
Samuel, Ens., d. Feb. 15, 1753	LR8	12
Samuel, s. Rev. Samuell, d. Feb. 2, 1756	LR11	577
Samuel, 2nd, s. Samuell & Mary, b. Apr. 11, 1758	LR11	586
Samuel, s. Thomas, 2nd., b. Jan. 2, 1774	LR21	548
Sarah, d. Thomas, b. Jan. 1, 1698	LR2	91
Sarah, d. Samuel, b. June 17, 1707	LR2	109
Sarah, d. Samuell, Jr., b. July 6, 1719	LR2	103
Sarah, m. Hezekiah **GRIDLEY**, b. of Farmington, [ ] 5, 1731	LR5	13
Sarah, d. Thomas, 2nd, d. July 23, 1736	LR5	50
Sarah, d. Nathan, b. Oct. 18, 1743	LR6	5
Sarah, d. Jeames, b. Nov. 8, 1744; d. Nov. 23, 1744	LR7	K
Sarah, d. David, b. Aug. 15, 1763	LR14	10
Sarah, d. Nathan, b. Oct. 18, [ ]	LR7	K
Seth, s. Nathan, b. Oct. 24, 1757	LR11	586
Seth, s. John, Jr., b. July 13, 1764	LR11	586
Simeon, s. Isaac, b. Feb. 5, 1748/9	LR7	K
Simeon, s. Isaac, b. Feb. 5, [ ]	LR7	L
Simon, s. Thomas, b. Apr. 1, 1683	LR2	91
Simon, m. Mehitibel **BIRD**, b. of Ffarmington, Mar. 22, 1711	LR2	123
Simon, m. Mary **WALLIS**, wid., b. of Farmington, May 3, 1733	LR5	300
Simon, d. Apr. 1, 1761	LR11	574
Solomon, s. Samuel, Jr., b. Nov. 30, 1728	LR4	395
Solomon, s. Asahael, b. Aug. 27, 1752	LR9	10-11
Susanna, d. Thomas, d. Sept. 21, 1704	LR1	3
Susanah, m. Matthew **WOODRUFF**, Jr., July 19, 1728	LR4	423
Susana, d. Nathan, b. Mar. 21, 1755	LR11	586
Sylvia, d. Thomas, b. [ ], 1764	LR17	437
Sylva, d. Thomas, b. Aug. 8, 1765	LR14	9
Silva, d. Oliver, b. Jan. 3, 1767	LR15	M
Theron, s. Elisha, b. Aug. 20, 1769	LR15	N
Thomas, m. Elizabeth **WROTHAM**, Nov. 5, 1679	LR1	5
Thomas, s. Thomas, b .Oct. 1, 1681	LR2	91
Thomas, the aged, d. Sept. 13, 1689	LR1	3
Thomas, s. Samuell, b. Mar. 1, 1690/1	LR1	2
Thomas, the aged, his w. [ ], d. Feb. 24, 1697/8	LR1	3
Thomas, of Farmington, m. Mary **LEE**, of Farmington, July 9, 1713	LR2	93
Thomas, 2nd, d. Oct. 25, 1723	LR2	66
Thomas, s. Jeames, b. Nov. 10, 1745	LR7	545
Thomas, "of T.", d. Dec. 19, 1755 (Perhaps "s. of J[ames]"?)	LR9	495
Thomas, s. Thomas, 2nd, b. Apr. 28, 1776	LR21	548
Timothy, s. Simon, b. Nov. 6, 1718	LR2	83
Timothy, s. Simon, d. Aug. 4, 1746	LR7	36
William, [s.] Nathan, [b.]	LR7	K
Zade, d. David, b. Dec. 10, 1773	LR17	437
NEWTON, NUTON, James, s. James, b. Apr. 18, 1724	LR2	69

	Vol.	Page
NEWTON, NUTON (cont.)		
Mehetibel, d. James, b. Feb. 25, 1723/4	LR2	69
Roger, 1st minister in Farmington, settled in 16[ ];		
afterwards dismissed and settled in Milford	LR1	2
Susana, d. Roger, b. Sept. 20, 16[ ]	LR2	330
NICHOLS, Abigail, d. Benjamin, b. Feb. 23, 1756	LR11	586
Benjamin, m. Huldah **GRIDLEY**, Jan. 2, 1754	LR11	575
Benjamin, d. Sept. 9, 1759	LR11	577
Elidia, d. Benjamin, b. Jan. 20, 1758	LR11	586
Lucy, d. Benjamin, b. May 23, 1754	LR11	586
NILES, Root Ezekiel, s. Filex Root, b. Oct. 20, 1761	LR15	N
NININS, W[illia]m, S. m. Emily **PORTER**, b. of Farmington,		
Nov. 22, 1826, by Rev. N. Porter	LR42	567
NOBLE, Sophia, m. Henry **LUCAS**, b. of Bristol, Apr. 17,		
1845, by William Wright	LR47	114
NORTH, Aaron, d. Nov. 20, 1776, in the 25th y. of his age	LR21	558-9
Abi, d. Timothy, b. Jan. 13, 1763	LR11	586
Abigail, d. Thomas, s. Samuell, b. Apr. 6, 1716/17	LR2	96
Abigail, m. Thomas **ANDRUSS**, June 18, 1744	LR7	46
Abigail, m. Thomas **ANDRUSS**, July 18, 1744	LR7	35
Abigail, [d. Daniel], b. July [ ]	LR7	K
Abijah, s. John, b. Oct. 2, 1741	LR6	5
Abiiah, s. John, b. Oct. 19, 1743	LR6	5
Abijah, s. Timothy, b. Feb. 8, 1759	LR11	586
Alvin, s. James, b. Sept. 4, 1781	LR21	548
Anne, d. Samuell, Jr., b. Sept. 4, 1771	LR17	437
Asahel, s .Timothy, b. Nov. 3, 1739	LR6	5
Asahel, s. Sam[ue]ll, Jr., b. Sept. 3, 1782	LR22	469
Ashbel, s. Ebenezer, b. Oct. 3, 17[ ]	LR5	5
Clarisse, d. Samuell, Jr., b. May 27, 1773	LR17	437
Clarissa, of Farmington, m. Rev. John B. **PRESTON**, of		
Ripley, N.Y., June 23, 1833, by David L. Ogden	LR42	A
Daniel, s. Thomas, s. Samuell, b. Mar. 20, 1702	LR2	111
Daniel, m. Mary **NORTHAWAY**, b. of Farmington, Feb.		
18, 1735/6	LR5	539
Daniel, m. Elidya **LEE**, Mar. 15, 1750	LR8	10
Daniel, s. [Daniel], b. Sept. [ ]	LR7	K
David, s. Nathaniel, b. Aug. 4, 1721	LR2	102
Ebenezer, m. Sible **CURTICE**, b. of Farmington, Dec.		
10, 1730	LR5	300
Eli, s. Timothy, b. May 11, 1743	LR6	5
Eli, m. Eunice **HART**, Oct. 3, 1765	LR11	594
Elidia, d. Daniel, b. Apr. 1, 1752	LR8	7
Elisha, s. Joseph, b. July 4, 1738	LR6	5
Elizabeth, w. John, d. Jan. 24, 1732/3	LR5	50
Esther, d. John (s. Nathaniell), b. May. 17, 1738/9	LR6	5
Eunice, d. John, b. Dec. 17, 1710	LR2	111
[E]unis, d. Timothy, b. Jan. 10, 1745/6	LR7	K
Eunice,* d. Timothy, d. Mar. 29, 1759 *(Arnold Copy		
has "Eunice Norton")	LR11	577
Eunice, d. Eli, b. June 24, 1767	LR15	N
Eunice, see Eunice **NORTON**	LR11	577
George, s. [Daniel], b. Mar. 11 [ ]; d. Apr. 9. [ ]	LR7	K

	Vol.	Page
NORTH (cont.)		
Hannah, d. John, b. Apr. 15, 1693	LR2	111
Hannah, m. Samuel **SEAYMOR**, b. of Ffarmington, May 10, 1706	LR2	123
Hannah, d. Thomas, s. Samuell, b. July 27, 1711	LR2	111
Hannah, d. Thomas, of Kensington, b. Sept. 6, 1722	LR4	375
Hannah, d. Nathaniel, b .May 14, 1727	LR4	395
Hannah, d. Thomas, m. Samuel **THOMSON**, Jr., May 3, 1738	LR6	27
Hannah, m. Timothy **NORTH**, b. of Farmington, Jan. 25, 1738/9	LR6	27
Hannah, m. Eleazer **ORUIS**, June 30, 1743	LR7	35
Hanah, w. Thomas, d. Nov. 4, 1757	LR11	577
Hannah, d. Daniel & Lidiah, b. Oct. 10, 1758	LR11	586
Henry S., m. Angelica Y. **MEIGS**, b. of Middletown, Sept. 5, 1831, by Rev. Noah Porter	LR42	560
Hezekiah, s. Thomas, s. Samuell, b. May 11, 1704	LR2	111
Hezekiah, m. Elizabeth **PORTTER**, b. of Farmington, Jan. 21, 1734/5	LR5	545
Isaac, s. Thomas, Jr., b. Sept. 27, 1703	LR2	97
Isaac, m. Mary **WOODFORD**, b. of Ffarmington, Feb. 27, 1727/8	LR4	423
Isaac, s. Joseph, b. Nov. 13, 1754	LR11	586
James, s. Thomas, Jr., b. Apr. 17, 1709	LR2	97
James, m. Rhodah **JUDD**, Sept. 29, 1774	LR21	557
James, s. James, b. Dec. 19, 1777	LR22	469
Jane, d. Josiah & Temperance, b. Nov. 25, 1735	LR5	6
Jane, d. Josiah, d. July 20, 1738	LR6	10
Johiel (?), d. Oct. 13, 1777, in the 72nd y. of his age	LR21	558-9
John, s. Samuell, of Ffarmington, m. Mary **WARNER**, May 16, 1692	LR2	145
John, s. Samuell, of Ffarmington, m. Mary **SEAMOR**, of Hartford, Apr. 25, 1700	LR2	145
John, m. Jane **STEBIN**, Mar. 19, 1707/8	LR1	6
John, s. Nathaniel, b. Mar. 13, 1710/11	LR2	96
John, Jr., s. John, d. Jan. 16, 1732/3	LR5	50
John, s. Samuell, m. Abigail **JUDD**, wid. Samuel, b. of Farmington; Mar. 20, 1733/4	LR5	300
John, s. Nathaniell, m. Easther **STANLEY**, b. of Farmington, Feb. 21, 1738/9	LR6	27
John, d. Apr. 20, 1745	LR7	36
John, s. Samuel, b. Nov. 10, 1750	LR8	7
Jonathan, s. John, b. Apr. 8, 1704	LR2	111
Joseph, s. John, bp. Mar. 18, 1659	LR2	327
Joseph, s. Thomas, of Kensington, b. June 2, 1720	LR4	375
Joseph, s. Nathaniel, b. Apr. 20, 1730	LR5	5
Joseph, of Farmington, m. Martha **SMITH**, of Simsbury, wid., July 17, 1734	LR5	300
Joseph, s. Joseph, b. July 1, 1736	LR6	5
Josiah, s. John, b. Feb. 11, 1705	LR2	111
Josiah, of Ffarmington, m. Temperance **BALDWIN**, of Milford, Nov. 22, 1726	LR2	104
Josiah, s. Josiah, b. Mar. 2, 1737/8	LR6	5

	Vol.	Page
NORTH (cont.)		
Lois, m. Samuel **SCOTT**, Aug. 30, 1770	LR17	G
Lois, w. Samuel, d. Sept. 15, 1783, in the 71st y. of her		
age	LR22	482
Lowes, d. [Nathan], b. [ ]	LR7	K
Lucy, d. Sam[ue]ll, Jr., b. Jan. 12, 1785	LR22	469
Lura, m. Mark **LEWIS**, b. of Farmington, May 4, 1835,		
by Rev. Noah Porter	LR47	89
Lydia, d. Nathaniel, b. Feb. 2, 1723/4	LR2	46
Lydia, m. Allin **GOODRICH**, June 15, 1748	LR7	46
Lidea, twin with Noah, d. Daniel, b. Mar. 23, 1754	LR9	10-11
Lynn, s. Samuell, Jr., b. Dec. 6, 1774	LR17	437
Marcus, s. Samuell, Jr., b. Sept. 18, 1776	LR21	548
Marcus, s. Sam[ue]l, Jr., b. Sept. 18, 1776	LR22	469
Margaret, d. John, b. Jan. 26, 1700/1	LR2	111
Margaret, d. Nathaniel, b. Jan. 2, 1713/14	LR2	96
Margaret, m. Joseph **WOODRUFF**, s. John, b. of		
Kensington, May 29, 1735	LR5	539
Martha, d. Thomas, Jr., b. June 30, 1700	LR2	97
Martha, wid., m. Matthew **WOODRUFF**, Sr., b. of		
Farmington, June 10, 173[ ]	LR5	13
Martha, d. Joseph, b. Aug. 4, 1740	LR6	5
Martin, s. Ebenezer, b. Dec. 13, 1734	LR6	5
Mary, d. John, b. Feb. 3, 1694/5	LR2	111
Mary, w. John, d. Mar. 1, 1694/5	LR2	141
Mary, d. Nathaniel, b. Mar. 18, 1716/17	LR2	81
Mary, w. John, d. Mar. 2, 1732/3	LR5	50
Mary, d. Ebenezer, b. Aug. 20, 1737	LR6	5
Mary, d. Daniel, d. Sept. 10, 1737	LR6	10
Mary, m. Zadock **HOGSKISS**, Dec. 22, 1743	LR6	305
Mary, w. Daniel, d. Aug. 3, 1748	LR8	11
Mary, m. Thomas **GILBERT**, Apr. 24, 1760	LR17	443
Mary, d. Daniel, b. Sept. 11, [ ]; d. Oct. 25, [ ]	LR7	K
Naomi, of Farmington, m. William K. **PECK**, of		
Harwinton, Jan. 21, 1821, by Ludovicus Robbins,		
V.D.M.	LR40	571
Nathan, s. Sam[ue]ll, Jr., b. Sept. 3, 1778	LR22	469
Nathaniel, m. Margaret **HOLCOM**, of Simsbury, June		
10, 1708	LR2	94
Nathaniel, s. Nathaniel, b. Apr. 14, 1709	LR2	96
Noah, s. Ebenezer, b. Jan. 10, 1732/3	LR5	307
Noah, s. Daniel, b. Jan. 2, 1750/1	LR8	7
Noah, s. Daniel & Elidia, d. Mar. 1, 1751	LR8	11
Noah, twin with Lidea, s. Daniel, b .Mar. 23, 1754	LR9	10-11
Noah, s. Daniel, d. July 16, 1769, in the 16th y. of his age	LR15	M
Oliver, s. Josiah & Temperance, b. Feb. 29, 1731/2	LR5	5
Oliver, s. Josiah, d. Aug. 26, 1737	LR6	10
Omri, m. Cybelia **NORTON**, Feb. 9, 1829, by Rev. Noah		
Porter	LR42	564
Omri M., m. Emma **WOODRUFF**, b. of Farmington,		
Oct. 8, 1823, by Noah Porter, V.D.M.	LR40	572
Pantha, m. John **BEACHER**, b. of Farmington, Sept. 27,		
1823, by Amasa Woodford, J.P.	LR40	572

	Vol.	Page
NORTH (cont.)		
Ruben, [s,] Samuel, b. May 23, [ ]	LR7	L
Rhoda, d. Timothy, b. Dec. 23, 1760	LR11	586
Rhoda, d. Timothy, d. Jan. 8, 1763	LR11	593
Rhoda, d. Asa, b. Mar. 13, 1771	LR17	437
Rhodah, d. James, b. Feb. 10, 1776	LR21	548
Ruth, d. John, b. Oct. 14, 1702	LR2	111
Ruth, d. [Daniel], b. May 4, [ ]	LR7	K
Samuell, m. Hannah NORTON, Jan. 3, 1666	LR1	5
Samuel, s. John, b. July 21, 1708	LR2	111
Samuell, s. Thomas (s. of Thomas), b. July 28, 1715	LR2	81
Samuel, s. Thomas, of Kensington, d. Apr. 11, 1725	LR2	148
Samuel, m. Lois PORTTER, b. of Farmington, Apr. 5, 1737	LR6	27
Samuel, Jr., m. Lucy DEMING, Nov. 29, 1770	LR17	G
Sam[ue]ll, s. Sam[ue]ll, Jr., b. Feb. 6, 1790	LR22	469
Samuel, his 1st s. [ ], b. Feb. 8, [ ]; d. [ ] his 1st d. [ ], b. Feb. 3, [ ]; d. [ ] 29, [ ]	LR7	L
Samuel, s. Samuel, b. July 27, [ ]	LR7	L
Sary, d. John, bp. [ ] 10, 1647	LR2	330
Sary, d. John, bp. Dec. 18, 1653	LR2	330
Sarah, d. Thomas (s. Thomas), b. Feb. 24, 1711/12	LR2	81
Sarah, d. Thomas, s. Samuell, b. June 26, 1717	LR2	84
Sarah, of Ffarmington, m. John WILLCOXON, of Simsbury, Dec. 14, 1724	LR2	52
Sarah, m. Joseph WOODRUFF, Jr., May 17, 1728	LR5	13
Sarah, d. Josiah, b. Dec. 21, 1729	LR5	5
Sarah, m. Abram WOODRUFF, b. of Farmington, Nov. 15, 1739	LR6	27
Sarah, m. Jonathan MILLER, Jr., Sept. 24, 1761	LR11	575
Sarah, d. Sam[ue]ll, Jr., b. Jan. 7, 1781	LR22	469
Seth, s. Timothy, b. Apr. 6, 1752	LR8	7
Seth Judd, s. James, b. Aug. 13, 1779	LR22	469
Solomon, s. Samuel, b. July 22, 1753	LR9	10-11
Solomon, d. Jan. 21, 1777, in the 24th y. of his age	LR21	558-9
Susanah, of Weathersfield, m. Benjamin JUDD, of Ffarmington, Jan. 18, 1693/4	LR2	123
Susanah, of Weathersfield, m. Benjamin JUDD, of Ffarmington, Jan. 18, 1693/4	LR3	553
Susannah, d. Thomas, s. Samuell, b. May 3, 1706	LR2	111
Sibbel, d. Josiah, b. Oct. 15, 1727	LR4	395
Cibble, d. Ebenezer, b. Sept. 24, 1736	LR6	5
Sibble, m. James GRIDLEY, Jr., Dec. 3, 1750	LR7	46
Sylvia, d. Samuell, Jr., b. Jan. 2, 1787	LR22	469
Thankfull, d. Thomas, s. Samuell, b. July 1, 1708	LR2	111
Thankful, m. James HART, b. of Farmington, Oct. 10, 1734	LR5	545
Thomas, of Ffarmington, s. Thomas, m. Martha RYCE, of Wallingford, Dec. 1, 1698	LR2	123
Thomas, of Ffarmington, s. Samuell, m. Hannah WOODFORD, of Ffarmington, Dec. 4, 1699	LR2	145
Thomas, s. Thomas, Jr., b. Oct. 27, 1705	LR2	97
Thomas, of Kensington, d. Mar. 2, 1724/5	LR2	148

	Vol.	Page

NORTH (cont.)

Thomas, d. Apr. 25, 1755	LR9	495
Timothy, s. Thomas, s. of Samuell, b. Sept. 10, 1714	LR2	95
Timothy, m. Hannah **NORTH**, b. of Farmington, Jan. 25, 1738/9	LR6	27
Timothy, s. Asa, b. Dec. 22, 1773	LR17	437
Timothy, of Candor, N.Y., m. Anna **DAY**, of Farmington, June 29, 1829, by Rev. Harry Bushnell	LR42	562
William, m. Jennet **WOODRUFF**, b. of Farmington, Aug. 31, 1834, by Rev. Noah Porter	LR42	E
-----, m. Margaret **LUSK**, Mar. 8, 1770	LR17	G
-----, [m.] Pomroy **STRONG**, [ ]	LR47	W-Y

NORTHAWAY, Ann, had s. Bissell **WOODFORD**, b. May

29, 1774	LR17	441
Elidia, d. [ ]	LR8	7
Frances, s. Samuel, b. July 20, 1756	LR11	586
George, s. Samuel, b. Sept. 1, 1754	LR11	586
Hannah, d. May 25, 1752	LR8	12
James, s. John, b. June 13, 1753	LR9	10-11
John, m. Susanah **WOODFORD**, b. of Farmington, May 17, 1741	LR6	304
John, s. John, b. Sept. 10, 1745	LR7	K
John, m. Mrs. Demaras **BURGE**, July 14, 1772	LR17	442
Josiah, s. Samuel, b. Jan. 13, 1749/50	LR8	7
Lydia, d. John, b. Nov. [ ]	LR7	J
Mary, m. Daniel **NORTH**, b. of Farmington, Feb. 18, 1735/6	LR5	539
Samuel, m. Anna **GARRET**, Oct. 5, 1746	LR7	35
Samuel, s. Samuell, b. Apr. 12, 1747	LR7	K
Samuel, s. Samuel, b. Dec. 5, 1752	LR11	586
Susanah, d. John & Susanah, b. Sept. 18, 1741	LR6	5
Susanna, w. John, d. Nov. 30, 1766	LR14	3

NORTON, NAUGHTON, [see also **ORTON**], Abigail, d.

Ens. Isaac, b. May. 25, 1716	LR2	96
Achsah, d. Isaac, b. June 10, 1721	LR2	102
Achsa, m. Jedediah **NORTON**, July 3, 1746	LR7	35
Alicksander, s. James, b. Apr. 3, 1728	LR5	5
Andrew, s. James, b. May 5, 1730	LR5	5
Andrew, m. Anne **GAYLORD**, Sept. 15, 1750	LR8	10
Ann, d. Roger, b .Aug. 13, 1758	LR14	9
Anna, d. John, Jr., b. Jan. 13, 1717/18	LR2	102
Anne, m. Jadah **HART**, b. of Farmington, Feb. 20, 1734/5	LR5	545
Anne, d. Andrew, Jr., b. Sept. 28, 1753	LR9	10-11
Ashble, d. Nov. 21, 1758	LR11	577
Ashbel, s. Bethuel, b. July 17, 1768	LR17	437
Belinda, w. Romanta, d. Feb. 20, 1792	LR29	580
Bethead,* twin with Martha, s. Ebenezer, b. Aug. 12, 1739 *("Bethuel")	LR6	5
Bethuel, m. Lois **HART**, Oct. 31, 1765	LR11	584
Charles, s. John, 3rd, b. Dec. 17, 1710	LR2	109
Charles, of Farmington, m. Rebeckah **MUNSON**, of New Haven, Aug. 9, 1738	LR6	27
Charles, s. Charles, b. May 17, 1742	LR6	5

	Vol.	Page
NORTON, NAUGHTON (cont.)		
Cybelia, m. Omri **NORTH**, Feb. 9, 1829, by Rev. Noah		
Porter	LR42	564
Delight, d. Ebenezer, b. Apr. 17, 1736	LR5	692
Delight, m. Timothy **UPTON**, Mar. 25, 1755	LR9	286
Dorothy, d. Thomas, b. June 6, 1763	LR14	9
Dorothy, d. Thomas, d. Sept. 2, 1764	LR14	3
Ebenezer, of Ffarmington, m. Sarah **SAVAGE**, of		
Middletown, July 7, 1726	LR2	257
Ebenezer, d. Mar. 21, 1750	LR11	577
Edward, s. Roger, b. Apr. 8, 1756	LR14	9
Eleziel,* s. James, b. Apr. 23, 1750 *(In pencil		
"Eliezer")	LR8	7
Elias, s. Sergt. John, b. Mar. 28, 17[ ]	LR5	5
Elias, s. Sergt. John, d. Apr. 9, 1732	LR5	50
Elidia, m. Ebenezer **ORVIS**, Oct. 1, 1747	LR7	46
Elizabeth, w. John, Sr., d. Nov. 5, 1702	LR1	3
Elizabeth, d. Thomas, b. July 27, 1703	LR1	2
Elizabeth, d. Isaac, b. June 20, 1708	LR2	111
Elizabeth, d. John (of Thomas), b. Dec. 7, 1725	LR2	69
Elizabeth, w. John (s. Thomas), d. Dec. 20, 1725	LR2	66
Elizabeth, d. Thomas, b. Feb. 6, 1729/30	LR5	5
Elizabeth, m. Simeon **JUDD**, Jan. 29, 1746	LR7	35
Elizabeth, m. Samuel **WOODRUFF**, Jan. 24, 1754	LR8	10
Elizabeth, d. Jedediah, b. Mar. 22, 1755	LR9	10-11
Elizabeth, d. Ichabod, b. Jan. 13, 1761	LR11	586
Eunice,* d. Timothy, d. Mar. 29, 1759 *(In pencil		
"Eunice **NORTH**")	LR11	577
Eunice Munson, d. Bethuel, b. Mar. 3, 1767	LR15	N
Ferlove, d. May 31, 1750	LR11	577
George, s. Thomas, b. Oct. 18, 1761	LR14	9
George, s. Thomas, d. Nov. 3, 1761	LR14	3
George, m. Elizabeth **FRISBIE**, b. of Farmington, Dec.		
20, 1820, by Bela Kellogg, V.D.M.	LR40	570
Gideon, s. Charles, b. [ ] 9, [ ]	LR7	L
Gideon, s. John, 3rd, b. Jan. 12, 1708/9	LR2	109
Gideon, 1st, s. John, 3rd, d. Oct. 1, 1712	LR2	62
Gideon, 2nd, s. John, 3rd, b. Sept. 5, 1713	LR2	95
Gideon, m. Martha **THOMSON**, b. of Farmington, Apr.		
15, 1736	LR5	692
Gideon, d. Mar. 26, 1742	LR6	305
Gideon, s. Stephen, b. Oct. 15, 1770	LR17	437
Gould Gift, s. Charles, b. Aug. 28, 1751	LR8	7
Hannah, m. Samuell **NORTH**, Jan. 3, 1666	LR1	5
Hannah, wid. of Thomas, m. Thomas **ROOT**, wid., of		
Lebanon, Dec. 28, 1732	LR5	300
Hannah, d. Roger, b. Sept. 27, 1747	LR8	7
Hannah, d. Roger, b. Sept. 27, 1747	LR14	9
Hannah, had d. Rachel Alvort, b. Dec. 22, 1761	LR22	460
Hannah, had s. Samuel **HORSINGTON**, b. Mar. 6, 1775	LR22	465
Hannah, had s. Samuel **HORSINGTON**, d. Sept. 17,		
1776, in the 2nd y. of his age	LR22	482
Hannah, see Jared **DAVIS**	LR22	462

	Vol.	Page
NORTON, NAUGHTON (cont.)		
Hart, s. Bethuel, b. Jan. 11, 1775	LR17	437
Huldah, d. Roger, b. Mar. 26, 1761	LR14	9
Ichabod, s. Thomas, b. Sept. 17, 1736	LR8	7
Icabod, m. Ruth **STRONG**, Feb. 21, 1760	LR11	592
Ichabod Porter, s. Romanta, b. Feb. 17, 1792	LR29	578
Isaac, of Ffarmington, m. Elizabeth **GALPIN**, of		
Stratford, May 6, 1707	LR2	145
Isaac, s. Isaac, b. Sept. 1, 1713	LR2	95
Isaac, Jr., of Farmington, m. Sarah **SAYMOUR**, of		
Hartford, July 1, 1740	LR6	27
Isaac, s. Roger, b. Feb. 11, 1752	LR14	9
Isaiah, s. Isaac, b. Mar. 22, 1782	LR22	469
Jeames, m. Sarah **KILLBORN**, Nov. 30, 1743	LR7	46
Jedediah, m. Achsa **NORTON**, July 3, 1746	LR7	35
Jedediah, Jr., m. Mary **MILLER**, Jan. 8, 1767	LR17	G
Jedediah, Jr., m. Elizabeth **KILLBORN**, Nov. 7, 1771	LR17	G
Jemima, d. Thomas, b. Oct. 7, 1744	LR8	7
Jemima, m. Sylvanus **CURTIS**, Oct. 22, 1762	LR11	594
Job, s. John, Jr., b. Feb. 19, 1719/20	LR2	102
Job, of Farmington, m. Susannah **OLMSTEAD**, of		
Hartford, Feb. 12, 1744	LR7	46
John, s. Thomas, b. June 5, 1701	LR1	2
John, 3rd, m. Anna **THOMSON**, May 6, 1708	LR1	6
John, Sergt., m. Anne **THOMSON**, b. of Farmington,		
May 6, 1708	LR5	300
John, s. John, 3rd, b. Nov. 16, 1715	LR2	95
John, s. Thomas, m. Thankfull **ROOT**, Dec. 5, 172[ ]	LR5	13
John, s. Thom[a]s, m. Elizabeth **HECOX**, Dec. 9, 1724	LR2	52
John, 2nd, d. Apr. 25, 1725	LR2	148
John, m. Ruth **BIRD**, b. of Farmington, Jan. 28, 1730/1	LR5	13
John, s. James, b. Jan. 10, 1739/40	LR6	5
John, m. Ruth **OWEN**, Nov. 14, 1750	LR8	10
John, [ ]	LR5	13
John Treadwell, of Albany, m. Mary Hillhouse **ATKINS**,		
of Farmington, Aug. 29, 1821, by N. S. Wheaton	LR40	571
Joseph, s. James, b. May 25, 1737	LR6	5
Josiah, s. Lieut. Isaac, b. June 26, 1726	LR2	242
Josiah, s. Lieut. Isaac, d. Nov. 24, 1726	LR2	66
Josiah, s. James, b. Nov. 28, 1752	LR9	10-11
Levy, s. James, b. Apr. 18, 1751	LR8	7
Lott, s. Thomas, b. Aug. 6, 1733	LR5	6
Luca, d. Sergt. John, b. Mar. 31, 1728	LR5	5
Martha, d. Gideon & Martha, b. Dec. 8, 1738	LR6	5
Martha, twin with Bethead, d. Ebenezer, b. Aug. 12, 1739	LR6	5
Martha, m. Nathaniel **HART**, Nov. 23, 1758	LR11	576
Mary, d. Sergt. John, b .May 20, 17[ ]	LR5	5
Mary, d. Thomas, b. Dec. 21, 1705	LR1	4
Mary, d. Sergt. John, b. May 20, 1730	LR5	5
Mary, d. John & Thankfull, b. Nov. 4, 1730	LR5	5
Mary, d. James, b. June 15, 1732	LR5	307
Mary, d. Roger, b. Feb. 28, 1754	LR14	9
Matthew, s. Samuel & Lydia, b. Feb. 4, 1738/9	LR6	5

	Vol.	Page
NORTON, NAUGHTON (cont.)		
Mathew, d. Oct. 23, 1759	LR11	577
Mercy, w. Jedediah, Jr., d. May 9, 1770	LR17	444
Nancy, d. Icabod, b. May 26, 1763	LR11	586
Neelow (?), d. Ebenezer, b. Apr. [ ], 1734	LR5	6
Norton, s. Roger, b. Feb. 11, 1752	LR8	7
Olive, d. Charles, b. Mar. 20, 1750	LR8	7
Phebe, d. Andrew, Jr., b. July 22, 1754	LR9	10-11
Porter, s. Bethuel, b. May 11, 1770	LR17	437
Rachel, w. Thomas, d. Sept. 16, 1751	LR8	12
Rebeckah, d. Charles, b. May 11, 1739	LR6	5
Rebeckah, d. Jedadiah, b. May 14, 1753	LR8	7
Roger, s. John, of Kinsington ,b. Mar. 15, 1722	LR2	46
Roger, of Farmington, m. Mary **PRATT**, of Hartford, Jan. 5, 1746/7	LR7	46
Roger, s. Roger, b. Jan. 25, 1749/50	LR8	7
Roger, s. Roger, b. Jan. 25, 1750	LR14	9
Roger, s. Isaac, b. Jan. 22, 1780	LR22	469
Romanta, m. Belinda **PORTER**, Mar. 2, 1791	LR29	576
Ruth, m. Noah **STANLEY**, [ ]	LR4	271
Ruth, d. Isaac, b. Jan. 6, 1710/11	LR2	111
Ruth, d. John (s. of John), b. Mar. 18, 1723/4	LR4	382
Ruth, d. John, of Kensington, b. Mar. 18, 1724	LR2	46
Ruth, d. Thomas, b. [ ], 1725/6	LR4	374
Ruth, d. Roger, b. Sept. 5, 1766	LR14	9
Salmon, s. Isaac, b. Mar. 17, 1776	LR22	469
Samuell, s. John, d. Aug. 20, 1659	LR2	319
Samuel, s. Thomas, b. Jan. 17, 1707/8	LR1	2
Samuel, m. Lydia **LEE**, b. of Farmington, Feb. 2, 1737/8	LR6	27
Samuel, s. Jedediah, b. Sept., last day, 1759	LR11	586
Sarah, m. Samuel **NEWEL**, Jr., b. of Ffarmington, Aug. 8, 1710	LR2	125
Sarah, d. John (s. of John), b. June 5, 1726	LR4	382
Sarah, d. Thomas, Jr., b. Sept. 28, 1727	LR4	395
Sarah, d. Ebenezer, b. Jan. 28, 1731/2	LR5	307
Sarah, d. Gideon, b. May 16, 1737	LR6	5
Sarah, d. Isaac, Jr., b. Aug. 5, 1741	LR6	5
Sarah, m. Phineas **LEWIS**, Nov. 27, 1746	LR7	35
Sarah, m. Thomas **UPTON**, Apr. 20, 1753	LR11	576
Sarah, m. Luke **STEBBINS**, May 1, 1755	LR11	576
Sarah, d. James, b. Nov. [ ], 1755	LR9	10-11
Sarah, m. Samuel **HOOKER**, Jr., Sept. 23, 1756	LR11	576
Sarah, d. Stephen, b. July 12, 1768	LR15	N
Sarah, d. Isaac, b. Feb. 18, 1778	LR22	469
Seth, s. Thomas, b. Aug. 10, 17[ ]	LR5	5
Stephen, s. Gideon, b. Aug. 4, 1740	LR6	5
Stephen, m. Lidia [ ], Nov. 26, 1766	LR15	A
Strong Asahel, s. Ichabod, b. Sept. 20, 1765	LR14	9
Susanah, d. James, b. Aug. 18, 1734	LR5	307
Susanah, w. Jeames, d. Apr. 15, 1742	LR6	305
Susana, d. Roger, b. July 29, 1763	LR14	9
Susanna S., m. David A. **SANFORD**, b. of Bristol, Oct. 19, 1836, by Rev. Noah Porter	LR47	94

	Vol.	Page
NORTON, NAUGHTON (cont.)		
Tabitha, d. Ens. Isaac, b. Dec. 20, 1718	LR2	83
Tabitha, of Weathersfield or Middletown, m. Isaac **LEE**,		
Jr., of Farmington, July 10, 1740	LR6	27
Thankfull, d. Sergt. John, b. Jan. 28, 17[ ]	LR5	5
Thankfull, d. John, b. July 19, 1782	LR8	7
Thomas, m. Hannah **ROSE**, June 7, 1700	LR1	4
Thomas, Jr., of Ffarmington, m. Elizabeth **MACUN**, of		
Stratford, Nov. 17, 1724	LR2	257
Thomas, of Farmington, m. wid. Rachel **PUMORY**, of		
Northampton, Dec. 11, 1739	LR6	27
Thomas, s. Thomas, b. Oct. 17, 1740	LR6	5
Thomas, m. Elizabeth **DEMING**, of Weathersfield, Sept.		
11, 1753	LR9	286
Thomas, m. Sarah **MARSH**, July 8, 1762	LR11	594
William, s. Jeames, b. Aug. 26, [ ]	LR7	K
Zenas Hart, s. Bethuel, b. Aug. 18, 1772	LR17	437
OLCOTT, Betsey, m. Linus **PARDY**, b. of Wolcott, Oct. 12,		
1831, by Rev. Noah Porter	LR42	559
OLIN, Elizabeth, of Farmington, m. Chauncey M. **FOX**, of		
New Hartford, Apr. 2, 1843, by Noah Porter	LR47	109
Mary Ann, m. Charles S. **GRANNIS**, b. of Farmington,		
Feb. 13, 1842, by Rev. Aaron S. Hill	LR47	106
OLMSTEAD, OLMSTID, Asher, s. Joseph, b. Feb. 6, 1738/9	LR6	5
Asher, s. Joseph, d. Aug. 7, 1753	LR8	12
Asher, d. Aug. 27, 1758	LR11	593
Joseph, m. [E]unice **DEMING**, b. of Farmington, Aug.		
11, 1737	LR6	27
Joseph, d. Sept. 21, 1756	LR11	593
Mary, d. John, b. Aug. 3, 1742	LR6	5
Mary, m. William **DICKENSON**, Apr. 4, 1765	LR15	A
Sarah, d. Sept. 27, 1767	LR11	593
Susannah, of Hartford, m. Job **NORTON**, of Farmington,		
Feb. 12, 1744	LR7	46
ORR, Esther, m. Julius **DORMAN**, Mar. 1, 1848, by Rev.		
William McAlister	LR47	122
ORTON, ORTEN [see also NORTON], Abigail, d. John, b.		
Sept. 3, 1751	LR8	7
Abigail, w. John, d. Oct. 21, 1754	LR9	495
Ann, d. Thomas, b. Feb. 19, 1702/3	LR1	2
Anna, w. Thomas, d. Mar. 22, 1735/6	LR5	50
Anne, d. Thomas, Jr., b. May 8, 1736	LR5	6
Elizabeth, d. Thomas, b. Nov. 8, 1732	LR5	6
Elizabeth, w. Thomas, Jr., d. May 16, 1738	LR6	10
Elizabeth R., m. George W. **BROWN**, of Bolton, May 6,		
1850, by William Wright	LR47	127
Esther, d. Thomas, b. Oct. 11, 1714	LR2	95
Esther, d. Thomas, d. Apr. 1, 1738	LR6	10
Esther, d. Thomas, Jr. & Elizabeth, b. May 12, 1738	LR6	5
Gideon, s. John, d. June 23, 1759, in the 11th y. of his age	LR11	577
Gideon Buckingham, s. John & Mary, b. May 19, 1759	LR11	586
Heman H., m. Jennet **CRAMPTON**, b. of Farmington,		
Nov. 28, 1839, by Rev. Noah Porter	LR47	101

	Vol.	Page
ORTON, ORTEN (cont.)		
Icabod, s. John, b. Oct. 15, 1754	LR9	12
James M., of Rome, N.Y., m. Ruby H. **GILLET**, of		
Farmington, Oct. 25, 1837, by Rev. Noah Porter	LR47	96
John, s. Thomas, b. Sept. 17, 1717	LR2	81
John, m. Abigail **WOODRUFF**, b. of Farmington, Dec.		
23, 1741	LR6	304
John, s. John, b. Dec. 31, 1742	LR6	5
John, of Farmington, m. Mary **SLAUGHTER**, of		
Simsbury, Dec. 11, 1755	LR9	286
Juliet, of Farmington, m. Samuel E. **TAYLOR**, of		
Colebrook, Feb. 18, 1841, by Rev. Noah Porter	LR47	104
Margaret, m. John **THOMSON**, Jr., Nov. 2, 1699	LR2	145
Margrit, d. Thomas, b. July 1, 1707	LR1	4
Margaret, d. Thomas, d. June 3, 1708	LR1	7
Margaret, d. Thomas, b. Mar. 31, 1712	LR2	98
Margaret, d. Thomas, b. Mar. 31, 1712	LR2	109
Margaret, d. Thomas & Sarah, b. Dec. 6, 1742	LR6	5
Mary, d. Thomas, b. Mar. 7, 1704/5	LR1	3
Mary, d. John & Mary, b. Mar. 21, 1757	LR11	586
Roger, s. Thomas, Jr. & Elizabeth, b. Mar. 11, 1730/1	LR5	6
Roger, s. Thomas, Jr., d. Sept 22, 1731	LR5	50
Samuel, of Wolcott, m. Patty **GAYLORD**, of Bristol,		
Apr. 3, 1833, by Rev. Noah Porter	LR42	558
Sarah, d. Thomas, b. Feb. 7, 1698/9	LR1	2
Sarah, m. Jonathan **HOLBERT**, b. of Ffarmington, July		
6, 1727	LR2	258
Thomas, m. An[n] **BUCKINGHAM**, May 9, 1698	LR1	4
Thomas, Jr., of Farmington, m. Elizabeth **SEDGWICH**,		
of Hartford, Jan. 12, 17[ ]	LR5	13
Thomas, s. Thomas, b. Jan. 4, 1701	LR1	2
Thomas, s. Thomas, d. May 18, 1706, ae about 5 1/2 y.	LR1	2
Thomas, s. Thomas, b. Apr. 30, 1709	LR2	109
Thomas, Sergt., m. Hephsibah **BEWEL**, Feb. 18, 1741/2	LR6	304
Thomas, d. May 13, 1744	LR7	36
ORVIS, ORUIS, ORUIC, ORUIE, Abiah, d. Roger, b. Nov.		
2, 1702	LR2	92
Amy H., of Farmington, m. David **BENTON**, of		
Litchfield, Apr. 25, 1831,by Rev. Noah Porter	LR42	560
Anna, m. Joseph **COGSWELL**, b. of Ffarmington, Aug.		
25, 1710	LR2	123
Azubath, d. Samuel, b. Nov. 22, 1725	LR2	34
Azubah, m. Ebenezer **GRIDLEY**, June 20, 1744	LR7	35
Bathiah, d. Roger, b. Jan. 13, 1698	LR2	92
Bathiah, d. Roger, b. Jan. 13, 1698; d. Nov. 1, 1702	LR2	141
Charles, s. Samuel, b. Oct. 11, 1711	LR2	34
Charles, m. Elizabeth **GRIDLEY**, d. Thomas, Jr., b.		
Farmington, Oct. 2, 1734	LR5	300
Charles, d. Oct. 15, 1743	LR7	36
Clarissa, A., m. Uriah **ALFORD**, Oct. 20, 1839, by		
Egbert Cowles, J.P.	LR47	110
David, s. Roger, b. Mar. 2, 1696/7	LR2	92

	Vol.	Page
ORVIS, ORUIS, ORUIC, ORUIE (cont.)		
David, of Farmington, m. Hannah **GAYLORD**, of		
Windsor, Feb. 5, 1718/19	LR2	101
David, s. David, b. Feb. 1, 173[4]/5	LR5	6
David, s. David, d. Dec. 16, 1745	LR7	36
Deborah, m. Ebenezer **BARNES**, b. of Ffarmington, Apr.		
8, 1699	LR2	123
Deborah, d. Samuel, b. June 10, 1715	LR2	34
Deborah, m. Jonathan **BARNES**, July 12, 1741	LR6	304
Dinah, d. Samuel, b. May 13, 1721	LR2	34
Ebenezer, s. Elezabeth, bp. Mar. 18, 1659	LR2	327
Ebenezer, s. Roger, b. Oct. 3, 1695	LR2	92
Ebenezer, s. Roger, b. Oct. 3, 1695; d. Feb. 13, 1695/6	LR2	141
Ebenezer, s. Roger, b. Oct. 3, 1705	LR2	92
Ebenezer, m. Elizabeth **ROOT**, b. of Farmington, Jan. 23,		
1732/3	LR5	300
Ebenezer, m. Elidia **NORTON**, Oct. 1, 1747	LR7	46
Eliezer, s. David, b. Nov. 14, 1719	LR2	102
Eleazer, m. Hannah **NORTH**, June 30, 1743	LR7	35
Elliner, d. Charles & Elizabeth, b. Mar. 24, 1737/8	LR6	5
Elidia, d. Ebenezer, b. Sept. 15, 1748	LR8	7
Elezabeth, had s. Ebenezer, bp. Mar. 18, 1659	LR2	327
Elizabeth, d. Roger, b. Oct. 1, 1693	LR2	92
Elizabeth, m. John **ANDRUS**, s. Benjamin, Apr. 26,		
1716	LR2	94
Elizabeth, d. Ebenezer & Elizabeth, b. Jan. 18, 1732/3	LR5	6
Elizabeth, w. Ebenezer, d. Jan. 27, 1745/6	LR8	11
Elizabeth, m. Timothy **PARKS**, Sept. 29, 1749	LR8	10
[E]unice, d. Samuel, Jr., b. Oct. 24, 1708	LR2	92
[E]unis, d. Charles, b. Feb. 26, 1739/40	LR6	5
Gershom, s. Samuel, b. Aug. 2, 1719	LR2	34
Hannah, d. David, b. Dec. 30, 1721	LR2	102
Gaziah, d. Ebenezer, b. Aug. 4, 1743	LR8	7
Lois, d. Ebenezer, b. Aug. 5, 1740	LR6	5
Lois, d. Ebenezer, b. Aug. 5, 1740	LR8	7
Lois L., of Farmington, m. Ruell **FULLER**, of Sherman,		
N.Y., Oct. 7, 1832, by Rev. Noah Porter	LR42	558
Lidia, m. Benjamin **HAWLEY**, June 21, 1773	LR17	G
Mary, m. Samuel **SCOTT**, b. of Ffarmington, Feb. [ ],		
1686/7	LR2	123
Mary, d. Roger, b. Oct. 18, 1707	LR2	92
Mary, m. Thomas **CATLIN**, b. of Farmington, Mar. 1,		
1843, by A. Benedict	LR47	109
Mary L., of Farmington ,m. Ransom **THOMSON**, of		
Hartford, Dec. 10, 1845, by Rev. Noah Porter	LR47	116
Mercy, d. Samuel, b. Apr. 24, 1717	LR2	34
Mercy, d. Charles, b. Sept. 29, 1742	LR6	5
Mercy, d. wid. Elizabeth, d. June 14, 1746	LR7	36
Meriam, d. Jan. 27, 1747/8	LR8	11
Merriam, wid., d. Dec. 26, 1747/8 [sic]	LR7	36
Richard, m. Mary S. **BROWN**, July 8, 1839, by Rev.		
Ezra S. Cook. Witnesses Ira W. Rowe & Richard		
Yale	LR47	100

	Vol.	Page
ORVIS, ORUIS, ORUIC, ORUIE (cont.)		
Roger, of Ffarmington, m. Mirryam **HANNISON**, of		
Hartford, Dec. 15, 1692	LR2	123
Roger, d. Jan. 14, 1736/7	LR8	11
Ruth, d. Charles, b. Oct. 2, 1735	LR5	6
Ruth, wid., m. Thomas **RICHARDS**, b. of Farmington,		
Dec. 28, 1738	LR6	27
Sally, of Farmington, m. Lucius **MUNSON**, of Litchfield,		
Apr. 11, 1832, by Rev. Noah Porter	LR42	559
Samuel, Jr., of Farmington, m. Rachel **ANDRUS**, of		
Waterbury, Sept. 5, 1707	LR2	123
Samuel, s. Samuel, b. Aug. 26, 1713	LR2	34
Silence, d. Samuel, b. June 17, 1723	LR2	34
William, s. Samuel, Jr., b. May 15, 1710	LR2	92
William A., m. Elizabeth **ROOT**, b. of Farmington ,May		
15, 1839, by Rev. Noah Porter	LR47	100
Zadoc, s. Ebenezer & Elizabeth, b. Jan. 27, 1737/8	LR6	5
Zadock, s. Ebeneer, b. Jan. 27, 1737/8	LR8	7
----en, s. Eleazer, b. Mar. 9, 1743	LR7	K
----er, [child of Eleazer], b. Jan. 14, 1744/5	LR7	K
OSBORN, John, of Windsor, m. Lucy **SWEET**, of		
Farmington, Jan. 31, 1821, by John Mix, J.P.	LR40	571
Noah H., m. Eliza A. **THOMSON**, b. of Farmington,		
Feb. 12, 1822, by Noah Porter, V.D.M.	LR40	571
OSGOOD, Louisa, of New Britain, m. James L. Philips, of		
Farmington, Aug. 7, 1845, by Rev. S. H. Clark	LR47	114
OULDS, Catharine, m. Samuel **BECKWITH**, b. of		
Farmington, Aug. 9, 1821, by Noah Porter, V.D.M.	LR40	571
OWEN, Daniel, m. Martha **HART**, Feb. 4, 1759	LR11	576
Daniel, d. Nov. 7, 1759	LR11	577
Martha, wid. had s. Daniel **MILLER**, b. Apr. 21, 1764	LR11	585
Obadiah, m. Mary **HART**, Nov. 27, 1760	LR11	575
Ruth, m. John **NORTON**, Nov. 14, 1750	LR8	10
Ruth, m. Elisha **PRATT**, Mar. 16, 1759	LR11	576
PADDEN, Asher, s. Robbard, b. Feb. 20, 1771	LR22	473
Benj[ami]n, s. Robert, b. Sept. 24, 1782	LR22	473
Beulah, d. Robbard, b. Oct. 5, 1772	LR22	473
Eunice, d. Robbard, b. Aug. 8, 1769	LR22	473
John, s. Robert, b. Feb. 6, 1778	LR22	473
Levi, s. Robert, b. Nov. 2, 1780	LR22	473
Simeon, s. Robert, b. Sept. 18, 1776	LR22	473
Tho[ma]s, s. Robert, b. June 4, 1774	LR22	473
William, s. Robert, b. Sept. 4, 1784	LR22	473
PAGE, Abigail, of Southington, m. John **CUSACK**, of Ireland,		
Aug. 10, 1826, by Rev. David L. Ogden	LR42	564
Ezra, of Windham, m. Margaret **GARDNER**, of Penn.,		
Mar. 19, 1827, by Rev. H. Bushnell	LR42	567
[PAINE], [see under **PAYNE**]		
PALMER, Cloe, m. Samuel **ROOT**, Mar. 22, 1758	LR11	575
Desire, m. John **HART**, s. Thomas, Apr. 10, 1755	LR10	6
Horace B., of Windsor, m. Sarah L. **DORMAN**, of		
Farmington, Dec. 2, 1849, by Rev. Noah Porter	LR47	126
Mary, d. Roswell, decd., b. June 26, 1776	LR21	549

	Vol.	Page

PALMER (cont.)

Rhoda, d. Enoch, b. May 9, 1764 — LR11 587

Roswell, of Farmington, m. Bathshebah **PECK**, of New
Haven, Sept. 18, 1775 — LR17 443

Roswell, d. Sept. 19, 1777, in the 26th y. of his age — LR21 558-9

Solomon, s. Enoch, b. May 10, 1766 — LR14 10

Viola, m. Charles **BLAKESLEY**, b. of Farmington, Aug.
5, 1849, by Rev. Henry J. Fox — LR47 125

PANTRY, Abigail, m. John **WHITMAN**, b. of Farmington,
Feb. 20, 1738/9 — LR6 27

PARCELLS, Mary S., of New Fairfield, m. Gideon W.
HART, of Avon, Dec. 10, 1844, by Rev. S. H.
Clark — LR47 113

PARDY, Linus, m. Betsey **OLCOTT**, b. of Wolcott, Oct. 12,
1831, by Rev. Noah Porter — LR42 559

PARKER, Mary J., m. Noah **POMROY**, b. of Bristol, June
13, 1843, by Rev. Noah Porter — LR47 110

Sarah, m. Simeon **STEADMAN**, May 10, 1770 — LR21 557

PARKS, Prudence, d. Timothy & Elizabeth, b. Feb. 15, 1749 — LR8 7

Timothy, m. Elizabeth **ORVIS**, Sept. 29, 1749 — LR8 10

PARMELEE, PARMERLEE, PALMERLE, PARMEL,

PARMELEY, PALMELEE, Amos, s. Jehiel, b. Jan. 2, 1759 — LR11 587

Ann, d. Jehiel, b. Sept. 29, 1766 — LR11 587

Charles, s. Jehial, b. Dec. 2, 17[ ] — LR7 L

Hanah, d. Jehiel, b. Jan. 26, 1752 — LR8 7

Huldah C., m. Franklin **HILLS**, b. of Farmington, June 2,
1840, by Rev. Noah Porter — LR47 102

Jane E., m. Charles A. **STEELE**, Sept. 11, 1839, by
Elisha C. Jones — LR47 101

Joel, s. Jehiel, b. Aug. 29, 1761 — LR11 587

Joshua, s. Jehiel, b. [ ] — LR7 L

Mary, d. Ishiel, b. June 10, 1742 — LR6 5

Mary, had illeg. d. Olive **NEVERS**, b. Sept. 10, 1758; f.
Samuel **NEAVERS** — LR11 586

Ruth, d. Jehiel, b. Jan. 30, 1757 — LR11 587

Sarah, d .[Jehial], b. Sept. 12, 17[ ] — LR7 L

Sible, m. Ethan **LEWIS**, June 18, 1746 — LR7 35

PARPOINT, Jeames, m. Mary **HOOKER**, July 26, 1698 — LR1 4

PARSONS, PARSON, PERSONS, Aaron, m. Sarah
CARINGTON, b. of Farmington, Sept. 18, 173[ ] — LR5 13

A[a]ron, s. John, b. Nov. 23, 1744 — LR8 7

Abigail, d. William, Jr., b. Aug. 8, 1721 — LR2 65

Abigail, d. William, d. Feb. 24, 1754 — LR8 12

Abigail, d. William, b. July 11, 1760 — LR11 587

Abigail, d. Thomas, b. May 1, 1762 — LR11 587

Abigail, d. William, Jr., d. Oct. 23, 1762 — LR11 593

Abigall, d. Moses, b. Feb. 9, 1766 — LR15 1

Abigail, d. Joshua, b. June 11, 1771 — LR17 437

Abigall, w. Joshua, d. May 26, 1773 — LR17 445

Amos, s. William, b. July 28, 1739 — LR6 5

Anne, d. Thomas, Jr., b. Oct. 13, 1780 — LR21 549

Asa, s. Thomas, b. Apr. 29, 1757 — LR11 587

Axsah Adkins, d. Isaac, b .May 8, 1767 — LR15 L

	Vol.	Page
PARSONS, PARSON, PERSONS (cont.)		
Benjamin, s. William, b. June 19, 1720	LR2	102
Bildad, s. Moses, b. Apr. 6, 1773	LR17	437
Daniel, s. Thomas, b. Feb. 20, 1760	LR11	587
David, s. William, Jr., b. Dec. 4, 1756	LR9	12
Dorcas, d. Moses, b. Sept. 30, 1764	LR14	10
Elenor, d. Tho[ma]s, b. [ ]	LR7	L
Elidia, d. Isaac, b. June 21, [ ]	LR7	L
Elijah, s. Moses, b. July 13, 1770	LR17	437
Elizabeth, [d. Thomas], b. Feb. [ ], 1749	LR7	L
Eunice, d. William, Jr., b. Mar. 25, 1759; d. 27th day of		
same month	LR11	587
Hannah, d. Isaac & Hannah, b. [ ] 4, 1729	LR4	396
Hannah, d. William, Jr., b. Feb. 28, 1733/4	LR5	6
Hannah, 2nd, d. Will[ia]m, d. July [ ], 1735	LR6	10
Hannah, d. Will[ia]m, 2nd, b. Sept. 2, 1737	LR6	5
Hannah, d. Joshua, b. Jan. 27, 1763	LR11	587
Isaac, of Ffarmington, m. Hannah **BARNES**, of		
Brookfield, Feb. 1, 1727/8	LR4	423
Isaac, s. Isaac, b. Mar. 12, 174[ ]	LR7	L
Isaac, s. Isaac, b. Mar. 10, 1743	LR6	5
Isaac, d. Sept. 14, 1756	LR11	577
Isaac, m. Mary **ADKINS**, July 17, 1766	LR15	N
Isaac, s. Isaac, b. Mar. 13, 1769	LR15	L
Joel, s. Joshua, b. Nov. 11, 1769	LR15	L
John, s. Aaron, b. Aug. 2, 1731	LR5	6
John, m. Ruth **PARSONS** (his cousin), b. of Farmington,		
Oct. 2, 1736	LR5	692
John, s. John, b. Apr. 10, 1739	LR6	5
John, Jr., m. Mercy **HILLS**, Oct. 27, 1757	LR11	576
Joshua, s. Isaac, b. Mar. 7, 1734; d. Oct. 27, 1735	LR5	7
Joshua, 2nd, [s.] Isaac, b. July 23, 1737	LR6	5
Joshua, m. Abigail **AGARD**, Apr. 29, 1762	LR11	592
Joshua, s. Joshua, b. Aug. 9, 1767	LR15	1
Joshua, m. Lois **WOODRUFF**, May 18, 1775	LR17	443
Julia Ann, m. Chester **DAYTON**, b. of Farmington, Oct.		
16, 1838, by Rev. S. H. Clark	LR47	97
Leah, w. Isaac, d. Apr. 8, 1766	LR15	M
Levi, s. Moses, b. Apr. 9, 1760	LR11	587
Marah, m. Andrew **GRIDLEY**, Oct. 10, 1749	LR7	46
Mary, d. William, Jr., b. Mar. 22, 1716/17	LR2	81
Mary, d. William, Jr., d. May 25, 1725	LR2	66
Mary, d. William, Jr., b. Oct. 8, 1727	LR4	395
Matthew, s. Thomas, b. Jan. 6, 1755	LR9	12
Mercy, m. Benjamin **BUCK**, b. of Ffarmington, Dec. 10,		
1728	LR4	423
Mercy, d. John, b. Jan. 14, 1750/1	LR8	7
Moses, s. Isaac, b. May 29, 1732	LR5	7
Moses, s. John, b. June 14, 1753	LR8	7
Moses, m. Abigail **HILLS**, Mar. 23, 1758	LR11	576
Moses, s. Moses, b. July 23, 1762	LR11	587
Olive, d. Thomas, Jr., b. Feb. 26, 1778	LR21	549
Phebe, d. Jacob, b. Feb. 14, 1725/6	LR2	242

	Vol.	Page
PARSONS, PARSON, PERSONS (cont.)		
Phebe, m. Zephaniah **BUCK**, Feb. 6, 1756	LR11	576
Phebe, d. William, Jr., b. Dec. 28, 1762	LR11	587
Phelps W., of Winsted, m. E. **WILSON**, of Harwinton,		
June 6, 1849, by Noah Porter	LR47	125
Rachel, d. William, Jr., b. June 8, 1724	LR2	65
Rachel, d. William, d. Oct. 30, 1727	LR4	396
Ruth, m. John **PARSONS** (her cousin), b. of Farmington,		
Oct. 2, 1736	LR5	692
Ruth, d. John, b. Mar. 22, 1747	LR8	7
Sarah, d. Isaac, b. Aug. 23, 1764	LR15	L
Simeon, s. Moses, b. Mar. 27, 1758	LR11	587
Stephen, s. Joshua, b. Mar. 9, 1765	LR11	587
Tibetha,* d. Thomas, b. Oct. 8, 1747 *(Tabitha)	LR7	L
Thankfull, d. Thomas, b. Jan. 4, 1765	LR17	437
Thomas, s. William, Jr., b. Feb. 15, 1718/19	LR2	65
Thomas, m. Rebeckah **BARNES**, Aug. 17, 1743	LR6	305
Thomas, m. Lydia **COLLINS**, Nov. 6, 1777	LR21	557
Thomas, s. [Thomas], b. Mar. [ ]	LR7	L
Tillese, d. John, b. June 13, 1739	LR6	5
William, Jr., m. Rachel **BARNES**, d. Joseph, Feb. 20,		
1715/16	LR2	94
William, s. William, Jr., b. Aug. 17, 1731	LR5	6
William, d. Oct. 2, 1735	LR5	500
William, Jr., m. Mary **BROWNSON** Apr. 4, 1755	LR9	286
PATTERSON, PATERSON, Anne, d. John, b. Dec. 27, 1736	LR6	5
David, s. William, b. Aug. 7, 1763	LR15	L
Elizabeth, d. William , b. Jan. 18, 1757	LR15	1
Esther, d. William, b. July 26, 1752	LR15	1
George, s. William, b. Jan. 7, 1765	LR15	L
John, s. John, b. Mar. 27, 1769	LR15	L
Mary, d. John & Ruth, b. Dec. 5, 1731	LR5	6
Ruth, d. John, b. June 16, 1739	LR6	5
Salmon, s. John, b. May 13, 1767	LR15	L
Sarah, d. John, b. June 13, 1734	LR5	6
Sarah, d. William, b. Nov. 21, 1758	LR15	1
Thomas, s. William, b. Mar. 7, 1762	LR15	L
William, s. William, b. Nov. 14, 1760	LR15	L
PAYNE, Andrew J., of Avon, m. Betsey **HART**, of		
Farmington, Oct. 17, 1838, by Rev. S. H. Clark	LR47	98
PECK, PEECK, PICK, Abel, s. Moses, b. May 5, 1743	LR6	5
Abell, s. Abell, 2nd, b. July 12, 1774	LR21	549
Abell, 2nd, d. Jan. 26, 1778, in the 33rd y. of his age	LR21	560
Abigail, m. Hezekiah **GRIDLEY**, Jr., Dec. 13, 1754	LR11	592
Abigail, m. Ozias **BROWNSON**, Oct. 23, 1762	LR11	592
Abigall, d. Abell, 2nd, b. May 13, 1776	LR21	549
Amos, m. Mary **HART**, July 26, 1750	LR7	46
Amos, s. Amos, b. Jan. 25, 1754	LR8	7
Amos, s. Amos & Mary, b. Jan. 25, 1754	LR11	587
Anne, d. Rev. Jeremiah, of Watterbury, m. Thomas		
STANLEY, s. Capt. John, May [ ], 1690; d. May		
23, 1718	LR4	271

	Vol.	Page
PECK, PEECK, PICK (cont.)		
Bathshebah, of New Haven, m. Roswell **PALMER**, of		
Farmington, Sept. 18, 1775	LR17	443
Candace, d. Abel, 2nd, b. Jan. 16, 1771	LR21	549
Charles, s. Eleanor, b. Nov. 8, 1727	LR4	395
Charles, of Burlington, m. Eunice **HINMAN**, of		
Farmington, Nov. 24, 1825, by Rev. Noah Porter	LR42	569
Charles, m. Laura **CHILDS**, b. of Farmington, Sept. 3,		
1826, by Rev. Noah Porter	LR42	567
David, m. Hannah **ROWLENSON**, June 1, 1749	LR7	46
Earl, of Cabotville, Mass., m. Elizabeth S. **BUNNEL**, of		
Farmington, June 10, 1844, by William Wright	LR47	113
Eldad, s. Samuel, b. Sept. 16, 1738	LR6	5
Eldad, m. Mary **FOSTER**, Feb. 9, 1764	LR11	594
Eleanor, had s. Charles, b. Nov. 8, 1727	LR4	395
Eleazer, s. Eleazer, b. July 7, 1710	LR5	6
Eleazer, m. Elizabeth **WOODRUFF**, Dec. 6, 1755	LR15	A
Elizabeth, m. Abell **HAWLEY**, Dec. 16, 1772	LR17	442
Eunice H., of Farmington, m. Shubert **THOMSON**, of		
Avon, Feb. 12, 1846, by Rev. Noah Porter	LR47	116
Hannah, m. James **BROWNSON**, b. of Farmington, Apr.		
26, 1737	LR6	27
Huldah, d. Amos, b. Sept. 18, 1762	LR11	587
Isaac, s. Eleazer, b. Aug. 21, 1756	LR15	1
Jemima, d. Eleazer, b. May 1, 1760	LR15	1
Julia E., of Farmington, m. Chester M. **KELLOGG**, of		
New Britain, May 12, 1851, by Rev. Samuel		
Rockwell, of New Britain	LR47	128
Levina, d. Samuel, b. Apr. 25, 1766	LR14	10
Lois, m. Lieut. Elijah **PORTER**, Apr. 14, 1775	LR17	443
Luce, d. Eleazer, b. Oct. 7, 1763	LR15	1
Lucy, d. Amos, b. Dec. 2, 1767	LR17	437
Maria, of Farmington, m. Carlos **WELTON**, of Bristol,		
Nov. 18, 1846, by Rev. William Watson, of		
Plymouth	LR47	119
Mary, d. Amos & Mary, b. Mar. 9, 1760	LR11	587
Mary, w. Amos, d. June 22, 1771	LR17	444
Mary, of Farmington, m. W[illia]m **FRISBIE**, of		
Westport, N.Y., Sept. 10, 1829, by Rev. Noah Porter	LR42	562
Mercy, m. Barnabus **THOMSON**, Nov. 30, 1775	LR21	557
Moses, of Middletown, m. Sarah **KELOG[G]**, of		
Hartford, Aug. 14, 1732	LR5	300
Oliver, s. Moses, b. Mar. 13, 1736/7	LR6	5
Oliver, m. Patience **CLARK**, Feb. 24, 1757	LR11	576
Reuben, s. Eleazer, b. Nov. 5, 1757	LR15	1
Rhoda, d. Moses & Sarah, b. Dec. 15, 1733	LR5	307
Rhoda, d. Moses, b. June 24, 1735	LR5	645
Rhoda, m. Rubin **HART**, Dec. 27, 1759	LR11	575
Ruth, d. Amos & Mary, b. Nov. 28, 1756	LR11	587
Ruth, w. Samuel, Jr., d. July 14, 1770	LR17	444
Salmon, s. Samuel, b. June 22, 1767	LR15	1
Samuel, m. Ruth **HOPKINS**, Mar. [ ], 1757	LR11	576
Samuel, s. Amos, b. Mar. 29, 1765	LR11	587

	Vol.	Page
PECK, PEECK, PICK (cont.)		
Samuel, s. Eleazer, b. Dec. 16, 1766	LR15	1
Samuel, s. Samuell, Jr., b. Sept. 25, 1768	LR17	437
Samuel, s. Abel, 2nd, b. Jan. 5, 1769	LR21	549
Sarah, d. Joseph, b. Aug. 11, 1747	LR6	5
Selah, s. Eleazer, b. Feb. 16, 1771	LR17	437
Seth, s. Eldad, b. May 4, 1770	LR17	437
Sophia, m. Henry J. **HART**, b. of Southington, Aug. 25,		
1842, by [ ]	LR47	108
Submitt, s. John, b. June 21, 1741	LR6	5
Submit, d. Samuell, d. Mar. 15, 1752	LR8	11
Submit, d. Eldad, b. Dec. 30, 1764	LR14	10
Thankfull, d. Samuell, Jr., b. Feb. 2, 1758	LR11	587
William K., of Harwinton, m. Naomi **NORTH**, of		
Farmington, Jan. 21, 1821, by Ludovicus Robbins,		
V.D.M.	LR40	571
Zebulon, s. Elieazer, b. Dec. 9, 1733	LR5	6
PEET, Mary, of Stratford, m. Daniel **BROWNSON**, of		
Ffarmington, Apr. 2, 1725	LR4	423
PENFIELD, Adelia, of Berlin, m. Edward **ANDRUS**, of		
Farmington, July 5, 1840, by Rev. Aaron S. Hill	LR47	102
Chester, of Berlin, m. Aurelia **CARRINGTON**, of		
Farmington, June 12, 1820, by Noah Porter, V.D.M.	LR40	570
PERCIVALL, PERSEVALL, Charlotte, d. James & Dorothy,		
b. July 6, 1773	LR17	437
Charlotte, d. James, d. Sept. 22, 1777	LR21	560
Charlotte, d. James, b. Feb. 9, 1782	LR22	473
Dorothy, d. James & Dorothy, b. Mar. 24, 1779	LR21	549
Ira, s. James & Dorothy, b. Sept. 22, 1770	LR17	437
Milton, s. James, b. Sept. 16, 1784	LR22	473
Timothy, s. James & Dorothy, b. Jan. 13, 1777	LR21	549
PERKINS, PIRKINS, Elizabeth, of Norwich, m. Daniel		
BUCK, of Wethersfield now of Farmington, June		
11, 1722	LR2	60
Louisa M., m. Steven B. **MUNN**, b. of Southington, Apr.		
12, 1846, by Rev. S. H. Clark	LR47	117
Phebe, m. Harvey **CURTIS**, b. of Farmington, Sept. 1,		
1822, by Noah Porter, V.D.M.	LR40	571
PETERSON, Charles, of New Haven, m. Sybel **JACKSON**,		
of Farmington, Jan. 31, 1831, by Rev. Noah Porter	LR42	560
PETTIBONE, PETIBONE, PETTEBONE, Abraham, s.		
Abraham, b. Nov. 6, 1751	LR11	587
Alexander, s. Abraham, b. Feb. 28, 1764	LR14	10
Chansey, s. Abraham, b. Apr. 29, 1766	LR14	10
Elizabeth, d. Abraham, d. Jan. 2, 1755	LR11	574
Elizabeth, d. Abraham, b. Oct. 17, 1756	LR11	587
Jerusha, d. Abraham, b. Feb. 25, 1753	LR11	587
Samuel, s. Abraham, b. Feb. 13, 1758	LR11	587
Theoda, s. Abraham, b. Oct. 13, 1761	LR14	10
Theoda, s. Abraham, b. Oct. 22, 1761	LR11	587
Theophilus, s. Abraham, b. Nov. 3, 1768	LR15	1
PHELPS, Abigail, wid., of Westfield, m. Samuel **JUDD**		
(Sergt.), of Ffarmington, May 27, 1725	LR2	52

	Vol.	Page
PHELPS (cont.)		
Abigail, of Hartford, m. William **HOOKER**, of		
Farmington, May 20, 1731	LR5	13
Abigail, m. Matthew **JUDD**, b. of Farmington, June 28,		
1733	LR5	300
Charlotte, m. George D. **COWLES**, b. of Farmington,		
Sept. 29, 1831, by Rev. Noah Porter	LR42	560
Elizabeth, of Windsor, m. [ ], of Ffarmington,		
Oct. 30, 17[ ]	LR5	13
Emeline, m. Timothy **PORTER**, b. of Farmington, Dec.		
26, 1833, by Rev. Noah Porter	LR42	D
Humphrey, of Barkhamsted, m. Clarinda **CADWELL**, of		
Farmington, Nov. 4, 1824, by Rev. Augustus Bolles	LR42	568
Phebe, d. Oct. 6, 1760, in the 64th y. of her age	LR11	593
Sary, m. John **WOODFORD**, Sept. 15, 1743	LR6	305
PHILLIPS, PHILIPS, Harriet Maria, m. Emerson		
STEDMAN, b. of Farmington, Nov. 2, 1845, by		
Rev. S. H. Clark	LR47	115
James L., of Farmington, m. Louisa **OSGOOD**, of New		
Britain, Aug. 7, 1845, by Rev. S. H. Clark	LR47	114
Jane, m. Richard **BLAKESLEE**, b. of Farmington, Aug.		
13, 1848, by Rev. Henry J. Fox	LR47	119
Roswell, of Burlington, m. Harriet **LEWIS**, of		
Farmington, Nov. 1, 1824, by Rev. Noah Porter	LR42	568
PHINNEY, Lucinda, of Farmington, m. Chauncey S. **LEWIS**,		
of Southington, Mar. 29, 1829, by Rev. Noah Porter	LR42	562
PIERCE, Edward N., m. Permelia F. **THOMPSON**, b. of		
[Farmington], Oct. 8, 1850, by William Wright	LR47	128
[PIERPOINT], [see under **PARPOINT**]		
PIERSON, Abraham, m. Sarah **BRAINARD**, Aug. 7, 1746	LR7	35
John, d. May 8, 1726 (transient person)	LR2	107
PIKE, David, s. David, decd., b. May 8, 1754	LR15	1
Jonathan, s. David, b. May 3, 1750	LR8	7
Samuel, s. James, b. Dec. 16, 1724	LR4	382
William, s. James, b. May 5, 1722	LR4	382
William, 2nd, s. James, d. Aug. 10, 1723	LR2	147
William, 2nd, s. James, b. Mar. 10, 1725/6	LR4	382
PINCHON, Mary, m. Samuel **SCOTT**, Jr., May 8, 1718	LR2	101
PINNEY, Mary, of Windsor, m. Jonathan **GRIDLEY**, of		
Ffarmington, Nov. 17, 1714	LR2	93
PITKIN, PIPTKIN, PITKINS, Elizabeth, d. Rev. Timothy, b.		
Sept. 19, 1761	LR11	587
Eunice, w. Rev. Timothy, d. Aug. 2, 1778, in the 37th y.		
of her age	LR22	482
Samuel, s. Timothy & Temperance, b. May 27, 1755	LR9	12
Samuel, s. Rev. Timothy, d. Sept. 9, 1777, in the 23rd y.		
of his age	LR21	560
Temperance, d. Rev. Timothy, b. May 3, 1772	LR17	437
Temperance, w. Rev. Timothy, d. May 19, 1772, in the		
41st y. of her age	LR17	444
Timothy, m. Mrs. Temperance **CLAP[P]**, Aug. 13, 1753	LR9	286
PLACE, Joel, of Burlington, m. Huldah **ADAMS**, of		
Farmington, Mar. 7, 1828, by Rev. Noah Porter	LR42	565

	Vol.	Page
PLUMB, PLUM, Azubah, d. Thankfull, b. Mar. 12, 1751	LR8	7
Gamaliel, s. Simeon, b. Jan. [ ], 1771	LR17	438
Joseph, s. Simeon, b. Mar. 29, 1774	LR17	438
Orlando, m. Sarah **WELTON**, b. of Wolcott, July 5, 1847, by William Wright	LR47	119
Sabra, d. Simeon, b. June 14, 1760	LR17	437
Samuel, s. Simeon, b. July 13, 1766	LR17	438
Sarah, d. Simeon, b. Oct. 24, 1775	LR17	438
Solomon, s. Simeon, b. June 12, 1769	LR17	438
Sibell, d. Simeon, b. June 7, 1764	LR17	437
Silva, d. Simeon, b. Feb. 27, 1762	LR17	437
Thankfull, had d. Azubah, b. Mar. 12, 1751	LR8	7
[POMEROY], POMROY, PUMORY, PUMMARY, Dorothy, of Northampton, m. John **TREADWELL**, Nov. 20, 1770	LR21	557
Noah, m. Mary J. **PARKER**, b. of Bristol, June 13, 1843, by Rev. Noah Porter	LR47	110
Rachel, wid. of Northampton, m. Thomas **NORTON**, of Farmington, Dec. 11, 1739	LR6	27
Rachel, of Northampton, m. Isaac **NEWEL**, May 15, 1741	LR6	304
POND, Aaron, d. Apr. 20, 1776, in the 58th y. of his age	LR21	558-9
PONTELS, William, m. Mary **RILEY**, Jan. 26, 1852, by Thomas Cowles, J.P.	LR47	130
PORTER, PORTTER, Abigail, d. Thomas, b. June 24, 1680	LR2	112
Abigail, d. Thomas (tailor), Mar. 2, 1689/90	LR2	141
Abigail, d. Thomas, b. July 8, 1694	LR2	112
Abigail, d. Dr. Samuel, b. Sept. 17, 1705	LR2	92
Abigail, d. Nathaniel, b. Nov. 1, 1719	LR2	102
Abigail, m. Stephen **ANDRUS**, s. Daniel, Dec. 29, 1720	LR2	101
Abigail, d. Dr. Samuel, m. Ephraim **THOMAS**, b. of Ffarmington, Dec. 1, 1726	LR2	257
Abigail, d. John, m. Aaron **BORWNSON**, Oct. 26, 1737	LR6	27
Abigail, d. Robert, b. Aug. 9, 1739	LR6	5
Abigail, d. Mehetable **LOVELAND**, b. Nov. 8, 1749	LR8	7
Abigail H., of Farmington, m. Jonathan **DONALDS**, of Canaan, May 29, 1839, by Rev. Noah Porter	LR47	100
Abigail Wadsworth, d. Joseph, b. Dec. 8, 1769	LR15	L
Alpheas, m. Mary D. **HATCH**, b. of Farmington, Nov. 13, 1850, by Rev. Noah Porter	LR47	129
Amos, s. John, b. July 9, 1763	LR11	587
Amzi, s. Lieut. Elijah, b. Nov. 17, 1775	LR17	438
Ann, d. Daniell, b. Mar. 7, 1660	LR1	2
Anna, d. John, b. Jan. 26, 1703/4	LR2	91
Anna, d. Samuel (s. Dr.* Samuel), b. Dec. 20, 1724 *(Perhaps "Deac.")	LR2	46
Anna, m. Isaac **BIDWELL**, June 5, 1744	LR7	35
Annah, wid., m. Ezekiel **LEWIS**, Mar. 9, 1758	LR11	576
Anna, w. Samuell, d. Sept. 13, 1758	LR14	3
Anna, d. Elijah, b. Mar. 6, 1759	LR14	10
Anna [d. Shubael & Roxy], b. June 17, 1793	LR47	A-B
Anna, d. David, b. July [ ]	LR7	L
Asa, [s. Jonathan], b. Sept. 15, 17[ ]	LR6	5

	Vol.	Page
PORTER, PORTTER (cont.)		
Asa, m. Lydia **ANDRUS**, June 13, 1764	LR11	594
Asahel, s. Asa, b. May 16, 1770	LR17	437
Asahel, s. [Benjamin], b. [ ]	LR7	L
Ashbill, s. Benijamin, b. Feb. 25, 1745/6	LR7	545
Belinda, m. Romanta **NORTON**, Mar. 2, 1791	LR29	576
Benjamin, s. Robbed, bp. Mar. 18, 1659	LR2	327
Benjamin, s. Thomas, b. Feb. 14, 1690/1	LR2	112
Benjamin, m. Esther **THOMSON**, b. of Ffarmington, Nov. 25, 1726	LR2	104
Benjamin, d. July 4, 1750	LR7	540
Caleb, s. Timothy, b. May 26, 1705	LR1	4
Caleb, s. Timothy, d. Dec. 24, 1707	LR1	3
Caleb, s. Dr. Timothy, b. June 7, 1723	LR2	88
Caleb, s. Dr. Timothy, d. June 14, 1723	LR2	61
Catharine E., m. Phineas **CURTIS**, b. of Bristol, Nov. 26, 1845, by Rev. Noah Porter	LR47	115
Charlotte, [d. Shubael & Roxy], b. Aug. 10, 1802; d. May 19, 1809	LR47	A-B
Cloe, d. John, b. July 25, 1779	LR22	473
Clarinda, w. John, d. Aug. 1, 1779, in the 43rd y. of her age	LR22	482
Synthia, d. Elijah, b. Sept. 1 ,1768	LR15	1
Daniell, s. Daniell, b. Feb. 2, 1652	LR1	2
David, s. William, b. May 9, 1712	LR2	99
David, m. wid. Anna **MOODEY**, July 26, 1744	LR7	46
David, s. Joseph & Abigail, b. Nov. 26, 1763	LR11	587
David, of Weathersfield, m. Olive **HADSELL**, of Farmington, Oct. 12, 1824, by Rev. Harry Bushnell	LR42	568
Dolly, of Farmington, m. Allison D. **MERRELL**, of Castleton, Vt., Aug. 12, 1823, by Noah Porter, V.D.M.	LR40	572
Ebenezer, m. Thankful [ ], Feb. 8, 1769	LR15	A
Ed, s. Noah, b. Apr. 15, 1765	LR15	1
Edward, of Farmington, m. Susannah **BUNNEL**,of Burlington, Apr. 5, 1852, at the house of Chauncey Porter, by Rev. P. G. Wightman, of Plainville	LR47	131
Eldad, [s. Jonathan], b. May 18, 1737	LR6	5
Elijiah, s. Samuel, Jr., b. Apr. 27, 1721	LR2	102
Elijah, m. Thankfull **BULL**, Sept. 21, 1748	LR7	46
Elijah, m. Thankful [ ], Sept. 22, 1748	LR14	10
Elijah, s. Elijah, b. Feb. 15, 1761	LR14	10
Elijah, Lieut., m. 2nd w. Lois **PECK**, Apr. 14, 1775	LR17	443
Elijah, Lieut., m. 3rd w. Margaret **WHAPLES**, Dec. 22, 1775	LR17	443
Eliza, of Farmington, m. Albert S. **UPSON**, of Waterbury, Oct. 12, 1851, by Rev. Noah Porter	LR47	130
Elizabeth, d. Robberd, bp., Jan. 15, 1653, being about four days old	LR2	330
Elizabeth, d. Thomas, b. June 1, 1699* *("1693"?)	LR2	112
Elizabeth, d. John, b. July 8, 1706	LR2	91
Elizabeth, m. Hezekiah **NORTH**, b. of Farmington, Jan. 21, 1734/5	LR5	545

	Vol.	Page
PORTER, PORTTER (cont.)		
Elizabeth, d. Ebeneer, b. Mar. 26, 1737/8	LR6	5
Elizabeth, m. David **HART**, Feb. 9, 1758	LR11	576
Elizabeth, m. Hezekiah **SCOTT**, Aug. 22, 1765	LR11	594
Emily, m. W[illia]m S. **NININS**, b. of Farmington, Nov.		
22, 1826, by Rev. N. Porter	LR42	567
Erastus, [s. Shubael & Roxy], b. Nov. 14, 1789	LR47	A-B
Erastus, m. Charlotte **WHITING**, b. of Farmington, Dec.		
5, 1826, by Rev. Noah Porter	LR42	567
Easther, d. Timothy, b. Apr. 19, 1699	LR1	2
Esther, d. Timothy, d. Sept. 14, 1699	LR1	2
Easther, d. John, b. Aug. 7, 1700	LR2	91
Easther, d. Nathaniel, b. Mar. 19, 1725/6	LR2	70
Esther, d. Benjamin, b. Aug. 25, 1734	LR6	5
Esther, m. Timothy **GRIDLEY**, b. of Farmington, Apr. 5,		
1737	LR6	27
[E]unic[e], d. Samuel, (Doctor), b. Feb. 24, 1711/12	LR2	97
[E]unice, m. John **WADSWORTH**, b. of Farmington,		
May 11, 1734	LR5	545
Eunice, d. Elijah, b. Aug. 6, 1750	LR7	L
Eunice, d. Elijah, b. Aug. 7, 1750	LR14	10
Eunice, d. Elijah, d. Sept. 28, 1751	LR8	13
Eunice, d. Elijah, d. Sept. 28, 1751*	LR14	3
Eunice, 2nd, d. Elijah, b. Apr. 6, 1754	LR11	587
Eunice, 2nd, d. Elijah, b. Apr. 6, 1754	LR14	10
Eunice, 2nd, d. Elijah, d. Sept. 18, 1755	LR8	13
Eunice, d. Elijah, d. Sept. 18, 1755	LR14	3
Ezekiel, s. Dr. Samuel, b. Aug. 2, 1707	LR2	92
Ezekiel, m. Almira **LANGDON**, Feb. 25, 1824, by Rev.		
Noah Porter	LR42	568
Gad, s. John, Jr., b. Dec. 16, 1760	LR11	587
George, s. Timothy, Jr., b. Sept. 20, 1767	LR15	1
Hannah, d. Samuel, drumer, b. June 17, 1688	LR1	7
Hannah, d. Nehemyah, b. May 11, 1694	LR2	232
Hannah, w. Nehemyah, d. May 27, 1710	LR2	142
Hannah, m. John **STANLEY**, Jr., b. of Ffarmington, Aug.		
[ ], 1710	LR2	123
Hannah, d. Sergt. William b. Nov. 3, 1722	LR2	88
Hanah, m. Joseph **WOODRUFF**, Mar. 1, 1744/5	LR11	576
Hanah, d. Joseph, b. Dec. 11, 1756	LR9	12
Heyshiba, d. Robert, b. Mar. 4, 1665/6	LR1	2
Hezekiah, s. Samuel, doctor, b. May 24, 1717	LR2	83
Isaac, s. Timothy, b. Dec. 30, 1704	LR1	3
Isaac, s. Timothy, Jr., b. Aug. 1, 1766	LR15	1
James, s. Samuel, doctor, b. Dec. 4, 1714	LR2	95
Johanna, d. Thomas, b. Jan. 6, 1655	LR2	328
John, s. Daniell, b. about Nov. 14, 1662	LR1	2
John, s. Thomas, b. July 18, 1686	LR2	112
John, s .Nehemyah, b. Jan. 11, 1687/8	LR2	232
John, m. Rebeckah **WOODFORD**, b. of Ffarmington,		
Jan. 2, 1695/6	LR2	123
John, s. Thomas (tailor), d. Nov. 4, 1709	LR2	141
John, s. Nathaniell & Ruth, b. Nov. 4, 1713	LR2	99

	Vol.	Page
PORTER, PORTTER (cont.)		
John, s. Nathan & Ruth, d. Dec. 1, 1713	LR2	62
John, s. William, b. June 20, 1718	LR2	84
John, [s. William], b. June 10, 1718; d. [ ], 27, 1726	LR4	396
John, s. Nathaniell, 2nd, b. Sept. 6, 1728	LR4	395
John, 2nd, s. William, b. May 6, 1730	LR5	6
John, of Kensington, d. Feb. 21, 1735/6	LR5	50
John, s. Ebenezer, b. May 11, 1735/6	LR6	5
John, m. Cloranah **WHITMAN**, Dec. 15, 1757	LR11	576
John, s. of Ebenezer, m. Mary **BARNES**, Feb. 9, 1758	LR11	576
John, m. Prodence **BRAYNARD**, Nov. 11, 1779	LR22	480
John, Sergt., m. [ ], b. of Farmington, [ ]	LR5	13
John C., m. Mary **ROOT**, b. of Farmington, Dec. 30,		
1841, by Rev. Noah Porter	LR47	106
Jonathan, s. Nehemyah, b. Apr. 28, 1700	LR2	232
Jonathan, d. Mar. 16, 1754	LR8	12
Joseph, s. Samuel, drumer, b. Dec. 12, 1702	LR1	7
Joseph, s. Sergt. William, b. May 28, 1725	LR2	65
Joseph, m. Hannah **HEART**, d. Deac. Ebenezer, July 11,		
1728	LR4	423
Joseph, s. Joseph, b. Aug. 23, 1766	LR14	10
Joshua, m. Mercy [ ], May 2, 1754	LR15	A
Josiah, s. Robert, b. Dec. 24, 1733	LR5	6
Lamuel, s. John, Jr., b. Mar. 4, 1766	LR15	1
Levi, s. [Benjamin], b. [ ]	LR7	L
Lois, d. Samuel, drumer, b. Mar. 18, 1704/5	LR1	7
Lois, m. Samuel **NORTH**, b. of Farmington, Apr. 5, 1737	LR6	27
Lois, d. Elijah, b. Mar. 2, 1752	LR11	587
Lois, d. Elijah, b. Mar. 2, 1752	LR14	10
Lois, 2nd, w. Lieut. Elijah, d. Aug. 20, 1774	LR17	445
Lorana, d. Joshua, b. May 12, 1757	LR15	1
Lucy, d. John & Clorinda, b. Sept. 15, 1770	LR15	L
Lydia, d. William, b. July 4, 1716	LR2	96
Lydia, m. John **LEE**, b. of Farmington, Jan. 6, 1741/2	LR6	304
Lydia Ann, m. Henry W. **WEBSTER**, b. of Watertown,		
Jan. 29, 1832, by Rev. Noah Porter	LR42	559
Marah,* had s. Isaac **HIGGARSON**, b. June 20, 1768		
*("Marah Potters"?)	LR15	F
Martha, d. Nehemyah, b. Jan. 28, 1692/3	LR2	232
Martha, d. Samuel, drumer, b. July 1, 1696	LR1	7
Martha, m. John **ASHMAN**, b. of Ffarmington, Jan. 7,		
1723/4	LR2	257
Martin, s. John (s. of Ebenezer) & Mary, b. Feb. 24, 1759	LR11	587
Mary, d. Robberd, b. Feb. 24, 1646	LR2	330
Mary, d. Daniell, b. Oct. 5, 1654	LR1	2
Mary, d. Thomas, b. July 2, 1689	LR2	112
Mary, d. Nehemyah, b. Sept. 16, 1689	LR2	232
Mary, d. Nehemyah, d. Mar. 10, 1690/1	LR2	142
Mary, d. John, b. Apr. 4, 1698	LR2	91
Mary, d. Samuel, drumer, b. Sept. [ ], 1700	LR1	7
Mary, d. Thomas (tailor), d. May 1, 1707	LR2	141
Mary, d. William, b. Dec. 12, 1713	LR2	99

	Vol.	Page
PORTER, PORTTER (cont.)		
Mary, d. Jno., m. John **COWLES**, s. Samuel, July 12, 1721	LR2	101
Mary, m. David **WOODRUFF**, Jan. 18, 1721/2	LR2	101
Marry, m. Ephraim **TREADWELL**, Apr. 30, 1741	LR6	304
Mary, d. John, b. Jan. 13, 1766	LR14	10
Matthew, s. Nehemyah, b. July 1, 1709	LR2	232
Matthew, s. Nehemyah, d. Sept. 9, 1709	LR2	142
Melete, d. Joshua, b. Feb. 17, 1759	LR15	1
Mercy, d. Benjamin & Easther, b. Dec. 24, 1730	LR5	6
Mercy, d. Joshua, b. Mar. 6, 1755	LR15	1
Mercy, d. Asa, b. Apr. 16, 1765	LR14	10
Nathan, m. Johannah **SMITH**, b. of Ffarmington, June 1, 1715	LR2	93
Nathaniel, s. Thomas, b. Mar. 28, 1692	LR2	112
Nathaniel, m. Ruth **WOODRUFF**, b. of Farmington, Jan. 1, 1712/13	LR2	125
Nathaniel, s. Nathaniell, b. Jan. 20, 1723/4	LR2	46
Nehemiah, s. Daniell, b. Oct. 24, 1656	LR1	2
Nehemyah, of Ffarmington, m. Hannah **LUMM**, of Woodbury, Jan. 21, 1686/7	LR2	125
Noah, m. Mercy **LEWIS**, May 10, 1764	LR11	592
Norman, m. Nancy **BRADLEY**, b. of Farmington, Sept. 23, 1828, by Rev. Noah Porter	LR42	564
Phebee, d. John, b. Sept. 28, 1773	LR17	437
Rachell, d. Thomas, bp. Dec. 26, 1658	LR2	328
Rachel, m. Samuell **COWLS**, s. Samuell, May 12, 1685	LR1	4
Rachel, d. Nehemyah, b. Mar. 28, 1702/3	LR2	232
Rachel, d. Samuel, b. Apr. 30, 1710	LR2	109
Rachel, m. Daniel **HANCOX**, b. of Ffarmington, June 4, 1724, by William Wadsworth, J.P.	LR2	258
Rachel, m. Ephraim **HOLISTER**, May 3, 1746	LR7	35
Rebeckah, d. John, b. Oct. 14, 1695	LR2	91
Rebeckah, d. Ebenezer, b. Oct. 20, 1731	LR5	6
Rebeckah, m. Samuel **WADSWORTH**, of Farmington, July 19, 1733	LR5	300
Rebecca Ann, of Farmington, m. John R. **KEEP**, of Franklin, N.Y., Aug. 31, 1842, by Rev. Noah Porter	LR47	108
Reuben, s. John, d. Dec. 15, 1782	LR22	482
Rhody, d. Robert & Sarah, b. July 20, 1729	LR5	6
Rhoda, m. Elihu **ROOT**, or Ezra, Apr. 30, 1750	LR7	35
Richard, s. Daniell, b. Mar. 24, 1658	LR1	2
Robberd, had s. [ ], b. Dec. 12, 1648	LR2	329
Robberd, s. Robberd, bp. Dec. 15, 1650	LR2	330
Robert, s. Thomas, b. May 16, 1697	LR2	112
Robert, m. Sarah **SMITH**, b. of Ffarmington, Oct. 17, 1728	LR4	423
Robert, s. Robert, b. Sept. 9, 1731	LR5	6
Robert, s. Robert, d. Nov. 14, 1736	LR6	10
Robert, s. Robert, b. June 23, 1742	LR6	5
Robert, s. Robert, d. June 15, 1767, ae 25 y.	LR14	3
Roxy, w. Shubael, d. [ ], 1812	LR47	A-B
Ruth, m. Samuell **SMITH**, Mar. 24, 1687	LR1	4

	Vol.	Page
PORTER, PORTTER (cont.)		
Ruth, d. Samuel, drumer, b. Jan. 22, 1698	LR1	7
Ruth, w. Nathan, d. Nov. 14, 1713	LR2	62
Ruth, d. Nathaniel, b. Dec. 1, 1717	LR2	84
Ruth, m. Daniel NEWEL, Oct. 31, 1721	LR2	101
Ruth, eldest, d. [Jonathan], b. Oct. 5, 1731	LR6	5
Ruth, d. Jonathan, d. Oct. 28, 1757	LR11	577
Ruth, d. Asa, b. May 16, 1767	LR17	437
Samuell, s. Daniell, b. Oct. 24, 1665	LR1	2
Samuell, m. Martha FREMAN, Feb. 18, 1685	LR1	5
Samuel, s. Samuel, drumer, b. Sept. 17, 1691	LR1	7
Samuel, s. Jonathan, b. Apr. 9, 17[ ]	LR6	5
Samuel, s. Nehemyah, b. July 16, 1702	LR2	232
Samuel, Dr., of Ffarmington, m. Abigail HUMPHRIES,		
sometime of Simsbury, [ ], 1702	LR2	123
Samuel, m. Anna HART, b. of Ffarmington, Dec. 23,		
1714	LR2	93
Samuel, s. Dr. Samuel, b. Mar. 16, 1719	LR2	83
Samuel, d. Oct. 8, 1768, in the 77th y. of his age	LR14	3
Sara, d. Robberd, bp. Dec. 20, 1657	LR2	328
Sarah, d. Samuel, drumer, b. about Nov. 15, 1693	LR1	7
Sarah, d. Dr. Samuel, b. Sept. 7, 1709	LR2	92
Sarah, m. Samuel THOMSON, s. Thomas, June 20, 1716	LR2	94
Sarah, d. Nathaniel, b. Feb. 27, 1721/2	LR2	102
Sarah, d. Robert, b. Oct. 14, 1736	LR6	5
Sarah, d. Joseph, d. Feb. 11, 1750/1	LR7	540
Sarah, d .Joshua, b. Mar. 9, 1756	LR15	1
Sarah, m. Oliver WOODRUFF, June 18, 1770	LR17	G
Selah, s. Timothy, Jr., b. July 30, 1772	LR17	437
Seth, s. Elijah, b. Mar. 6, 1756	LR11	587
Seth, s. Elijah, b. Mar. 25, 1756	LR14	10
Shubael, b. Aug. 18, 1763; m. Roxy CURTIS, Jan. 9,		
1786; d. [ ], 1825	LR47	A-B
Shuball, s. Elijah, b. Aug. 18, 1763	LR14	10
Simeon, s. John, Jr., b. June 12, 1768	LR15	1
Stephen, s. Samuel, drumer, b. Jan. 17, 1706/7	LR1	7
Stephen, s. Elijah, b. July 2, 174[ ]	LR7	L
Stephen, s. Elijah, b. July 12, 1749	LR14	10
Stephen, s. Elijah, d. Sept. 28, 1749	LR14	3
Stephen, s. Elijah, d. Sept. 28, 1749	LR7	36
Stephen, s. Samuell, b. Apr. 4, [ ]	LR1	2
Susan, [d. Shubael & Roxy], b. June 23, 1787	LR47	A-B
Susan, m. Daniel TILLOTSON, b. of Farmington, June		
8, 1835, by Noah Porter	LR47	89
Susannah, d. Ebenezer, b. Oct. 5, 1729	LR5	6
Susannah, m. Daniel NEWEL, Feb. 13, 1753	LR8	10
Thankfull, w. Lieut. Elijah, d. Sept. 28, 1768, ae 39 y.	LR14	3
Thomas, s. Robberd, b. Oct. 25, 1650	LR2	329
Thomas, s. Robert, m. Abigail COWLES, b. of		
Ffarmington, May [ ], 1678	LR2	145
Thomas, s. Nehemyah, b. Dec. 25, 1697	LR2	232
Thomas, s. Timothy, b. Aug. 17, 1700	LR1	2
Thomas, s. Robert, d. Dec. 19, 1718	LR2	61

	Vol.	Page
PORTER, PORTTER (cont.)		
Thomas, s. Nathaniell, b. July 22, 1730	LR5	6
Thomas, s. Benjamin & Easther, b. Oct. 3, 1732	LR5	6
Thomas, s. Benjamin & Easther, d. Oct. 4, 1732	LR5	50
Thomas, s. Ebenezer, b. Feb. 4, 1733/4	LR5	6
Timothy, s. Thomas, b. Nov. 4, 1672	LR1	2
Timothy, m. Juanah **BULL**, Apr. 22, 1697	LR1	4
Timothy, s. Timothy, b. Sept. 14, 1702	LR1	2
Timothy, Dea., m. Silence **CHAPMAN**, Oct. 10, 1750	LR7	46
Timothy, m. Emeline **PHELPS**, b. of Farmington, Dec.		
26, 1833, by Rev. Noah Porter	LR42	D
Wells, s. Benjamin, b. Feb. 18, 17[ ]	LR7	L
Wells, s. Benjamin, d. June 24, 1748	LR7	540
William, s. Thomas, b. Oct. 28, 1682	LR2	112
William, m. Mary **SMITH**, b. of Farmington, June 14,		
1711	LR2	125
William, s. Sergt. William, b. Sept. 12, 1720	LR2	88
William, [s, William], b. Sept. 22, 1720; d. [ ] 27, 1726	LR4	396
Zube, d. Benjamin, b. Sept. 6, 17[ ]	LR6	5
Zube, d. Benjamin, b. June 23, 1737	LR6	5
Zubae, d. Benjamin, d. July 1, 1737	LR6	10
Zube, d. Beniamin, b. Sept. 6, 1740; d. July 27, 1742	LR7	545
Zube, d. Benjamin, b. Sept. [ ]	LR7	L
-----, m. Hezekiah **LEE**, b. of Ffarmington, [ ],		
1728	LR4	423
POSEY, Alexander, m. Emily Maria **DEMING**, b. of		
Farmington, Dec. 8, 1840, by Rev. Aaron S. Hill	LR47	103
POST, Cynthia L., of Batavia, N.Y., m. Stephen **GLADDING**,		
of Farmington, Aug. 3, 1845, by Rev. S. H. Clark	LR47	114
POTMER, Fanny, m. Jonathan Floyd **COOK**, Mar. 21, 1848,		
by Rev. Joel Grant, of Avon	LR47	122
POTTER, Abigail, m. Gideon **ANDRUSS**, b. of Farmington,		
Apr. 11, 1743/4	LR7	46
Marah,* had s. Isaac **HIGGARSON**, b. June 20, 1768		
*(Perhaps "Marah **PORTER**"?)	LR15	F
Minerva, m. Zerah **WOODFORD**, b. of Farmington,		
Aug. 10, 1820, by Ludovicus Robbins, V.D.M.	LR40	570
PRATT, Daniel, s. Elisha, b. Sept. 1, 1761	LR11	587
Elisha, s. John, d. Aug. 15, 1731	LR5	50
Elisha, s. John, b. May 15, 1736	LR5	6
Elisha, s. John & Mary, b. Aug. 10, 1735	LR5	307
Elisha, m. Ruth **OWEN**, Mar. 15, 1759	LR11	576
Elisha, s. Elisha, b. July 27, 1768	LR17	437
Elizabeth, of Saybroook, m. Ezra **WARNER**, of		
Farmington, May 4, 1738	LR6	27
John, of Weathersfield, m. Mary **ROOT**, of Ffarmington,		
Nov. 8, 1721	LR2	60
John, s. John, b. Aug. 6, 1739	LR6	5
Mary, d. John & Mary, b. May 1, 1723	LR2	87
Mary, d. John, d. Nov. 8, 1736	LR6	10
Mary, of Hartford, m. Roger **NORTON**, of Farmington,		
Jan. 5, 1746/7	LR7	46
Mary, d. Elisha, b. Oct. 29, 1763	LR11	587

	Vol.	Page
PRATT (cont.)		
Ogden C., of Middletown, m. Clarissa **FAIRCHILD**, of		
Farmington, Nov. 24, 1831, by Rev. Noah Porter	LR42	559
Sarah, d. John, b. Sept. 17, 1726	LR2	34
Sarah, d. John & Mary, b. June 14, 1732	LR5	6
Sarah, m. Elnathan **GRIDLEY**, Feb. 27, 1753	LR8	10
Welcome A., m. Maria **WELLS**, Aug. 23, 1825, at the		
house of wid. Wells, of Northington Soc., by Luther		
Higley, J.P.	LR42	569
PRESTON, John B., Rev. of Ripley, N.Y., m. Clarissa		
NORTH, of Farmington, June 23, 1833, by David		
L. Ogden	LR42	A
PRINCE, Cartini, lately of Norfolk, m. John H. **ADAMS**,		
lately of Hartford, Dec. 24, 1849, by Rev. Noah		
Porter	LR47	126
Charles, of Canton, m. Hannah **SEIGNOR**, of		
Farmington, Nov. 24, 1825, by Rev. Noah Porter	LR42	569
Mary Ann, m. Hiram **SMITH**, Oct. 17, 1839, by Rev.		
Ezra S. Cook	LR47	101
PRINDLE, Daniel, of Simsbury, m. Lydia **ANDREWS**, of		
Farmington, May 28, 1829, by Rev. Noah Porter	LR42	562
PROSSEE, Levi, of Bloomfield, m. Harriet **WILCOX**, of		
Farmington ,Oct. 11, 1848, by Rev. Noah Porter	LR47	123
PURDY, Charlotte, of Plymouth, m. William **HILLS**, of		
Farmington, Feb. 25, 1833, by Rev. Noah Porter	LR42	558
[PYNCHON], [see under **PINCHOW**]		
RAMSEY, Charles, s. John & Etta, b. June 11, 1821	LR41	A
Charles, of Springfield, Mass., m. Harriet S. **HAWLEY**,		
of Farmington, Apr. 20, 1846, by Rev. Noah Porter	LR47	117
George, s. John & Etta, b. Mar. 9, 1823	LR41	A
RECOR, Anne, of Farmington, m. Henry **VOSBURG**, of		
Bristol, Dec. 30, 1849, by William Wright	LR47	127
Augusta, of New Britain, m. Samuel C. **DUNHAM**, of		
Farmington, Aug. 29, 1847, by William Wright	LR47	121
REED, Catharine, m. James **McDONALD**, b. of Hartford,		
Dec. 6, 1835, by Rev. Noah Porter	LR47	91
REES, Margaret, w. John, d. Sept. 9, 1751	LR8	12
REW, John, s. Memucan, b. Aug. 21, 1787	LR35	[ ]
RICE, RYC, RYCE, [see also **ROYCE**], Martha, of		
Wallingford, m. Thomas **NORTH**, of Ffarmington,		
S. Thomas, Dec. 1, 1698	LR2	123
Mary,* of Wallingford, m. Joseph **SMITH**, Jr., of		
Ffarmington, Jan. 19, 1707/8 *(In pencil "Mary		
ROYCE")	LR2	125
Sedgwick, m. Caroline **CASE**, Jan. 20, 1823, by Elisha		
Cushman	LR40	572
Tryphenia, of Barkhamsted, m. Joseph **HART**, of		
Farmington, July 26, 1826, by Harry Bushnell	LR42	569
RICH, Elizabeth, d. David, b. Aug. 20, 1751	LR8	8
Elizabeth, d. David, d. Mar. 21, 1752	LR8	11
Jerusha, d. David, b. Mar. 4, 1757	LR11	588
John, s. William, b. Nov. 14, 1763	LR11	588
Josiah, s. David, b. Sept. 6, 1744	LR8	8

	Vol.	Page
RICH (cont.)		
Mary, d. William & Mary, b. Mar. 13, 1755	LR9	12
Mehetabel, d. David, b. Nov. 12, 1749	LR8	8
Mahetabel, w. David, d. July 22, 1757	LR11	577
Mehetebel, m. Ebenezer **HAWLEY**, Nov. 29, 1769	LR15	A
Phebe, d. David, b. Dec. 22, 1747	LR8	8
Rebeckah, d. David, b. Jan. 21, 1746	LR8	8
Samuel, s. David, b. Feb. 26, 1753	LR8	9
William, s. William, b. July 17, 1753	LR8	8
RICHARDS, Aaron, s. Samuel, b. May 20, 1749	LR8	8
Abigail, w. Thomas, d. Sept. 24, 1736	LR6	10
Abigail, m. Thomas **LANGHTON**, Dec. 9, 1742	LR6	305
Amos, s. John, b. Apr. 7, 1759	LR11	588
Charles, m. Martha **HAWLEY**, b. of Farmington, Dec. 2, 1840, by Rev. Noah Porter	LR47	103
Charles, m. Lucy A. **HAWLEY**, b. of Farmington, Mar. 1, 1849, by Rev. D. M. Seward, of West Hartford	LR47	125
Cornelia, of Farmington, m. John L. **BUTLER**, of Wilkesbarrie, Pa., Nov. 9, 1826, by Rev. Noah Porter	LR42	567
Ebenezer, m. wid. Mercy **BUCK**, b. of Farmington, Dec. 6, 1736	LR6	27
Ebenezer, d. Jan. 7, 1755	LR9	495
Elidia, d. John, b. Apr. 10, 1754	LR9	12
Elijah, s. John, b. July 10, 1756	LR11	588
Elijah, s. John, b. Nov. 11, 1777	LR21	549
Elizabeth, m. James **HORSINGTON**, Dec. 24, 1750	LR7	46
Elizabeth, d. Samuel, b. Feb. 26, 1751	LR8	8
Esther, d. John, b. May 15, 1764	LR14	10
James, s. Lemuel, Jr., b. May 24, 1783	LR22	473
John, s. Thomas, b. Mar. 21, 1730/1	LR5	6
John, m. Marah **FRENCH**, Apr. 14, 1752	LR8	10
John, m. Elizabeth **DICKENSON**, Dec. 26, 1776	LR21	557
John, Rev. of Woodstock, Vt., m. Emily **COWLES**, of Farmington, June 16, 1828, by Rev. N. Porter	LR42	564
Lucretia, d. Dr. Samuel, b. June 4, 1762	LR11	588
Lurina, m. Asaph **HURD**, b. of Farmington, Feb. 6, 1828, by Amasa Woodford, J.P.	LR42	564
Lydia, d. Thomas, b. Mar. 23, 1732/3	LR5	6
Lydia, of Bristol, m. Daniel **MERRELL**, of Canton, Mar. 30, 1830, by Rev. Noah Porter	LR42	561
Mary, d. Ebenezer, b. Dec. 14, 1737	LR6	6
Mary, of Farmington, m. Joseph **BROWN**, of Crum Elbow Precinct, Dutchess Cty., N.Y., Mar. 20, 1760	LR11	575
Mercy, d. Aug. 30, 1758	LR11	577
Peletiah, s. Samuel, b. Feb. 8, 1758	LR11	588
Peletiah, s. Samuell, d. Nov. 19, 1758	LR11	577
Samuel, m. Lidia **BUCK**, Dec. 8, 1747	LR8	10
Sarah, d. Lemuel, Jr., b. Jan. 13, 1789	LR22	473
Seth, s. Dr. Samuel, b. Oct. 4, 1764	LR11	588
Susanah, m. Jonathan **ANDRUS**, b. of Farmington, June 5, 1735	LR5	692

	Vol.	Page
RICHARDS (cont.)		
Thomas, his d. [ ], b. [ ], 1728	LR4	396
Thomas, m. wid. Ruth **ORUIS**, b. of Farmington, Dec.		
28, 1738	LR6	27
William, s. Samuell, b. Oct. 9, 1756	LR11	588
RICHARDSON, RICHASON, John, [s. Thomas], b. Apr. 15,		
1672	LR1	2
Mary, d, Thomas, b. Dec. 25, 1667	LR1	2
Rachel, of Wallingford, m. John **LEWIS**, of Farmington,		
Dec. 2, 1736	LR6	27
Sarah, [d. Thomas], b. Mar. 25, 1669	LR1	2
RIGHT, [see under **WRIGHT**]		
RILEY, Mary, m. William **PONTELS**, Jan. 26, 1852, by		
Thomas Cowles, J.P.	LR47	130
RISTER, George W., of Flemington, N.Y., m. Mary		
Ann **BARBER**, of Farmington, July 2, 1844, by		
Rev. Noah Porter	LR47	112
ROBBINS, ROBINS, Cornelia, of Farmington, m. Augustus		
A. **ALLEN**, of New Britain, Nov. 5, 1848, by		
William Wright	LR47	123
Evinice, d. Thomas, b. Apr. 13, 1752	LR8	9
Lowrey, m. Emily **FOOT**, Oct. 19, 1835, by David G.		
Ogden	LR47	92
Mary, m. Hiram **HART**, b. of Farmington, May 22, 1827,		
by Rev. Harvey Bushnell	LR42	565
[Thom]as, s. Thomas, b. Nov. 21, 1743	LR7	M
Thomas, had d. [ ], b. Sept. 14, 1748	LR7	M
-----h, d. [Thomas], b. June 2, 1746	LR7	M
ROBERTS, ROBARDS, ROBBARDS, Aaron, of		
Berlin, m. Mary **WADSWORTH**, May 20, 1829 by		
Rev. Noah Porter	LR42	562
Abial, m. Martha **HULL**, Aug. 14, 1750	LR7	35
Abial, m. Martha **HULL**, Aug. 14, 1750	LR8	8
Abial, had, s. Moses, b. May 23, 1751	LR8	8
Abigail, d. Jabez, b. Dec. 13, 1753	LR8	8
Benjamin, s. Jacob, b. Mar. 10, 1759	LR11	588
David, s. Jabish, b. Apr. 14, 1748	LR8	8
Dudley, s. Jacob, b. July 20, 1756	LR11	588
Garry H., of Bristol, m. Betsey **CLARK**, of Farmington,		
Jan. 24, 1837, by Rev. Noah Porter	LR47	95
Gideon, s. Elias, b. Mar. 5, 1749	LR7	M
Hephzibah, d. Abial & Martha, b. Feb. 9, 1755	LR9	12
Jabash, m. Abigail **COOPER**, Feb. 2, 1744	LR8	10
Jabez, s. Jabez, b. Dec. 29, 1759	LR11	588
James, of Hartford, m. Ann **CABLE**, of Burlington, Oct.		
11, 1835, by Rev. Noah Porter	LR47	90
Joseph, m. Anne **LEAMING**, Jan. 6, 1773	LR17	442
Mary, d. Jabish, b. Oct. 8, 1746	LR8	8
Meriam, d. Abial & Martha, b. Feb. 8, 1753	LR9	12
Moses, s. Abial, b. May 23, 1751	LR8	8
Rosina A., of Hartford, m. Jaurus D. **GILBERT**, of New		
Haven, Oct. 2, 1821, by Noah Porter, V.D.M.	LR40	571
Samuel, d. Nov. 7, 1776, in the 52nd y. of his age	LR21	558-9

	Vol.	Page
ROBERTS, ROBARDS, ROBBARDS (cont.)		
Thankfull, d. Jabish, b. Mar. 7, 1751	LR8	8
Thankfull, m. Nathaniel Hun **ROOT**, Oct. 11, 1770	LR17	442
ROBINSON, Eunice, of Farmington, m Frederick C.		
THOMAS, of Avon, Apr. 28, 1841, by Rev. Noah		
Porter	LR47	104
George, m. Sarah B. **COWLES**, Nov. 30, 1820, by Noah		
Porter, V.D.M.	LR40	570
Julia, m. Samuel K. **LOOMIS**, b. of Farmington, Nov.		
16, 1826, by Rev. Noah Porter	LR42	567
ROCKWELL, Philo G., of New Britain, m. Elizabeth A.		
WADSWORTH, of Farmington, Oct. 30, 1850, by		
Rev. Noah Porter	LR47	129
ROGERS, Elidia, d. David, b. Jan. 29, 1750/1	LR8	8
Eunice, d. David, b. Mar. 23, 1749	LR8	8
ROLY, Catharine, of Farmington, m. Orrin L. **BOOTH**, of		
Avon, Feb. 23, 1846, by Rev. S. H. Clark	LR47	116
ROOT, Abigail, d. Samuel, b. Aug. 29, 1721	LR2	65
Abigail, d. Joseph, Jr., b. July 6, 1734	LR5	6
Abigail, w. Samuel, d. June 27, 1748	LR7	36
Abigail, d. Job, b. Sept. 17, 1754	LR9	12
Abigail, m. Timothy **ANDRUS**, Apr. 18, 1764	LR11	594
Alfred, m. Sibbel E. **DOOLITTLE**, b. of Farmington,		
Nov. 18, 1838, by Rev. Noah Porter	LR47	98
Amzi, m. Ann **JONES**, Aug. 10, 1821, by Noah Porter,		
V.D.M.	LR40	571
Amzi Francis, of Farmington, m. Mary **THORP**, of		
Southington, Apr. 10, 1842, by Rev. Aaron S. Hill	LR47	107
Anvie, m. Julia **MUNN**, Oct. 7, 1850, by Rev. Charles		
Kelsey	LR47	127
Asahel, s. Caleb, b. Jan. 17, 1732/3	LR5	6
[A]sahel, [s. Caleb], b. Feb. 26, 1741	LR7	M
Asahel, s. John, b. Feb. 11, 1766	LR14	10
Asahel, s. Daniel, b. Mar. 3, 1768	LR17	438
Caleb, of Farmington, m. Elizabeth **SALMON**, of		
Westfield, Aug. 9, 1693	LR2	93
Caleb, s. Caleb, b. Mar. 14, 1697/8	LR2	95
Caleb, d. June 10, 1712	LR2	62
Caleb, of Farmington, m. Johannah **SHAW**, of Windham,		
July 12, 1721	LR2	101
Caleb, s. Caleb, b. Oct. 26, 1725	LR2	70
Caleb, his s. [ ], b. July 24, 1735	LR7	M
Daniel, s. Thomas (s. of Caleb), b. Apr. 3, 1735	LR5	307
Daniel, m. Esther **ANDRUS**, Apr. 27, 1757	LR11	576
Daniel, m. Sarah **ROOT**, Feb. 3, 1762	LR11	575
David, s. Stephen, b. Jan. 23, 1751	LR8	8
Edward, m. Mary **ROW**, b. of Farmington, Aug. 13,		
1822, by Noah Porter, V.D.M.	LR40	571
Eleazer, d. Feb. 22, 1769, in the 49th y. of his age	LR15	M
Elias, m. Electa **ALVORD**, May 16, 1827, by Rev. Noah		
Porter	LR42	565
Elidia, d. Thomas, Jr., b. Dec. 29, 1758	LR11	588
Elihu or Ezra, m. Rhoda **PORTTER**, Apr. 30, 1750	LR7	35

	Vol.	Page
ROOT (cont.)		
Elisha, m. Lucy **CURTIS**, Jan. 16, 1764	LR17	G
Elizabeth, d. Joseph, b. June 22, 1692	LR2	99
Elizabeth, d. Caleb, b. Apr. 8, 1706	LR2	95
Elizabeth, m. Ebenezer **ORUIS**, b. of Farmington, Jan. 23, 1732/3	LR5	300
Elizabeth, d. Job, b. Jan. 3, 1763	LR11	588
Elizabeth, m. William A. **ORVIS**, b. of Farmington, May 15, 1839, by Rev. Noah Porter	LR47	100
Emeline E., of Farmington, m. Isaac S. **CLOUGH**, of Waltham, Mass., [ ] 1, 1848, by Rev. J. Sykes	LR47	122
Emily, m. Edward **LANGDON**, b. of Farmington, June 10, 1834, by Rev. Noah Porter	LR42	E
Easther, w. Job, d. Feb. 26, 1758	LR11	593
[E]unic[e], d. John, s. Stephen [& Margaret], b. May 4, 1718	LR2	104
Ezekiel, s. Joseph, Jr., b. Feb. 1, 1731/2	LR5	6
Ezekiel, s. Joseph, Jr., d. May 6, 1735	LR5	50
Ezekiel, twin with Hannah, s. Joseph, b. Aug. 27, 1741	LR6	6
Ezekiel, see also Root Ezekiel Niles		
Ezra, see Elihu Root	LR7	35
Hannah, twin, with Ezekiel, d. Joseph, b. Aug. 27, 1741	LR6	6
Hannah, w. Joseph, d. Aug. 31, 1741	LR6	10
Hannah, d. Job, b. May 21, 1761	LR11	588
Hannah, wid., d. Jan. 23, 1762	LR11	574
Hannah, d. Elisha, b. Mar. 1, 1765	LR17	438
Hannah, b. Nov. 7, 1785; m. Joseph **HAWLEY**, Feb. 16, 1816	LR47	W-Y
Henry, m. Mary **GAY**, b. of Farmington, Oct. 12, 1825, by Rev. Noah Porter	LR42	569
Hezekiah, s. John, b. Aug. 18, 1705	LR1	4
Hezekiah, s. John, s. Jno & Martha, b. Nov. 6, 1715	LR2	87
Huldah, d. Samuel & Abigail, b. Apr. 10, 1726	LR2	69
Huldah, d. Elezier, b. Mar. 26, 1754	LR9	12
Huldah, d. Eleizer, d. Oct. 13, 1756	LR9	495
Huldah, d. Eleazer, b. June 17, 1763	LR11	588
Jeames, s. Stephen, b. Feb. 23, 1726	LR7	546
James, s. Elihu, b. Nov. 19, 1750	LR8	8
James, m. Mercy **STEDMAN**, July 22, 1772	LR17	443
James & Mercy, had s. [ ], b. Apr. 16, 1773	LR17	438
James, his s. [ ], d. Apr. 16, 1773	LR17	445
Johannah, d. Caleb, 2nd, b. May 5, 1728	LR5	6
Job, s. Thomas, of Kensington, b. Apr. 6, 1728	LR4	395
Job, m. Elizabeth **BARNES**, Jan. 3, 1754	LR8	10
Job & Easther, had d. [ ], s. b. [Feb. 25], 1758	LR11	593
Joel, s. Thomas, Jr., b. May 4, 1755	LR9	12
Joel, s. Elisha & Lucy, b. Aug. 31, 1770	LR17	438
John, s. John, m. Martha **HUNN**, wid. Nathaniell, b. of Ffarmington, Dec. 9, 1714	LR2	93
John, s. Stephen, m. Margaret **STRONG**, July 10, 1716	LR2	104
John, s .John, s. Jno & Martha, b. Oct. 11, 1718	LR2	87
John, s. John, s. of Stephen [& Margaret], b. Mar. 21, 1722/3	LR2	104

	Vol.	Page
ROOT (cont.)		
John, m. Ann **STEEL**, May 26, 1762	LR11	592
John, s. John, b. Apr. 4, 1764	LR11	588
John, d. Nov. 16, 1764, in the 80th y. of his age	LR11	593
John, d. Nov. 8, 1781, in the 59th y. of his age	LR21	560
Jonathan, s. Timothy, b. Dec. 20, 1707	LR2	109
Jonathan, s. Thomas, Jr., d. Jan. 29, 1757	LR11	577
Jonathan, s. Thomas, Jr., b. Dec. 30, 1757	LR11	588
Joseph, of Farmington, m. Elizabeth **WARNER**,		
sometime of Middletown, Sept. 17, 1691	LR2	125
Joseph, s. John, b. Mar. 17, 1693	LR1	4
Joseph, s. Joseph, b. Aug. 27, 1699	LR2	99
Joseph, Jr., m. Hannah **WADSWORTH**, Sept. 23, 1726	LR2	100
Joseph, Sr., m. Ruth **SMITH**, wid., b. of Farmington,		
May 3, 1727	LR2	258
Joseph, s. Joseph, Jr., b. Apr. 2, 1738	LR6	6
Joseph, Sr., d. Dec. 18, 1739	LR6	10
Joseph, s. John, d. Oct. 15, 1747	LR7	36
Joseph, d. Nov. 4, 1783, in the 46th y. of his age	LR22	482
Joseph A., m. Elizabeth **MOSES**, b. of Canton, Nov. 1,		
1846, by Rev. Noah Porter	LR47	118
Joshua, s. Caleb, b. Apr. 13, 1723	LR2	87
Josiah, s. John (s. of Jno (?)), b. Aug. 25, 1724	LR2	46
Josiah, m. Keziah **SMITH**, June 23, 1746	LR8	10
Josiah, d. Oct. 1, 1752, in the 29th y. of his age	LR8	12
Josiah, s. Josiah, b. Nov. 17, 1752	LR9	12
Josiah, m. Martha **MOOR**, Dec. 14, 1760	LR11	575
Julia, m. William A. **IVES**, Nov. 21, 1832, by Rev. David		
L. Parmelee	LR42	558
Julia Ann, of Farmington, m. Franklin **WILCOX**, of		
Bershire, Mass., Feb. 18, 1822, by Noah Porter,		
V.D.M.	LR40	571
Julia Ann., m. Lewis **HART**, b. of Farmington, Apr. 10,		
1842, by Rev. Aaron S. Hill	LR47	107
Keziah, m. Ebenezer **HAWLEY**, Oct. 19, 1757	LR11	575
Lois, d. John, s. of Stephen [& Margaret], b. Jan. 24,		
1725/6	LR2	104
Lucy, d. Elisha & Lucy, b. May [ ], 1768	LR17	438
Lydia, m. Romanta **BARBER**, b. of Farmington, May 3,		
1829, by Rev. H. Bushnell	LR42	562
Margaret, m. John **ROW**, b. of Ffarmington, Jan. 22,		
1717/18	LR2	93
Margaret, d. John, s. of Stephen & [Margaret], b. July 5,		
1720	LR2	104
Margarit, w. John, d. Apr. 20, 1751, in the 60th y. of her		
age	LR8	11
Mark, s. Timothy, b. Nov. 29, 1764	LR14	10
Martha, d. John, s. Jno & Martha, b. May 4, 1721	LR2	87
Martha, d. Josiah, b. May 28, 1750	LR9	12
Martha, m. Jesse **CURTIS**, Dec. 2, 1772	LR17	442
Mary, d. Joseph, b. Jan. 22, 1693/4	LR2	99
Mary, d. Caleb, b. Mar. 6, 1694/5	LR2	95
Mary, d. John, b. Mar. 23, 1699	LR1	4

	Vol.	Page
ROOT (cont.)		
Mary, d. Stephen, m. William **JUDD**, s. Thomas, b. of		
Farmington, Jan. 21, 1712/13	LR2	125
Mary, m. Jonathan **LEE**, b. of Farmington, June 4, 1713	LR2	125
Mary, of Ffarmington, m. John **PRATT**, of		
Weathersfield, Nov. 8, 1721	LR2	60
Mary, m. John **BURR**, Jr., of Ffarmington, Nov. 15, 1722	LR2	51
Mary, d. Joseph, Jr., b. Oct. 21, 1727	LR4	395
Mary, d. John, s. Stephen, b. Sept. 11, 1728	LR4	395
Mary, m. Azarah **SMITH**, b. of Kensington, Aug. 14,		
1740	LR6	27
Mary, m. Aezariah **SMITH**, Aug. 14, 1740	LR8	10
Mary, Mrs., m. Rev. Samuel **NEWELL**, May 4, 1749	LR7	35
Mary, d. Noah, b. Dec. 12, 1762	LR9	12
Mary, m. John C. **PORTER**, b. of Farmington, Dec. 30,		
1841, by Rev. Noah Porter	LR47	106
Mary L., m. Francis W. **COWLES**, b. of Farmington,		
Sept. 9, 1835, by Rev. Noah Porter	LR47	90
Nancy J., of Farmington, m. Joseph M. **BASSET**, of		
Rowe, Mass., Nov. 3, 1844, by Rev. S. H. Clark	LR47	113
Nathaniel Hun, s. Josiah, b. Nov. 6, 1747	LR9	12
Nathaniel Hun, m. Thankfull **ROBBARDS**, Oct. 11, 1770	LR17	442
Noah, s. Thomas, b. Sept. 5, 1731	LR5	6
Noah, m. Mary **GRIDLEY**, June 10, 1762	LR9	12
Olive, d. Samuel & Sarah, b. Nov. 7, 1754	LR11	588
Oliver, s. Samuel, d. Feb. 24, 1749/50	LR7	540
Oren, s. Joseph, b. Sept. 14, 1766	LR15	M
Ozias, s. Samuel & Cloe, b. Jan. 18, 1759	LR11	588
Phebe, d. Joseph, Jr., b. Mar. 21, 1730	LR5	6
Phelix,* d. Joseph, Jr., b. Mar. 21, 1730 *(In pencil		
"Phebe"?)	LR5	6
Phelix, d. Joseph, Jr., b. Mar. 21, 1730	LR5	6
Phineas, s. Caleb, b. July 22, 1735	LR5	2
Polly, of Bristol, m. Jeremiah H. **BARTHOLOMEW**, of		
Farmington, Sept. 15, 1834, by Rev. Noah Porter	LR42	E
Roxy, m. Edward **MORSE**, b. of Farmington, Aug. 22,		
1820, by Noah Porter, V.D.M.	LR40	570
Ruth, d. Nathaniell Hun, b. July 26, 1771	LR17	438
Salmon, s. Joseph, b. May 14, 1764	LR15	M
Samuel, s. John, b. Aug. 15, 1696	LR1	4
Samuel, s. Caleb, b. Nov. 20, 1712	LR2	95
Samuel, s. Samuel, b. Jan. 8, 1723/4	LR2	65
Samuel, s. Joseph, d. Oct. 27, 1747	LR7	36
Samuel, Jr., had s. [ ], b. Feb. 10, 1747/8	LR7	M
Samuel, d. June 22, 1748	LR7	36
Samuel, m. Cloe **PALMER**, Mar. 22, 1758	LR11	575
Samuel, s. Eleazer & Rhoda, b. July 7, 1759	LR11	588
Samuel H., m. Catharine A. **WINSHIP**, b. of Farmington,		
Sept. 28, 1848, by Rev. Noah Porter	LR47	123
Sarah, d. John (s. of Stephen), b. Oct. 11, 1731	LR5	6
Sarah, d. Thomas, b. June 5, 1733	LR5	3
Sarah, m. Thomas **GRIDLEY**, blacksmith, b. of		
Farmington, Dec. 5, 1734	LR5	539

	Vol.	Page
ROOT (cont.)		
Sarah, wid. Stephen, d. Mar. 28, 1740	LR6	10
Sarah, d. Samuel & Sarah, b. Dec. 15, 1750	LR11	588
Sarah, wid., m. Capt. Eldad **LEWIS**, Apr. 11, 1754	LR10	6
Sarah, m. Daniel **ROOT**, Feb. 3, 1762	LR11	575
Sarah, d. Daniell, b. July 5, 1770	LR17	438
Sarah, d. James, b. June 17, 1774	LR17	438
Sarah, m. Hiram N. **GLEASON**, [Feb.] 3, 1825, by Rev. Noah Porter	LR42	568
Sarah, of Farmington, m .Nathan **WOODRUFF**, of Southington, May 30, 1832, by Rev. Noah Porter	LR42	559
Sarah, of Farmington, m. Joel **BEECHER**, of Cheshire, July 21, 1833, by Rev. Noah Porter	LR42	A
Seth, s. Joseph, b. May 13, 1762	LR11	588
Seth, s. [ ]	LR11	588
Simmeon, s. Caleb, b. Feb. 25, 1731	LR5	6
Stephen, s. Timothy, b. Mar. 18, 1710/11	LR2	92
Stephen, d. Jan. 6, 1716/17	LR2	62
Stephen, m. Sarah **HART**, d. Dea. Jno, June 19, 1740	LR6	27
Stephen, s. Stephen & Sarah, b. Oct. 20, 1740	LR6	6
Stephen, his d. [ ], b. Sept. 30, 1743	LR7	M
Stephen, had d. [ ], b. [ ] 9, 1748	LR7	M
Stephen, d. Sept. 5, 1752	LR8	12
Stephen, s. Noah, b. Mar. 12, 1764	LR9	12
Stephen, s. Timothy, b. Aug. 19, 1768	LR15	M
Susannah, m. Joseph **LANGTON**, 1st, b. of Ffarmington, Oct. [ ], 1683	LR2	257
Temperance, m. Job **BROWNSON**, Oct. 8, 1752	LR8	10
Thankfull, d. John, b. Sept. 16, 1702	LR1	4
Thankfull, m. John **NORTON**, s. Thomas, Dec. 5, 172[ ]	LR5	13
Thankfull, d. Nathaniell **HUN**, b. June 22, 1773	LR17	438
Theodus, s. Timothy, b. July 17, 1742	LR6	6
Thomas, s. Caleb, b. Jan. 16, 1701/2	LR2	95
Thomas, of Farmington, m. Sarah **DUDLEY**, of Saybrook, Feb. 15, 1726/7	LR2	258
Thomas, s. Thomas, b. Jan. 8, 1729/30	LR5	6
Thomas, wid. of Lebanon, m. Hannah **NORTON**, wid. of Thomas, Dec. 28, 1732	LR5	300
Thomas, Jr., formerly of Lebanon, d. May 24, 1734	LR5	50
Thomas, Jr., m. Elida **HENSDEL**, Apr. 3, 1755	LR8	10
Timothy, of Ffarmington, m. Margaret **SEAMOR**, sometime of Hartford, Mar. 20, 1707	LR2	145
Timothy, m. Mary **HART**, d. Dea. Jno, b. of Farmington, Dec. 6, 1739	LR6	27
Timothy, s. Timothy, b. Oct. 16, 1740	LR6	6
Timothy, Lieut., d. Aug. 24, 1746, at Cape Britton	LR7	36
William, s. Caleb, b. July 22, 1737	LR7	M
W[illia]m M., m. Lucinda **BROWNSON**, b. of Farmington, Sept. 21, 1829, by Rev. Noah Porter	LR42	562
-----ch, [child of Caleb], b. Apr. 7, 1743	LR7	M
-----er, d. Timothy, b. June 9, 1744	LR7	M
-----kiah, s. John, b. Apr. 14, 1747	LR7	M
ROSE, Hannah, m. Thomas **NORTON**, June 7, 1700	LR1	4

	Vol.	Page
ROSE (cont.)		
Lucy, of Middlebury, Vt., m. Loyal W. **CARTER**, of Leyden, N.Y., Jan. 6, 1839, by Rev. S. H. Clark	LR47	99
ROSS, Frederick, m. Nancy **SHARP**, Feb. 2, 1851, by Egbert Cowles, J.P.	LR47	128
ROWE, ROW, Almira, m. Erastus H. **ADAMS**, Dec. 9, 1828, by Rev. Noah Porter	LR42	564
Caroline A., [d. Ira & Julia C.], b. Jan. 25, 1824; d. Feb. 29, 1828	LR47	W-Y
Caroline A., [d. Ira & Julia C.], b. Mar. 29, 1828	LR47	W-Y
Chauncey, m. Susan **DICKINSON**, b. of Farmington, Oct. 9, 1839, by Rev. Noah Porter	LR47	101
Esther, w. Lieut. John, d. Aug. 25, 1756	LR11	577
Ira, b. Dec. 25, 1784; m. Julia C. **MILLER**, Sept. 18, 1814	LR47	W-Y
Ira M., [s. Ira & Julia C.], b. Sept. 18, 1822	LR47	W-Y
James H., [s. Ira & Julia C.], b. Jan. 14, 1821	LR47	W-Y
Joan, had s. Memucun, b. Nov. 27, 1753	LR8	8
John, m. Margaret **ROOT**, b. of Ffarmington, Jan. 22, 1717/18	LR2	93
John, Lieut., m. Sarah **DEMING**, Feb. 15, 1759	LR11	576
John G., [s. Ira & Julia C.], b. Sept. 25, 1830	LR47	W-Y
Mary, m. Edward **ROOT**, b. of Farmington, Aug. 13, 1822, by Noah Porter, V.D.M.	LR40	571
Matilda M., [d. Ira & Julia C.], b. May 6, 1826	LR47	W-Y
Matilda M., of Farmington, m. Cyrrel **BULLOCK**, of Rehobath, Mass., Mar. 8, 1843, by S. W. Smith, Elder	LR47	110
Memucun, s. Joan Row, b. Nov. 27, 1753	LR8	8
William G., m. Amelia F. **MILLER**, Sept. 19, 1832, by Rev. Noah Porter	LR42	559
ROWLENSON, Hannah, m. David **PICK**, June 1, 1749	LR7	46
ROWLEY, Eliza G., of Farmington, m .Chester **SNATH**, of Burlington, Feb. 15, 1825, by Rev. Noah Porter	LR42	568
Fidelia J., of Farmington, m. John W. **HILLS**, of East Hartford, Aug. 6, 1837, by Rev. S. H. Clark	LR47	95
Philo, of Farmington, m. Julian **LEWIS**, of Berlin, [Feb.] 11, [1830], by Rev. Noah Porter	LR42	561
Simeon, of Farmington, m. Marinda **BRUNSON**, of Berlin, July 27, 1836, by Rev. Noah Porter	LR47	93
Simeon A., m. Eliza **WOODRUFF**, b. of Farmington, Sept. 19, 1830, by Rev. Noah Porter	LR42	560
ROYCE, ROYS, ROYSE, [see also **RICE**], Abel, had d. [ ], b. [ ] 1, 1745	LR7	M
Abel, had child, b. Dec. 5, 1748	LR7	M
Abel, s. Nehemiah, b. Sept. 27, 1752	LR8	9
Abigail, m. Abel **HAWLEY**, Nov. 13, 1754	LR9	286
Abigail, d. Ephraim, b. Jan. 24, 1783	LR22	473
Amos, s. Jacob, b. May 4, 1758	LR11	588
Asaph, s. Nehemiah, b. Dec. 11, 1763	LR11	588
Chancey, s. Ephraim, b. Oct. 28, 1781	LR22	473
Cloe, m. John **MATHEWS**, Nov. 30, 1769	LR17	G
Desire, m. Enos **CLARK**, Dec. 11, 1760	LR11	575

	Vol.	Page
ROYCE, ROYS, ROYSE (cont.)		
Dimend, s. Benedict, b. Jan. 12, 1767	LR15	M
Elizabeth, of Wallingford, m. Stephen LEE, of		
Ffarmington, Oct. 1,1690	LR2	125
Ephraim, m. Abigail ANDRUS, Nov. 9, 1780	LR22	480
Easther, m. John BULL, Nov. 23, 1698	LR1	4
Hannah, d. Nehemiah, b. Feb. 1, 1747/8	LR7	K
Jacob, m. Thankfull HAMLIN, Oct. 10, 1753	LR11	576
Jane, d. Benedict, b. Mar. 23, 1765	LR15	M
Joel, s. Jacob, b. Feb. 24, 1755	LR11	588
Lent, s. Nehemiah, b. Mar. 22, 1767	LR15	M
Mary, of Wallingford, m. Joseph LANGTON, 1st, of		
Ffarmington, Oct. 18, 1714	LR2	257
Mehetable, m. Jesse BUNEL, Apr. 19, 1757	LR11	576
Nehemiah, s. Nehemiahi, b. Dec. 8, 1754	LR9	12
Phebe, d. Nehemiah & Rhody, b. Dec. 22, 1751	LR8	8
Rebeckah, d. Abel, b. June 11, 1745	LR7	M
RUGGLES, Abigaile, m. Nathaniel WINCHEL, Jr., Mar. 2,		
1720/1	LR2	100
RUNSMEL, Loring, m. Susan F. FISKE, b. of Hartford, Sept.		
14, 1830, by Rev. Noah Porter	LR42	560
RUSS, Elisha, s. John & Esther, b. Dec. 31, 1737	LR6	6
John, m. Esther BUCK, b. of Farmington, Nov. 25, 1736	LR6	27
RUSSELL, RUSSEL, RUSIL [E]unis, m. Enos CLARK,		
Dec. 7, 1743/4	LR7	35
Samuel, of Burlington, m. Catharine H. MERRELL, of		
Unionville, Apr. 27, 1842, by R. Woodruff	LR47	107
Sarah, m. Selah GRIDLEY, Jan. 1, 1779	LR22	480
RUST, Ester, m. Joseph BRONSON, Mar. 4, 1741	LR7	35
Roseannah, m. Moses BACON, Dec. 25, 1777	LR21	557
SAGE, Lucy, m. Amos GAYLORD, Feb. 15, 1773	LR17	442
Sary, m. Ebenezer STEEL, Aug. 10, 1749	LR7	35
SALMON, Elizabeth, of Westfield, m. Caleb ROOT, of		
Farmington, Aug. 9, 1693	LR2	93
SAMMADY, Samuel, m. Lucinda BROWN, b. of Farmington,		
Sept. 4, 1834, by Rev. Noah Porter	LR42	E
SANFORD, David A., m. Susanna S. NORTON, b. of Bristol,		
Oct. 19, 1836, by Rev. Noah Porter	LR47	94
Mehetable, m. Thaddeus L. THOMSON, b. of		
Farmington, Oct. 21, 1829, by Rev. Harry Bushnell	LR42	562
Thomas, of Milford, m. Rebeckah BARNES, of		
Ffarmington, Sept. 29, 1713	LR2	60
SAVAGE, Sarah, of Middletown, m. Ebenezer NORTON, of		
Ffarmington, July 7, 1726	LR2	257
SCOTT, SCOOT, SCOT, Abigall, d. Ezekiel, b. Mar. 14,		
1770	LR17	441
Abigall, d. Ezekiel, b. Mar. 14, 1770	LR21	550
Anner, of Waterbury, m. Philemon BARNS, June 10,		
1779	LR22	480
Bulah, m. Nathaniel COGSWELL, Sept. 11, 1760	LR11	575
Cornelia, m. Samuel DICKINSON, Oct. 17, 1849, by		
Noah Porter, Jr.	LR47	125
Ebenezer, s. Samuel, b. Aug. 10, 1694	LR2	91

	Vol.	Page
SCOTT, SCOOT, SCOT (cont.)		
Ebenezer, s. Samuel, Sr., d. June 10, 1715	LR2	107
Ebenezer, s. Samuel, Jr., b. Aug. 2, 1723	LR2	46
Ebenezer, m. Susannah WEBSTER, Nov. 1, 1746	LR8	10
Elidia, m. John LOWREE, Apr. 5, 1758	LR11	575
Elisha, s. Hezekiah, Jr., b. July 26, 1732	LR5	307
Elisha, s. Ebenezer, b. Jan. 8, 1751	LR8	8
Elisha, m. Mercy [ ], Apr. 21, 1766	LR15	A
Elizabeth, d. Hezekiah, b. Nov. 12, 1734	LR5	307
Ezekiel, s. Hezekiah, b. June 26, 1738	LR6	6
Ezekiel, of Farmington, m. Catharine MILLS, of		
Wallingford, June 23, 1763	LR11	592
Ezekiel, Jr., s. Ezekiel, b. June 10, 1772	LR17	441
Ezekiel, s. Ezekiel, b. June 10, 1772	LR21	560
George, s. Ezekiel, b. Oct. 6, 1774	LR21	550
Hezekiah, s. Samuell, b. Sept. [ ], 1703	LR2	91
Hezekiah, s. Hezekiah & Mercy, b. Oct. 7, 1729	LR5	7
Hezekiah, d. Jan. 17, 1765	LR14	3
Hezekiah, m. Elizabeth PORTTER, Aug. 22, 1765	LR11	594
Hezekiah, d. May 16, 1787, in the 58th y. of his age	LR21	560
James, s. Ezekiel, b. Jan. 6, 1763	LR17	441
James, s. Ezekiel, b. Jan. 6, 1763	LR21	550
Jerusha, d. Ebenezer, b. Mar. 10, 1753	LR8	8
Jonathan, s. Ezekiel, b. Jan. 20, 1780	LR21	550
Lucy, d. Ebenezer, b. Apr. 20, 1749	LR8	8
Lyda, d. Zache, b. Feb. 14, 174[ ]	LR7	N
Margaret, d. Samuel, Jr., b. Oct. 21, 1729	LR5	7
Martha, d. Samuel, b. Dec. [ ], 1687	LR2	91
Martha, of Farmington, m. Thomas WARNER, s. Daniel,		
June 5, 1711	LR2	60
Martha, d. Samuell, Jr., b. July 2 ,1735	LR5	7
Martha, m. Nathaniel COOK, Mar. 8, 1754	LR8	10
Mary, d. Samuell, b. Mar. 1, 1699/1700	LR2	91
Mary, m. Samuel ANDRUS, Nov. 8, 1721	LR2	101
Mary, d. Samuel, Jr., b. Mar. 30, 1732	LR5	7
Mary, m. Josiah COWLES, Nov. 23, 1748	LR7	35
Mercy, d. Ezekiel, b. Dec. 1, 1765	LR14	11
Mercy, d. Ezekiel, b. Dec. 1, 1765	LR17	441
Mercy, d. Ezekiel, b. Dec. 1, 1765	LR21	550
Phebe, d. Ezekiel, b. Oct. 7, 1767	LR17	441
Phebe, d. Ezekiel, b. Oct. 7, 1767	LR21	550
Samuel, m. Mary ORUIE, b. of Ffarmington, Feb. [ ],		
1686/7	LR2	123
Samuel, s. Samuel, b. Oct. 7, 1696	LR2	91
Samuel, Jr., m. Mary PINCHON, May 8, 1718	LR2	101
Samuel, s. Hezekiah, b. Mar. 12, 1746	LR7	N
Samuel, s. Ebenezer, b. Sept. 2, 1747	LR8	8
Samuel, m. Lois NORTH, Aug. 30, 1770	LR17	G
Sarah, d. Samuel, Jr., b .May 2, 1727	LR4	395
Seth, s. Ezekiel, b. May 12, 1777	LR21	550
Simeon, s. Ezekiel, b. Jan. 6, 1764	LR14	11
Tabitha, d. Samuell, Jr., b. Jan. 28, 1718/19	LR2	83
Temperance, d. Elisha, b. Sept. 27, 1766	LR15	L

	Vol.	Page
SCOTT, SCOOT, SCOT (cont.)		
Zacheus, s. Samuel, Jr., b. Sept. 5, 1721	LR2	102
SCOVILLE, SCOVEL, SCOBELL, SCOVILL, Elizabeth, d.		
Abigail, b. Jan. 1, 1774	LR17	441
John, m. Sarah **BARNES**, Mar. 29, 1666	LR1	5
Mabel, m. Caleb **HOPKINS**, Feb. 21, 1765	LR11	594
William C., of Harwinton, m. Mary Ann **HINMAN**, of		
Farmington, Jan. 1, 1840, by Rev. Noah Porter	LR47	102
SEARLE, J. C., Rev., m. Emmeline C. **YOUNGS**, b. of		
Farmington, Apr. 8, 1850, by Rev. Noah Porter	LR47	129
SECOUR, * Martha, of Simsbury, m. Jeames **THOMSON**, of		
Ffarmington, Nov. 19, 1741 *(Perhaps		
"LECOUR"?)	LR6	304
SEDGWICK, SEDGWICH, Amanda, d. Stephen, b. Feb. 12,		
1777	LR21	550
Amos, s. Stephen, b. Aug. 21, 1773	LR17	439
Amos, s. Stephen, d. Apr. 18, 1775	LR17	445
Amos, s. Stephen, b. June 12, 1779	LR21	550
Dorcas, d. Stephen, b. Dec. 24, 1734	LR5	307
Elizabeth, of Hartford, m. Thomas **ORTON**, Jr., of		
Farmington ,Jan. 13, 17[ ]	LR5	13
Gad, s. Stephen, b. Oct. 24, 1769	LR15	L
Hannah, d. Stephen, b. Dec. 16, 1736	LR6	6
Hannah, d. Stephen ,Jr., b. Dec. 15, 1767	LR15	L
Lucy, d. Stephen [ ]	LR17	439
Sarah, d. Stephen, Jr., b. Sept. 5, 1762	LR11	589
Stephen & Mary, had d. [ ], b. [ ], 1728	LR4	396
Stephen, s. Stephen, b. June 3, 1731	LR5	7
Stephen, s. Stephen, d. Mar. 18, 1765	LR14	3
Stephen, Jr., m. wid. Lucy **WOODFORD**, Sept. 10, 1761	LR11	592
Stephen, s. Stephen, Jr., b. Aug. 10, 1764	LR11	589
Stephen, s. Stephen, Jr., b. Dec. 28, 1765	LR15	L
Stephen, d. Aug. 13, 1768	LR15	M
SEELEY, Raymond H., Rev. of Bristol, m. Catharine L.		
COWLES, of Farmington, Oct. 9, 1843, by Noah		
Porter, Int. Pub.	LR47	111
SEIGNOR, Hannah, of Farmington, m. Charles **PRINCE**, of		
Canton, Nov. 24, 1825, by Rev. Noah Porter	LR42	569
SELDEN, Catharine, [d. John & Hannah], b. May 30, 1797	LR47	W-Y
Edward, [s. Hezekiah & Eunice}, b. Aug. 8, 1813	LR47	W-Y
Eunice, [d. Hezekiah & Eunice], b. [ ]; d. May		
[ ], 1826	LR47	W-Y
Fanny W., [d. Hezekiah & Eunice], b. Dec. 26, 1791	LR47	W-Y
Harriet, [d. John & Hannah], b. Jan. 3, 1808	LR47	W-Y
Henry, [s. Hezekiah & Eunice], b. Feb. 27, 1815	LR47	W-Y
Henry P., [s. John & Hannah], b. Oct. 18, 1820	LR47	W-Y
Hezekiah, b. Mar. 15, 1783; m. Eunice **STANLEY**, Oct.		
19, 1806	LR47	W-Y
Hez[ekiah], m. Fanny **WOODRUFF**, June 13, 1827	LR47	W-Y
John, b. Feb. 4, 1777; m. Hannah **HURLBUT** , [ ]	LR47	W-Y
John C., [s. John & Hannah], b. Oct. 16, 1813	LR47	W-Y
Joseph, [s. Hezekiah &Eunice], b. Oct. 17, 1823	LR47	W-Y
Julia, [d. Hezekiah & Eunice], b. Mar. 20, 1807	LR47	W-Y

	Vol.	Page
SELDEN (cont.)		
Lemuel, [s. John & Hannah], b. June 20, 1811	LR47	W-Y
Mary N., [d. John & Hannah], b. Feb. 9, 1803	LR47	W-Y
Susan, [d. John & Hannah], b. Mar. 21, 1816	LR47	W-Y
Thomas Hurlbut, [s. John & Hannah], b. July 9, 1799	LR47	W-Y
SEYMOUR, SAYMOR, SEAMOR, SEAYMOR,		
SEAMOUR, SAYMORE, SEMER, Abigail, d. Ebenezer, b.		
Mar. 3, 1710/11	LR2	97
Anna, d. Ebenezer, b. July 28, 1712	LR2	232
Ebenezer, m. Abigail HOLLISTER, Dec. 29, 1709	LR2	123
Elizabeth, d. Ebenezer, b. Apr. 28, 1714	LR2	81
[E]unice, d. Jonathan, b. Jan. 1, 1713	LR2	81
Gideon, s. Ebenezer, d. Oct. 20, 1736	LR6	10
Hannah, d. Samuel, b. Mar. 28, 1706/7	LR2	97
Hannah, wid. Richard, d. Sept. 16, 1712	LR2	142
Hannah, m. Allen GOODRICH, Dec. 10, 1729	LR5	13
Jerusha, d. Jonathan, b. Aug. 23, 1717	LR2	81
Jerusha, m. James NEWEL, Nov. 19, 1739	LR6	27
Jonathan, of Ffarmington, m. [E]unice HOLLISTER, of		
Weathersfield, Dec. 23, 1714	LR2	94
Margaret, sometime of Hartford, m. Timothy ROOT, of		
Ffarmington, Mar. 20, 1707	LR2	145
Martha, m. Solomon COWLES, Dec. 22, 1742	LR6	305
Mary, m. John STEEL, Nov. 25, 1655	LR2	331
Mary, of Hartford, m. John NORTH, s. Samuell, of		
Ffarmington, Aug. 25, 1700	LR2	145
Mary, d. Samuel, b. Nov. 13, 1708	LR2	97
Mercy, m. George HUBBARD, b. of Ffarmington, Feb.		
[ ], 1710/11	LR2	123
Mercy, d. Samuell, b. Sept. 11, 1715	LR2	81
Mercy, m. Uriah JUDD, Feb. 19, 1747	LR7	46
Rebeckah, d. Samuel, b. June 23, 1711	LR2	232
Rebeckah, m. Elisha GOODRICH, b. of Farmington,		
Nov. 21, 1734	LR5	545
Richard, s. Ebenezer, b. Oct. 16, 1716	LR2	81
Samuel, m. Hannah NORTH, b. of Ffarmington, May 10,		
1706	LR2	123
Sarah, of Hartford, m. Isaac NORTON, Jr., of		
Farmington, July 1, 1740	LR6	27
SHARP, Nancy, m. Frederick ROSS, Feb. 2, 1851, by Egbert		
Cowles, J.P.	LR47	128
SHAW, Johannah, of Windham, m. Caleb ROOT, of		
Ffarmington, July 12, 1721	LR2	101
Mehitabel, of Windham, m. Gideon BARNES, of		
Farmington, Nov. 2, 1732	LR6	27
SHELDON, Henry O., of Farmington, m. Elizabeth		
WILLIAMS, of Weathersfield, May 30, 1825, by		
Rev. Noah Porter	LR42	569
SHEPARD, SHEPERD, Lucinda, m. William EATON, b. of		
Bristol, May 6, 1841, by Rev. Aaron S. Hill	LR47	104
Lucy, m. William R. JACKWAY, b. of Farmington ,Oct.		
11, 1827, by Rev. Noah Porter	LR42	565

	Vol.	Page
SHERWOOD, Rachel, of Simsbury, m. Timothy **HAWLEY**,		
of Farmington, Jan. 5, 1736/7	LR6	27
SKINNER, Joseph P., of Springfield, Mass., m. Jane A.		
WARREN, of Farmington, Aug. 4, 1850, by Rev.		
Noah Porter	LR47	129
SLAUGHTER, Mary, of Simsbury, m. John **ORTON**, of		
Farmington, Dec. 11, 1755	LR9	286
SLOPER, Daniel, m. Rachel **LANKTON**, Jan. 9, 1752	LR8	10
Daniel, s. Daniel, b. Apr. 20, 1756	LR11	589
Ezekiel, s. Daniel, b. June 5, 1762	LR11	589
Rachel, d. Daniel, b. Dec. 1, 1759	LR11	589
SMALLAGE (?), Julia A., m. J. **BENNET**, Jan. 5, 1847, by		
Rev. B. Creagh	LR47	119
SMITH, Abel, s. Hezekiah, b. Apr. 19, 1740	LR9	12
Abigail, d. John, b. July 20, 1729	LR5	7
Abigail, w. John, d. July 29, 1729	LR5	50
Abigail, d. Joseph, Jr., b. Apr. 15, 1752	LR11	589
Abigail, d. Ebenezer, Jr., b. Mar. 10, 1755	LR11	589
Abigail, d. Samuel, b. Feb. 28, 1760	LR11	589
Abigail, d. Samuell, [s. of James], d. Mar. 10, 1762	LR11	574
Abigail, d. Samuel [s. of James], b. May 25, 1762	LR11	589
Abigall, m. Samuel **ANDRUS**, Dec. 17, 1769	LR17	442
Abigail, of Hartford, m. William H. **STODDARD**, of		
Weathersfield, Mar. 3, 1831, by Rev. Quartus		
Stewart	LR42	560
Abijah, s. William, d. Sept. 12, 1728	LR4	396
Abijah, s. Samuel, b. Nov. 14, 1767	LR14	11
Ayllen, s. Noah, b. Aug. 23, 1744	LR7	N
Alma, d. Hester **CARRINGTON**, b. Aug. 6, 1780	LR21	550
Amasa, s. Joseph, of Neeambridge Parish, b. Sept. 4, 1756	LR9	12
Anna, d. Noah, b. June 20, 1740	LR6	1
Anna, d. Jedediah, b. Nov. 1, 1744	LR7	N
Anne, d. Noah, b. June 20, 1740	LR6	6
Anne, m. Joseph **HOPKINS**, Jr., Apr. 15, 1760	LR11	575
Asaph, s. Noah, b. June 9, 1750	LR8	8
Azeriah, s. Joseph, Jr., b. Dec. 28, 1712	LR2	81
Azarah, m. Mary **ROOT**, b. of Kensington, Aug. 14,		
1740	LR6	27
Aezariah, m. Mary **ROOT**, Aug. 14, 1740	LR8	10
Azubah, d. James & Ruth, b. Sept. 4, 1732	LR6	6
Benjamin, s. Ephraim, b. Apr. 10, 1706	LR2	112
Benjamin, m. Agnes **HUGG**, wid., Nov. 5, 1740	LR6	304
Calvin, s. Samuel, b. Apr. 18, 1771	LR17	439
Chloe, d. Elnathan, b. May 23, 1776	LR21	550
Cyrenus, of Chatham, m. Angeline M. **HAMLIN**, of		
Farmington, Sept. 6, 1844, by William Wright	LR47	113
David, s. David, b. Nov. 3, 1744	LR7	N
Deswell, s. Steel, b. Oct. 19, 1754	LR9	12
Ebenezer, s. Jonathan, b. Sept. 2, 1702	LR2	88
Ebenezer, of Ffarmington, m. Mary **WHITTLESLEY**, of		
Weathersfield, July 2, 1724	LR2	52
Ebenezer, s. Ebenezer, b. July 1, 1725	LR2	70

	Vol.	Page
SMITH (cont.)		
Ebenezer, Jr., m. Mehetabel **BRECK**, of Weathersfield, Oct. 18, 1750	LR11	575
Eber, s. Samuell, b. Mar. 26, 1771	LR17	439
Elihu, s. Jonathan, b. Nov. 14, 1726	LR2	34
Elijah, s. Joseph, b. Oct. 29, 1721	LR2	102
Elijah, s. William, b .May 1, 1726	LR2	69
Elijah, m. Sarah **GRIMES**, Apr. 6, 1752	LR8	10
Elijah, s. Elijah, b. May 30, 1753	LR9	12
Elisha, s. Ebenezer, b. Aug. 14, 1751	LR11	589
Eliza, m. Marcus **BUNNEL**, b. of Farmington, May 1, 1831, by Rev. Noah Porter	LR42	560
Eliza D., Mrs. of Farmington, m. Leonard **COTTON**, of Middletown, Apr. 22, 1841, by Rev. Aaron S. Hill	LR47	104
Elizabeth, d. Samuel, weaver, b. July 25, 1713	LR2	99
Elizabeth, m. Isaac **COWLES**, b. of Ffarmington, Dec. 27, 1716	LR2	94
Elizabeth, d. Jonathan, b. Apr. 2, 1721	LR2	34
Elizabeth, m. Ephraim **SMITH**, Jr., Jan. 24, 1744/5	LR7	46
Elizabeth, d. Thomas, b. June 26, 1749	LR7	N
Elizabeth, d. Joseph, b. Mar. 7, 1754	LR8	9
Elizabeth, d. Ebenezer, Jr., b. Feb. 4, 1757	LR11	589
Elizabeth, d. Elijah, b. Mar. 2, 1760	LR15	L
Elnathan, m. Cloe [ ], July 9, 1767	LR15	A
Elnathan, s. Elnathan, b. May 6, 1768	LR15	L
Ephraim & w. Rachel, see John **COLE**, 1st	LR5	50
Ephraim, m. Rachel **COLE**, b. of Ffarmington, Apr. [ ], 1686	LR2	145
Ephraim, s. Ephraim, b. Dec. 16, 1690	LR2	112
Ephraim, Jr., m. Sarah **HART**, d. Stephen, Jan. 19, 1720/1	LR2	101
Ephraim, s. Benjamin, b. Sept. 9, 1741	LR6	6
Ephraim, s. Beniamin, d. Oct. 8, 1743	LR7	36
Ephraim, Jr., m. Elizabeth **SMITH**, Jan. 24, 1744/5	LR7	46
Ephraim, s. Ephraim, b. Nov. 2, 1745	LR7	546
Ephraim, d. Jan. 12, 1753	LR8	12
Esther, d. Jonathan, b. Sept. 28, 1713	LR2	34
Esther, d. Joseph, Sr., d. May 18, 1725	LR2	148
[E]unice, d. Samuel, s. of Jonathan, b. Sept. 10, 1707	LR2	92
Evarie,* d. Joseph, b. June 16, 1756 *("Eunice"?)	LR8	9
Fanne, m. Nathan **BOOTH**, Jr., June 24, 1773	LR17	432
Fanna, m. Nathan **BOOTH**, Jr., June 24, 1773	LR17	442
Frances, d. Ebenezer, Jr., b. Mar. 3, 1753	LR11	589
Geria,* m. Jonathan **GILBERT**, June 24, 1742 *(In pencil "Keziah")	LR7	35
Gideon, s. Joseph, Jr., b. Dec. 1, 1740	LR7	N
Gideon, s. David, b. Aug. 6, 1753	LR9	12
Gurdon, s. Joseph, Jr., b. Aug. 12, 1749	LR11	589
Guidon, s. [Joseph], b. Aug. 12, 1749	LR7	N
Hannah, d. Jonathan, Jr., b. Aug. 10, 1709	LR2	109
Hannah, m. Ezekiel **LEWIS**, b. of Farmington, Dec. 14, 1733	LR5	300
Hannah, d. Thomas, b. Sept. 14, 1742; d. Dec. 25, 1742	LR6	6

	Vol.	Page
SMITH (cont.)		
Helinah, d. William b. Sept. 28, 1717	LR5	7
Heman, s. Stephen, d. Oct. 2, 1749	LR7	540
Heman, 2nd, s. Stephen, b. Nov. 29, 1753	LR9	12
Hervy, s. David, b. Feb. 8, 1766	LR14	11
Hesther, d. Joseph, b. Oct. 30, 1705	LR1	3
Hiram, m. Mary Ann **PRINCE**, Oct. 17, 1839, by Rev.		
Ezra S. Cook	LR47	101
Huldah, d. Jedediah, b. Jan. 4 ,1749/50	LR7	N
Huldah, d. Steel, b. July 8, [ ]; d. Aug. 4, 1750	LR8	8
Huldah, d. Samuell & Huldah, b. Jan. 16, 1772	LR17	439
Isaac, s. David, b. Jan. 20, 1748	LR8	8
Ithamer, s. Stephen, b. Nov. 22, 1742	LR7	N
James, s. Samuel, b. Oct. 9, 1704	LR1	3
James, of Ffarmington, m. Ruth **JUDD**, of Watterbury,		
Apr. 26, 1727	LR2	258
James, s. Samuel, b. July 29, 1753	LR8	8
Jedadiah, s. Joseph, Jr., b. Feb. 12, 1715/16	LR2	81
Jedadiah, m. Susanah **COGSWEL**, b. of Farmington, Jan.		
1, 1740/1	LR6	304
Jemimah, m. John **WELLS**, June 18, 1731	LR6	304
Jemimah, see Jemimah **WELLS**	LR6	305
Joel, s. Elijah, b. Aug. 5, 1757	LR11	589
Johannah, d. Joseph, b. Oct. 15, 1692	LR1	3
Johannah, m. Nathan **PORTTER**, b. of Ffarmington,		
June 1, 1715	LR2	93
John, s. Samuel, b. Feb. 4, 1701/2	LR1	3
John, s. Ephraim, b. Apr. 16, 1709	LR2	112
John, weaver, m. Abigail **WADSWORTH**, b. of		
Farmington, Aug. 28, 1728	LR6	27
John, m. Abigail **WADSWORTH**, Dec. 28, 1728	LR4	423
John, weaver, of Farmington, m. Abigail **MERREL**, of		
Hartford, Jan. 18, 1733/4	LR6	27
John, s. David, b. Mar. 4, 1749	LR8	8
John, m. Julian **MIX**, b. of Farmington, Oct.9, 1831, by		
Rev. Noah Porter	LR42	560
Jonathan, s. Jonathan, m. Hannah **BODURTHA**, of		
Springfield, June 30, 1708	LR2	145
Jonathan, s. Jonathan, b. Nov. 18, 1718	LR2	34
Jonathan, Sr., d. Apr. 25, 1721	LR2	66
Jonathan, s. Ephraim, Jr., b. Feb. 9, 1747/8	LR7	N
Joseph, m. Johanah **LOMIS**, Nov. 20, 1691	LR1	6
Joseph, Jr., of Ffarmington, m. Mary **RYC**,* of		
Wallingford, Jan. 19, 1707/8 *(In pencil		
"ROYCE")	LR2	125
Joseph, s. Joseph, Jr., b. July 13, 1710	LR2	97
Joseph, Jr., of Farmington, m. Thankfull **HUBBERT**, of		
Middletown, Mar. 2, 1737/8	LR6	27
Joseph, s. Joseph, b. Oct. 11, 1744	LR7	N
Joseph, s. Elnathan, b. May 28, 1779	LR21	550
Jullian, m. Henry **NASH**, July 13, 1834, by Rev. Noah		
Porter	LR42	E
Gaziah,* d. James, b. Apr. 28, 1728 *("Keziah")	LR4	395

	Vol.	Page
SMITH (cont.)		
Keziah,* m. Jonathan GILBERT, June 24, 1742		
*(Arnold Copy has "Geria")	LR7	35
Keziah, m. Josiah ROOT, June 23, 1746	LR8	10
Lamantah, d. Abigail, b. Feb. 26, 1755	LR11	589
Lemuel, s. Ebenezer, Jr., b. Mar. 11, 1759	LR11	589
Levi, s. Samuell, b. Sept. 29, 1773	LR17	439
Levi, of Burlington, m. Elizabeth WELLS, of Berlin,		
Oct. 26, 1825, by Rev. Noah Porter	LR42	569
Lorenzo, of Farmington, m. Eleanor HINMAN, of		
Bristol, Apr. 7, 1830, by Rev. Noah Porter	LR42	561
Lucy, d. Thomas & Mary, b. Feb. 19, 1735/6	LR5	7
Lucy, d. Azakiah, b. Dec. 12, 1746	LR9	12
Lucy, m. Amos BULL, Oct. 5, 1767	LR15	A
Lucy Ann, d. Samuel, b. Dec. 20, 1765	LR14	11
Lucy J., m. William BROWN, b. of Farmington, Sept. 1,		
1834, by Rev. Noah Porter	LR42	E
Lydia, d. Ephraim, b. Nov. 20, 1697	LR2	112
Lidya, m. Joseph WOODFORD, b. of Ffarmington ,Jan.		
23, 1699	LR2	125
Lydia, m. Daniel WOODRUFF, b. of Ffarmington, Oct.		
15, 1719	LR2	101
Lydia, d. Azakiah, b. Nov. 17, 1742	LR9	12
Lydia, m. Jonathan CHURCHEL, Nov. [ ], 1746	LR7	35
Lydia, m. Ichabod ANDRUS, Nov. 17, 1763	LR11	594
Lydia, d. David, b. Feb. 16, 1765	LR14	11
Lydia, d. Elnathan, b. Mar. 28, 1782	LR22	475
Mamry, s. Samuell, b. July 29, 1767	LR17	439
Marcy, d. Joseph, b. Aug. 6, 1702	LR1	3
Mareb, d. Samuel, b. Aug. 29, 1764	LR14	11
Margaret, d. Jonathan, b. Aug. 7, 1711	LR2	34
Martha, d. Samuel, b. Jan. 20, 1696	LR1	2
Martha, m. Timothy STANLEY, b. of Ffarmington, Dec.		
25, 1718	LR2	101
Martha, wid. of Simsbury, m. Joseph NORTH, of		
Farmington, July 17, 1734	LR5	300
Martha, d. John, weaver, & Abigail, b. Feb. 10, 1734/5	LR6	6
Mary, m. Beniamin ANDRUSS, May, about 26, 1682	LR1	5
Mary, d. Ephraim, b. Apr. 11, 1703	LR2	112
Mary, d. Jonathan, m. Samuel COLE, b. of Ffarmington,		
Mar. 17, 1707/8	LR2	145
Mary, m. William PORTTER, b. of Farmington, June 14,		
1711	LR2	125
Mary, d. Jonathan, b. Apr. 14, 1724	LR2	34
Mary, d. Jedidiah, b. Jan. 22, 1741/2	LR6	6
Mary, d. Beniamin, b. Jan. 14, 1744/5	LR7	N
Mary, d. Azariah, b. Oct. 30, 1748	LR9	12
Mary, d. Joseph, b. May 9, 1752	LR8	9
Mary, m. Isaac GLEASON, Oct. 18, 1759	LR11	592
Mary, 2nd w. William, d. June 30, 1774, in the 60th y. of		
her age	LR17	445
Mary, d. Samuell, of New Brittain, b .Sept. 9, 1777	LR21	550

	Vol.	Page
SMITH (cont.)		
Mary, m. Nelson **HOWARD**, b. of Farmington, Sept. 5, 1842, by Noah Porter, V.D.M.	LR47	108
Mary Ann Steele, d. Sam[ue]ll, b. Feb. 16, 1784	LR22	475
Matthew, s. Stephen, b. Jan. 1, 1739/40	LR6	6
Moses, s. William, b. Sept. 21, 1735	LR5	307
Moses, s. William, d. Oct. 19, 1756	LR8	13
Moses, s. William, d. Oct. 19, 1756	LR9	495
Moses, s. Samuel, b. Jan. 1, 1766	LR14	11
Nancy, d. Elnathan, b. Mar. 17, 1770	LR15	L
Noah, s. Samuel, s. Jonathan, b. Aug. 12, 1710	LR2	92
Noah, s. Noah, b. Nov. 21, 1738	LR6	6
Noah, s. Noah, d. Sept. 23, 1758	LR11	577
Noah, s. Noah, b. [ ]	LR11	589
Olive, d. Noah, b. Dec. 13, 1749	LR8	8
Phebe, d. Samuel, s. Jonathan, b. Aug. 5, 1715	LR2	95
Polly, d. Elnathan, b. July 1, 1784	LR22	475
Prudence, twin with Ruth, d. John, weaver, & Abigail, b. Oct. [ ], 1736	LR6	6
Prudence, twin with Ruth, d. John, weaver, & Abigail, d. Oct. latter end, 1736	LR6	10
Prudence, 2nd, d. John & Abigail, b. Apr. 18, 1740	LR6	6
Rachel, d. Ephraim, b. Feb. 10, 1694/5	LR2	112
Rachel, d. Jonathan, b. June 2, 1716	LR2	34
Rachel, m. Daniel **WARNER**, b. of Farmington, July 25, 1738	LR6	27
Rachel, w. Ephraim, d. Apr. 5, 1751	LR8	12
Rebeckah, d. William, b. June 1, 1716	LR2	95
Rebeckah, d. Stephen, b. Apr. 18, 1748	LR7	N
Rebecka, w. William, d. Feb. 23, 1771, in the 74th y. of her age	LR17	444
Reuben, s. Thomas & Mary, b. Feb. 19, 1737	LR6	6
Reuben, s. James & Ruth, b. July 12, 1737	LR6	6
Rubin, d. May 26, 1760	LR11	577
Reubin, s. Steel, b. Feb. 8, 1761	LR11	589
Rhoda, d. Joseph, Jr., b. Sept. 15, 1752	LR11	589
Rhoda, m. Matthew **COLE**, Jr., Dec. 9, 1756	LR11	576
Rollin, of West Hartford, m. Eliza A. **WARREN**, of Farmington, Nov. 25, 1841, by Rev. Aaron S. Hill	LR47	106
Ruth, d. Samuell, b. Feb. 24, 1692	LR1	2
Ruth, d. Samuel, d. Apr. 25, 1693	LR1	2
Ruth, d. Joseph, b. Dec. 1, 1695	LR1	3
Ruth, d. Samuel, b. July 12, 1710	LR2	109
Ruth, wid. m. Joseph **ROOT**, Sr., b. of Farmington, May 3, 1727	LR2	258
Ruth, d. Stephen, b. Sept. 13, 1734	LR6	6
Ruth, twin with Prudence, d. John, weaver, & Abigail, b. Oct. [ ], 1736	LR6	6
Ruth, twin with Prudence, d. John, weaver, & Abigail, d. Oct. latter end, 1736	LR6	10
Ruth, d. Stephen, d. Sept. 28, 1749	LR7	540
Ruth, d. Stephen, b. Apr. 29, 1750	LR7	N
Ruth, d. Samuel & Abigail, b. Nov. 7, 1755	LR9	12

	Vol.	Page

SMITH (cont.)

	Vol.	Page
Ruth, m. Stephen **JOHNSON**, [ ], 1779	LR22	480
Samuell, m. Ruth **PORTER**, Mar. 24, 1687	LR1	4
Samuell, s. Samuell, b. Feb. 26, 1693	LR1	2
Samuell, s. Jonathan, m. Sarah **LEWIS**, Aug. 15, 1706	LR1	4
Samuel, s. Samuel, d. May 25, 1712	LR2	141
Samuel, s. Samuel (s. of Jonathan), b. Aug. 7, 1722	LR2	34
Samuel, weaver, d. Jan. 6, 1724/5	LR2	66
Samuel, s. Thomas, b. Feb. 7, 1727/8	LR4	395
Samuel, s. Thomas, d. Apr. 27, 1729	LR5	50
Samuel, s. William, b. Sept. 7, 1732	LR5	7
Samuel, s. James & Ruth, b. Apr. 9, 1733	LR5	7
Samuel, 2nd, s. Thomas & Mary, b. Nov. 19, 1733	LR5	7
Samuel, s. Jonathan, d. Apr. 30, 1735	LR5	50
Samuel, m. Ruth **HIGHBY**, June 3, 1752	LR9	286
Samuel, m. Mary **GOODRICH**, Dec. 6, 1759	LR11	575
Samuel, s. Samuel, b. Apr. 22, 1760	LR11	589
Samuel, m. Huldah **MARTHA**, Feb. 25, 1771	LR17	G
Sarah, d. Samuell, b. Aug. 2, 1690	LR1	2
Sarah, d. Ephraim, b. Aug. 6, 1700	LR2	112
Sarah, m. Nathaniel **STANLEY**, b. of Ffarmington, Dec. 2, 1714	LR2	93
Sarah, d. Samuell, s. of Jonathan, b. Feb. 2, 1718/19	LR2	83
Sarah, d. William, b. Mar. 2, 1727/8	LR4	395
Sarah, m. Robert **PORTTER**, b. of Ffarmington, Oct. 17, 1728	LR4	423
Sarah, m. Nathaniel **MESSENGER**, b. of Hartford, Jan. 1, 1729/30	LR5	300
Sarah, m. Nathaniel **MESSENGER**, b. of Hartford, Jan. 1, 1729/30	LR5	307
Sarah, d. Thomas, b. Aug. 10, 1731	LR5	7
Sarah, d. William, d. Jan. 14, 1731/2	LR5	50
Sarah, w. Ephraim, Jr., d. Aug. 31, 1744	LR7	36
Sarah, d. Noah, b. Mar. 3, 1747	LR7	N
Sarah, d, Noah, d. Mar. 8, 1750	LR8	12
Sarah, d. Ephraim, Jr., b. Mar. 10, 1752	LR8	8
Sarah, d. Elijah, b. Sept. 1, 1755	LR9	12
Sarah, d. Samuell (s. of William), b. Apr. 5, 1761	LR11	589
Sarah, d. Samuel, b. Apr. 13, 1769	LR15	L
Sarah, m. Collen **LUDINGTON**, Feb. 9, 1775	LR21	557
Seth R., of Southington, m. Esther **ANDREWS**, of Farmington, Dec. 11, 1831, by Rev. Noah Porter	LR42	559
Simeon, s. David, b. May 15, 1751	LR8	8
Solomon, s. Elijah, b. Sept. 2, 1767	LR15	L
Steel, s. Thomas & Mary, b. Feb. 14, 1725/6	LR2	69
Steel, s. Thomas, d. May 11, 1729	LR5	50
Steel, s. Thomas & Mary, b. Sept. 20, 1729	LR5	7
Stephen, s. Samuel, weaver, b Apr. 3, 1707	LR1	4
Stephen, m. Mary **CLARK**, b. of Farmington, Nov. 1, 1733	LR5	300
Susannah, d. Joseph, b. Apr. 20, 1698	LR1	3
Susannah, m. James **GRIDLEY**, Nov. 26, 1719	LR2	101
Susanah, d. Samuel, b. Oct. 5, 1764	LR11	589

	Vol.	Page
SMITH (cont.)		
Cibble,* d. Stephen, b .May 5, 1737 *("Sibble")	LR6	6
Sibbel, d. Azariah, b. Feb. 17, 1751	LR9	12
Sylvia, d. Elnathan, b. May 23, 1772	LR17	439
Sylvia, d. Elnathan, d. Apr. 26, 1773	LR17	445
Sylvia, d. Elnathan, b. Apr. 5, 1774	LR17	439
Thankfull, d. Joseph, b. Nov. 4, 1700	LR1	3
Thankfull, d. Joseph, b. Nov. 17, 1746	LR7	N
Thomas, s. Samuell, b. Oct. 12, 1699	LR1	2
Thomas, m. Mary **STEEL**, b. of Ffarmington, Jan. 14, 1724/5	LR2	52
Thomas, s. Thomas, b. Oct. 19, 1743	LR6	6
Thomas, m. Anne **HOOKER**, Dec. 31, 1767	LR15	A
Timothy, 6th, s. Ebenezer, Jr., b. Mar. 3, 1761	LR11	589
Timothy, of New Haven, m. Sarah **HART**, of Farmington, June 1, 1850, by William Wright	LR47	127
Welthena, d. Samuell, b. Sept. 11, 1766	LR11	589
William, s. Samuell, b. Jan. 8, 1687* *("1690" written in parentheses)	LR1	2
William, s. Jonathan, b. Mar. 30, 1699	LR2	87
William, m. Rebeckah **WOODRUFF**, b. of Ffarmington, Nov. 18, 1714	LR2	93
William, d. July 26, 1718	LR5	50
William, of Ffarmington, m. Rebeckah **HUN**, of Weathersfield, July 22, 1725, by David Goodrich, J.P.	LR2	51
William, of Farmington, m. Rebeckah **HUNN**, of Weathersfield, July 22, 1725	LR6	27
William, s. John, weaver, & Abigail, b. Jan. 12, 1737/8	LR6	6
William, s. Thomas, b. Apr. 24, 1746	LR7	N
William, s. Samuel, b. Sept. 2, 1770	LR17	439
William, Sr., d. Jan. 9, 1779, in the 80th y. of his age	LR22	482
Zephaniah, s. Joseph, b. Feb. 16, 1710/11	LR2	97
---lian, m. Mary **WILLS**, July 11, 1771	LR17	G
SNATH, Chester, of Burlington, m. Eliza G. **ROWLEY**, of Farmington, Feb. 15, 1825, by Rev. Noah Porter	LR42	568
SNOW, Levi, of Ellington, m. Almira **BRACE**, of Farmington, Sept. 3, 1822, by Pierpoint Brockett	LR40	572
SOPER, Emily D., m. John **CHIDSEY**, b. of Farmington, Apr. 26, 1829, by Henry Bushnell	LR42	562
SOUTHERGILL, James, m. Eliza **LAWRENCE**, [ ], by Rev. William McAlister	LR47	122
SPARROW, Roxana, of Tolland, Conn., m. Jonathan H. **CLARK**, of Chester Cty. of Hampden, Mass., Apr. 28, 1839, by Rev. S. H. Clark	LR47	99
SPAULDING, George, m. Helen **COWLES**, Feb. 25, 1824, by Henry M. Mason	LR42	568
SPENCER, Caleb C., of Windsor, m. Clarissa B. **BURR**, of Farmington, Jan. 23, 1822, by Rev. Augustus Bolles, of Wentonbury	LR40	571
Daniel, s. Joseph, b. Apr. 1, 1761	LR11	589

	Vol.	Page
SPENCER (cont.)		
Dwight, of New Hartford, m. Abby **BUTLER**, of Burlington, Sept. 1, 1850, by Rev. Peter Tatro, Jr., of Bristol	LR47	127
Elizabeth, m. Samuel **CULVER**, Dec. 22, 1763	LR11	594
Joseph, m. Mary **JEROME**, Oct. 12, 1758	LR11	576
Mamree, d. Joseph, b. Oct. 29, 1759	LR11	589
Rachel, m. Matthew **HUNGERFORD**, Feb. 26, 1756	LR11	576
Thankfull, m. Nathaniel **BUNEL**, Sept. 8, 1755	LR9	286
SPERRY, Eli, m. Charlotte **DIX**, b. of Farmington, Nov. 3, 1824, by Amasa Woodford, J.P.	LR42	568
Joel, Jr., m. Sarah **WOODRUFF**, Aug. 5, 1824, by Amasa Woodford, J.P.	LR42	568
SQUIRE, SQUIER, SQUIERS, Elisha, m. Rachel **BROWNSON**, Apr. 11, 1767	LR15	A
Elizabeth, of Woodbury, m. Michael **BROWNSON**, of Farmington, May 8, 1735	LR5	539
Ephraim, d. Oct. 29, 1758	LR11	577
Harriet A., of Hartford, m. Eli **MAYNARD**, of Ellington, Apr. 10, 1839, by Rev. Noah Porter	LR47	99
Mabel, d. Ephraim, b. Nov. 17, 1754	LR11	589
Solomon, s. Elisha, b. Oct. 23, 1767	LR15	L
STANLEY, STANDLE, STANDLEE, STANDLEY, STANDLY, STANLY, Abi, d. Timothy, b. Aug. 9, 1765	LR14	11
Abigall, m. Samuell **COALES**, June 14, 1660	LR1	5
Abigail, d. John, b. July 25, 1669	LR1	2
Abagall, m. John **HOOKER**, Nov. 24, 1687	LR1	5
Amzi, s. Gad, b. Oct. 23, 1770	LR15	L
Ann, d. Nathaniell, b. Jan. 15, 1731/2	LR5	7
Anna, d. Thomas, b. May 14, 1699	LR1	2
Anna, d. Thomas, 2nd, b. May 14, 1699	LR4	271
Anna, d. Thomas, b. Oct. 30, 1718	LR2	83
Anna, d. Thomas, 2nd, b. Oct. 30, 1718	LR2	102
Anna, d. Thomas & Esther, b. Oct. 30, 1718	LR4	271
Anna, m. Thomas **HART**, s. Sergt. Thomas, Mar. 16, 1720/1	LR2	101
Anna, d. Thomas & Esther, b. Mar. 7, 1729/30	LR4	271
Anna, d. Thomas, Jr., b. Aug. 8, 1742	LR6	6
Anne, wid. Thomas, d. May 23, 1718	LR2	62
Anne, [w. Thomas], d. May 23, 1718	LR4	271
Anne, d. Samuel, Jr., b. July 6, 1728	LR4	395
Anne, d. Thomas, d. Nov. 6, 1732	LR4	271
Asa, s. Noah, b. Dec. 6, 1766	LR14	11
Asa, s. Noah, d. Dec. 12, 1766	LR14	3
Asa, s. Seth, b. Nov. 21, 1774	LR17	439
Cate, d. Seth, b. Jan. 15, 1782	LR22	475
Cruger, s. Seth, b. Nov. 19, 1775	LR17	439
Cynthia, d. Noah, b. Dec. 9, 1767	LR15	L
Elidrat, d .Timothy, b. Apr. 26, 1763	LR11	589
Elijah, s. John, b. May 28, 1754	LR11	589
Elizabeth, d. John, b. Apr. 1, 1657	LR1	2
Elizabeth, d .John, bp. May 5, 1657	LR2	328
Elizabeth, d. John, b. Nov. 28, 1672	LR1	2

	Vol.	Page
STANLEY, STANDLE, STANDLEE, STANDLEY, STANDLY, STANLY (cont.)		
Elizabeth, m. John **WADSWORTH**, Aug. 20, 1696	LR1	5
Elizabeth, d. Samuell, b. Mar. 13, 1714/15	LR2	81
Elizabeth, d. Nathaniel, b. Jan. 16, 1719/20	LR2	102
Elizabeth, m. George **BIRD**, b. of Farmington, Dec. 15, 1825, by Rev. Noah Porter	LR42	569
Elizabeth N., of Berlin, m. Azmon **WOODRUFF**, of Farmington, Dec. 9, 1824, by Rev. Noah Porter	LR42	568
Erastus, s. Seth, b. Oct. 22, 1776	LR21	550
Easther, m. John **NORTH**, s. Nathaniell, b. of Farmington, Feb. 21, 1738/9	LR6	27
Esther, wid. Dea. John, d. Jan. 29, 1739/40	LR6	10
Esther, d. Gad, b. Sept. 2, 1768	LR15	L
Esther, wid., d. July 22, 1776, in the 81st y. of her age	LR21	558-9
Eunice, b. Aug. 15, 1786; m. Hezekiah **SELDEN**, Oct. 19, 1806	LR47	W-Y
Frances A.M., m. Elisha P. **WHITNEY**, b. of Amhurst, Mass., July 9, 1843, by Rev. R. A. Chalker	LR47	111
Frances W., m. Allen W. **MILLER**, b. of Ffarmington, May 29, 1823, by Noah Porter, V.D.M.	LR40	572
Gad, s. Thomas & Easther, b. Mar. 21, 1734/5	LR4	271
Gad, m. Marah **JUDD**, Oct. 29, 1767	LR15	A
Gad, s. Maj. Gad, b. Aug. 13, 1776	LR21	550
Hezekiah, s. John, b. July 15, 1749	LR8	8
Horatio, s. Seth, b. Nov. 24, 1777	LR21	550
Isack, s. John, b. Sept. 22, 1660	LR1	2
James, s. Thomas, Jr. & Mary, b. Feb. 14, 1748/9	LR4	271
Jane, d. Seth, b. Mar. 7, 1783	LR22	475
Jane, of Farmington, m. Lucas H. **CARTER**, of Wolcott, Sept. 11, 1833, by Rev. Noah Porter	LR42	A
Jesse, s. Timothy, b. Oct. 26, 1777	LR21	550
Job, s. Thomas & Easther, b. Aug. 4, 1732	LR4	271
Job, s. Thomas [& Easther], d. July 5, 1740	LR4	271
John, s. John, b. Nov. [ ], 1647	LR1	2
John, Capt. d. Dec. 19, 1706	LR1	3
John, Jr., m. Hannah **PORTTER**, b. of Ffarmington, Aug. [ ], 1710	LR2	123
John, Jr., of Ffarmington, m. Mary **RIGHT**, of Weathersfield, Dec. 9, 1714	LR2	93
John, m. Sarah **MIX**, May 11, 1743	LR7	46
John, s. John, b. Oct. 23, 1746	LR7	N
John, d. Sept. 8, 1748	LR7	36
John, his w. [ ], gave up her [ ], June 26, 1[ ]	LR1	2
Josiah, s. Samuell, b. Aug. 10, 1717	LR2	81
Lois, d. Timothy, b. Sept. 28, 1731	LR5	7
Lott, s. Thomas, Jr. & Mary, b. Mar. 3, 1752	LR4	271
Luce, w. John, joined church, Apr. 20, 1663	LR2	327
Lucy, d. Thomas, Jr. & Mary, b. July 14, 1744	LR4	271
Marah, w. Thomas, d. Jan. 3, 1763	LR11	593
Mary, m. Nathaniell **HOOKER**, Dec. 23, 1698	LR1	4
Mary, d. Nathaniel, b. Dec. 4, 1722	LR2	34
Mary, d. John, b. Mar. 11, 1745	LR7	N

	Vol.	Page
STANLEY, STANDLE, STANDLEE, STANDLEY,		
STANDLY, STANLY (cont.)		
Mary, d. Gad, b. Aug. 2, 1772	LR17	439
Mercy, d. Timothy, b. Aug. 5, 1726	LR4	374
Nancy, d. Seth, b. Jan. 2, 1781	LR21	550
Nathaniel, m. Sarah **SMITH**, b. of Ffarmington, Dec. 2,		
1714	LR2	93
Nathaniel, s. Nathaniel, b. Jan. 8, 1724/5	LR2	65
Noah, s. Thomas, 2nd & Esther, b. Jan. 16, 1723/4	LR4	271
Noah, 2nd, s. Noah [& Ruth], b. Apr. 25, 1759	LR4	271
Noah, d. May 5, 1778, in the 55th y. of his age	LR21	560
Noah, m. Ruth **NORTON**, [ ]	LR4	271
Oliver, s. John, b. July 17, 1751	LR8	8
Oliver, s. Timothy, b. July 3, 1758	LR11	589
Oliver, s. Timothy, d. Aug. 5, 1758	LR11	577
Oliver, s. Timothy, b. May 1, 1775	LR17	439
Phebe, d. Maj. Gad, b. Aug. 28, 1778	LR21	550
Rette, m. Joseph **LEE**, Feb. 1, 1743/4	LR7	35
Roxana, b. Dec. 1, 1783; m. Asahel **THOMSON**, [s. of		
Abel], Oct. 29, 1806; d. Nov. 24, 1807	LR22	476
Ruth, d. Samuel, b. July 19, 1719	LR2	102
Ruth, d. Thomas, 2nd & Esther, b. July 8, 1726; d. Aug.		
3, 1726	LR4	271
Ruth, d. Nathaniell, b. Jan. 13, 1726/7	LR4	382
Ruth, d. Noah & Ruth, b. July 11, 1756	LR4	271
Salma, s. Seth, b. Oct. 10, 1779	LR21	550
Salmon, s. John, b. Feb. 2, 1753	LR11	589
Samuel, Jr., of Ffarmington, m. Anne **BRACY**, of		
Hartford, Sept. 1, 1727	LR4	423
Sarah, d. John, b. Feb. [ ], 1651	LR1	2
Sara, d. John, b. Feb. 18, 1651	LR2	330
Sarah, wid. Capt. John, d. May 15, 1713	LR2	142
Sarah, d. Nathaniel, b. Nov. 21, 1715	LR2	96
Sarah, Jr., m. Stephen **TUTTLE**, b. of Farmington, Jan.		
23, 1734/5	LR5	545
Selah, s. Thomas, b. June 1, 1762	LR14	11
Seth, s. Noah & Ruth, b. Mar. 18, 1750/1	LR4	271
Seth, s. Thomas, of Kensington, b. May 6, 1755	LR11	589
Seth, m. Ruth **CLARK**, Jan. 6, 1774	LR17	442
Sybel, d. Thomas, b. Oct. 17, 1757	LR14	11
Sylvea, d. Noah & Ruth, b. Oct. 24, 1753	LR4	271
Thomas, s. Capt. John, b .Nov. 1, 1649; d. Apr. 15, 1713	LR4	271
Thomas, s. John, b. Dec. 10, 16[49]	LR2	330
Thomas, s. John, b. [ ], 1649	LR1	2
Thomas, s. Capt. John, m. Anne **PECK**, d. Rev. Jeremiah,		
of Watterbury, May [ ], 1690	LR4	271
Thomas, s. Thomas, b. Oct. 31, 1696	LR1	2
Thomas, 2nd, s. Thomas, 1st, b. Oct. 31, 1696	LR4	271
Thomas, d. Apr. 14, 1713	LR2	62
Thomas, s. Thomas, m. Easther **COWLES**, b. of		
Ffarmington, Jan. 2, 1717/18	LR2	87
Thomas, 2nd, m. Esther **COWLES**, d. Samuel, Jan. 2,		
1717/18	LR4	271

	Vol.	Page
STANLEY, STANDLE, STANDLEE, STANDLEY,		
STANDLY, STANLY (cont.)		
Thomas, 3rd, s. Thomas, b .Nov. 27, 1720	LR2	102
Thomas, s. Thomas, 2nd & Esther, b. Nov. 27, 1720	LR4	271
Thomas, s. John, Jr., b. June 20, 1726	LR2	282
Thomas, 3rd, of Farmington, m. Mary **FRANCIS**, of		
Weathersfield, d. James, of Newington Parish, May		
22, 1740	LR4	271
Thomas, d. Oct. 13, 1756	LR9	495
Thomas, m. wid. Sarah **GRIDLEY**, Feb. 28, 1765	LR11	594
Timothy, s. John, b. Mar. 17, 1653	LR1	2
Timothy, m. Martha **SMITH**, b. of Ffarmington, Dec. 25,		
1718	LR2	101
Timothy, s. Timothy, b. Dec. 16, 1719	LR2	102
Timothy, his 2nd child d. July 6, 1722 (A son); his 3rd		
child d. June 9, 1723 (A d.); his 4th child d. Feb. 3,		
1724/5 (A son)	LR2	107
Timothy, his 2nd child b. July 6, 1722; his 3rd child b.		
June 9, 1723; his 4th child b. Jan. 25, 1724/5	LR4	374
Timothy, s. Timothy, d. Sept. 3, 1723	LR2	107
Timothy, s. Thomas & Easther, b. Aug. 13, 1727	LR4	271
Timothy, s. Timothy, b. June 8, 1729	LR5	7
Timothy, m. Elidiah **NEWELL**, May, 5, 1757	LR11	576
Timothy, s. Timothy, b. June 29, 1771	LR17	439
William, s. Nathaniel & Sarah, b. Nov. 18, 1729	LR5	7
----el, m. Rhoda **WADSWORTH**, Aug. 6, 1771	LR17	G
STARR, William Henry, of New York, m. Frances Cowles		
CAMP, of Farmington, Mar. 2, 1836, by Rev. Noah		
Porter	LR47	93
STEARNS, Isaac, of Lanesborough, Mass., m. Lucy **HART**, of		
Berlin, Sept. 19, 1831, by Rev. Noah Porter	LR42	560
STEBBINS, STEBIN, Eleanor, d. Luke & Sarah, b. Aug. 3,		
1756	LR11	589
Jane, m. John **NORTH**, Mar. 19, 1707/8	LR1	6
Luke, m. Sarah **NORTON**, May 1, 1755	LR11	576
Samuel, s. Seth & Sarah, b. Aug. 5, 1758	LR11	589
Sarah, w. Luke, d. Feb. 18, 1764	LR11	593
STEDMAN, STEADMAN, Abigail, d. John, b. Jan. 19, 1704	LR5	307
Anne, s. Hezekiah **ANDRUS**, May 20, 1757	LR11	576
Azuba, of Berlin, m. Walter H. **COWLES**, of		
Farmington, July 10, 1822, by W. Eli, V.D.M.	LR40	571
Damaris, d. John, b. Apr. 7, 1713	LR5	307
Daniel, s. John, b. Jan. 14, 1722	LR5	307
Elisha Stoddard, s. Lemuel, b. Aug. 13, 1783	LR22	475
Elizabeth, d. John, b. Aug. 22, 1709	LR5	307
Elizabeth, d. Thomas, b. May 5, 1778	LR21	550
Elizabeth C., m. Charles **HINSDALE**, b. of Hartford,		
Nov. 2, 1845, by Rev. S. H. Clark	LR47	115
Emerson, m. Harriet Maria **PHILLIPS**, b. of Farmington,		
Nov. 2, 1845, by Rev. S. H. Clark	LR47	115
Irena, d. Samuell, Jr., b. Jan. 2, 1771	LR17	439
Jerusha, d. John, b. Aug. 1, 1711	LR5	307
John, s. John, b. Mar. 2, 1706	LR5	307

	Vol.	Page
STEDMAN, STEADMAN (cont.)		
John, Jr., m. [E]unice [ ], Sept. 5, 1733	LR5	545
Lydia, d. John, b. Mar. 29, 1725	LR5	307
Lyman, s. Thomas, b. Apr. 20, 1780	LR21	550
Mary, d. John, b. Apr. 12, 1717	LR5	307
Mercy, m. James **ROOT**, July 22, 1772	LR17	443
Nabbee, d. Samuell, Jr., b. Apr. 28, 1769	LR15	L
Samuel, s. John, b. Dec. 28, 1714	LR5	307
Samuel, m. Keziah [ ], July 6, 1768	LR15	N
Simeon, m. Sarah **PARKER**, May 10, 1770	LR21	557
Simeon, s. Simeon, b. May 13, 1771	LR21	550
Simeon, s. Simeon, b. Feb. 16, 1773	LR21	550
Simeon, m. Lucy Ann **HART**, b. of Farmington, Mar. 2,		
1845, by Rev. S. H. Clark	LR47	113
Timothy, s. John, b. May 2, 1719	LR5	307
Violet, d. John, b. Jan. 2, 1708	LR5	307
STEELE, STEAL, STEEL, STEELL, Abigail, d. Joseph, b.		
Jan. 5, 1720/1	LR2	282
Ann, m. John **ROOT**, May 26, 1762	LR11	592
Anna, d. Joseph, b. Jan. 23, 1724/5	LR2	282
Anna, of Weathersfield, m. William **HOOKER**, of		
Ffarmington, July 16, 1724	LR2	52
Betsey, d. James, b. June 17, 1792	LR29	578
Celestial M., of Farmington, m. William **BALDWIN**, of		
New Haven, Nov. 16, 1845, by Rev. S. H. Clark	LR47	115
Charles A., m. Jane E. **PARMELEE**, Sept. 11, 1839, by		
Elisha C. Jones	LR47	101
Charles T., of Farmington, m. Mary S. **CLARK**, of		
Hartford, Nov. 27, 1845, by William Wright	LR47	116
Daniel, s. John, Jr. & Mary, b. Mar. 8, 1730/1	LR5	7
David, s. James, b. Nov. 23, 1789	LR29	578
Ebenezer, s. Samuell, b. Apr., last, 1671	LR1	2
Ebenezer, m. Sarah **HART**, Feb. 15, 1704/5	LR2	145
Ebenezer, Capt., d. Oct. 6, 1722	LR2	61
Ebenezer, s. Joseph, b. May 18, 1727	LR4	395
Ebenezer, m. Sary **SAGE**, Aug. 10, 1749	LR7	35
Edmond, m. Lucy **NEWELL**, Oct. 10, 1830, by David L.		
Ogden	LR42	560
Eldad, s. Ens. John, b. Oct. 1, 1736	LR6	6
Elisha, s. John, Jr., b. Nov. 13, 1726	LR2	242
Elizabeth, d. Joseph, b. Dec. 16, 1715	LR2	282
Elizabeth, d. John, Jr., b. Oct. 23, 1719	LR2	102
Ezekiel, s. John, Jr., b. Dec. 15, 1732	LR5	7
Hanna, d. John, d. July 17, 1655	LR2	320
Hannah, d. Samuel, b. Aug. [ ], 1668	LR1	2
Henry, m. Harriet **SWEET**, b. of Farmington, Dec. 19,		
1832, by Rev. Noah Porter	LR42	558
Honour, d. Samuell & Honour, b. July 14, 1759	LR11	589
James, s. Samuel, b. Aug. last, 1662	LR1	2
James, s. Samuell, bp. Aug. 27, 1664	LR2	327
James, s. Joseph, b. May 18, 1719	LR2	282
John, s. John, b. Nov. 5, 16[ ]	LR2	330
John, Jr., d. Mar. 8, 1653	LR2	320

	Vol.	Page
STEELE, STEAL, STEEL, STEELL (cont.)		
John, m. Mary **SEMER**, Nov. 25, 1655	LR2	331
John, d. Feb. 27, 1664* *(First written "1666")	LR2	319
John, Jr., m. Mary **NEWEL**, b. of Ffarmington, Dec. 27,		
1716	LR2	94
John, s. John, Jr., b. Nov. 15, 1724	LR2	46
John, Sr., d. Aug. 26, 1738	LR6	10
John, s. Samuel, b. May 19, 1753	LR8	8
John, s. Samuel, b. May 19, 1753	LR9	12
John, 2nd, s. Samuel, b. Jan. 24, 1757	LR11	589
John, s. James, b. Apr. 16, 1787	LR29	578
Levi, s. Joseph, b. Dec. 10, 1731	LR5	7
Lucina, of Berlin, m. Noble **ANDRUS**, of Farmington,		
Apr. 13, 1838, by Rev. S. H. Clark	LR47	97
Lucy, d. Joseph, b. June 24, 1737	LR6	6
Lucy, d. Ebenezer, Jr., b. Mar. 3, 1776	LR21	550
Ledia, m. James **BIRD**, Mar. 31, 1657	LR2	331
Mary, d. Samuell, b. Dec. 5, 1652	LR2	330
Mary, m. William **JUDD**, Mar. 31, 1657	LR2	331
Mary, m. John **THOMSON**, s. of Thomas, Oct. 24, 1670	LR2	5
Mary, d. Ebenezer, b. June 15, 1706	LR2	109
Mary, d. John, Jr., b. Sept. 20, 1722	LR2	102
Mary, m. Thomas **SMITH**, b. of Ffarmington, Jan. 14,		
1724/5	LR2	52
Rachell, w. John, Sr., d. Oct. 24, 1653	LR2	320
Ruth, m. John **THOMSON**, Sr., b. of Farmington, June		
18, 1724	LR2	52
Samuell, s. John, b. Mar. 26, 1652 *("March" written in		
pencil and "born" written over "baptized")	LR2	330
Samuell, s. Samuell, bp. Mar. 20, 1658	LR2	328
Samuel, s. John, Jr., b. Nov. 4, 1717	LR2	84
Samuel, s. Joseph, b. Feb. 24, 1722/3	LR2	282
Samuel, m. Honour **DEMING**, May 4, 1749	LR7	46
Sarah, d. Ebenezer, b. May 15, 1708	LR2	109
Sarah, d. Joseph, b. July 17, 1717	LR2	282
Sarah, m. Nathaniel **COLE**, of Kensington, May 15, 1748	LR7	46
Sarah, Mrs., d. Feb. 26, 1751	LR8	11
Solomon, s. John, Jr., b. Nov. 15, 1728	LR4	395
Thomas, s. James, b. Aug. 21, 1794	LR29	578
STEVENS, STEPHENS, Acsah, d. Benjamin, b. June 13,		
1743	LR7	N
Achael, m. Eldad **HART**, July 8, 1761	LR11	592
Anna, d. John & Thankfull, b. Feb. 23, 1772	LR17	441
Benjamin, m. Comfort **KELLSEY**, Oct. 20, 1740	LR6	304
Edward, of Kensington, m. Mary E. **JOHNSON**, of N.Y.,		
Oct. 15, 1848, by William Wright	LR47	123
Henry, m. Catharine **ANDRUS**, b. of Farmington, Nov.		
25, 1841, by Rev. Aaron S. Hill	LR47	106
Lemuel, s. Benjamin, b. June 13, 1745	LR8	8
Lemuel, s. [Benjamin], b. Aug. 22, 1745	LR7	N
Levy, s. Benjamin, b. Oct. 20, 1749	LR8	8
Perudah, twin with Phebe, s. Benjamin, b. Sept. 25, 1754	LR9	12
Phebe, twin with Perudah, d. Benjamin, b. Sept. 25, 1754	LR9	12

	Vol.	Page
STEVENS, STEPHENS (cont.)		
Roswell, s. Benjamin, b. Aug. 22, 1747	LR8	8
Sarah, d. Benjamin, b. Oct. 20, 1751	LR8	8
Tamasa, d. Benjamin, b. Aug. 24, 1741	LR6	6
Thankfull, had d. Bulah **FRANK**, b. June 27, 1778 or		
1788	LR21	543
STEVERY, Hopkins, of Waterbury, m. Rachel **HILLS**, of		
Farmington, Apr. 11, 1826, by Rev. Noah Porter	LR42	569
STILES, Lydia A., m. John B. **WHEELER**, b. of Bristol, Dec.		
30, 1839, by Rev. Noah Porter	LR47	102
Albert, [s. Giles & Sally], b. Dec. 29, 1840	LR47	W-Y
Eliza Loveland, [d. Giles & Sally], b. Feb. 18, 1839	LR47	W-Y
Ellen Elizabeth, [d. Giles & Sally], b. Apr. 22, 1837; d.		
Oct. 4, 1839	LR47	W-Y
Giles, m. Sally **LOVELAND**, Nov. 27, 1822	LR47	W-Y
Giles, [s. Giles & Sally], b. July 9, 1830	LR47	W-Y
James Allen, [s. Giles & Sally], b. Feb. 14, 1833	LR47	W-Y
Jane Maria, [d. Giles & Sally], b. Oct. 18, 1824	LR47	W-Y
Jane Maria, [d. Giles & Sally], d. Aug. 9, 1845	LR47	W-Y
John Webster, [s. Giles & Sally], b. Nov. 21, 1826	LR47	W-Y
Sarah Ann, [d. Giles & Sally], b. July 27, 1823	LR47	W-Y
Sarah Ann, m. Edward E. **WARREN**, b. of Farmington,		
Dec. 7, 1842, by Noah Porter, V.D.M.	LR47	109
Walter, [s. Giles & Sally], b. Aug. 27, 1828	LR47	W-Y
STIMSON, Mary, had d. Mary **BISEL**, b. July 17, 1749	LR8	3
Mary, had d. Mary Bisel, d. Aug. 13, 1751	LR8	11
Mary, m. Eliphas **ANDRUS**, Sept. 3, 1752	LR8	10
STOCKING, Thomas R., of Buffalo, N.Y., m. Julia Ann		
BIDWELL, of Farmington, May 6, 1835, by Rev.		
Noah Porter	LR47	89
STODDARD, David E., of Avon, m. Clarissa **HART**, of		
Farmington, Nov. 16, 1846, by Noah Porter	LR47	118
Sarah, Mrs. of Northampton, m. Samuel **WHITTMAN**,		
Mar. 9, 1708/9	LR2	145
William H., of Weathersfield, m. Abigail **SMITH**, of		
Hartford, Mar. 3, 1831, by Rev. Quartus Stewart	LR42	560
STONE, Abigall, d. Nathaniell, b. Dec. 20, 1774	LR17	439
Antonette, m. Henry **CLARK**, b. of Farmington, June 26,		
1847, by Rev. Noah Porter	LR47	121
George, of Harwinton, m. Abigail **COUCH**, of Bristol,		
Jan. 3, 1827, by Rev. Rodney Rosseter, of Plymouth	LR42	567
Nathaniel, m. Temperance **JEROME**, Apr. 30, 1772	LR17	443
STOUGHTON, Alice, d. John, b. Apr. 21, 1769	LR17	439
Ann, d. John, b. July 23, 1771	LR17	439
Gustavus, s. John, b. Jan. 31, 1763	LR17	439
John, m. Ann **LEWIS**, July 29, 1762	LR17	442
Lucy, d. John, b. May 11, 1767	LR17	439
Roxana, d. John, b. Mar. 14, 1765	LR17	439
STOW, Charles K., of Middletown, m. Mary W. **BATES**, of		
Farmington, June 8, 1826, by Rev. Noah Porter	LR42	567
Lucy, m. Oliver **HUNGERFORD**, Dec. 24, 1767	LR17	443
Sarah Jane, of Farmington, m. Alphonso **BOARDMAN**,		
of Bristol, Apr. 8, 1849, by William Wright	LR47	125

	Vol.	Page
STREET, Anne, d. Nehemiah, b. May 6, 1773	LR17	441
Sinthe, d. Nehemiah, b. May 20, 1774 (Cynthia)	LR17	441
Nehemiah, m. Thankfull **MOODEY**, Apr. 16, 1772	LR17	443
Samuel, s. Nehemiah, b. [ ], 1776	LR21	550
STRICKLAND, Elizabeth, of Hartford, m. Samuel **NEAL**, of		
Farmington, May 11, 1735	LR5	300
STRONG, Abi, d. Elisha, b. Sept. 27, 1756	LR14	11
Achsah, d. Elisha, b. Dec. 29, 1754	LR14	11
Asahel, of Northampton, m. Margaret **HART**, of		
Ffarmington, June 11, 1689	LR2	257
Asahel, s. Asahel, b. Oct. 8, 1702	LR4	382
Asahel, Jr., m. Ruth **HOOKER**, b. of Ffarmington, June		
8, 173[ ]	LR5	13
Asahel, Sr., d. Oct. 8, 1739	LR6	10
Asahel, Capt., d. Mar. 31, 1751	LR8	11
Syprian, s. Asahel, b. May 26, 1743	LR7	N
Elijah, s. Elisha, b. Nov. 6, 1762	LR14	11
Elizabeth, d. Asahel, b. Nov. 22, 1696	LR4	382
Elizabeth, d. Asahel, d. Apr. 14, 1706	LR2	148
Elizabeth, d. Asahel, b. Nov. 30, 1746	LR7	N
Ellen A., of Farmington, m. John N. **BARTLETT**, of		
Avon, Sept. 7, 1846, by Noah Porter	LR47	118
Ellen Root (d. Pomroy), b. Nov. 13, 1822	LR47	W-Y
Elnathan, s. Asahel & Ruth, b. Oct. 13, 1730	LR5	7
Elnathan, s. Asahel, Jr. & Ruth, d. Sept. 25, 1736	LR5	500
Elnathan, m. Lucretia **CURTISS**, Nov. 15, 1764	LR11	592
Ephraim, s. Asahel, b. Feb. 16, 1741/2	LR6	6
Eunis, d. John, b. Feb. 9, 1741/2	LR6	6
John, s. Asahel, b. Mar. [ ], 1705/6	LR4	382
John, m. [E]unice **WHITMAN**, b. of Farmington, Feb. 7,		
1733/4	LR5	300
John, s. John & [E]unis, Dec. 22, 1739	LR6	6
John, s. John, d. Nov. 20, 1745	LR7	36
John, s. John, b. June 3, 1750	LR8	8
John M., [s. Pomroy], b. Aug. 23, 1813	LR47	W-Y
Jonathan, s. Asahel, Jr., d. Sept. 15, 1736	LR5	49
Julia, [d. Pomroy], b. Dec. 30, 1815	LR47	W-Y
Julia M., m. Chauncey **BROWN**, b. of Farmington, Aug.		
10, 1836, by Rev. Noah Porter	LR47	93
Lois, d. Asahel, b. Feb. 8, 1698/9	LR4	382
Lois, d. Asahel, Jr. & Ruth, b. Dec. 22, 1732	LR5	7
Lois, single, d. Dec. 13, 1733	LR5	50
Lois, twin with Ruth, d. Asahel, Jr., d. Sept. 6, 1736	LR5	50
Lois, d. Asahel, Jr. & Ruth, d. Sept. 6, 1736	LR5	500
Lois, 2nd, d. Ashel, Jr., b. May 3, 1737	LR6	6
Luce, d. John, b. May 20, 1744	LR7	N
Lucy, m. Nathaniel **WINCHEL**, Jr., Dec. 15, 1759	LR11	575
Marah, d. John, b. Aug. 21, 1749	LR7	N
Margaret, d. Asahel, b. Apr. 22, 1690	LR4	382
Margaret, m. John **ROOT**, s. Stephen, July 10, 1716	LR2	104
Margaret, w. Asahel, Sr., d. May 29, 1735	LR5	50
Mary, d Asahel, b. Jan. 22, 1692/3	LR4	382
Mary, m. Daniel **LEWIS**, b. of Ffarmington, May 1, 1718	LR2	101

	Vol.	Page
STRONG (cont.)		
Mary, d. Elisha, b. Aug. 1, 1751	LR14	11
Mellecent, d. John, b. Nov. 6, 1755; d. Nov. 6, 1755	LR9	12
Naome, d. Elisha, b. Nov. 26, 1760	LR14	11
Philip, [s. Pomroy], b. Oct. 28, 1805	LR47	W-Y
Philip, [s. Pomroy], b. Jan. 9, 1809	LR47	W-Y
Pomroy, [m.] [ ] **NORTH**, [ ]	LR47	W-Y
Ruth, d. Asahel, Jr. & Ruth, b. Apr. 7, 1735	LR5	306
Ruth, d. Asahel & Ruth, b. Apr. 10, 1735	LR5	7
Ruth, twin with Lois, d. Asahel, Jr., d. Sept. 6, 1736	LR5	50
Ruth, d. Asahel, Jr. & Ruth, d. Sept. 6, 1736	LR5	500
Ruth, d. Asahel, b. Sept. 3, 1739	LR6	3
Ruth, 2nd, d. Asahel, b. Sept. 3, 1739	LR6	6
Ruth, m. Icabod **NORTON**, Feb. 21, 1760	LR11	592
Ruth, Mrs., m. Solomon **WHITMAN**, Nov. 19, 1772	LR17	442
Sarah, d. John & [E]unice, b. Nov. 25, 1737	LR6	6
Sarah, d. Elisha, b. Feb. 2, 1750	LR14	11
Simeon, s. John & [E]unice, b. May 8, 1735	LR5	307
Simeon, Major, d. Oct. 15, 1776, in the 42nd y. of his age	LR21	558-9
Susan M., [d. Pomroy], b. Jan. 22, 1804	LR47	W-Y
SUMMADY, Fanny, m. Alanson **FREEMAN**, b. of		
Farmington, Nov. 29, 1838, by Rev. Noah Porter	LR47	98
SUTLIFF, Frederick B., m. Polly Emeline **ALLEN**, b. of		
Bristol, Nov. 28, 1834, by Rev. Noah Porter	LR47	88
John H., of Plymouth, m. Harriet J. **WARNER**, of		
Farmington, Dec. 16, 1832, by Rev. Noah Porter	LR42	558
SWEET, Abigail, m. Alvin B. **HURLBURT**, b. of		
Farmington, Nov. 7, 1823, by Noah Porter, V.D.M.	LR40	573
Edwin, m. Julia **HART**, b. of Farmington, Oct. 12, 1823,		
by Noah Porter, V.D.M.	LR40	572
Harriet, m. Henry **STEELE**, b. of Farmington, Dec. 19,		
1832, by Rev. Noah Porter	LR42	558
James, Jr., of Farmington, m. Susan M. **BUNNEL**, of		
Southington, Dec. 10, 1843, by William Wright	LR47	112
Jane, of Farmington, m. G. W. **WOOD**, of Camden, N.Y.,		
Dec. 1, 1828, by Rev. Noah Porter	LR42	564
Lucy, of Farmington, m. John **OSBORN**, of Windsor,		
Jan. 31, 1821, by John Mix, J.P.	LR40	571
Maria, m. Emory **FARR**, b. of Farmington, Sept. 18,		
1838, by Rev. Noah Porter	LR47	97
Milo, of Farmington, m. Eliza **MOODEY**, of Burlington,		
Sept. 28, 1823, by Noah Porter, V.D.M.	LR40	572
SWEETLAND, Walter B., of Hartford, m. Clarissa A.		
MITCHELL, of Farmington, May 22, 1828, by		
Rev. Noah Porter	LR42	564
SWERES (?), Bidwell, m. Jennet **DOUGLASS**, b. of		
Farmington, Nov. 10, 1829, by Rev. Noah Porter	LR42	561
SYKES, Amaziah, s. John, b. Dec. 17, 1724/5	LR4	374
TAFT, Charlotte, of Burlington, m. John **ALDERMAN**, Jr.,		
July 4, 1843, by Rev. B. Creagh	LR47	110
TALCOTT, William, of Coventry, m. Matilda W. **MILLER**,		
of Farmington, Nov. 30, 1846, by Rev. Noah Porter	LR47	118

	Vol.	Page
TALMAGE, TAMAGE, Asa, s. Tho[ma]s W[illia]m, b. Dec.		
30, 1775	LR21	551
David, s. Ichabod, b. Nov. 30, 1774	LR17	439
Deborah, of New Haven, m. Timothy **BRONSON,** of		
Farmington, Jan. 14, 1747/8	LR7	35
Hannah, m. Philemon **BRADLEY,** Dec. 20, 1774	LR21	557
Ichabod, m. Hannah **MINOR,** Mar. 9, 1774	LR17	443
Polle, d. Thomas W[illia]m, b. Dec. 21, 1776	LR21	551
Statira, d. Thomas W., b. Nov. 13, 1774	LR21	551
Stephen T., m. Lucetta **BARTHOLOMEW,** May 8,		
1842, by Rev. C. D. Cowles	LR47	107
Tho[ma]s Will[ia]m, m. Eunice **ATKINS,** Jan. 27, 1774	LR21	557
TAYLOR, Emily, of Glastonbury, m. Alfred **DORMAN,** of		
Farmington, Oct. 19, 1836, by Rev. Noah Porter	LR47	90
Jane, of Glastonbury, m. Henry **HART,** of Farmington,		
Dec. 7, 1834, by Rev. Noah Porter	LR47	88
Julia, of Burlington, m. Erastus **LEE,** of Farmington,		
Mar. 6, 1825, by Rev. Noah Porter	LR42	568
Samuel E., of Colebrook, m. Juliet **ORTON,** of		
Farmington, Feb. 18, 1841, by Rev. Noah Porter	LR47	104
TEMPLER, Sarah, of Wallingford, m. John **HESSINGTON,**		
of Farmington, Nov. 3, 1735	LR5	539
TERRY, John B., of Plymouth, m. Amanda **HARRISON,** of		
Waterbury, June 16, 1828, by Rev. Noah Porter	LR42	564
THATCHER, Nelson E., of Burlington, m. Lydia **BOOTH,**		
of Farmington, Sept. 8, 1850, by Rev. Charles		
Kelsey	LR47	127
THOMAS, Abigail, d. Ephraim & Abigail, b. Feb. 19. 1728/9	LR5	7
Asahel, s. Ephraim, b. Apr. 18, 1732	LR5	7
Enoch, s. Enoch, b. May 27, 1743	LR11	590
Ephraim, m. Abigail **PORTTER,** d. Dr. Samuel, b. of		
Ffarmington, Dec. 1, 1726	LR2	257
Ezekiel, s. Ephraim & Abigail, b. Aug. 19, 1730	LR5	7
Frederick C., of Avon, m. Eunice **ROBINSON,** of		
Farmington, Apr. 28, 1841, by Rev. Noah Porter	LR47	104
Jeremiah S., of Terryville, m. Sarah **BARTHOLOMEW,**		
of [Plainville], Oct. 20, 1847, by William Wright	LR47	121
Leverett, s. Enoch, b. June 16, 1737	LR11	590
Samuel, s. Ephraim, b. Oct. 8, 1727	LR4	395
Sary, d. Sept. 26, 1740	LR6	10
[S]arah, d. Samuell, b. Dec. 16, 1746	LR7	M
Sarah, m. Thomas **HART,** Jr., Aug. 21, 1750	LR7	35
Tredwell, d,* Enoch, b. Apr. 3, 1740 *(A son?)	LR11	590
Zebulon, s. John, b. Dec. 27, 1755	LR8	8
THOMSON, THOMPSON, TOMSON, Abel, s. James, b.		
Feb. 19, 1749	LR7	F
Abel, b. Feb. 19, O.S., 1749; m. Ruth **GRIDLEY,** Dec. 7,		
1775; m. 2nd w. Sybel **HART,** Nov. 14, 1793	LR22	476
Abell, m. Ruth **GRIDLEY,** Dec. 7, 1775	LR21	557
Abigail, d. Thomas, s. of Thomas, b. Sept. 3, 1710	LR2	109
Abigail, w. Thomas (s. of Thomas), d. Aug. 6, 1720	LR2	61
Abigail, m. Daniel **HART,** b. of Farmington, July 18,		
1734	LR5	300

	Vol.	Page
THOMSON, THOMPSON, TOMSON (cont.)		
Abigaile, d. Timothy, b. Mar. 2, 1747	LR7	M
Ann, d. Hezekiah, b. Feb. 10, 1762	LR11	590
Ann, [d. Asahel & Ruth], b. Jan. 13, 1815	LR22	476
Ann, m. Augustus L. **BARBER**, b. of Farmington, Sept. 28, 1836, by Rev. Noah Porter	LR47	94
Anna, m. John **NORTON**, 3rd, May 6, 1708	LR1	6
Anna, w. Timothy, d. May 11, 1793, in the 77th y. of her age	LR29	580
Anne, m. Sergt. John **NORTON**, b. of Farmington, May 6, 1708	LR5	300
Anne, d. Thomas, b. Mar. 27, 1715	LR2	95
Anne, d. Thomas (s. of Thomas), d. May 7, 1718	LR2	62
Anne, d. Samuel, b. Mar. 1, 1728/9	LR4	396
Anson, s. John, b. Dec. 28, 1676	LR1	2
Asa, s. Barnabas, b. Mar. 23, 1759	LR11	590
Asahel, s. Abell, b. Mar. 13, 1783	LR22	476
Asahel, s. Abel, b. [Mar. 13, 1783]; m. Roxana **STANLEY**, Oct. 29, 1806	LR22	476
Asahel, m. Ruth **WHITMAN**, Nov. 14, 1809	LR22	476
Asahel, d. [ ], 1841	LR22	476
Barnibus, s. Samuel, b. Nov. 13, 1723	LR2	70
Barnebus, m. Ruth **HART**, June 16, 1748	LR7	46
Barnebuss, had d. [ ], b. May 5, 1749	LR7	M
Barnibus, his d. [ ], d. May 9, 1749	LR7	36
Barnabus, s. Barnabus, b. Aug. 7, 1752	LR8	8
Barnabus, m. Mercy **PEAK**, Nov. 30, 1775	LR21	557
Barnabus, d. Sept. 18, 1776, in the 53rd y. of his age	LR21	558-9
Bathiah, d. Samuel, b. May 1, 1721	LR2	70
Charles, of New York, m. Harriet E. **COWLES**, of Farmington, Nov. 10, 1841, by Rev. Noah Porter	LR47	106
Cloe, d. Timothy, b. May 3, 1743	LR6	7
Cyrus, b. Apr. 18, 1791; d. Sept. 8, 1796	LR22	476
Daniel, s. Samuel, b. Aug. 9, 1716	LR2	70
Daniel, m. Sarah **BROWNSON**, b. of Ffarmington, Sept. 21, 1727	LR4	423
Daniel, of Ffarmington, m. Ruth **HOPKINS**, of Farmington, or Hartford, June 28, 1729	LR5	13
Delightfull, d. Solomon, b. Mar. 8, 1757	LR11	590
Dolle, d. John, Jr., b. Feb. 28, 1774	LR17	439
Dolle, d. John, Jr., d. Aug. 24, 1775, in the 2nd y. of her age	LR17	445
Ebenezer, s. Samuell, b. Jan. 9, 1710/11	LR2	98
Ebenezer, s. Samuel, b. Aug. 4, 1755	LR11	590
Elezier, s. Daniel, b. Apr. 1, 1731	LR5	7
Elijah, s. Daniel, b. Dec. 21, 1732	LR5	7
Eliza A., m. Noah H. **OSBORN**, b. of Farmington, Feb. 12, 1822, by Noah Porter, V.D.M.	LR40	571
Elizabeth, d. Thomas, (s. of Thomas), b. Aug. 8, 1706	LR1	4
Elizabeth, w. Thomas, d. Nov. 4, 1727	LR4	396
Elizabeth, m. Samuel **HART**, s. Thomas, Feb. 25, 1729/30	LR5	13

	Vol.	Page
THOMSON, THOMPSON, TOMSON (cont.)		
Elizabeth, d. Samuel, b. July 12, [probably 1743]; d. Aug. 17, 1743	LR6	7
Elizabeth, eldest, d. Ezekiel, b. Apr. 4, 1747	LR7	M
Elizabeth, see Elizabeth WOODRUFF,	LR1	3
Ellen Maria, d. Horace, b. June 14, 1836	LR47	119
Emmeline M., b. Aug. 1, 1802; d. Dec. 16, 1825	LR22	476
Emeline M., m. Selah MILLER, July 15, 1824, by Rev. Noah Porter	LR42	568
Easther, d. Dr. Thomas, b. July 13, 1710	LR2	111
Esther, m. Benjamin PORTTER, b. of Ffarmington, Nov. 25, 1726	LR2	104
Ethan, s. Solomon, b. Oct. 8, 1746	LR7	F
Ethan, s. Solomon, d. Feb. 3, 1749/50	LR7	540
[E]unice, d. John, b. Apr. 17, 1721	LR2	102
[E]unice, m. James JUDD, b. of Farmington, Jan. 29, 1740/1	LR6	304
Ezekiel, s. John, b. Sept. 5, 1713	LR2	99
Ezekiel, m. Catharine HITCHCOX, Sept. 2, 1746	LR7	35
Flora, b. Mar. 3, 1788; m. Amon HAWLEY, Oct. 27, 1814	LR47	W-Y
Hannah, d. John, Jr., b. Oct. 6, 1708	LR2	109
Hannah, twin with Sarah, d. Samuell, s. of Thomas, b. Mar. 10, 1721/2	LR2	102
Hannah, d. Samuell (s. Thomas), d. Mar. 19, 1721/2	LR2	61
Hannah, d. Samuel, b. Aug. 30, 1725	LR2	70
Hannah, d. Hezekiah, b. Apr. 14, 174[ ]	LR7	K
Hannah, d. Samuel & Hannah, b. Dec. 10, 1740	LR6	7
Hannah, d. Samuel & Sarah, d. Jan. 9, 1740/1	LR6	10
Hanah, d. Samuell, b. May 10, 1742	LR6	7
Hannah, m. Hezekiah THOMSON, Sept. 20, 1744	LR7	46
Hannah, d. Hezekiah, d. Sept. 4, 1748	LR7	36
Hannah, d. Hezekiah, b. Sept. 4, 1756	LR8	8
Harriet L., [d. Horace & Mercy], b. Nov. 29, 1832	LR22	476
Harriet S., of Farmington, m. Harry P. MATHEWS, of Southington, Jan. 30, 1832, by Rev. Irenus Atkins, of Southington	LR42	559
Henry, b. Oct. 14, 1808	LR47	W-Y
Hesther, d. Thomas, b. June 17, 1655	LR2	329
Hezekiah, m. Hannah THOMSON, Sept. 20, 1744	LR7	46
Hezekiah, s. Hezekiah, b. June 28, 1754	LR9	12
Horace, [s. Abel], b. Oct. 16, 1804; m. Mercy GRIDLEY, Dec. 10, 1828; d. Dec. [ ], 1844	LR22	476
Huldah, d. Jeames, b. Dec. 15, 1746	LR7	K
Huldah, d. James, d. Oct. 5, 1749	LR7	36
Huldah, d. James, b. June 27, 1758	LR11	590
James, s. John, b. Jan. 29, 1710/11	LR2	111
James, of Farmington, m. Mary JUDSON, of Woodbury, Apr. 12, 1739	LR6	27
James, m. Mary LEWIS, b. of Farmington, Oct. 30, 1741	LR6	304
Jeames, of Ffarmington, m. Martha SECOUR,* of Simsbury, Nov. 19, 1741 *(Perhaps "Lecour"?)	LR6	304
Jeames, s. Jeames, b. June 15, 1744	LR7	K

	Vol.	Page
THOMSON, THOMPSON, TOMSON (cont.)		
James, s .James, d. Oct. 8, 1749	LR7	36
James, s. Abell, b. Feb. 23, 1777	LR21	551
James, [s. Abel], b. Feb. 23, 1777	LR22	476
James, d. Dec. 16, 1785, ae 76	LR22	476
James, d. Dec. 16, 1785, in the 75th y. of his age	LR22	482
James, b. Feb. 5, 1822	LR47	W-Y
Jane, [d. Asahel & Ruth], b. Mar. 30, 1819	LR22	476
Johannah, m. Eli **ANDRUS**, Sept. 3, 1753	LR9	286
John, s. Thomas, m. Mary **STEELE**, Oct. 24, 1670	LR1	5
John, had s. [ ], b. Dec. 29, 1671	LR1	2
John, had s. [ ], b. June 30, 1674	LR1	2
John, had s. [ ], b. Mar. 25, 1678/9	LR1	2
John, his s. [ ]. d. May 14, 1679	LR1	2
John, Jr., m. Margaret **ORTEN**, Nov. 2, 1699	LR2	145
John, s. John, Jr., b. Apr. 5, 1704	LR2	109
John, Sr., d. Nov. 21, 1711	LR2	141
John, Sr., m. Ruth **STEEL**, b. of Ffarmington, June 18, 1724	LR2	52
John, Jr., m. Joannah **GRIDLEY**, d. Thomas, blacksmith, b. of Farmington, June 7, 1731	LR5	13
John, Sr., b. Aug. 7, 1736; m. Mary **THOMSON**, Sr., [ ]; d. Feb. 20, 1828	LR47	W-Y
John, 2nd, d. Aug. 9, 1741	LR6	10
John, Jr., m. Mary **MERRELLS**, Apr. 29, 1773	LR17	443
John, d. Sept. 18, 1775, in the 71st y. of his age	LR17	445
John, Jr., [s. John, Sr. & Mary], b. Apr. 6, 1778; d. Nov. 28, 1843	LR47	W-Y
John, b. Sept. 23, 1815	LR47	W-Y
John, m. Sarah **COWLES**, b. of Farmington, July 29, 1827, by Rev. Noah Porter	LR42	565
John, m. Ann **McCLINTOCK**, b. of Farmington, Nov. 15, 1849, by Rev. Noah Porter	LR47	126
John W., [s. Asahel & Ruth], b. Nov. 11, 1821	LR22	476
Jonathan, s. Daniell, b. May 8, 1750	LR8	8
Joseph, s. John, Jr., b. June 18, 1706	LR2	109
Joseph, s. John, d. Apr. 18, 1735	LR5	50
Joseph,'s. Hezekiah, b. June 24, 1745	LR7	F
Joseph, s. Hezekiah, d. July 6, 1747	LR7	36
Joseph, 2nd, s. Hezekiah, b. Oct. 20, 1751	LR8	8
Justus F., of Avon, m. Charlotte E. **ANDREWS**, of Farmington, Feb. 4, 1846, by Rev. Noah Porter	LR47	116
Levi, s. Barnabus, b. Sept. 13, 1755	LR8	8
Lothrop, s. Hezekiah, b. Sept. 3, 1760	LR11	590
Lott, s. Samuel, b. May 4, 1752	LR8	8
Lucy, m. Samuel **WOODFORD**, Mar. 18, 1757	LR11	576
Lucy, [d. John, Sr. & Mary], b. Aug. 13, 1783; d. Nov. 3, 1826	LR47	W-Y
Lucy, m. Fisher **GAY**, b. of Farmington, Sept. 28, 1830, by Rev. Noah Porter	LR42	560
Luther G., [s. Horace & Mercy], b. Feb. 3, 1830	LR22	476
Mable, d. Hezekiah, b. June 7, 1849	LR7	M
Marah, d. James, d. Oct. 10, 1749	LR7	36

	Vol.	Page

THOMSON, THOMPSON, TOMSON (cont.)

	Vol.	Page
Margaret, d .John, Jr., b. Oct. 11, 1700	LR2	109
Maria S., [d. Asahel & Ruth], b. Nov. 25, 1810	LR22	476
Martha, d. Samuell, s. Thomas, b. Dec. 17, 1717	LR2	84
Martha, m. Gideon NORTON, b. of Farmington, Apr. 15, 1736	LR5	692
Martha, d. James, b. Oct. 13, 1753	LR11	590
Mary, d. Thomas, bp. June 7, 1653	LR2	330
Mary, m. Thomas HART, s. Capt. [ ], Dec. 17, 1702	LR1	4
Mary, d. Dr. Thomas, b. Dec. 26, 1707	LR2	111
Mary, d. Thomas, [s. of John], d. Mar. 3, 1712/13	LR2	142
Mary, d. Samuel, b. July 26, 1714	LR2	70
Mary, m. Samuel WOODRUFF, b. of Farmington, Mar. 12, 1734/5	LR5	539
Mary, w. James, d. Apr. 24, 1740	LR6	10
Mary, d .Jeames, b. Oct. 7, 1742	LR6	7
Mary, Sr., b. Oct. 9, 1743; m. John THOMSON, Sr., [ ]; d. May 17, 1810	LR47	W-Y
Mary, d. James, b. Apr. 26, 1751	LR8	8
Mary, m. Solomon WHITMAN, Jr., Feb. 20, 1772	LR17	G
Mary, d. John, Jr., b. May 15, 1775	LR17	439
Mary, Sr., w. John, Sr., d. May 17, 1810	LR47	W-Y
Mary, of Farmington, m. John S. BANCROFT, of East Windsor, Nov. 20, 1834, by Rev. Noah Porter	LR47	88
Mary, b. Oct. 4, 1817; d. May 25, 1841	LR47	W-Y
Mercy, d. Samuel, b. Jan. 23, 1738/9	LR6	7
Nancy, d. Abel, b. Jan. 21, 1779	LR22	476
Nancy C., b. June 18, 1828	LR47	W-Y
Nathaniel, s. John, Jr., b. Feb. 20, 1701/2	LR2	109
Nathaniel, s. Solomon, b. Nov. 21, 1753	LR9	12
Nathaniel, d. June 16, 1766, ae 65	LR14	3
Permelia F., m. Edward N. PIERCE, b. of [Farmington], Oct. 8, 1850, by William Wright	LR47	128
Phebe, d. Thomas (s. of Thomas), b. June 25, 1717	LR2	81
Phebe, d. Nov. 26, 1747	LR7	36
Priscilla, d. John, Jr., b. Apr. 18, 1732	LR5	7
Priscilla, d. John, Jr., d. Jan. 18, 1733/4	LR5	50
Ransom, of Hartford, m. Mary L. ORVIS, of Farmington, Dec. 10, 1845, by Rev. Noah Porter	LR47	116
Rhoda, d. Timothy, b. Sept. 4, 1751	LR8	8
Rhoda Ann, of Southington, m. Oliver BELDEN, of Vienna, O., Dec. 30, 1830, by Rev. Irenus Atkins, of Southington	LR42	560
Richard, b. Mar. 26, 1812	LR47	W-Y
Roxana, w. Asahel, d. Nov. 24, 1807	LR22	476
Roxana, m. Truman BRACE, b. of Farmington, Nov. 15, 1825, by Rev. Noah Porter	LR42	569
Roxana S., [d. Asahel & Roxana], b. Nov. 16, 1807; d. Nov. 24, [1807]	LR22	476
Ruth, d. Samuel, b. Sept. 11, 1712	LR2	232
Ruth, m. Joseph JUDD, Jr., b. of Farmington, Dec. 25, 1734	LR5	539
Ruth, d. Barnabus, b. July 11, 1750	LR8	8

	Vol.	Page
THOMSON, THOMPSON, TOMSON (cont.)		
Ruth, m. Daniel **WOODFORD**, May 30, 1771	LR21	557
Ruth, w. Abel, d. Jan. 11, 1793	LR22	476
Samuel, of Ffarmington, m. Hannah **LATHROP**, of		
Wallingford, Feb. 17, 1706/7	LR2	125
Samuel & w. Hannah, had d. [ ], b. May 27, 1708; d.		
June 4, 1708	LR2	125
Samuel, s. Samuell, b. Apr. 13, 1709	LR2	98
Samuel, s. Thomas, m. Sarah **PORTTER**, June 20, 1716	LR2	94
Samuel, s. Samuell (s. of Thomas), b. Mar. 24, 1725/6	LR2	242
Samuell, s. Thomas, twin), d. Apr. 7, 1726	LR2	66
Samuel, Jr., m. Hannah **NORTH**, d. Thomas, May 3,		
1738	LR6	27
Samuel, Sr., d. Jan. 18, 1738/9	LR6	10
Samuel, s. Samuell, b. June 29, 1744	LR7	M
Sarah, d. Thomas, b. July 3, 1708	LR1	4
Sarah, twin with Hannah, d. Samuell, s. of Thomas, b.		
Mar. 10, 1721/2	LR2	102
Sarah, d. Samuel (s. of Thomas), d. May 1, 1725	LR2	66
Sarah, d. Daniel, b. June 28, 1728	LR5	7
Sarah, m. Timothy **HAWLEY**, b. of Farmington ,Oct. 15,		
1730	LR5	13
Sarah, d. Timothy & Anne, b. June 14, 1741	LR6	7
Sarah, m. Elijah **ANDRUS**, Aug. 4, 1761	LR11	592
Sarah, m. Roger **GRIDLEY**, June 1, 1775	LR21	557
Sarah, [d. John, Sr. & Mary], b. Aug. 31, 1788	LR47	W-Y
Sarah J., [d. Horace & Mercy], b. June 16, 1831	LR22	476
Seth, s. James, b. Aug. 2, 1755	LR11	590
Seth, d. May 11, 1776, in the 21st y. of his age	LR21	558-9
Seth, s. Abell, b. Jan. 22, 1781	LR22	476
Seth, d. Mar. 4, 1811	LR22	476
Seth W., [s. Asahel & Ruth], b. Apr. 10, 1813; d. Jan. 28,		
1814	LR22	476
Shubert, of Avon, m. Eunice H. **PECK**, of Farmington,		
Feb. 12, 1846, by Rev. Noah Porter	LR47	116
Solomon, s. John, b. Apr. 11, 1716	LR2	96
Solomon, m. Susannah **GRIDLEY**, Dec. 26, 1745	LR7	35
Solomon & Susannah, had s. [ ], b. June 19, 1761; d.		
same day	LR11	574
Stephen, s. Samuell (s. of Thomas), b. Mar. 24, 1725/6	LR2	242
Stephen, s. Sam[ue]ll, d. Mar. 13, 1736/7	LR6	10
Susanah, d. Samuel, [b.] May 26, 1749	LR7	F
Susanah, d. Samuell, d. Sept. 3, 1751	LR8	11
Susannah, d. Solomon, b. Jan. 10, 1752	LR8	8
Susannah, w. Solomon, d. June 19, 1761	LR11	574
Sybel, 2nd w. Abel, d. May 2, 1822	LR22	476
Thaddeus L., m. Mehetable **SANFORD**, b. of		
Farmington, Oct. 21, 1829, by Rev. Harry Bushnell	LR42	562
Theoditca, d. Solomon, b. Dec. 9, 1759	LR11	590
Theodosia, m. Thomas **LEE**, June 7, 1780, by [ ]	LR47	99
Thomas, d. Apr. 25, 1655	LR2	320
Thomas, s. Thomas, b. Abigail **WOODRUFF**, Nov. 16,		
1705	LR1	4

	Vol.	Page
THOMSON, THOMPSON, TOMSON (cont.)		
Thomas, Sr., d. Jan. 3, 1706/7	LR1	3
Thomas, Dr., of Ffarmington, m. Elizabeth **COWLES**, of		
Ffarmington, Jan. 15, 1706/7	LR2	145
Thomas, s. Samuel, b. Oct. 6, 1718	LR2	70
Thomas, s. Thomas, 2nd, b. July 15, 1720	LR2	102
Thomas, s. Thomas, m. Elizabeth **JUDD**, May 25, 1721	LR2	101
Thomas, d. Mar. 29, 1735	LR5	50
Thomas, [s. of] Thomas, d. Dec. 19, 1745	LR7	36
Thomas, s. Timothy, b. May 15, 1749	LR7	M
Thomas, Dr., d. July 17, 1750	LR7	540
Timothy, s. Thomas, s. Thomas, b. Oct. 31, 1712	LR2	109
Timothy, m. Anne **DEMING**, b. of Farmington, Feb. 1,		
1738/9	LR6	27
Timothy, had d. [ ], b. Dec. 2, 1744	LR7	M
Tryphena, d. Timothy, b. Apr. 13, 1756	LR9	12
William L., of Hartford, m. Jane T. **LEWIS**, of		
Farmington, Jan. 8, 1850, by Rev. Noah Porter	LR47	126
THORN, Olive, m. Thomas **CLARK**, Jan. 6, 1824, by Rev.		
Rufus Hawley	LR42	568
THORP, Asahel, s. Samuell, Jr., b. Aug. 7, 1773	LR17	439
Caroline, d. Samuell, Jr., b. Jan. 23, 1775	LR17	439
Elnathan, s. Lines, b. May 20, 1768	LR17	439
Lois, m. Elnathan **JUDD**, Mar. 2, 1758	LR11	576
Lucy, d. Lines, b. July 15, 1773	LR17	439
Mary, d. Lines, b. Aug. 3, 1771	LR17	439
Mary, of Southington, m. Amzi Francis **ROOT**, of		
Farmington, Apr. 10, 1842, by Rev. Aaron S. Hill	LR47	107
Mary E., m. Martin H. **BLINN**, Sept. 24, [1850], by Rev.		
Charles Kelsey	LR47	127
Miles, of Bristol, m. Rhoda **LEWIS**, of Farmington, Mar.		
31, 1828, by Rev. Noah Porter	LR42	564
Molly, d. Samuel, b. Oct. 12, 1777	LR21	551
Nabby, d. Lines, b. May 13, 1778	LR21	551
Tripheny, d. Lines, b. Mar. 22, 1776	LR17	439
TILLOTSON, Charlotte, m. Edward **WOODFORD**, b. of		
Farmington, Nov. 30, 1826, by Rev. Harry Bushnell	LR42	567
Daniel, m. Susan **PORTER**, b. of Farmington, June 8,		
1835, by Noah Porter	LR47	89
Elisha, s. Elisha, b. Feb. 28, 1752	LR14	11
Joseph, m. Theodosey **YOUNGS**, Feb. 15, 1759	LR11	576
Oliver, m. Julia **DAY**, b. of Ffarmington, Jan. 12, 1825,		
by Rev. Harry Bushnell	LR42	568
Ruth, m. Elijah T. **MILLER**, b. of Farmington, Sept. 16,		
1824, by Rev. Harry Bushnell	LR42	568
Sarah G., of Farmington, m. Henry W. **EVERS**, of		
Manlius, N.Y., Oct. 5, 1824, by Rev. Noah Porter	LR42	568
Seth, m. Frances **WHITMAN**, b. of Farmington, Jan. 28,		
1823, by Noah Porter, V.D.M.	LR40	572
TINKER, Maria S., of Farmington, m. Horatio N.		
BRINSMADE, of Hartford, Sept. 29, 1825, by Rev.		
Noah Porter	LR42	569

	Vol.	Page
TINKHAM, Joseph, of Farmington, m. Mrs. Nancy WESTCOTT, of Weathersfield, Mar. 4, 1834, by Rev. L. C. Cheney	LR42	D
TODD, Maria, of Plymouth, m. Stephen L. LOVELAND, of Farmington, Sept. 5, 1847, by William Wright	LR47	121
Sarah A., of Mereden, m. Lucius BURNHAM, of New Hartford, Oct. 10, 1852, at the house of her father, in Plainville, by Rev. P. G. Wightman, of Plainville	LR47	131
TOLLES, Harry, m. Harriet M. HITCHCOCK, b. of Southington, Aug. 13, 1844, by Rev. William Wright	LR47	113
TOMPKINS, Charles F., of Bristol, m. Pauline LEE, of Farmington, Nov. 9, 1845, by Rev. S. H. Clark	LR47	115
Enos, of New York, m. Rebecca NEWELL, of Farmington, June 6, 1824, by Rev. Harry Bushnell	LR42	568
TRASK, Jared H., of Camden, N.Y., m. Francis HILLS, of Farmington, Sept. 22, 1829, by Rev. Noah Porter	LR42	562
TREADWELL, TREDWELL, TREADWEL, Dolle, 1st d. John, b. Nov. 28, 1771	LR21	551
Dolle, 1st d. John, d. Mar. 18, 1774, in the 3rd y. of her age	LR21	558-9
Dolle, 2nd d. John, b. Mar. 22, 1774	LR21	551
Ephraim, m. Marry PORTTER, Apr. 30, 1741	LR6	304
Ephraim, s. Ephraim, b. Mar. 4, 1748	LR7	K
Ephraim, had s. [ ], b. [ ] 9, 1750	LR7	F
Ephraim, s. Ephraim, d. Aug. 19, 1751	LR8	11
Ephraim, 2nd, s. Capt. Ephraim, b. Nov. 24, 1753	LR8	8
Eunice, 3rd d. John, b. July 13, 1776	LR21	551
John, s. Ephraim, b. Oct. 11, [1744]; d. [Oct.] 30, [1744]	LR7	F
John, s. Ephraim, b. Nov. 23, 1745	LR7	F
John, m. Dorothy POMROY, of Northampton, Nov. 20, 1770	LR21	557
John, s. John, b. Oct. 19, 1778	LR21	551
Joseph, s. Ephraim, d. July 24, 1751	LR8	11
Luce, d. Ephraim, b. Sept. 3, 1742	LR6	7
Lucy, m. Timothy WOODRUFF, Apr. 21, 1761	LR11	591
Mary, d. Ephraim, b. July 17, 1752	LR8	8
Mary, d. Ephraim, d. Dec. 6, 1752	LR8	11
TREAT, TREET, Hannah, wid. sometime of Weathersfield, m. John HART, s. Stephen, of Ffarmington, Apr. 12, 1694	LR2	123
Isaac Norton, d. Jan. 10, 1763, in the 84th y. of his age	LR14	3
TRYON, Ruth, m. William CHURCHILL, Sept. 25, 1760	lr17	442
TUBBS, Bulah, m. John CLARK, 3rd, Sept. 23, 1773	LR17	442
Chloe Eliza, [d. Sylvanus], b. July 3, 1803	LR32	566
Elias, [s. Sylvanus], b. May 27, 1796	LR32	566
Eliza C., of Farmington, m. Lemuel LEWIS, of Wolcott, Nov. 24, 1827, by Rev. Noah Porter	LR42	565
Enos Clark, [s. Sylvanus], b. Aug. 1, 1800	LR32	566
Silvester, [s. Sylvanus], b. Mar. 15, 1794	LR32	566
Ursula, [child of Sylvanus], b. Jan. 30, 1798	LR32	566
Ursula, of Farmington, m. Joseph HUBBELL, of Wolcott, Vt., Oct. 3, 1826, by Stephen Crosby	LR42	567

	Vol.	Page
TUCKER, Edwin, m. Maria **DARROW**, b. of Farmington,		
May 1, 1839, by Rev. Noah Porter	LR47	99
TURREL, Jeremiah, of Winchester, m. Mary **TURREL**, of		
New Haven, Nov. 1, 1841, by Rev. Aaron S. Hill	LR47	105
Mary, of New Haven, m. Jeremiah **TURREL**, of		
Winchester, Nov. 1, 1841, by Rev. Aaron S. Hill	LR47	105
TUSOO, Peter, negro, d. Mar. 17, 1767	LR14	3
TUTTLE, TUTTEL, TUTTELL, Amos, s. Simon, b. Sept.		
2, 1758	LR11	590
Anne, d. Simon, b. Apr. 24, 1760	LR11	590
Christian, d. Simon, b. Apr. last day, 1751	LR8	8
Daniel, s. Simeon (?), b. Aug. 10, 1747	LR7	K
Easther, d. Simeon, b. Nov. 5, 1764	LR15	K
Eunis, d. Gershom, b. Apr. 23, 1743	LR7	K
Gershom, s. Gershom, b. Aug. 22, 1738	LR6	7
Hanah, d. Gershom, b. Mar. 25, 1745	LR7	K
Hannah, m. Asa **JOHNSON**, May 12, 1763	LR11	594
Hannah, d. Oliver, b. Feb. 18, 1765	LR11	590
Huldah, d. Gershom, b. June 21, 1749	LR7	F
Joel, s. Simeon, b. May 27, 1749	LR7	K
Julia, d. Oliver, b. Mar. 23, 1767	LR15	K
Lois, d. Oliver, b. Jan. 6, 1762	LR11	590
Lola, d. Simeon, b. Apr. 18, 1769	LR15	K
Oliver, s. Gershom, b. Dec. 28, 1739	LR6	7
Oliver, s. Oliver, b. Feb. 10, 1769	LR15	K
Salina B., m. William P. **BRASON**, b. of Brimfield,		
Mass., Apr. 10, 1828, by Rev. Noah Porter	LR42	564
Samuel, s. Gershom, b. Feb. 15, 1747	LR7	K
Sarah, wid. Stephen, d. July 20, 1736	LR5	49
Solomon, s. Gershom, Jr., b. Nov. 10, 1760	LR11	590
Solomon, s. Gershom, b. Mar. 31, 1762	LR11	590
Stephen, m. Sarah **STANLEY**, Jr., b. of Farmington, Jan.		
23, 1734/5	LR5	545
Stephen, d. June 25, 1735	LR5	50
Stephen, s. Stephen, b. Oct. 14, 1735	LR5	307
Thankfull, d. Simon, b. Mar. 20, 1753	LR8	8
Theoderit, s. Gershom, b. Nov. 27, 1763	LR11	590
Ziba, s. Simeon, b. Mar. 29, 1767	LR15	K
TWIST, Joseph, m. Mahetabel **BURR**, Sept. 3, 1751	LR8	10
Susannah, d. Joseph, b. Dec. 26, 1752	LR8	8
TYLER, Ephraim, s. Benjamin, b. Apr. 11, 1760	LR11	590
Patience, d. Benjamin, b. May 20, 1762	LR11	590
UPSON, [see also **UPTON**], Adah, d. Asa, b. June 14, 1770	LR15	N
Albert S., of Waterbury, m Eliza **PORTER**, of		
Farmington, Oct. 12, 1851, by Rev. Noah Porter	LR47	130
Amasa, s. Ezekiel, b. July 26, 1775	LR17	440
Amos, m. Sarah [ ], Feb. 27, 1766	LR15	N
Amos, s. Amos, b. Mar. 14, 1771	LR17	440
Asa, m. Mary **NEWELL**, Jan. 17, 1750/1	LR7	35
Ashbel, s. Timothy, b. May 19, 1764	LR11	590
Charles, m. Amanda **HUMPHREY**, b. of Burlington,		
Mar. 22, 1832, by Rev. Noah Porter	LR42	559
Delight, d. Timothy, b. Mar. 11, 1769	LR11	590

	Vol.	Page
UPSON (cont.)		
Elizabeth, d. July 20, 1655	LR2	320
Ezekiel, m. Mary **BROWNSON**, Sept. 17, 1772	LR17	442
Freelove, d. Timothy, b. Mar. 22, 1759	LR11	590
George, s. Asa, b. Feb. 4, 1760	LR11	590
Job, s. Asa, b. June 5, 1764	LR11	590
Job, s. Asa, d. July 11, 1764	LR11	593
John, Jr., m. Lois **ATWATER**, Dec. 14, 1768	LR15	N
Joseph, s. Ezekiel, b. Aug. 17, 1773	LR17	440
Levi, s. Amos, b. Jan. 2, 1777	LR21	552
Lucia, d. Asa, b. Sept. 14, 1767	LR15	N
Lucy, d. Amos, b. Nov. 19, 1766	LR15	N
Mark, s. Amos, b. Aug. 2, 1772	LR17	440
Martin, s. Timothy, b. Mar. 29, 1774	LR17	440
Mary, m. Josiah **NEWEL**, Feb. 18, 1745/6	LR7	35
Mary, d. Asa, b. Jan. 28, 1762	LR11	590
Moses H., Capt. of Burlington, m. Delight **BEECHER**, of		
Wolcott, Jan. 14, 1830, by Erastus Scranton, V.D.M.	LR42	561
Samuel,* m. Ruth **COWLES**, Apr. 5, 1759 *(Written		
"Samuel UPTON")	LR11	575
Sarah, d. Timothy, b. June 20, 1761	LR11	590
Sarah, d. Amos, b. Mar. 18, 1769	LR15	N
Sarah, d. Amos, d. Sept. 13, 1773	LR17	445
Saul, s. Asa, b. Jan. 24, 1758	LR11	590
Selah, s. Timothy, b. May 20, 1776	LR21	552
Seth, s. Timothy, b. June 21, 1771	LR17	440
Shebell, s. Amos, b. Nov. 15, 1767	LR15	N
Sibbell, d. Amos, d. Aug. 20, 1773	LR17	445
Silva, d. Asa, b. Aug. 10, 1765	LR15	N
Thomas, d. July 19, 1655	LR2	320
Timothy, s. Timothy, b. Sept. 21, 1766	LR15	J
Triphena, d. Timothy, b. Sept. 1, 1756	LR11	590
Truman, s. John, Jr., b. Oct. 6, 1769	LR15	N
UPTON, [see also **UPSON**], Daniel, m. Hannah **JUDD**, [ ],		
1751	LR9	286
Elizabeth, d. Daniel, b. Mar. 3, 1752	LR9	12
Jefer, s. Daniel, b. Sept. 10, 1754	LR9	12
Martha, m. William **BARNES**, Jan. [ ], 1757	LR11	576
Rachel, d Asa, b. Dec. 26, 1753	LR8	9
Thomas, m. Sarah **NORTON**, Apr. 20, 1753	LR11	576
Timothy, m. Delight **NORTON**, Mar. 25, 1755	LR9	286
Treman, s. Asa, b. Dec. 20, 1751	LR8	9
VENTRES, VENTERES, VENTRUS, John, s. William, b.		
Dec. 8, 1657	LR2	328
Mare, d. William, b. Oct. 20, 1654	LR2	329
Moses, Jr., d. Sept. 20, 1721	LR2	61
William, s. William, b. Jan. 28, 1655	LR2	328
VIBBERTS, George N., of East Hartford, m. Harriet		
DAILEY, of Farmington, July 26, 1840, by Rev.		
Aaron S. Hill	LR47	103
VIETS, J. Jay, of East Granby, m. Jane **WADSWORTH**, of		
Farmington, May 6, 1851, by Rev. G. M. Porter	LR47	128

	Vol.	Page
WADSWORTH, WADSWORT (cont.)		
Hezekiah, s. Nathaniell, b. Sept. 16, 1722	LR4	375
Hezekiah, d. Oct. 20, 1740	LR7	36
Hezekiah, m. Lois **JUDD**, Dec. 13, 1744	LR7	35
James, s. Samuel, Jr., b. Dec. 12, 1729	LR5	8
James, m. Abigail **LEWIS**, Nov. 2, 1749	LR7	35
Jane, of Farmington, m. J. Jay **VIETS**, of East Granby,		
May 6, 1851, by Rev. G. M. Porter	LR47	128
John, s. John, b. Apr. 14, 1662	LR1	2
John, m. Elizabeth **STANLEY**, Aug. 20, 1696	LR1	5
John, s. John, b. Oct. 9, 1702	LR1	2
John, Sergt., m. Mary **GRIDLEY**, b. of Ffarmington,		
Sept. 2, 1714	LR2	93
John, m. [E]unice **PORTTER**, b. of Farmington ,May 11,		
1734	LR5	545
John, d. Nov. 9, 1760	LR11	574
Lucy, d. James, b. June 28, 1772	LR17	440
Luke, s. James, b. Aug. 23, 1754	LR8	9
Luke, s. James, d. Apr. 4, 1758	LR11	577
Luke, s. James, b. Oct. 21, 1759	LR11	591
Lydia, d. John, b. Oct. 6, 1706	LR1	3
Lydia, d. John, b. May 28, 1736	LR6	7
Manna, s. Asahel, b. Oct. 19, 1769	LR15	N
Mariann, w. Thomas, d. July 4, 1759	LR11	577
Mary, d. John, b. Nov. 13, 1665	LR1	2
Mary, d. Nathaniell, b. Apr. 14, 1720	LR4	375
Mary, d. Capt. William, d. Apr. 20, 1722	LR2	61
Mary, w. Timothy, d. Feb. 25, 1755	LR11	577
Mary, d. Timothy, b. July 31, 1763	LR11	591
Mary, of Farmington, m. Aaron **ROBERTS**, of Berlin,		
May 20, 1829, by Rev. Noah Porter	LR42	562
Mercy, d. John & Elizabeth, b. Sept. 11, 1713	LR2	99
Mercy, d. Sergt. John, d. June 29, 1715	LR2	62
Nathaniell, of Ffarmington, m. Dorothy **BALL**, of New		
Haven, Mar. 21, 1705	LR2	123
Nathaniell, s. Nathaniell, b. Sept. 6, 1718	LR4	374
Nathaniel, Jr., m. Hannah **GRIDLEY**, June 12, 1746	LR7	46
Nathaniel, m. Esther **COWLES**, May 16, 1754	LR9	286
Nathaniell, Ens., d. Dec. 20, 1761	LR11	574
Nathaniel, d. Nov. 7, 1789, in the 72nd y. of his age	LR22	482
Oraney, d. James, b. July 11, 1766	LR14	11
Rebeckah, w. Lieut. Samuel, d. Sept. 28, 1756	LR8	12
Rhoda, d. Timothy & Mary, b. Sept. 22, 1755	LR11	591
Rhoda, m. [ ]el **STANLEY**, Aug. 6, 1771	LR17	G
Romao, s. William, Jr., b. Apr. 2, 1769	LR15	N
Ruth, d. John, b. Apr. 14, 1711	LR2	97
Ruth, m. Elisha **LEWIS**, b. of Farmington, Apr. 18, 1739	LR6	27
Ruth, d. John, b. Nov. 27, 1750	LR8	9
Ruth, Mrs., m. Solomon **WHITMAN**, July 30, 1778	LR22	480
Samuel, s. John, b. Jan. 13, 1659	LR1	2
Samuel, of Ffarmington, m. Hannah **JUDSON**, of		
Woodbury, June 12, 1689	LR2	125
Samuel, s. Samuell, b. June 23, 1698	LR2	97

	Vol.	Page
WADSWORTH, WADSWORT (cont.)		
Samuel, Jr., of Farmington, m. Susannah **FFENN**, of		
Milford, Aug. 15, 1728	LR4	423
Samuel, Lieut., d. May 29, 1731	LR5	50
Samuel, s. Samuel, b. Sept. 20, 1732	LR5	8
Samuel, m. Rebeckah **PORTTER**, b. of Farmington, July		
19, 1738	LR5	300
Samuel, Lieut., d. Oct. 3, 1745	LR8	12
Sarah, d. John, b. Nov. 1, 1657	LR1	2
Sarah, d. John, b. July 3, 1697	LR1	2
Sarah, m. Samuel **COWLES**, Jr., b. of Farmington, Nov.		
28, 1716	LR2	94
Sarah, d. Nathaniell, b. Apr. 26, 1716/17	LR4	374
Sarah, m. Samuel **GRIDLEY**, Feb. 14, 1744/5	LR7	35
Susannah, w. Samuel, 2nd, d. Dec. 5, 1732	LR5	50
Susana, d. James, b. May 13, 1764	LR11	591
Susannah, d. James, d. Jan. 12, 1768 ae 3 y. [1] month	LR14	3
Susanna, d. James, b. June 11, 1768	LR15	K
Tenn, s. James, b. Feb. 11, 1752	LR8	9
Theada, s. Timothy, b. Oct. 7, 1753	LR8	9
Thomas, m. Meriam **BECKLEY**, b. of Farmington, Dec.		
5, 1745	LR7	35
Thomas, d. Feb. 21, 1771, in the 92nd y. of his age	LR17	444
Timothy, s. Ens. Nathaniell, b. Nov. 27, 1727	LR5	8
Timothy, m. Mary **COWLES**, Sept. 20, 1750	LR7	46
Timothy, m. Hopey **KILBORN**, Nov. 16, 1753	LR11	576
William, m. Abigell **LEWIS**, Dec. 10, 1696	LR1	5
William, s. William, b. Dec. 7, 1697	LR1	2
William, s. William, d. July 21, 1699	LR1	3
William, his d. [ ], b. [ ] 4, 1699/1700	LR1	2
William, s. Will[iam], d. July 28, 1705	LR1	2
William, m. Sarah **BUNSE**, Jan. 13, 1708/9	LR2	145
William, s. William, b. Dec. 2, 1709	LR2	109
William, Jr., m. Ruth **HART**, b. of Farmington, May 15,		
1740	LR6	27
William, s. Capt. William, b. Feb. 16, 1742	LR8	9
William, Capt., d. Oct. 26, 1751	LR8	11
William, d. Aug. 7, 1769, in the 60th y. of his age	LR17	444
WALE, Caroline, d. Eleazer, b. Oct. 26, 1758	LR11	591
WALLACE, WALLIS, Andrew L., of Berlin, m. Abigail H.		
G. **DOOLITTLE**, of Farmington, Nov. 30, 1837, at		
the house of Amos Doolittle, by Rev. J. Goodwin	LR47	96
Mary, wid., m. Simon **NEWEL**, b. of Farmington, May 3,		
1733	LR5	300
WARD, Augustus, of Berlin, m. Susan **COWLES**, of		
Farmington, May 19, 1840, by Rev. Noah Porter	LR47	102
WARNER, Abigail, m. Jedediah **BARNES**, b. of Farmington,		
Dec. 3, 1730	LR5	13
Benjamin, s. Demas, b. Mar. 3, 1774	LR17	440
Charles A., m. Matilda **CLARK**, b. of Berlin, Dec. 12,		
1836, by Rev. Noah Porter	LR47	95
Cloe, d. Thomas (s. of Thomas), b. Aug. 12, 1738	LR6	7
Cloe, d. Demas, b. Apr. 16, 1767	LR17	440

	Vol.	Page

WARNER (cont.)

Daniel, s. Thomas & Martha, b. June 1, 1716	LR2	87
Daniel, m. Rachel **SMITH**, b. of Farmington, July 25, 1738	LR6	27
Demas, s. Thomas, b. Jan. 13, 1745/6	LR7	E
Demas, m. Rhoda [ ], Apr. 15, 1767	LR17	G
Elizabeth, sometime of Middletown, m. Joseph **ROOT**, of Farmington, Sept. 17, 1691	LR2	125
Ezra, s. Thomas & Martha, b. July 27, 1712	LR2	87
Ezra, of Farmington, m. Elizabeth **PRATT**, of Saybrook, May 4, 1738	LR6	27
Hannah, d. Thomas (s. Daniel), b. Dec. 25, 1727	LR4	395
Harriet J., of Farmington ,m. John H. **SUTLIFF**, of Plymouth, Dec. 16, 1832, by Rev. Noah Porter	LR42	558
Joel, s. Demas. b. Apr. 25, 1772	LR17	440
John, d. Mar. 1, 1706/7	LR1	2
Lydia, of Farmington, m. W[illia]m B. **COFFIN**, of Easton, N.Y., July 12, [1833], by Rev. Noah Porter	LR42	A
Mara, d. Thomas, Jr., of Southington, b. Sept. 2, 1748	LR7	F
Martha, twin with Thomas, d. Thomas & Martha, b. June 7, 1722	LR2	87
Mary, m. John **NORTH**, s. Samuell, May 16, 1692	LR2	145
Obadiah, s. Ephraim, b. Jan. 5, 17[ ]	LR6	7
Phebe, d. Daniel, b. Dec. 11, 1738	LR6	7
Phebe, d. Thomas, Jr., of Southington, b. June 25, 1753	LR8	9
Rebeckah, d. Thomas, b. [ ]	LR7	F
Rhodah, d. Demas, b. Jan. 19, 1776	LR21	563
Sarah, d. Thomas (s. Thomas), b. Dec. 30, 1735/6	LR6	7
Susanah, m. Nathan **COGSWEL**, Nov. 24, 1737	LR6	27
Thomas, s. Daniel, m. Martha **SCOTT**, of Farmington, June 5, 1711	LR2	60
Thomas, twin with Martha, s. Thomas & Martha, b. June 7, 1722	LR2	87
Thomas, s. Thomas, m. Abigail **BARNES**, b. of Farmington, Jan. 2, 1728/9	LR5	545
Thomas, s. Demas, b. Sept. 23, 1770	LR17	440
Winthrop, m. Harriet Louisa **ALLEN**, b. of Farmington, Jan. 23, 1839, by Rev. S. H. Clark	LR47	99
Zebulon, s. Ezra, b. June 15, 1739	LR6	7
Zubah, d. Demas, b. Oct. 4, 1778	LR21	553

WARREN, WARRIN, WARIEN, Abigail S., m. Allan **WEBSTER**, b. of Farmington, Oct. 4, 1835, by Rev. Noah Porter

Rev. Noah Porter	LR47	90
Abraham, d. Mar. 19, 1756	LR8	12
Abraham, d. Mar. 19, 1756	LR11	577
Edward E., m. Sarah Ann **STILLMAN**, b. of Farmington, Dec. 7, 1842, by Noah Porter, V.D.M.	LR47	109
Eliza A., of Farmington, m. Rollin **SMITH**, of West Hartford, Nov. 25, 1841, by Rev. Aaron S. Hill	LR47	106
Experience, m. Jonathan **GRISWOLD**, Oct. 6, 1748	LR7	46
Experience, m. Jonathan **GRISWOLD**, Oct. 6, 1748	LR9	286
Franklin, m. Mary Jane **LEE**, b. of Farmington, Oct. 6 [probably 1852], by Rev. Cephas Brainerd	LR47	131

	Vol.	Page
WARREN, WARRIN, WARIEN (cont.)		
George C., m. Amelia **FULLER**, Aug. 27, 1834, by Rev.		
Noah Porter	LR42	E
Hannah, of Glastenbury, m. Josiah **LEE**, of Farmington,		
Nov. 3, 1737	LR6	27
Harriet N., of Farmington, m. Hubert F. **WIGHTMAN**,		
of Bristol, Mar. 17, 1852, by Rev. Noah Porter	LR47	130
Jane A., of Farmington, m. Joseph P. **SKINNER**, of		
Springfield, Mass., Aug. 4, 1850, by Rev. Noah		
Porter	LR47	129
Lucy, m. Lyman **HURLBUT**, b. of Farmington, May 5,		
1828, by Noadiah Woodruff, J.P.	LR42	564
Mary, d. Elisah, b. Feb. 28, 1761	LR11	591
Samuel, m. Phila **GLADDING**, Nov. [ ], 1847, by		
Egbert Cowles, J.P.	LR47	128
William, of New Hartford, m. Polly **WAY**, of		
Farmington, Feb. 16, 1831, by Rev. Noah Porter	LR42	560
William, m. Lucina **WILLIAMS**, June [ ], 1849, by		
Egbert Cowles, J.P.	LR47	128
WASHBURN, Esther M., of Hartford, m. Albert **GALPIN**, of		
Weathersfield, July 4, 1843, by Rev. Horace		
Bushnell, of Hartford	LR47	110
WATEROUS, George W., of Hartford, m. Hannah M.		
ANDRUS, of Farmington, Dec. 25, 1850, by Rev.		
Charles Kelsey	LR47	128
WATERS, WARTERS, Levicy, of Hartford, m. Joseph		
HOLLISTER, of Farmington, July 3, 1820, by		
Noah Porter, V.D.M.	LR40	570
Lois, d. Abraham, b. Oct. 15, 1764	LR15	K
Loisa, m. Ozias **LANDON**, Feb. 18, 1824, by Rev. Noah		
Porter	LR42	568
Lusina, d. Abraham, b. Oct. 30, 1766	LR15	K
WATSON, Heman, m. Mary **HAWLEY**, Feb. 14, 1770	LR17	G
Mary, d. Heman, b. Apr. 2, 1771	LR17	440
Mary, d. Heman, d. Apr. 15, 1771	LR17	444
WAY, Polly, of Farmington, m. William **WARREN**, of New		
Hartford, Feb. 16, 1831, by Rev. Noah Porter	LR42	560
WEBSTER, Aaron, s. Aaron, b. Feb. 2, 1753	LR14	11
Abial, s. Aaron, b. Feb. 6, 1750	LR14	11
Abigail, d. Capt. John, b. Sept. 23, 1731	LR5	8
Abigail, m. John **DUTTON**, Mar. 14, 1754	LR9	286
Allan, m. Abigail S. **WARREN**, b. of Farmington, Oct. 4,		
1835, by Rev. Noah Porter	LR47	90
Anne, d. Asee, b. May 28, 1771	LR21	553
Anne, d. Robert, b. Oct. 8, 1775	LR21	553
Asa, s. Asa, b. Feb. 20, 1763	LR11	591
Cyrus, s. Asee, b. Mar. 24, 1765	LR21	553
Elisha, s. Aaron, b. Nov. 22, 1758	LR14	11
Elizabeth, m. Joseph **HAWLEY**, Jan. 21, 1781	LR22	480
Eunice, Mrs., m. Lucien W. **HILLS**, b. of Farmington,		
May 1, 1842, by Rev. Aaron S. Hill	LR47	107
Hannah, d. Aaron, b. Oct. 20, 1748	LR14	11
Hannah, m. Jared **HARRISON**, Dec. 27, 1769	LR15	N

	Vol.	Page
WEBSTER (cont.)		
Hannah Lewis, d. John, b. May 20, 1762	LR14	11
Henry W., m. Lydia Ann **PORTER**, b. of Watertown,		
Jan. 29, 1832, by Rev. Noah Porter	LR42	559
Jerusha, d. Aaron, b. Dec. 14, 1756	LR14	11
Jerusha, m. Lieut. Daniel **BARNS**, Jan. 13, 1779	LR22	480
John, m. Rhoda **LEWIS**, Nov. 3, 1755	LR9	286
John, s. Asee, b. Aug. 14, 1769	LR21	553
Joshua, m. Abigall **BOOTH**, Mar. 24, 1773	LR17	443
Lee, s. Capt. John & Abiah, b. Apr. 1, 1734	LR5	8
Lydia 2nd, d. Aaron, b. Oct. 7, 1746	LR14	11
Mathew, his w. [ ], d. July 16, 1655	LR2	320
Mercy, m. Abell **CARTER**, Apr. 17, 1777	LR22	480
Philogus, s. John, b. Apr. 24, 1759	LR14	11
Rhoda, d. John, b. Oct. 3, 1769	LR14	11
Robert, s. Capt. John, b. Apr. 8, 1736	LR6	7
Robert, s. Aaron, b. Dec. 14, 1752	LR14	11
Robert, m. Jerusha **ATKINS**, Feb. 23, 1775	LR21	557
Ruth B., of Harwinton, m. Leonard **BEECHER**, June 6,		
1841, by Rev. Noah Porter	LR47	105
Sarah, d. Asee, b. May 6, 1767	LR21	553
Sarah, d. Aaron, b. Aug. 7, 1767	LR17	440
Seth, s. Asee, b. Feb. 6, 1774	LR21	553
Susannah, m. Ebenezer **SCOTT**, Nov. 1, 1746	LR8	10
Theodosia, s. John, b. Aug. 19, 1756	LR14	11
Usula, d. John, b. Mar. 17, 1765	LR14	11
Vashti, d. John, b. Dec. 19, 1767	LR14	11
Wells, of Windsor, m. Sarah J. **GRIMES**, of Simsbury,		
Oct. 12, 1835, by Rev. Noah Porter	LR47	90
WELCH, Laura, of Canton, m. Edwin C. **VINING**, of		
Simsbury, Sept. 16, 1829, by Smith Dayton, Elder	LR42	562
Mary, m. Samuel **MARSHALL**, Dec. 22, 1848, by Rev.		
Henry J. Fox	LR47	124
WELLES, WEELS, WELLS, WILLS, Anna, w. Richard, d.		
July about 10, 1659	LR2	319
Elizabeth, of Berlin, m. Levi **SMITH**, of Burlington, Oct.		
26, 1825, by Rev. Noah Porter	LR42	569
Jemimah, alias **SMITH**, d. Dec. [ ], 1734	LR6	305
John, m. Jemimah **SMITH**, June 18, 1731	LR6	304
John, s. John, b. Dec. [ ], 1734	LR6	7
John, s. John, d. Dec. [ ], 1734	LR6	305
John, m. Sarah **GAILER**, Dec. [ ], 1735	LR6	304
John, m. Hannah **COKER**,* July 20, 1738 *(Should be		
"**BAKER**")	LR6	304
John, s. John, b. Aug. 23, 1740	LR6	7
Joseph, Dr., m. Mary **HART**, Jan. 17, 1754	LR9	286
Joseph, s. Dr. Joseph & Mary, b. Nov. 12, 1754	LR9	12
Lendae, d. John, b. Sept. 6, 1739	LR6	7
Maria, m. Welcome A. **PRATT**, Aug. 23, 1825, at the		
house of wid. Wells, of Northington Soc., by Luther		
Higley, J.P.	LR42	569
Mary, d. Dr. Joseph & Mary, b. July 16, 1759	LR11	591
Mary m. [ ]lian **SMITH**, July 11, 1771	LR17	G

	Vol.	Page
WELLES, WEELS, WELLS, WILLS (cont.)		
Rhoda, d. Dr. Joseph, b. Apr. 17, 1764	LR11	590
Richard, joined church, Sept. 17, 1659	LR2	327
Rosalender, d. John, b. June 24, 1732	LR6	7
Rosalenda, d. John, d. Sept. 19, 1738	LR6	305
Russell, of Farmington, m. Roxy Emeline **MARSHALL**, of Windsor, Nov. 17, 1822, by Amasa Woodford, J.P.	LR40	572
Sarah, d. John, b. Oct. 31, 1735	LR6	7
Sarah, w. John, d. Dec. 2, 1735	LR6	305
Silvester, s. Dr. Joseph & Mary, b. May 20, 1762	LR11	591
Susanah, d. John, b. May 3, 1742	LR6	7
WELTON, WELLTON, Arnold, s. Solomon, b. Oct. 18, 1780	LR21	553
Benjamin, m. Elizabeth **AUSTIN**, Feb. 12, 1776	LR17	443
Billey, s. Solomon, b. Oct. 17, 1774	LR21	553
Caleb Abanathar, s. Solomon, b. Aug. 6, 1788	LR29	578
Carlos, of Bristol, m. Maria **PECK**, of Farmington, Nov. 18, 1846, by Rev. William Watson, of Plymouth	LR47	119
George, m. Sary **HOSINGTON**, Nov. 23, 1738, by [ ]	LR6	305
Hannery, s. Solomon, b. Sept. 27, 1772	LR17	440
Loraney, d. Solomon, b. Nov. 7, 1784	LR22	478
Sarah, d. George, b. June (?)28, 1739	LR6	7
Sarah, m. Orlando **PLUMB**, b. of Wolcott, July 5, 1847, by William Wright	LR47	119
Silence, d. George, b. Nov. 5, 1741	LR6	7
Solomon, m. Lois **ABERNATHY**, Nov. 28, 1771	LR17	G
Solomon, s. Solomon, b. Oct. 18, 1781	LR21	553
Sophronia, d. Solomon, b. Sept. 1, 1796	LR29	578
WEST, Hezekiah, m. Experience **DAVIS**, Nov. 20. 1777	LR22	480
Mary, m. Thomas **DAVIS**, Nov. 20, 1777	LR22	480
WESTCOTT, Nancy Mrs. of Weathersfield, m. Joseph **TINKHAM**, of Farmington, Mar. 4, 1834, by Rev. L. C. Cheney	LR42	D
Selah, m. Catharine L. **DORMAN**, Nov. 17, 1842, by Rev. C. D. Cowles	LR47	109
WETHENBURY, Benjamin, of Hartford, m. Elizabeth **WOODRUFF**, of Farmington, Apr. 15, 1829, by Harry Bushnell	LR42	562
WETMORE, WETTMORE, Dorcas, wid. of Middletown, m. Benjamin **ANDRUS**, Sr., of Ffarmington, June 14, 1710	LR2	123
Mehetable, d. Feb. 16, 1768, in the 78th y. of her age	LR15	M
WHAPLES, WHEPLES, Elisha, of Weathersfield, m. Amanda **HART**, of Farmington, Oct. 11, 1826, by Rev. Harry Bushnell	LR42	567
Elizabeth, m. Sergt. Isaac **HART**, Nov. 24, 1721	LR2	60
Elizabeth, m. John **COLE**, Nov. 11, 1737	LR6	27
Honor, m. Zebulon **GOODRICH**, Jr., Oct. 4, 1769	LR17	442
Hope, of Weathersfield, m. Elias **HART**, of Farmington, Oct. 17, 1753	LR9	286
Mabel, m Ebenezer **DICKENSON**, June 2, 1757	LR11	576
Margaret, m. Lieut. Elijah **PORTER**, Dec. 22, 1775	LR17	443
WHEDON, -----, m. Titus **BROWNSON**, Mar. 20, 1761	LR11	592

	Vol.	Page
WHEELER, WHELER, Daniel, of Bristol, m. Hannah ELTON, of Burlington, July 16, 1827, by Rev. Noah Porter	LR42	565
Emma, m. Evelin **WOODFORD**, b. of Farmington, Jan. 1, 1827, by Rev. Bela Kellogg	LR42	567
John B., m. Lydia A. **STILES**, b. of Bristol, Dec. 30, 1839, by Rev. Noah Porter	LR47	102
Leonard A., of Spencer of Tioga Cty., N.Y., m. Julia **MILLS**, of Farmington, June 30, 1842, by Rev. C. D. Cowles	LR47	107
Rachel, of Hartford, m. Benjamin **DENTON**, of Ffarmington, Dec. 1, 1724	LR2	52
Seth, m. Harriet **WOODFORD**, Mar. 29, 1825, by Rev. Bela Kellogg	LR42	569
William, m. Elizabeth **COWLES**, b. of Farmington, Feb. 6, 1834, by Rev. Noah Porter	LR42	D
WHITE, Catharine, of Bolton, m. Harvey **MERCHANT**, of Plainville, Dec. 3, 1848, by William Wright	LR47	124
WHITEHOUSE, Daniel, m. Almyra Ann **BURRUS**, Nov. 29, 1839, by Rev. Ezra S. Cook	LR47	101
WHITING, Charlotte, m. Erastus **PORTER**, b. of Farmington, Dec. 5, 1826, by Rev. Noah Porter	LR42	567
James H., m. Emma Ann **LANE**, b. of Farmington, May 21, 1849, by William Wright	LR47	125
Lucinda, of Farmington, m. William **WHITING**, of Warsaw, N.Y., Feb. 12, 1833, by Rev. Henry Stanwood, of Bristol	LR42	558
William, of Warsaw, N.Y., m. Lucinda **WHITING**, of Farmington, Feb. 12, 1833, by Rev. Henry Stanwood, of Bristol	LR42	558
WHITMAN, WHITTMAN, WHITMER, Ann Sophia, of Farmington, m. Henry **FARNUM**, of New Haven, Dec. 1, 1839, by Rev. Noah Porter	LR47	102
Cate, d. Elnathan, b. Jan. 21, 1787	LR22	478
Cloe, d. Elnathan, b. Dec. 16, 1784	LR22	478
Cloranah, m. John **PORTTER**, Dec. 15, 1757	LR11	576
Elizabeth, d. Samuel, b. Jan. 17, 1720/1	LR2	102
Elizabeth, of Farmington, m. William T. G. **MORTON**, of Boston, May [ ], 1844, by Rev. Noah Porter	LR47	112
Elnathan, s. Samuel, b. Jan. 12, 1708/9	LR2	111
Elnathan, s. Solomon, b. Mar. 21, 1746	LR7	E
[E]unice, d. Samuell & Sarah, b. Feb. 24, 1711/12	LR2	99
[E]unice, m. John **STRONG**, b. of Farmington, Feb. 7, 1733/4	LR5	300
Frances, m. Seth **TILLOTSON**, b. of Farmington, Jan. 28, 1823, by Noah Porter, V.D.M.	LR40	572
John, s. Samuell & Sarah, b. Dec. 23, 1713	LR2	99
John, m. Abigail **PANTRY**, b. of Farmington, Feb. 20, 1738/9	LR6	27
Lemuel, s. Solomon, b. Aug. 1, 1739	LR6	7
Lemuel, s. Solomon, Jr., b. June 15, 1780	LR17	441
Louisa, m. Lucius S. **COWLES**, b. of Farmington, Sept. 20, 1848, by Rev. Noah Porter	LR47	123

	Vol.	Page
WHITMAN, WHITTMAN, WHITMER (cont.)		
Mary, d. Solomon, d. Aug. 10, 1751	LR8	11
Mary, d. Solomon, d. Aug. 10, 1751	LR8	12
Mary, d. Solomon, b. [ ]	LR7	F
Mary A., m. John **HILLS**, Aug. 5, 1846, by Noah Porter	LR47	117
Mira, d. Solomon, Jr., b. May 6, 1773	LR17	441
Nancy, d. Solomon, Jr., b. Oct. 3, 1786	LR17	441
Polly, d. Solomon, Jr., b. Nov. 18, 1777	LR17	441
Ruth, w. Solomon, d. Sept. 18, 1777, in the 70th y. of her age	LR21	558-9
Ruth, b. Sept. 28, 1784; m. Asahel **THOMSON**, Nov. 14, 1809	LR22	476
Samuel, Rev., settled in [ ], 1706	LR1	2
Samuel, m. Mrs. Sarah **STODDARD**, of Northampton, Mar. 9, 1708/9	LR2	145
Samuel, s. Rev. Samuell, b. Jan. 13, 1715/16	LR2	95
Samuel, Rev., d. July 31, 1751	LR8	11
Samuel, s. Solomon, b. Sept. 29, 1752	LR8	9
Samuel, s. Solomon, Jr., b. Jan. 24, 1783	LR17	441
Sarah, d. Samuell, b. Mar. 12, 1717/18	LR2	84
Solomon, s. Samuel, b. Apr. 20, 1710	LR2	111
Solomon, m. Susannah **COLE**, b. of Farmington, Dec. 17, 1736	LR6	27
Solomon, Jr., m. Mary **THOMSON**, Feb. 20, 1772	LR17	G
Solomon, m. Mrs. Ruth **STRONG**, Nov. 19, 1772	LR17	442
Solomon, m. Mrs. Ruth **WADSWORTH**, July 30, 1778	LR22	480
Solomon, 3rd, s. Solomon, b. Sept. 19, 1789	LR17	441
Solomon, s. Solomon, b. Jan. 2, 17[ ]	LR6	7
Susannah, w. Solomon, d. Mar. 19, 1772, in the 57th y. of her age	LR17	444
Susannah, d. Solomon, Jr., b. Nov. 26, 1775	LR17	441
William, s. Elnathan, b. July 11, 1783	LR22	478
William H., m. Absarah **WOODRUFF**, b. of Farmington, Oct. 3, 1847, by Noah Porter	LR47	121
WHITNEY, Ebenezer H., of Hampton, N.Y., m. Candace N. **HOTCHKISS**, of Farmington, Nov. 20, 1823, by Noah Porter, V.D.M.	LR40	573
Elisha P., m. Frances A. M. **STANLEY**, b. of Amhurst, Mass., July 9, 1843, by Rev. R. A. Chalker	LR47	111
WHITTLESEY, WHETTESEY, Abner, m. Harriet A. **NEWELL**, b. of Farmington, May 24, 1848, by Noah Porter	LR47	122
Ann A., of Farmington, m. Daniel W. **YOUNG**, of Barkhamseted, Dec. 9, 1840, by Rev. Noah Porter	LR47	104
Ellen R., of Farmington, m. George L. **COGSWELL**, of New Preston, May 21, 1851, by Rev. Noah Porter	LR47	129
Ellen R., of Farmington, m. George Lyman **COGSWELL**, of New Preston, May 21, 1851, by Rev. Noah Porter	LR47	130
Hannah, m. Elijah **GRIDLEY**, Nov. 26, 1793	LR29	576
Mary, of Weathersfield, m. Ebenezer **SMITH**, of Ffarmington, July 2, 1724	LR2	52

	Vol.	Page
WIARD, WYARD, WEIRD [see also **WIAT**], Darius, s.		
Elisha, b. June 12, 1761	LR15	K
Dorcas, d. Seth, b. Feb. 9, 1780	LR17	441
Huldah, d. John, b. Jan. 4, 1755	LR9	12
John, m. Martha NEWEL, Mar. 1, 1744	LR7	35
John, s Elisha, b. May 29, 1765	LR15	K
John, s. Seth, b. Feb. 14, 1773	LR17	440
Lemuel, s. Elisha, b. Feb. 14, 1754	LR15	K
Lois, d. John, b. July 8, 1752	LR8	9
Lois, d. Seth, b. Sept. 21, 1777	LR17	441
Lois, d. Seth, b. Sept. 21, 1777	LR22	478
Martha, d. Elisha, b. Mar. 1, 1756	LR15	K
Noble P., m. Celia Ann Fuller, Oct. 6, 1845, by Rev. J.		
Burton Beach	LR47	115
Phebe, d. Seth, b. July 31, 1775	LR17	441
Phebee, d. Seth, b. July 31, 1775	LR22	478
Rhoda, d. Seth, b. Mar. 27, 1771	LR17	440
Sarah, m. Eldad LEWIS, Mar. 10, 1737	LR7	46
Sarah, d. John, b. Nov. 25, 1745	LR7	E
Seth, s. John, b. Sept. 24, 1749	LR7	F
-----, m. Dorcas HOPKINS, June 20, 1770	LR17	G
WIAT, [see under **WYATT**]		
WICKS, Montgomery, m. Almira MURRAY, b. of		
Farmington, Nov. 15, 1838, by Rev. S. H. Clark	LR47	98
WIGHTMAN, Hubert F., of Bristol, m. Harriet N. WARREN,		
of Farmington, Mar. 17, 1852, by Rev. Noah Porter	LR47	130
WILCOX, WILLCOCKS, WILLCOX, Anne, w. Josiah, d.		
Dec. 17, 1749	LR7	540
Charles, of Harwinton, m. Charlotte HART, of		
Farmington, Oct. 14, 1845, by William Wright	LR47	116
Clarissa, of Farmington, m. Sylvester FITTS, of East		
Windsor, July 4, 1827, by Rev. Bela Kellogg	LR42	565
Eleazer, m. Jemima MUNSON, Mar. 16, 1790	LR22	480
Eleazer Curtiss, s. Eleazer, b. May 21, 1780	LR21	553
Elias, m. Prudence LEWIS, Apr. 9, 1777	LR22	480
Ezra, s. Josiah, b. June 16, 1753	LR8	9
Franklin, of Bershire, Mass., m. Julia Ann ROOT, of		
Farmington, Feb. 18, 1822, by Noah Porter, V.D.M.	LR40	571
Harriet, of Farmington, m. Levi PROSSEE, of		
Bloomfield, Oct. 11, 1848, by Rev. Noah Porter	LR47	123
Josiah, m. Elizabeth CURTIS, Jan. 1, 1750/1	LR7	35
Josiah, s. Josiah, b. Apr. 10, 1752	LR8	9
Mary, m. David ANDRUSS, Sept. 6, 1744	LR7	35
Miranda, of Granby, m. Virgil CORNISH, of Hartford,		
July 30, 1839, by Isaac Porter	LR47	100
Rachel, d. Eleazer, b. Apr. 28, 1782	LR22	478
Ruth, m. Amos WILKINSON, Mar. 14, 1765	LR11	592
WILKINSON, WILCASON, WILLCOXSON,		
WILCOKSON, WILCOXON, Amos, m. Ruth WILLCOX,		
Mar. 14, 1765	LR11	592
Amos, s. Amos, b. Dec. 24, 1776	LR22	478
Amos, s. Josiah, b. Dec. 26, 1765	LR14	11
Birzaveth, s. Amos, b. Jan. 28, 1770	LR15	N

	Vol.	Page

WINCHELL, WINCHEL, Abigail, d. Nathaniel, Jr., b. Jan.

15, 1721/2	LR2	102
Abigail, m. Elijah **BROWNSON,** Apr. 13, 1739	LR6	27
Abigaile, w. Nathaniel, d. Sept. 11, 1745	LR7	36
Abigail, d. Nathaniel, Jr., b. June 1, 1747	LR7	E
Anne, d. Nathaniell, Jr., b. June 11, 1733	LR5	8
Applica, d .Nathaniell, Jr., b. Dec. 26, 1735	LR5	692
Asa, s. Hezekiah, b. Oct. 14, 1763	LR11	590
Benjamin, s. Nathaniel, Jr., b. June 10, 1730	· LR5	8
Dan, m. Lois **CURTISE,** Oct. 9, 1755	LR11	576
Daniel, s. Hezekiah, b. Nov. 20, 1736	LR6	7
Ezekiel, s. Hezekiah & Mary, b. Dec. 11, 1732	LR5	8
Ezekiel, s. Hezekiah, d. Nov. 4, 1737	LR6	10
Ezekiel, s. Dan, b. Oct. 7, 1758	LR11	591
Hannah, w. Nathaniel, Jr., d. May 6, 1755	LR8	12
Hezekiah, m. Mary **COLE,** b. of Ffarmington, Feb. 10,		
1724/5	LR2	257
Hezekiah, s. Hezekiah & Mary, b. Mar. 1, 1729/30	LR5	8
Hezekiah, m. Rachel **MIGALE,** Jan. 10, 1758	LR11	576
Hezekiah, d. Dec. 27, 1760	LR11	574
Ira, s. Dan, b. Dec. 22, 1759	LR11	591
Lois, d. Dan, b. June 6, 1756	LR11	591
Mary, m. Asa **BROWNSON,** Aug. 22, 1765	LR12	513
Mercy, d. Nathaniel, Jr. & Mercy, b. Nov. 15, 1723	LR2	46
Mercy, m. Amos **BRONSON,** June 13, 1748	LR7	35
Nabby, d. Temperance, b. Aug. 20, 1765	LR21	553
Nathaniel, Jr., m. Abigaile **RUGGLES,** Mar. 2, 1720/1	LR2	100
Nathaniel, s. Nathaniel, Jr., b. Mar. [ ], 1725/6	LR4	374
Nathaniel, Sergt., d. Feb. 4, 1741	LR6	305
Nathaniel, Jr., m. Hannah **COWLES,** [d. of] Caleb, June		
8, 1746	LR7	35
Nathaniel, Jr., m. Hannah **COWLES,** June 9, 1746	LR7	46
Nathaniel, Jr., m. Lucy **STRONG,** Dec. 15, 1759	LR11	575
Nathaniel, Dr., d. Feb. 21, 1768	LR14	3
Owen, of Berlin, m. Sophia **CARRINGTON,** of		
Farmington ,Nov. 8, 1825, by Rev. Noah Porter	LR42	569
Rhoda, d. Hezekiah, b. Nov. 30, 1753	LR11	591
Robert, s. Temperance b. Mar. 10, 1767	LR21	553
Roger, s. Hezekiah, b. Apr. 12, 1762	LR11	590
Sabary, d. Dan, b. Feb. 26, 1760	LR11	591
Sarah, of Windsor, m. Joseph **JUDD,** of Farmington, June		
3, 1713	LR2	125
Sarah, m. Josiah **BRONSON,** Nov. 12, 1747	LR7	35
Sarah, d. Dan., b. June 25, 1757	LR11	591
Solomon, s. Hezekiah, b. Feb. 3, 17278	LR4	395
Solomon, m. Sibel **HOOKER,** Aug. 23, 1753	LR9	286
Solomon, s. Solomon, b. Jan. 30, 1755	LR11	591
Stephen, s. Nathaniell, Jr., b. June 18, 1738	LR6	7
Temperance, had d. Nabby, b. Aug. 20, 1765	LR21	553
Temperance, had s. Robert, b. Mar. 10, 1767	LR21	553
Thankfull, m. James **BOOTH,** Nov. 23, 1775	LR21	557

WINSHIP, Catharine A., m. Samuel H. **ROOT,** b. of

Farmington, Sept. 28, 1848, by Rev. Noah Porter	LR47	123

	Vol.	Page
WINSTON, Abigail, d. John, b. Nov. 6, 1754	LR9	12
Daniel Grackson, s. Stephen, b. Feb. 27, 1768	LR15	N
Elidia, d. John, b. Dec. 7, 1757	LR11	591
Jemima, d. Stephen, b. Feb. 7, 1761	LR15	N
Johannah, d. Stephen, b. Nov. 13, 1765	LR15	N
John, m. Elydya **BRISTOW**, Mar. 12, 1752	LR8	10
Patience, d. John, b. July 17, 1753	LR8	9
Rosannah, d. Stephen, b. Jan. 2 ,1759	LR15	N
Stephen, s. Stephen, b. Apr. 8, 1763	LR15	N
WINTTENE (?), Hanah, m. Thomas **ANDRUS**, Nov. 7, 1751	LR7	46
WOLCOTT, WOOLCOT, Charlotte, of Farmington, m.		
Samuel **HADSELL**, of Burlington, Nov. 2, 1827,		
by Harvey Bushnell	LR42	565
Marah, m. Moses **BARNES**, Sept. 7, 1748	LR7	35
WONG (?), Phebe, m. Sergt. Nehemiah **LEWIS**, Sept. 19,		
1749	LR7	35
WOOD, WOODS, Abigail, d. John, b. Oct. 10, 1766	LR15	K
Catharine, d. John, b. Apr. 21, 1763	LR11	591
Eli, s. John, b. Oct. 22, 1753	LR8	9
G. W. of Camden, N.Y., m. Jane **SWEET**, of		
Farmington, Dec. 1, 1828, by Rev. Noah Porter	LR42	564
Hephzibah, d. John, b. Jan. 8, 1756	LR11	591
Hephsibah, m. Judah **BARNES**, Nov. 3, 1774	LR21	557
Huldah, d. John, b. Oct. 13, 1754	LR11	591
Huldah, m. Daniel **CLARK**, June 11, 1772	LR22	480
John, s. Elexander, b. Oct. 15, 1728	LR8	9
John, m. Hephzibah **BECKLEY**, Jan. 18, 1753	LR8	10
John, s. John, b. Apr. 1, 1768	LR15	K
John, s. John, d. Aug. 22, 1769, in the 2nd y. of his age	LR15	M
Joseph L., of Burlington, m. Julia A. **LEE**, of Farmington,		
Sept. 3, 1843, by Noah Porter, Int. Pub.	LR47	111
Ruth, d. John, b. Mar. 13, 1757	LR11	591
Silas, s. John, b. Feb. 7, 1759	LR11	591
Silas, s. John, d. June 15, 1760	LR11	574
Silence d. John, b. Oct. 10, 1764	LR14	11
WOODEN, Alva L., m. Sophronia **GAYLORD**, b. of Bristol,		
May 4, 1831, by Rev. Noah Porter	LR42	560
WOODFORD, Abigail, m. Caleb **COWLES**, b. of Woodford,		
Aug. 8, 1710	LR2	125
Almira, m. Edward **MILLER**, b. of Farmington, Sept. 12,		
1826, by Rev. Bela Kellogg	LR42	567
Amos, s. Joseph, b. Aug. 2, 1737	LR6	7
Anne, d. William, b. Oct. 12, 1758	LR11	591
Bisel, s. John, b. Apr. 9, 1754	LR8	9
Bissell, s. Ann **NORTHAWAY**, b. May 29, 1774	LR17	441
Daniel, m. Ruth **THOMSON**, May 30, 1771	LR21	557
Daniel, d. Apr. 12, 1777	LR31	560
Daniel, s. Samuell, b. [ ]	LR7	F
Dinah, d. Joseph, 3rd, b. Mar. 1, 1754	LR9	13
Dolly, m. Jeffrey **BISHOP**, b. of Farmington, May 18,		
1822, by Bela Kellogg, V.D.M.	LR48	571
Dorothy, d. John, b. Oct. 7, 1759	LR11	591
Dudley, s. William, b. Feb. 20, 1753	LR9	12

	Vol.	Page

WOODFORD (cont.)

	Vol.	Page
Edward, m. Charlotte **TILLOTSON**, b. of Farmington, Nov. 30, 1826, by Rev. Harry Bushnell	LR42	567
Elydya, had illeg. s. John **GARRET**, b. July 21, 1751, f. John **GARRET**	LR8	5
Elidia, m. Thomas **ANDRUS**, Jan. 13, 1753	LR8	10
Elidia, d. William, b. Oct. 27, 1754	LR8	9
Elijah, s. William, b. May 30, 1751	LR9	12
Elisha, s. Joseph, 3rd, b. Nov. 1, 1752; d. Nov. 29, 1752	LR9	12
Elizabeth, m. Nathaniel **COLE**, b. of Ffarmington, June 11, 1707	LR2	123
Elizabeth, d. Joseph, b. July 22, 1707	LR2	97
Esther, m. Samuel **BIRD**, b. of Ffarmington, Jan. 2, 1695/6	LR2	123
Esther, d. William, b. Sept. 7 [ ]	LR7	F
Evelin, m. Emma **WHEELER**, b. of Farmington, Jan. 1, 1827, by Rev. Bela Kellogg	LR42	567
Ezekiel, s. John, [ ]	LR7	F
Hannah, m. Thomas **NORTH**, s. Samuell, b. of Ffarmington, Dec. 4, 1699	LR2	145
Hannah, d. Joseph, Jr., b. July 17, 1737	LR6	7
Hannah, d. Samuell, b. July 22, 1753	LR11	590
Harriet, m. Seth **WHELER**, Mar. 29, 1825, by Rev. Bela Kellogg	LR42	569
Harvey, m. Alma **CHIDSEY**, b. of Avon, May 2, [1833], by Noah Porter, V.D.M.	LR42	A
Henry, m. Huldah **ANDRUS**, b. of Farmington, Sept. 20, 1826, by Rev. Noah Porter	LR42	567
John, s. Joseph, b. June 2, 1718	LR2	84
John, m. Sary **PHELPS**, Sept. 15, 1743	LR6	305
John, s. John, b. July [ ], 1744	LR7	E
Joseph, m. Lidya **SMITH**, b. of Ffarmington, Jan. 23, 1699	LR2	125
Joseph, s. Joseph, b. Aug. 22, 1705	LR2	97
Joseph, s. Joseph, Jr., b. Mar. 12, 1731/2	LR5	8
Joseph, 3rd, m. Elizabeth **HART**, Aug. 1, 1751	LR10	6
Lucy, d. William, b. Oct. 12, 1756	LR8	9
Lucy, wid., m. Stephen **SEDGWICK**, Jr., Sept. 10, 1761	LR11	592
Lidya, d. Joseph, b. Sept. 22, 1702	LR2	97
Lidya, m. William **HOOKER**, b. of Ffarmington, Feb. 15, 1721/2	LR2	100
Mary, m. Thomas **BIRD**, b. of Farmington, July 3, 1693	LR2	125
Mary, d. Joseph, b. June 26, 1704	LR2	97
Mary, d. Joseph, b. Mar. 2, 1708/9	LR2	97
Mary, m. Isaac **NORTH**, b. of Ffarmington, Feb. 27, 1727/8	LR4	423
Mary, d. Samuel & Mary, b. Sept. 15, 1741	LR6	7
Mary Bird, d. Daniel, b. Sept. 30, 1771	LR21	553
Nancy, m. Leffort **HART**, b. of Farmington, Sept. 12, 1826, by Rev. Bela Kellogg	LR42	567
Orrin, m. Diana **DERRIN**, b. of Farmington, Apr. 4, 1830, by Rev. Harry Bushnell	LR42	561

	Vol.	Page
WOODFORD (cont.)		
Rebeckah, m. John **PORTTER**, b. of Ffarmington, Jan. 2, 1695/6	LR2	123
Rebeckah, d. Joseph, b. Apr. 22, 1711	LR2	97
Rebeckah, d. Joseph, d. May 9, 1711	LR2	141
Rebeckah, d. Joseph, b. May 20, 1716	LR2	96
Rebeckah, m. Joshua **WOODRUFF**, b. of Farmington, May 4, 1738	LR6	27
Roger, s. John, b. Nov. 9, 1746	LR7	E
Rosanah, d. John, b. Apr. 10, 1759	LR11	591
Ruth, d. Samuel, b. Nov. 4, 1744	LR7	E
Ruth, d. Daniell, b. Aug. 30, 1774	LR21	553
Samuel, s. Joseph, b. Mar. 30, 1712	LR8	98
Samuel, had d. [ ], b. Aug. 28, 1745	LR7	E
Samuel, s. Samuel, b. Sept. 11, 1751	LR8	9
Samuel, m. Lucy **THOMSON**, Mar. 18, 1757	LR11	576
Samuel, d. July 19, 1759	LR11	577
Sarah, d .Joseph, b. June 4, 1714	LR2	99
Sarah, m. Jonah **WOODRUFF**, b. of Farmington, Dec. 19, 1733	LR5	300
Sarah, d. Joseph, Jr., b. May 6, 1734	LR5	8
Sarah, d. Joseph, Jr. & Sarah, b. Mar. 19, 1740/1	LR6	7
Sarah, m. Hiram **HUNT**, b. of Farmington, Apr. 25, 1821, by Noah Porter, V.D.M.	LR40	571
Solomon, s. Samuel, b. Mar. 8, 1751	LR8	9
Susan, m. Nathan **LEWIS**, b. of Farmington, Nov. 11, 1829, by Rev. Noah Porter	LR42	561
Susanah, m. Anthony **JUDD**, b. of Ffarmington, June 26, 1707	LR2	125
Susanah, m. John **NORTHAWAY**, b. of Farmington, May 17, 1741	LR6	304
Susanah, d. Samuel, b. July 24, 1746	LR7	E
Timothy, s. Samuel, Jr., b. Dec. 29, 1757	LR11	591
William, s. Joseph, b. Nov. 13, 1722	LR2	34
William, m. Susannah **GARRETT**, Oct. 31, 1745	LR7	35
William, had s. [ ], b. Nov. 12, 1747	LR7	E
Zerah, m. Minerva **POTTER**, b. of Farmington, Aug. 10, 1820, by Ludovicus Robbins, V.D.M.	LR40	570
WOODRUFF, Aaron, s. Matthew, b. Oct. 25, 1715	LR2	95
Aaron, m. Mary **MILLS**. of Simsbury, Aug. 5, 1743	LR6	305
Aron, d. [ ]	LR6	305
Abell, m. Abigall **WOODRUFF**, Jan. 7, 1779	LR22	480
Abi, d. Joshua, Jr., b. Oct. 3, 1769	LR17	440
Abigail, d. Samuell, b. Feb. 26, 1705	LR2	111
Abigail, m. Thomas **THOMSON**, s. Thomas, Nov. 16, 1705	LR1	4
Abigail, d. Samuel, d. Nov. 8, 1707	LR2	141
Abigail, twin with Anne, d. John, b. Jan. 3, 1713/14	LR2	99
Abigail, d. Samuell (cordwainer), b. Sept. 24, 1717	LR2	81
Abigail, d. Sergt. Joseph, b. Feb. 24, 1719/20	LR2	102
Abigail, d. Samuel, Jr., b. Nov. 1, 1723	LR2	87
Abigail, d. Josiah, b. Mar. 28, 1736	LR6	7
Abigail, d. John, of Kensington, b. Feb. 12, 1737/8	LR6	7

	Vol.	Page
WOODRUFF (cont.)		
Abigail, m. David **CURTIS**, Jr., b. of Farmington, Apr. 27, 1738	LR6	27
Abigail, m. John **ORTON**, b. of Farmington, Dec. 23, 1741	LR6	304
Abigail, d. Samuell, b. Aug. [ ], 1768	LR15	K
Abigall, m. Abell **WOODRUFF**, Jan. 7, 1779	LR22	480
Abigail R., of Avon, m. John S. **BARNES**, of Hartford, Jan. 6, 1850, by J. C. Searle	LR47	127
Abijah, s. Joshua, b. Dec. 11, 1753	LR8	9
Abraham, s. Matthew, b. Feb. 15, 1710/11	LR2	92
Abraham, d. Dec. 7, 1768, in the 59th y. of his age	LR17	444
Abram, m. Sarah **NORTH**, b. of Farmington, Nov. 15, 1739	LR6	27
Abzarah, m. William H. **WHITMAN**, b. of Farmington, Oct. 3, 1847, by Noah Porter	LR47	121
Alanson, s. Abell, b. Dec. 18, 1782	LR22	478
Almira, d. Elijah, b. Jan. 21, 1768	LR15	K
Alson T., of Avon, m. Harriet **ATKINS**, of Plymouth, Mar. 19, 1849, by J. C. Searle	LR47	124
Alvin, s. Micah, b. Oct. 17, 1774	LR17	441
Amasa, s. Samuell, b. Oct. 25, 1764	LR15	K
Ame, d. Elisha, b. Nov. 6, 1769	LR15	N
Amon, of Southington, m. Eliza **HILLS**, of Farmington, Feb. 9, 1837, by Rev. Noah Porter	LR47	95
Ann, d. Ezekiel, b. Jan. 15, 1735/6	LR5	8
Ann, m. Matthew **WOODRUFF**, Nov. 27, 1755	LR9	286
Anne, twin with Abigail, d. John, b. Jan. 3, 1713/14	LR2	99
Anne, d. Samuell, b. Sept. 23, 1762	LR15	K
Aphia, of Farmington, m. Jeremiah **ELIS**, of Litchfield, Jan. 3, 1827, by Rev. Harvey Bushnell	LR42	567
Appleton, m. Dinah **HART**, Mar. 27, 1758	LR11	576
Appleton, Jr., s. Appleton, b. June 17, 1771	LR22	478
Ard, m. Orpha **COWLES**, b. of Southington, July 13, 1842, by Rev. C. D. Cowles	LR47	108
Arden, s. Abell, b. Feb. 14, 1785	LR22	478
Arden, s. Abel, d. May 20, 1789, in the 5th y. of his age	LR29	580
Asah, s. Ebenezer, b. Dec. 31, 1729	LR5	8
Asa, s. Simmons, b. Dec. 10, 1745	LR7	E
Asahel, s. James, b. Dec. 31, 1743	LR8	9
Asenath, d. Judah, b. Aug. 19, 1753	LR17	440
Augustus B., m. Belinda D. **JONES**, b. of Farmington, Sept. 11, 1831, by Rev. Noah Porter	LR42	560
Azmon, of Farmington, m. Elizabeth N. **STANLEY**, of Berlin, Dec. 9, 1824, by Rev. Noah Porter	LR42	568
Azuba, d. Samuell, b. July 16, 1766	LR15	K
Benjamin, s. Nathan[ie]ll, b. Nov. 24, 1715	LR2	95
Caltha, m. Wilson **HURD**, b. of Farmington, Dec. 31, 1829, by George Norten, J.P.	LR42	561
Charles, s. Nathaniel, b. Apr. 19, 1720	LR2	102
Charles, s. Capt. Judah & Eunice, b. Nov. 9, 1757	LR17	440
Synthe, d. Oliver, b. Feb. 18, 1772	LR17	440
Daniel, s. Samuell, b. Nov. 2, 1696	LR2	111

	Vol.	Page
WOODRUFF (cont.)		
Daniel, m. Lydia **SMITH**, b. of Ffarmington, Oct. 15,		
1719	LR2	101
Daniell, his 2nd d. [ ], b. [ ], 1727	LR4	396
Daniel, s. Daniel, b. Oct. 28, 1728	LR4	395
Daniel, s. Aaron, b. Aug. 6, 1751	LR8	9
David, s. Samuell, b. Feb. 27, 1698	LR2	111
David, m. Mary **PORTTER**, Jan. 18, 1721/2	LR2	101
David Brown, s. Thomas, b. June 4, 1765	LR11	590
Dinah, d. Nathaniel, b. Jan. 27, 1711/12	LR2	98
Dinah, d. Appleton, b. Jan. 9, 1759	LR22	478
Dinah, d. Apleton, b. Dec. 29, 1759	LR11	591
Dorcas, d. Joseph, of Kensington, b. Apr. 8, 1739	LR6	7
Dorkus, d. Robert, b. Feb. 13, 1760	LR11	591
Ebenezer, s. Samuell, b. Dec. 27, 1694	LR2	111
Elijah, s. John, b. Nov. 25, 1718	LR2	83
Elijah, s. Matthew, Jr. & Susanah, b. Nov. 12, 1735	LR5	8
Elijah, m. Mary [ ], Dec. 17, 1766	LR15	A
Elisha, s. Aaron, b. Mar. 14, 1746	LR7	E
Elisha, s. Hezekiah, b. May 1, 1746	LR7	E
Eliza, m. Simeon A. **ROWLEY**, b. of Farmington, Sept.		
19, 1830, by Rev. Noah Porter	LR42	560
Elizabeth, d. John, b. Apr. 17, 1697	LR1	2
Elizabeth, w. John & d. Thomas **THOMSON**, d. Dec. 30,		
1705	LR1	3
Elizabeth, d. Matthew, b. May 10, 1713	LR2	99
Elizabeth, w. Matthew, d. Feb. 5, 1727/8	LR4	396
Elizabeth, m. William **HART**, b. of Farmington, Feb. 2,		
1737/8	LR6	27
Elizabeth, d. Hezekiah, b. May 1, 1738	LR6	7
Elizabeth, d. Jonathan, b. Mar. 2, 1745	LR7	E
Elizabeth, m. Eleazer **PECK**, Dec. 6, 1755	LR15	A
Elizabeth, d. Noah, b. Aug. 15, 1760	LR11	591
Elizabeth, of Farmington, m. Benjamin		
WETHENBURY, of Hartford, Apr. 15, 1829, by		
Harry Bushnell	LR42	562
Elizabeth Hall, d. Micah, b. Jan. 5, 1773	LR17	441
Elizabeth Hall, d. July 5, 1776, in the 4th y. of her age	LR21	558-9
Elizabeth Hall, d. Micah, b. Apr. 7, 1777	LR22	478
Eluia, d. Micah, b. July 13, 1770	LR17	441
Emma, m. Omri M. **NORTH**, b. of Farmington, Oct. 8,		
1823, by Noah Porter, V.D.M.	LR40	572
Esther, d. Samuel, Jr., b. May 8, 1721	LR2	102
[E]unie, d. Nathaniel, b. Apr. 7, 1710	LR2	109
Eunice, twin with Judah, d. Capt. Judah, b. Nov. 6, 1763	LR17	440
Ezekiel, s. Samuell (cordwainer), b. Jan. 15, 1706/7	LR1	4
Ezekiel, m. Anne **COWLES**, b. of Farmington, Feb. 20,		
1734/5	LR5	539
Fanny, m. Hez[ekiah] **SELDEN**, June 13, 1827	LR47	W-Y
Fanny, of Farmington, m. Amon **ANDREWS**, of		
Mereden, June 24, 1846, by Rev. Noah Porter	LR47	117
Flora, d. Abell, b. Sept. 27, 1780	LR22	478
Gad, s. Mathew, b. Mar. 28, 1759	LR11	591

	Vol.	Page
WOODRUFF (cont.)		
George, m. Harriet **LOOMIS**, b. of Farmington, Mar. 13, 1845, by Noah Porter	LR47	113
George S., m. Jane **DUNHAM**, b. of Farmington, July 4, 1847, by William Wright	LR47	119
Gurdian, s. Simmons, b. July 14, 1755	LR11	591
Hannah, d. Joseph, s. Jo[natha]n, b. Aug. 29, 1704	LR2	84
Hannah, w. Joseph, d. Aug. [ ], 1726	LR2	148
Hannah, d. Daniel, b. July 7, 1731	LR5	8
Hannah, d. Noah (s. of David), b. Oct. 4, 1753	LR11	591
Hannah, d. Noah [s. of David], d. Sept. 16, 1757	LR11	593
Hannah, m. Solomon **CURTIS**, Dec. 6, 1764	LR11	592
Hannah, d. Oliver, b. Nov. 11, 1770	LR17	437
Hawkins, s. James, b. Oct. 20, 1750	LR8	9
Henna, had s. Samuell, b. Aug. 2, 1661	LR2	327
Hezekiah, s. Samuell, b. Aug. 9 ,1701	LR2	111
Hezekiah, of Farmington, m. Sarah **MACUN**,* of Stratford, Dec. 3, 1730 *("MACUN" – McEWEN)	LR5	13
Hezekiah, d. David, b. Feb. 20, 1734/5	LR6	7
Hezekiah, s. Hezekiah, b. Mar. 16, 1735/6	LR6	7
Hezekiah, Jr., m. Ruth **BORDMAN**, Oct. 15, 1761	LR11	575
Hezekiah, s. Hezekiah, Jr., b. Feb. 5, 1774	LR17	441
Huldah, m. Hawkins **HART**, Apr. 17, 1758	LR11	575
Huldah, m. Joel **HART**, Mar. 15, 1781	LR22	480
Isaiah, s. Hezekiah, Jr., b. Oct. 17, 1764	LR15	K
Isaiah, s. Noah, b. Aug. 15, 1766	LR14	11
Jacob, s. Nathaniel, b. Aug. 13, 1717	LR2	81
James, s. Samuel, b. May 23, 1708	LR1	7
James, of Farmington, m. Geziah **MUNN**, of Windsor, Nov. 19, 1735	LR5	539
Jeames, m. Lydia **CURTIS**, Feb. 4, 1742	LR6	305
James, s. James, b. Nov. 19, 1747	LR8	9
James, s. James, d. Jan. 17, 1748	LR8	11
James, 2nd, s. James, b. Nov. 11, 1748	LR8	9
James H., of Watertown, m. Mary Ann **HALL**, of Plymouth, Jan. 12, 1835, by Rev. Noah Porter	LR47	88
Jane M., of Farmington, m. Hiram **BUTLER**, of Mereden, July 25, 1843, by Rev. Noah Porter	LR47	110
Jason, s. Samuel, b. Aug. 21, 1758	LR15	K
Jennet, m. William **NORTH**, b. of Farmington, Aug. 31, 1834, by Rev. Noah Porter	LR42	E
Jha(?), m. Abigail [ ], Feb. 9, 1769	LR15	N
John, s. Samuell, b. Apr. 5, 1708	LR2	111
John, twin with Joseph, s. John, b. Mar. 5, 1708/9	LR2	109
John, s .John (s. of Samuell), b. Oct. 18, 1732	LR5	8
John, of Kensington, s. John, m. Abigail **CURTICE**, of Newington, b. of Farmington, Nov. 28, 1734	LR5	539
John, s. John & Abigail, b. July 12, 1735	LR5	8
John, s. Elijah, b. Mar. 16, 1750	LR11	591
John, s. Oliver, b. Apr. 21, 1774	LR17	441
John, s. John, b. Jan. 27, 1775	LR23	478
John, d. Mar. 7, 1793, in the 42nd y. of his age	LR29	580

	Vol.	Page
WOODRUFF (cont.)		
Jonah, m. Sarah **WOODFORD**, b. of Farmington, Dec. 19, 1733	LR5	300
Jonathan, s. Samuell, b. Nov., last, 1688	LR1	2
Jonathan, m. Sarah **LANGTON**, b. of Farmington, July 10, 1711	LR2	125
Jonathan, s. Samuell, d. Apr. 29, 1712	LR2	141
Jonathan, s. Joseph, s. Jo[natha]n, b. June 13, 1714	LR2	84
Jonathan, s. Daniel, b. Oct. 30, 1720	LR2	102
Joseph, of Ffarmington, s. John, m. Elizabeth **CURTICE**, of Weathersfield, Apr. 15, 1708	LR2	101
Joseph, twin with John, b. Mar. 5, 1708/9	LR2	109
Joseph, s. Joseph, s. Jo[natha]n, b. July 7, 1716	LR2	84
Joseph, s. Matthew, m. Easther **BROWN**, of Arther Cull, Oct. 24, 1717	LR2	94
Joseph, s. John, m. Hannah **CLARK**, b. of Ffarmington, Dec. 17, 1722	LR2	257
Joseph, Jr., m. Sarah **NORTH**, May 17, 1728	LR5	13
Joseph, s. John, m. Margaret **NORTH**, b. of Kensington, May 29, 1735	LR5	539
Joseph, Capt., d. Jan. 23, 1736/7	LR6	10
Joseph, m .Hanah **PORTTER**, Mar. 1, 1744/5	LR11	576
Joseph, s. Thomas, b. Apr. 13, 1749	LR7	F
Joseph, s. Joseph, b. Sept. 4, 1753	LR11	591
Joshua, s. Matthew, b. Nov. 7, 1708	LR1	7
Joshua, m. Rebeckah **WOODFORD**, b. of Farmington, May 4, 1738	LR6	27
Joshua, had s. [ ], b. July 11, 1744	LR7	E
Joshua, s. Joshua, b. June 20, 1748	LR8	9
Joshua, Jr., m. Prudence [ ], Oct. 20, 1768	LR15	A
Josiah, s. Joseph, s. Jonathan, b. Aug. 18, 1706	LR2	84
Judah, s. Sergt. Joseph, b. Sept. 30, 1722	LR2	102
Judah, twin with Eunice, s. Capt. Judah, b. Nov. 6, 1763	LR17	440
Julia, of Farmington, m. Alfred S. **GRANT**, of Bristol, Dec. 16, 1840, by Rev. Noah Porter	LR47	104
Kaziah, w. James, d. Aug. 22, 1736	LR6	10
Gaziah, d. Jeames, b. Oct. 27, 1742	LR6	7
Levi, s. Oliver, b. Mar. 26, 1784	LR29	578
Louis, d. Aaron, b. May 3, 1744	LR7	E
Lois, d. Appleton, b. Sept. 5, 1767	LR22	478
Lois, m. Joshua **PARSONS**, May 18, 1775	LR17	443
Lot, s. Oliver, b. Feb. 14, 1779	LR29	578
Lucy, d. John, b. Nov. 1, 1782	LR22	478
Lidya, d. Joseph, s. Jo[natha]n, b. Apr. 11, 1710	LR2	84
Lydia, d. Daniel, b. Mar. 5, 1722/3	LR2	88
Lydia, d. Josiah, b. Jan. 8, 1740/1	LR6	7
Lydia, d. James, b. Apr. 29, 1745	LR8	9
Lydia, d. James, d. Sept. 9, 1751	LR8	11
Manty, s. John, b. Sept. 29, 1787	LR29	578
Margaret, d. June 6, 1711	LR2	141
Margaret, d. John, b. July 18, 1712	LR2	99
Margaret, d. Joseph, of Kensington, b. Apr. 11, 1736	LR6	7
Margaret, d. Jonathan, b. Feb. 11, 1739	LR7	E

	Vol.	Page
WOODRUFF (cont.)		
Mark, d. Aug. 31, 1776, in the 20th y. of his age	LR21	558-9
Martha, d. Joseph, s. of Matthew, b. July 22, 1719	LR2	102
Martha, m. Thomas **ANDRUSS**, July 3, 1751	LR7	46
Martha, s. Simmons, b. Oct. 19, 1757	LR11	591
Mary, d. John, b. Jan. 31, 1699	LR1	2
Mary, d. Samuel, cordwainer, b. Oct. 12, 1712	LR2	98
Mary, d. Matthew, 2nd, d. Sept. 27, 1713	LR2	107
Mary, d. Matthew, d. Sept. 27, 1713	LR2	142
Mary, d. David, b. Mar. 25, 1724/5	LR2	70
Mary, m. Daniel **GRIDLEY**, b. of Farmington ,Feb. 14, 1732/3	LR5	300
Mary, m. David **COGSWELL**, July 10, 1749	LR8	10
Mary, d. Summans, b. Jan. 5, 1750/1	LR8	9
Mary, d. Phinehas, b. Mar. 31, 1763	LR15	K
Mary, d. Asa, b. Dec. 22, 1763	LR11	591
Mary, d. Appleton, b. Sept. 24, 1779	LR22	478
Matilda, m. James H. **MILLER**, b. of Farmington, Sept. 24, 1828, by Rev. Noah Porter	LR42	564
Matthew, m. Elizabeth **BALDING**, Sept. 15, 1694	LR1	4
Matthew, s. Matthew, b. Oct. 1, 1697	LR1	2
Matthew, Jr., m. Susanah **NEWEL**, July 10, 1728	LR4	423
Matthew, Sr., m. wid. Martha **NORTH**, b. of Farmington, June 10, 173[ ]	LR5	13
Matthew, s. Matthew, Jr. & Susanah, b. Nov. 11, 1730	LR5	8
Matthew, m. Ann **WOODRUFF**, Nov. 27, 1755	LR9	286
Medad, s. Thomas, b. Dec. 15, 1751	LR8	9
Mercy, [twin with Ruth], d. Matthew, Jr., b. Mar. 23, 1741	LR6	7
Mercy, m. Asahell **WADSWORTH**, Feb. 2, 1769	LR15	A
Micah, s. Zebulon, b. Apr. 25, 1745	LR7	E
Micah, m. Elizabeth [ ], May 14, 1767	LR15	A
Micah, s. Micah, b. Feb. 5, 1779	LR22	478
Molly, d. John, b. July 22, 1777	LR22	478
Moses, s. Thomas, b. Sept. 6, 1753	LR8	9
Moses, m. Orpha **FRANCIS**, Oct. 4, 1824, by Rev. Harry Bushnell	LR42	568
Nabby, d. Abel, b. Dec. 26, 1789	LR29	578
Nansee, d. Micah, b. Apr. 22, 1768	LR15	K
Nancy, d. John, b. Jan. 15, 1790	LR29	578
Nancy, m. Henry **LEWIS**, Aug. 25, 1841, by Rev. Aaron S. Hill	LR47	105
Nathan, d. Sept. 11, 1766, in the 36th y. of his age	LR14	3
Nathan, of Southington, m. Sarah **ROOT**, of Farmington, May 30, 1832, by Rev. Noah Porter	LR42	559
Nathaniel, m. Thankfull **RIGHT**, July 6, 1709	LR2	145
Nodiah, s. Salvanus, b. June 19, 1738	LR6	7
Nodiah, s. Selvanus, d. July 19, 1738	LR6	10
Noahdiah, s. Capt. Judah, b. Nov. 2, 1760	LR17	440
Noadiah, s. Hawkins, b. Nov. 10, 1778	LR22	478
Noah, s. Samuell, shoemaker, b. Mar. 2, 1714/15	LR2	95
Noah, s. David, b. Jan. 15, 1730/1	LR5	8
Noah, m. Mary **BARNS**, Dec. 5, 1752	LR11	592

	Vol.	Page
WOODRUFF (cont.)		
Noah, m. Mary **CADWELL**, Jan. 3, 1760	LR11	575
Noah, s. Noah, b. Dec. 27, 1761	LR11	591
Obedience, d. Josiah, b. Feb. 12, 1755	LR9	12
Olive, d. Matthew, b. Nov. 2, 1761	LR11	591
Olive, d. Hezekiah, Jr., b. Apr. 17, 1763	LR11	591
Oliver, s. Matthew, Jr., b. Mar. 24, 1739/40	LR6	7
Oliver, s. Matthew, Jr., d. May 16, 1740, ae about 2 m.	LR6	10
Oliver, s. Joshua, b. Sept. 23, 1750	LR8	9
Oliver, m. Sarah **PORTTER**, June 18, 1770	LR17	G
Oliver, s. Oliver, b. July 23, 1786	LR29	578
Oliver, s. Oliver, d. Oct. 10, 1786	LR29	580
Oliver, s. Oliver, b. Feb. 27, 1790	LR29	578
Phebe, m. Nathaniel **COWLES**, b. of Farmington, Feb. 11, 1696/7	LR2	93
Phebe, d. John, b. May 31, 1702	LR1	2
Phebe, d. Joseph, s. Jo[natha]n, b. May 5, 1712	LR2	84
Phebe, m. Benony **MOSES**, b. of Farmington, Jan. 3, 1736/7	LR6	27
Phebe, d. Josiah, b. Sept. 24, 1738	LR6	7
Phebe, d. Matthew, b. Nov. 7, 1746; d. Jan. 23, 1747/8	LR7	35
Phineas, s. Hezekiah, b. Oct. 27, 1733	LR5	8
Phinehas, m. Sarah **DEING**, June 10, 1762	LR11	575
Rachel, d. Samuell, b. Nov. 20, 1703	LR2	111
Rachel, d. Daniel, b. Nov. 25, 1725	LR2	70
Rachel, m. John **BELL**, b. of Ffarmington, Dec. 7, 1727	LR4	423
Rachel, d. David, b. Mar. 22, 1732/3	LR5	8
Rebeckah, d. Samuell, b. Feb. 4, 1690	LR2	111
Rebeka, d. Joshua, b. Sept. 8, 17[ ]	LR6	7
Rebeckah, m. William **SMITH**, b. of Ffarmington, Nov. 18, 1714	LR2	93
Rebeckah, d. Samuel, Jr., b. Aug. 1, 1726	LR2	242
Rebeckah, w. Samuel, Sr., d. Aug. 24, 1737	LR6	10
Rebeckah, d. Oliver, b. Feb. 7, 1776	LR21	553
Rhoda, d. Joshua, b. July 7, 1746	LR7	E
Rhoda, m. Timothy **GRIDLEY**, May 8, 1766	LR17	G
Rhoda, d. Hezekiah, b. Nov. 29, 1767	LR15	N
Robert, s. Samuel, cordwainer, b. Oct. 8, 1710	LR2	92
Robert, s. Hezekiah, b. Feb. 21, 1731/2	LR5	8
Robert, m. Jerusha **BROWNSON**, Feb. 17, 1757	LR11	575
Rocela, d. Appleton, b. July 22, 1762	LR22	478
Roger, s. Jonathan, b. Dec. 18, 1743	LR7	E
Roger Hooker, s. Appleton, b. Oct. 16, 1773	LR22	478
Rosanah, d. James, b. Sept. 14, 1746	LR8	9
Rosannah, d. James, d. Sept. 28, 1746	LR8	11
Roswell, s. Noah, b. June 6, 1768	LR15	N
Ruth, d. Samuell, b. Feb. 15, 1692	LR2	111
Ruth, m. Nathaniel **PORTTER**, b. of Farmington, Jan. 1, 1712/13	LR2	125
Ruth, d. Samuel, Jr., b. May 1, 1719	LR2	102
Ruth, [twin with Mercy], d. Matthew, Jr., b. Mar. 23, 1741	LR6	7
Ruth, d. Robert, b. Apr. 10, 1751	LR9	12

	Vol.	Page
WOODRUFF (cont.)		
Ruth, d. Hezekiah, b. May 17, 1769	LR15	N
Ruth, d. Oliver, b. Sept. 29, 1787	LR29	578
Sally, d. Oliver, b. Feb. 27, 1778	LR29	578
Sally, d. Oliver, d. Apr. 5, 1778	LR29	580
Sally, d. Oliver, b. July 5, 1781	LR29	578
Samuell, s. Henna, b. Aug. 2, 1661	LR2	327
Samuel, s. Samuell, b. Jan. 20, 1686	LR1	2
Samuel, Jr., m. Easther **BIRD**, b. of Ffarmington, July 10, 1718	LR2	101
Samuel, s. Samuel, cordwainer, b. Jan. 13, 1722/3	LR2	87
Samuel, Capt., had d. [ ], b. [ ], 1728	LR4	396
Samuel, cordwainer, d. Nov. 27, 1732	LR5	50
Samuel, s. Samuel, Jr., b. Oct. 3, 1734	LR5	8
Samuel, m. Mary **THOMSON**, b. of Farmington, Mar. 12, 1734/5	LR5	539
Samuel, s. Samuel & Mary, b. Dec. 20, 1735	LR5	8
Samuel, m. Elizabeth **NORTON**, Jan. 24, 1754	LR8	10
Samuel, m. Ruth [ ], Feb. 2, 1758	LR15	A
Samuell, s. Samuell, b. Feb. 19, 1760	LR15	K
Samuel, d. Apr. 10, 1777, in the 54th y. of his age	LR21	558-9
Sarah, d. Matthew, b. June 16, 1703	LR1	2
Sarah, d. John, b. Oct. 15, 1715	LR2	95
Sarah, d. Matthew, 3rd, d. July 10, 1725	LR2	107
Sarah, d. Samuel, cordwainer, b. Aug. 11, 1726	LR2	242
Sarah, d. Joseph, glazier, b. Nov. 15, 1728	LR4	395
Sarah, d. Matthew, Jr., [b.], 1729	LR4	396
Sarah, d. John & [E]unice, b. Sept. 10, 1730	LR5	8
Sarah, d. Josiah, b. Sept. 19, 1735	LR6	7
Sarah, w. Ebenezer, d. Feb. 5, 1743/4	LR7	36
Sarah, d. Abraham, b. June 3, 1748	LR7	F
Sarah, d. Robert, b. Oct. 6, 1749	LR9	12
Sarah, d. May 21, 1751, ae 67	LR8	11
Sarah, d. Simmons, b. June 26, 1753	LR11	591
Sarah, d. Elijah, b. Nov. 1, 1753	LR11	591
Sarah, d. Asa, b. Apr. 7, 1761	LR11	591
Sarah, d. Phineas, b. Apr. 7, 1764	LR15	K
Sarah, d. Hezekiah, Jr., b. May 11, 1766	LR15	K
Sarah, m. Marvin **CLARK**, Jan. 18, 1773	LR17	443
Sarah, d. Micah, b. Nov. 5, 1787	LR22	478
Sarah, m. Joel **SPERRY**, Jr., Aug. 5, 1824, by Amasa Woodford, J.P.	LR42	568
Sarah, m. Henry **MYGOTT**, b. of Farmington, June 23, 1830, by Rev. Noah Porter	LR42	561
Seeth, s. Ezekiel, b .May 1, 1738	LR6	7
Seth, of Avon, m. Anne E. **GILBERT**, of Farmington, Nov. 5, 1848, by Rev. Noah Porter	LR47	123
Shubel, s. Josiah, Jr., b. Sept. 26, 1763	LR11	590
Sibbel, d. Asa, b. Sept. 13, 1755	LR9	12
Silvanus, s. Matthew, b. Mar. 16, 1699/1700	LR1	2
Silvanus, m. Elizabeth **HART**, d. Sergt. Thomas, b. of Farmington, May 27, 17[ ]	LR5	13
Simeons, s. John, b. Jan. 5, 1710/11	LR2	92

	Vol.	Page
WOODRUFF (cont.)		
Solomon, s. Hezekiah, b. Apr. 3, 17[ ]	LR6	7
Solomon, s. David, b. May 11, 1723	LR2	87
Solomon, s. David, d. Dec. 31, 1736	LR6	10
Solomon, s. Joshua, b. Sept. 14, 1739	LR6	7
Solomon, s. Noah, b. Dec. 11, 1763	LR11	591
Susanah, d. John, b. June 26, 1706	LR2	109
Susannah, d. Matthew, d. Apr. 21, 1748	LR7	35
Susanah, d. Matthew, b. Mar. 2, 1757	LR11	591
Sylvester, m. Nancy **ANDRUS**, b. of Farmington ,Mar. 7, 1828, by Rev. Noah Porter	LR42	564
Thankfull, d. Nathaniell, b. June 22, 1714	LR2	95
Thankfull, d. Nathaniell, b. Apr. 14, 1722	LR2	88
Theode, d. Joshua, Jr., b. Oct. 25, 1771	LR17	440
Thomas, s. Joseph, glasser, b. June 6, 1725	LR2	70
Thomas, m. Rebeckah **LOOMIS**, June 26, 1748	LR7	46
Timothy, s. Matthew, b. Feb. 23, 1705/6	LR1	4
Timothy, s. Matthew, 3rd, d. Mar. 14, 1725	LR2	107
Timothy, s. Nathaniell, b. Nov. 7, 1727	LR6	7
Timothy, s. Ebenezer, b. Aug. 14, 1731	LR5	8
Timothy, s. Matthew, Jr., b. Dec. 20, 1732	LR5	8
Timothy, m. Lucy **TREADWELL**, Apr. 21, 1761	LR11	592
Timothy, s. Appleton, b. May 24, 1776	LR22	478
Timothy, d. Sept. 24, 1788, in the 57th y. of his age	LR22	482
Uriah, s. Josiah, b. Mar. 16, 1766	LR14	11
William, s. Joshua, b. Nov. 9, 1760	LR11	591
Zebulon, s. Joseph, s. Jo[natha]n, b. Mar. 11, 1717/18	LR2	84
Zebulon, m. Sarah **JUDD**, Oct. 25, 1744	LR7	46
Zebulon, s. Micah, b. Dec. 27, 1782	LR22	478
-----, s. [ ], b. Feb. 11, 1746/7	LR7	E
WOODSON, Rachel, d. William, b. [ ], 1728/9	LR4	396
WOODWARD, Anne, of Bristol, m. Joshua W. **BOLLES**, of Colebrook, Jan. 11, 1825, by Rev. Noah Porter	LR42	569
WRIGHT, RIGHT, Aaron, s. Judah, b. [ ] 25, [ ]	LR7	E
Agnes Louisa, b. Dec. 10, 1843	LR47	447
Betsey, of Hartland, m. George **KILLBOURNE**, of Litchfield, now of Unionville, July 4, 1839, by John Bartlett	LR47	100
Charles H., of Milledgeville, Ga., m. Martha E. **MORSE**, of Plainville, Oct. 2, 1843, by Rev. William Wright	LR47	111
Daniel, s. Amos, b. Mar. 22, 1763	LR11	590
Daniel, s. Daniell, b. Mar. 21, 1764	LR15	N
Ezekiel, m. Eunice **NEAL**, Jan. 26, 1761	LR11	575
Gad, s. Reuben, b. Sept. 30, 1780	LR21	553
Isabel, d. Amos, b. Dec. 11, 1769	LR15	N
John, of Berlin, m. Emeline **CAMERON**, of Farmington, Sept. 22, 1829, by Rev. Noah Porter	LR42	562
Joseph, s. Judah, b. Oct. 11, [ ]	LR7	R
Judah, s. Daniell, b. June 13, 1767	LR15	N
Keziah, m. Daniel **LEWIS**, Oct. 12, 1753	LR8	10
Louis, d. Judah, b. Sept. 23, 1744	LR7	E
Lucy, d. Ezekiel, b. Mar. 25, 1763	LR11	591
Lidia, d. Amos, b. Jan. 17, 1771	LR22	478

	Vol.	Page
WRIGHT, RIGHT (cont.)		
Mary, of Weathersfield, m. John **STANDLEY**, Jr., of		
Ffarmington, Dec. 9, 1714	LR2	93
Oliver, s. Amos, b. Feb. 25, 1779	LR22	478
Reuben, m. Matha **GRIDLEY**, Mar. 12, 1780	LR21	557
Sarah, of Hatfield, m. Ezekiel **LEWIS**, of Farmington,		
July 27, 1747	LR7	35
Thankfull, m. Nathaniel **WOODRUFF**, July 6, 1709	LR2	145
Thankfull, m. Nathan **JUDD**, Feb. 3, 1742	LR6	305
WROTHAM, Elizabeth, m. Thomas **NEWELL**, Nov. 5, 1679	LR1	5
Susana, m. Samuell **HOUGH**, Nov. 25, 1679	LR1	5
-----h, w. Simon, d. Nov. 30, 1684	LR1	2
[**WYATT**], **WIAT**, Sary, d. John, bp. Mar. 20, 1658	LR2	328
YALE, Abel, m. Sarah **JEROME**, July 20, 1759	LR11	575
Ether, d. Abel, b. May 14, 1760	LR11	592
Harriet, of Farmington, m. James S. **YOUNG**, of		
Southington, Nov. 19, 1840, by Rev. Noah Porter	LR47	103
Ruth, m. Samuel **LEWIS**, Jr., Aug. 12, 1756	LR11	576
Thomas, s. Abel, b. Nov. 6, 1761	LR11	592
YEOMANS, YEOMAN, Gad, m. Emma **ANDRUS**, June 11,		
1824, by Rev. Noah Porter	LR42	568
Joseph, m. Rosannah **HART**, b. of Farmington, Jan. 18,		
1826, by Rev. Harvey Bushnell	LR42	569
Martin, m. Eliza **DANIELS**, b. of Farmington, Sept. 15,		
1822, by Amzi Benedict	LR40	572
Rosanna, m. Moses **BACHELDOR**, b. of Farmington,		
June 15, 1834, by Rev. Noah Porter	LR42	E
YOUNG, YOUNGS, Almyran, m. Maria **CRAMPTON**, Mar.		
12, 1833, by Rev. David L. Parmelee	LR42	A
Anna, d. Stedman, b. Jan. 27, 1755	LR8	9
Daniel W., of Barkhamsted, m. Ann A. **WHITTLESEY**,		
of Farmington, Dec. 9, 1840, by Rev. Noah Porter	LR47	104
Emmeline C., m. Rev. J. C. **SEARLE**, b. of Farmington,		
Apr. 8, 1850, by Rev. Noah Porter	LR47	129
Esther, d. Stedman, b. May 21, 1749	LR8	9
James S., of Southington, m. Harriet **YALE**, of		
Farmington, Nov. 19, 1840, by Rev. Noah Porter	LR47	103
Nathaniel, s. Stedman, b. July 1, 1752	LR8	9
Sarah, d. Stedman, b. June 8, 1746	LR8	9
Theodosey, m. Joseph **TILLOTSON**, Feb. 15, 1759	LR11	576
NO SURNAME		
Abigail, m. William **HART**, Oct. 13, 1768	LR15	A
Abigail, m. Jha(?) **WOODRUFF**, Feb. 9, 1769	LR15	N
Ann, m. Amos **BURR**, Dec. 30, 1761	LR15	N
Annah, m. Caleb **MATTHEW**, Jr., Jan. 1, 1766	LR15	A
Anna, m. [ ]an **JUDD**, Nov. 15, 1767	LR17	G
Ashbel, negro, m. Phebe **HENRY**, Mar. 1, 1750/1	LR7	35
Catharine, negro, d. Levergale, b. Feb. 2, 1768	LR15	N
Dinah, colored, m. Noah [ ], May 12, 1736, by Justice		
Yale of Wallingford	LR6	27
Elenor, d. Ezekiel, b. Aug. 9, 1748	LR7	F
Elizabeth, m. Jonathan **BARNS**, Aug. 4, 1757	LR15	A
Elizabeth, m. Micah **WOODRUFF**, May 14, 1767	LR15	A

	Vol.	Page
NO SURNAME (cont.)		
Elizabeth, m. Enos **CLARK**, Jr., May 21, 1767	LR15	A
Elizabeth, m. Martin **BULL**, Nov. 9, 1768	LR15	A
Esther, m. Benjamin **KILLBORN**, Apr. 25, 1770	LR15	N
[E]unice, m. John **STEDMAN**, Jr., Sept. 5, 1733	LR5	545
Hannah, m. Elijah **FRANCIS**, Apr. 22, 1755	LR15	A
Hannah, m. William **LEWIS**, Oct. 1, 1767	LR15	A
Jemima, m. [ ]than **LEWIS**, Jr., Dec. 15, 1769	LR17	G
Jesse, negro s. Noah & Dinah, d. Dec. 18, 1738	LR6	10
Keziah, m. Samuel **STEDMAN**, July 6, 1768	LR15	N
Lidia, m. Stephen **NORTON**, Nov. 26, 1766	LR15	A
Margaret, m. Samuel **CURTIS**, May 13, 1766	LR15	A
Mary, m. John **CURTISS**, Dec. 3, 1762	LR15	A
Mary, m. Elijah **WOODRUFF**, Dec. 17, 1766	LR15	A
Mary, m. Thomas **GRIDLEY**, June 23, 1768	LR15	N
Marty, m. David **NEAL**, Oct. 31, 1769	LR17	G
Mahitabel,* m. Oliver **ELLSWORTH**, May 28, 1767		
*(Mehitabel)	LR15	A
Mercy, m. Joshua **PORTTER**, May 2, 1754	LR15	A
Mercy, m. Richard **KILLBORN**, Dec. 8, 1763	LR14	8
Mercy, m. Elisha **SCOTT**, Apr. 21, 1766	LR15	A
Noah, negro, m. Dinah [ ], May 12, 1736, by Justice		
Yale, of Wallingford	LR6	27
Phebe, m. Abraham **GRIDLEY**, July 7, 1768	LR15	A
Prudence, m. Joshua **WOODRUFF**, Jr., Oct. 20, 1768	LR15	A
Rachel, d. Jonathan, b. [ ], 1729	LR4	396
Rhoda, m. John **BARNES**, Jr., Aug. 11, 1766	LR17	G
Rhoda, m. Demas **WARNER**, Apr. 15, 1767	LR17	G
Rhodah, m. Stephen **HART**, 3rd, Oct. 6, 1767	LR15	N
Richard, negro formerly of Mr. Wadsworth, m. Rebeckah		
D. **SAMPSON**, negro, May 13, 1719	LR2	101
Rodes, m. Daniel **COWLES**, Jr., Apr. 25, 1766	LR22	480
Ruth, m. Samuel **WOODRUFF**, Feb. 2, 1758	LR15	A
Sarah, m. David **NEWELL**, Dec. 10, 1761	LR14	10
Sarah, m. Amos **UPSON**, Feb. 27, 1766	LR15	N
Sham, negro s. Noah & Dinah, b. Sept. 4, 1737	LR6	5
Sible, m. Job **GRIDLEY**, May 10, 1768	LR15	A
Thankful, m. Elijah **PORTTER**, Sept. 22, 1748	LR14	10
Thankfull, m. Ebenezer **PORTTER**, Feb. 8, 1769	LR15	A
Thankfull, [ ]	LR6	1
Thomas, Sr., d. May 10, 1729	LR4	396
-----, m. Sarah **BARNS**, Feb. 11, 1768	LR17	G
-----, d. Sept. 7, 1682	LR1	2

www.ingramcontent.com/pod-product-compliance
Lightning Source LLC
Chambersburg PA
CBHW072044020426
42334CB00017B/1389